The Christian Tradition

The Christian Tradition

A History of the Development of Doctrine

Jaroslav Pelikan

3

The Growth of Medieval Theology (600-1300)

The University of Chicago Press

Chicago and London

The University of Chicago Press, Chicago 60637
The University of Chicago Press, Ltd., London

93 92 91 90 89 88 87 86 85 84   8 7 6 5 4

Library of Congress Cataloging in Publication Data

Pelikan, Jaroslav Jan, 1923-
    The growth of medieval theology (600-1300)

    (His The Christian tradition; 3)
    Bibliography: p.
    Includes indexes.
    I.   Theology, Doctrinal—History—Middle Ages, 600-
1500.   I. Title.

BT21.2.P42 vol. 3   [BT26]   230s   [230'.09'02]
ISBN 0-226-65374-9 (cloth)
ISBN 0-226-65375-7 (paper)

Contents

Preface

The completion of *The Growth of Medieval Theology* has brought my history of the development of Christian doctrine well past the halfway point, with the period of the Reformation and the modern era reserved for the two remaining volumes. In the present volume, even more than in either of the preceding ones, it has been necessary to adhere strictly to the definition of the work as a whole set down in the introduction to volume 1. Most histories of medieval doctrine have been histories of Christian thought, or even histories of philosophical thought, rather than histories of what the church believed, taught, and confessed on the basis of the word of God. For that reason certain issues (for example, the question of universals) and certain thinkers (above all, Thomas Aquinas) have been far more prominent in such histories than they are here. Although I was, as my earlier publications indicate, better prepared to write about Thomas than about any of the other authors on whom I have drawn in the present volume, the limitations I have imposed on the subject matter of *The Christian Tradition* made a detailed exposition of Thomistic thought unjustifiable, despite its obvious attractions.

As I have sought to show in the introduction to this volume, even the word "theology" is used in the title (as it was often used in the Middle Ages) in a sense different from that in which we generally use it. To us, the word tends to mean what individual theologians do and how they develop their systems, but I am employing it almost as a synonym for "church doctrine." Therefore the outline of *The Growth of Medieval Theology* is shaped primarily

by the evolution of the doctrines and only secondarily by
the controversies or the speculations of the doctors. Like
its two predecessors, this volume is arranged chronologically, even though the titles of the chapters are topical
rather than chronological. The date of the classic formulation of a doctrine or the consummation of an important
stage of the development of a doctrine has determined
where I have discussed that doctrine, including earlier
stages of its development—Anselm's *Why God Became
Man* for chapter 3, the definition of the real presence and
the establishment of the seven sacraments for chapter 4,
Abelard's *Sic et non* for part of chapter 5, the "five ways"
of Thomas for part of chapter 6. Even the discussions of
heresy and of other religions in chapter 5 appear where
they do in the narrative because of the prominence of
those questions in the life and teaching of the church of
the twelfth century.

The setting of this volume within the context of the
entire work has helped to give such issues as the doctrine
of the Trinity and christology a prominence that they
often lack in histories of medieval thought. Above all, it
has been responsible for my attention to the question of
tradition. There is, at least since the apostles, no figure in
Christian history who has so dominated a millennium
with his teachings as Augustine did. How he was understood (or misunderstood) and how he was transmitted
(or superseded) is, therefore, a central element in the
story. I have also made connections between this volume
and the first two in other and more trivial ways. I have, for
example, often rendered the Latin term "verbum" as
"Logos" when it was clearly a reference to the second
person of the Trinity, and have used "Theotokos" to
translate such Latin formulas as "Dei genitrix" or "mater
Dei" or (in two or three texts) "Teothocos." This I have
done not to claim for Latin writers a greater command of
Greek than they possessed, but to facilitate the comparison and contrast that are so interesting and important a
feature of doctrinal development. Cross-references to
previous volumes, as well as cross-references within this
volume, are also intended to serve that end.

Once again, I am obliged—and delighted—to acknowledge the help I have received from others. A series of
dissertations I directed on topics in medieval doctrine,
notably that of Patrick Geary on relics and that of E. Ann

Matter on Mary, made me aware of issues and of texts that I might otherwise have overlooked. Several lecture invitations gave me the opportunity to try out most of these chapters on a living audience and on colleagues in medieval studies who gave me the benefit of their criticism and advice. The host institutions for those lectures were (in alphabetical order): The University of Calgary; the Catholic University of America; the University of Chicago; Princeton University; Saint Mary's College at Notre Dame; the University of Toronto (the Centre for Medieval Studies and the Pontifical Institute of Mediaeval Studies); and Yale University. I have likewise benefited from several distinguished library collections, above all from the Sterling Memorial Library and the Beinecke Rare Book and Manuscript Library at Yale, but also from the Library of Congress, the Widener Library at Harvard, and the library of the Medieval Institute of the University of Notre Dame. Most of all, of course, I have learned from the primary sources listed at the beginning of the book and from the secondary works listed at the end of the book, as well as from other writings in both categories not specifically identified. Nancy Wellins assisted me with verifying citations. The devoted and accurate transcription of a difficult manuscript into its final form was the work of my secretary, Mrs. Candace Bryce.

Primary Sources

Authors and Texts

xi

Alex.Hal.	Alexander of Hales
Quaest.disp.	*Disputed Questions*
S.T.	*Summa Theologica*
Sent.	*Commentary on the Sentences*
Alg.	Alger of Liège
Mis.et just.	*On Mercy and Justice {De misericordia et justitia}*
Sacr.	*On the Sacraments*
Alterc.syn.	*Altercation between the Church and the Synagogue*
Amal.	Amalarius of Metz
Bapt.	*On Baptism*
Off.	*Book of Offices*
Ord.	*On the Days of Ordinances*
Ambr.	Ambrose of Milan
Inc.	*On the Mystery of the Lord's Incarnation*
Is.et an.	*On Isaac and the Soul {De Isaac et anima}*
Myst.	*On the Mysteries*
Ps.118	*Exposition of Psalm 118*
Sacr.	*On the Sacraments*
Spir.	*On the Holy Spirit*
Ambr.Aut.	Ambrose Autpert
Apoc.	*Commentary on the Apocalypse*
Assump.	*On the Feast of the Assumption*
Luc.	*On the Birthday of Saint Luke*
Mts.	*On Saint Matthias*
Nat.Virg.	*On the Nativity of the Virgin Mary*
Purif.	*On the Purification of the Virgin*
Sanct.	*On All Saints' Day*
Trans.	*On the Transfiguration of the Lord*
Vit.virt.	*On the Conflict of Vices and Virtues*
V.Pald.	*Life of Paldo*
Amul.	Amolo of Lyons
Ep.	*Epistles*
Grat.	*On the Grace and Foreknowledge of God*
Anast.Clun.*Ep.Ger.*	Anastasius of Cluny. *Epistle to Gerald*
Andr.Cr.*Or.*	Andrew of Crete. *Orations*
Ang.*Gen.*	Angelomus of Luxeuil. *Commentary on Genesis*
Ann.Bert.	*The Annals of Saint-Bertin*
Ans.	Anselm of Canterbury
Cas.diab.	*On the Fall of the Devil {De casu diaboli}*
Conc.	*On the Harmony of the Foreknowledge, Predestination, and Grace of God with Free Will {De concordia praescientiae et praedestinationis et gratiae dei cum libero arbitrio}*
Concept.virg.	*On the Virginal Conception and on Original Sin*
Cur d.h.	*Why God Became Man {Cur deus homo}*
Ep.	*Epistles*
Inc.	*Epistle on the Incarnation of the Word*
Lib.arb.	*On the Freedom of the Will {De libertate arbitrii}*
Med.	*Meditations*
Mon.	*Monologion*
Orat.	*Prayers {Orationes}*
Pros.	*Proslogion*
Sacr.eccl.	*On the Sacraments of the Church*
Ver.	*On Truth {De veritate}*

Ans.Hav.*Dial.*	Anselm of Havelberg. *Dialogues in Constantinople with Nicetas of Nicomedia*
Ans.L.	Anselm of Laon
Sent.Ans.	*Sentences of Anselm*
Sent.div.pag.	*Sentences of the Divine Page*
Att.Verc.	Atto of Vercelli
Ep.	*Epistles*
Serm.	*Sermons*
Aud.*V.Elig.*	Audoin. *Life of Eligius*
Aug.	Augustine of Hippo
Civ.	*City of God {De civitate dei}*
Conf.	*Confessions*
Doctr.christ.	*On Christian Doctrine*
Enchir.	*Enchiridion*
Ep.	*Epistles*
Ev.Joh.	*Exposition of the Gospel of John*
Fid.et symb.	*On Faith and the Creed {De fide et symbolo}*
Gen.ad litt.	*Exposition of Genesis according to the Letter {De Genesi ad litteram}*
Mor.eccl.	*On the Morals of the Catholic Church*
Nat.et grat.	*On Nature and Grace {De natura et gratia}*
Parm.	*Against the Epistle of Parmenianus*
Persev.	*On the Gift of Perseverance*
Praed.sanct.	*On the Predestination of the Saints {De praedestinatione sanctorum}*
Ps.	*Exposition of the Psalms*
Retract.	*Retractations*
Rom.	*Exposition of Certain Propositions from the Epistle to the Romans*
Spir.et litt.	*On the Spirit and the Letter {De spiritu et littera}*
Trin.	*On the Trinity*
Ps.Aug.*Hypomn.*	Pseudo-Augustine. *Memorandum against the Pelagians and Celestians {Hypomnesticon}*
Bald.	Baldwin of Ford
Comm.fid.	*On the Commendation of Faith*
Sacr.alt.	*The Sacrament of the Altar*
Tract.	*Tractates*
Beat.	Beatus of Liébana
Apoc.	*Commentary on the Apocalypse*
Elip.	*Against Elipandus*
Bed.	The Venerable Bede
Act.	*Exposition of the Acts of the Apostles*
Cant.	*Allegorical Exposition of the Song of Songs*
E.et N.	*Commentary on Ezra and Nehemiah*
Ep.	*Epistles*
Ep.Ecg.	*Epistle to Egbert*
Ep.Joh.	*Exposition of 1 John*
Gen.	*Commentary on Genesis*
H.e.	*Ecclesiastical History*
Hist.ab.	*History of the Abbots*
Hom.	*Homilies*
Luc.	*Exposition of the Gospel of Luke*
Marc.	*On the Gospel of Mark*

1 Pet.	*Exposition of 1 Peter*
Sam.	*On the First Part of Samuel*
Tabern.	*On the Tabernacle*
Temp.	*On the Building of the Temple*
Ben.A.*Fel.*	Benedict of Aniane. *Against the Impiety of Felix*
Ben.N.*Reg.*	Benedict of Nursia. *Rule*
Bern.Reich.	Berno of Reichenau
Dial.	*Dialogue on Fasting*
Ep.	*Epistles*
Miss.off.	*The Office of the Mass*
Modul.	*On Various Modulations of the Psalms and of Chants*
V.Udal.	*Life of Ulrich of Augsburg {Vita S. Udalrici}*
Bernl.Const.*Lib.*	Bernold of Constance. *Treatises {Libelli}*
Boeth.*Trin.*	Boethius. *On the Trinity*
Bonac.*Manif.*	Bonacorsi of Milan. *Manifestation of the Heresy of the Cathars*
Bonav.	Bonaventure
Brev.	*Breviloquium*
Hex.	*Collations on the Hexaemeron*
Itin.	*The Journey of the Mind to God {Itinerarium mentis in deum}*
Quaest.disp.	*Disputed Questions*
Red.	*The Reduction of the Arts to Theology*
Sent.	*Commentary on the Sentences*
Trip.	*On the Threefold Way {De triplici via}*
Bonif.*Serm.*	Boniface (Wynfrith). *Sermons*
Brd.Clr.	Bernard of Clairvaux
Adv.	*Advent Sermons*
Apol.	*Apologia*
Assump.	*Sermons on the Assumption*
Cant.	*Sermons on the Song of Songs*
Cons.	*On Consideration*
Conv.	*On Conversion*
Dil.	*On the Love of God {De diligendo deo}*
Div.	*Sermons on Diverse Topics*
Ep.	*Epistles*
Grad.	*On the Steps of Humility and Pride {De gradibus humilitatis et superbiae}*
Grat.	*On Grace and Free Will*
Laud.Virg.	*In Laud of the Virgin Mother*
Nat.	*Sermons on the Nativity*
Ps.90	*Exposition of Psalm 90*
Purif.Mar.	*On the Purification of Saint Mary*
Sanct.	*On All Saints' Day*
V.Mal.	*Life of Saint Malachy*
Vig.Nat.	*On the Vigil of the Nativity*
Brd.Schol.*Mirac.Fid.*	Bernard Scholasticus. *On the Miracles of Saint Faith*
Brngr.Tr.	Berengar of Tours
Apol.	*Apologia*
Coen.	*On the Holy Supper {De sacra coena}*
Ep.	*Epistles*
Ep.Adel.	*Epistle to Adelmannus*
fr.	*Fragments*
Opusc.	*Opusculum*

Brnld.*Brngr.*	Bernold of Constance. *On the Multiple Condemnation of Berengar the Heresiarch*
Brun.Col.*1 Cor.*	Bruno of Cologne. *Exposition of 1 Corinthians*
Brun.S.	Bruno of Segni
Apoc.	*Exposition of the Apocalypse*
Az.	*On the Sacrifice of the Azymes*
Ep.	*Epistles*
Ex.	*Exposition of Exodus*
Gen.	*Exposition of Genesis*
Inc.	*On the Incarnation of the Lord and His Burial*
Joh.	*Commentary on the Gospel of John*
Laud.Mar.	*In Laud of Saint Mary*
Lev.	*Exposition of Leviticus*
Luc.	*Commentary on Luke*
Num.	*Exposition of Numbers*
Sacr.	*The Sacraments of the Church*
Sent.	*Sentences*
Sym.	*On Simoniacs*
Cant.parth.	*Hymns of the Virginity {Cantiones partheniae}*
Car.M.	Charlemagne [Carolus Magnus]
Ep.	*Epistles*
Ep.Elip.	*Epistle to Elipandus of Toledo and the Bishops of Spain*
CAut.(670)	Second Council of Autun
CCar.(853)	Synod of Quiercy
CCP(681)	Third Council of Constantinople
CFr.(794)	Council of Frankfurt
Cap.	*Capitulary*
Syn.	*Synodical Epistle*
Chart.univ.Par.	*Chartulary of the University of Paris*
CHat.(680)	Council of Hatfield
CLater.(1215)	Fourth Lateran Council
CLing.(859)	Synod of Langres
CRem.(1148)	Synod of Reims
CSen.(1140)	Synod of Sens
CTol.(633)	Fourth Council of Toledo
CTol.(653)	Eighth Council of Toledo
CTrid.(1545–63)	Council of Trent
CVal.(855)	Synod of Valence
Cyn.*Chr.*	Cynewulf. *Christ*
Cypr.*Domin.orat.*	Cyprian. *On the Lord's Prayer {De dominica oratione}*
Ps.Cypr.*Abus.*	Pseudo-Cyprian. *On Twelve Abuses of the Age*
Cyr.H.*Catech.*	Cyril of Jerusalem. *Catechetical Lectures*
Dant.	Dante Alighieri
Inf.	*Inferno*
Purg.	*Purgatorio*
Deusd.	Deusdedit
Coll.can.	*Collection of Canons*
Inv.sym.	*Against Invaders and Simoniacs*
Dion.Ar.*C.h.*	Pseudo-Dionysius the Areopagite
	Celestial Hierarchy
Drm.*Rd.*	*The Dream of the Rood*
Dur.Tr.*Corp.*	Durandus of Troarn. *On the Body and Blood of Christ {De corpore et sanguine Christi}*

Eadm.*V.Ans.*	Eadmer. *Life of Anselm*
Ebr.*Antihaer.*	Ebrard of Béthune. *Against Heresy*
Ecb.*Cathar.*	Ekbert of Schönau. *Twelve Sermons against the Cathars*
Ein.*V.Car.M.*	Einhard. *Life of Charlemagne*
Elip.	Elipandus of Toledo
Ep.	*Epistles*
Ep.Alc.	*Epistle to Alcuin*
Ep.Car.M.	*Epistle to Charlemagne*
Ep.episc.Fr.	*Epistle to the Bishops of Francia*
Symb.fid.	*Confession of Faith {Symbolum fidei}*
Ep.Traj.	*Epistle of the Clergy of Utrecht {Epistola ecclesiae Trajectensis}*
Episc.Fr.*Ep.Elip.*	Bishops of Francia. *Epistle to Elipandus*
Ermeng.*Tract.*	Ermengaud. *Treatise against the Heretics*
Fel.	Felix of Urgel
Flor.	Florus of Lyons
Amal.	*Against Amalarius*
Exp.miss.	*Exposition of the Mass*
Jud.	*Against the Jews*
Praed.	*On Predestination*
Quaest.	*Resolution of a Question*
Scot.Er.	*Against John Scotus Erigena*
Tr.ep.	*On Three Epistles*
Ver.	*On Holding Immovably to the Truth of Scripture*
Fred.*Nih.*	Fredegisius. *On Nothing and on Darkness*
Fulb.	Fulbert of Chartres
Ep.	*Epistles*
Hymn.	*Hymns*
Jud.	*Against the Jews*
Serm.	*Sermon*
V.Aut.	*Life of Saint Autbert*
Gand.*Sent.*	Gandulph of Bologna. *Sentences*
Gez.*Corp.*	Geza of Saint Martian. *On the Body and Blood of Christ {De corpore et sanguine Christi}*
Gisl.Crisp.	Gilbert Crispin
Gent.	*Disputation of a Christian with a Gentile*
Jud.	*Disputation of a Jew with a Christian*
Sim.	*On Simoniacs*
V.Herl.	*Life of Herluin of Bec*
Gisl.Por.	Gilbert de La Porrée
Com.Eut.	*Commentary on Boethius: "Against Eutyches and Nestorius"*
Com.Trin.	*Commentary on Boethius: "On the Trinity"*
Ep.Matt.	*Epistle to Matthew*
Goff.Clr.*Lib.*	Geoffrey of Clairvaux. *Treatise against Gilbert {Libellus contra Gilbertum}*
Goff.Vind.	Geoffrey of Vêndome
Lib.	*Treatises {Libelli}*
Opusc.	*Opuscula*
Serm.	*Sermons*
Goth.	Gottschalk of Orbais
Conv.brev.	*Brief Confession*
Conf.prol.	*Prolix Confession*
Corp.	*On the Body and Blood of the Lord {De corpore et sanguine Domini}*

Deit.	*That It Is Permissible to Speak of the Deity as Trine*
Div.	*On Diverse Matters*
fr.	*Fragments*
Praed.	*On Predestination*
Redempt.	*How Many Ways Redemption Is Spoken of*
Resp.	*Responses*
Sched.	*A Slip of Paper {Schedula}*
Trin.	*On the Trinity*
Goz.Ep.Val.	Gozechinus. *Epistle to Valcherus*
Gr.M.	Gregory the Great
Dial.	*Dialogues*
Ev.	*Homilies on the Gospels {In evangelia homiliae}*
Mor.	*Moral Discourses on Job*
Ps.Gr.M.Lib.antiph.	Pseudo-Gregory the Great. *Antiphonary*
Gr.Tr.	Gregory of Tours
Hist.Franc.	*History of the Franks*
Mirac.	*On Miracles*
Gualt.Torn.Jud.	Walter of Tournai. *Against the Jews*
Gualt.S.Vict.Lab.	Walter of Saint-Victor. *Against the Four Labyrinths of France*
Guib.Nog.	Guibert of Nogent
Corp.	*Epistle on the Morsel Given to Judas and on the Reality of the Lord's Body {Epistola de buccella Judae data et de veritate dominici corporis}*
Gest.	*The Deeds of God through the Franks {Gesta dei per Francos}*
Inc.	*On the Incarnation*
Laud.Mar.	*In Laud of Saint Mary*
Mor.	*Moral Discourses on Genesis*
Ord.serm.	*The Order of a Sermon*
Pign.	*On the Relics of the Saints {De pignoribus sanctorum}*
Virg.	*On Virginity*
Vita sua	*Autobiography {De vita sua}*
Guit.Av.	Guitmond of Aversa
Conf.	*Confession*
Corp.	*On the Reality of the Body and Blood of Christ in the Eucharist {De corporis et sanguinis Christi veritate in eucharistia}*
Hadr.I.Ep.episc.Hisp.	Pope Hadrian I. *Epistle to the Bishops of Spain*
Haer.Cathar.	*The Heresy of the Cathars*
Ps.Haim.Halb.Corp.	Pseudo-Haimo of Halberstadt. *On the Body and Blood of the Lord {De corpore et sanguine Domini}*
Her.	Heriger of Lobbes
Corp.	*On the Body and Blood of the Lord {De corpore et sanguine Domini}*
Ep.Hug.	*Epistle to Hugh*
Episc.Leod.	*History of the Bishops of Liège {Gesta pontificum Tungrensium sive Leodicensium}*
V.Had.	*Life of Saint Hadalinus*
V.Land.	*Life of Saint Landoald*
V.Rem.	*Life of Saint Remaclus*
Herb.Los.Serm.	Herbert of Losinga. *Sermons*
Herib.Haer.	Heribert. *Epistle on the Heretics*
Herm.Mag.Epit.	Master Herman. *Epitome of Christian Theology*
Herm.Sched.Conv.	Herman of Scheda. *On His Conversion*

Herm.Torn.*Rest.Mart.*	Herman of Tournai. *On the Restoration of the Monastery of Saint Martin*
Hier.	Jerome [Hieronymus]
Ep.	*Epistles*
Esai.	*Commentary on Isaiah*
Gal.	*Commentary on the Epistle to the Galatians*
Hebr.nom.	*The Interpretation of Hebrew Names*
Hebr.quaest.	*Hebrew Questions on the Book of Genesis*
Matt.	*Commentary on Matthew*
Ps.Hier.*Indur.*	Pseudo-Jerome. *On the Hardening of the Heart of Pharaoh {De induratione cordis Pharaonis}*
Hil.*Trin.*	Hilary of Poitiers. *On the Trinity*
Hild.*Ep.*	Hildegarde of Bingen. *Epistles*
Hild.Tr.*Mah.*	Hildebert of Tours. *History of Mohammed*
Hinc.R.	Hincmar of Reims
Deit.	*On the Deity as One and Not Three*
Div.	*On the Divorce of Lothair and Tetberga*
Ep.	*Epistles*
Metrop.	*On the Rights of Metropolitans*
Perv.	*To those Who Seize Church Property and Rob the Poor {Ad rerum ecclesiasticarum pervasores et pauperum praedatores}*
Praed.	*On Predestination*
Recl.	*To the Recluses and the Simple*
Reg.	*On the Person of the King and the Royal Ministry {De regis persona et regio ministerio}*
Hon.Aug.	Honorius of Autun [Honorius Augustodunensis]
Eluc.	*Elucidation*
Inev.	*Inevitability*
Hrot.	Roswitha of Gandersheim [Hrotsvitha]
Asc.	*The Ascension of the Lord*
Dion.	*The Passion of Saint Dionysius*
Gall.	*Gallicanus*
Mar.	*Mary*
Pel.	*Pelagius*
Hug.Am.*Haer.*	Hugh of Amiens. *Against the Heretics of His Time*
Hug.Bret.*Corp.*	Hugh of Breteuil. *On the Body and Blood of Christ {De corpore et sanguine Christi}*
Hug.Met.*Ep.*	Hugh of Metellus. *Epistles*
Hug.S.Vict.	Hugh of Saint-Victor
Did.	*Didascalion*
Sacr.	*The Sacraments of the Christian Faith*
Scrip.	*On Sacred Writings and Writers {De scripturis et scriptoribus sacris}*
Sum.Sent.	*Summa of the Sentences*
Verb.	*On the Word of God {De verbo dei}*
Hug.Sper.	Hugh of Speroni
Hymn.lat.	*Latin Hymnographers*
Hymn.temp.	*Hymns on the Time {Hymni de tempore}*
Ildef.	Ildefonsus of Toledo
Cog.bapt.	*On the Knowledge of Baptism {De cognitione baptismi}*
Itin.des.	*Journey through the Desert {De itinere deserti}*
Virg.Mar.	*The Virginity of Mary*
Ps.Ildef.	Pseudo-Ildefonsus

Cor.Virg.	*The Crown of the Virgin {De corona Virginis}*
Serm.	*Sermons*
Is.St.*Serm.*	Isaac of Stella. *Sermons*
Isid.Sev.	Isidore of Seville
Diff.	*Differences*
Eccl.off.	*Ecclesiastical Offices*
Exp.sac.	*Expositions of the Mystical Sacraments*
Gen.	*Commentary on Genesis*
Goth.	*History of the Goths*
Jud.	*Against the Jews*
Orig.	*Origins*
Proëm.	*Prefaces to the Books of the Old and New Testaments {In libros veteris ac novi testamenti proëmia}*
Sent.	*Sentences*
Ps.Isid.Sev.*Ep.Red.*	Pseudo-Isidore of Seville. *Epistle to Redemptus*
Iv.	Ivo of Chartres
Decr.	*Decree*
Ep.	*Epistles*
Pan.	*Panormia*
Prol.	*Prologue*
Serm.	*Sermons*
Joach.	Joachim of Fiore
Apoc.	*Exposition of the Apocalypse.* Venice, 1527. Facsimile edition, Frankfurt, 1964
Art.fid.	*On the Articles of the Faith {De articulis fidei}*
Conc.	*The Harmony of the New and the Old Testaments {Concordia novi et veteris testamenti}.* Venice, 1519. Facsimile edition, Frankfurt, 1964
Ev.	*Treatise on the Four Gospels {Tractatus super quatuor evangelia}*
Jud.	*Against the Jews*
Joh.Abr.*Off.eccl.*	John of Avranches. *Ecclesiastical Offices*
Joh.Lod.*V.Petr.Dam.*	John of Lodi. *Life of Peter Damian*
Joh.Saler.*V.Od.Clun.*	John of Salerno. *Life of Odo of Cluny*
Joh.Salis.*Hist.pont.*	John of Salisbury. *Pontifical History*
Jon.Aur.*Inst.laic.*	Jonas of Orléans. *On Lay Instruction*
Jul.Pom.*fr.*	Julian Pomerius. *Fragments*
Jul.Tol.	Julian of Toledo
Aet.sext.	*The Sixth Age {De comprobatione aetatis sextae}*
Antikeim.	*Antitheses {Antikeimena}*
Nah.	*Commentary on Nahum*
Prog.fut.	*Prognostications of the Future*
Lanf.	Lanfranc of Bec
Corp.	*On the Body and Blood of the Lord {De corpore et sanguine Domini}*
Ep.	*Epistles*
Leand.Sev.*Laud.eccl.*	Leander of Seville. *In Laud of the Church {In laudem ecclesiae}*
Leo.M.*Serm.*	Leo the Great [Leo Magnus]. *Sermons*
Lib.Car.	*Caroline Books {Libri Carolini}*
Lib.princ.	*Book of Two Principles*
Lud.P.*Ep.Hild.*	Louis the Pious. *Epistle to Hilduin*
Mar.Vict.*Ar.*	Marius Victorinus. *Against Arius*
Monet.Crem.*Cathar.*	Moneta of Cremona. *Summa against the Cathars and Waldenses*

Nicol.I.*Ep.*	Pope Nicholas I. *Epistles*
Nicol.Clr.*Serm.*	Nicholas of Clairvaux. *Sermons*
Od.Cambr.	Odo of Cambrai
Jud.	*Against a Jew Named Leo*
Pecc.orig.	*On Original Sin {De peccato originali}*
Od.Clun.	Odo of Cluny
Coll.	*Conferences {Collationes}*
Hymn.	*Hymns*
Occup.	*Occupation*
Serm.	*Sermons*
V.Ger.	*Life of Saint Gerald of Aurillac*
Ot.Fr.*Gest.Frid.*	Otto of Freising. *Deeds of Frederick Barbarossa*
Othl.	Othlo of Sankt Emmeram
Curs.	*On the Spiritual Course*
Dial.	*Dialogue on Three Questions*
Doctr.spir.	*On Spiritual Doctrine*
Man.	*Manual*
Prov.	*Proverbs*
Tent.	*On His Temptations {De suis tentationibus}*
V.Bonif.	*Life of Saint Boniface*
V.Wolf.	*Life of Saint Wolfgang*
Visib.	*On Visible Things*
Ov.*Fast.*	Ovid. *Fasti*
Pard.	Pardulus
Paul.Alb.*Ep.*	(Paul) Albar of Cordova. *Epistles*
Paul.Diac.*Homil.*	Paul the Deacon. *Homiliary*
Paulin.Aquil.	Paulinus of Aquileia
Ep.	*Epistles*
Fel.	*Against Felix*
Lib.sac.	*Sacred Book {Libellus sacrosyllabus}*
Petr.Ab.	Peter Abelard
Apol.	*Apologia*
Conf.	*Confession of Faith*
Dial.	*Dialogue between a Philosopher, a Jew, and a Christian*
Ep.	*Epistles*
Eth.	*Ethics*
Int.theol.	*Introduction to Theology*
Prob.Hel.	*Problems of Heloise*
Rom.	*Exposition of the Epistle to the Romans*
Serm.	*Sermons*
Sic et non	*Yes and No*
Symb.Apost.	*Exposition of the Creed Known as the Apostles' {Expositio symboli quod dicitur Apostolorum}*
Theol.chr.	*Christian Theology*
Theol.schol.	*Theology for Scholars*
Theol.S.b.	*Theology of the "Summum Bonum"*
Petr.Alf.*Dial.*	Peter Alfonsi. *Dialogues*
Petr.Bl.*Perf.Jud.*	Peter of Blois. *Against the Perfidy of the Jews*
Petr.Cant.*Verb.abbr.*	Peter Cantor. *Abbreviated Word {Verbum abbreviatum}*
Petr.Dam.	Peter Damian
Carm.	*Hymns {Carmina}*
Lib.grat.	*Gracious Book {Liber gratissimus}*
Off.B.V.M.	*Office of the Blessed Virgin Mary*

Omnip.	*On Divine Omnipotence*
Opusc.	*Opuscula*
Perf.mon.	*On the Perfection of Monks*
Serm.	*Sermons*
V.Rad.Dom.Lor.	*Life of Saints Ralph and Dominic Loricatus*
V.Rom.	*Life of Saint Romuald*
Ps.Petr.Dam.	Pseudo-Peter Damian
Exp.can.miss.	*Exposition of the Canon of the Mass*
Serm.	*Sermons*
Petr.Lomb.	Peter Lombard
Coll.	*Collections on the Epistles of Saint Paul*
Ps.	*Commentary on the Psalms of David*
Sent.	*Sentences*
Serm.	*Sermons*
Petr.Mart.*Patar.*	Peter Martyr. *Summa against the Patarenes*
Petr.Mon.*Hist.Alb.*	Peter the Monk. *History of the Albigenses*
Petr.Pict.	Peter of Poitiers [Petrus Pictaviensis]
Ep.Petr.Ven.	*Epistle to Peter the Venerable*
Sent.	*Sentences*
Petr.Ven.	Peter the Venerable
Ep.	*Epistles*
Jud.	*Against the Hardness of the Jews*
Mirac.	*On Miracles*
Petrob.	*Against the Petrobrusians*
Sect.Sar.	*Against the Sect or Heresy of the Saracens*
Serm.	*Sermons*
Sum.Sar.	*Summa against the Saracens*
Prim.*Scar.*	Priminius. *Scarapsus*
Prud.Tr.	Prudentius of Troyes
Hinc.et. Pard.	*Epistle to Hincmar and Pardulus*
Praed.	*On Predestination against John Scotus Erigena*
Rab.	Rabanus Maurus
Ecclus.	*Commentary on Ecclesiasticus*
Ep.	*Epistles*
Gen.	*Commentary on Genesis*
Inst.cler.	*The Instruction of the Clergy*
Reg.	*Commentary on the Books of Kings {Commentaria in libros quatuor Regum}*
Rad.Ard.	Ralph the Ardent
Hom.	*Homilies*
Hom.ep.ev.	*Homilies on the Sunday Epistles and Gospels {In epistolas et evangelia dominicalia homiliae}*
Radb.	Paschasius Radbertus
Cog.	*You Compel Me {Cogitis me}*
Corp.	*On the Body and Blood of the Lord {De corpore et sanguine Domini}*
Ep.Fr.	*Epistle to Frudegard*
Matt.	*Exposition of Matthew*
Part.Mar.	*On the Parturition of Saint Mary*
Rain.Sacc.*Cathar.*	Rainerius Sacconi. *Summa on the Cathars and the Paupers of Lyons*
Rath.	Ratherius of Verona
Dial.conf.	*Confessional Dialogue*

Ep.	*Epistles*
Exh.prec.	*Exhortations and Prayers {Exhortationes et preces}*
Metr.	*On the Translation of Saint Metro*
Ot.serm.	*On the Vain Word {De otioso sermone}*
Prael.	*Forewords {Praeloquia}*
Serm.Asc.	*Sermons on the Ascension*
Serm.Cen.Dom.	*Sermon on the Lord's Supper {Sermo in cena Domini}*
Serm.Mar.Marth.	*Sermon on Mary and Martha*
Serm.Pasch.	*Post-Paschal Sermons*
Serm.Pent.	*Sermons on Pentecost*
Serm.Quad.	*Sermons on Quadragesima*
Ratr.	Ratramnus
Corp.	*On the Body and Blood of the Lord {De corpore et sanguine Domini}*
Part.Mar.	*On the Parturition of Saint Mary*
Praed.	*On the Predestination of God*
Reg.Pr.*Eccl.disc.*	Regino of Prüm. *Ecclesiastical Discipline*
Rem.Aux.	Remigius of Auxerre
Cel.miss.	*The Celebration of the Mass*
Gen.	*Exposition of Genesis*
Matt.	*Homilies on Matthew*
Quaest.	*On Two Questions*
Rich.S.Vict.	Richard of Saint-Victor
Apoc.	*Commentary on the Apocalypse*
Ben.maj.	*Benjamin Major*
Ben.min.	*Benjamin Minor*
Comp.	*The Comparison of Christ to a Flower and of Mary to a Branch*
Diff.sacr.	*On the Difference between the Sacrifice of Abraham and the Sacrifice of the Blessed Virgin Mary*
Edict.	*An Edict Went Out*
Em.	*On Emmanuel*
Erud.hom.	*On the Erudition of the Inner Man*
Except.	*Book of Exceptions*
Grad.car.	*The Four Steps of Violent Love {De quatuor gradibus violentae caritatis}*
Pot.lig.solv.	*On the Power of Binding and Loosing {De potestate ligandi et solvendi}*
Seir	*One Is Calling to Me from Seir* [Isa. 21:11]
Serm.cent.	*One Hundred Sermons {Sermones centum}*
Stat.hom.	*On the State of the Inner Man*
Tabern.	*The Tabernacle of the Covenant*
Trin.	*On the Trinity*
Robt.Pull.*Sent.*	Robert Pullen. *Sentences*
Rom.ord.	*Roman Orders of Service*
Rosc.*Ep.Ab.*	Roscellinus. *Epistle to Abelard*
Rufin.As.*Bon.pac.*	Rufinus of Assisi. *On the Good of Peace {De bono pacis}*
Rup.	Rupert of Deutz
Ann.	*Annulus*
Div.off.	*On Divine Offices*
Ev.Joh.	*Commentary on the Gospel of John*
Job	*Commentary on the Book of Job*

Sacr.Gel.	Gelasian Sacramentary
Sacr.Greg.	Gregorian Sacramentary
Sanct.merit.	The Merits of the Saints
Scot.Er.	John Scotus Erigena
Carm.	Hymns {Carmina}
Ev.Joh.	Commentary on the Gospel of John
Exp.C.h.	Exposition of the "Celestial Hierarchy"
Periph.	On Natures {Periphyseon}
Praed.	On Predestination
Prol.Ev.Joh.	Homily on the Prologue of the Gospel of John
Vers.Dion.Ar.	Version of Dionysius the Areopagite
Vers.Max.	Version of Maximus Confessor
Sent.div.	Sentences of Divinity
Sent.Flor.	Sentences of Florian
Seq.trans.	Transitory Sequences
Serv.Lup.	Servatus Lupus of Ferrières
Coll.	Collection on Three Questions
Ep.	Epistles
Ep.Add.	Additional Epistles
Quaest.	Book on Three Questions
Sig.*Vir.ill.*	Sigebert. *On Illustrious Men {De viris illustribus}*
Steph.Aug.*Sacr.alt.*	Stephen of Autun [Stephanus Augustodunensis]. *On the Sacrament of the Altar*
Symb.Apost.	Apostles' Creed {Symbolum Apostolorum}
Symb.Ath.	Athanasian Creed {Symbolum Athanasianum}
Symb.Nic.-CP	Niceno-Constantinopolitan Creed {Symbolum Nicaeno-Constantinopolitanum}
Tert.*Paenit.*	Tertullian. *On Penitence*
Thdr.Stud.*Nat.Mar.*	Theodore of Studios. *The Nativity of Mary*
Thes.Hymn.	Thesaurus of Hymns
Thos.Aq.	Thomas Aquinas
Gent.	Summa against the Gentiles
Graec.	Against the Greeks
S.T.	Summa Theologica
Sent.	Commentary on the Sentences
Sep.sub.	On Separate Substances
Un.int.	The Unity of the Intellect
V.Mauril.	Life of Saint Maurilius
Vac.Err.	Vacarius. *Against Many and Various Errors*
Verg.*Aen.*	Vergil. *Aeneid*
Wand.*Creat.*	Wandalbert. *On Creation*
Ps.Wm.Camp.*Dial.*	Pseudo-William of Champeaux. *Dialogue between a Christian and a Jew*
Wm.Mon.*Henr.Mon.*	William the Monk. *Against Henry the Monk*
Wm.S.Th.	William of Saint-Thierry
Am.	On the Nature and the Dignity of Love {De natura et dignitate amoris}
Cant.	Exposition of the Song of Songs
Disp.Ab.	Disputation against Peter Abelard
Med.	Meditative Prayers
Sacr.alt.	On the Sacrament of the Altar
Zen.Ver.*Tract.*	Zeno of Verona. *Tractate*

Editions and Collections

AFP	*Archivum Fratrum Praedicatorum.* Rome, 1931–.
Alberigo	Alberigo, Giuseppe, and others, eds. *Conciliorum oecumenicorum decreta.* New York, 1962.
Anal.Hymn.	*Analecta Hymnica Medii Aevi.* Leipzig, 1886–1922.
Andrieu	Andrieu, Michel, ed. *Les Ordines Romani du haut Moyen-âge.* Louvain, 1931–57.
Beekenkamp	Beekenkamp, Willem Hermanus, ed. *Berengarii Turonensis de sacra coena adversus Lanfrancum liber posterior.* The Hague, 1941.
BFS	*Bibliotheca Franciscana scholastica medii aevi.* Quaracchi, 1903–.
BGPM	*Beiträge zur Geschichte der Philosophie {und Theologie} des Mittelalters.* Münster, 1891–.
Bliemetzrieder	Bliemetzrieder, Franz Plazidus, ed. *Anselmus von Laon systematische Sentenzen.* Münster, 1919.
Blumenkranz	Blumenkranz, Bernhard, ed. *Altercatio aecclesie contra synagogam.* Strasbourg, 1954.
Borgnet	Borgnet, Auguste, ed. *B. Alberti Magni . . . Opera omnia.* Paris, 1890–99.
Boyer-McKeon	Boyer, Blanche, and McKeon, Richard, eds. Peter Abailard. *Sic et Non.* Chicago, 1976–77.
Brezzi	Brezzi, Paolo, ed. S. Pier Damiani. *De divina omnipotentia e altri opuscoli.* Florence, 1943.
Brink	Brink, J. N. Bakhuizen van den, ed. Ratramnus. *De corpore et sanguine Domini.* Amsterdam, 1954.
Buttimer	Buttimer, Charles Henry, ed. *Hugonis de Sancto Victore Didascalion: De studio legendi.* Washington, 1939.
Canal	Canal, J. M. "La virginidad de María según Ratramno y Radberto, monjes de Corbie. Nueva edición de los textos." *Marianum* 30 (1968): 53–160.
CCCM	*Corpus christianorum. Continuatio mediaevalis.* Turnhout, Belgium. 1966–.
CCSL	*Corpus christianorum. Series latina.* Turnhout, Belgium, 1953–.
Châtillon-Tulloch	Châtillon, Jean, and Tulloch, William-Joseph, eds. Richard de Saint-Victor. *Sermons et opuscules spirituels inédits.* Bruges, 1951.
Constable	Constable, Giles, ed. *The Letters of Peter the Venerable.* Volume 1: Text. Cambridge, Mass., 1967.
Cook	Cook, Albert Stanburrough, ed. *The "Christ" of Cynewulf.* Reprint edition. Hamden, Conn., 1964.
CSEL	*Corpus scriptorum ecclesiasticorum latinorum.* Vienna, 1866–.
Denifle-Châtelain	Denifle, Heinrich, and Châtelain, Emile, eds. *Chartularium universitatis Parisiensis.* Paris, 1889–97.
Dondaine	Dondaine, Antoine, ed. *Un traité néo-manichéen du XIIIe siècle: Le "Liber de duobus principiis," suivi d'un fragment de rituel Cathare.* Rome, 1939.
Ed.Leon.	*S. Thomae Aquinatis opera omnia, iussu Leonis XIII edita.* Rome, 1882–.
Fredericq	Fredericq, Paul, ed. *Corpus documentorum inquisitionis haereticae pravitatis neederlandicae.* Volume 1. Ghent and The Hague, 1889.
FSI	*Fonti per la storia d'Italia.* Rome, 1887–.

Geyer Geyer, Bernhard, ed. *Die Sententiae divinitatis, ein Sentenzbuch der Gilbertinischen Schule.* Münster, 1909.

Gietl Gietl, Ambrosius M., ed. *Die Sentenzen Rolands, nachmals Papstes Alexander III.* Reprint edition, Amsterdam, 1969.

Glanvell Glanvell, Viktor Wolf von, ed. *Die Kanonessammlung des Kardinals Deusdedit: Die Kanonessammlung selbst.* Paderborn, 1905.

Glorieux Glorieux, Palémon, ed. "Le *Contra quatuor labyrinthos Franciae* de Gauthier de Saint-Victor. Edition critique." *Archive d'histoire doctrinale et littéraire du Moyen-âge* 19 (1952): 187–335.

Goulburn-Symonds Goulburn, Edward Meyrick, and Symonds, Henry, eds. *The Life, Letters and Sermons of Bishop Herbert de Losinga.* Volume 2: *The Sermons.* Oxford, 1878.

Gundlach Gundlach, Wilhelm, ed. "Zwei Schriften des Erzbischofs Hinkmar von Reims." *Zeitschrift für Kirchengeschichte* 10 (1889): 92–145, 258–310.

Häring Häring, Nikolaus Martin, ed. *The Commentaries on Boethius by Gilbert of Poitiers.* Toronto, 1966.

Heurtevent Heurtevent, Raoul. *Durand de Troarn et les origines de l'hérésie bérengarienne.* Paris, 1912.

Homeyer Homeyer, Helene, ed. *Hrotsvithae opera. Mit Einleitungen und Kommentar.* Munich, 1970.

Jecker Jecker, Gallus. *Die Heimat des hl. Pirmin des Apostels der Alamannen.* Münster, 1927.

Keeler Keeler, Leo William, ed. *Sancti Thomae Aquinatis Tractatus de unitate intellectus contra Averroistas.* Rome, 1936.

Klumper *Doctoris irrefragabilis Alexandri de Hales . . . Summa theologica iussu . . . Bernardini Klumper . . . edita.* Quaracchi, 1924–48.

Knoepfler Knoepfler, Alois, ed. *Rabani Mauri De institutione clericorum libri tres.* Munich, 1900.

Korfmacher Korfmacher, William Charles, ed. *Othloni Libellus Proverbiorum.* Chicago, 1936.

Kritzeck Kritzeck, James. *Peter the Venerable and Islam.* Princeton, 1964.

Laistner Laistner, Max Ludwig Wolfram, ed. *Bedae Venerabilis expositio actuum apostolorum et retractatio.* Cambridge, Mass., 1939.

Lambot Lambot, Cyrille, ed. *Oeuvres théologiques et grammaticales de Godescalc d'Orbais.* Louvain, 1945.

LCL *Loeb Classical Library.* Cambridge, Mass., 1912–.

Leclercq-Rochais Leclercq, Jean, and Rochais, Henri, eds. *Sancti Bernardi Opera.* Rome, 1957–.

Lescoe Lescoe, Francis J., ed. *Saint Thomas Aquinas: Treatise on Separate Substances.* West Hartford, Conn., 1963.

Levison Levison, Wilhelm. *England and the Continent in the Eighth Century.* Oxford, 1946.

Lokrantz Lokrantz, Maragareta, ed. *L'opera poetica di S. Pier Damiani.* Uppsala, 1964.

Luscombe Luscombe, David Edward, ed. *Peter Abelard's Ethics.* Oxford, 1971.

Mandonnet Mandonnet, Pierre, ed. *S. Thomae Aquinatis . . . Scriptum super libros Sententiarum Magistri Petri Lombardi.* Paris, 1929–47.

Manselli Manselli, Raoul. "Il monaco Enrico e la sua eresia." *Bullettino dell' Istituto Storico Italiano per il Medio Evo e Archivio Muratoriano* 65 (1953): 1–63.

Mansi	Mansi, J. D., ed. *Sacrorum conciliorum nova et amplissima collectio*. Florence, 1759–98.
Matronola	Matronola, Martinio, ed. *Un testo inedito di Berengario di Tours e il Concilio Romano del 1079*. Milan, 1936.
MGH	*Monumenta Germaniae Historica*. Berlin, 1826–.
Auct.Ant.	*Auctores Antiquissimi.*
BDK	*Die Briefe der deutschen Kaiserzeit.*
Conc.	*Concilia.*
Conc.Sup.	*Conciliorum Supplementa.*
Ep.	*Epistolae.*
Lib.lit.	*Libelli de lite.*
Poet.	*Poetae Latini.*
Scrip.	*Scriptores.*
Scrip.Ger.	*Scriptores rerum Germanicarum.*
Scrip.Lang.	*Scriptores rerum Langobardicarum.*
Scrip.Mer.	*Scriptores rerum Merovingicarum.*
Mohlberg	Mohlberg, Cunibert, ed. *Das fränkische Sacramentarium Gelasianum in alamannischer Überlieferung.* 2d ed. Münster, 1939.
Montclos	Montclos, Jean de. *Lanfranc et Bérenger: La controverse eucharistique du XIe siècle.* Louvain, 1971.
Ostlender	Ostlender, Heinrich, ed. *Sententiae Florianenses.* Bonn, 1929.
PG	*Patrologia Graeca.* Paris, 1857–66.
PL	*Patrologia Latina.* Paris, 1878–90.
Plummer	Plummer, Charles. *Venerabilis Baedae opera historica.* Volume 1: Text. Oxford, 1896.
PMS	*Publications in Medieval Studies of the University of Notre Dame.* Notre Dame, Indiana, 1936–.
Quaracchi	*Doctoris seraphici S. Bonaventurae . . . opera omnia.* Quaracchi, 1882–1902.
Reischl-Rupp	Reischl, W. K., and Rupp, J., eds. Cyril of Jerusalem. *Opera.* Munich, 1848–60.
Ricchini	Ricchini, Thomas Augustin, ed. *Venerabilis Patris Monetae Cremonensis . . . adversus Catharos et Valdenses libri quinque.* Rome, 1743.
Ripberger	Ripberger, Albert, ed. *Der Pseudo-Hieronymus-Brief IX "Cogitis me." Ein erster marianischer Traktat des Mittelalters von Paschasius Radbert.* Freiburg in der Schweiz, 1962.
Robinson	Robinson, Joseph Armitage. *Gilbert Crispin, Abbot of Westminster. A Study of the Abbey under Norman Rule.* Cambridge, 1911.
Sanders	Sanders, Henry Arthur, ed. *Beati in Apocalipsin libri duodecim.* Rome, 1930.
SC	*Sources chrétiennes.* Paris, 1940–.
Schaff	Schaff, Philip, ed. *Creeds of Christendom.* 6th ed. New York, 1919.
Schmitt	Schmitt, F. S., ed. *Sancti Anselmi opera omnia.* Seckau, Rome, Edinburgh, 1938–61.
SLH	*Scriptores Latini Hiberniae.* Dublin, 1955–.
Southern	Southern, Richard William, ed. *The Life of St Anselm, Archbishop of Canterbury, by Eadmer.* 2d ed. Oxford, 1972.
SPE	*Santos padres españoles.* Madrid, 1971–.
Spic.Bon.	*Magistri Petri Lombardi Parisiensis episcopi Sententiae in IV*

	libros distinctae. 3d ed. Volume 4 of *Spicilegium Bona-* *venturianum.* Quaracchi, 1971–.
ST	*Studi e testi.* Rome, 1900–.
Sudendorf	Sudendorf, Hans Friedrich Georg Julius, ed. *Berengarius Tu-ronensis, oder eine Sammlung ihn betreffender Briefe.* Hamburg and Gotha, 1950.
Swanton	Swanton, Michael, ed. *The Dream of the Rood.* Manchester and New York, 1970.
Swoboda	Swoboda, Antonius, ed. *Odonis abbatis Cluniacensis Occupatio.* Leipzig, 1900.
Thaner	Thaner, Friedrich, ed. *Summa Magistri Rolandi.* Innsbruck, 1874.
Thomas	Thomas, Rudolf, ed. Petrus Abaelardus. *Dialogus inter Philoso-phum, Iudaeum, et Christianum.* Stuttgart, 1970.
TPMA	*Textes philosophiques du moyen âge.* Paris, 1955–.
TU	*Texte und Untersuchungen zur Geschichte der altchristlichen Literatur.* Leipzig. 1882–.
Walter	Walter, Johannes Wilhelm von. *Magistri Gandulphi Bononien-sis Sententiarum libri quatuor.* Vienna and Breslau, 1924.
Webb	Webb, Clement Charles Julian, ed. "Dispute of a Christian with a Heathen touching the Faith of Christ." *Medieval and Renaissance Studies* 3 (1954): 55–77.

The Middle Ages as "Age of Faith"

See vol.1:9

In a passage quoted in the introduction to the first volume of this work, the most influential twentieth-century historian of medieval philosophy has declared that "the general tendency among historians of medieval thought has been to imagine the middle ages as peopled by phi-

Gilson (1957) 156

losophers rather than theologians." In part because of this overemphasis on medieval philosophy, the complaint of the most influential twentieth-century historian of medieval theology also continues to be valid: "In the Thomistic movement . . . the continuity between the patristic period and the scholastic period has not received adequate at-

Grabmann (1957) 1:22

tention." It is a primary purpose of the present volume to seek to rectify those imbalances by recounting "the growth of medieval theology."

Each of the three terms in that title calls for some clarification. It has become a truism that *medieval* man was not aware of belonging to an age that stood in the "middle" between the ancient and the modern periods. Medieval theologians themselves spoke of being part of the "modern" era. Thus a ninth-century scholar, in the course of the debate over the doctrine of predestination, contrasted the age of the church fathers with "the modern time," in

Flor.Tr.ep.8 (PL 121:1002)

which he knew himself to be living. In the eleventh century, "modern" was a term of opprobrium, so that, in refuting the theories about the Eucharist that were current, it was possible to attack "modern dogmaticians" and "the

Dur.Tr.Corp.1.1; 5.12 (PL 149:1378; 1393)

inciters of modern heresy." Writing at the same time, another theologian attacked the tendency of "those who in the modern era do not shrink from" dangerous opin-

Her.Corp. 1; 4 (PL 139: 180; 182)

ions, and he described "modern" times, as distinguished

I

Her.*Episc*.*Leod*.1 (*MGH Scrip.* 7:164)

Ans.L.*Sent.Ans.*5 (Bliemetzrieder 112)

Alan.Ins.*Haer*.1.1 (*PL* 210: 307)

Thos. Aq. *S.T.*1–II.107.1 ob.1 (*Ed.Leon.*7:278)

Aug.*Civ.*11.1 (*CCSL* 48:321–22)

Jul.Tol.*Antikeim*.2.69 (*PL* 96: 697)

Hab.3:2

Alb.M.*Proph.min.*Hab.3.2 (Borgnet 19:433)

Gordon (1925) 25

See p. 99 below

Ambr.Aut.*Apoc.*8 (*CCCM* 27: 636)

from "ancient" times, as a period when rational faith had yielded to "credulity." A twelfth-century canonist and theologian could speak of "the holy modern fathers" as authorities on marital legislation, while another writer of that century lamented the lack of "moderns" who could refute heresy as the fathers had; and the dominant theological figure of the thirteenth century could assert that "the faith of the ancients and that of the moderns are identical."

Yet that does not mean that the idea of belonging to "the middle age" was unknown to these centuries. Augustine himself had spoken of living "in this age that comes in the middle [in hoc interim saeculo]," but this was a reference to the two cities, the city of God and the city of man, which were intermingled until the Last Judgment. It was a similar view of history when the seventh-century archbishop of Toledo, Julian, spoke of "a middle age [tempus medium]" that came "between the two comings of Christ, the first in the incarnation and the second in judgment." At the other end of the period covered by this volume, Albertus Magnus, commenting on the passage "Revive thy work in the midst of the years," declared: "He calls it 'the midst of the years' because, as great works have been manifested since the beginning of the world and will be manifested at the end in the condemnation of the world, so now he prays that in the middle age [in medio tempore], in which the saints are being troubled by the wicked, [God] may revive his work in the destruction of those who are evil." When we speak in this volume of "medieval" theology, of course, we are following the usage of recent times; for such words were largely "a product of the artistic and especially the architectural revival of the Middle Ages which animated the early decades of the Victorian age, and the first examples recorded occur invariably in that context."

Whatever connotations the term "medieval" may have in architecture or literature, it suggests certain characteristics of Christian teaching in this period that are distinctive. One such characteristic, noted by medieval men themselves, was that most of them had received the Greek and even the Latin classics through the fathers' use of ancient texts rather than through their own reading and study. Some of them also noted another contrast with the patristic period, the identification of the Eucharist rather than of baptism as the most important sacrament in the church. It was a recognition of this contrast when defenders of the doctrine of the real presence felt obliged to account for the omission of the Eucharist from the creeds, which did refer to baptism; this was, they said, due to the absence of attacks on the faith of the church in the real presence. That neglect was evident above all in the writings of Augustine, so that, for the Eucharist as well as for several other doctrines, it is possible to view the medieval development as "a series of footnotes" to Augustine and at the same time as a series of efforts to amplify and correct the Augustinian legacy. One Augustinian doctrine that required amplification was the doctrine of redemption through Christ; the Middle Ages may be seen as the period when the primary focus of Christian thought about Christ shifted from what he was to what he did, from the person of Christ to the work of Christ.

Recently historians of the Middle Ages have begun employing the phrase "age of faith" in referring to the period. At least two histories of the time intended for the general reader, one of them published in 1950 and the other in 1965, have taken this as their title. As the introduction to the second of these has noted, "The thousand medieval years were not solely an 'age of faith,' nor is faith a uniquely medieval phenomenon. But the cathedrals were the most impressive monuments of that era; its greatest poem was a description of Hell, Purgatory, and Paradise; crusades were the only collective enterprises which temporarily rallied all nations; there were heretics and infidels but agnosticism was nonexistent or cowed into silence; the clergy was more numerous and influential in politics, economics, philosophy and other intellectual pursuits than it has ever been since." Or, in the words of another distinguished scholar, "if by that phrase ["age of faith"] we mean that any conception of the world from which the supernatural was excluded was profoundly alien to the minds of that age, that in fact the picture which they formed of the destinies of man and the universe was in almost every case a projection of the pattern traced by a Westernized Christian theology and eschatology, nothing could be more true." As yet another interpreter of medieval thought has put it, "If I were to sum up in two words what I believe is the essential message of medieval thought, I would say: It is the spirit in

Wm.S.Th.*Sacr.alt.*11 (*PL* 180:359)

See vol.1:330

See vol.1:258

Lopez (1965) 6

Bloch (1964) 82

Curtius (1953) 598

which it restated tradition; and this spirit is Faith and Joy."

It is essential, however, in speaking about the Middle Ages as "age of faith," to note the specific senses in which the term "faith" was used in the Middle Ages. Although the technical distinction between "the faith by which one believes [fides qua creditur]" and "the faith which one believes [fides quae creditur]" was a later one, it expressed what Rupert of Deutz was saying when he asserted the superiority of "believing in Christ," that is, "venerating and loving the Logos," to merely "believing Christ," that is, affirming "that he speaks what is true." Yet when medieval theologians spoke of "the faith," it was the latter, objective sense of the word that often predominated over the subjective sense. The Christian gospel as "the one true faith" or as "the apostolic faith, which alone is the true faith" or as "the true and catholic faith" was the object of "faith" as an act or as a virtue. Therefore even an unbelieving priest could administer "the faith" to others, because it was an objectively given truth, whether the individual himself accepted it or not. The content of this "catholic faith" was summarized in the Athanasian Creed. For our purposes here, "age of faith" refers primarily to faith in the sense of "that which is believed."

Rup.Div.off.10.8 (CCCM 7: 341)

See pp. 215–16 below
Guit.Av.Corp.3 (PL 149: 1485)
Brun.S.Apoc.5.16 (PL 165: 693)

Ecb.Cathar.4.3 (PL 195:26)

See p. 11 below

See vol.1:1

Brd.Clr.Ps.90.11.1 (Leclercq-Rochais 4:448); Guib.Nog. Ord.serm. (PL 156:21)

Robt.Pull.Sent.7.17 (PL 186: 928)
Rich.S.Vict.Ben.min.80 (PL 196:57)

Bern.Reich.Dial.2 (PL 142: 1090)

Ps.116:10;2 Cor.4:13

Brd.Clr.Grad.4.15 (Leclercq-Rochais 3:28)

Rich.S.Vict.Serm.cent.25 (PL 177:950)

See vol. 2:5

A synonym for such "faith" would be "doctrine," as defined at the very beginning of this work. In medieval usage, the word "doctrine [doctrina]" could simply mean "instruction," or it could even be a summary of the entire Christian imperative, as when Robert Pullen stated: "The doctrine of a priest consists in two things, namely, purity of faith and honesty of morals." But it also meant "the doctrine that teaches about heavenly things," "the right faith and sound doctrine" whose boundaries had been set by the catholic fathers from the beginning of the church. This was the doctrine that was believed, taught, and confessed on the basis of the word of God. The biblical formula, "I believed, and so I spoke," linked believing the truth and confessing the truth as inseparable parts of the same response to Christ. Thus Augustine was notable for "the faith of his heart" and for "the confession of his mouth." While for Eastern Christians the conflict with Islam was the occasion for affirming what they believed, taught, and confessed, Western theologians came closest to such affirmations when they were setting forth their doctrine of the real presence in the Eucharist: in the ninth century Gottschalk stated what "everyone ought to believe, know, hold, and confess"; a treatise ascribed to another ninth-century figure, Haimo of Halberstadt, but probably written during the tenth or the eleventh century, opened its statement of eucharistic doctrine with the words "Therefore we believe and faithfully confess and hold"; and Baldwin, archbishop of Canterbury in the final quarter of the twelfth century, declared his faith in the reality of the eucharistic miracle by admonishing, "Simply and confidently, firmly and constantly, therefore, let us hold, believe, and confess."

That way of speaking about "faith" or about "doctrine" is likewise central in the medieval use of the term *theology,* which has determined how the title of this volume employs the word. For "it was only very slowly that 'theology' acquired the specific sense of an organized and learned understanding of the data of revelation." The preponderant tendency of the Middle Ages was reflected in the use of the term "theologize" to describe the evangelization of the heathen, or in the decree of the Fourth Lateran Council in 1215, establishing the office of "theologian" as that of "one who is to teach priests and others about the Sacred Page and above all to inform them of those things that are known to pertain to the cure of souls." There were times when certain medieval writers deviated from that tendency and came closer to our present-day use of the word. As part of his program of reflection and speculation, John Scotus Erigena proposed a fourfold division of wisdom, in which "theology" was to take its part alongside other branches of knowledge; it dealt, solely or at least chiefly, with "speculation about the divine nature." From Greek thought he had learned that "theology" was, strictly speaking, this "contemplation of the divine nature"; it was, in short, as Dionysius had said, "the reason of God." Yet Erigena, too, followed the more general practice when he spoke of the Old Testament prophets as "theologians" or when he spoke mystically about "the wings of intimate theology." A later force for innovation in the understanding of the term was the thought of Peter Abelard, or at any rate that of some of his followers, who gave his treatises such titles as *Christian Theology, Theology of*

Goth.*Corp.* (Lambot 324)

Ps.Haim.Halb.*Corp.* (*PL* 118: 815–16)

Bald.*Sacr.alt.*2.1.3 (*SC* 93:210)

Chenu (1966) 376

ap.DuCange (1883) 8:96

CLater.(1215) *Const.* 11 (Alberigo 216)

Hug.S.Vict.*Did.*2.2 (Buttimer 25)

Scot.Er.*Periph.*3.29 (*PL* 122: 705)
Scot.Er.*Periph.*2.30 (*SLH* 9: 166)

Scot. Er.*Prol.Ev.Joh.*14 (*SC* 151:270–72)
Scot.Er.*Exp.C.h.*6.2 (*CCCM* 31:89)

Scot.Er.*Exp.C.h.*7.3 (*CCCM* 31:108)

Scot.Er.*Prol.Ev.Joh.*1 (*SC* 151: 202)

Scholars, and *Theology of the "Summum Bonum."* It remains true, in any case, that "well into the twelfth century and even beyond, the use of 'theology' as a synonym for 'the Sacred Page' or 'the Divine Page,' that is, Holy Scripture" maintained itself, while such terms as "sacred doctrine" and "divine science" came to designate the intellectual activity to which we now assign the name "theology."

Although, for a modern reader, the medieval significance of "theology" may be the most problematical issue in the terminology of our title, there would seem to be no doubt that the term *growth* in that title would be far more problematical to a medieval reader. The apostolic and catholic faith was "one faith" because it was a faith that had been delivered once and for all and had been transmitted by apostolic tradition. Therefore it was unchanging and unchangeable, and the very suggestion that it had undergone change or development or growth seemed to strike at the foundations of apostolic continuity. Heretics could, and did, accuse the orthodox of having added such doctrines as transubstantiation to the original deposit of the faith, since it was not mentioned in any of the ancient creeds; to this the orthodox were obliged to reply that the doctrine had indeed been present from the beginning, but had not been asserted because it was accepted by everyone without question. To be sure, there were "some matters that are held but are not taught," open questions on which there was no clear witness of Scripture and tradition. Several such questions appeared in the doctrine of Mary, including the beginning of her life (whether or not she had been immaculately conceived) and the end of her life (whether or not she had been raised from the dead). On such questions "we do not dare to speak," one theologian asserted, while another, refusing to assert the doctrine of the immaculate conception or to sanction festivals in its honor, reserved to "the authority of the apostolic see" the right to speak on the matter. Such judgments seemed to assume that there could be some sort of development or growth; on the basis of patristic suggestions about how the doctrine of the Holy Spirit had developed, Thomas Aquinas defended the legitimacy of the Filioque by explaining that it "was contained implicitly in the faith that the Holy

Ghellinck (1948) 92

Petr.Ven.*Petrob*.29 (*CCCM* 10: 25)

Alan.Ins.*Haer*.1.59 (*PL* 210: 263)
Guib.Nog.*Pign*.1.1 (*PL* 156: 612)

See pp. 171–73 below
Guib.Nog.*Pign*.1.3 (*PL* 156: 623–24)

Brd.Clr.*Ep*.174.9 (Leclercq-Rochais 7:392)
Alex.Hal.*Quaest.disp*.36.3 (*BFS* 20:636–38)

See vol.1:211

Thos.Aq.*S.T*.1.36.2 ad 2 (*Ed. Leon.* 4:378)

Spirit proceeds from the Father" and that it had now been made explicit.

When we speak of "the growth of medieval theology," therefore, we are at one and the same time attempting, in our use of the term "theology," to replace the modern connotations of the term with those that were more congenial to medieval Christians, and yet superimposing the modern conceptions of what was "medieval" and, above all, the modern notion of "growth" as change and development upon the ideas and teachings of the Middle Ages. We are also continuing our practice in the first two volumes of paying attention only to the history of doctrine,

See vol.1:173; vol.2:4–5

even at the expense of fascinating and important questions outside the area of doctrine. To mention only a few examples, we shall not discuss the role of the conflict of personality in the stormy career of Peter Abelard; nor the threats of barbarian invasion that were believed to have

Bern.Reich.*V.Udal*.14 (*PL* 142:1191)

been repulsed by the power of the Virgin Mary; nor the habit of Berengar of Tours of consistently referring to his

Lanf.*Corp*.16 (*PL* 150:426); Brngr.Tr.*Coen*.12 (Beekenkamp 19)

opponent, Humbert of Silva Candida, as "that Burgundian"; nor the chilling account given by Hincmar of Reims about the death of Gottschalk, concluding with the words: "And when his end was approaching, his brethren who were present sought to persuade him to recant his wicked ideas and perverse beliefs and to accept Holy Communion. He replied that he could not recant his ideas and beliefs and that by authority he could not accept Communion. And so he concluded an unworthy life with a death that was worthy of it, and he departed into his own

Hinc.R.*Deit*.19 (*PL* 125:618)

place." Even the Crusades belong to our story only as a part of the confrontation between Western Christianity and the faiths of other men.

Within the scheme of the work as a whole, the present volume resumes the history of doctrine in the West with the seventh century, as the second volume did with the East in the same century. But in the Western church this was perceived to be a time when "the study of letters is dying, and no one is capable of preserving in writing the

Gr.Tr.*Hist.Franc*.pr. (*MGH Scrip.Mer*.1B:1)

Auerbach (1971) 84–85

doings of the present." Modern scholars, while deploring the excesses of that characterization, join in asserting that the point at which we begin here "was low tide on the

Waddell (1955) 30

Laistner (1966) 136

Continent of Europe," when "the continent of Western Europe was withered by a blight of intellectual sterility"

Lot (1961) 371

and by "a decadence which is incurable." The volume closes with the thirteenth century, at which point volume 4 will begin. Western developments, therefore, will require two volumes for the same period that has been covered by a single volume for the East. The Reformation itself would be justification enough for that disparity, which is also made necessary by the complexity of the history being recounted here in volume 3. The chronological division is necessarily arbitrary, as is the decision to include in volume 4 certain doctrinal movements that began in the twelfth or thirteenth century but that bear so close a relation to the history of the fourteenth and fifteenth centuries as to warrant treatment there. This is, in short, the history of what we have called "orthodox catholicism in the West" from the seventh century until the time when both its orthodoxy and its catholicity were fundamentally called into question by protest, by heresy, and ultimately by the Reformation.

See vol.1:349–57

The Integrity
of the
Catholic Tradition

In the Latin West, no less than in the Greek or the Syriac East, the seventh and eighth centuries were a time when the definition of Christian doctrine was set by the authority of tradition. "This," said the conclusion of a seventh-century treatise for Christian initiates, "is the true integrity of the catholic tradition of the faith; if any single part of it is denied, the power of the faith as a whole will be lost." The treatise was a compilation of quotations from the church fathers. As the author asserted at the very beginning, he was "not proposing novelties to our neophytes, but either making clear or noting for the future the admonitions of the fathers." "The integrity of the apostolic tradition" and "the integrity of the faith" continued to be a matter of concern to all theological parties. A "solicitude for integrity . . . in the truth of the catholic faith" meant to Alcuin, at the end of the eighth century, an adherence to the teachings of Christian antiquity. His imperial patron, following some of Alcuin's very words, urged that "the truth of the catholic faith be investigated," but such "investigation" meant to him that the faith should be "supported by the most solid testimonies of the holy fathers" and thus "maintained without any doubting." Later in the same epistle, Charlemagne echoed an Augustinian formula when he declared: "This is the catholic faith, and therefore it is ours."

Underlying such declarations of loyalty to the catholic tradition was the assumption that it was a unified whole, resting on the consensus of the orthodox teachers of the church. "To agree with the catholic consensus in every respect" was a mark of Christian modesty, according to a

Ildef.*Cog.bapt*.96 (*SPE* 1:324)

Ildef.*Cog.bapt*.pr. (*SPE* 1:238) Nicol.I.*Ep*.82 (*MGH Ep.* 6: 434) Agob.*Fel*.1 (*PL* 104:34); Radb.*Matt*.2.3 (*PL* 120:182); Scot.Er.*Ev.Joh*.3.1 (*SC* 180: 200)

Alc.*Fel.haer*.1 (*PL* 101:87–88); Rab.*Inst.cler*.pr. (Knoepfler 3)

Alc.*Ep.* 201 (*MGH Ep.* 4:334)

Car.M.*Ep.Elip.* (*MGH Conc.* 2:160)

Aug.*Trin*.1.5 (*CCSL* 50:36) Car.M.*Ep.Elip.* (*MGH Conc.* 2:164)

Ps.Cypr.*Abus*.5 (*TU* 34:42)

Bed.*Gen*.pr. (*CCSL* 118A:1–2)
Bed.*H.e*.4.17 (Plummer 239)

Alc.*Fel*.3.14 (*PL* 101:170)

Alc.*Ep*.23 (*MGH Ep*.4:61)

Alc.*Elip*.4.2 (*PL* 101:287)

Alc.*Fel*.1.6 (*PL* 101:132–33)

Isid.Sev.*Exp.sac*.pr.5 (*PL* 83:209)

Ogara (1936) 141

Bed.*Luc*.pr. (*CCSL* 120:5)

Laistner (1966) 163

Southern (1970) 7

Bed.*Luc*.pr. (*CCSL* 120:7–8)

Ambr.Aut.*Apoc*.pr. (*CCCM* 27:5)

seventh-century manual. Bede made an effort to set forth "the meaning of . . . the catholic fathers" in his commentaries, and he spoke of "the unanimous consensus of all in the catholic faith." By the time of Alcuin it was customary to refer to "the total unanimity of the catholic church" as the criterion of orthodox doctrine. This true doctrine of the gospel, taught and preached unanimously by the church, was "shining brightly through the whole world." To his opponents Alcuin set forth the contrast between this unanimous consensus and their theological isolation; "you alone," he charged, "are opposed to all of these, you alone have usurped the distinctive title of 'master.'" He challenged them to produce a single nation or city that agreed with them rather than with the universal church, whose spokesman he was. Other Western spokesmen in these centuries—whether British or Spanish, Italian or Frankish—would have agreed.

Yet it would be a mistake to conclude from this that all the theologians of these centuries were content to do no more than simply to repeat and transmit the patristic consensus. Isidore of Seville was so devoted to such repetition and transmission of "the ancients" that it has become almost obligatory for a modern work on him to identify him as a "compiler." Nevertheless, even his theological imagination, although skillfully concealed, was operative in the selection and arrangement of his material into an "immense farrago of the ancient world." In the case of Bede, the creative element was permitted to make its presence more evident. He styled himself a "compiler" of what had been said by the theological genius of the church fathers, but he "knit the whole together in a way which raises his theological works well above the level of mere compilation or catenae." Even amid his disclaimers of originality he "aimed not only at copying the thoughts of greater men, but at completing them," for he admitted that he had "added some tokens of his own effort as the Author of light revealed them." Ambrose Autpert, a Benedictine of the eighth century, while asserting that he was "following the faith and the ideas of catholics," also acknowledged that he had "added from my own resources, or rather from the gift of the grace of God, many things in which [the church fathers] seem to be deficient" in the interpretation of the Apocalypse of John. Another commentary on the Apocalypse included the prayer that

Beat.*Apoc*.1.3.6 (Sanders 54)

the Holy Spirit would make the author worthy of adding something to what his ancestors had said about the book. Alcuin was likewise an industrious and encyclopedic collector of ancient authorities, one who followed the consensus of the fathers, "introducing nothing novel and accepting nothing but what is to be found in their catholic

Alc.*Fel*.1.4 (*PL* 101:131)

writings." Yet it was his "study of earlier authors" that "opened the way for comparison of texts" and for "the reawakening of dialectical exercises in the field of theol-

Levison (1946) 157

ogy." This combination of adherence to authority (auctoritas) with independent critical reflection (ratio), in widely varying proportions, was to characterize Western theology throughout the Middle Ages.

The Faith and the Creed

Symb.Ath.1 (Schaff 2:66)

See vol.1:351
CTol. (633) *Cap*.1 (Mansi 10: 615–16)

CAut. (670) (*MGH Conc*.1: 220)

"Whoever wants to be saved, it is necessary above all that he hold the catholic faith." This opening declaration of the Athanasian Creed was restated in the confession of faith adopted by the Fourth Council of Toledo in 633; the authority of the Creed was also affirmed at the Second Synod of Autun in about 670; and the collection of ser-

Bonif.*Serm*.1.1 (*PL* 89:843)

mons attributed to Boniface the missionary, near the middle of the next century, paraphrased this opening declaration in its own first paragraph. These words meant that the standard of orthodox doctrine defined by the

Bed.*Gen*.2 (*CCSL* 118A:105);
Hinc.R.*Deit*.2 (*PL* 125:514)

fathers and councils of the church was the measure of authentic Christian believing. To this "rule of catholic faith and truth" every true believer had to conform. The integrity of the catholic tradition was safeguarded by the rule of faith.

See vol.1:117

Whatever the term "rule of faith" may have meant in patristic usage, it seems that by this time it was usually identified with the several creeds confessed by the church.

Ambr.Aut.*Apoc*.2 (*CCCM* 27: 102)

A common name for creed was "symbol," as in the title of Augustine's work *The Faith and the Creed* {De fide et

Aug.*Fid.et symb.* (*PL* 40:181–96)

symbolo}, which was frequently quoted in the early Middle Ages. The name was known to have come from the Greek and to mean "sign." As the disciples were about to be scattered abroad throughout the world, they had been

Beat.*Elip*.1.87 (*PL* 96:946–47)

moved to formulate this sign for their preaching; it contained "the confession of the Trinity, the unity of the

Isid.Sev.*Orig*.6:57–58 (*PL* 82: 257)

church, and the entire mystery of Christian dogma." What Christ in the days of his flesh had handed on by tradition to his disciples, they had in turn handed on by tradition

Bed.*H.e.*4.17 (Plummer 239)

Hinc.R.*Deit.*11 (*PL* 125:561)

Ildef.*Cog.bapt.*133 (*SPE* 1:
366–68)
Prim.*Scar.*32 (Jecker 70)
Bonif.*Serm.*5.3; 15.4 (*PL* 89:
853;870); Aud.*V.Elig.*2.16
(*MGH Scrip.Mer.*4:705)
Isid.Sev.*Sent.*1.21.1 (*SPE* 2:
287); Beat.*Elip.*1.36 (*PL* 96:
913–14); CFr. (794)
*Cap.*33 (*MGH Conc.*2–I:169)

Alc.*Ep.Beat.* (Levison 320)

Ps.111:3 (Vulg.)

Isid.Sev.*Sent.*2.5.2 (*SPE* 2:
310)

Alc.*Fel.*2.3 (*PL* 101:148)

Radb.*Ep.Fr.* (*CCCM* 16:157)
Ambr.Aut.*Apoc.*2 (*CCCM* 27:
166–67)

Isid.Sev.*Orig.*8.2.4 (*PL* 82:
296)

Jul.Tol.*Aet.sext.*2.14 (*PL* 96:
568)

Ambr.Aut.*Vit.virt.*11 (*PL*
40:1097)

Ambr.Aut.*Apoc.*1 (*CCCM* 27:
28)

Isid.Sev.*Sent.*2.2.13 (*SPE* 2:
307); Ambr.Aut.*Apoc.*2
(*CCCM* 27:119)

Bed.*Ep.*15 (*PL* 94:709); Bonif.
*Serm.*6.2 (*PL* 89:856)

to the church in the form of the creedal symbol, and "their successors, apostolic men, in six ecumenical councils . . . and in other catholic synods, confirmed by the holy see," had carried it on. The missionary literature of the eighth century commended the symbol together with the Lord's Prayer (which continued to receive expositions of its own) as the content of what converts to Christianity were to learn. In the brief compass of these two texts "the entire breadth of the Scriptures is embraced," so that they sufficed for the children of the church as an epitome of the entire law of the gospel. One way to refer to the creed could therefore be "the symbol of catholic peace," as it was sung and confessed in the church. The function of the symbol as something confessed served to give it its status as a doctrinal authority. The psalmist had said that "confession and magnificence are [God's] work," which meant that the ability to make a confession of faith did not lie within human power, since no one had contributed any good work by which to merit receiving the confession of faith; it must be a gift of divine grace.

What the church confessed and believed was "the faith of all catholics," which was, in turn, what it had been taught by the apostles. Believing, teaching, and confessing belonged together. To believe meant to accept that which one could not see, so that "faith" could be defined as "that by which we truly believe what we are completely incapable of seeing." From this subjective definition it was easy to move to the use of the word "faith" not for the act of believing, but for its content, the relation between God and man. The "definition of the Christian faith" pertained to past things that were narrated in the gospel message and to future things for which believers hoped. "Those who consent to the Christian faith" was a title that could be applied even to those members of the church who negated such consent by their mode of life, and "those who do not violate the faith concerning Christ and the church" was a term for orthodox believers. Although it was possible to distinguish between "faith" and "doctrine," as when Isidore spoke of those who "are Christians only in their faith, but in their work dissent from Christian doctrine," the pattern of usage was determined by the practice of calling Christian doctrine "the faith" or "the catholic faith" in the sense of that with which one's speaking and writing had to agree. Alcuin composed a

Alc.*Ep*.268 (*MGH Ep*.4:426)

Heb.11:6
Alc.*Trin*.1.1 (*PL* 101:14)
Alc.*Fel*.6.8 (*PL* 101:209);
Car.M.*Ep.Elip*. (*MGH Conc.*
2:158)

Alc.*Fel*.1.3 (*PL* 101:130)

Alc.*Ep.Beat*. (Levison 321)

Alc.*Ep*.23 (*MGH Ep*.4:61)

Acts 2:42

Jul.Tol.*Nah*.22 (*PL* 96:717)

Ildef.*Itin.des*.9 (*SPE* 1:386)

Ambr.Aut.*Luc*. (*PL* 95:1530–31)

Isid.Sev.*Sent*.3.36.1 (*SPE* 2:473)

Ps.Cypr.*Abus*.10 (*TU* 34:56);
Alc.*Ep*.280 (*MGH Ep*.4:437)

Ps.Cypr.*Abus*.1 (*TU* 34:33)

Bed.*Act*.1 (Laistner 6)
See vol.2:254

Isid.Sev.*Sent*.3.10.1 (*SPE* 2:432)

Aldh.*Virg*.2 (*MGH Auct.Ant.*
15:230)
Isid.Sev.*Orig*.8.2.1 (*PL* 82:295)
Isid.Sev.*Orig*.6.19.58 (*PL* 82:257); Ambr.Aut.*V.Pald*.3
(*MGH Scrip.Lang*.549); Beat.
Elip.1.62 (*PL* 96:931)
Ambr.Aut.*Apoc*.4 (*CCCM* 27:361); Beat.*Apoc*.2.1.54
(Sanders 168)

See vol.2:68–75

treatise (now lost) on "the catholic faith," and he identified faith in this dogmatic sense as that of which the New Testament said: "Without faith it is impossible to please [God]." He spoke of being "inside the walls of the catholic faith" as the only assurance of avoiding error. The sanctity of this catholic faith was to be defended against heresy.

The relation between "faith" and "doctrine" in Alcuin's language can be seen from such a formula as "catholic doctrine believes" or from his term for heresy: "any doctrine that is found outside the walls of the faith of the church and the doctrine of the apostles." Even where there was no such discrimination of terms, however, "the doctrine of the apostles," a New Testament concept, was coordinated with the "decrees and canons of the orthodox fathers" in the structure of church authority. The apostles were the wellsprings from which the church was to drink its doctrine. An important constituent in the definition of the term "doctrine" was the distinction between it and "deeds" or "life" or "work." The preacher was to be "a shining example both in doctrine and in life," for the former without the latter made a man arrogant while the latter without the former made him useless. The bishop was to exhibit "in his work" what he taught others "in his language about doctrine." A discrepancy between the works of the preacher and the words of his preaching could cause his hearers to despise his "doctrine." Bede reminded his hearers that in the New Testament the rule was: "First do, and then teach"; for as earlier theologians had also said, practice was the basis of theory. To be effective, doctrine needed the assistance of divine grace, without which it would remain in the ears but never penetrate to the heart. But with the help of grace, "divine dogmas" were a means of fostering the spiritual life of the children of the church. Thus the word "dogma," which had been used as a term for philosophical opinions, could now become a synonym for "Christian doctrine," although it was also customary to speak of the "perverse dogmas" of the heretics.

Christian doctrine was handed on from one generation of the church to the next in the form of the orthodox tradition. The British prelates assembled at the Council of Hatfield in 680 invoked the tradition in support of the position defined as orthodox over against Monotheletism, "as our incarnate Lord Jesus Christ handed on by tradition to his disciples, those who saw him in person and heard his sermons, and as the symbol of the holy fathers handed on by tradition, as well as all the holy and universal councils in concert and the chorus of all the eminent teachers of the catholic church." It was this decree that Bede identified as "the unanimous consensus of all in the catholic faith." When he himself came to the task of expounding Scripture, he insisted on presenting the explanation that had been "handed on by tradition from the fathers." Moreover, he laid it down as a requirement for anyone sent to preach to Jews or to heathen that he "teach those things that the church has received and learned through the apostles," for anyone who took it upon himself "on his own initiative" to teach something new and different was not fit to be a teacher and preacher in the church. An orthodox teacher was, by Isidore's definition, "one who believes correctly and who lives as he believes." Such a teacher, according to the Greek origin of the word "orthodox," was "a man who is correct in how he gives glory [to God], a name to which someone is not entitled if he lives otherwise than he believes."

Greek etymology was also the source for Isidore's definition of the word "catholic," which was, he said, synonymous with "universal or general." A bit later in his *Origins* he elaborated: "Catholic [means] universal, that is, according to the whole." The difference between the catholic church and "the conventicles of the heretics" was that the church extended through the whole world, while the adherents of a particular false doctrine were confined to a few regions. This distinction was eventually to be cited by the defenders of catholic doctrine against Isidore's Spanish successors, who for their part would declare: "We believe and confess the holy catholic church, spread throughout the world by the preaching of the apostles . . . among the catholics, not the heretics." In Bede's England, the conflict between universal and particular, while different dogmatically from that in Spain, did involve the issue of catholicity, so that "in the *Ecclesiastical History* his short sketches of men and women are concerned mainly with the two problems: Are they 'Catholici' and do their works conform to their belief?" In evaluating a theologian of the past, Ambrose Autpert said, "one should not be prejudiced by the period in which he wrote, but should

CHat. (680) ap.Bed.*H.e*.4.17 (Plummer 239)

See p. 10 above

Bed.*Luc*.pr. (*CCSL* 120:7–8)

Bed.*Temp*. (*CCSL* 119A:200); Beat.*Elip*.1.15 (*PL* 96:903)

Isid.Sev.*Orig*.7.14.5 (*PL* 82:294)

Isid.Sev.*Orig*.7.14.4 (*PL* 82:294); Ambr.Aut.*Apoc*.7 (*CCCM* 27:570); Beat.*Apoc*.2.pr.1.2 (Sanders 102)

Isid.Sev.*Orig*.8.1.1 (*PL* 82:293–94); Isid.Sev.*Sent*.1.16.6 (*SPE* 2:271)

See p. 52 below

Fel.ap.Alc.*Fel*.1.4 (*PL* 101:130)

Carroll (1946) 67

Ambr.Aut.*Apoc*.6 (*CCCM* 27:465)

Bed.*Gen*.1 (*CCSL* 118A:69)

Alc.*Elip*.1.14 (*PL* 101:250);
Alc.*Ep*.166 (*MGH Ep*.4:269)

Alc.*Elip*.3.12 (*PL* 101:279)

Kleinclausz (1948) 212

Alc.*Ep.Beat*. (Levison 322);
Episc.Fr.*Ep.Elip*. (*MGH Conc*.
2–I:156); Ambr.Aut.*Apoc*.9
(*CCCM* 27:761)

Alc.*Fel*.pr. (*MGH Ep*.4:337)

Alc.*Ep*.137 (*MGH Ep*.4:211)

See vol. 2:19–20

Jul.Tol.*Prog.fut*.2.36 (*PL* 96:495–96);
Jul.Tol.*Prog.fut*.1.13–15 (*PL* 96:467–72)

seek to discern only whether what he wrote is true and catholic or false and heretical." For, according to Bede, it was "only in that unity which is called 'catholic' that the gate of life is open to all." Bede's spiritual descendant, Alcuin of York, proudly identified himself as "a catholic, born and reared in the catholic church," and he was convinced that apart from the "truth of the church" there could be no salvation.

To Alcuin, as to his predecessors in the seventh and eighth centuries, this "truth of the church" was that which had been defined by the fathers of the church. What has been called "the self-effacement of Alcuin in relation to the fathers" was the dominant theme and method of his theology. In all questions of doctrine, he said, "I wish to follow the footsteps of the holy fathers, neither adding to nor subtracting from their most sacred writings." They had become the fathers of the church by virtue of their having "begotten us in Christ" through their fidelity to authentic Christian teaching. Therefore one would not err if one resolved to abide "in the company of such men within the camp of the catholic faith," for outside that camp were the enemies of the faith. Or, to shift the metaphor, the testimony of the church fathers was "the public highway of apostolic doctrine," in fact "the royal road." The pilgrim could travel safely on this road; but if he strayed "to the right or to the left" away from it, he would be lost in "the detours of one or another sort of novelty." The compilation of quotations from the fathers could be taken as the proper method of theology because of the authoritarian system of doctrinal verification within which they were thought to hold the position of harmonious and unimpeachable witnesses to orthodox doctrine.

A catalog of the specific fathers employed as witnesses would, if pressed far enough, probably include most of the names, if not all of the writings, that appeared in similar compilations of patristic texts in the East. In view of the widespread incapacity of East and West to read each other's languages and to understand each other's writers, it is not surprising to find that the Latin fathers predominated in the Western compilations. Thus Cyprian, "the renowned doctor and wonder-working master" of the church, was a source to be quoted at considerable length. When a particular Latin father, such as Jerome,

Beat.*Apoc*.pr.2–3 (Sanders 2–5); Alc.*Ep*.251 (*MGH Ep*.4: 407)

See vol. 2:64–65

Alc.*Fel.haer*.39 (*PL* 101:103)
See vol.1:320–24
See vol.1:338–39
Alc.*Fel*.1.19 (*PL* 101:143)

Harnack (1931) 3:259
Ambr.Aut.*Apoc*.7 (*CCCM* 27:602)

Paulin.Aquil.*Fel*.3.2.7 (*PL* 99: 463); Hadr.I.*Ep.episc.Hisp.* (*MGH Conc.* 2–I:125)
Radb.*Corp*.9 (*CCCM* 16:60)
Radb.*Corp*.9 (*CCCM* 16:53–54); Rup.*Div.off*.3.20 (*CCCM* 7:93)

CTol. (653) (Mansi 10:1215)
Alc.*Elip*.2.8 (*PL* 101:266)

Ambr.Aut.*Assump*.3 (*PL* 39: 2130)

Jul.Tol.*Prog.fut*.3.5 (*PL* 96: 499–500); Elip.*Ep*.1.10 (*PL* 96:865)

Bed.*Gen*.1 (*CCSL* 118A:53)

Alc.*Trin*.pr. (*MGH Ep*.4:415)
Hinc.R.*Deit*.1 (*PL* 125:489)

Bed.*Luc*.pr. (*CCSL* 120:10)

had expounded a book of the Bible, a commentary on that book would draw copiously from his work. Pope Leo I, a Latin author who was also much beloved of the Greek theologians of this period, was hailed as "a man of the utmost fidelity to the catholic faith and of outstanding reputation for his eloquence in speaking of the relation between the divine and the human natures in Christ." Despite his polemic against Augustine, Cassian was quoted, because of his espousal of the consensus of the church, as an authority for "the catholic faith." But the most notable characteristic of the appeal to patristic authority in these centuries was the pattern by which one generation's echo became the next generation's voice: theologians who had wanted to do no more than to repeat the fathers were themselves elevated to the company of the fathers. Gregory the Great, for all his repetition of Augustine, was "the most widely read of the Western church fathers." He was "outstanding among the writers of the church," praised for his eloquence and his faith. In the controversies of the ninth century over the Eucharist Gregory came to be cited as an authority in his own right, as did the Venerable Bede. Less than two decades after his death, Isidore of Seville, the docile "compiler" of earlier authorities, was being designated "the most recent ornament of the catholic church" and "the most learned of men now at the end of the ages," and his theological works were held in "the highest veneration" by the centuries that followed.

Although the fathers being cited included the orthodox teachers of both East and West, among them for example Chrysostom, it was principally Augustine, either directly or indirectly, upon whom the seventh and eighth centuries—as well as the ninth and those that followed—drew for their understanding of church doctrine, "very often without even mentioning his name." When the doctrine to be discussed was the dogma of the Trinity, it was natural to cite "the reasons that Father Augustine in his books on the Holy Trinity regarded as of primary importance," or to cite "Augustine and the other orthodox theologians" as authorities in trinitarian doctrine. But in the exegesis of Scripture it was no less necessary, as Bede said, to include "testimonies from the blessed Augustine," as well as from other church fathers. So, for example, one entire book of Bede's *Allegorical Exposition of the Song* of Songs was compiled from the writings of Gregory the Great, who had, in turn, depended on the writings of Augustine. Julian of Toledo, "the most competent theologian among the Visigothic bishops of Spain," affirmed the standing of Augustine as "the eminent doctor"; and when he came to write his examination of apparent contradictions in the Old and New Testaments, he gathered quotations from Augustine and Gregory. From such quotations and from the catalogs of manuscripts in monastic libraries it is evident how dominant a place Augustine held in the intellectual and theological life of the early Middle Ages. In the Carolingian era he was hailed by Servatus Lupus as "an author of utmost sweetness and reputation," as "a man possessed of a genius that was divine," and as "Augustine, of whom I cannot say whether he was more admirable for his content or for his style."

The quality that marked Augustine and the other orthodox fathers was their loyalty to the received tradition. The apostolic anathema pronounced against anyone, even "an angel from heaven," who preached "a gospel contrary to that which you have received" by tradition was, as in the East so also in the West, a prohibition of any kind of theological novelty. The Latin text of the New Testament urged that "novelties of terminology [novitates vocum]" be avoided. One definition of heretics could be "those who now take pleasure in making up new terminology for themselves and who are not content with the dogma of the holy fathers." Fathers of the stature of Leo had asserted that "the birth . . . of Christ . . . passes all understanding," and therefore "what is it that these new scrutinizers of the secrets of God suppose that they understand" when such secrets had been hidden from "the ancient fathers and the catholic doctors?" One who denied the consensus of such catholic doctors on the doctrine of Mary was dismissed as "the fabricator of a new error." But even those who were eventually denounced as heretics shared a fidelity to "apostolic doctrine" and "catholic faith" and an antipathy to "all novelties," and it was possible to appeal to them "to permit nothing new, nothing contrary to apostolic traditions, to arise."

Etymologically, the word "heresy" had come from the Greek word for "choice," so that the heretics were those who chose a "perverse dogma" and for its sake withdrew from the fellowship of the orthodox church. Such with-

Bed.*Cant*.7 (*PL* 91:1223–36)

See vol.1:350–51

Murphy (1951) 361
Jul.Tol.*Prog.fut*.1.9–12 (*PL* 96:464–66)

Jul.Tol.*Antikeim.* (*PL* 96:595–704)

Serv.Lup.*Ep*.4 (*MGH Ep*.6:14)
Serv.Lup.*Ep*.5 (*MGH Ep*.6:15–16)
Serv.Lup.*Quaest.* (*PL* 119:634)

Gal.1:8–9

See vol.2:9

Ambr.Aut.*Apoc*.pr. (*CCCM* 27:7); Alc.*Ep.Beat.* (Levison 318–19)

1 Tim.6:20 (Vulg.)

Alc.*Ep*. 166 (*MGH Ep*.4:272)

Alc.*Ep.Beat.* (Levison 322)

Leo M.*Serm*.10.4 (*SC* 22:174)

Alc.*Fel.haer*.41 (*PL* 101:104)

Ildef.*Virg.Mar*.2 (*SPE* 1:57)

Alc.*Ep.Beat.* (Levison 318–19)

Isid.Sev.*Orig*.8.3.1 (*PL* 82:296); Rab.*Inst.cler*.2.58 (Knoepfler 175)

Aldh.*Virg*.8 (*MGH Auct.Ant.*
15:236)
See vol.1:69
Beat.*Apoc*.2.pr.7.1–7 (Sanders
129–30); Beat.*Elip*.2.30 (*PL*
96:995); Ambr.Aut.*Apoc*.9
(*CCCM* 27:726); Hinc.R.
Deit.11 (*PL* 125:561–62)

Jul.Tol.*Nab*.61 (*PL* 96: 734);
Ambr.Aut.*Apoc*.4 (*CCCM* 27:
333)

Leand.Sev.*Laud.eccl.* (*PL* 72:
896)

Isid.Sev.*Proëm.* (*PL* 83:163)

Isid.Sev.*Sent*.1.16.3 (*SPE* 2:
270); Agob.*Fel*.2 (*PL* 104:35)

Jul.Tol.*Nab*.51 (*PL* 96:730);
Bed.*Marc*.3 (*CCSL* 120:552);
Ambr.Aut.*Apoc*.6 (*CCCM* 27:
508–9)

Isid.Sev.*Sent*.3.12.7 (*SPE* 2:
435)

Bed.*E.et N*.3 (*CCSL* 119A:
377); Isid.Sev.*Sent*.1.16.5 (*SPE*
2:270–71); Hinc.R.*Deit*.pr.
(*PL* 125:481–82); Scot.Er.
Praed.1.3 (*PL* 122:359)

Ambr.Aut.*Apoc*.pr. (*CCCM*
27:5)

Alc.*Fel*.pr. (*MGH Ep*.4:337);
Alc.*Fel*.2.8 (*PL* 101:152–53)
Ambr.Aut.*Apoc*.1; 6 (*CCCM*
27:52; 544–45)
See vol.1:151–52

Ildef.*Cog.bapt*.96 (*SPE* 1:
324); Beat.*Apoc*.11.4.13–14
(Sanders 601)

Jul.Tol.*Prog.fut*.2.28 (*PL* 96:
490)
Jul.Tol.*Antikeim*.1.37 (*PL* 96:
614); Amal.*Off*.3.44.1 (*ST*
139:381); Guib.Nog.*Laud.
Mar*.6 (*PL* 156:554)

drawal from catholic unity was also characteristic of "schismatics," and the distinction between schism and heresy was sometimes, but not always, observed; it was even possible to refer to simony as "heresy." Heresy was the second of the storms that had raged against the church, the first having been that of the heathen and the third having been that of false Christians. As those who violated catholic unity and who therefore "love Christ with an adulterous love," heretics did not deserve a legitimate place in the Christian family. Like the friends of Job, they were hypocrites and teachers of "perverse dogmas." And while the church "patiently tolerates those in her midst who lead an evil life," she rejected and excommunicated those "who believe an evil faith." Some enemies of the church lived without her sacraments and outside her fellowship, some outside her fellowship but within her sacraments. But the most dangerous were those who lived within the church and within her sacraments, but were enemies nonetheless; such were the heretics. They did not stop short of interpolating their doctrines into books by orthodox fathers. Nevertheless, it was important to recognize that the rise of heresy had sometimes provoked the orthodox church into clarification of its doctrine that might never have been possible had not its enemies made such clarification necessary.

Nor was a heretic always consistent in his treatment of the catholic faith, for sometimes a theologian who erred gravely on fundamental doctrines could, by mixing "honey" with his "poison," also be a witness to orthodoxy. Writing against a position that he denounced as heretical, Alcuin felt able to use the writings of Origen, but only where he had been in agreement with the orthodox fathers. Among Spanish theologians, as among orthodox theologians generally, such Origenist doctrines as the restoration of all creatures, including the devil, to their original dignity were rejected as "sacrilegious disputation." But in Spain one could also speak of what "Origen, the doctor, teaches in his dogmas" even in the area of eschatology. Various theologians could resolve exegetical difficulties by quoting what "we find to have been explained in this way by Origen." It would seem that the definition of the rule of faith was thought to be so clear and so secure that even a heretic such as Origen could be studied and quoted without becoming a threat to the integrity of the catholic tradition.

*Symb.Ath.*1 (Schaff 2:66)

After affirming that "whoever wants to be saved, it is necessary above all that he hold the catholic faith," the Athanasian Creed had gone on to specify the two cardinal dogmas that formed the main content of that faith. "And the catholic faith is this," it continued, "that we worship

*Symb.Ath.*3 (Schaff 2:66)

one God in Trinity"; and in a later article it added: "Furthermore it is necessary to eternal salvation that one faithfully believe the incarnation of our Lord Jesus

*Symb.Ath.*29 (Schaff 2:68)

Christ." The mysteries of the Trinity and of the person of the God-man constituted the rule of faith of the church catholic, and orthodox adherence to them determined the

Agob.*Fel.*3 (*PL* 104:35)

integrity of the catholic tradition. The mark of the genuine "catholic Christian," then, was that "he preserves the true faith of the Trinity with a firm readiness to believe, and that he repudiates the thinking of heretical perversion." The church catholic was that society "which remains

Ambr.Aut.*Purif.*5 (*PL* 89: 1295–96)

faithful to one Lord as to its legitimate husband." A concern for the preservation of this trinitarian loyalty—as, for example, when Bede, on the basis of patristic precedent, found the doctrine of the Trinity in the first two

Bed.*Gen.*1 (*CCSL* 118A:7)

verses of the Bible—pervaded Western Latin Christendom during the early Middle Ages, partly because of the persistence of indigenous Arianism among the Visigoths and other Germanic tribes.

Because of this threat, but even more because of Byzantine theology, Charlemagne commissioned Alcuin to undertake a thorough exposition of the faith of the church on this fundamental issue. Except for its presenta-

Alc.*Ep.*257 (*MGH Ep.*4:414– 15)

tion of the distinctive Western theologoumenon on the procession of the Holy Spirit from both the Father and the Son rather than from the Father only, Alcuin's summary was a thoroughly conventional recitation of what the Christians in the East as well as in the West taught about the Trinity. For example, he repeated the standard principle—which had special importance in the polemical context in which he was writing—that "wherever in Holy Scripture we read, 'God alone,' this should not be taken as referring to any one person in the Holy Trinity, but to

Alc.*Trin.*2.18 (*PL* 101:35)

the entire Holy Trinity." Even when, later in the ninth century, the theological discussion turned to the question of the real presence in the Eucharist, "the footsteps of the

Radb.*Corp*.9 (*CCCM* 16:56)

Hinc.R.*Ep*.1 (*MGH Ep*. 8:1)

Ambr.Aut.*Apoc*.3; 7; 9 (*CCCM* 27:181; 628; 678)

Isid.Sev.*Sent*.1.1.1 (*SPE* 2: 226)

Isid.Sev.*Sent*.1.6.1 (*SPE* 2: 236)

See vol.1:54

Ex.3:14
Jul.Tol.*Antikeim*.1.24 (*PL* 96: 607)
Alc.*Ep*.268 (*MGH Ep*.4:426);
Paulin.Aquil.*Fel*.1.14 (*PL* 99: 366); Scot.Er.*Praed*.9.4 (*PL* 122:391)

Alc.*Trin*.1.9–10 (*PL* 101:19)

Alc.*Trin*.2.6 (*PL* 101:27);
Hinc.R.*Recl*.1
(Gundlach 302); Beat.*Apoc*. 4.5.121 (Sanders 388)

John 17:21
Alc.*Trin*.2.1 (*PL* 101:23–24)

Alc.*Ep*.163 (*MGH Ep*.4:263)

See vol.2:264–65

Isid.Sev.*Sent*.2.1.5 (*SPE* 2: 304)

Isid.Sev.*Sent*.1.2.4 (*SPE* 2:229)

Jul.Tol.*Antikeim*.1.24 (*PL* 96:607)

fathers" in the doctrine of the Trinity were a continuing point of theological reference; and a typical ordination vow of the ninth century opened with a trinitarian confession of faith.

Underlying the trinitarian dogma now, as in its origins, were certain axioms about the unchangeable nature of the divine, which continued to be asserted as self-evident long after their philosophical presuppositions were no longer consciously affirmed as such. The opening article of Isidore's *Sentences* was a discussion of the absoluteness of God, who could not be changed; for while the mutable creature was good, it was not the highest good, which only the immutable God could be. As immutable and eternal, God transcended time, having neither past nor future but only an eternal present within himself, since in his eternal awareness all things were included. The basic passage cited by the fathers in proof of this doctrine of God was the word of God to Moses: "I am who I am." This text continued to be "a sign of the divine essence" and to serve as proof that in his eternal essence God was "immutable." In the Godhead one must not assume that anything was "accidental" to the divine essence, since God was utterly immutable. Biblical language about such apparently mutable divine characteristics as "wrath" was not to be understood in an anthropopathic way, since "God is wrathful without any possibility or disturbance of his simple nature, nor of course any change." The ontological distinction between Creator and creature was to be preserved even in the most intimate of biblical statements about the union of God and man through Christ. While the human soul was immortal, it was not immutable, for only God was "truly and properly eternal." All of this suggested what the East called "apophatic theology," the principle that one could speak of the divine only in negative terms. "God is known correctly only when we deny that he can be known perfectly" at all. For even as theology spoke about God, it had to acknowledge that no human language was capable of speaking properly about the ineffable mystery of God.

It is, however, important to recognize that all such affirmations, whatever their affinities to Eastern theology, were in fact articulated "on the basis of the distinctions stated by Augustine." So much was this the case that some Augustinian distinctions in the doctrine of the Trinity

Alc.*Trin*.1.3 (*PL* 101:16)

Aug.*Trin*.15.17.27 (*CCSL* 50: 501)

Ildef.*Cog.bapt*.65 (*SPE* 1:298); Beat.*Apoc*.12.2.17 (Sanders 621); Radb.*Matt*.2.1 (*PL* 120: 111)

Aug.*Trin*.14.4.6 (*CCSL* 40: 428)

Jul.Tol.*Nah*.38 (*PL* 96:725)

See vol.2:183–98

Ildef.*Cog.bapt*.3; 55 (*SPE* 1: 240; 293)

Hymn.*lat*.2.144 (*Anal.Hymn*. 50:193–94); Cyn.*Chr*. 357–58 (Cook 14); Od.Clun.*Occup*. 6.621–36 (Swoboda 137); Fulb.*Hymn*.26 (*PL* 141:351)

Ildef.*Cog.bapt*.59 (*SPE* 1:295); Ildef.*Virg.Mar*.8 (*SPE* 1:106)

were not so much asserted as taken for granted by the main body of Western theology, for example, the crucial distinction between what was said of God "according to his essence" and what was said of him "according to the relations among the three persons." As part of his trinitarian speculations, Augustine had come to view the Holy Spirit as "the mutual love by which the Father and the Son love each other reciprocally." This identification had become part of the way Western theologians understood orthodox trinitarianism, so that "the Holy Spirit is properly called 'love,' probably because by nature he joins those from whom he proceeds." Another idiosyncratic theme of Augustine's *On the Trinity* was its exploration of psychological analogues within human experience for the transcendent relations between the divine persons. Since the human soul was created in the image not of a lonely single God but in that of the Trinity, there had to be some analogous relation between the soul and the Trinity. This analogous relation was found, on the basis of Augustine's trinitarian view of the world and of the soul, in "human consciousness," where a human trinity of "mind, intellect, and love" served as a way of acknowledging the divine Trinity.

The most striking, and ecumenically the most fateful, example of the pervasive authority of Augustine in Latin trinitarian theology was the almost automatic manner in which Western theologians accepted the idea of the Filioque. It seems clear that if Eastern theology had not challenged this idea as an unwarranted tampering with the text of the Nicene Creed and as a unilateral act of dogmatic legislation by one of the five apostolic patriarchs, the West would have gone on teaching it as a part of the undisputed (and therefore indisputable) heritage of the orthodox faith. Before such challenges from the East, the Filioque was merely stated, not argued. Its place in Western theology and worship is evident from its repeated appearance as a commonplace in liturgical and devotional poetry. In the seventh century it was taught that the difference between the Son and the Spirit in the Trinity lay in the former's being eternally begotten only by the Father and the latter's proceeding from both the Father and the Son. A creed adopted at Rome in that century and reaffirmed by the English church glorified "God the Father . . . and the Son . . . and the Holy Spirit, who proceeds in an ineffable way from the Father and the Son." Because the Holy Spirit was the Spirit "both of the Father and of the Son," the Father and the Son were one in their possessing the Spirit, who proceeded from them both. Soon thereafter, "the catholic faith" was asserted to be trinitarian in the sense that "the Father has the Son, the Son has the Father, and the Holy Spirit proceeds from the Father and the Son," since "the Father is the principle [principium] of the Godhead." By the time of the Carolingian disputes with the East, it was altogether natural for Western teachers to assert that the Holy Spirit "proceeds completely from the Father, and completely from the Son," or even that "the Holy Spirit . . . proceeds from the Father and the Son according to the essence" of the Godhead. This equation of the Augustinian version of the trinitarian dogma with the universal faith of the church helps to explain the response of the West to the Greek attacks upon its theory of Filioque. Only much later in the Middle Ages, and then only rarely, was it suggested that the entire issue was merely a dispute over words.

The other major component in the integrity of the catholic tradition was the doctrine of the person of Christ. Like the trinitarian dogma, it had come from the councils of the early church, which were no longer subject to dispute. Yet in the Syriac and the Greek East it continued to be a major issue of theological debate, with significant participation also by the Latin West in the outcome of the disputes. The distinctive achievement of Western theology in the Middle Ages was to consist in a further development of the doctrine of the work of Christ rather than of the doctrine of the person of Christ, but at this point of our narrative it needs only to be noted that for the seventh and eighth centuries the formal authority of the christological dogma stood alongside that of the trinitarian dogma as part of the catholic rule of faith. Homiletically, one asserted that "by the mercy of the Lord, God descended to men, so that men might be able by obedience to ascend to God." The only-begotten Son of the Father had become incarnate to lead men to faith. As the entire orthodox church, whether of East or West, declared, the one incarnate Christ was the proper subject of all christological predications, so that it was not appro-

ap.Bed.*H.e.*4.17 (Plummer 240)

Isid.Sev.*Sent.*1.15.2 (*SPE* 2: 267)

Bonif.*Serm.*1.2 (*PL* 89:844–45)

Alc.*Trin.*2.19 (*PL* 101:25–36); Beat.*Elip.* 2.53 (*PL* 96:1008)

Hadr.I.*Ep.episc.Hisp.* (*MGH Conc.*2–I:128)

Sent.*Flor.*18 (Ostlender 7–8)

Hinc.R.*Ep.*1 (*MGH Ep.* 8:1)

See vol.2:37–90

Bonif.*Serm.*2.2 (*PL* 89:847)

Bonif.*Serm.*10.1 (*PL* 89:862)

Ambr.Aut.*Purif*.10 (*PL* 89: 1299)

priate to speak of him as "one and another [alius et alius]," but as a single hypostasis, divine and human in one. These and similar declarations of dogmatic solidarity between the orthodoxy of the East and that of the West were sufficient to make clear that the West stood with all of Christendom in its loyalty to the catholic tradition, but they were not enough to preclude further dogmatic disputes about the person of Christ.

Faith, Hope, and Love

Ambr.Aut.*Purif*.5 (*PL* 89: 1295-96)

Prim.*Scarap*.13 (Jecker 44); Beat.*Elip*.1.46 (*PL* 96:920); Beat.*Apoc*.8.7.20 (Sanders 548)

1 Cor.13:13

See vol.1:142-46

Brun.S.*Sent*.2.1-3 (*PL* 165: 901-11)

Aug.*Enchir*. (*CCSL* 46:49-114) Aug.*Retract*.2.63.89 (*CSEL* 36: 202)

Auerbach (1965) 43 Rich.S.Vict.*Grad.car*.43 (*TPMA* 3:171)

Ambr.Aut.*Trans*.5 (*PL* 89: 1308)

Ambr.Aut.*Vit.virt*.2 (*PL* 40: 1093); Ambr.Aut.*Apoc*.2 (*CCCM* 27:149-50)

Isid.Sev.*Sent*.1.14.4 (*SPE* 2: 262-63)

Bonif.*Serm*.4.8 (*PL* 89:852)

A catholic Christian, according to Ambrose Autpert, was one who "preserves the true faith of the Trinity with a firm readiness to believe." But Priminius, an eighth-century abbot, was no less accurate when he formulated this definition: "A Christian is one who imitates and follows Christ in all things." Such a definition, with its concentration on faith, hope, and love as the content of the Christian way of life and on the life and teachings of Jesus as its norm, had been part of the understanding of salvation since the earliest days of the church, and the definition of Christianity as faith, hope, and love continued to shape medieval theology. Thanks largely to the piety and thought of Augustine—whose handbook of Christian teaching, commonly called *Enchiridion* by medieval (and modern) writers, originally bore the title *Faith, Hope, and Love*—it had taken deep root in Western Christendom, where "the lowliness of the sublime, the historical humiliation of the godhead" shaped language and life throughout the Latin Middle Ages. Thus the same Ambrose Autpert spoke of how Christ "set forth an example in himself for [our] imitation," and elsewhere he admonished, on the basis of Philippians 2:6-8: "If the divine majesty lowers itself in such great humility, does human weakness have the right to make boast of anything?" In this he was carrying on a way of speaking characteristic of his fathers and brethren, who took delight in the paradox of the incarnation. Christ, the Son of God, had undergone humiliation in order to save mankind, and it was only fitting that his followers should imitate his humble suffering.

The summons of the gospel to the imitation of Christ and to the Christian way of life took on a special urgency in this period because the conflict between Christendom

Rab.*Inst.cler.*1.27 (Knoepfler 46–49)

Episc.Fr.*Ep.Elip.* (*MGH Conc.* 2–I:157)

McNeill-Gamer (1938) 43

Prim.*Scarap.*22 (Jecker 54–55)

Bonif.*Serm.*6.1; 8.2; 15.1 (*PL* 89:855; 859; 870); Othl.*V. Bonif.*21 (*MGH Scrip.Ger.* 50:162–63)

Acts 1:26
Ambr.Aut.*Mts.*6 (*PL* 129: 1027)
Rab.*Ecclus.*8.1 (*PL* 109:1005–8)

Alc.*Ep.*124 (*MGH Ep.*4:183)

Alc.*Ep.*267 (*MGH Ep.*4:426)

Agob.*Grand.*1; 3 (*PL* 104:147; 148)
Agob.*Grand.*16 (*PL* 104:158)
Agob.*Grand.*15 (*PL* 104:157)
Serv.Lup.*Ep.*20 (*MGH Ep.* 6:28)

Ildef.*Itin.des.* (*SPE* I:381)

Bonif.*Serm.*8.1 (*PL* 89:858)

and heathendom was a real and an intense one. Upon becoming a Christian, a pagan was required to renounce the devil and all his works, and the interpretation of the Christian message had to be careful to avoid any "offense to pagan nations." Significantly, much of the material that we have been citing was originally produced in the setting of the church's mission to the pagan tribes. Even after these tribes had been baptized and formally incorporated into the catholic church, pastoral responsibility combined with apologetic interest to make the relation between Christian and pre-Christian ways of life an insistent issue. This is evident from the penitential collections of the period, in which "clauses on superstition form a constituent part of most" of the church's legislation, and also from its teaching. The *Dicta* of Priminius, for example, made a point of prohibiting not only idolatry, as would be expected of almost any manual of Christian believing and living, but also the practice of incantation. The sermons bearing the name of Boniface, "the apostle of Germany," repeatedly attacked "the auguries of the pagans" as a capital sin. The casting of lots in Scripture was not to be taken as a justification for such methods of making choices now. Such prohibitions and denunications continued to be necessary. Thus Alcuin, asking "What has Ingeld to do with Christ?" warned that "auguries and [divination through] the songs of birds and [omens by] sneezing and many other such things must be avoided altogether." At about the same time Agobard of Lyons spoke out, citing the authority of Scripture as well as that of reason, against superstition as "a not insignificant feature of unbelief," and Servatus Lupus expressed his misgivings about the practice of regarding comets as portents.

Because of this persistent threat, the bond between doctrinal orthodoxy and moral obedience was seen to be a close one. Ildefonsus of Toledo, after writing his textbook on the meaning of baptism, followed it with a guidebook entitled *Book on the Journey through the Desert on Which One Continues after Baptism,* which was intended to pick up where the textbook had left off. The very definition of salvation was shaped by this bond between orthodoxy and morality. "Salvation," according to the sermons of Boniface, meant "obeying the commandments of God and always doing singlemindedly the will of Him

1 Tim.2:4

Isid.Sev.*Orig.*6.2.7 (*PL* 82:230)
See vol.1:38–39

Beat.*Apoc.*3.4.41 (Sanders 314)

Rom.10:4

Ps.Cypr.*Abus.*12 (*TU* 34:59)

Isid.Sev.*Sent.*1.18.1 (*SPE* 2:276)

Ps.Cypr.*Abus.*12 (*TU* 34:59)

Bed.*Cant.*1 (*PL* 91:1071)

Bed.*Gen.*2 (*CCSL* 118A:91)
Bed.*Cant.*1 (*PL* 91:1065–84)

See vol.1:313

Bed.*Cant.*1 (*PL* 91:1069)

Bed.*Luc.*1 (*CCSL* 120:62)

who 'desires all men to be saved' and none to perish." The gospel as a way of life was identified as a "new law" or as "the evangelical law," as it had been in the early centuries of the church. Christians also recognized that they had to come to the Old Testament through the New, so that they had "not learned the gospel through the law, but the law through the holy gospel." So close was the identification of law and gospel that the statement of the apostle Paul, "Christ is the end of the law," was taken to mean that "those who are without the law come to be without Christ." According to Isidore, "the path by which one goes to Christ is the law, through which those who understand it accurately travel to God." Although such statements about the gospel as law and about salvation as moral obedience were not meant to negate the character of grace as a divine gift rather than as a human achievement, since it was known that the law was useless without the gospel, they did shift the emphasis in the understanding of salvation. Believers were admonished, therefore: "Let us not be without Christ here in this transient time, lest Christ begin to be without us in the future."

Accompanying such moral admonition was a continuing definition of salvation as a free gift of unmerited grace. In this, as in his thought generally, Bede showed himself to be a thoroughgoing disciple of Augustine, "the doctor of grace." It was the motto of Bede's life and of his theology that "grace should be the starting point, grace should be the consummation, grace should be the crown" of all human existence. The birth by which a human being entered this world was a good gift of God, but the "grace of new birth" was to be preferred to it. It is noteworthy that Bede wrote only one polemical treatise, a defense of the Augustinian doctrine of grace against the writings of the Pelagian theologian Julian of Eclanum, whom he accused of exaggerating the innate goodness of man in such a way that grace was assigned only the role of "a supervenient auxiliary" rather than that of "a prevenient inspirer and author of good efforts and merits in us." But grace was in fact the source to which the beginning of every good action and thought in the human heart was to be ascribed. "Not this or that good, but all good" had come from "the plenitude of our Creator" and from his

Bed.*Hom*.1.2 (CCSL 122:8)

unmerited generosity. As the accounts in the Gospels showed, the grace of the Holy Spirit sometimes conferred miraculous powers on the faithful and sometimes withheld them; but for the daily way of life of Christians— the way of faith, of hope, and of love toward God and the neighbor—the grace of the Holy Spirit was always

Bed.*Marc*.1 (CCSL 120:443)

present.

Laistner (1966) 160

In his unequivocal loyalty to the Augustinian doctrine of grace, as in his "numerous and fierce . . . warnings against Pelagianism," Bede stood out among the theologians of these centuries. Yet even those who were more ambiguous in their interpretation of the gratuitous character of grace retained much of the common property of Augustinism, for example, the familiar distinction be-

See vol.1:300–301

tween "nature" and "grace." The relation of God to men by "nature" was expressed in his "both filling and containing all that he has made," his relation to them by "grace" in his "revealing himself by the gratuitous gift of his mercy to those who are to be saved." When applied to

Alc.*Trin*.2.7 (PL 101:27)

christology, this distinction meant that by "nature" Christ was the only-begotten Son of God, while it was by "grace" that he had assumed humanity in order to save it. This

Alc.*Trin*.3.2 (PL 101:39)

Augustinian distinction of nature and grace continued to be a theological tool in the Carolingian era, and the re-

Radb.*Corp*.1 (CCCM 16:16)

statement of it was to serve as the key to the solution of various theological dilemmas in the thirteenth century.

See pp. 284–92 below

The other component of the Augustinian theology of grace that was repeated by every summary of Christian doctrine in this period was the relation between grace and original sin. Of his own power man was able to "walk in the way of iniquity," but he could not return to the right

Jul.Tol.*Antikeim*.1.104 (PL 96:646)
Isid.Sev.*Sent*.1.11.1 (SPE 2: 254)

way except by divine grace. Although everything under heaven had been created for man's sake, the fall had put him under sin and the condemnation of death. So funda-

Bonif.*Serm*.2.1 (PL 89:845)

mental was the Augustinian doctrine of original sin that, for example, Julian of Toledo began his work on eschatology with the words: "Through the sin of the first man

Jul.Tol.*Prog.fut*.1.1 (PL 96: 461)

it came about that death entered into the world."

For Augustine himself, this interpretation of the relation between sin and grace had led to a rather equivocal

See vol.1:320–21

position on the freedom of the will. The Augustinians of the early Middle Ages did not resolve the paradox either. "Without the grace of God," according to Ildefonsus, "the free will is not capable of anything good." The prevenient grace of God brought it about that an unwilling person came to desire what was good, and so "grace prevenes free will." Wherever such a doctrine may have left the freedom of the will and the moral responsibility of man outside the state of conversion, it did exalt and extol the gift of grace. The salvation of the saints and their membership in the church was accomplished "by no . . . preceding merits of theirs, but by the gracious will of God alone." Grace alone, without human merit, brought men back to God. Anyone who pondered his true condition must recognize his utter incapacity and his total lack of any merits of his own. He must "put his hope solely in God, who both prepares the will and grants the ability." God restored men by his gifts; he did not confer merits on them because of what they had deserved. His mercy had to come first, and only on that basis would he later crown good works with his rewards.

Occasionally this idea of "grace alone" could even lead to the corollary of "faith alone," as when Julian of Toledo declared that "all effort of human argument must be postponed where faith alone is sufficient." "The righteousness of faith, by which we are justified" consisted in this, "that we believe in him whom we do not see, and that, being cleansed by faith, we shall eventually see him in whom we now believe." His predecessor on the episcopal throne of Toledo, Ildefonsus, spoke even more strongly when he prayed: "God, who dost make the unclean clean and who by taking away sins dost justify the sinner without works." Because this passage sounded so much like the teachings of the Protestant Reformers of the sixteenth century, it was expunged from some manuscripts of Ildefonsus's *On the Virginity of Mary* by "readers who 'were more pious than learned' [and] who feared that by the misinterpretation of these words Ildefonsus could be accused of the heretical teaching that men could be saved by faith alone." Elsewhere in his writings Ildefonsus did insist that just as a metallic object became beautiful not only by the beauty of its material but by the craftsmanship of the artisan, so also "faith unadorned with works is not only lacking in beauty, but is in fact dead." Yet a little later in the same work he quoted Romans 5:1 to prove that "the beginning of human salvation comes from faith . . . which, when it is in Christ, is justification for the believer." And Julian, attempting, as others did, to harmonize the teach-

Ildef.*Cog.bapt.*100 (*SPE* 1: 328) ; Ildef.*Itin.des.*74 (*SPE* 1:424)

Ambr.Aut.*Apoc.*1 (*CCCM* 27: 38)

Ildef.*Itin.des.*19 (*SPE* 1:395)

Serv.Lup.*Quaest.* (*PL* 119: 641)

Jul.Tol.*Aet.sext.*2.14 (*PL* 96: 569–70)

Ildef.*Virg.Mar.*pr. (*SPE* 1:43)

Braegelmann (1942) 138

Ildef.*Itin.des.*83 (*SPE* 1:429)

Ildef.*Itin.des.*89 (*SPE* 1:432) Hinc.R.*Praed.*34 (*PL* 125: 350)

ings of the Epistle to the Romans with those of the Epistle of James, recognized a sense in which "if someone believes in Christ . . . he can be saved by faith alone," but James was saying that this must not be used as license to "refuse to do good works."

Much more common, also in Spanish theology, was the warning against anyone who "flatters himself uselessly about faith alone if it is not adorned with good works." It was necessary to warn against those "who presume that they can attain eternal bliss solely by the confession of faith, even if they do not have the works of faith." For the word of the Epistle of James about the faith of demons meant that "if it were enough for faith alone to save without love, the demons, too, could be saved." The collection of sermons bearing the name of the missionary Boniface would appear to be typical of Christian preaching and teaching. The righteousness of the believer, said a sermon on the Beatitudes, was not a state that was reached once and for all, but a process of growth, "so that we never suppose that we are righteous enough, but constantly beseech God to increase our merits." According to the next sermon, hearers needed to be reminded of what they had promised God in their baptism: to believe in him as Father, Son, and Holy Spirit. "But because it is written, 'Faith apart from works is dead,' and because he who knows God ought to observe his commandments, these are the commandments of God, which we are announcing to you, for you to keep and observe." There followed an enumeration of such commandments. And in a later sermon on the nature of faith, he asserted its primacy in the Christian life, "because the comprehension of divinity and the knowledge of truth must be learned through the catholic faith." While it was true, therefore, that faith without good works was vain, it was no less true that good works availed nothing apart from true faith; and true faith was an assent to the true doctrine taught by the catholic church in its tradition. Neither faith alone nor works alone could be called the basis of salvation, for neither could actually be alone; hence the most accurate and complete way to describe salvation was to say that those who were saved were "righteous by faith and by action." It was by grace, to be sure; but the term "grace" could be used either for the gift of God, which was received by faith, or for the effects of that gift in man, which were expressed by works.

Rom.3:28;Jas.2:24

Jul.Tol.*Antikeim*.2.77 (*PL* 96: 701)

Isid.Sev.*Sent*.2.2.8 (*SPE* 2:306)

Ambr.Aut.*Apoc*.2 (*CCCM* 27: 132; 158)

Jas.2:19

Beat.*Elip*.1.62 (*PL* 96:931); Beat.*Apoc*.1.5.93 (Sanders 100)

Bonif.*Serm*.4.4 (*PL* 89:851)

Jas.2:26

Bonif.*Serm*.5.1 (*PL* 89:852)

Bonif.*Serm*.7.2 (*PL* 89:857)

Beat.*Apoc*.12.2.60 (Sanders 628); Agob.*Fel*.2 (*PL* 104:34–35)

Bonif.*Serm*.7.2 (*PL* 89:857)

Ambr.Aut.*Purif*.6 (*PL* 89: 1296)

See vol.1:155-56

As in earlier centuries, the connection between the doctrine of grace and the doctrine of the means of grace continued to be in need of clarification. Perhaps because of the emphasis of many theologians on the primacy of faith, just recounted, the role of the preaching of the word of God as a means of grace assumed considerable importance. An additional factor accounting for this importance was the missionary program of the church during the seventh, eighth, and ninth centuries. In the missionary literature Christ was portrayed as the great preacher, who had "preached to the Jews and to the Gentiles to forsake all their evil and diabolical works, to do penance, to accept baptism, and to keep his commandments, which are the four Gospels and the other Sacred Scriptures." The missionary—and, indeed, every pastor—was to follow this example; for, according to Bede, "the pastors of the church have been ordained primarily for the task of preaching the mysteries of the word of God." These mysteries included the sacraments but were not simply to be identified with them. Ordination, then, was not only the conferral of authority to celebrate and administer the sacraments, but also and chiefly the commission to proclaim the word—an emphasis that continued to appear in the treatment accorded to the reading of the Gospel as part of the celebration of the Mass. "This is your task, my holy lord," wrote Alcuin to a bishop, "this is your reward, this is your everlasting praise and glory, that you preach the word of God to all with great confidence." The word was a means of grace.

Prim.*Scar*.7 (Jecker 37)

Bed.*Hom*.1.7 (*CCSL* 122:49)

See p. 124 below

Alc.*Ep*.89 (*MGH Ep*.4:133)

Despite this stress on the doctrine of the word, most of the doctrinal development in the understanding of the means of grace took place in the interpretation of the sacraments, through which the church, as the mother of all those who lived on earth, was herself born and nourished. Sometimes the sacraments and "the proclamation of the truth" through the word were coordinated, but even this coordination was cast in the Augustinian framework, according to which the word was added to the elements to make a sacrament. From the sacramental theology of Augustine there had likewise come the teaching that the objective efficacy of the sacraments did not depend on the subjective state of the minister. As in Augustine himself, so in these Augustinians, this theory was formulated principally in relation to baptism; but its eventual appli-

Bed.*Gen*.1 (*CCSL* 118A:38); Bed.*Luc*.6 (*CCSL* 120:423)

Jul.Tol.*Nah*.50 (*PL* 96:729)

Aug.*Ev.Joh*.80.3 (*CCSL* 36:529)

See vol.1:311

See p. 197, pp. 212–13 below

Ildef.*Cog.bapt*.16 (*SPE* 1:253)

Radb.*Corp*.12 (*CCCM* 16:76)

Bonif.*Serm*.12.4 (*PL* 89:866)

Ildef.*Cog.bapt*.23 (*SPE* 1: 260)

Jon.Aur.*Inst.laic*.3.14 (*PL* 106:260–61); Reg.Pr.*Eccl. disc*.1.118 (*PL* 132:214–15)

See vol.1:304–6

See pp. 204–6 below

Bed.*Gen*.2 (*CCSL* 118A:90); Bed.*Luc*.1 (*CCSL* 120:84); Ambr.Aut.*Apoc*.7 (*CCCM* 27: 621)

Bed.*1 Pet*.1 (*PL* 93:46)

Bed.*Luc*.3 (*CCSL* 120:224) Isid.Sev.*Sent*.1.22.1 (*SPE* 2:288)
See vol.1:158
Bed.*Gen*.2 (*CCSL* 118A:124)

cation to the Eucharist and then to ordination was to determine the outcome of various medieval theological controversies. It was Christ himself, as one external to the physical act, who actually did the baptizing, and he did so regardless of the moral or religious condition of the priest; for "the power of this sacrament is not in the office of the minister, but in the power of the Master." As a ninth-century theologian summarized it, this doctrine taught that the validity of the sacrament did not depend "on the merit of the consecrator, but on the word . . . of the Creator and on the power of the Holy Spirit." This applied not only to baptism, penance, and the Eucharist, but to other sacramental or semisacramental actions, for example, to the use of the sign of the cross. Exorcism, which never became a sacrament in its own right but depended on baptism for its function, was a means of replacing demonic with divine power. Bede's formulation of the sacramental significance of the anointing of the sick was sufficiently clear to give it a place in ninth-century compilations of proof texts for the developing sacramental doctrine of the West.

The Augustinism of the seventh and eighth centuries is evident above all in their concentration on the doctrine of baptism as the key to sacramental theology. Following their teacher, the Augustinian theologians of the early Middle Ages based their doctrine of the sacraments principally on baptism, while later medieval doctrine, beginning in the ninth century, went beyond Augustine in assigning to the Eucharist the paradigmatic function in sacramental teaching. Like preaching, baptism was interpreted in relation to the ministry of Christ himself. The baptism and the passion of Christ had been the means by which he had opened the gate of the kingdom of heaven and had restored the eternal life that had been lost in the fall of Adam. Baptism as a means of grace and the suffering of Christ as the means of redemption were "so mutually connected that neither of them can grant us salvation without the other." Therefore it was impossible for anyone to become a member of the church without baptism. Likewise it was only the catholic church that had the legitimate sacrament of baptism, although it was also true, as Cyprian had insisted, that a baptism administered by a heretic was valid. If someone had been baptized in the name of the Trinity, he was not to be rebaptized

Ildef.*Cog.bapt*.121 (*SPE* 1: 352–53)

when he moved from heresy and schism to the communion of the catholic church. But if in the administration of baptism, whether by a catholic or by a heretic, the name of one of the persons of the Trinity were omitted, this would invalidate the baptism; on the other hand, a grammatical or linguistic error in the ceremony was apparently not sufficient grounds for invalidating the sacrament—a view that continued to prevail in later centuries.

Ildef.*Cog.bapt*.112 (*SPE* 1: 344)
Bonif.*Ep*.68 (*MGH Ep*.3: 141); Othl.*V.Bonif*.1.34 (*MGH Scrip.Ger*.50:147)
Alex.III.*Sent.Rol*. (Gietl 205); Ans.L.*Sent.div.pag*.5 (Bliemetzrieder 44)

The place of baptism in the plan of salvation was attested also by the special miracles that sometimes attended it. Even though miracles were an important means of testifying to a sacrament, the most important means was the evidence of the benefits conferred by it. Baptism enabled infants to be saved through the faith and confession of others, provided that "when they come to the proper age, they preserve the integrity of the faith that has been confessed for them." The content of the gift of baptism could be variously described: it was citizenship in the eternal homeland given to one who was only a guest in this temporal life; it was adoption as a member of the body of Christ; it was the forgiveness not only of original sin but also of "actual sins, whether committed by the heart or the mouth, in deed or thought or word." One of the most striking ways of speaking about baptism was the description of it as a "compact [pactum]" made with God. A compact, according to commonly accepted etymology, was an agreement of "peace [pax]" between two parties. The term may also have connoted the new covenant conveyed by baptism, as a parallel to and a fulfillment of the old covenant conveyed by circumcision, and also as a replacement for the old compact with the devil. Summarizing the compact and the other benefits of the sacrament, Priminius called upon his readers: "Behold, what a compact and promise and confession you have with God. As a believer, you have been baptized in the name of the Father and of the Son and of the Holy Spirit for the forgiveness of all your sins, and you have been anointed by the priest with the chrism of salvation for eternal life. Your body has been clothed in a white garment, and Christ has clothed your soul with heavenly grace. A holy angel has been assigned to protect you; and, having accepted the name of 'Christian,' you have been numbered in the catholic church and have been made a member of Christ."

Ildef.*Cog.bapt*.105 (*SPE* 1: 333–35)

Alc.*Ep*.110 (*MGH Ep*.4:158)

Alc.*Ep*.34 (*MGH Ep*.4:76)
Radb.*Corp*.3 (*CCCM* 16:25)

Ildef.*Cog.bapt*.81 (*SPE* 1:309)

Prim.*Scar*.12 (Jecker 43)

Isid.Sev.*Orig*.5.24.18 (*PL* 82: 205)

Isid.Sev.*Jud*.2.16.5; 2.24.1 (*PL* 83:525;530)

Ambr.Aut.*Apoc*.1 (*CCCM* 27: 48)

Prim.*Scar*.12 (Jecker 43–44)

See vol.1:163–66

The principal lineaments of this catholic doctrine of baptism had been clearly visible almost from the beginning of patristic theology. The doctrine of penance, by contrast, had followed a zigzag path through the history of the Latin church, as the seemingly contradictory themes of unlimited forgiveness and ascetic discipline had alternated in dominance. As infant baptism became the normal procedure, except for those converted by the missions, the idea that baptism forgave actual sins lost much of its practical significance, and penance became the "second form of cleansing after the sacrament of baptism, so that the evils we do after the washing of baptism may be healed by the medicines of penance." The tears of penance were "a second baptism." It was, however, only after this period that the sacramental character of penance was clarified. Bede, for example, laid down the requirement that "those who have withdrawn from the society of the holy church by sinning should be reconciled to her by doing penance through the official action of the priests." Yet it does seem that "in his writings . . . the predominant meaning of *paenitentia* is 'repentance' rather than 'penance.'" It is likewise evident that "Bede does not designate penance by the term sacrament," even though he did include in his discussions of it most of the elements that eventually qualified it as a sacrament. It was the consensus of early medieval theologians that since there was no forgiveness of sins apart from the church, the minister of the church had the right to impose set times of public penance on sinners as a means of rendering satisfaction to the church. What was needed was the conceptual framework of an entire sacramental system, within which penance, together with the other rites that conveyed divine grace through earthly means, could be defined.

Ildef.*Cog.bapt.*81 (*SPE* 1:309)

Bonif.*Serm.*8.1 (*PL* 89:858); Beat.*Apoc.*3.3.67 (Sanders 291) Ambr.Aut.*Apoc.*1; 2; 7 (*CCCM* 27:48; 164; 621); Beat.*Apoc.* 3.2.43 (Sanders 275)

Bed.*E.et N.*2 (*CCSL* 119A:321)

Laistner (1938) 268

Carroll (1946) 170

Ildef.*Cog.bapt.*82 (*SPE* 1:310–11)

One rite whose doctrinal significance was specified much more clearly after Augustine than it had been by him was the offering of masses on behalf of the faithful departed. Because sacrifice for the dead was the practice of the universal church throughout the world, it was fitting to conclude that the practice had come down by tradition from the apostles themselves; but the corollary of such a practice was the belief that the sins of the departed could be forgiven, which implied some sort of intermediate state between heaven and hell. The doctrine of purgatory as the intermediate state had been proposed

Jul.Tol.*Prog.fut.*1.20 (*PL* 96:474)

Beat.*Elip.*1.80 (*PL* 96:942)

Isid.Sev.*Eccl.off.*1.18.11 (*PL* 83:757)

See vol.1:355–56

Jul.Tol.*Prog.fut*.2.19 (*PL* 96:483)

Bed.*Marc*.1 (*CCSL* 120:477)

Bed.*Luc*.1 (*CCSL* 120:81)

Isid.Sev.*Sent*.3.62.8 (*SPE* 2:524)
Alc.*Trin*.3.21 (*PL* 101:53)

Hinc.R.*Recl*. (Gundlach 263); Serv.Lup.*Ep*.30 (*MGH Ep*.6:36)

ap.Alc.*Ep*.139 (*MGH Ep*.4: 221)

Luke 23:43

Jul.Pom.*fr*.ap.Jul.Tol.*Prog. fut*.2.1 (*PL* 96:475)
Gr.M.*Dial*.4.25 (*PL* 77:357)

Jul.Tol.*Prog.fut*.2.8 (*PL* 96: 478–79)

Jul.Tol.*Prog.fut*.2.12 (*PL* 96: 480)

Bed.*Luc*.2 (*CCSL* 120:155–56)
Jul.Tol.*Prog.fut*.2.26 (*PL* 96: 488)

Luke 16:19–31

Bed.*H.e*.5.12 (Plummer 308)

See vol.2:279–80

tentatively by Augustine and set forth definitely by Gregory I. Quoting these two authorities, Julian of Toledo asserted the doctrine as one "defined by the statements of many treatises" of the fathers, as well as by such biblical passages as Matthew 12:32 and 1 Corinthians 3:12-15. The first of these passages meant that "some kinds of guilt are forgiven in this age, but other kinds in the age to come." The second meant that the fires of purgatory could not consume metal, "that is, the greater and harder sins," but that they could consume wood, hay, and straw, "that is, the lesser and milder sins." From these "milder sins" the elect could eventually be purged, so that "at the end they enjoy the contemplation of eternal goods." Purgatory was therefore "a transitory fire," and one over which the church on earth, through its power to bind sins and to loose them, had authority and jurisdiction.

Exact details concerning the state of the souls of the saints before the final judgment continued to be a matter of puzzlement and speculation, with some expressing doubts whether or not "the souls of the holy apostles and martyrs and of others who were perfect are received into the heavenly kingdom before the day of judgment." The words of Christ to the thief on the cross, "Today you will be with me in Paradise," were taken to be "unambiguous" proof that the souls of the blest, once they had left their bodies, were taken up into Paradise "without any interval of time." Yet it was clear from the teaching of Gregory the Great that this was not true of all, for there were some who needed further purification after death. A special case was the condition of the Old Testament patriarchs before the descent of Christ to the abode of the dead to open the gates of Paradise for them. But just as prayers on behalf of the faithful departed belonged to the universal usage of the church, so also it was widely believed that "the outstanding men of the church who have preceded us to the Lord" acted as "patrons." They prayed for the salvation of the living, whom they had loved while in this world, as Dives had prayed even in hell. The schematization of the afterlife made possible by the definition of purgatory as "the place in which the souls of those who . . . in the hour of death take refuge in penance are examined and chastised" not only became a crucial point of difference between East and West, but also helped to provide the late Middle Ages with the basic framework for their most characteristic and most profound artistic expression, Dante's *Divine Comedy*.

In Dante no less than in his predecessors at the beginning of the medieval period, purgatory formed part of a total picture and world view. For "though in itself inseparable from any Christian representation of the Universe, the image of the final catastrophe had seldom impinged so strongly on the consciousness of men as at this time." Near the end of his *Sentences* Isidore of Seville directed his readers away from their quest for a long life, which was a "mortal life," to "that life for whose sake you are a Christian, namely, life eternal . . . , the vital life." "The kingdom of the future" had preeminence over "the kingdom of time," and "the heavenly fatherland" over "this present age." The death of a good man was not an end but a beginning, "a migration to a better life." Therefore the hope and happiness of the elect were not to be found anywhere this side of "the future Sabbath" in heaven, where their "remuneration . . . is the vision of God." Many of the signs of the end of the world had already been fulfilled, and others were in the process of coming true. Yet to come were such signs as the conversion of Israel prophesied by the apostle Paul, but they would come surely and could come soon. This hope joined with faith and love to constitute the three fundamental components of the Christian way of life.

The Spirit and the Letter

The inclusion of "the faith of the people of Israel" in Christ as a sign of the end of the world was a part not only of the continuing Christian effort to come to terms with the meaning of Romans 9-11 but of the ineluctable demand that the church make sense of Judaism and clarify its relation to the ancient people of God. That demand was expressed, for example, in the summary of a Jewish-Christian dispute recited by Gregory of Tours, or in the treatise of Ildefonsus *On the Virginity of Mary*, which was directed "against three unbelievers" but which actually devoted the bulk of its discussion to an argument with a Jew. Like their contemporaries in the East during these centuries, Western theologians, as the heirs of patristic thought, repeated the standard theological and biblical arguments of the earlier disputes with Jewish spokes-

Bloch (1964) 84

Isid.Sev.*Sent*.3.61.5 (*SPE* 2: 522)

Bonif.*Serm*.11 (*PL* 89:863)
Ambr.Aut.*Vit.virt*.26 (*PL* 40: 1103)
Alc.*Ep*.198 (*MGH Ep*.4:327)

Bed.*Gen*.2 (*CCSL* 118A:86)
Jul.Tol.*Prog.fut*.3.50 (*PL* 96: 519)

Ambr.Aut.*Apoc*.1 (*CCCM* 27: 53)

Rom.11:25-26

Alc.*Trin*.3.19 (*PL* 101:51)

1 Cor.13:13
Ambr.Aut.*Apoc*.6; 10 (*CCCM* 27:476; 808-9)

Alc.*Trin*.3.19 (*PL* 101:51)

See vol.1:23

Gr.Tr.*Hist.Franc*.6.5 (*MGH Scrip.Mer*.1B:268-72)

Ildef.*Virg.Mar*.3-12 (*SPE* 1: 62-154)
See vol.2:200-215

2 Cor.3:6
Goth.*Praed*.15 (Lambot 240–42)
Aug.*Spir.et litt*.8.13; 27.48 (*CSEL* 60:164–66; 202–3)

Beat.*Elip*.1.98 (*PL* 96:955)
Beat.*Apoc*.9.1.10–11 (Sanders 532–33); Amal.*Off*.2.16.6 (*ST* 139:239)

Gen.49:10

See vol.1:55–56

See vol.2:205–6
Isid.Sev.*Jud*.1.8.1 (*PL* 83:464); Aldh.*Virg*.8 (*MGH Auct.Ant*.15:236); Beat.*Apoc*.2.pr.2.7 (Sanders 110)

Ildef.*Virg.Mar*.5 (*SPE* 1:78); Od.Clun.*Occup*.5.44–46 (Swoboda 95)

Jul.Tol.*Aet.sext*.1.10 (*PL* 96:546)

Jul.Tol.*Aet.sext*.1.18–19 (*PL* 96:552–53)

See vol.1:16–20

Beat.*Apoc*.3.4.50 (Sanders 315); Flor.*Ver*.15 (*PL* 121:1130)

Isid.Sev.*Jud*.11–56 (*PL* 83:470–95)

Gen.1:26

See vol.1:197; vol.2:203–4

Isid.Sev.*Jud*.1.3.5 (*PL* 83:455)

See vol.1:59–60
Beat.*Elip*.1.105 (*PL* 96:959); Hinc.R.*Praed*.34 (*PL* 125:352)
Isid.Sev.*Jud*.2.15 (*PL* 83:522–24)

Deut.6:4

ap.Isid.Sev.*Jud*.1.4.1 (*PL* 83:457)

Alc.*Trin*.1.2 (*PL* 101:14)

Isa.42:13
Isid.Sev.*Jud*.1.61.2 (*PL* 83:497)

men. The Pauline distinction between the spirit and the letter had served Augustine, in his oft-quoted treatise *On the Spirit and the Letter,* as the basis for a discussion of the contrast between Christianity and Judaism; and it continued to be used for this purpose, as well as for the defense of spiritual against literal exegesis. The prophecy of Jacob about Judah, which had provided the historical framework within which the church fathers had defined the place of Judaism in the divine economy as important but transitory, was also a standard part of the Eastern theological arsenal against Jewish claims. In Latin theology, too, this passage was quoted over and over. It was used to prove to the Jews that the Christ whom they were awaiting had now come. Its prophecy that the scepter would not depart from Judah until the coming of the one for whom it had been prepared meant that the line of Herod ended at the coming of Christ and that the historic vocation of the people of Israel had now been accomplished.

Other proof texts and "Christian midrashim" assembled in the "testimonies" of the early fathers against Judaism were also rehearsed in the medieval treatises. Isidore of Seville reviewed the life and career of Christ, from his birth to his ascension into heaven, and cited proofs from the Old Testament for each of the events. Certain individual passages came in for special consideration. The statement in the creation story, "Let us make man," which had long been used to prove that the Trinity was the Maker of all things and especially of man, could not be taken to mean, as the rabbis maintained, that God had consulted with the angels when he called humanity into existence. Although the Decalogue, as a part of Christian teaching, was to be obeyed just as it stood, its commandment of the Sabbath could not refer to the Jewish observance of Saturday. The confession of the Shema, "Hear, O Israel: The Lord our God is one Lord," was used by the Jewish critics of Christian doctrine as a refutation of the dogma of the Trinity; but actually, "all divinely inspired Scripture, Old and New Testament alike, if it is understood in a catholic sense, teaches Father, Son, and Holy Spirit" as one God in Trinity. The writings of the prophets were also to be understood "in a catholic sense": the statement of Isaiah about the Lord's "going forth" was to be taken as a reference "to the second coming" of Christ; his de-

Isa.53

Isid.Sev.*Jud.*1.44.3 (*PL* 83: 488); Flor.*Jud.*12 (*PL* 116: 148)
Dan.7:1-7
Jul.Tol.*Aet.sext.*1.21 (*PL* 96: 554); Ambr.Aut.*Apoc.*8 (*CCCM* 27:659)

scription of the suffering servant served to refute the Jewish hope of a Messiah who was to come but was not to die; and Daniel's prophecy of the four kingdoms meant that the fifth kingdom, which would overthrow them all, would be that of Jesus Christ.

Alc.*Trin.*1.2 (*PL* 101:14)

A recurrent theme in these exegetical disputes was the contrast between Jewish particularism and Christian universalism. To be "understood in a catholic sense," the Old Testament Scriptures must be read as a witness not only to catholic dogma but to catholicity itself. Of all the proofs that the Messiah had come, the "truest" was the calling of the Gentiles and their acceptance of him, which showed that he was "the expectation of the nations." For even the nations that did not believe in him "still do not escape the lordship of Christ, so long as there is pressure being put on them from those princes in whose hearts Christ himself is known to dwell by faith," so that there was probably "no nation remaining that is ignorant of the name of Christ." This universalism proved the superiority of Christianity to Judaism, which remained confined to one small nation. Although there was "one church in all his saints, the same faith of all the elect, that is, of those preceding and those following his coming in the flesh" (which suggested that the Jews had a chronological priority), the Gentiles, by being the first to believe in Christ, had taken precedence over the Jews, who had now lost the right to be called "Jews," which meant "confessors." The early church had made a gradual transition from Jewish particularity to Christian universality, as the circumcision of Timothy by Paul showed, but it was clear that all such specifically Jewish observances were to cease with the coming of Christ. Yet there remained many Jews who did not believe in Christ, and their punishment for having rejected him still rested on them.

Jul.Tol.*Aet.sext.*1.13 (*PL* 96: 548)

Gen.49:10

Jul.Tol.*Aet.sext.*1.14 (*PL* 96: 549)

Bed.*Hom.*2.15 (*CCSL* 122:280)

Isid.Sev.*Jud.*2.4.1 (*PL* 83:508)

Ambr.Aut.*Apoc.*2 (*CCCM* 27: 118); Beat.*Apoc.*1.5.86 (Sanders 98)

Acts 16:3

Jul.Tol.*Antikeim.*2.60 (*PL* 96: 693)

Isid.Sev.*Jud.*2.6.1 (*PL* 83:510)
Jul.Tol.*Aet.sext.*1.16 (*PL* 96: 549)

Although such assertions of Christian universalism easily became defenses of Christian imperialism, as the reference to "Christian princes" showed, there was also a persistent, if less effectual, recognition that the Christian case in relation to Judaism was not to be carried by princes and warriors, but by preachers of the gospel. As Isidore put it, "faith is not in any sense achieved under duress, but by the persuasion of reason and of evidence. In those on whom it is forced by violence it is not permanent." He criticized a kind of conversion of Jews that

Isid.Sev.*Sent.*2.2.4 (*SPE* 2:306)

had been brought about "not according to knowledge, because it forced by constraint those whom it should have persuaded by a rational presentation of the faith." Under his chairmanship a council at Toledo decreed in 633 that Jews must not be compelled to join the church, but be persuaded to join it of their own free will. The sword with which the church conquered its enemies was not physical coercion, but the preaching of the word. In keeping with this principle, Isidore's treatise *On the Catholic Faith against the Jews* "is perhaps the ablest and most logical of all the early attempts to present Christ to the Jews." Other attempts, too, claimed to put their case "without the prejudice of the Christian faith," but not always very successfully. Following Isidore and his patristic sources, Alcuin declared that "faith . . . is a voluntary matter, not a compulsory one," and he "inveighed tirelessly against compulsory missionary methods [and] . . . the abuse of royal power in the treatment of conquered nations," including also the Jews.

To the Judaism that had antedated the coming of Christ, Christian theologians were quite willing to apply the title of "church." The entire congregation of the elect, whether before Christ or after Christ, was called "church," but for the sake of precision it had become customary to use the term "synagogue" for "that portion of the faithful that preceded the time of the Lord's incarnation" and to reserve the term "church" for that portion that followed the incarnation. Applied to pre-Christian believers, "synagogue" was an honorific title. It was a way of identifying the congregation of believing Jews as "the mother of the church," which could mean either that "Christ, who deigned to be called the brother of the elect, was born of its flesh" or that "the church is procreated by the books of the law and the prophets." But "synagogue" could also carry a pejorative connotation, as when Isidore prophesied that in the age of Antichrist "the synagogue will rage against the church even more terribly than it persecuted the Christians at the time of the coming of the Savior." Viewed in this light, as the community that had rejected the Messiah and that had been the implacable enemy of the church ever since, Judaism was seen as heresy and was identified as "the synagogue of Satan," and the contrast of church and synagogue was taken to be one not merely of chronology but of opposition. In the

Isid.Sev.*Goth*.60 (*MGH Auct. Ant*.11:291)

CTol. (633) *Cap*.57 (Mansi 10:633)
Ambr.Aut.*Apoc*.5 (*CCCM* 27:417–18); Flor.*Jud*.48 (*PL* 116:175)

A.L.Williams (1935) 217
Jul.Tol.*Aet.sext*.1.3 (*PL* 96:541)

Alc.*Ep*.111; 113 (*MGH Ep*.4:160; 164)

Wallach (1959) 27

Bed.*Hom*.2.15 (*CCSL* 122:280)

Bed.*Cant*.2 (*PL* 91:1083); Beat.*Apoc*.2.pr.6.1–2 (Sanders 126)

Ambr.Aut.*Apoc*.1 (*CCCM* 27:32)

Isid.Sev.*Sent*.1.25.6 (*SPE* 2:294)

Flor.*Jud*.4 (*PL* 116:143)
Bed.*Sam*.4 (*CCSL* 119:255)

Bed.*Gen*.1 (*CCSL* 118A:58)

eleven th and twelfth centuries the Christian opposition to
Judaism, together with the Christian opposition to Islam,
took on a new form, when the commonplaces of conventional apologetics had to yield to a deeper theological
encounter.

See pp. 242–55 below

It was, however, not chiefly the place of the Jewish
religious community, but rather the meaning of the
Jewish Bible, that concerned the theologians of the
seventh, eighth, and ninth centuries. One of these theologians could declare, concerning the writers of the Jewish

Ildef.*Virg.Mar*.6 (*SPE* 1:91)

Bible, "Their truth is my faith." But by this he was not
in any sense identifying his outlook with that of the
Jews; he was rather laying claim to the Jewish Bible as

See vol.1:58–62

the Christian Old Testament. As in the early church, this
often implied that the Old Testament held an inferior
place in comparison with the New. Thus "the new
prophecy [of the Book of Revelation] excels the old
prophecies just as the gospel excels the observance of the
law." It did so because it presented as already fulfilled
those "mysteries regarding Christ and the church which
[the old prophecies], seeing them from afar, discerned

Ambr.Aut.*Apoc*.pr. (*CCCM* 27:7)

as yet to come in the future." The correct term for the
Old Testament was "figure," but for the New it was

Radb.*Corp*.5 (*CCCM* 16:33)
Isid.Sev.*Sent*.1.20.3 (*SPE* 2:286)

"reality." Or one could contrast "the shadow of reality"
in the Old with "reality" in the New. In the proper order
of things, "new deeds fulfill ancient promises, reality
casts out the shadow, revelation makes known what was
uncertain and hidden, and the new faith opens up the

Ildef.*Virg.Mar*.6 (*SPE* 1:88)

arcane mysteries of antiquity." The inferiority of the Old
Testament to the gospel was especially visible in its ethical standards; it was not legitimate to cite the cruelties
of the Israelites against their enemies as justification for

Rab.*Reg*.1.15 (*PL* 109:49)

similar atrocities, since what was commanded then could
not be even permitted now, and with the birth of Christ

Jul.Tol.*Aet.sext*.1.8 (*PL* 96:545)

"wars have come to an end throughout the world."
As in the early church the Old Testament, while treated

See vol.1:58

as obsolete, was nevertheless read as Christian Scripture,
so in the Middle Ages it was the latter way of dealing
with the Jewish Bible that dominated the teaching of
the church: "The Old and the New Testaments are one

Ambr.Aut.*Apoc*.3 (*CCCM* 27:231)

book." Statements from the Book of Psalms could take
their place alongside the sayings of Jesus in the Gospels,
because "the Psalmist is speaking affirmatively in the

Jul.Tol.*Antikeim.*1.63 (*PL* 96: 623)

Isid.Sev.*Proëm.*34 (*PL* 83:163)

Bed.*Sam.*3 (*CCSL* 119:186)

Alc.*Trin.*1.2 (*PL* 101:14)

Bed.*Retr.Act.*10.5 (Laistner 125)
Isid.Sev.*Jud.*1.6.1 (*PL* 83:463)
See vol.2:209
Ildef.*Virg.Mar.*6 (*SPE* 1:85)

See vol.1:60–62

Isid.Sev.*Sent.*3.12.3 (*SPE* 2:434)

Isid.Sev.*Jud.*2.20.1 (*PL* 83: 528); Ambr.Aut.*Apoc.*1 (*CCCM* 27:50–51)

Bed.*Gen.*1 (*CCSL* 118A:3)

name of Christ [ex persona Christi], as though this were being addressed by the voice of the Son of God to God the Father." The Psalter was principally devoted to the theme of the birth, death, and resurrection of Christ. To be sure, this theme was not automatically visible to every reader. "When unbelievers read the Scriptures, the place of Christ there appears to be empty. The reason is that by failing to review the total context of the Old Testament, they cannot find Him whom a scribe educated in the matters of the kingdom of heaven knows how to find in almost all the sacred pages." Read in this way, "all divinely inspired Scripture, Old and New Testament," bore witness to the catholic and orthodox faith of the church. Everything in the Scripture, "even the names and the geography," was to be understood as "filled with spiritual figures." Not only such familiar parallels as "Joshua" and "Jesus," which had figured in Christian apologetics since early times, but "all these prophecies find their summation in" the Christian gospel.

To discern the deeper and truer meaning of such passages, it was necessary to understand that biblical words and biblical narratives meant more than they said. Recapitulating the hermeneutics of the church fathers, Isidore set down the rule that "anyone who runs through the words of the law in a carnal way does not understand the law at all, but only he who looks at it with the perception of his inner understanding, for those who concentrate on the letter of the law cannot penetrate its secrets." A failure to observe this rule had brought many down the path to heresy and error. In fact, "neither a Jew nor a heretic can understand it, since he is not a disciple of Christ." Against Jews and heretics it was necessary to insist that the language of Scripture "is to be understood not only historically, but also according to its mystical sense, that is, spiritually." The reliance on the spiritual interpretation of Scripture did not imply a demeaning of the historical sense. Bede was particularly insistent on the importance of the historical sense, urging that anyone who undertook to interpret the Bible allegorically take diligent care lest "by his allegorizing he desert the explicit faith based on history." The historical references in Scripture were less in need of explanation than were other passages; or if they were not clear, it did not matter as

Bed.*Ep*.14 (*PL* 94:699)

much. But this did not give the exegete the right to ignore such references, for the historical sense continued to be basic to the task of biblical interpretation.

Although the development of the principles and methods of biblical interpretation is not a matter of direct concern to us in this work, they do pertain to our narrative to the extent that the "fourfold norm of the ecclesiastical tradition" and the "fourfold structure of the evangelical narrative" were thought to provide justification for a fourfold sense of Scripture: historical, allegorical, tropological, and anagogical. This meant that one should pay attention in the study of the Bible to its narrative of events, its intimation of eternal truths, its prescription of moral duties, and its anticipation of future happenings. Sometimes the hermeneutical principle could be reduced to a threefold sense—historical, tropological, and mystical—but this difference was more technical than substantive. Eventually it became possible to speak even of a sevenfold sense of Scripture rather than merely a fourfold sense. The fundamental issue, however, was the emphasis on the difference between the letter and the spirit, which implied that the literal and historical meaning of a passage did not exhaust the intention of the word of God being spoken through it.

Aldh.*Virg*.4 (*MGH Auct.Ant.* 15:232)

Bed.*Tabern*.1 (*CCSL* 119A:25)

Isid.Sev.*Sent*.1.18.12 (*SPE* 2:278); Isid.Sev.*Jud*.2.20.2 (*PL* 83:528–29); Beat.*Apoc*.2.3.65 (Sanders 200)

The doctrinal importance of these hermeneutical questions lay in their contribution to the authority of Scripture, for it was a Scripture interpreted in this way that was regarded as authoritative for the teaching of the church. Inspiration by the Holy Spirit was attributed to the Bible on this basis. The writers of Scripture had not spoken on their own authority or from their own knowledge but had received their witness from "the supreme Spirit, who gives life to all, and whose work it is to speak through the mouth of all the prophets." To be precise, therefore, one had to say that the true author of Scripture was the Holy Spirit himself, who had dictated to the prophets what they were to write on his authority, though not necessarily "the physical words in their mouths." This was how they had become "the writers of the Sacred Books, speaking by divine inspiration and dispensing the heavenly commandments for our instruction." These commandments pertained not only to the rule of Christian living, but also to "the rule of believing." Authority in the church, therefore, was to be ascribed to "the apostles of God," for they

Ambr.Aut.*Apoc*.1 (*CCCM* 27:25)

Agob.*Fred*.12 (*PL* 104:177)

Isid.Sev.*Eccl.off*.1.12.13 (*PL* 83:750)

Isid.Sev.*Orig*.6.2.50 (*PL* 82:235)

Isid.Sev.*Orig*.8.3 (*PL* 82:296)

Aldh.*Carm*.1.12 (*MGH Auct. Ant*.15:12)

Flor.*Ver*.15 (*PL* 121:1130)

Jul.Tol.*Antikeim*.2.5 (*PL* 96:666)

Isid.Sev.*Sent*.1.16.8 (*SPE* 2:271)

Isid.Sev.*Sent*.1.18.6 (*SPE* 2:277)

Jul.Tol.*Aet.sext*.1.3 (*PL* 96:541)

Ildef.*Cog.bapt*.26 (*SPE* 1:264)

Alc.*Fel.haer*.3 (*PL* 101:88)

Alc.*Fel*.4.8 (*PL* 101:181)

Prim.*Scarap*.1 (Jecker 34)

Radb.*Ep.Fr*. (*CCCM* 16:161)

Alc.*Elip*.1.2 (*PL* 101:243)

had not carried to the nations the results of their own reflection, but had faithfully transmitted "the discipline that they had received from Christ." Thus the apostle Paul was "the greatest of teachers," as a member of this apostolic college.

There could not be any opposition between Paul and other apostles, for there could not be any opposition in Scripture anywhere. It was axiomatic that one "should understand two true statements of the Lord in such a way that we do not predicate any contradictions of them at all." This did not mean that everything in Scripture was equally clear. The very cultivation of a multiple sense implied that one must go beyond the explicit language of the Bible to its deeper intent. Scripture was, then, an obscure book to superficial or heretical readers, who used its obscurity as a cover for their distortion of its true and orthodox interpretation. Some things in Scripture were admittedly more obscure than others, as a way of sharpening the understanding of the reader. But the intent of Scripture was clear, so that anyone who understood its central message was also in a position to deal with its less easily intelligible portions. Thus the authority of the Bible was the same as the authority of Christ himself, and "ignorance of the Scriptures is ignorance of Christ."

Even though it was possible, in the name of this understanding of authority, to set Scripture against patristic antiquity and to dismiss ancient usage as having "no claim" where it lacked "evident documentation from Holy Scripture," the assumption underlying the entire method of interpreting the Bible was the agreement between Scripture and tradition. The language of Scripture about Christ was quite clear in itself, but the interpretation "of the holy fathers and catholic doctors" served to reinforce it. "The brightness of this catholic faith" was the light that illumined all of Scripture. The Holy Spirit had spoken through the prophets and priests of the Old Testament and through "all the doctors of the catholic church" of the New Testament. The decrees of the Council of Ephesus in 431 and the statements of the Gospels were put on the same level. In making a theological point against heresy, one could refer to "the authority of the Holy Scriptures and the truth of the catholic faith," which were in complete harmony. The law and the prophets in the Old Testament and the Gospels and the apostles in the New Testament were the inspired authority of the church, but it was by "the tradition of the elders" and "the monuments of the fathers" that this authority was endorsed for the church. While later centuries were to set the authority of Scripture and the authority of church and tradition into opposition, it was characteristic of the integrity of the catholic tradition as this was received by the seventh and eighth centuries in the West that any such opposition was regarded a priori as inconceivable.

The City of God

Contradiction between Scripture and church was impossible because "the church, as the bride of Christ, the temple of the Most High, and the city of the Most High, and the city of the great King, flourishes with such great power, dignity, and wisdom that it cannot be conquered by any enemy nor led astray by any friend." Among these prerogatives and titles of the church, the one most explicitly identified with the Augustinian tradition was "city." Augustine's *City of God* had developed the idea that throughout human history there would be two cities, one from God and the other from the devil, the first founded by Abel and the second founded by Cain. They were both to continue until the resurrection and the last judgment. One source for Augustine's conception had been "the holy city, new Jerusalem" in the Book of Revelation. Early medieval exegesis of Revelation took it for granted that this "is to be understood as nothing other than the church of the elect," since "the city . . . is the church of God." If the church was the city of God, its "ramparts are the Holy Scriptures." Each of the three books of the seventh-century *Prognostications of the Future* by Julian of Toledo expounded quotations from Augustine's *City of God,* which thus continued to exercise its role as the normative schematization of world history from a Christian perspective.

Another political metaphor for the church, and one with much more extensive documentation in the Bible, was "kingdom." The term had never lost its eschatological connotations, and these became even more prominent when the awareness of the end was aroused. But there was also the sense that "between the two comings of Christ, the first in the incarnation, the second in the judgment, there is a middle age." It was this that the Book

Marginal notes (left column):

Ildef.*Cog.bapt.*77 (*SPE* 1: 305)

Jul.Tol.*Nah.*18 (*PL* 96:716)

Aug.*Civ.*15.1 (*CCSL* 48:453–54)

Ambr.Aut.*Apoc.*7 (*CCCM* 27: 627); Beat.*Apoc.*10.2.4–12 (Sanders 585–86)

Ildef.*Cog.bapt.*95 (*SPE* 1:320–21)

Rev.21:2
Ambr.Aut.*Apoc.*9 (*CCCM* 27: 776)
Ambr.Aut.*Apoc.*7 (*CCCM* 27: 559); Beat.*Apoc.*7.1.5 (Sanders 515)
Alc.*Fel.*1.7 (*PL* 101:133); Car. M.*Ep.Elip.* (*MGH Conc.*2–I: 160)

Jul.Tol.*Prog.fut.*1.12; 2.21; 3.3 (*PL* 96:466; 485; 498)

See vol.1:40–41

See vol.1:19

See p. 2 above

of Revelation had meant when it spoke of the thousand years during which Christ and the saints would reign on earth. The millennium referred to "the church of God, which, by the diffusion of its faith and works, is spread out as a kingdom of faith from the time of the incarnation of Christ until the time of the coming judgment." The promise of Christ that he would eat and drink with his disciples in the kingdom of his Father did not apply to the millennium nor even to heaven, but to "the present church;" it meant "the kingdom of the Father, that is, the church, as often as we either eat or drink him [in the Eucharist] worthily." The equation of church and kingdom was such that one could simply speak of "his kingdom, which is the church." Neither as the kingdom of God nor as the city of God, however, was the empirical church completely free of sin or of sinners. The Augustinian doctrine that the holiness of the church did not imply moral perfection was reiterated in the warning that saints and sinners were mixed together in "the total body of the church." Holiness was an appropriate predicate for the church because it was in the church, through sacramental grace, that one received the forgiveness of sins.

As the city of God and the kingdom of God, in spite of the sinfulness of its members, the church was closely identified with Christ. Christ and the church, according to Bede, had "one nature." The church had come from the side of Christ, just as Eve had been taken from the side of Adam. It was important in any such identification between Christ and the church to note the difference between the two as objects of faith: in the Nicene Creed one affirmed a faith "in" God and Christ, but only a faith "that his holy church is." Therefore the glory of the church was derived from its relation to Christ. "The church," in Bede's phrase, would "never be deserted by Christ," and its solidity would never be destroyed. As Christ in the days of his flesh had taught the crowds from the bark of Peter, so now "the bark of Simon is the primitive church" and "to the present day he teaches the nations from the authority of the church." This authority was correlated closely with the authority of Scripture and with that of the dogmatic tradition. The entire authority of the Gospels proclaimed what all the statements of the apostles affirmed, and this was also what the great broad world believed and

Rev.20:1–6

Jul.Tol.*Antikeim*.2.69 *(PL* 96: 697)

Matt.26:29

Beat.*Apoc*.10.3.11–14 (Sanders 589)

Radb.*Corp*.21 *(CCCM* 16:113)

Ambr.Aut.*Apoc*.1 *(CCCM* 27: 64)

See vol.1:308–13

Ambr.Aut.*Apoc*.2; 1 *(CCCM* 27:96; 66); Beat.*Apoc*.4.3.7 (Sanders 352–53)

Ildef.*Cog.bapt*.82 *(SPE* 1: 310–11)

Beat.*Apoc*.2.6.50 (Sanders 238)

Bed.*Cant*.3 *(PL* 91:11) Ildef.*Cog.bapt*.7 *(SPE* 1: 243–44)

Gen.2:21–22

Ildef.*Cog.bapt*.37 *(SPE* 1: 276); Alc.*Fel*.2.17 *(PL* 101: 158–59)

Bed.*Sam*.1 *(CCSL* 119:28); Jul.Tol.*Antikeim*.2.14 *(PL* 96: 672)

Bed.*Marc*.4 *(CCSL* 120:623)

Luke 5:3

Bed.*Luc*.2 *(CCSL* 120:114)

Beat.*Elip*.1.1 *(PL* 96:895)

Alc.*Ep*.23 *(MGH Ep*.4:62)

Hinc.R.*Praed*.pr. *(PL* 125:65)

Isid.Sev.*Proëm*.8 *(PL* 83:158);
Ambr.Aut.*Apoc*.10 *(CCCM* 27:
868)

ap.Bed.*H.e*.2.4 (Plummer 87)

Bed.*H.e*.2.2 (Plummer 81)

Bed.*Marc*.2 *(CCSL* 120:513)

Bed.*Luc*.6 *(CCSL* 120:422)

Leand.Sev.*Laud.eccl.* *(PL* 72:
894)

Isid.Sev.*Jud*.1.55.4 *(PL* 83:
494); Leand.Sev. *Laud.eccl.*
(PL 72:893)

Isa.45:22-23

Isid.Sev.*Jud*.2.1.6 *(PL* 83:500)

John 10:16

Leand.Sev.*Laud.eccl.* *(PL* 72:
895)

Bed.*Ep.Joh.* *(PL* 93:106)

Isid.Sev.*Jud*.2.1.3 *(PL* 83:499)

See vol.2:146

John 19:23-24

Ps.Cypr.*Abus*.11 *(TU* 34:57-
58)

what the Roman church declared. Hincmar of Reims lined up "the authority of the Holy Scriptures" with that of "the orthodox teachers" and that of the Roman see as witnesses to the truth of Christ and of his church. This also implied that it was up to the church to decide which books belonged to the canon of Scripture.

The authority of the church was derived from its universality. Lawrence of Canterbury urged the Scots "to observe the unity of peace and a conformity with the church of Christ spread throughout the world." Those who differed from this conformity were guilty of preferring their own traditions to those of the universal church. There were, of course, "diverse groupings of churches throughout the world," but taken together these formed "the one catholic church." All nations participated in this one church, which was both true and catholic, having come from Jerusalem to the nations but having nevertheless remained "both there and here." What made the church catholic was its dissemination throughout the world and the inclusion of all the nations in its association. The apostles had preached the gospel through all the earth, converting the various peoples of the earth to Christ. Therefore the prophecies of the Old Testament about the universality of the dominion exercised by the God of Israel had not been fulfilled in the history of Israel but in that of the catholic church, and the prophecy of Christ about "other sheep" had likewise been fulfilled when the entire world had received the opportunity to believe in Christ and to come together into the one catholic church. It was possible to cite the authority of the church because it was thought to represent the consensus of a single and universal Christian community.

As a result, one could go so far as to charge that "anyone who disturbs the unity of that holy church which Jesus came to bring together is striving as far as he can to undermine Jesus himself." The church was one, made up of Jews and Gentiles, who had been brought together into one faith, one people, and one kingdom. Following an idea set forth by Cyprian and repeatedly propounded by theologians, a treatise bearing his name spoke of the church as the "seamless robe" of Christ and accused schismatics of an audacity more overweening than that of the soldiers at the crucifixion, who had been unwilling to tear the undivided garment of the Lord. So fundamental was the unity of the catholic church to Christian faith and life that apart from its fellowship all faith was vain and all good works were devoid of reward; only within "the unity of the catholic church and the concord of the Christian religion" could either faith or works have any value. Those who set themselves against this unity, not only in questions of dogma but also in matters of church discipline and practice, were without excuse, even if they claimed to adhere to the authority of Old and New Testaments and to that of the trinitarian dogma of the church; for "the catholic faith and the concord of fraternal love move inseparably along the same path," from which none could deviate without threatening catholic unity.

Aldh.*Ep*.4 (*MGH Auct.Ant.* 15:481)

Ps.Cypr.*Abus*.7 (*TU* 34:46)

Aldh.*Ep*.4 (*MGH Auct.Ant.* 15:485–86)

The authority of this one catholic church was guaranteed and maintained by those who held ecclesiastical office. Christ had ordained offices of varying dignity in the church. In Christ, as the one foundation of the church, the twelve foundations of the church, the apostles, were established; and in these twelve, in turn, all the administrators of the church in all ages were joined together. The twelve apostles were the origin of the office of bishop, and the seventy disciples sent forth by Christ represented the priests of the church. This identification of Christian ministers as priests in the Levitical succession, which had begun in the early church, did not obliterate the teaching, likewise a part of early Christian doctrine, that by virtue of their baptism all Christian believers participated in a priestly ministry. The "royal priesthood" described in the New Testament pertained to all, not only to the ordained clergy, for "all those who have been elected by grace are called priests." Neither functionally nor doctrinally however, did this idea of the universal priesthood of believers modify the concentration of theologians and churchmen on the ordained priesthood and its qualifications for the ministry of preaching and administering the sacraments.

Beat.*Apoc*.3.2.27 (Sanders 271–72)

Ambr.Aut.*Apoc*.10 (*CCCM* 27:800)

Luke 10:1
Bed.*Tabern*.3 (*CCSL* 119A: 112)

See vol.1:25

See vol.1:160

1 Pet.2:9
Bed.*1 Pet*.2 (*PL* 93:50–51); Ambr.Aut.*Apoc*.3; 1 (*CCCM* 27:267; 48) Beat.*Apoc*.12.4.4 (Sanders 638)

Isid.Sev.*Sent*.3.35.1 (*SPE* 2: 472)

In their doctrine of the priesthood, as in their doctrine of the church generally, many of the thinkers of this early medieval period may aptly be termed "systematic theologians of canon law rather than of dogma." The subject of such ecclesiological predicates as "one" or "catholic" was the institutional, hierarchical church, more specifically, the body of those who acknowledged the authority of the see of Rome. To be a catholic rather than a schismatic, one

Betz (1965) 229

had to follow the well-established authority of the Roman church. Those who had separated themselves from this authority were accused of supposing that Christ had a church no broader than their own sect, and hence of believing that power in the church had been taken away from its legitimate incumbents and transferred to the few who belonged to this "new church." Outside the borders of the true church it was useless to make a boast of one's orthodoxy or of adherence to the catholic faith. Authentic orthodoxy and legitimate church membership were inseparable. "For our part," Alcuin announced, "we take our stand firmly within the borders of the apostolic doctrine and of the holy Roman church, following their established authority and clinging to their sacred doctrine, introducing nothing new and accepting nothing apart from what we find in their catholic writings." This was the only reliable guarantee of believing correctly and thereby of attaining salvation in the kingdom of heaven.

Standing behind the guarantee was the apostle Peter, to whom the keys of the kingdom of heaven had been entrusted. He was, in a title originally applied to the Roman god Janus, "the heavenly wielder of the keys, who throws open the gate of heaven." In his descriptions of Peter, Bede likewise made use of traditional prerogatives. He called Peter "the patron of the entire church" and "the first pastor of the church," as well as "the prince of the apostles." He acknowledged that the command of Christ to Peter, "Feed my sheep," had been spoken not only to him, but to all the disciples. This meant that "the other apostles were the same as what Peter was, but the primacy was given to Peter for the purpose of commending the unity of the church." All the apostles and their successors were shepherds, but there was to be only one flock, whose unity was represented by Peter. Elsewhere Bede could take the commission to Peter to mean that "the Lord commanded Saint Peter to take care of his entire flock, that is, of the church," adding that Peter had in turn conveyed this order to the pastors of the church who followed him in the governance of the flock. The charge of Christ to Peter was an argument against the date of Easter observed in England, because such an observance conflicted with "the universal church of Christ throughout the world." But when he came to identify the "rock" on which

Alc.Ep.137 (MGH Ep.4:215)

Alc.Ep.23 (MGH Ep.4:61–62)

Aldh.Ep.4 (MGH Auct.Ant. 15:486)

Alc.Fel.1.4 (PL 101:131)

Matt.16:19
Ov.Fast.1.228
Aldh.Carm.1.6; 4.1.2 (MGH Auct.Ant.15:11; 19); Aldh.Ep. 4 (MGH Auct.Ant.15:485)

Bed.Hom.1.16 (CCSL 122:115; 117)

Bed.Hist.ab.1; 2 (Plummer 364; 366)

John 21:17

Bed.Hom.2.22 (CCSL 122:347)

Bed.1 Pet.5 (PL 93:64–65)

Bed.H.e.3.25 (Plummer 188)

Beat.*Apoc*.12.2.47 (Sanders 626)

See vol.2:157; 160

Bed.*Marc*.3 (*CCSL* 120:551)

Bed.*Hom*.1.20 (*CCSL* 122:144–45)

Fröhlich (1963) 123

Carroll (1946) 88
Bed.*H.e*.1.29; 2.1 (Plummer 63; 73)

Bed.*H.e*.3.25 (Plummer 188)

Aldh.*Ep*.4 (*MGH Auct.Ant.* 15:482)

Alc.*Ep*.137 (*MGH Ep*.4:211)

Ambr.Aut.*Mts*.12 (*PL* 129:1031)
Ambr.Aut.*Apoc*.9 (*CCCM* 27:749)

Christ had promised to build his church, Bede, together with other Latin theologians of the period, seemed to come closer to the Eastern exegesis of Mathew 16:18–19 than to the Western; for he spoke of the church as being founded "on the rock of faith, from which [Peter] received his name," and he stated that "upon this rock" meant "upon the Lord, the Savior, who conferred upon his knowing and loving confessor a participation in his name" by calling him "Peter." In this interpretation of the "rock," Bede was joined by biblical interpreters of his own and of later periods; for "the most astonishing fact" is that "in the specifically exegetical literature of the entire Middle Ages one looks in vain for the equation 'petra = Peter,'" which was so prominent in the polemical and canonical literature.

It appears that "in the texts on the powers accorded Peter, Bede nowhere speaks of his particular successors, though he does specify the successors of all the apostles. But in other works there is apparent a special attention to the succession in the Roman see." He customarily referred to Rome as "the holy and apostolic see," and he supported the authority of Roman doctrine and practice as catholic against local deviations from it. His countryman and contemporary, Aldhelm, used the words of Christ to Peter in Matthew 16:18–19 to argue that "if the keys of the kingdom of heaven have been conferred on Peter by Christ..., who can triumphantly enter into the gates of the heavenly Paradise if he scorns the chief statutes of [Peter's] church and despises the commandments of its doctrine" about the date of Easter? It was a violation of "the rule of the catholic faith on the basis of the commandments of Scripture" for English monks not to conform to "the tonsure of Saint Peter, the prince of the apostles." A century or so later, another scion of the English church objected to the use of salt in the celebration of the Eucharist on the grounds that "this custom is neither observed by the universal church nor validated by the authority of Rome." The primacy of Peter meant to Ambrose Autpert that there was "a prerogative of excellence in apostolic dignity, not above all the others but with all the others," and that Peter was "the bearer of the person of the church," which had become the coregent of Christ. Although the reluctance of the patristic period

See vol.1:119; 159

to isolate the primacy of Peter from the authority of the apostolic college as a whole continued in the seventh and eighth centuries, the Western doctrine had already moved unmistakably in the direction of papal monarchy, which was to reach its climax in the thirteenth century. In Isidore's formula, the pope, as supreme pontiff, was "the chief of priests . . . the highest priest"; it was he who appointed all other priests in the church and who had all ecclesiastical offices at his disposal. Therefore even so vigorous a proponent of the special claims and administrative autonomy of metropolitans as Hincmar, the archbishop of Reims in the ninth century, pointed out, in his very defense of these claims, that "solicitude for all the churches has been committed to the holy Roman church, in Peter, the prince of the apostles." His quarrels were with individual incumbents of the papacy over particular matters of policy and ecclesiastical administration, never with the status of Rome as the principal see of Christendom. The church of Rome was "the mother and the teacher [mater et magistra]," whose authority was to be consulted on all questions of faith and morals, and her instructions were to be obeyed. Elaborating on the metaphor of the church as mother, he characterized "the catholic, apostolic, and holy Roman church" as the one who had "given birth to us in faith, fed us with catholic milk, nourished us with breasts full of heaven until we were ready for solid food, and led us by her orthodox discipline to perfect manhood." To those who were faithful and pious members of the catholic church, the validity of a doctrine could be established simply by showing what this church taught. Not only did the church decide which books belonged in the catholic canon of Scripture; it was also the attestation of "the holy see of Rome" that provided credentials for the church fathers, so that "if there are some who are called doctors [of the church], we do not accept or cite their statements in proof of the purity of the faith unless that same catholic mother church has decreed that their statements are sound."

It is likewise on the basis of the writings and the career of Hincmar that we may understand how the Augustinian theory of the relation between the city of God and the city of man was applied to the relation between the catholic church and the Christian kingdom of the Franks. Like the contemporary Byzantine theory of

Isid.Sev.Orig.7.12.13 (PL 82:291); Beat.Apoc.2.pr.4.11 (Sanders 119)

Hinc.R.Metrop.18 (PL 126:199)

Hinc.R.Metrop.4 (PL 126:190)

Hinc.R.Ep.169 (MGH Ep. 8:154)

Hinc.R.Div.pr. (PL 125:623)

Hinc.R.Praed.4 (PL 125:88)

Hinc.R.Praed.24 (PL 125:214)

Hinc.R.Ep.99 (MGH Ep. 8:48)

See vol.2:144; 168

Schrörs (1884) 443
Hinc.R.*Reg*.5 (*PL* 125:839)

Aug.*Civ*.5.24 (*CCSL* 47:160)
Aug.*Civ*.1.6 (*CCSL* 47:5)
Verg.*Aen*.6.853

Alc.*Ep*.178 (*MGH Ep*.4:294)

Ex.17:11–12
Car.M.*Ep*.93 (*MGH Ep*.4:137–38)

Alc.*Ep*.308 (*MGH Ep*.4:471)

Wallach (1959) 25

Ein.*V.Car.M*.24 (*MGH Scrip. Ger*.1:29)

church and state, Western political ideology is relevant to our narrative only as it serves to illumine the doctrine of the church. Hincmar's conception of the ideal form of association was "a division of secular and spiritual authority, a restriction of each to its own territory, but in such a way that they both support each other amicably in their tasks, and that the church, which stands higher in dignity, provides the state with the immutable laws of religion and morality as a norm." In expounding this conception of church and state, he drew for his picture of the model secular ruler on the description of the Christian emperor in the fifth book of Augustine's *City of God*. The *City of God* was also the source for Alcuin's admonition to Charlemagne that he should, in the words of Vergil, "spare those whom he conquers and vanquish those who are proud." Apparently from Alcuin's pen came Charlemagne's description of the relative roles of emperor and pope: the former was to defend the church from the attacks of its pagan foes and to foster the catholic faith within the church; the latter was to assist the imperial armies by lifting up his hands to God, as Moses did for the hosts of Israel, assuring victory for the catholic empire over the enemies of God and of his church. God had given him imperial power, Alcuin told Charlemagne, chiefly for the protection of the church.

From these and many other statements it is evident that "Alcuin saw in Charlemagne Augustine's ideal Christian emperor, the *felix imperator*," and from the report of his biographer Einhard that Augustine's *City of God* was Charlemagne's favorite book it would seem that the emperor accepted this identification. Not only in this reinterpretation of *The City of God,* but throughout the definition of what constituted Christian doctrine, the Augustinian synthesis of the early Middle Ages articulated "the integrity of the catholic tradition" in the form that was to be normative for medieval theology in subsequent centuries. Nevertheless, it could not be transmitted to those centuries without further critical examination. The clarification of what it meant—and of what it did not mean—was an assignment taken up by the theological culture that owed its founding to the emperor Charlemagne.

Beyond the Augustinian Synthesis

Goth.*Praed*.11 (Lambot 220)

Hinc.R.*Deit*.17 (*PL* 125:593)

Between the end of the eighth century and the end of the ninth, the comfortable assumption of an Augustinian synthesis that could be accepted by all as the catholic tradition was called into question on several basic counts. So dominant were the thought and the vocabulary of Augustine in defining "the integrity of the catholic tradition" that it has been possible to use titles of his works as subheads in our first chapter. But when one participant in a controversy could consistently refer to him as "our Augustine" while another countered that "although he speaks of 'our Augustine,' he has wandered far away from him," it became clear that simply invoking his name or even quoting proof texts from his writings would not suffice as a guarantee of catholicity and of orthodoxy. The growing recognition that the Augustinian synthesis must be interpreted, and that perhaps it must even be transcended, provoked controversy, stimulated research, and nurtured reflection; and out of these three elements would be shaped the distinctive character of medieval theology.

Flor.*Scot.Er*.11 (*PL* 119:163)

Alc.*Ep*.280 (*MGH Ep*.4:437)

Alc.*Fel*.1.7 (*PL* 101:133)

"The error of the modern period" came as a shock to the spokesmen for the church. Controversy had "suddenly erupted" after what seemed to have been a period of doctrinal tranquility. Was it not true, Alcuin asked his opponents, that "the entire church of Christ, once the heresies of Eutyches and Nestorius had been condemned, was at peace for a long time, with nothing disturbing it, until this new sect, unheard of in ancient times, arose all at once as a result of your insolence?" "Until the present time," according to Paschasius Radbertus, "no one has erred on [the doctrine of the Eucharist] except for those

Radb.*Ep.Fr.* (*CCCM* 16:169)

who have also erred on the doctrine of Christ." And Hincmar, attacking what he regarded as heretical innovation on the doctrine of predestination, listed the dogma of the Trinity and the doctrine of the Eucharist as areas where his contemporaries were "stirring up idle chatter

Hinc.R.*Praed.*31 (*PL* 125:296)

in opposition to the truth of the catholic faith." In a catalog of christological heretics, an author would enumerate false teachers from the fourth and fifth centuries and then move immediately to one who had appeared "just now, during our own times." The fathers and

Beat.*Elip.*2.94 (*PL* 96:1025)

doctors of Christian antiquity, it was believed, had successfully routed the various heresies with which the archenemy of the faith had sought to subvert the church; but "now," in the ninth century, the devil was "attempting to undermine the fortified walls of the faith with a new

Scot.Er.*Praed.*1.4 (*PL* 122:359)
Ratr.*Part.Mar.*1.1 (Canal 84)

engine of war." He was spreading "new poisons of unbelief" in an attempt to destroy the catholic faith. So widespread was the devastation caused by this apostasy and controversy that "the study of doctrine, by which faith and the knowledge of God ought to be nourished and

Flor.*Ver.*1 (*PL* 121:1083)

to grow day by day, is extinct almost everywhere."

Not all of these prophets of doom were on the same side in the various doctrinal controversies of the age, but all of them were beneficiaries of the spiritual and intellectual revival inaugurated by the emperor Charlemagne; for "on the disintegrated ruins of the ancient world it built an empire which lacked the strength and the balance of the old *respublica,* but which contained

Lopez (1959) 1
Amal.*Bapt.*1–3 (*ST* 138:236–37)
Alc.*Ep.*163 (*MGH Ep.*4:263–65)

durable spiritual values." With his own interest and curiosity about theological questions, even the most abstruse ones, the emperor took up a role as patron of humanistic and theological studies. Paraphrasing the words

Verg.*Aen.*12.59

of Vergil, his court theologians hailed him as the one "on whom alone rests the entire welfare of the churches of

Alc.*Ep.*174 (*MGH Ep.*4:288)
Paulin.Aquil.*Lib.sac.*14 (*MGH Conc.*2–I:142)

Christ"; and they made apostrophes to him a part of their dogmatic treatises in defense of orthodoxy, thanking him for having commissioned them to undertake such a de-

Alc.*Ep.*172 (*MGH Ep.*4:284)

fense. He himself intervened actively in the disputes between East and West over images and over the pro-

See vol.2:155–56; 186–87

cession of the Holy Spirit. In response to a warning not to corrupt Charles, Alcuin replied: "It would be impossible for him to be corrupted by anyone, for he is a catholic in faith, a king in power, a pontiff in preaching, a judge in equity, a philosopher in liberal studies, a model in

Alc.*Elip*.1.16 (*PL* 101:251)

morals." Whatever may have been the literal accuracy of such panegyrics, Charlemagne did gather together in his own lifetime and stimulate for the lifetimes of his immediate successors an assemblage of scholars and authors without peer in the Latin West during the surrounding centuries. Among these were also many of the thinkers who found it necessary to go beyond the Augustinian synthesis.

The Reconsideration of Dogma

The encomium of Charlemagne by Alcuin was evoked by a warning from Elipandus, archbishop of Toledo, who was accused, together with Felix of Urgel, of "false doctrine in asserting that there was an adoption of the Son of God." Although it was acknowledged even by his adversaries that Felix lived an exemplary Christian life and that he had written much that was consonant with the catholic faith, he had "diverged from the holy apostolic church solely in the use of this one word, 'adoption.'" What he had confessed and then recanted and then—as became evident to his opponents in a series of questions and answers found among his literary remains after his death— confessed again was a "Spanish error" with which others, including especially Elipandus, were thought to have been infected. For while throughout the Middle Ages many of "the seminal ideas . . . came out of Spain," the eighth and ninth centuries saw Spain as a seedbed, first of tyrants and now of schismatics, as well as of apostates; for rumors of the heresy of adoptionism had spread through all of Spain and even beyond its borders into the kingdom of the Franks. The Spanish origins of the heresy, particularly its sources in the idiosyncracies of Spanish liturgy (whose variations from other liturgies continued to interest Western theologians), became an issue in the controversy, as did the relative authority of the see of Rome and the see of Toledo.

As stated by the principal Spanish opponent of Elipandus in the controversy, the issue was that "one party of [Spanish] bishops says that Jesus Christ is adopted according to his humanity and in no way adopted according to his divinity," while the other party said that "unless he is the proper and only Son of God the Father according to both natures rather than the adopted Son," one could not call the crucified one the true Son of God, since

CFr. (794) *Cap*.1 (*MGH Conc*.2–1:165)

Alc.*Ep*.166 (*MGH Ep*.4:271)

Alc.*Ep*.23 (*MGH Ep*.4:62; 65)

Agob.*Fel*.1 (*PL* 104:33)

Alc.*Elip*.1.8 (*PL* 101:247)
Southern (1962) 19
Alc.*Ep*.137 (*MGH Ep*.4:212)
Flor.*Jud*.42 (*PL* 116:171)

Beat.*Elip*.1.13 (*PL* 96:901–2)
Alc.*Elip*.2.7 (*PL* 101:264)
Bern.Reich.*Miss.off*.1 (*PL* 142: 1057–58); Guit.Av.*Corp*.3 (*PL* 149:1484)

Alc.*Fel*.7.13 (*PL* 101:226)

Beat.*Elip*.13 (*PL* 96:902)

See vol.1:175–76

Elip.*Ep*.5 (*MGH Ep*.4:308);
Fel.ap.Agob.*Fel*.36 (*PL* 104:
60)

Elip.*Ep.episc.Fr*.2 (*MGH Conc*.2–I:111*)

Elip.*Ep.episc.Fr*.18 (*MGH Conc*.2–I:119)

Fel.ap.Alc.*Fel*.1.15 (*PL* 101:
140)

Fel.ap.Paulin.Aquil.*Fel*.1.55
(*PL* 99:412)

Fel.ap.Paulin.Aquil.*Fel*.2.12
(*PL* 99:432); Fel.ap.Alc.*Fel*.
5.8 (*PL* 101:195)

Matt.17:5; Matt.16:15
Elip.ap.Paulin.Aquil.*Lib.sac*.6
(*MGH Conc*.2–I:135); Elip.ap.
Alc.*Elip*.1.20 (*PL* 101:255)

See vol.1:189–90

Elip.*Ep. episc.Fr*.15 (*MGH Conc*.2–I:118); Fel.ap.Paulin.
Aquil.*Fel*.1.27 (*PL* 99:379)
Ps.22:1; Matt.27:46
See vol.1:244; vol.2:59

Jul.Tol.*Antikeim*.2.55 (*PL* 96:
690)
Elip.*Ep.Alc.* (*MGH Ep*.4:
304)
Elip.*Ep.episc.Fr*.15 (*MGH Conc*.2–I:118)

See vol.1:89–90

Fel.ap.Alc.*Fel*.2.12 (*PL* 101:
155)

his humanity had been adopted. It was important to note that neither party was attempting to revive the teaching that the divine in Christ had been adopted. Elipandus and Felix both believed themselves to be in harmony with the orthodox catholic faith of the church. Elipandus explicitly declared that the Son of God had been begotten by the Father "not by adoption but by birth, not by grace but by nature," and he anathematized as blasphemy the teaching that "the Son of God, begotten outside time, was adopted"; Felix likewise asserted that "we believe that he was adopted by the Father in that [nature] according to which he was the son of David, but not in that according to which he exists as Lord." According to the divine nature, Felix said, "he must be believed to be true God and the true Son of God." But nowhere in the Gospels was it said that the Son of God had been "given over for us" to suffering and death, but only the Son of man; on the other hand, the attestations of the Son of God by the voice of God the Father from the cloud or by the confession of Peter referred only to his divinity as Son of God, not to his humanity.

The purpose of introducing (or reintroducing) the category of adoption into the christological discussion was to clarify the right of the humanity of Christ to the title "Son of God," the most common and most comprehensive name for Jesus Christ, as a right acquired not by nature but by adoption. According to Elipandus and Felix, a denial that according to his humanity Christ was the adoptive Son of God would amount to a denial that he was true man. Once again, the cry of dereliction on the cross, "My God, my God, why hast thou forsaken me," served as a touchstone; following a Spanish predecessor of unquestioned orthodoxy, Elipandus attributed it to the humanity of Christ. The alternative was to relapse into the docetist heresy of the Gnostics and Manicheans, condemned by the ancient church. "For if in his flesh, which he took upon himself at his very conception from the womb of the Virgin, our Redeemer is not the adoptive [Son] of the Father but is the true and proper Son, then how can you avoid saying that this flesh of his was not created and made from the mass of the human race nor from the flesh of his mother, but was begotten from the essence of his Father, just as his divinity was?" And that, according to Elipandus, was the very heresy into which his

Elip.*Ep.Car.M.* (*MGH Conc.* 2–I:121)
Elip.*Ep.episc.Fr.*1 (*MGH Conc.* 2–I:111)

Fel.ap.Alc.*Fel.*1.8 (*PL* 101: 133)

Alc.*Fel.*3.17 (*PL* 101:172)
Alc.*Elip.*1.9 (*PL* 101:247)

Paulin.Aquil.*Fel.*1.27 (*PL* 99: 379); Alc.*Fel.*3.11 (*PL* 101: 169)

Paulin.Aquil.*Fel.*1.37 (*PL* 99: 391)

Elip.*Symb.fid.*ap.Beat.*Elip.* 1.40–41 (*PL* 96:917)

Elip.*Ep.Alc.* (*MGH Ep.*4:305)

Fel.ap.Paulin.Aquil.*Fel.*2.9 (*PL* 99:429)

Rom.8:29
Elip.*Ep.episc.Fr.*9 (*MGH Conc.*2–I:113)

Isid.Sev.*Orig.*9.5.20 (*PL* 82: 355)

Fel.ap.Alc.*Fel.*7.3 (*PL* 101: 215)

Ben.An.*Fel.* (*PL* 103:1399)

Paulin.Aquil.*Fel.*1.22 (*PL* 99: 375)

Alc.*Fel.haer.*69 (*PL* 101:116)

Alc.*Ep.*166 (*MGH Ep.*4:269); Alc.*Fel.*3.8 (*PL* 101:167)

opponents had fallen; they taught "that the Son of God did not assume from the Virgin a flesh like ours, except for sin," and even "that he did not take upon himself a visible form from the Virgin." Thus they taught "that the two natures of Christ are mixed together like wine and water." These charges were vigorously denied. Rejection of the idea of adoption as applied to the human nature of Christ did not amount to a confusion of the two natures or to a denial of his true humanity. Not confusing the natures and not dividing them, the opponents of adoptionism said of the entire person of the God-man: "I confess him to be true man, but I also proclaim him to be true God and I reverently adore him." But there was a great difference between confessing him to be true man and calling him an ordinary man, which was the unavoidable implication of the position that his humanity was adopted to be the Son of God.

Advocates of that position insisted, on the contrary, that adoption was the only way to be able to say simultaneously that the Father "created all visible things, not through him who was born of the Virgin but through him who [is Son of God] by being begotten, not by being adopted" and that the Father "redeemed the world through the same [Son], at once Son of God and Son of man, adoptive in his humanity and not adoptive in his divinity." If according to his humanity he was the son of David, this humanity must be the Son of God by adoption, not by nature. For as the Son of man he had not been eternally with the Father in heaven. Therefore he was "only-begotten by nature" as Son of God, but also, as Son of man, 'first-born among many brethren," but this "by adoption and grace," not by nature. Adoption was the most appropriate term, for according to the definition of Isidore an adopted son bore both the name that was his by nature and that which he acquired by adoption. Therefore the title "Son of God" was shared jointly by the humanity that had been assumed and by the divinity that had assumed it. "In other words, they say that 'assumption' and 'adoption' are one and the same." This equation of adoption with assumption—and sometimes with "conjunction" as well—was identified by the critics of adoptionism as its chief source and was rejected on the grounds that not every assumption was properly called adoption, even though every adoption was some sort of assumption. For

Ben.An.*Fel.* (*PL* 103:1401)

Paulin.Aquil.*Lib.sac*.3 (*MGH Conc*.2–I:133)

Deut.18:15; Acts 3:22

Elip.*Ep.Alc.* (*MGH Ep*.4:303)

Ex.2:10

Paulin.Aquil.*Lib.sac*.7 (*MGH Conc*.2–I:135–36)

Radb.*Matt*.1.1 (*PL* 120:79)

Paulin.Aquil.*Fel*.1.26 (*PL* 99:378–79)
Elip.*Ep.episc.Fr*.9 (*MGH Conc*.2–I:113)

Ps.82:6;John 10:34
Beat.*Elip*.2.100 (*PL* 96:1027);
Hinc.R.*Deit*.2 (*PL* 125:518)

Eph.2:3
Paulin.Aquil.*Fel*.1.44 (*PL* 99:397)

Alc.*Ep*.166 (*MGH Ep*.4:270)

Alc.*Ep*.2.17 (*PL* 101:158)

Agob.*Fel*.34 (*PL* 104:60)

Aug.*Ev.Joh*.2.13 (*CCSL* 36:17)

Hadr.I.*Ep.episc.Hisp.* (*MGH Conc*.2–I:125); Radb.*Part.Mar*.2.73 (Canal 154)

Scot.Er.*Prol.Ev.Joh*.21 (*SC* 151:306); Prud.Tr.*Praed*.16 (*PL* 115:1253); Rup.*Div.off*.11.4 (*CCCM* 7:373); Bald.*Sacr.alt*.2.1.2 (*SC* 93:154); Rich.S.Vict.*Except*.2.10 (*TPMA* 5:120)

that matter, even "assumption" was not altogether precise, for the Son of God had descended from heaven to become incarnate as man, not to assume a man. Adoptionism had to say either that the humanity of Christ had been adopted in the womb of Mary or that the adoption had come later, after he had lived a perfect life as man. Either alternative led to heresy. On the basis of the biblical parallel between Moses and Christ, Elipandus argued that Christ was the adoptive Son of God; but to his opponents the adoption of Moses by the daughter of Pharaoh was proof that "one who is adopted is called 'son' in an improper and not in an essential sense," and that therefore the term was not a fitting one for Christ, except, of course, as it applied to his "adoption" by Joseph, who was not his true father.

It was, however, a fitting term for the Christian. Christ was the adopter, not the adoptee, while the believers were the adoptees. When Elipandus compared the human Christ as adopted with "the other saints," he overlooked the fundamental difference between them: "Even though the saints are called 'gods,' they are not worshiped; only Christ is called 'God' and is worshiped." The baptism of Christ by John the Baptist manifested the difference. For believers, baptism was the means by which they were changed from "children of wrath" to sons of God through "the grace of adoption," but this was not true of Christ. Felix appeared to be teaching that Christ, too, had needed to be baptized in order to become the Son of God. But the baptism administered by John was not a means of regeneration even for those who needed it, much less for Christ, who did not need it. Indeed, precisely because Christ did not need to be adopted but was the Son of God by nature, he could confer the grace of adoption on his faithful adherents. On the basis of the words of Augustine that "we have not been born of God, as the Only-begotten was, but have been adopted through his grace," it was argued that Christ could not have conferred this grace if he himself had been in need of it. The adoptionist controversy may well have stimulated more careful consideration—in this and in subsequent centuries—of the difference between the "natural" sonship of Christ and the "adoptive" sonship of believers. Thus Beatus of Liébana, leader of the Spanish opposition to Felix and Elipandus, not only made the polemical point that "adopted" was

Beat.*Elip*.2.33 (*PL* 96:998)

Beat.*Apoc*.2.pr.9.13 (Sanders 145)
Beat.*Apoc*.3.3.23 (Sanders 282)

Beat.*Apoc*.2.pr.1.12 (Sanders 104)

Beat.*Apoc*.12.2.103–4 (Sanders 634)

Beat.*Elip*.2.51 (*PL* 96:1007)

Beat.*Elip*.2.50 (*PL* 96:1006)

Beat.*Elip*.1.118 (*PL* 96:968)

Beat.*Elip*.1.49 (*PL* 96:929)

Beat.*Apoc*.1.2.42 (Sanders 51)

Alc.*Fel.haer*.70 (*PL* 101:117)

Phil.2:7
Hadr.I.*Ep.episc.Hisp.* (*MGH Conc*.2–I:126–27)

Paulin.Aquil.*Fel*.3.5 (*PL* 99:438–39)

See vol.2:88–89

Paulin.Aquil.*Fel*.1.13 (*PL* 99:365)

Alc.*Fel*.2.12 (*PL* 101:155–56)

See vol.2:83–84
See vol.1:249–51

the right term not for the one who did the choosing, but for those who were chosen; he also developed the exegetical point in his commentary on the Apocalypse. The church was "adopted by God as a daughter" and through its adoption came to share in the humility of Christ. Christ was the firstborn among his brethren because they were the ones who had been adopted, and the likeness between him and them had to be interpreted in the light of the difference.

For there was, Beatus wrote against Elipandus, "a great difference between Christ as man and the whole multitude of the saints," a difference that came down to the axiom that "Christ could exist without them, all by himself, but they could neither live nor exist without Christ." Therefore such titles as "Christ" and "Lord" were used of him "in a singular sense," to show that when they were applied to the saints they were intended in a derivative sense. By his failure to observe this distinction, Elipandus was, in effect, making Christ and the Christian the same, nullifying the uniqueness of Christ, who alone among all men was God himself and whom therefore "we segregate from other men." No one was really like him because even those who were adopted as sons of God did not thereby "begin to be God by nature." And "how could he be unique," Alcuin asked, "if he were adopted, just as we are?" Strictly speaking, the term "servant" did not apply to him, even though "the form of a servant" was a biblical term for his humiliation. For the same reason, the anguish in Gethsemane must mean that he was giving an example of how to suffer and pray. What the Western defenders of orthodoxy did in response to adoptionism was to assert their equivalent of the Eastern doctrine of "enhypostaton," according to which "the hypostasis of the Logos, who previously was simple, becomes composite." Because Christ had not first been a mere man and then one in whom God dwelt, his human nature from its inception had been "one person with God." By the incarnation, therefore, "the humanity entered into the unity of the person of the Son of God. . . . In the assumption of the flesh by God, what is absent is the person of a man, but not the nature of a man."

A corollary—or, to be more precise, at least chronologically, a presupposition—of the idea of "enhypostaton" was the communication of properties between the two natures in the one person of Christ. The proponents of adoptionism were obliged to affirm such a communication of properties, as when Felix, echoing an earlier Spanish source, asserted that "because of the singularity of the person in which the divinity of the Son of God and his humanity have actions in common, the things that are divine are sometimes referred to the human and the human things that are done are from time to time ascribed to the divine." As an example he quoted the passage: "No one has ascended into heaven but he who descended from heaven, the Son of man, who is in heaven"; for it was obvious "that the Son of man did not descend from heaven and he was not there before he was born on earth." Felix's interpretation seemed to imply, however, that the communication of properties was chiefly verbal, since no one in the controversy took such a passage of the New Testament to be saying that the humanity of Christ had existed in heaven before being born of the Virgin. When Felix said that "the Son of God in the Son of man is sometimes called Son of man" and that "the Son of man in the Son of God is titled Son of God," Agobard replied: "Do you mean 'is called' rather than 'is'?" and "Do you mean 'is titled' rather than 'is'?" As in the case of the Nestorian doctrine of the person of Christ, so also in the case of the adoptionist doctrine, there was a suspicion that the communication of properties was merely an attribution of properties but not a genuine exchange.

For Beatus and his allies, there was a real exchange, so that one could say, in accents reminiscent of early Christian language, "My God suffered for me, my God was crucified for me," but could not say, "The man died, and God raised him up." For all such predicates belonged to "the single person" of the God-man, not to one or the other nature. Thus "the decisive mistake of the Spanish theologians," according to their opponents, "consists in their making sonship a predicate of the nature rather than of the person." This seemed to lead to two Sons of God, perhaps even to two Gods. For although Felix averred, "I am not dividing the persons, I am merely distinguishing the natures," there seemed in fact to be "no way to avoid saying two persons in Christ," because everything that would have been required for a duality of persons was found in Felix's writings. If Christ was a natural Son of God and an adoptive Son of God, he must be

Ildef.*Virg.Mar*.3 (*SPE* 1:65)

Fel.ap.Agob.*Fel*.33 (*PL* 104:59)

John 3:13(Vulg.)

Fel.ap.Paulin.Aquil.*Fel*.2.6 (*PL* 99:426)

Agob.*Fel*.33 (*PL* 104:59)
See vol.2:48–49

See vol.1:177
Beat.*Elip*.1.8 (*PL* 96:898)
Beat.*Elip*.1.123 (*PL* 96:971)

Beat.*Elip*.1.60 (*PL* 96:930)

Boshof (1969) 65
Paulin.Aquil.*Fel*.1.7 (*PL* 99:358); Paulin.Aquil. *Ep*.17 (*MGH Ep*.4:523)
Fel.ap.Paulin.Aquil.*Fel*.1.9 (*PL* 99:361)
Alc.*Ep.Beat*. (Levison 319)

Alc.*Fel*.7.11 (*PL* 101:223)

Alc.*Fel*.1.11 (*PL* 101:136)

Paulin.Aquil.*Fel*.1.20 (*PL* 99: 373)

Alc.*Elip*.4.5 (*PL* 101:290)

Agob.*Fel*.19 (*PL* 104:45)

Hinc.R.*Deit*.9 (*PL* 125:553); Alc.*Elip*.1.22 (*PL* 101:257)

"one person and another person [alter et alter]." But orthodox dogma taught that "he was born of his Father not as another person [alter] than the one born of his mother, but in another manner [aliter]." The alternative, regardless of how one avoided the formula itself, was "duality," the specter of a divided Christ, whom no one "could very well put back together with mere empty words." As Hincmar summarized the case against adoptionism, "there are not two Christs, nor two Sons, but one Christ, one Son, both God and man, because God, the Son of God, assumed a human nature, not a [human] person."

Hincmar's assertion of the unity of Christ was part of a treatise devoted to the unity of God the Trinity. For although the primary intent of the adoptionist movement was to safeguard the integrity of the humanity of Christ, some of its opponents, in their defense of what they defined as Chalcedonian and Nicene orthodoxy, believed that the divine in Christ was also at issue in the controversy over adoption. The polemical stand against adoptionism may have been a factor in the official affirmation of the doctrine of the procession of the Holy Spirit from the Son as well as from the Father. Paulinus made his case against Felix a trinitarian as well as a christological one, and Beatus attacked Elipandus first for "that Trinity of yours, which we do not accept," and then for "that Christ of yours, whom we do not believe to be as you teach." Arius had made the three persons of the Trinity into three Gods, Sabellius had made the one nature of the Trinity into one person, and Elipandus had confused the three persons with one another. The opponents of adoptionism were not sure whether it was descended from Arianism or whether it was guilty of Sabellianism; but they were convinced that despite its protestations of Nicene orthodoxy and its explicit disclaimers of both the Arian and the Sabellian heresies, adoptionism could not purge itself of the taint of error with which the very term "adoption," when applied to Christ, had been marked since the early church. And therefore adoptionism was condemned at the Synod of Frankfurt in 794.

At least in the case of Elipandus, the use of this term did bear some relation to the dogma of the Trinity, for he himself connected his christological opponents with

See vol.2:185–86

Paulin.Aquil.*Fel*.1.24 (*PL* 99: 377)

Beat.*Elip*.1.48 (*PL* 96:921)

Beat.*Elip*.2.23–24 (*PL* 96:992)
Paulin.Aquil.*Fel*.1.12 (*PL* 99: 363)
Beat.*Elip*.1.47 (*PL* 96:921)

See vol.1:175–76;253; vol.2:42
CFr. (794) *Syn.* (*MGH Conc.* 2–I:143–57)

Elip.*Ep.episc.Fr.*17 (*MGH Conc.*2–I:119)

the rather bizarre trinitarian doctrine of Migetius, against which he also contended. According to Elipandus, Migetius taught a doctrine of the Trinity in which the Father was believed to be David the king and the Holy Spirit

Elip.*Ep.*1.3 (*PL* 96:860–61)

was said to be Paul the apostle. As for the person of the Son of God in the Trinity, Migetius was said to have identified him as the descendant of David according to the

Elip.*Ep.*1.4 (*PL* 96:861–62)

flesh. In opposition to this version of the dogma of the Trinity, Elipandus recited the orthodox teaching that there were "three persons, Father, Son, and Holy Spirit, spiritual, incorporeal, undivided, unconfused, coessential, consubstantial, coeternal in one divinity, power, and majesty,

Elip.*Ep.*1.9 (*PL* 96:864)

having no beginning and no end, but abiding forever." The person of the Son in this Trinity was not, as Migetius said, the same as the son of David, born on earth within human history, but the one born of the Father without

Elip.*Ep.*1.7 (*PL* 96:863)

any beginning and outside time and history. This was the catholic and orthodox faith "in accordance with the tradi-

Elip.*Ep.*1.6 (*PL* 96:863)

tions of the fathers," and this had to be defended against any confusion between the Son of God and the son of David, whether such confusion be that of Beatus, who denied that the son of David had been adopted in the incarnation, or that of Migetius, who equated the son of David with the Son of God in the Trinity.

A more significant discussion of the dogma of the Trinity than that between Elipandus and Migetius was the controversy provoked by the trinitarian doctrines of Gottschalk of Orbais, who seems to have been supported

Hinc.R.*Deit.*pr. (*PL* 125:475)

by Ratramnus. The issue in the controversy was the propriety of speaking about "trine deity [trina deitas],"

Hinc.R.*Deit.*pr. (*PL* 125:473–74)

as Gottschalk did. The controversy arose, according to Gottschalk's opponent, as a question about the appropriateness of "a hymn whose author is completely unknown, in which the words appear: 'We entreat thee, O trine

Sanct.merit. (*Anal.Hymn.* 2:75)

and single Deity.'" With the memory of the conflict over adoption still vivid, some theologians appeared to dismiss the matter with a reference to the condemnation of Felix

Rab.*Ep.*43 (*MGH Ep.*5:488–89)

by Alcuin and the Synod of Frankfurt in 794. But while some of the polemics developed in that condemnation were pertinent also here, it was also possible for Gott-

Hinc.R.*Deit.*9 (*PL* 125:552)

schalk to quote the orthodox case against Felix in support of his position. In addition to the verse from the hymn,

Goth.*Div.*1 (Lambot 295) Wand.*Creat.*13 (*MGH Poet.* 2:619)

as well as similar words in other hymns, another occasion

for the dispute was the statement of Jerome that in the Trinity the Father was "the principal Spirit" and the Son "the right Spirit" and the Holy Spirit "the Spirit according to the proper name," which seemed to mean that there were "three Spirits." Instead, Gottschalk argued that Christian monotheism precluded the use of such terms as "three Spirits" or "three deities" for the three persons of the Trinity, but that it was not inconsistent with this monotheism to say that "God, [who is] Lord and Spirit, is trine in person and one in nature."

Even in his doctrine of the Holy Spirit, however, Gottschalk was concerned with the "essential questions of trinitarian theology and of the theology of the incarnation." In arguing for the notion of trine deity he was concerned to find a formula that would avoid the implication "that the humanity was assumed not only by the Son, but at the same time by the Father and the Holy Spirit, since it was evidently the divinity that assumed the humanity." "Trine deity" was such a formula, for it meant that "each person of the Trinity has its own deity and divinity." In the incarnation, therefore, only the deity of the second person of the Trinity assumed a human nature. Each person of the Trinity, moreover, was "in itself [per se] a primary power," so that in the Godhead "power," "principle," and "fullness" were all both single and trine. Gottschalk's adversaries attacked this formula as inconsistent with Scripture and the catholic faith. For Scripture did not divide the Trinity in this manner, but taught "a single and identical action of [the Trinity] everywhere"; in the story of the annunciation, for example, the angel Gabriel prophesied that the incarnation of the Son was to take place when "the Holy Spirit will come upon [Mary], and the power of the Most High [the Father] will overshadow [her]," thus naming the entire Trinity as participant in the action. Ascribing to each person of the Trinity "its own and special deity" instead of saying that the deity was common to the three persons and was therefore single could not avoid tritheism, for it meant that there were "three deities," one for each person of the Trinity.

The only alternative to tritheism, if "trine deity" were to be accepted, was a separation of the divine nature into three parts, which likewise would be a surrender of trinitarian monotheism. Arguing that, to the contrary,

Hier.*Gal*.2.3 (*PL* 26:399)
Goth.*Trin*. (Lambot 259)

Goth.*Trin*. (Lambot 264)

Jolivet (1958) 151

Goth.*Deit*.1 (Lambot 85)

Goth.*Sched*. (Lambot 24)

Goth.*Deit*.3 (Lambot 94)

Luke 1:35
Hinc.R.*Deit*.9 (*PL* 125:552)

Hinc.R.*Deit*.7 (*PL* 125:540)

Hinc.R.*Deit*.5 (*PL* 125:533)

Goth.*Resp*.3 (Lambot 137)
Goth.*Trin*. (Lambot 261)
Goth.*Deit*.1 (Lambot 90)

Goth.*Sched*. (Lambot 22)

Goth.*Trin*. (Lambot 270)

Hinc.R.*Deit*.pr. (PL 125:480)

Goth.*Deit*.4 (Lambot 101)

Goth.*Sched*. (Lambot 20–21)

Hinc.R.*Deit*.4 (PL 125:531)
Deut.6:4

Hinc.R.*Deit*.1; 18 (PL 125:484;
601–2)
Boeth.*Trin*.3 (LCL 12)

Hinc.R.*Deit*.8; 16 (PL 125:542;
587)

Hinc.R.*Deit*.6 (PL 125:537)

Hinc.R.*Deit*.16; 8 (PL 125:588;
541)

Hinc.R.*Deit*.2 (PL 125:513)

"God would not be one, true, and living unless he had been and were a trine God," Gottschalk insisted that he was introducing "no plurality at all" into God and that his theory would safeguard monotheism. It was, to be sure, a special sort of monotheism, fundamentally different from "the poverty-stricken doctrine of the Jews, [who worship] a Majesty singular in loneliness and one in person." Gottschalk's monotheism was opposed to the teachings of the Arians about "three gods" as well as to the ideas of the Sabellians about a "God one in person." But the suspicion of his opponents that Gottschalk, despite this conventional rejection of both heresies, was closer to the Arian than to the Sabellian extreme of trinitarian error found some substantiation in his own words; for while he repudiated Arianism with the deprecation "Far be it from me," his rejection of Sabellianism was accompanied with the stronger formula "Farther still be it from me." It was, he maintained, Sabellian to "believe and confess that the deity is personally one." To the chief opponent of Gottschalk, Hincmar, it was nonsense to speak of the deity as "personally trine," since "deity" was the same as the divine essence or nature, which must be single. The Shema, "Hear, O Israel: The Lord our God is one Lord," meant that there could be no plurality and no numbering in the deity. From Boethius he quoted the axiom that oneness excluded numbering and that the repetition of oneness without differentiation did not introduce plurality. Another word for "Trinity" would be "Triunity, that is, unity three times but not trine unity [ter unitas, et non trina unitas]." Hence it would be permissible to speak of "God trine in persons" or of "trine Trinity," but not of "trine deity." Hincmar's case against Gottschalk prevailed, and the formula "trine deity" was condemned at the Synod of Soissons in 853.

Both the teaching that the humanity of Christ was "adopted" and the idea that the deity was "trine" were accused of violating the authority of tradition. The accusation would, of course, reappear in all the controversies of the ninth century—and beyond. But in these controversies it acquired special significance because it involved dogmas universally accepted throughout the church. Therefore the problem of tradition would appear to merit more formal consideration here. "I ask, therefore," Paulinus inquired of Felix, "who was that teacher of error,

Paulin.Aquil.*Fel*.1.39 (*PL* 99: 393)

Alc.*Elip*.4.2 (*PL* 101:286)
Alc.*Ep*.23 (*MGH Ep*. 4:61);
Alc.*Fel*.2.5 (*PL* 101:150);
Paulin.Aquil.*Fel*.1.40 (*PL* 99: 394)

Beat.*Elip*.2.9 (*PL* 96:983);
Alc.*Fel*.1.2 (*PL* 101:129);
Alc.*Ep*.166 (*MGH Ep*.4:269)

Hadr.I.*Ep.episc.Hisp*. (*MGH Conc*.2–I:123)
CFr. (794) *Syn*. (*MGH Conc*. 2–I:153)

Hinc.R.*Deit*.pr.;10 (*PL* 125: 475;554)

Hinc.R.*Deit*.16 (*PL* 125:588)

Agob.*Fel*.pr. (*PL* 104:31);
Paulin.Aquil.*Lib.sac*.13 (*MGH Conc*.2–I:140); Ratr.*Matt*.5.8 (*PL* 120:351)
Hinc.R.*Deit*.pr. (*PL* 125:480)
Paulin.Aquil.*Fel*.1.8 (*PL* 99: 359)
Épisc.Fr.*Ep.Elip*. (*MGH Conc*. 2–I:154); Alc.*Fel.haer*.2 (*PL* 101:88); Alc.*Fel*.1.11 (*PL* 101:136); Agob.*Fel*.6 (*PL* 104: 38)

Elip.*Ep.Car.M*. (*MGH Conc*. 2–I:121);
Épisc.Fr.*Ep.Elip*. (*MGH Conc*. 2–I:155)

ap.Alc.*Ep*.166 (*MGH Ep*.4: 274)

ap.Alc.*Elip*.2.7 (*PL* 101:264)

Elip.*Ep.Alc*. (*MGH Ep*.4:305);
Elip.*Ep.episc.Fr*.8 (*MGH Conc*. 2–I:113)

one who had never been a disciple of the truth, from whom you learned that Christ was 'God by name' and 'an adoptive son'?" Alcuin demanded to know where such terms had been hiding for so long. They certainly had not come from Scripture. At no other place in the world and at no other time in history since apostolic times had the church taught any such thing. "The catholic church has never believed this, has never taught this, and has never yielded her assent to those who believe wrongly," asserted Pope Hadrian, as had the Synod of Frankfurt before him. Gottschalk's version of the dogma of the Trinity was no less an innovation. It was, according to Hincmar, Gottschalk's "custom to invent new and unheard of things, which are contrary to the ancient understanding of the orthodox." Therefore one should not be surprised at his teaching, for "ever since childhood he has always sought out novel ways of expression and is still always trying to find out how he can say things that no one else says." Yet it was not quite accurate to say that these several theories were completely unheard of. To the defenders of orthodoxy they represented the rise of "a new heresy, or rather the recrudescence of an old one." Gottschalk had been inspired by Arius; Felix, too, was sometimes accused of embracing Arianism, but it was much more common to identify him and Elipandus with the Nestorian heresy. This implied, of course, that the weight of the orthodox tradition, originally directed against these earlier heresies, was now overwhelmingly on the side of the party opposing the modern heresies.

Sometimes the controversy seemed to become a matter of pitting one part of the tradition against another. Felix maintained that it was customary among Spanish theologians to refer to Christ as "adopted," and Elipandus quoted a eucharistic prayer from the liturgy used in Spain that spoke of "the passion of the adoptive man." Other passages from the Mozarabic Rite also appeared to refer to the humanity of Christ this way. The counterclaim that, if "your Ildefonsus in his prayers called Christ 'adoptive,' our Gregory, the pontiff of the Roman see and the brilliant teacher of the whole earth, in his prayers did not hesitate always to call him 'only-begotten,'" seemed to assume a greater uniformity of liturgical usage than the language of the Latin fathers or even of the anti-adoptionists themselves would bear out. Although the

See vol.1:182–84; 197–98
Isid.Sev.*Jud*.1.1.16 (*PL* 83:
451); Isid.Sev.*Sent*.1.10 (*SPE*
2:253); Ambr.Aut.*Apoc*.5; 9
(*CCCM* 27:385; 741)
Ildef.*Cog.bapt*.39 (*SPE* 2:
279)

Beat.*Elip*.1.71 (*PL* 96:938)

Beat.*Apoc*.1.2.36–37 (Sanders 50)
Alc.*Elip*.1.3 (*PL* 101:244)

Alc.*Fel*.3.16 (*PL* 101:171)
Aug.*Trin*.1.7.14 (*CCSL* 50:46)

Alc.*Fel*.1.10 (*PL* 101:136);
Goth.*Div*.1 (Lambot 296)
Radb.*Ep.Fr.* (*CCCM* 16:170; 172)

Ambr.Aut.*Apoc*.1 (*CCCM* 27: 44)

Alc.*Ep*.166 (*MGH Ep*.4:274)

Alc.*Elip*.3.19 (*PL* 101:285)
Hadr.I.*Ep.episc.Hisp.* (*MGH Conc*.2–I:124–25)

Alc.*Elip*.4.5 (*PL* 101:289);
Alc.*Fel*.4.3 (*PL* 101:175)

Alc.*Fel*.7.5 (*PL* 101:216)
Episc.Fr.*Ep.Elip.* (*MGH Conc*. 2–I:150)

Ambr.*Inc*.8.87 (*PL* 16:840)

Elip.*Ep.Alc.* (*MGH Ep*.4: 303); Alc.*Elip*.2.5 (*PL* 101: 261)

ap.Paulin.Aquil.*Fel*.3.21 (*PL* 99:454–55)

Alc.*Elip*.4.9 (*PL* 101:292–93)

term "angel" for Christ had long been under a cloud of suspicion, it continued to be used by orthodox theologians in Spain, but also elsewhere. It was also possible in Spain to speak of "Christ clothed in a man." Yet similar expressions could be found in other orthodox writers as well, including the writers who attacked Felix and Elipandus. Although he was writing against Elipandus, Beatus of Liébana was not restrained from saying: "You know that the Logos himself assumed a man [assumpsit hominem], that is, a rational soul and the flesh of a man, and was made man while yet remaining God." Elsewhere he could refer in one sentence to "the humanity of the assumed flesh" and in the next to "the man who had been taken up" in the incarnation. Also writing against Elipandus, Alcuin employed the title "the assumed man," which he likewise applied to Christ in his works against Felix. On the basis of a quotation from Augustine, both Alcuin and Gottschalk called the humanity of Christ "the man who had been taken up." Similar language appeared in the works of other orthodox theologians as well, and Ambrose Autpert was even able to distinguish between "the assumed man" and "the Son."

Significantly, however, the term "adopted" did not seem to appear in these sources, whether patristic or Carolingian, with the possible exception of the Spanish liturgy. Isidore had proliferated titles and metaphors for Christ, but "adoptive" was not among them; on the contrary, Isidore could be quoted in opposition to adoptionism. So could many other church fathers, including Greeks, such as Gregory Nazianzus or Cyril of Alexandria in his conflict with Nestorius. Felix attempted to invoke the authority of Athanasius, but this was turned against him, with the charge that he had omitted some words that would have been embarrassing to his position. Chiefly, of course, it was "the ecclesiastical usage" of the Latin fathers that was being contested by the two sides. A passage from Ambrose, "by our very own usage [in ipso usu nostro] an adoptive son is also a true son," was quoted by Elipandus to prove that humanity of Christ had been adopted; it was charged that Felix quoted it in the form, "by our usage He Himself [ipse usu nostro] is an adoptive son and a true son." Marius Victorinus appeared in the lists of patristic authorities cited in opposition to adoptionism, although he had in fact said of Christ: "He

Mar.Vict.*Ar*.1.10 (*SC* 68:208)

Hil.*Trin*.2.27 (*PL* 10:68)
Elip.*Ep.episc.Fr*.4 (*MGH Conc.*
2–I:112)

Alc.*Fel*.6.6 (*PL* 101:206);
Hinc.R.*Deit*.2 (*PL* 125:527);
Hinc.R. *Praed*.pr. (*PL* 125:55)

Agob.*Fel*.39–40 (*PL* 104:65–67)

Hil.*Trin*.6.45 (*PL* 10:194)
Paulin.Aquil.*Fel*.3.19 (*PL* 99:
452); Alc.*Fel.haer*.4–9 (*PL*
101:89–91)
Hil.*Trin*.6.23;12.15 (*PL* 10:
174–75; 441–42)

See vol.2:70–75

Goth.*Sched*. (Lambot 20–21)
CCP (681) *Act*.11 (Mansi 11:
470;503)

CCP (681) *Act*.18 (Mansi 11:
710)

Hinc.R.*Deit*.2 (*PL* 125:512)

Hinc.R.*Deit*.6 (*PL* 125:538)

Hinc.R.*Deit*.2 (*PL* 125:527)

is not a son in the same way that we are, for we are sons by adoption, he by nature. Yet Christ, too, is a son by a kind of adoption, but only according to the flesh." There was a more serious problem in the works of Hilary, who had written: "The dignity of [Christ's] power is not forfeited when the lowliness of the flesh is adopted [adoptatur]." This served Elipandus as proof for his doctrine of the adoption of the flesh. But because the previous sentence of the quotation read, "God is adored [Deus adoratur]," Alcuin and Hincmar accused the adoptionists of tampering with the text of Hilary, which according to them, should have read: "The dignity of [Christ's] power is not forfeited when the lowliness of the flesh is adored." As textual critics, the adoptionists were right and the orthodox were wrong; but when it came to the interpretation of the text, it was the other way around: "adopt" was no more than a synonym for "assume" or "take up." Hilary had explicitly rejected the idea that salvation came through the offering of an adopted Son for those who were to be adopted, and in other passages, quoted by the critics of adoptionism, had attacked the use of "adoption" as a term for Christ.

In the controversy with Gottschalk over "trine deity," similar claims and counterclaims were exchanged. In defense of the hymn verse on which his doctrine was based, Gottschalk compiled a catena of passages from the fathers where the term "trine" had appeared, including the *Acts* of the Third Council of Constantinople, held in 680–81, at which the orthodox teaching of two actions and two wills in Christ had been defined. In the Latin version of these *Acts* Gottschalk found an anathema pronounced against the Arians for teaching "three deities," but also an edict affirming that "the trine deity is to be glorified together." Hincmar replied that the manuscript of the *Acts* of the council had been "adulterated" by Gottschalk through the addition of "this noun of feminine gender and this adjective," namely, "trine deity [trina deitas]." Later he did allow that because of the complexity of Greek theological vocabulary (which, he admitted, he himself could not read), someone might have rendered the Greek text of the *Acts* this way, "by interpreting word for word." But on the basis of his experience with Gottschalk in the predestinarian controversy, Hincmar was quite ready to charge his opponent with falsifying patristic texts, as well as with quoting them out of context, distorting their meaning, and failing to identify his quotations by title and chapter. This last charge was directed also at Elipandus by his opponents; "you have," they said, "failed to mention the names of the books and the numbers of the chapters, so as to make it more difficult to investigate your error." Hincmar attacked Gottschalk with other patristic authorities, too, such as the Athanasian Creed.

Yet Hincmar's primary authority in this as in other theological matters was Augustine. Alcuin's compilation of passages from Augustine on the dogma of the Trinity served Hincmar as a polemical resource. It was all the more appropriate to rely on Augustine's interpretation of this dogma because Hincmar's opponents were "mutilating" and "distorting" Augustine's teachings. Hence the first book of *On the Trinity* seemed almost to have been written to refute those who were misapplying these teachings. Augustine had written there that "deity . . . is the incorporeal unity of the Trinity," a formula that Hincmar quoted as: "The unity of the Trinity is the incorporeal deity." Gottschalk claimed that Augustine had frequently used the term "trine unity," which meant "neither the solitary singularity of one person nor the plurality of three gods"; and he did have irrefutable support in the writings of Augustine for this claim. But Hincmar retorted that his detailed collation of various manuscripts showed "trine deity" to be a heretical interpolation into the text of Augustine, who had never used the term. In fact, Hincmar alleged, the forger who had tampered with the manuscripts of Augustine had not had the temerity to insert the phrase "trine and single deity," which would have been too obvious, but had put in the words "trine and single truth" instead.

In the same way, the adoptionists were accused of "feigning that [Augustine] says something that we do not find among his statements." They "mistakenly count him among the partisans of [their] sect." This they did, according to Alcuin, by attributing to Augustine entire letters in which the term "adoption" was used, so as to give the impression that he had taught the exact opposite of his genuine doctrine. Elipandus's confession of faith made a point of citing several testimonies from "the eloquence of Saint Augustine." "Who is this Augustine,

Hinc.R.*Deit*.13 (*PL* 125:577)

Episc.Fr.*Ep.Elip*.3 (*MGH Conc*.2–I:144)

Hinc.R.*Deit*.18 (*PL* 125:603)

Hinc.R.*Deit*.9 (*PL* 125:552)

Hinc.R.*Deit*.pr. (*PL* 125:475)

Aug.*Trin*.1.8 (*CCSL* 50:47)

Hinc.R.*Deit*.1 (*PL* 125:499)

Goth.*Trin*. (Lambot 265) Aug.*Conf*.12.7.7 (*CSEL* 33: 314); Aug.*Mor.eccl*.1.14.24 (*PL* 32:1321)

Hinc.R.*Deit*.2 (*PL* 125:512–14)

Hinc.R.*Deit*.2 (*PL* 125:525)

Episc.Fr.*Ep.Elip*.17 (*MGH Conc*.2–I:151)

Alc.*Elip*.3.17 (*PL* 101:281)

Alc.*Elip*.2.10 (*PL* 101:267)

Elip.*Ep.episc.Fr*.10 (*MGH Conc*.2–I:114–16)

who is supposed to have said that the voice of the Father [at the baptism of Christ] thundered out over an adoptive son?" Paulinus asked, adding: "But I will not demean myself by acknowledging this Augustine with you." Although it had to be conceded that many of the adoptionists' formulas had come from the authentic sermons of Augustine, "something has been added by heretical perversity." Where Augustine had referred to the believer as "adopted man," Elipandus quoted him as saying that Christ "according to his humanity is called an adopted man"; and where Augustine had said that "he [Christ] is called Son of God together with the man He had assumed," Elipandus rendered the passage as: "He is called Son of God together with the adoptive man, and the adoptive man is called Son of man together with the Logos." Such statements as these, Alcuin retorted, had never come from Augustine or from any other catholic theologian. For he had taught "that the man became one person with God and is the one Son of God and is God."

Although Western thinkers had been assuming for centuries that there was complete unanimity among them on the dogma of the Trinity and the dogma of the two natures in Christ and had been quoting Augustine as the principal spokesman for that unanimity, it became evident in the controversy over adoptionism and in the controversy over "trine deity" that even these two dogmas were subject to serious reconsideration. As the basis for the assumption of unanimity in dogma had been the Augustinian synthesis, so it was also an unconventional reading of Augustine that underlay the reconsideration. Despite the contemporary anathemas pronounced on the adoptionists and on Gottschalk, the problems raised over the doctrine of the two natures were not to be resolved until the doctrine of the person of Christ was incorporated into a comprehensive interpretation of the work of Christ, in which the redemptive function of the human nature received its due; and the status of Augustine as a theological authority required for its clarification a more thorough investigation of how the disparate elements of the patristic tradition, including his writings, could be brought together into a new orthodox synthesis.

The Rule of Prayer

In his attack on Gottschalk's idea of "trine deity," Hincmar cited not only the authority of the church fathers

Paulin.Aquil.Fel.2.23 (PL 99:458)

Episc.Fr.Ep.Elip.3 (MGH Conc.2–I:144)
Aug.Ev.Joh.29.8 (CCSL 36:288)

Elip.Ep.Alc. (MGH Ep.4:303)

Aug.Ep.169.2.7 (CSEL 44:617)

Elip.Ep.Alc. (MGH Ep.4:306)

Alc.Elip.2.13 (PL 101:270)

Agob.Fel.23 (PL 104:51)

See vol.1:339

Hinc.R.*Deit*.19 (*PL* 125:614)
Hinc.R.*Praed*.35; 38 (*PL* 125:379; 473)

Hinc.R.*Deit*.pr. (*PL* 125:473–74)
Hymn.temp.12.4 (*Anal.Hymn.* 51:14)

Goth.*Deit*.1 (Lambot 86)

Goth.*Deit*.4 (Lambot 99)

Ps.Gr.M.*Lib.antiph*. (*PL* 78:721)

Goth.*Sched*. (Lambot 23)

See vol.1:270–71; vol.2:59–60; 78–79

Goth.*Sched*. (Lambot 22)

Hinc.R.*Deit*.3; 16 (*PL* 125:529–30;588)

Eph.4:5

Goth.*Redempt*. (Lambot 282)

Hinc.R. *Deit*.10 (*PL* 125:557)

Hinc.R.*Deit*.11; 12 (*PL* 125:564; 567)
Hinc.R.*Deit*.1 (*PL* 125:498)

Hinc.R.*Deit*.17; 18 (*PL* 125:591; 611)

Goth.*fr*.8 (Lambot 33)

See vol 1:198–99

and Scripture, but also that of the liturgy. He quoted the axiom of Prosper of Aquitaine, which by now was being attributed to Pope Celestine I, that "the rule of prayer should lay down the rule of faith." It was a principle that he found useful in another controversy with Gottschalk. For his part, Gottschalk also relied on the rule of prayer as a doctrinal authority. It was "from the conclusion of a hymn" that the controversial phrase "trine deity" had come. From another hymn Gottschalk argued that since "Lord" and "divinity" were used interchangeably, it was as proper to speak of "trine divinity" as it was of "the trine Lord." It was equally proper when a hymn spoke of the humanity of Christ as "the flesh of God." The language of the church's worship was proof that the term "trine" did not compromise the oneness of God, for the church used the singular number when it prayed: "Blessed be [Benedicta sit] the Holy Trinity." The Trisagion, whose theological interpretation had been an issue in the christological controversies of the East, was translated by Gottschalk as "trine holiness"; but Hincmar objected that this was a mistranslation, since the term really meant "thrice holy." On the basis of the liturgical practice of trine immersion in what was nevertheless, by apostolic precedent, called "one baptism," Gottschalk maintained that Father, Son, and Holy Spirit were "one in nature and trine in person." In reply Hincmar pointed out that trine immersion was by no means a universal observance, for in some provinces a single immersion had become the practice as a witness against Arianism; and such a "difference of custom does not jeopardize the one faith of the holy church." Hincmar also sought to restrain the practice of drawing theological conclusions from the rule of prayer by ascribing some instances of "trine" in Christian poetry to the exigencies of Latin meter. But the best of Christian poetry—notably the hymns of Ambrose—conformed to the principles of trinitarian orthodoxy in showing "that one God, the Holy Trinity of a single deity, is always . . . to be understood, believed, and preached."

Replying to Gottschalk's use of the liturgical formula from collects addressed to the Son, "who livest and reignest with God the Father," Hincmar took the formula as the exception that proved the rule set down by ancient canons, "that when one is officiating at the altar, prayer should always be addressed to the Father through the

Hinc.R.*Deit*.18 (*PL* 125:603-4)

Beat.*Elip*.2.56 (*PL* 96:1010)

Son" rather than directly to the Son. These same canons were also quoted in the controversy over adoptionism. The advocates of adoptionism laid great stress on the use of the terms "adoption" and "adoptive" in the Spanish liturgies, whose rule of prayer seemed to lay down their rule of faith. But in opposition to such local usage there stood the universal rule of prayer as set down by the

Episc.Fr.*Ep.Elip*.7 (*MGH Conc*.2–I:145)

church of Rome. Its liturgical tradition went back to Peter and Paul themselves, and therefore its usage was

Hinc.R.*Deit*.13 (*PL* 125:573)

authoritative. Hence it was appropriate to quote from the Roman liturgy in establishing the orthodoxy of the anti-

Alc.*Fel*.7.13 (*PL* 101:227)

adoptionist postion. The conclusion appended to most collects, in the Roman liturgy but not only there, "through Jesus Christ, our Lord, who lives and reigns as God with thee in the unity of the Holy Spirit," was a reference to "the Jesus Christ who was born of the Virgin," who therefore was not the adoptive Son of God, but the true Son. For the fundamental issue between adoptionism and

Alc.*Fel*.4.5 (*PL* 101:177-78)

orthodoxy came down to worship. "One has to ask," Alcuin said, "whether we are to adore or worship anything except the true God. If not, the inference must be drawn: 'How is it that you worship the Son of the

Alc.*Ep*.204 (*MGH Ep*.4:339)

Virgin if he is not true God?' "

The most important liturgical component in the case against adoptionism was the appropriateness of calling the Virgin Mary "Theotokos," although by now this was

See vol.1:261; vol.2:139-41

the usage of both liturgy and dogma. The apparent parallels between adoptionism and Nestorianism gave prominence to this title. Felix was quoted as having said of Mary: "By nature she is properly the mother of the assumed humanity, but by grace and honor she has become the mother

ap.Agob.*Fel*.14 (*PL* 104:43)

of the divinity." This contradicted the practice of the catholic church throughout the world, "which does not cease confessing with a free and public voice that the blessed

Paulin.Aquil.*Fel*.1.15 (*PL* 99:367)

Virgin Mary is Theotokos, that is, God-bearer." In opposition to Felix it was necessary to assert that Mary was the

Ben.An.*Fel*. (*PL* 103:1400)

Theotokos; to say, as Elipandus did, that God had not created the world through him who was born of the

Beat.*Elip*.2.59 (*PL* 96:1010);
Alc.*Elip*.1.13 (*PL* 101:250)

Virgin was to deny the doctrine of Theotokos. The orthodox use of this name was proof that the entire incarnate

Alc.*Fel*.1.13; 3.17 (*PL* 101:138; 173)

Christ was the one Son of God. Gottschalk was, for once,

Goth.*Div*.15 (Lambot 318)

a spokesman for orthodoxy when he affirmed the title and declared that "Saint Mary, ever-Virgin, is not only the bearer of the man Christ, but is also, by virtue of the unity of his person, Theotokos, that is, God-bearer." As a result of the conflict over adoptionism, the Carolingian period was "an epoch in which the doctrine of the Council of Ephesus about the 'God-bearer' was worked out" for Western theology.

It was such an epoch, however, because during the eighth and ninth centuries the Western doctrine of Mary, which, except for the thought of Jerome and Ambrose, was largely dependent on that of the East, resumed a development of its own. As in the dogmas of the Trinity and the incarnation, so in this doctrine there was a sudden eruption of discussion and debate after centuries of a rather static harmony. So thoroughly had the church fathers beat down those who taught falsely about the Virgin that "from then until the present there has not arisen any revival of error about her"; but "now, by the imprudence of certain brethren," questions were being raised for the first time concerning the doctrine of Mary. It had been emphasized already in the seventh century that this doctrine had to be considered as a unit, so that someone who became confused on any part of it would be confused about all of it. It is noteworthy that the author of that judgment, Ildefonsus of Toledo, "not only defended the virginity of Mary, but was certainly instrumental in furthering her cult." For as the very title "Theotokos" suggested, this was a doctrine in which the rule of prayer played an even more prominent part than usual in laying down the rule of faith.

Evidence to support this contention comes from the prayers and hymns that were addressed to Mary. While in the patristic period in the West "nobody observed the day of the Mother of God . . . [and] everyone prayed to St. Stephen, but no one turned to Mary," apostrophes to her now become increasingly common in Western devotion and liturgy. "I pray thee, I pray thee, O holy Virgin," Ildefonsus wrote, "that I may have Jesus by the same Spirit by whom thou didst give birth to Jesus." Admonishing his brethren to pray to the Virgin, Ambrose Autpert expressed the petition that "through her what we have done wrong may be excused, what we offer she may accept, what we ask she may grant, and what we fear she may excuse." To this same petition he elsewhere appended the words: "because we cannot find anyone more powerful in merits than thou art for placating the wrath

Ambr.Aut.*Assump*.11 (*PL* 39: 2134)

Alc.*Ep*.296 (*MGH Ep*.4:455)

Radb.*Matt*.6.11 (*PL* 120:440)

Radb.*Part.Mar*.1.17 (Canal 122)

Radb.*Cog*.81 (Ripberger 95)

Ildef.*Virg.Mar*.12 (*SPE* 1:150)

Ildef.*Virg.Mar*.1 (*SPE* 1:49)

See vol.2:139–41

Ambr.Aut.*Nat.Virg.* (*PL* 101: 1303)

Ambr.Aut.*Sanct.* (*PL* 94:453)
Ambr.Aut.*Apoc*.5 (*CCCM* 27: 369)
Ambr.Aut.*Nat.Virg.* (*PL* 101: 1306)
Thdr.Stud.*Nat.Mar*.7
(*PG* 96:689)
Ambr.Aut.*Apoc*.5 (*CCCM* 27: 369); Ambr.Aut.*Purif*.3 (*PL* 89:1294); Ratr.*Part.Mar*.3.12 (Canal 93)

Hier.*Ep*.49.21 (*CSEL* 54:386)
Cant.4:12
Aldh.*Carm*.2.20–21 (*MGH Auct.Ant*.15:13); Radb.*Part. Mar*.1.27 (Canal 127–28)

See vol.1:241
Ambr.Aut.*Assump*.4 (*PL* 39: 2130–31)
Ambr.Aut.*Purif*.4; 13 (*PL* 89: 1294–95; 1301);
Ambr.Aut.*Apoc*.5 (*CCCM* 27: 443–44)

Rev.12:1

Kamlah (1935) 130

Radb.*Matt*.2.1 (*PL* 120:106)

of the Judge, thou who didst merit to become the mother of the Redeemer and Judge." Nor was it only individual piety that directed its prayers to Mary. Although qualified with the condition, "if it so please someone," there were, according to Alcuin, celebrations of "the mass of the holy Theotokos and ever-Virgin Mary on certain days." A half-century or so later, Paschasius Radbertus cited "the authority of the church and the tradition of the holy fathers" to prove that "the blessed and glorious Virgin Mary is sung and proclaimed everywhere as the one who has been exalted in great glory above the choirs of the angels." Only Christ, John the Baptist, and Mary, he said, were honored by having their birthdays commemorated in the calendar of the church, and he used "the festival [of Mary] that you are celebrating today" as the basis for an exhortation to humility. Everyone insisted, of course, that such liturgical celebration of Mary did not detract from, but enhanced, the honor paid to her Son.

Another part of the same process was the invention of titles and prerogatives for Mary, analogous to those of Eastern liturgy and theology. To Ambrose Autpert she was "higher than heaven, deeper than the abyss, one who deserves to be called mistress of the angels, terror of hell, and mother of the nations"; again, "the temple of the Lord, the shrine of the Holy Spirit," "the promised land," and "the ladder of heaven on which God descends to earth." From such passages as Isaiah 11:1 came the designation of Mary as "branch [virga]," which, while present also in Greek theology, had a special appeal to Latins because it was a homonym for "virgin [virgo]." The patristic identification of Mary as the "garden locked" and "fountain sealed" continued to be a way of speaking about her perpetual virginity. Like the familiar parallel between Mary and Eve, most of these titles were based on a typological interpretation of the Old Testament in relation to Mary, but Mary, in turn, was seen as a type of the church. Therefore "the mariological interpretation" of the vision of "a woman clothed with the sun" in the Apocalypse, "which we take for granted, occurs only as an exception in the commentaries of the early Middle Ages," since the passage was usually applied to the church. This and other titles could sometimes be taken as referring "specifically to her, although generally to the church."

Ps.Ildef.*Serm*.1 (*PL* 96:250)

Bed.*Luc*.1 (*CCSL* 120:48)

Gen.3:15 (Vulg.)

Bed.*Gen*.1 (*CCSL* 118A:66);
Ambr.Aut.*Apoc*.2 (*CCCM* 27:
122); Alc.*Gen*.76 (*PL* 100:524)

Isid.Sev.*Gen*.1.3.15 (*PL* 50:
914); Ang.*Gen*.3.15 (*PL* 115:
141); Rab.*Gen*.1.18 (*PL* 107:
495–96)

See pp. 165–68 below

Paulin.Aquil.*Lib.sac*.14 (*MGH
Conc*.2–I:141)

Ambr.Aut.*Nat.Virg*. (*PL* 101:
1300; 1302)

Ps.Ildef.*Cor.Virg*.3 (*PL* 96:
289)

Ildef.*Virg.Mar*.12 (*SPE* 1:147)

Bed.*H.e*.5.19 (Plummer 329)

Ambr.Aut.*Apoc*.2 (*CCCM* 27:
116–17)

Alc.*Trin*.3.14 (*PL* 101:46)

Bed.*Luc*.4 (*CCSL* 120:237)
Luke 1:48

Luke 2:22

Matt.5:18
Rab.*Inst.cler*.2.33 (Knoepfler
122)

Bed.*Luc*.1 (*CCSL* 120:36)

Ambr.Aut.*Assump*.7 (*PL* 39:
2132)
Bed.*Hom*.1.3 (*CCSL* 112:18);
Hinc.R.*Praed*.24 (*PL* 125:
214); Prud.Tr.*Praed*.5 (*PL* 115:
1090)
Radb.*Part.Mar*.1.14 (Canal
120)
Sacr.Gel.214.1157–58
(Mohlberg 178)

Radb.*Part.Mar*.1.16 (Canal
121)

Like Mary, the church could be called "Theotokos," for the church was "simultaneously a bride and an immaculate virgin, as a virgin conceiving us by the Holy Spirit and as a virgin giving birth to us without pain." The "first gospel," translated into Latin as "she shall crush [ipsa conteret] your head," was part of this typology, for it was fulfilled when the church destroyed the temptations of the devil as soon as they arose; but it was also beginning to be seen as a prophecy of Mary, the woman through whose obedience the disobedience of the first woman would be undone.

Assigning to Mary so prominent a role in salvation meant that she was in some sense a mediatrix between God and man. "Through her we have merited to receive the Author of life," Paulinus wrote, and Ambrose Autpert spoke of "the world redeemed through her" and of "the life of our race repaired through her." She was hailed as the one who "repairs earthly things and restores heavenly things." Her mediation obtained the forgiveness of sins and the purification of the sinner, and her intercession healed the sick. As one whose humility had "merited the union of God and man" in her Son by "drawing down the Holy Spirit upon her," she had been the only woman deemed worthy of receiving into herself the divinity of the Son of God and of giving birth to him; for this, but even more for her continuing attendance upon her Son, she deserved the title "blessed." Her obedience to the Old Testament law of purification after the birth of Christ was not evidence that she needed such purification, but rather that her Son, as he said, had come to fulfill the law. Yet the same authors who spoke this way about Mary also represented her as in need of salvation herself. Christ had begun his work of redemption by conferring salvation on his mother, who "was not saved from iniquity by any of her own preceding merits, but redeemed by the blood of Christ solely through the gratuitous goodness of God." For it was widely held that Christ had been the only one who was conceived without original sin. If, then, she had been "born and procreated of the flesh of sin" and yet was hailed in the rule of prayer as "happy [felix]" and "blessed [beata]," this had to mean that, though conceived in sin, she "was not subject to any transgressions when she was born and did not contract original sin in the sanctified womb." In these words

Balić (1958) 165

Ratr.*Part.Mar*.2.6 (Canal 88)

See p. 171 below

Ambr.Aut.*Nat.Virg.* (*PL*
101:1301)

Ambr.Aut.*Assump*.2 (*PL* 39:
2130)

Radb.*Cog*.7–9 (Ripberger
60–61); Radb.*Matt*.1.1 (*PL*
120:97)

Ambr.Aut.*Assump*.3 (*PL* 39:
2130)

Radb.*Cog*.81 (Ripberger 95–
96)
Ambr.Aut.*Assump*.1 (*PL* 39:
2130)

2 Cor.12:2
Ambr.Aut.*Assump*.3 (*PL* 39:
2130)

"Paschasius makes one of the first efforts among western theologians to discover the doctrine of the Immaculate Conception," but he was prevented by "obscure, incomplete and imperfect terminology" from formulating this doctrine. Other writers spoke of a sanctification of the womb in Mary's giving birth to Christ, not of a sanctification in her own conception or birth; and the question of the immaculate conception of Mary was to linger throughout the Middle Ages and to erupt into open controversy in the twelfth and thirteenth centuries, without achieving definitive formulation until the nineteenth century.

There was a similar absence of consensus regarding the end of Mary's life, on which dogmatic determination came only in the twentieth century. It was recognized that the principal accounts both of her beginning and of her end were apocryphal and did not enjoy acceptance as canonical by the church, and that "no catholic history gives an account of the way she ascended to the heavenly realm." It was a mistake, Paschasius Radbertus warned, to "accept doubtful things as certain," for on the basis of reliable accounts, as distinguished from apocryphal ones, it was certain only that Mary had "left the body," but not how she had done so. In part, therefore, the case for the doctrine of the assumption had to be an argument from silence, since there did not exist an explicit theological tradition concerning the death of Mary. The proper basis for an understanding of Mary's end was the liturgical one, and the feast of her assumption was "a day that excels the solemnities in honor of all the [other] saints." By its commemoration of the feast, the church confessed that Mary had been assumed into heaven, but it did not specify the manner of her assumption; hence "the correct position regarding her assumption is shown to be this, that—without knowing 'whether in the body or out of the body,' as the apostle says—we believe that she was assumed higher than the angels."

Yet it was neither the way in which Mary was conceived nor the mode in which she was assumed into heaven but the manner in which she gave birth to Christ that became an issue between Radbertus and his monastic confrere, Ratramnus. On this issue the patristic tradition was ambiguous, for "it is clear that the fathers paid atten-

Canal (1968) 91

Hinc.R.*Div*.12 (*PL* 125:694)

Radb.*Matt*.2.1 (*PL* 120:106)
Alc.*Trin*.3.14 (*PL* 101:47);
Ambr.Aut.*Nat.Virg.* (*PL* 101:
47); Ratr.*Part.Mar.*1.4 (Canal
86–87)

Ratr.*Part.Mar.*1.1 (Canal 85)

Ratr.*Part.Mar.*3.10 (Canal 91)

Isid.Sev.*Jud*.1.10.9–10 (*PL*
83:470); Ildef.*Virg.Mar.* (*SPE*
1:67)

Ezek.44:3

Ratr.*Part.Mar.*3.14 (Canal 94)

Ratr.*Part.Mar.*3.20 (Canal 98)

Gal.4:4
Radb.*Part.Mar.*1.32 (Canal
130)
Radb.*Part.Mar.*1.40 (Canal
134)
Radb.*Part.Mar.*2.69 (Canal
152)

Radb.*Part.Mar.*1.14 (Canal
120); Ambr.Aut.*Nat.Virg.* (*PL*
101:1302)
Radb.*Part.Mar.*1.7 (Canal
116)
Radb.*Part.Mar.*1.47 (Canal
138)

Radb.*Part.Mar.*1.5 (Canal
138)

Ratr.*Part.Mar.*2.5 (Canal 87)

Ratr.*Part.Mar.*3.18 (Canal 97)

tion to the virginal conception, not to the miraculous birth" of Christ; but the details of the parturition had to be part of the doctrine of Mary's perpetual virginity. Any alternative to the perpetual virginity was unthinkable. The formula, "virgin before giving birth, virgin while giving birth, virgin after giving birth," was universally accepted. Ratramnus took this to mean that "her inviolate virginity conceived as a woman and gave birth as a mother." The miracle consisted in the preservation of her virginity in conception and in birth, but this did not imply that the physical act of birth was abnormal in other ways, as Ratramnus understood his opponents to be saying. Their position was a threat to the true humanity of Christ. Ezekiel 44:2 was a standard proof for the perpetual virginity of Mary, but Ratramnus read the following verse as evidence that Christ had come "into the house of the world" by the same way as other men: the purification of Mary in the temple proved the same thing. Paschasius Radbertus, on the other hand, interpreted the purification only as a demonstration that Christ was "born of woman, born under the law," thus as an analogy to the circumcision of Christ. To Radbertus the mode of Christ's birth was more significant than the manner of his conception. The chief interest in the mode of Christ's birth was to insist that it had taken place "without sorrow and without pain," since these were consequences of the curse pronounced on Eve; but Mary gave birth as Eve would have if she had not fallen. Apparently with Ratramnus in mind, he attacked those who, while not saying that Mary had lost her virginity in giving birth to Christ, nevertheless "deny the very thing they confess when they say that she gave birth to her Son according to the common law of nature."

In many ways Ratramnus and Radbertus were arguing past each other, for the former did not teach that the virginity of Mary had been violated in the birth of Christ and the latter did not deny that Christ had been born in a normal manner. Underlying this exchange, however, was a basic difference of attitude. Urging that "by nature nothing is shameful," Ratramnus maintained that what was "unusual" was "the order of conception, not the law of birth." A preoccupation with the miraculous aspects of Christ's nativity beyond "established nature or the

Ratr.*Part.Mar*.2.9 (Canal 90–91)
Ratr.*Part.Mar*.1.4; 1.1 (Canal 87; 84)
Radb.*Part.Mar*.1.49 (Canal 139)

Radb.*Part.Mar*.2.64 (Canal 148)

John 21:19; 26
Radb.*Part.Mar*.1.51 (Canal 141)

Radb.*Part.Mar*.1.21 (Canal 125)
Radb.*Matt*.2.1 (*PL* 120:105; 107)

Radb.*Part.Mar*.1.11 (Canal 119)

Radb.*Part.Mar*.1.6 (Canal 116)

Ambr.*Myst*.9.53 (*SC* 25–II: 186–88)

Cristiani (1968) 169
Radb.*Corp*.4 (*CCCM* 16:30);
Ratr.*Corp*.53 (Brink 47)
Radb.*Part.Mar*.2.53 (Canal 143);
Radb.*Corp*.4; 12 (*CCCM* 16: 30; 77)

Ratr.*Corp*.28 (Brink 41)

Goth.*Corp*. (Lambot 324)
Ratr.*Corp*.15 (Brink 37)

Peltier (1938) 76

authority of Holy Scripture" was a concession to "heathen superstition," by which the virgin birth would not have been a genuine birth but a "monstrosity." "We do not say, as they charge, that he was born in a montrous way," Radbertus answered, only that Mary "gave birth in the same way that she conceived." As Christ, according to the Gospel account, had passed through closed doors, so also he had passed through the closed womb of the Virgin. For the birth of Christ belonged to the order of mystery rather than to the order of nature; it was "contrary to nature, or rather beyond nature." Laws of nature—even the original law of man's creation before the fall, not to speak of the law governing man's sinful condition— did not apply to it. Radbertus discerned in his opponents' position an inversion of the proper relation between God and nature, for they seemed to forget that "the laws of God do not depend on the nature of things, but the laws about the nature of things flow from the laws of God."

This basic difference between Ratramnus and Radbertus expressed itself also in their conflict over the presence of the body and blood of Christ in the Eucharist. On the basis of a passage from Ambrose about "the order of nature," which was "the only true 'authority' on which his theory is founded," but which was quoted by both sides in the conflict, Radbertus drew a parallel between "the temerity of certain brethren" regarding the birth of Christ and their error regarding the eucharistic presence. It was certainly the statement of a consensus when Ratramnus asserted that "we do not think that any of the faithful doubts that the bread which Christ gave to his disciples had been made his body" or when one of his supporters declared that "everyone ought to believe that the body and blood of the Lord [in the Eucharist] is his true flesh and blood." His opponents "faithfully confess the body and blood of Christ," Ratramnus acknowledged. But as one "who on nearly all the theological questions agitating this epoch held to an opinion different from that of Radbertus," Ratramnus identified two alternative theories within this consensus: that which held "that in the mystery of the body and blood of Christ, daily celebrated in the church, nothing takes place under a figure, under a hidden symbol, but it is performed with a naked manifestation of reality itself"; and his own view, "that these elements are contained in the figure of a mystery, and that it is one thing which appears to the bodily sense and another which faith beholds."

Ratr.*Corp*.2 (Brink 33)

It was, as he added, "no small divergence." Two questions were involved, and it was characteristic of the controversy that Ratramnus was the one who identified them as two questions, not simply two versions of the same question. One was the nature of the presence in the Eucharist, the other the relation of the eucharistic body of Christ to the historical body of Christ. For Radbertus the two questions were closely intertwined, and his answer to the second determined his answer to the first. For the flesh that Christ gave for the life of the world in the Eucharist was "obviously none other than the one that was born of Mary, suffered on the cross, and rose from the grave." The relation between the eucharistic body and the historical body was one of identity, not merely one of continuity. What was created by the words of institution in the Eucharist was "neither some other blood nor the blood of someone else, but the blood of Jesus Christ." To sharpen the language of identity still more, Radbertus continued: "And therefore, O man, whenever you drink this cup or eat this bread, you should keep in mind that you are not drinking any other blood than the one that was poured out for you and for all for the forgiveness of sins, and that this is no other flesh than the one that was given up for you and for all and that hung on the cross." When challenged, he only repeated this formula, adding with emphasis that the flesh was Christ's "very own." Indeed, he turned one objection to his position—namely, that Christ had not yet suffered and died when he instituted the Lord's Supper and that therefore it could not be his historical body—into an argument in favor of his position by asserting that if Christ had waited until after the resurrection, "the heretics would have said that Christ is now incorruptible and located in heaven and that therefore his flesh cannot be eaten on earth by the faithful."

Ratr.*Corp*.5–6; 50 (Brink 34; 46)

John 6:51

Radb.*Corp*.1 (CCCM 16:15)

Radb.*Corp*.15 (CCCM 16:95)

1 Cor.11:26

Matt.26:28
Rom.8:32
Radb.*Corp*.15 (CCCM 16:96)

Radb.*Ep.Fr.* (CCCM 16:145)

Ratr.*Corp*.27–28 (Brink 40–41)

Radb.*Corp*.18 (CCCM 16:100)

Because of this identity between the eucharistic and the historical body, it was necessary to distinguish between "figure" and "reality." There could be no question that the body and blood of Christ was present "according to reality, even though it is received in the sacrament through faith." Christ had not said, "This is the figure of my body," but, "This is my body," and Radbertus expressed his

Radb.*Corp*.2 (CCCM 16:21)

Radb.*Matt*.12.26 (*PL* 120:890)

amazement that anyone would say that "it is not in fact the reality of the flesh and blood of Christ" present in the sacrament. To be quite precise and complete, one had to say that the Eucharist was "properly called 'reality' and 'figure' at one and the same time," since its appearance was that of bread and wine but its true reality was that of

Radb.*Corp*.4 (*CCCM* 16:28–29)

the body and blood of Christ. In the Old Testament era there had been only "the hope and the figure, in which the promise of reality was present," but now "we enjoy only

Radb.*Corp*.5 (*CCCM* 16:33)
Radb.*Corp*.10 (*CCCM* 16:68–69)

the reality," namely, "the true flesh and blood of Christ." The color and taste of bread and wine were not changed; but this was merely "the figure of bread and wine,"

Radb.*Corp*.1; 11 (*CCCM* 16:14–15; 75)

and what was in fact present after the consecration was "nothing other than the flesh and blood of Christ." This took place by the will of God, by which also "the divine Judge covers reality with figures, conceals it under sacra-

Radb.*Matt*.7.13 (*PL* 120:492)

ments, obscures it by mysteries." The presence of the body and blood of Christ was an objective reality, so that even

1 Cor.11:27

someone who received them "in an unworthy manner"

Radb.*Corp*.22 (*CCCM* 16:127)

was nonetheless receiving the true body and blood. For the reality or truth [veritas] of the presence was guaranteed by "the only-begotten Son of God, who is truth [veritas] himself, not by grace, but by nature." Therefore

Radb.*Matt*.2.2 (*PL* 120:139)
Radb.*Matt*.12.26 (*PL* 120:890)

"when truth itself says, 'This is my body,'" this was to be believed, because "the words of Christ are as efficacious as they are divine, so that nothing else comes forth than

Radb.*Corp*.15 (*CCCM* 16:93)

what they command."

Ratramnus based his interpretation of the eucharistic presence on a different definition of "figure" and "reality" from that of Radbertus. "The most simple and comprehensive statement that can be made of Ratramnus's Eucharistic beliefs is that he thought the Eucharist to be in

Fahey (1951) 77

the real order what a metaphor is in the logical order." To him, "reality" meant empirical reality, a "representation of clear fact, not obscured by any shadowy images, but uttered ... in natural meanings. ... Nothing else may

Ratr.*Corp*.8 (Brink 34–35)

be understood than what is said." "Figure," on the other hand, referred to "a kind of overshadowing that reveals its

Ratr.*Corp*.7 (Brink 34)

intent under some sort of veil." Now if the question arose as to which of those categories was the proper one for the presence of the body and blood of Christ in the Eucharist, the answer was obviously "figure"; for the Eucharist was a "mystery," an action which "exhibits one thing outwardly to the human senses and proclaims another thing

Ratr.*Corp*.9 (Brink 35)

Ratr.*Corp*.11 (Brink 35–36)

Ratr.*Corp*.48 (Brink 46)

Ratr.*Corp*.16 (Brink 37)
Ratr.*Corp*.15 (Brink 37)

Ratr.*Corp*.50 (Brink 46)

Ratr.*Corp*. 8; 92 (Brink 35; 57)

Ratr.*Corp*.37 (Brink 43–44)

Ratr.*Corp*.57 (Brink 48)
Ratr.*Corp*.69 (Brink 51)
Ratr.*Corp*.72 (Brink 52)

Ratr.*Corp*.89 (Brink 56)

Ratr.*Corp*.101 (Brink 60)

See vol.1:304–6

inwardly to the minds of the faithful." To say that "nothing is being received here figuratively, but it is all being viewed in its reality" would be to substitute sense experience for faith. Another term for reality in the vocabulary of Ratramnus was "outward appearance [species]," according to which bread and wine remained what they were; but according to their "divine force" or "as far as their power is concerned," they had become the body and blood of Christ, and it was "not permissible even to think, much less to say" that they had not.

On the basis of this schema Ratramnus proceeded to a consideration of "the second question," that is, "whether that very body which was born of Mary, suffered, died, and was buried, and which sits at the right hand of the Father is what is daily eaten in the church by the mouth of the faithful through the mystery of the sacraments," and his answer had to be in the negative. The historical body of Christ—the one that was born of Mary and that suffered on the cross—belonged to the order of empirical reality, where what was said was what was meant. But what was "called Christ's body and blood" in the Eucharist bore a certain "resemblance" to his historical body and blood and therefore could be so designated, just as Easter Sunday each year was called "the day of the Lord's resurrection" even though he had been raised historically "only once." The historical body was properly called "the real flesh of Christ," the eucharistic body "the sacrament of that real flesh." Thus there was truly "a great difference" between the two bodies, and "they are not the same." The difference between them was "as great as that which exists between a pledge and the thing for which it is pledged, between an image and the thing of which it is an image, appearance and reality." Yet Ratramnus could warn that "it should not be supposed that in the mystery of the sacrament either the body of the Lord or his blood is not received by the faithful"; by "body" and "blood," however, he meant the eucharistic "figure," not the historical and empirical reality.

In his use of the term "figure" for the body in the Eucharist and in his refusal to identify it unequivocally with the body born of Mary, Ratramnus could claim the support of a long and distinguished Augustinian tradition, in which the concept "body of Christ" itself and the idea of "eating" it in the Eucharist were part of a broader

Amal.*Off*.3.35.1–2 (*ST* 139: 367–68)

Flor.*Amal*.2.7 (*PL* 119:87)

Radb.*Ep.Fr.* (*CCCM* 16:173)

Radb.*Corp*.7 (*CCCM* 16:37–39)

Goth.*Corp*. (Lambot 327)

Goth.*Corp*. (Lambot 335)

John 6:53–58

Jul.Tol.*Antikeim*.1.16 (*PL* 96: 602)

Ildef.*Cog.bapt*.136 (*SPE* 1: 371)

Radb.*Corp*.6 (*CCCM* 16:34)

Beat.*Elip*.1.97 (*PL* 96:954)

See vol.1:356

and more "spiritual" way of speaking and thinking that went far beyond the Eucharist. One of his contemporaries, Amalarius of Metz, set forth the thesis that "the body of Christ is triform . . . : first, the holy and immaculate [body], assumed from the Virgin Mary; second, that which walks on the earth; third, that which lies in the sepulcher." The first was represented by the eucharistic host when it was dipped in the chalice, the second by the host when it was eaten by priest or people, the third by the host when it was reserved on the altar. Although this distinction evoked criticism, from Paschasius Radbertus among others, Radbertus also had to recognize that "body of Christ" could mean the church or the Eucharist or the body born of Mary. Pointing out "that we who are the body of Christ eat the body of Christ [ut nos qui sumus corpus Christi sumamus corpus Christi]," Gottschalk of Orbais distinguished between a "natural" and a "special" sense of the word. Just as it was impossible to confine "body" to the Eucharist, so also "eating" and "drinking" could be seen as referring in the first instance to faith itself and only then to the Communion. Julian of Toledo, for example, had taken the words of Jesus about "eating" and "drinking" to mean that "we say we drink the blood of Christ not only in the sacramental rite, but also when we receive his saying, in which there is life," and his predecessor, Ildefonsus, had said that "to eat this food and to drink this drink is to abide in Christ." Even Radbertus had paraphrased these words of Christ in similar fashion: "To eat his flesh and drink his blood means that one abides in Christ and Christ in him." This way of speaking could easily move from the explicit identification of the Eucharist as "the body of Christ," not one crumb of which must be permitted to fall for fear of punishment, to the equation of "the Eucharist" with the preaching of the gospel.

Although the language of the "rule of faith" as interpreted by the theologians was in many ways on the side of Ratramnus in the dispute, it was eventually the "rule of prayer" that was to "lay down the rule of faith" in the area of eucharistic doctrine; and this was working in favor of Radbertus. Not what the fathers had said about the eating and drinking of the body and blood of Christ, but what they had said about the sacrifice of the Mass would determine the teaching of the church also about the presence. The fanciful extremes to which Amalarius took his principle that there was "nothing superfluous" in the liturgy did not deter even his severest critics from compiling the exegesis of the several steps in the rite of the Mass from various sources. Ratramnus, too, found justification in the liturgy for his use of the terms "pledge" and "image," as well as for his use of the distinction between "appearance" and "reality" in speaking about the body and blood of Christ in the Eucharist. Nevertheless, the tenor of the rule of prayer was moving in the opposite direction. For Radbertus, the practice of prayer was a source of authoritative teaching not only about the doctrine of prayer itself, but also more generally about what "we believe" and what "the entire church in every nation . . . confesses," for example, regarding the Virgin Mary. After citing the daily celebration of the Eucharist as a reason for giving attention to its meaning, he went on to quote the words of the canon of the Mass, which had been quoted already by Ambrose: "Command that these things be borne by the hands of thy angel to thy sublime altar in the presence of thy divine majesty." But if what was borne was worthy of such an altar, "consider if anything corporeal can be more sublime than when the substance of bread and wine is efficaciously changed within into the flesh and blood of Christ, in such a way that after the consecration the true flesh and blood of Christ is truly believed [to be present]."

As this reference to the "sublime altar" in heaven suggests, the most important aspect of the Eucharist for Radbertus was the sacrifice, while Ratramnus, even according to his modern interpreters, did "not distinguish . . . between the sacramental reality and what we might call the sacrificial reality" and "certainly denied that the action of the Mass is a real, true and proper sacrifice." When the Epistle to the Hebrews said that Christ had made his sacrifice "once for all," this proved that "what he did once for all he does not repeat daily." Alluding to the very same passages, Radbertus taught that "although Christ, having suffered once for all in the flesh, saved the world once for all through one and the same suffering unto death, this offering is nevertheless repeated daily." For since there was daily sin, there had to be a daily sacrifice for sin. Elsewhere he suggested that if the "daily bread" sought in the Lord's Prayer referred to "the body

Amal.*Ord*.36 (*ST* 138:348)

Flor.*Exp.miss*.1.1 (*PL* 119: 15–16)

Ratr.*Corp*.85 (Brink 55–56) *Sacr.Gel*.173.983 (Mohlberg 151)

Ratr.*Corp*.88 (Brink 56) *Sacr.Gel*.229.1231 (Mohlberg 189)

Radb.*Matt*.4.6 (*PL* 120:292)

Radb.*Ep.Fr*. (*CCCM* 16:170)

Radb.*Corp*.2 (*CCCM* 16:20)

Ambr.*Sacr*.4.27 (*SC* 25–II:116)

Sacr.Gel.291.1558 (Mohlberg 240)

Radb.*Corp*.8 (*CCCM* 16:41–43)

Gliozzo (1945) 114

Fahey (1951) 80

Heb.7:27; 9:26 Ratr.*Corp*.39 (Brink 44); Goth.*Corp*. (Lambot 332)

Radb.*Corp*.9 (*CCCM* 16:52–53)

Matt.6:11

Radb.*Matt*.4.6 (*PL* 120:291)

Prim.*Scarap*.23; 25 (Jecker 56–57; 58)

Jul.Tol.*Prog.fut.* (*PL* 96:476) Bed.*H.e*.4.22 (Plummer 252); Bed.*Ep.Ecg*.17 (Plummer 422)

John 1:29 Bed.*Hom*.1.15 (*CCSL* 122: 105–6)

Bed.*E.et N*.2 (*CCSL* 119A: 329); Bed.*Tabern*.2 (*CCSL* 119A:48)

See vol.2:133–34

Isid.Sev.*Eccl.off*.1.15.3 (*PL* 83:753)

See pp. 185–86 below

Brink (1954) 64

of Christ" in the Eucharist, this could not mean that "we eat him daily," but that "he is sacrificed daily." In exhortations to the faithful, attendance at the sacrifice of the Mass was urged much more earnestly than the reception of Communion was. Similarly, the sacrificial interpretation of the Eucharist was embedded much more firmly in the church than was the idea of the real presence —so firmly that "even if it were not mentioned anywhere at all in the ancient Scriptures, the authority of the universal church, which is evident in this practice, must not be regarded lightly." Bede was confident that the "offering" of the Mass availed for the dead and that Christ "daily takes away the sins of the world" for the living in the eucharistic sacrifice, and therefore that "the Lord has offered the sacrifice of his flesh and blood to the Father and has commanded us to make our offering in bread and wine." In the Eastern iconoclastic controversy during this same century the sacrifice of the Eucharist had been a proof for the reality of the body of Christ. Now in the West it became necessary to draw the implications of the sacrifice for the doctrine of the real presence, "so that," as Isidore of Seville had said, "the sacrifice that is offered to God, sanctified by the Spirit, might be conformed to the body and blood of Christ."

There was still much that remained unresolved. A more appropriate set of concepts and terms than those available in the ninth century would have been needed to state the doctrine of the presence clearly. Nor would clarity be possible until the doctrine of the Eucharist acquired the context of an entire sacramental system, within which it could take its place. Both these needs reflected the confused state of the Augustinian synthesis itself, as the use of Augustine and of Ambrose by both sides showed. When the conflict was resumed in the eleventh century, some of the issues and even some of the names in the ninth-century debate had been forgotten. The treatise of Ratramnus was to come out of the shadows even later than that, when it became "a sort of shibboleth on the subject of eucharistic doctrine" during the controversies of the Reformation in the sixteenth century.

The Sovereignty of Grace

On no Christian doctrine was the Augustinian synthesis inherited by the ninth century as ambiguous as on

See vol.1:297–98

Cappuyns (1964) 102

See vol.1:318–27

See vol.1:327–29

Hinc.R.*Praed*.12; 22 (*PL* 125:
120; 197–201); Flor.*Tr.ep*.13
(*PL* 121:1010); Flor.*Ver*.3 (*PL*
121:1090); Flor.*Jud*.56 (*PL*
116:182); Goth.*Praed*.7
(Lambot 189); Amul.*Ep*.2
(*MGH Ep*.5:378)

Prud.Tr.*Praed*.2; 12 (*PL* 115:
1032; 1171–72)

Aug.*Enchir*.26.100 (*CCSL* 46:
103)

Amann (1937) 320
Ann.Bert. 849 (*MGH Scrip.
Ger*.31:36–37); Rab.*Ep*.22
(*MGH Ep*.5:428)

Hinc.R.*Praed*.34 (*PL* 125:353)

Hinc.R.*Ep*.188 (*MGH Ep*.8:
196)
Rab.*Ep*.43 (*MGH Ep*.5:488)

Serv.Lup.*Quaest*. (*PL* 119:639)

Flor.*Tr.ep*.pr. (*PL* 121:985–
86); Flor.*Ver*.2 (*PL* 121:1085)

Flor.*Tr.ep*.10 (*PL* 121:1004–
5)

Mauguin (1650) 2:42–43

predestination, and on no doctrine was the theological controversy as bitter. It was "the most animated controversy of the ninth century." What was embarrassing about Augustine on the real presence in the Eucharist was his vagueness; what was embarrassing about him on predestination was his clarity. The controversies over his predestinarianism during the last years of his life and during the century following his death had led, at the Council of Orange and in the thought of its leading spokesman, Caesarius of Arles, to a position that vindicated Augustine's essential teaching on grace but muffled his views on predestination to punishment. That combination was defined as normative Augustinism, and the authority of Caesarius and of the Council of Orange was so firmly established that all the various combatants in the predestinarian controversy of the ninth century had to acknowledge it. But it was inevitable, in an age when the writings of the fathers were being copied and studied more than they had been for centuries, that someone would discover in the works of Augustine, alongside his constant stress on the centrality of grace, his much less frequent but still undeniable acceptance of the corollary to this stress on sovereign grace, namely, that God acted "for the damnation of those whom he had justly predestined to punishment and for the salvation of those whom he had kindly predestined to grace."

This discovery was the achievement of "the strict constructionists among the Augustinians," notably of Gottschalk of Orbais. His implacable adversary, Hincmar of Reims, dismissed "these modern predestinarians" as "not amounting to even ten in number," but soon thereafter he had to admit that "Gottschalk . . . is said to have many patrons." One of these was Ratramnus; Servatus Lupus, abbot of Ferrières, also came to his support against those whom he sarcastically termed "certain brilliant lights," meaning Hincmar, Rabanus Maurus, and their party; and Florus of Lyons, one of the leading scholars of the time, writing on behalf of the church of Lyons, sought to distinguish between Gottschalk's personal failings and "the divine truth" that Gottschalk had articulated. On the basis of some such distinction, as restated by a later historian of the movement, we may turn to "the matter of the doctrine alone." These issues were identified by various of the participants in different ways; but Hincmar, Florus,

Hinc.R.*Recl.* (Gundlach 261);
Flor.*Tr.ep.*1 (*PL* 121:987–89);
Serv.Lup.*Quaest.* (*PL* 119:
644–45)

Alc.*Trin.*2.8 (*PL* 101:28);
Ratr.*Praed.*2 (*PL* 121:64);
Scot.Er.*Praed.*4.3 (*PL* 122:
371)

Hinc.R.*Recl.* (Gundlach 292;
261)

Goth.*Praed.*7.3 (Lambot 181)

Goth.*Praed.*7.8 (Lambot 185)

Hinc.R.*Perv.* (*PL* 126:122)

Goth.*Praed.*13 (Lambot 234)

CCar. (853) *Cap.*1 (Mansi 14:
920)

Flor.*Ver.*3 (*PL* 121:1087)

CCar. (853) *Cap.*1 (Mansi 14:
920)

Flor.*Ver.*3 (*PL* 121:1091)

Serv.Lup.*Quaest.* (*PL* 119:
637)

Hinc.R.*Recl.* (Gundlach 294)

Goth.*Praed.*13 (Lambot 234)
Flor.*Ver.*12 (*PL* 121:1115);
Prud.Tr.*Hinc.et Pard.* (*PL*
115:1010)
Flor.*Quaest.* (*PL* 121:1075)

and Servatus Lupus, opponents though they were, all enumerated three questions as the fundamental ones, albeit each in his own order. The three questions were, in the order given by Servatus Lupus: free will, predestination, and redemption.

Central in the Augustinian synthesis was the universally accepted principle that "we ought to believe both the grace of God and the free will of man," neither without the other. But Gottschalk, according to Hincmar, "confuses grace and free will" and "teaches the doctrine of grace without teaching the doctrine of free will, with the result that, under the pretense of piety, he preaches sheer negligence . . . and produces a vicious complacency." Hincmar in turn, according to Gottschalk, had "given nature preference over grace." But "no one in his right mind can say that nature is in any way greater than grace, since in fact grace is God" himself. While Hincmar stressed that God had conferred free will on angels (as well as on men) because otherwise they would have been more "like stones" than "like God," Gottschalk made the point that "every rational creature, not only the human but also the angelic, must be acknowledged as always in need of divine grace in order to be pleasing to God." When the Council of Quiercy in 853, controlled by Hincmar, asserted that "God Almighty created him righteous, without sin, and endowed with free will," Florus objected that this assertion of free will was "utterly devoid of any reference to the grace of God." And when the same council went on to declare that "God, the good and just, elected, on the basis of his foreknowledge, those from the mass of perdition whom he by grace predestined to life," Florus once more found the definition inadequate because it ignored the prior role of grace in election and seemed to make grace a consequence of divine foreknowledge; but "election was by grace alone," without respect to any merit that was to come. Such views of free will and of merit threatened to "make of no effect the gift of divine grace." No one, of course, was denying the need for grace; but it does seem clear that Hincmar, even when extolling grace, stressed its auxiliary function in relation to the free will, and that the predestinarians stressed its primacy as the divine initiative for the beginning of faith and salvation. This stress on grace, they maintained, had been the chief burden of Augustine's theology.

Aug.*Nat.et grat.*26.29 (*CSEL* 60:255)

Goth.*Resp.*6 (Lambot 153)
Aug.*Ep.*157.3.16 (*CSEL* 44:465)
Goth.*Resp.*6 (Lambot 148)

Goth.*Praed.*15 (Lambot 242)

ap.Flor.*Tr.ep.*21 (*PL* 121:1022–23)

Flor.*Tr.ep.*24 (*PL* 121:1029)

Flor.*Ver.*10 (*PL* 121:1112)

Flor.*Tr.ep.*22 (*PL* 121:1025)

Flor.*Ver.*11 (*PL* 121:1112)

Flor.*Tr.ep.*38 (*PL* 121:1050);
Serv.Lup.*Ep.Add.*4 (*MGH Ep.* 6:112)
Flor.*Praed.* (*PL* 119:100);
Serv.Lup.*Quaest.* (*PL* 119:630–31)
Flor.*Ver.*3 (*PL* 121:1091);
Serv.Lup.*Quaest.* (*PL* 119:627)

Serv.Lup.*Ep.Add.*3 (*MGH Ep.* 6:110)
Flor.*Tr.ep.*21 (*PL* 119:1024);
Serv.Lup.*Quaest.* (*PL* 119:638)

Flor.*Ver.*10 (*PL* 121:1111)

Hinc.R.*Praed.*23 (*PL* 125:209)

Hinc.R.*Praed.*21 (*PL* 125:194)

CCar. (853) *Cap.*2 (Mansi 14:921)

Hinc.R.*Praed.*21 (*PL* 125:194)

It was likewise on the basis of a passage from Augustine, comparing free will without grace to an eye that is blind, that Gottschalk denied to the free will any capacity to do anything good apart from the grace of God. Without grace, Augustine had said, freedom was not truly freedom at all, but rebellion, and Gottschalk agreed. Only after receiving the grace of Christ and being made alive by it did a person receive a truly free will. From this Gottschalk drew the conclusion that "none of us is able to use free will to do good, but only to do evil." This seemed even to his supporters to be going too far. It was essential not to deny free will, lest such a denial provide the unbelievers with an excuse. "By some sort of natural good" a human being was capable of "certain good works and certain virtues." Therefore "all men, even those who are alien from Christ, have free will," that is, "a rational and intellectual mind by which they can discern and judge . . . between good and evil." This enabled them to do certain good acts that were socially beneficial and upright. Failure to perform these acts meant that they could be held accountable, and accountability required that there be free will. But if free will referred to what man had possessed before the fall, the ability to cling to God of his own accord, then that will was dead. Free will in man after the fall "is sufficient to enable man to do evil." Adam had been born with a free will that was a gift of grace, but the fundamental Augustinian doctrine was that "we are not born in the condition in which Adam was created, but as sinners in our origin" and hence without his kind of free will. This did not mean a loss of human nature as such, but of "the good of nature." In a set of five theses Florus sought to clarify the issue by showing in what sense "the holy fathers do not deny that free will is present in men." Hincmar described free will after the fall as "sluggish and weak as far as anything good is concerned" rather than as dead; and although he spoke of men as having "our affection captive without the grace of Christ," what he meant by this was made clear at the Council of Quiercy, which equated the free will lost in Adam with the free will regained in Christ, clearly implying, he insisted, that it was solely "this free will, not any other" that had been lost.

Otherwise, Hincmar maintained, it would be not only human accountability, but divine justice that would be

Hinc.R.*Praed*.26 (*PL* 125: 270)

Rab.*Ep*.42 (*MGH Ep*.5:481)

Serv.Lup.*Ep.Add*.3 (*MGH Ep*. 6:110)
Serv.Lup.*Ep.Add*.4 (*MGH Ep*. 6:112)

Ratr.*Praed*.2 (*PL* 121:69)
Ratr.*Praed*.2 (*PL* 121:54)
Goth.*Praed*.8 (Lambot 199)
John 12:32

Goth.*Praed*.13 (Lambot 232)

John 6:44

Amul.*Grat.* (*PL* 116:101)

Amul.*Grat.* (*PL* 116:100)
Flor.*Ver*.6 (*PL* 121:1096);
Flor.*Scot.Er*.13 (*PL* 119: 178–83)
See vol.1:323

Ambr.Aut.*Apoc*.5; 7 (*CCCM* 27:411;573)
Ex.9:12

Rom.9:21 (Vulg.)
Ps.Hier.*Indur*.ap.Hinc.R.
Recl. (Gundlach 280)

Hinc.R.*Praed*.3.1 (*PL* 125:74);
Hinc.R.*Ep*.37b (*MGH Ep*. 8:19)

Flor.*Tr.ep*.39 (*PL* 121:1053)
ap.Rab.*Ep*.44 (*MGH Ep*. 5: 493)

Rom.9:18

undercut. If "these modern predestinarians" were right, then "the necessity of salvation has been imposed on those who are saved and the necessity of damnation has been imposed on those who perish." Gottschalk was teaching that God "constrains every man" in such a way that it was "vain and useless" for him, by his free will, to do any works of his own for salvation. Writing to Hincmar in rebuttal, Servatus Lupus objected to the insinuation that "there is a fatalistic necessity imposed by the truth of the doctrine of predestination . . . to the exclusion of the freedom of the will." Augustine had rejected any such insinuation. Ratramnus, who had said that the will of God acted in the hearts of men to produce in them the "movement of the will" that he wanted, expressed his surprise that "some people" concluded that this took place "by some sort of necessity and that this necessity cannot be changed in any way." But "the predestination [of God] does not compel anyone." What did it mean then for Christ to say, in a text quoted by Gottschalk, "I, when I am lifted up from the earth, will draw all men to myself"? This "drawing" put the impulse for human action in God, so that "we run in a way that befits our salvation when we are drawn by God." And when Christ said, "No one can come to me unless the Father who sent me has drawn him," this was to be understood as meaning that "he draws, not by necessity, but by his delightful will and love." This was not fatalism, for "not only could [men] have been otherwise, but they have been." As a test case it was possible to cite Judas, as Augustine had, but more attention was given to Pharaoh, whose heart had been hardened by God. There seems to have arisen a treatise, since lost, bearing the name of Jerome and entitled *The Hardening of the Heart of Pharaoh*. It maintained that "every vessel makes itself a vessel of honor or of shame by the freedom of the will in accordance with the reason with which we have been created." Hincmar repeatedly quoted the treatise as authentic; but Florus was unwilling to accept its authority sight unseen, and Ratramnus denied that it was a genuine work of Jerome's.

Yet it was difficult to evade the words of the apostle, that God "has mercy upon whomever he desires, and he hardens the heart of whomever he desires," which seemed to say that both those whom God hardened and those on

Serv.Lup.*Ep.Add.*3 (*MGH Ep.* 6:110)

Goth.*Praed.*14 (Lambot 239)

Bonif.*Serm.*2.1 (*PL* 89:846); Jul.Tol.*Nab.*38 (*PL* 96:723)

Flor.*Ver.*6 (*PL* 121:1096)

Ratr.*Praed.*1 (*PL* 121:15)

CCar. (853) *Cap.*1 (Mansi 14:920); Hinc.R.*Praed.*16 (*PL* 125:130)

Goth.*Conf.brev.* (Lambot 54)

Goth.*Conf.prol.* (Lambot 70)

Flor.*Tr.ep.*24 (*PL* 121:1028)

Flor.*Tr.ep.*28 (*PL* 121:1034) Prud.*Tr.Praed.*epil. (*PL* 115:1349–50)

Goth.*Conf.prol.* (Lambot 68)

Goth.*Conf.brev.* (Lambot 52)

Goth.*Div.*6 (Lambot 308–9); Serv.Lup.*Quaest.* (*PL* 119:623–24)

Goth.*Resp.*7 (Lambot 157); Goth.*Conf.prol.* (Lambot 56)

Flor.*Tr.ep.*2 (*PL* 121:989); Ratr.*Praed.*2 (*PL* 121:71)

Jas.1:17 Ratr.*Praed.*2 (*PL* 121:70); Goth.*Conf.prol.* (Lambot 59)

Flor.*Quaest.* (*PL* 121:1072)

whom he had mercy had been predestined to their eventual condition. Any other interpretation, according to Gottschalk, amounted to a denial of the grace and the omnipotence of God. Although the term "predestination" had sometimes been used loosely as a synonym for "providence," it referred here to "what has been predetermined, decreed, preestablished, foreordained," so that "the predestination of the acts of God is the arrangement of his eternal counsel." While they differed with the authors of this definition about whether predestination was single or double, Hincmar and his party shared the definition itself with them. In setting forth his doctrine of predestination, Gottschalk believed that he was confessing the catholic faith and that it was not he, but his opponents, who were the heretics. Speaking for the church of Lyons, Florus agreed that Gottschalk's doctrine was the truly catholic one and that Hincmar's doctrine "is very clearly contrary to the faith." Prudentius recited a catalog of orthodox fathers supporting double predestination. Gottschalk attempted to base his idea of "double predestination" on his doctrine of "trine deity," but the foundation of his distinctive teaching lay in other aspects of his doctrine of God, above all in his doctrine of divine immutability.

"I believe and confess that God, omnipotent and unchangeable, has foreknown and predestined": so Gottschalk opened a confession of his faith. The conclusion of another statement of faith was an apostrophe extolling the transcendence of God beyond time and beyond change. If God had not foreordained the damnation of the devils and of the wicked, they could not be damned; for "if he does something that he has not done by predestination, he will simply have to change," which was blasphemous. There was in God no new counsel, no new decision, consequently also no new judgment; therefore his judgment was predestined. The words of the New Testament, that "with [God] there is no variation or shadow due to change," ruled out the possibility that God could have decided on hell only after the devil had fallen. The same text from the New Testament provided a gloss on the passages where the Old Testament said that God had "changed his will":"not that by his just severity he had decreed that he would relax [his judgment]." Such pas-

Flor.*Tr.ep*.2 (*PL* 121:992)

Heb.6:13–18

Flor.*Ver*.6 (*PL* 121:1094)

See vol.1:229–32

Hinc.R.*Perv.* (*PL* 126:122)

Hinc.R.*Ep*.37a (*MGH Ep.* 8:14)

Hinc.R.*Recl.* (Gundlach 269–70)

Hinc.R.*Praed*.19 (*PL* 125: 172–73); Radb.*Matt*.2.1 (*PL* 120: 112–115); Rup.*Div.off*.3.14 (*CCCM* 7:85)

Ps.Aug.*Hypomn*.6.2. (*PL* 45: 1657)

Hinc.R.*Ep*.37b (*MGH Ep.* 8: 17–18)
Goth.*Resp*.6 (Lambot 151);
Goth.*Redempt.* (Lambot 279)
Prud.Tr.*Praed*.14 (*PL* 115: 1200); ap.Rab.*Ep*.43 (*MGH Ep*.5:489); ap.Hinc.R.*Praed*. 1 (*PL* 125:73)

Flor.*Tr.ep*.35 (*PL* 121:1044–47); Flor.*Ver*.9 (*PL* 121:1108–9); Flor.*Scot.Er*.18 (*PL* 119: 238)

sages were not proof of divine mutability, but an accommodation to human mutability. For when Scripture said that God "swore," this oath was "nothing other than the eternal and unchangeable predestination of the immovable counsel of God." As in the christological controversies of the early church, so here both sides unequivocally affirmed the absoluteness and unchangeability of God—Hincmar, too, opened a confession of faith with a statement of this tenet—but it was the predestinarians who based their doctrine on it.

Hincmar's doctrine of predestination was based rather on the distinction between predestination and foreknowledge: "If [Gottschalk] had had the knowledge and the will to distinguish between foreknowledge and predestination on the basis of the teachings of Holy Scripture and the catholic fathers, he need not have fallen into error." God had foreknown that "some, through the freedom of the will assisted by grace, would be good," and these he had predestined to salvation; he had foreknown that others would remain in their sins, but these "were not predestined to be wicked . . . or to remain in their iniquity." Therefore foreknowledge and predestination must be distinguished. A chief source of the distinction was a pseudo-Augustinian treatise from the sixth century, the *Memorandum against the Pelagians and Celestians,* which taught: "Not everything that [God] foreknew did he predestine. What is evil he only foreknew, but what is good he both foreknew and predestined." Quoting the treatise as "Saint Augustine's book on predestination," Hincmar accused Gottschalk of misinterpreting Augustine. Apparently Gottschalk himself had no difficulty in ascribing the work to Augustine, but there were others who denied its Augustinian authorship. Because of its absence from the catalog of Augustine's writings discussed in his *Retractations* and on the basis of a careful comparison with the literary style as well as with the theological content of the genuine works, Florus of Lyons demonstrated that the treatise could not have been written by Augustine.

The reason for Hincmar's insistence upon the distinction between foreknowledge and predestination, according to his opponents, was that "he does not want predestination to be understood as applying to any but the elect

Flor.*Tr.ep*.34 (*PL* 121:1043)

Prud.Tr.*Praed*.10 (*PL* 115:1126)

Goth.*Conf.prol.* (Lambot 61);
Flor.*Praed.* (*PL* 119:98)
Jul.Tol.*Antikeim*.1.100 (*PL* 96:645)

Amul.*Grat.* (*PL* 116:102)

Goth.*Praed*.24.1 (Lambot 339)

Ratr.*Praed*.2 (*PL* 121:76);
Prud.Tr.*Praed*.10 (*PL* 115:1135–39)
Hinc.R.*Praed*.19 (*PL* 125:171)

Flor.*Tr.ep*.1 (*PL* 121:989)

Flor.*Tr.ep*.2 (*PL* 121:989)

Flor.*Tr.ep*.3 (*PL* 121:993);
Flor.*Scot.Er*.17 (*PL* 119:216)

Flor.*Tr.ep*.3 (*PL* 121:994)

Flor.*Tr.ep*.3 (*PL* 121:994–95);
Flor.*Scot.Er*.2 (*PL* 119:112–14)

Flor.*Tr.ep*.4 (*PL* 121:995);
Flor.*Scot.Er*.3 (*PL* 119:121)

Flor.*Tr.ep*.46 (*PL* 121:1064);
Flor.*Scot.Er*.11 (*PL* 119:169)
Flor.*Tr.ep*.5 (*PL* 121:997)

Flor.*Tr.ep*.6 (*PL* 121:998)

Ratr.*Praed*.1 (*PL* 121:24)

Isa.45:11(Vulg.)

and wants only foreknowledge to apply to the damned." They themselves did make use of the distinction when they, in turn, accused some of Gottschalk's enemies of confusing foreknowledge and predestination, and when they identified God's foreknowledge of sin as the basis for predestination to damnation; but in keeping with earlier theologians they would not make God's foreknowledge of human merit a basis for predestination to salvation, for this was by grace. Strictly speaking, it was not accurate to refer to "*fore*knowledge" in God, with whom there was no before or after and therefore no "interval" of time between foreknowledge and predestination, as Hincmar also had to agree. In the most careful and thorough analysis of foreknowledge and predestination to have come from any of the participants in the controversy, Florus set down "seven rules of faith": "The foreknowledge and predestination [of God] is eternal and unchangeable"; "There is nothing . . . in the acts of God . . . that he himself . . . has not foreknown and immovably foreordained"; "In the works of God Almighty there are not some that are foreknown and others that are predestined"; "Good works belong to the creature itself in such a way that they are altogether . . . the works of the Creator, but the evil works of that same creature . . . can be said to be foreknown by God, but not predestined"; "By his foreknowledge and predestination God . . . has not imposed necessity on anyone"; "Wherever the idea of foreknowledge and of predestination appears [in Scripture, even though the words themselves are not used], foreknowledge and predestination are meant"; "We believe that none of the elect can perish, and we maintain that none of the damned can ever be saved."

The possible consequences of blurring the distinction between foreknowledge and predestination became evident when, for example, Ratramnus wrote: "Nothing that happens to men in this world takes place apart from the secret counsel of God Almighty. For God, foreknowing all things that are to follow, decreed before the ages how they are to be arranged through the ages." It was easy for such a doctrine of divine omnipotence to become a thoroughgoing determinism, according to which God did all things, both evil and good. The crux of interpretation was the passage: "He has done the things that are to be."

It had been cited by Augustine in his explanation of pre-destination, and it recurred throughout the writings of the predestinarians. Gottschalk used it as a proof text in his detailed confession of faith; Ratramnus took it to mean that "the things that are to be done by God through intervals of time have already been done in the counsel of [his] predestination," so that "those whom he is going to condemn to punishment he has already condemned in predestination"; Prudentius paraphrased it to say that God had "created, ordained, disposed, dispensed, destined, and predestined" all his deeds; Servatus Lupus, on the basis of these words, argued that, for God, "predestined" and "perfected" were identical, since what God had decreed could not be changed; and Florus quoted the passage to demonstrate that all the actions of God already existed "eternally and immovably in his eternal and unchangeable counsel." From the words "He has done the things that are to be" came also the way out of the difficulty, the thesis that it was the actions of God himself that were predestined, not the actions of his creatures, as it was written in the prophet: "I the Lord have spoken, and I have done it." God was "the author and orderer" of good, and the orderer but not the author of evil.

If God's "ordering" of evil included the actions that he was going to take in history but had already taken in eternity, his eternal act of predestination must pertain to the evil as well as to the good and must therefore be dual, not single. The classic statement of dual predestination had not come from Augustine directly, but had been formulated by Isidore on the basis of Augustine: "There is a double predestination, whether of the elect to rest or of the damned to death. Both are caused by divine judg-ment." Nor was this statement an isolated lapse in Isidore's writings. Not only did he speak, in Augustinian fashion, of "those who now seem to be elect and holy" but who would be damned on the Day of Judgment; but he con-fined the gift of grace "solely to the elect," and taught that the others had been "predestined to punishment and had been damned," so that, being forsaken by God, "they could not deplore their evils even if they wanted to." Such was "the hidden order of predestination," which surpassed hu-man understanding. It was not surprising, therefore, when, as Hincmar reported with dismay, his opponents quoted "as an authority Isidore, the Spanish bishop, a learned

Aug.*Praed.sanct.*10.19 (*PL* 44: 974)
Goth.*Conf.prol.* (Lambot 56; 63); Goth.*Praed.*7.5 (Lambot 182)

Ratr.*Praed.*2 (*PL* 121:68)

Ratr.*Praed.*1 (*PL* 121:33)

Prud.Tr.*Praed.*1 (*PL* 115:1022)

Serv.Lup.*Quaest.* (*PL* 119: 643); Serv.Lup.*Ep.Add.*4 (*MGH Ep.*6:112)

Flor.*Quaest.* (*PL* 121:1067); Flor.*Tr.ep.*28 (*PL* 121:1034)

Flor.*Tr.ep.*2 (*PL* 121:989); Flor.*Praed.* (*PL* 119:99–100); Ratr.*Praed.*2 (*PL* 121:80)

Ezek.17:24(Vulg.)

Ratr.*Praed.*1 (*PL* 121:15)

Isid.Sev.*Sent.*2.6.1 (*SPE* 2: 314)

Isid.Sev.*Sent.*1.29.7 (*SPE* 2: 301)
Isid.Sev.*Sent.*2.5.6 (*SPE* 2: 311–12)

Isid.Sev.*Diff.*2.32.117–18 (*PL* 83:88)
Isid.Sev.*Sent.*2.15.1 (*SPE* 2: 335)

Isid.Sev.*Sent.*2.6.6 (*SPE* 2:315)

Hinc.R.*Praed.*9 (*PL* 125:96)

Goth.*Conf.brev.* (Lambot 54);
Goth.*Conf.prol.* (Lambot 67);
Goth.*Resp.*7 (Lambot 154–55)
Ratr.*Praed.*2 (*PL* 121:55–60);
Prud.Tr.*Praed.*2 (*PL* 115:1029)

Hinc.R.*Praed.*9 (*PL* 125:97–98)

Hinc.R.*Praed.*19 (*PL* 125:174; 177)

Goth.*Praed.*24.1 (Lambot 339);
Flor.*Scot.Er.*2 (*PL* 119:111)

CCar. (853) *Cap.*1 (Mansi 14:920)

Ps.Aug.*Hypomn.*6.6.8 (*PL* 45:1661–62)

Hinc.R.*Ep.*37b (*MGH Ep.*8:19)

Hinc.R.*Recl.* (Gundlach 272)

Hinc.R.*Recl.* (Gundlach 269)
Goth.*Resp.*7 (Lambot 155)

Flor.Tr.*ep.*30 (*PL* 121:1038);
Ratr.*Praed.*2 (*PL* 121:53)
Flor.Tr.*ep.*6; 32 (*PL* 121:998; 1040)

man and one who is in many ways beneficial to those who read him, who in his book of *Sentences* says that predestination is double." Gottschalk quoted these words of Isidore at length and often, and so did his supporters. Hincmar's defense against the barrage of patristic testimony was to disengage the language of Isidore from that of others, including especially Gregory the Great; and, since Isidore's statements still stood, he explained that the term "double predestination" could be taken in a catholic sense if it were understood to mean that God's grace granted to the elect what they did not merit and that his justice granted to the damned what they did deserve.

Although "double predestination" thus had a certain patristic legitimacy, it was, according to Hincmar and his party (and, for that matter, according to Gottschalk and his party also) preferable to speak of "one predestination of God, which pertains either to the gift of grace or to the retribution of justice." This still left the question of how to deal with "predestination to punishment." The answer came from Pseudo-Augustine, who set down "this rule of argument made clear in the divine testimonies: that the sinners who have been foreknown in their own sins before they were in the world have not been predestined, but their punishment has been predestined for them on the basis of their having been foreknown." Hincmar made this answer his own, declaring that "God has predestined what divine equity was going to render, not what human iniquity was going to commit." Therefore punishment had been predestined for the devil and for all those who, by their own free will, would join themselves to him. This was opposed to the teaching of the predestinarians, whom Hincmar understood to be saying that some "had been predestined to punishment and had been created so that they might go to eternal fire." Gottschalk and his supporters maintained that they did not teach this, but that Hincmar's distinction between predestination *to* punishment and predestination *of* punishment was an evasion; for "just as [God] has predestined certain punishments for those who deserve them, so most certainly he has predestined for those punishments those same ones who deserve them." Those who were predestined to punishment could not be saved, not because they could not be converted but because they

Serv.Lup.*Quaest.* (PL 119: 628); Flor.*Praed.* (PL 119: 98)
Goth.*Conf.prol.* (Lambot 55–56); Flor.*Praed.* (PL 119: 99)

Prud.Tr.*Hinc.et Pard.*3 (PL 115:976); Ratr.*Praed.*2 (PL 121:49)
Goth.*Praed.*7.9 (Lambot 190)

Serv.Lup.*Quaest.* (PL 119:629)

See vol.1:321

1 Tim.2:4
See vol.1:325–27

Hinc.R.*Recl.* (Gundlach 276)

Hinc.R.*Recl.* (Gundlach 294–95); Hinc.R.*Praed.*34 (PL 125:367)

Flor.*Tr.ep.*11 (PL 121:1005)

Prud.Tr.*Hinc.et Pard.*3 (PL 115:976–77); Flor.*Tr.ep.*11–12 (PL 121:1005–9); Serv.Lup. *Quaest.* (PL 119:636–37)

Goth.*Praed.*14 (Lambot 238)

Serv.Lup.*Quaest.* (PL 119: 646)

Serv.Lup.*Quaest.* (PL 119: 646)

Hinc.R.*Ep.*37a (MGH Ep.8: 14)

refused to be. Their damnation—and their predestination to damnation—was just. God had not predestined evil things, but only good things, one of which, however, was his justice, which did not leave sin unpunished. He did not predestine anyone to sin, but to the punishment merited by sin. It was better even for the wicked that they be condemned than that they be permitted to go on sinning; indeed, it was good for everyone, "so that the boasting of the proud might be put down, the devotion of the humble might grow, and the praise of God by both might be increased."

For these latter-day Augustinians, as for their master, the most serious crux of interpretation raised by such a view of predestination was the statement of the apostle Paul that God "desires all men to be saved and to come to the knowledge of the truth," which had been explained by Augustine's apologist, Prosper, and was now being explained by such theologians as Hincmar on the basis of Prosper, to mean that "because no one is saved without his own will . . . [God] desires that we desire the good and, when we desire it, he desires to fulfill in us his plan." This statement of Paul's, the predestinarians had to admit, was "extremely perplexing and much discussed in the writings of the holy fathers and explained in many different ways." Therefore its interpretation was "not to be settled precipitately, but very cautiously." They rehearsed Augustine's various attempts to circumvent the text's affirmation of the universal salvific will of God. From the use of the identical word "desires" in 1 Timothy 2:4, "who desires all men to be saved," and in Romans 9:18, "He has mercy upon whomever he desires," Gottschalk strove to demonstrate that "truly God has not in any way desired to save with eternal salvation those whom, as Scripture testifies, he hardens." The "all men" in the text must mean "all men who are saved" rather than "all men" in general.

Logically, such a line of argumentation had to lead to the even larger question: Did it imply that "not all men are redeemed" by the death of Christ, as well as that "not all men are saved" eventually? Hincmar cited as one of Gottschalk's errors "that the suffering of Christ was not offered up for the salvation of the whole world and that original sin is not washed away through the grace of baptism for the nonpredestined." In opposition to this

Hinc.R.*Praed*.27 (*PL* 125:282)

restriction of the death of Christ to the elect, the Council of Quiercy in 853, and Hincmar in support of Quiercy, declared that "just as there is not, has not been, and will not be any human being whose nature was not assumed in our Lord Jesus Christ, so there is not, has not been, and will not be any human being for whom He has not suffered, even though not all are redeemed by the mystery of His suffering." Although Gottschalk's supporters retorted that such sharing of their human nature by Christ was of no avail to unbelievers, they, too, had to accept a christological basis for the doctrine of predestination. Partly as a consequence of the controversy over the "adoption" of the human nature of Christ, the statement of the apostle Paul that Christ had been "predestined to be the Son of God" was interpreted by both Gottschalk and Hincmar as a reference to the human nature of Christ, predestined for the work of redemption.

CCar. (853) *Cap*.4 (Mansi 14:921)

Flor.*Ver*.13 (*PL* 121:1122)

Paulin.Aquil.*Fel*.2.1 (*PL* 99:417); Alc.*Fel*.2.13 (*PL* 101:156); Agob.*Fel*.17 (*PL* 104:44)

Rom.1:4(Vulg.)

Goth.*Praed*.24.3 (Lambot 344); Hinc.R.*Recl*. (Gundlach 268–69)

Both of them likewise agreed that this "redemption" in the strict sense of the word was not shared by all men and that therefore Christ could not be said to have redeemed all men. But it was quite another matter to say that Christ had not suffered for all men. If someone who accepted the gift of redemption, and then rejected it and perished, could be called by the New Testament one "for whom Christ died," Hincmar maintained, then Christ had suffered and died also for those who refused ever to accept the gift. "As far as the kindness of the Redeemer, the greatness and power of the price [he paid], and the richness of the redemption are concerned, Christ died for all men." For if Christ had died only for the elect, God could be accused of injustice. Turning this argument about the richness of the redemption against Hincmar, the predestinarians charged that by his view it would have to be concluded that the blood of Christ, shed also for those who refused it, had been wasted. But it had not been wasted, because "the body of Christ was sacrificed for the body of Christ," that is, for the church, made up of "all believers in Christ who have been or are or ever will be." The sins of those outside the church were not weighed in the balance of the death of Christ. All those whom God desired to save were saved through redemption by the blood of Christ, and none of them would perish. For the saving will of God always accomplished its ends. To say that Christ had suffered for

Goth.*Redempt*. (Lambot 279–80); Hinc.R.*Praed*.34 (*PL* 125:366)

1 Cor.8.11

Hinc.R.*Praed*.32 (*PL* 125:309); Hinc.R.*Recl*. (Gundlach 290–91)

Hinc.R.*Recl*. (Gundlach 291–92)
Hinc.R.*Praed*.34 (*PL* 125:350)

Goth.*Praed*.10.1 (Lambot 214)

Flor.*Tr.ep*.16 (*PL* 121:1015)

Flor.*Ver*.14 (*PL* 121:1129)
Goth.*Praed*.16 (Lambot 243–44)

Goth.*Deit*.3 (Lambot 98); Goth.*Praed*.10.1 (Lambot 214)
Prud.Tr.*Hinc.et Pard*.4 (*PL* 115:979)

Flor.*Ver*.14 (*PL* 121:1123–24);
Goth.*Praed*.7.9 (Lambot 188–89)

See vol.1:151

Goth.*Praed*.18 (Lambot 249)

Hinc.R.*Recl.* (Gundlach 261)

Goth.*Redempt.* (Lambot 281)
Flor.*Tr.ep*.15–16 (*PL* 121: 1012–13)

2 Cor.5:19

1 John 2:2

Goth.*Praed*.9.3 (Lambot 204)

John 12:32

Serv.Lup.*Quaest.* (*PL* 119:645)

1 Tim.2:6

Flor.*Ver*.14 (*PL* 121:1124)

Matt.20:28

Flor.*Tr.ep*.27 (*PL* 121:1032)

Flor.*Tr.ep*.20 (*PL* 121:1021–22)
Matt.26:28

Prud.Tr.*Hinc.et Pard*.3 (*PL* 115:976)

Goth.*Praed*.7.9; 9.3; 12 (Lambot 189; 205; 226)

Hinc.R.*Recl.* (Gundlach 290)

See vol.1:309–11

all men, including even Antichrist, was an unheard-of novelty and presumption. Even Origen's universalism was preferable to the idea that Christ had died for those who were damned, for at least it did not say that the death of Christ had gone to waste.

Any answer to the question of whether Christ had suffered for all men or only for the elect had to be squared, even by those who contended that Scripture dealt only with the predestined, with the various statements of Scripture about redemption. On the basis of a concordance study, Gottschalk listed ten senses in which the word "redemption" was used in the Bible, and he put his argument into that context; Florus devised a different set of categories for his argument. In this framework it was possible to argue that such New Testament phraseology as "reconciling the world" and "expiation for the sins of the whole world" referred only to the elect rather than to all men, since God had "elected a world from out of the world." The frequently discussed words of Christ, "I will draw all men to myself," must be understood to be using "all men" to mean only the elect, "gathered together from all classes of men." The statement of the apostle Paul that Christ "gave himself as a ransom for all" was speaking of all who were truly regenerate. It had to be interpreted in the light of the parallel statement of Christ himself about "a ransom for many." By saying that he was shedding his blood "for many," Christ showed that "all men" identified "those many for whom the Lord . . . says that his blood was shed." In instituting the sacrament, Christ had explicitly said "not 'for all' but 'for many,' not 'for others' but 'for you.' " The most that Hincmar could reply to this sacramental argument, as stated several times by Gottschalk, was to claim that since Judas had been present when the words "for many" and "for you" had been spoken, they did include someone who was not a true believer.

A more serious sacramental argument against Gottschalk's position was based on the historic Augustinian defense of the objective efficacy of the sacraments regardless of the moral and religious condition of either the minister or the recipient. Amolo of Lyons stated his displeasure at Gottschalk's idea that no one who had been redeemed by the blood of Christ could perish. "All those who faithfully come to the baptism of Christ," he wrote to Gottschalk, "have been redeemed by no other price than the blood of Christ. But when some of them make this grace to be of no effect in them and thus perish forever, in what way is it true that no one can perish who has been redeemed by the blood of Christ?" The same was true of the other sacraments, which Gottschalk's doctrine made "perfunctory and useless" in those who believed and then fell away. This was, Hincmar charged, a negation of the cross of Christ and of the sacrament of baptism. He accused Gottschalk of teaching that "the grace of baptism does not take away original sin from those who have not been predestined to life." Consideration of this difficulty required a refinement of the predestinarian doctrine. For while it was true that the death of Christ was of no avail for those who were baptized and then fell away, there was a sense in which one was obliged to speak of "a redemption that is common to the elect and to the damned," namely, "the redemption that takes place through the grace of baptism," "which washes away past sins, but does not redeem from future sins." In this sense Christ could be said to have been crucified for the redemption also of those who temporarily became "participants in his redemption" but later forsook the state of grace. The sacrifice of the Mass was offered up for "no one except the one who has been reborn by the grace of baptism." As an Augustinian, Gottschalk urged that he, not his opponents, was the champion of the doctrine of baptism by his stress on the sovereignty of grace and the divine initiative carried out in infant baptism. It was also consistent with Augustinian sacramentalism when unbaptized infants were denied salvation and when heathen who had not heard the gospel were said to be damned—both of these because of original sin.

Like the ninth-century controversy over the Eucharist, the ninth-century debate over predestination "lacked many later distinctions and theological definitions" and could not be settled at this time. In 853 at Quiercy Hincmar convoked a synod of his supporters, who decreed a doctrine of predestination based on the distinction between foreknowledge and predestination and on a predestination of punishment but not a predestination to punishment. Two years later a synod at Valence condemned the actions of Quiercy and decreed "a predestination of the elect to life and of the damned to death." This was confirmed in 859 at a synod held in Langres. In that same year, according to *The Annals of Saint-Bertin,*

Margin notes

Amul.*Ep*.2 (*MGH Ep*.5:371)
Hinc.R.*Praed*.34 (*PL* 125:365)

Hinc.R.*Recl*. (Gundlach 285)

Goth.*Praed*.12 (Lambot 229)

Goth.*Praed*.11 (Lambot 222)

Flor.*Tr.ep*.15–16 (*PL* 121:1012–13)

Flor.*Ver*.14 (*PL* 121:1126)

See vol.1:302
Goth.*Praed*.14 (Lambot 239)

See vol.1:304
Flor.*Tr.ep*.6 (*PL* 121:999)

Flor.*Ver*.12 (*PL* 121:1118)

Vielhaber (1956) 71

CCar. (853) *Cap*.1 (Mansi 14:920)

CVal. (855) *Can*.3 (Mansi 15:4)
CLing. (859) *Can*.3 (Mansi 15:537–8)

"Nicholas, the Roman pontiff, issues a faithful confirmation and catholic determination about the grace of God and free will, about the truth of double predestination, and about the doctrine that the blood of Christ was shed

Ann.Bert.859 (MGH Scrip. Ger.31:53)

[only] for all believers." Hincmar attributed this entry in the chronicle to Prudentius and, writing in 866, claimed that he had not heard or read of the pope's action from any

Hinc.R.Ep.187 (MGH Ep.8: 196)

other source. Although theologians and historians have debated the question since, there seems to be no other definite evidence regarding the action of Pope Nicholas in 859. Gottschalk's refusal to be reconciled even on his

Hinc.R.Deit.19 (PL 125:618)

Flor.Tr.ep.10 (PL 121:1004–5)

deathbed and Hincmar's prosecution of the case against Gottschalk even after the death of "the miserable monk" suggest not only the role of personal factors in the controversy, but also the unresolved character of the theological issues themselves.

At least two of these issues had to be clarified in the centuries that followed. One issue was the doctrine of the atonement, which was, in Gottschalk's theology, a corollary of predestination. Yet all the parties to the debate maintained that the doctrine of redemption was fundamental to it, so that there could be no answer to the question of whether Christ had suffered for all men or only for the elect until the prior question had been addressed: What was redemptive about the suffering and death of Christ? Gottschalk's doctrine of predestination was an attempt to harmonize the "kindness" and the

Goth.Conf.prol. (Lambot 56)

"judgment" of God; and Florus formulated the paradox of justice and mercy even more sharply when he noted that in biblical passages where God was said to have changed his mind, "he decreed one thing by his justice and did another thing by his goodness, and yet he, being both just and merciful, did not do anything that was

Flor.Quaest. (PL 121:1072);
Flor.Scot.Er.1 (PL 119:104–5)

self-contradictory." The relation of the justice of God to the mercy of God, and of both to redemption through the death of Christ, was to be the theme of Anselm's work, in which the doctrine of predestination, precisely because it was not the main point, could be dealt with as part of the total doctrine of redemption.

The other issue raised by Gottschalk was the one implicit in all the debates of the ninth century, namely, the authority of the fathers and especially of Augustine. Was the attack on Gottschalk, Florus asked, "a hidden way

Flor.Scot.Er.4 (PL 119:126)

of charging Augustine with heresy"? And were Gott-

Prud.Tr.*Praed*.5 (*PL* 115: 1078)
Rab.*Ep*.42 (*MGH Ep*.5:481–82); Hinc.R.*Praed*.5 (*PL* 125: 89)
Goth.*Conf.brev*. (Lambot 52–53); Goth.*Conf.prol*. (Lambot 57–58)
Prud.Tr.*Hinc.et Pard*.6–7; 13 (*PL* 115:980–89; 1004–10); Serv.Lup.*Coll*. (*PL* 119:647–66)

Flor.*Sent*.pr. (*PL* 116:107)

Hinc.R.*Praed*.35 (*PL* 125:381)

Hinc.R.*Ep*.37b (*MGH Ep*.8: 16)

Cappuyns (1964) 385

Alc.*Trin*.pr. (*MGH Ep*.4:415)
Rab.*Inst.cler*.3.20 (Knoepfler 228)

Hinc.R.*Ep*.37a (*MGH Ep*.8: 16)

Scot.Er.*Periph*.5.4 (*PL* 122: 868–70)

Flor.*Scot.Er*.pr. (*PL* 119:101–3)

schalk's critics claiming, Prudentius asked, that "no one but you has either read or understood the books of the celebrated Augustine"? Gottschalk's opponents were unanimous in attacking him for distorting Augustine; but he was able to counter with many quotations from Augustine in defense of his doctrine, and his supporters provided more of the same. It was, according to Florus, easy for "the devoted and simple reader" to become confused by "the great and multiple arguments" of Augustine and to weary of the question. Even Hincmar had to admit that it was "superfluous" to enumerate patristic quotations, since his opponents, too, "collect and accumulate many testimonies from many sources." Rather one must recognize that "it is not the number of the testimonies but their authority that counts." Determining this authority, he said elsewhere, called for historical scholarship and interpretive skill. But it was only when the status of patristic authority was moved to the center of theological inquiry that such scholarship and such skill became available to the theological enterprise. This was to be the work of the twelfth century.

The Claims of Reason

The Augustinian synthesis contained, at least inchoately, another way out of the dilemma posed by the doctrine of predestination, and, for that matter, out of the paradox of the eucharistic presence. It was to transpose the entire structure of nature and grace into an "exemplaristic monism" in which these theological tenets, and ultimately all Christian theological tenets, could be seen as little more than particular instances of certain universal ontological principles. Even the most orthodox of ninth-century theologians spoke of "the principles of dialectic" by which such doctrines as the Trinity could be "explained." They called dialectic "the discipline of disciplines," and they criticized Gottschalk and his ilk for failing to understand that "Augustine and the other doctors, in their conflicts against the heretics, were speaking dialectically." Now a theological system arose in which dialectic, as "the mother of the arts," was applied to Christian thought in a fashion that seemed to the orthodox to be a presumptuous denial of Scripture and tradition. This was the system of John Scotus Erigena. To him "that art which is called dialectic is not the product of human invention, but has been

Scot.Er.*Periph*.4.4 (*PL* 122: 748–49)

Hinc.R.*Praed*.31 (*PL* 125:296)

Scot.Er.*Periph*.5.3 (*PL* 122: 865–66)

Scot.Er.*Exp.C.h*.1.3 (*CCCM* 31:16–17)

Scot.Er.*Exp.C.h*.7.2 (*CCCM* 31:105)
Scot.Er.*Periph*.4.20 (*PL* 122: 836)

Scot.Er.*Ev.Joh*.1.30 (*SC* 180: 162)

Scot.Er.*Ev.Joh*.6.5–6 (*SC* 180: 352–58)

Scot.Er.*Exp.C.h*.7.2 (*CCCM* 31:103–4); Scot.Er.*Carm*. 2.3.61–65 (*MGH Poet.* 3:533)

See vol.1:249–51; 270–74; vol. 2:83–84
Scot.Er.*Periph*.2.11 (*SLH* 9: 34)
Scot.Er.*Periph*.5.38 (*PL* 122: 994)
Scot.Er.*Exp.C.h*.1.3 (*CCCM* 31:17)

Scot.Er.*Ev.Joh*.1.31 (*SC* 180: 178)

Walker (1966) 158

Pard.ap.Flor.*Tr.ep*.39 (*PL* 121:1052); Scot.Er.*Praed*.pr. (*MGH Ep.* 5:630–31)

established in the nature of things by the Author of all the arts."

Applying the techniques of dialectical analysis to the Eucharist, Erigena composed a treatise in which he taught, according to Hincmar, "that the Sacrament of the Altar is not the true body and the true blood of the Lord, but only a memorial of his true body and blood." The treatise itself has been lost, but from his other writings it is evident that the framework for his thinking about the Eucharist was an interpretation of the universe according to which "there is nothing among visible and corporeal things that does not signify something incorporeal and intelligible." Hence "this visible Eucharist, which the priests of the church confect daily on the altar from the sensible material of bread and wine . . . is a type and an analogy of spiritual participation in Jesus." He taught that the church—unlike the heavenly powers, which needed no such mediation—was formed by the sacraments of blood and water, the Eucharist and baptism, to which elsewhere he added chrism as the third of "the symbols of the New Testament." Sometimes he seemed to be saying that the historical content of the Eucharist made the term "symbol" inappropriate for it, but elsewhere he was also quite willing to use the term for the Eucharist and the other sacraments of the New Testament. Yet it was not a "mere symbol" for Erigena; nothing really was. For what it symbolized and memorialized was the reality of a presence of Christ, through the communication of properties, "according to the flesh . . . always and everywhere, yet neither local nor temporal," in both his natures. Of this "unity of the human and the divine substance" the Eucharist was a "truth-bearing sign," in which, beyond all that was physical, believers "spiritually sacrifice [Christ] and eat him not dentally but mentally [mente non dente]." Thus to some of his contemporaries and to some later interpreters, "it is chiefly in his conception of the Eucharist that Erigena's unorthodoxy appears."

Because his treatise on the Eucharist was destroyed while his treatise on predestination was preserved, together with some responses to it, it is much less difficult to reconstruct Erigena's role in the predestinarian controversy than in the eucharistic controversy. At the behest of bishops Hincmar and Pardulus, he undertook to reply to Gottschalk's doctrine, even though "the doctrine of

Dörries (1925) 98

Scot.Er.*Praed*.2.5; 12.1 (*PL* 122:363; 401–2)
Scot.Er.*Periph*.2.2; 2.20 (*SLH* 9:14; 76)

Scot.Er.*Periph*.3.9 (*PL* 122: 645)
Isa.45:11(Vulg.)
Scot.Er.*Periph*.4.14 (*PL* 122: 807)

Scot.Er.*Praed*.9.6 (*PL* 122: 392–93)
Scot.Er.*Praed*.2.1 (*PL* 122: 360)
Scot.Er.*Praed*.3.1 (*PL* 122: 364)

Scot.Er.*Praed*.9.1 (*PL* 122: 390)

Scot.Er.*Praed*.2.6 (*PL* 122: 363–64)
Scot.Er.*Praed*.11.3 (*PL* 122: 398)

Scot.Er.*Praed*.11.4 (*PL* 122: 399–401)

Scot.Er.*Praed*.14.1 (*PL* 122: 408)

Scot.Er.*Praed*.15.3 (*PL* 122: 413)

Scot.Er.*Praed*.10.5 (*PL* 122: 396)
Scot.Er.*Praed*.10.3; 15.9 (*PL* 122:394; 416)

Scot.Er.*Praed*.12.5 (*PL* 122: 405)

Scot.Er.*Praed*.16.6 (*PL* 122: 423)

Scot.Er.*Praed*.18.7 (*PL* 122: 434)

Scot.Er.*Praed*.3.7 (*PL* 122: 369)
Scot.Er.*Praed*.12.4 (*PL* 122: 403)

Scot.Er.*Praed*.1.2 (*PL* 122: 358)

election has no place in Erigena's world of thought." Predestination for him was synonymous with God's foreknowledge of his own works, the "primordial causes" or prototypes of all existing things. There was then no distinction between "providence" and "cause," for both referred to God. "He has done the things that are to be" meant that God had done all things at the same time. Hence "predestination" was not a completely precise term to use of God, for whom preparing an action and carrying it out were identical. "For him it is not one thing to be and another to will, but being and willing are the same," and so was "predestinating." Indeed, all such terms as "wisdom" or "power," although none of them was completely precise, referred to "the single immutable essence of God"; and because this essence was single, it was "wicked" to speak of two wills or of two powers or of two predestinations. There could be only one predestination, that to eternal salvation.

As for damnation, it had to be acknowledged that in some of his works Augustine had spoken of a predestination to punishment. But such statements could be explained away, and it would be clear that "he did not in any way teach two predestinations." It was likewise the usage of Scripture, when speaking about punishment, to speak of foreknowledge, not of predestination. Even the foreknowledge of God, however, pertained only to existing things, not to things that did not exist. Sin and evil, as "nothing," did not exist and therefore were neither predestined nor even foreknown by God. For if "no one is elected to punishment, how can the punishment be predestined"? It was axiomatic that no nature could be punished by another nature, and therefore no punishment could come from God or be predestined or foreknown by him. When Scripture or Augustine spoke about the predestination of the wicked to punishment, this was to be taken to mean that God "has circumscribed them with his immutable laws, which their wickedness is not permitted to evade." God, who was both "just and merciful," had, "by a single predestination," determined to give eternal salvation to the blessed, so that "all divine predestination is a preparation of his gifts." Gottschalk, with his doctrine of a double predestination, was a heretic, to be repudiated in the name of "true reason and the authority of the holy fathers."

All of this was intended to be a statement of "the royal

Scot.Er.*Praed*.4.3 (*PL* 122:371)

Scot.Er.*Praed*.pr. (*MGH Ep.* 5:631)
Hinc.R.*Praed*.2 (*PL* 125:84); *Ann.Bert*.849 (*MGH Scrip. Ger*.31:53)

Flor.*Scot.Er*.19 (*PL* 119:241)

Prud.Tr.*Praed*.3 (*PL* 115:1043)

Flor.*Scot.Er*.18 (*PL* 119:231)

Flor.*Scot.Er*.pr. (*PL* 119:102)

1 Tim.4:7
CVal. (855) *Can*.6 (Mansi 15:6)

Burch (1951) 30

Scot.Er.*Praed*.3 (*PL* 122:364–69)
Scot.Er.*Ev.Joh*.1.28 (*SC* 180:144)

Scot.Er.*Exp.C.h*.1.1 (*CCCM* 31:4)

Scot.Er.*Ev.Joh*.1.29 (*SC* 180:156)

Alc.*Fel*.1.8; 6.1 (*PL* 101:134; 200)

Radb.*Corp*.2 (*CCCM* 16:20)

Scot.Er.*Prol.Ev.Joh*.19 (*SC* 151:296); Scot.Er.*Praed*.1.4 (*PL* 122:360)

Scot.Er.*Periph*.2.36 (*SLH* 9:206)

Scot.Er.*Periph*.1.69 (*SLH* 7:198)
Scot.Er.*Periph*.1.56 (*SLH* 7:164)
Scot.Er.*Periph*.1.66 (*SLH* 7:194)

road" of orthodoxy, which did not stray "either to the right or to the left." It was written "as a testimony to the orthodox confession" of the faith of the catholic church against Gottschalk. But those who thought Gottschalk's doctrine "noxious" or "pestiferous" soon found such an antidote worse than the disease. It was a denial of the apostolic faith of the church. Its author was utterly devoid of any official standing in the church and had proved himself to be "a master of error" who discussed "the truth of God and the integrity of the faith . . . without a knowledge of the true faith, without the utterly faithful authority of Holy Scripure, without a thorough instruction in the doctrine of the fathers." He had relied solely on "human and, as he himself boasts, philosophical arguments." The same synod that condemned Hincmar and his colleagues for going too far in their opposition to Gottschalk also anathematized "the silly questions and old wives' tales . . . , which are abhorrent to the purity of the faith." In the history of philosophy, "Erigena was not so much the first medieval as the last ancient philosopher"; but he was nevertheless the theologian who decisively raised, for the first time in the Middle Ages, the theological question of the claims of reason in the formulation of Christian doctrine, especially in the interpretation of the relation of God and the world. As such, he merits attention here, together with his opponents.

The error of double predestination, according to Erigena, was that it was contrary to reason as well as to Scripture and tradition. The "path" to true understanding lay in "the cooperation of divine grace and the power of reason in the hearts of wise believers"; to sit at the feet of Christ the Logos was to learn from these two, reason and revelation. Other thinkers of the time stressed the superiority of faith to reason in the understanding of such mysteries as the incarnation, as well as the need for both faith and knowledge. But Erigena saw evidence for the harmony between the two in the violation of both by sinners and heretics, since "there is nothing that fits better with sound reason than the unshakable and proven authority of the holy fathers." This was because "true authority is nothing other than the truth that has been discovered by the power of reason and committed to writing by the holy fathers." Discovering the truth depended on reason and authority, which could not contradict each other, having a single

Scot.Er.*Periph*.1.71 (*SLH* 7: 204)
Scot.Er.*Ev.Joh*.4.4 (*SC* 180: 300)
Isa.7:9

See pp. 258–60 below
Scot.Er.*Prol.Ev.Joh*.3 (*SC* 151: 214); Scot.Er.*Ev.Joh*.6.3 (*SC* 180:338); Scot.Er.*Periph*.1.67 (*SLH* 7:194)
Scot.Er.*Exp.C.h*.4.3 (*CCCM* 31:76–77); Scot.Er.*Ev.Joh*.1.25 (*SC* 180:124); Scot.Er.*Periph*.4.7 (*PL* 122:763)

Scot.Er.*Praed*.1.1 (*PL* 122: 357–58)
Gr.Tr.*Mirac*.3.pr. (*MGH Scrip.Mer*.1–II:586)
Beat.*Apoc*.2.6.36 (Sanders 236); Beat.
Elip.1.51 (*PL* 96:924); Prud.Tr.*Praed*.18 (*PL* 115: 1303); Hinc.R.*Deit*.11 (*PL* 125:564)
Hier.*Ep*.22.30 (*CSEL* 54:189–91)
Prud.Tr.*Praed*.1 (*PL* 115: 1017–19)
Ecclus.3:21–22
Paulin.Aquil.*Fel*.1.11 (*PL* 99: 362); Episc.Fr.*Ep.Elip*.2 (*MGH Conc*.2–I:143); Hinc.R.*Recl*. (Gundlach 263)
See vol.2:34; 31

Scot.Er.*Periph*.1.9 (*SLH* 7: 52)
Serv.Lup.*Ep*.119 (*MGH Ep*. 6:101)

Alc.*Ep*.170 (*MGH Ep*.4:279)

Scot.Er.*Exp.C.h*.1.3 (*CCCM* 31:16)
Flor.*Scot.Er*.18 (*PL* 119:230–31)
Scot.Er.*Praed*.18 (*PL* 122: 430–36)

Verg.*Aen*.1.1
Radb.*Matt*.3.pr. (*MGH Ep*. 6:143); Paul.Alb.*Ep*.4.10 (*PL* 121:433)
Radb.*Matt*.2.2 (*PL* 120:123)

Ambr.Aut.*Apoc*.8 (*CCCM* 27: 636)

Prud.Tr.*Praed*.18 (*PL* 115: 1312)

source in common. Faith was the "beginning" from which the church ascended to "theological reasons." The words of the prophet, "Unless you believe, you will not understand," which were to provide the motto for "faith in search of understanding" in later medieval theology, proved the chronological priority of faith but the theological superiority of understanding. Revelation or "theophany," however, was not confined to Scripture, but was present in every creature in which God disclosed himself.

Erigena was unique in his assertion that true philosophy was true religion, and vice versa. His opponents, echoing earlier writers, reminded him that it has not been through philosophers and orators but through fishermen that Christ had conquered his enemies. They cited the example of Jerome's repudiation of Cicero as a cautionary tale to Erigena. The admonition of Sirach, "Seek not what is too difficult for you, nor investigate what is beyond your power," was embedded in the tradition of medieval thought; Erigena quoted it, too, but took it (as had Maximus Confessor, his spiritual master) also as a command that justified "human investigations" of the deep things of God. Other thinkers of the time discussed the seven liberal arts, and in a letter to Charlemagne Alcuin hailed their rebirth and transformation through the sevenfold gift of the Holy Spirit; but Erigena declared them indispensable to the Christian philosopher in his understanding of God and the world, and, much to the distress of his critics, he attributed Gottschalk's heresy to his neglect of the liberal arts. "We do not deal with Vergil's 'Arms and the man,' finding our condiment in the Greek salt of fables," Radbertus boasted, although he did attribute the *Fourth Eclogue* to the Holy Spirit; and Ambrose Autpert, exclaiming, "Plato is nothing to me, nor Cicero, nor Homer, nor Vergil," pointed out that the difference between his age and the patristic age was that the fathers had absorbed the classics directly, while he had to "admit that if I by chance seem to have any of this, I have received it from the granary of the Lord's preaching." In opposition to Erigena's identification of philosophy as the way of salvation, the defenders of orthodoxy, while conceding that God was the source of all truth, insisted that "the philosophers of the world did not have the Holy Spirit" and that therefore they could not be indispensable to theology.

Bed.*Sam*.2 (*CCSL* 119:121);
Aldh.*Ep*.3 (*MGH Auct.Ant.*
15:479–80); Beat.*Apoc*.5.3.3
(Sanders 416); Radb.*Matt.*
6.12 (*PL* 120:482); Rab.*Inst.*
cler.3.2 (Knoepfler 191)

Prud.Tr.*Praed*.3 (*PL* 115:
1042–43)

Scot.Er.*Periph*.1.31 (*SLH* 7:
114)
Scot.Er.*Periph*.1.14 (*SLH* 7:
84)

Scot.Er.*Periph*.4.7 (*PL* 122:
762)

Scot.Er.*Periph*.1.14 (*SLH* 7:
84)
Scot.Er.*Periph*.1.64 (*SLH* 7:
188)
Scot.Er.*Prol.Ev.Joh*.3 (*SC* 151:
212)

Scot.Er.*Ev.Joh*.3.12 (*SC* 180:
272)

Scot.Er.*Periph*.3.24–4.27 (*PL*
122:690–860)

Scot.Er.*Periph*.4.5 (*PL* 122:
749); Scot.Er.*Exp.C.h*.4.1
(*CCCM* 31:66)

Scot.Er.*Periph*.1.58 (*SLH* 7:
170)
Scot.Er.*Periph*.4.16 (*PL* 122:
818)
Scot.Er.*Ev.Joh*.4.1; 6.2 (*SC*
180:284; 332)

Scot.Er.*Periph*.4.26 (*PL* 122:
859)

Scot.Er.*Ev.Joh*.6.6 (*SC* 180:
366)

Scot.Er.*Periph*.1.65 (*SLH* 7:
190)

Scot.Er.*Praed*.11.6 (*PL* 122:
400–401)

Mathon (1954) 427

Flor.*Scot.Er*.17 (*PL* 119:148)

Usually such disparagement of classical philosophy and rhetoric was intended to emphasize, by means of contrast, the authority of the apostolic Scripture. Erigena's opponents attacked him for not supporting his statements with "the testimonies of the divine oracles" but substituting his own "petty ratiocinations." Erigena himself, who spoke of Plato as "the greatest of those who philosophized about the world" and of Aristotle as "the shrewdest among the Greeks," could assert, after quoting Plato, that "what we cannot prove by the authority of Holy Scripture and of the holy fathers . . . we ought not accept" and, after quoting Aristotle, that "when it comes to theology, that is, to the investigation of the divine essence," the categorial system of Aristotle did not apply. It was necessary to follow the authority of Scripture, where "the mysteries [of Christ] are safeguarded"; for "the words of the prophets and apostles are the words of God, because they spoke the words of God, and the Holy Spirit spoke in them." When he undertook to discuss the relation between Creator and creature, he did so by instituting a lengthy exegesis of the creation story in the Book of Genesis. It was essential to take account of the multiplicity of biblical language and of the several levels at which Scripture spoke. One of these levels was the historical. The heights of theoretical speculation must not obliterate "the truth of history," also called "the truth of the things that have been done" or "the faith of the things that have happened." But the only way to keep the authority of Scripture was to remember that not everything in Scripture was meant to be taken at this historical level. While being careful "not to contradict the simplicity of those who take this passage of divine Scripture [the creation story] historically," one had to recognize that there were passages where "nothing is to be understood historically."

The proof for this version of biblical authority came from the fathers of the church. At the time that he wrote his treatise on predestination, Erigena was working on the basis only of the Latin fathers, above all of Augustine, whom he defended against the "heretical" distortions of Gottschalk; but "the Augustinian ideas and texts are very often subordinate to the dialectical procedures, to reasonings that lead to conclusions which are quite alien to the thought of the master of Hippo." Erigena's critics charged him with failing to heed Augustine's "caution" and with

Prud.Tr.*Praed*.8; 14 (*PL* 115: 1110; 1194)

Scot.Er.*Periph*.2.16 (*SLH* 9: 54)
Scot.Er.*Vers.Dion.Ar*.pr. (*PL* 122:1031); Scot.Er.*Vers.Max*. pr. (*PL* 122:1196)

Prud.Tr.*Praed*.18 (*PL* 115: 1305)
Scot.Er.*Periph*.4.17; 5.8 (*PL* 122:830; 880)
See vol.2:181
Scot.Er.*Periph*.3.38; 4.26 (*PL* 122:735; 860)

Scot.Er.*Vers.Dion.Ar*. (*PL* 122:1039–1194)
See vol.1:344–48
Scot.Er.*Periph*.3.9 (*PL* 122: 644)
Lud.P.*Ep.Hild*. (*MGH Ep*.5: 327)

Théry (1931) 186
Hinc.R.*Praed*.25; 33; 34 (*PL* 125:225–26; 313; 353); Radb.*Matt*.7.14 (*PL* 120:529)
Scot.Er.*Periph*.1.70 (*SLH* 7: 200)

See vol.2:8–36

Dräseke (1902) 52

Scot.Er.*Periph*.1.13 (*SLH* 7: 74)
Scot.Er.*Exp.C.h*.2.3 (*CCCM* 31:33)

Scot.Er.*Ev.Joh*.1.25 (*SC* 180: 116)
Scot.Er.*Periph*.1.66 (*SLH* 7: 190)

Scot.Er.*Exp.C.h*.2.3 (*CCCM* 31:33)

Scot.Er.*Periph*.1.14 (*SLH* 7: 84)
Scot.Er.*Praed*.9.7 (*PL* 122: 393); Scot.Er.*Periph*.1.14 (*SLH* 7:76–78)
Scot.Er.*Periph*.3.8 (*PL* 122: 639)
Scot.Er.*Periph*.1.71 (*SLH* 7: 204)

using him as an excuse for his own heresy by attributing to him ideas that he had never had. When Erigena was faced with an apparent contradiction between Augustine and Basil, he disclaimed the right "to adjudicate between the interpretations of the holy fathers"; but by the time he said this, he was already discovering his deep affinity with the Greek fathers (although he had been chided all along for his Hellenizing tendencies and continued to try to explain them). Like other Latin theologians, he identified Gregory of Nazianzus with Gregory of Nyssa, although he had translated a work of the latter from Greek into Latin. It was, however, another translation from the Greek that made him influential, that of "the supreme theologian, Dionysius the Areopagite, the celebrated bishop of Athens," correcting an earlier version by Hilduin of Saint-Denis. This translation as well as his commentaries made Erigena "without any doubt the one who really introduced the Dionysian writings in the West." His opponents too, quoted these writings as authoritative. To Dionysius must be added another Greek theologian, "the venerable Maximus," who provided the starting point for many of "the principal and central elements of [Erigena's] teaching."

Of all these elements, the most important was the doctrine of God. Dionysius and Maximus, his Greek masters, taught Erigena to distinguish between two parts of theology: the apophatic or negative, which "denies that the divine essence or substance is any of the things that are," and the cataphatic or positive, which "predicates of [the divine essence] all the things that are." Of the two, the negative was "the more appropriate and more valid," for even the angels were unable to know God in his true nature. By this way of negation, on which reason and revelation agreed, one came to the recognition that God was "not any kind of essence nor any kind of goodness, since he is superessential and is more than goodness and is exalted above all that can be spoken or understood." Calling God "superessential" did not say "what he is, but what he is not." Such terms as "foreknowledge" and "predestination" applied temporal notions to a God who transcended time as well as every other category. For "his nature is simple, and more than simple; absolute beyond all accidents, and more than absolute," and therefore of course "utterly impassible." But then, as Erigena himself

Scot.Er.*Periph*.1.62 (*SLH* 7: 178)
Scot.Er.*Periph*.1.68 (*SLH* 7: 196)

Scot.Er.*Exp.C.h*.2.4 (*CCCM* 31:42)
Scot.Er.*Periph*.1.75 (*SLH* 7: 216)
Scot.Er.*Exp.C.h*.1.1; 7.2 (*CCCM* 31:5; 102)

Scot.Er.*Exp.C.h*.4.1 (*CCCM* 31:67)
Scot.Er.*Periph*.1.72 (*SLH* 7: 206)
Scot.Er.*Prol.Ev.Joh*.11 (*SC* 151:256); Scot.Er.*Periph*.3.28 (*PL* 122:704)

Scot.Er.*Periph*.3.10 (*PL* 122: 650)

Scot.Er.*Praed*.2.6 (*PL* 122: 364)

Scot.Er.*Periph*.1.12 (*SLH* 7:64)

Scot.Er.*Periph*.1.3 (*SLH* 7:38)

Scot.Er.*Exp.C.h*.9.2 (*CCCM* 31:138)

Flor.*Scot.Er*.4 (*PL* 119:130–31)

Scot.Er.*Periph*.3.9 (*PL* 122: 642)
Scot.Er.*Periph*.5.15 (*PL* 122: 887)
Scot.Er.*Prol.Ev.Joh*.9 (*SC* 151: 244)

asked, "if he neither acts nor suffers, how is he said to love all things and to be loved by all the things that have been made by him?" The answer was that "God is called 'love' by a metaphor." If love was defined as "a laudable desire for that immateriality which surpasses all reason and understanding," then God as love could only be "love-in-himself," just as he was "both motion and stability, stable motion and mobile stability."

Because this conception of a transcendence beyond all existence and even beyond love seemed to make the very name "God" meaningless, it was necessary to emphasize the other half of the same truth: that God was not only "nothing," but also "everything." "All things are in him, since he himself is all things," and therefore "in all things that are, whatever is, he himself is." Thus the obverse side of absolute transcendence was absolute immanence. But this, in turn, opened up at least two questions. First, "if this is the way it is [that God is the beginning and the end of all things], who would not immediately burst out in speech and declare: 'Then God is all things, and all things are God'?" It was this perspective on the relation between God and the world that underlay his generalized definition of predestination: "The things that [God] wills to be are, and they are just because he has willed that they come into being." In its more refined form, it became the principle that "everything that is said to exist does not exist in itself, but by participation in that nature which truly exists." In addition to the question of pantheism, Erigena's ontology also raised the problem of diversity among creatures. For if "he who alone truly is, is the essence of all things," why should there be differences among them? Erigena's answer, based on Dionysius, was that "if God had made the universe to be created equal, without any differentiation of various orders [of being], ... there would be no order in the republic of natures. If there were no order, there would be no harmony. And if there were no harmony, there would be no beauty."

There was another question about this cosmology, for orthodox Christianity at any rate: What did it imply for the plan of salvation? The function of the Logos was to be "the simple and multiple and most principal reason of all things." All things had their "most general causes" in the Logos, and they "exist in him causally" before existing in themselves. In this sense creatures "were before they

Scot.Er.*Exp.C.h.*4.1 (*CCCM* 31:68)

Scot.Er.*Periph.*2.20 (*SLH* 9: 70)
Gen.1:1
Scot.Er.*Periph.*2.15 (*SLH* 9: 48–50)
Scot.Er.*Periph.*1.59 (*SLH* 7: 170)

Scot.Er.*Prol.Ev.Joh.*11 (*SC* 151:258)

Scot.Er.*Ev.Joh.*1.25 (*SC* 180: 116–18); Scot.Er.*Periph.*5.25 (*PL* 122:912)
See vol.1:141–55
Scot.Er.*Praed.*9.4 (*PL* 122: 392); Scot.Er.*Periph.*5.36 (*PL* 122:981)
Scot.Er.*Ev.Joh.*1.30 (*SC* 180: 166); Scot.Er.*Periph.*5.38 (*PL* 122:1003)
Scot.Er.*Periph.*4.4 (*PL* 122: 748); Scot.Er.*Ev.Joh.*1.29 (*SC* 180:150–52)

Gal.3:28

Scot.Er.*Periph.*2.6; 2.10 (*SLH* 9:22; 32)
See vol.2:224

Scot.Er.*Ev.Joh.*1.31 (*SC* 180: 174); Scot.Er.*Periph.*4.13; 16 (*PL* 122:799; 817)

Scot.Er.*Prol.Ev.Joh.*21 (*SC* 151:306)

Prud.Tr.*Praed.*4 (*PL* 115: 1077)
Jas.1:17
Scot.Er.*Exp.C.h.*1.1 (*CCCM* 31:1); Scot.Er.*Ev.Joh.*3.9 (*SC* 180:252–54)

Scot.Er.*Periph.*1.pr. (*SLH* 7: 36)

Scot.Er.*Prol.Ev.Joh.*13 (*SC* 151:262–64)

are, that is, they existed in the providence of God before they came to be in the act of creation." The doctrine of the Logos made it possible to say that the primordial causes of all things, the Platonic "forms," were coeternal with the eternal generation of the Logos, who, as the "beginning" spoken of in the first verse of the Bible, could be seen as "the form of all forms." It was less clear what the relation of the preexistent Logos was to the incarnate person of Jesus Christ and to the redemption wrought by him. "The light of men," Erigena wrote, "is our Lord Jesus Christ, who in his human nature has manifested himself to every rational and intellectual creature." This included men as the "rational creatures" and angels as the "intellectual creatures," the former because their nature needed to be set free "from death, from servitude to the devil, and from ignorance of the truth," the latter because they needed "to recognize their Cause, of whom they were ignorant before." To describe this reconciliation, Erigena made use of various metaphors from the history of the doctrine of the atonement: Christ was a sacrifice; he was the one who had fulfilled the law for all men by his suffering and death; he was the one whom death could not hold captive and who, by his resurrection, had restored all of human nature to its "pristine state"; he was the universal man beyond all gender, "in whom there is neither male nor female," who rose from the dead "without physical sexuality but simply as a human being," since, according to Erigena and his sources, "the division of nature into two sexes . . . is a punishment of sin" in the fall of Adam.

Christ was all of this, and more, as incarnate Logos and Savior. Yet Erigena's definition of reason and revelation had as its necessary corollary a schematization of the relation between nature and grace that was bound to cast doubt on his doctrine of salvation. The distinction between nature and grace was based on the text: "Every good endowment [nature] and every perfect gift [grace] is from above." "Nature" in Erigena's metaphysical thought was the universal category, embracing "all the things that are and that are not." In his theological thought, as applied to the doctrine of man, "nature" meant that created endowment by which man was capable of participating in the wisdom of God and by which, in fact, he did participate in the Summum Bonum even after

Scot.Er.*Exp.C.h.*2.3 (*CCCM* 31:39)
Scot.Er.*Ev.Joh.*3.9 (*SC* 180: 264)

Scot.Er.*Praed.*16.1 (*PL* 122: 417)

Flor.*Scot.Er.*7 (*PL* 119:145)

Scot.Er.*Exp.C.h.*15.5 (*CCCM* 31:204)

Scot.Er.*Periph.*5.27 (*PL* 122: 921)

Prud.Tr.*Praed.*5; 17 (*PL* 115: 1087; 1289)

See vol.1:151–52

Scot.Er.*Periph.*5.27 (*PL* 122: 928–31)

Scot.Er.*Carm.*2.7.15–18 (*MGH Poet.* 3:537); Scot.Er.*Prol.Ev. Joh.*23 (*SC* 151:310)

Scot.Er.*Periph.*5.27 (*PL* 122: 924)

1 Cor.15:56

1 Cor.15:25

Scot.Er.*Periph.*5.28 (*PL* 122: 935)

1 Cor.15:28

Scot.Er.*Periph.*5.8 (*PL* 122: 876)
Scot.Er.*Periph.*5.25 (*PL* 122: 912)
Flor.*Scot.Er.*16; 19 (*PL* 119: 201; 246)
Scot.Er.*Periph.*2.28 (*SLH* 9: 158)
Scot.Er.*Periph.*5.27 (*PL* 122: 925–27)
Scot.Er.*Periph.*5.28 (*PL* 122: 935); Scot.Er.*Exp.C.h.*8.2 (*CCCM* 31:129)

Scot.Er.*Periph.*5.19 (*PL* 122: 891)
Scot.Er.*Exp.C.h.*2.1 (*CCCM* 31:24)

the fall. For "there is truly no rational nature that is utterly lacking in any gift of grace"; even the damned retained in their nature a notion of eternal beatitude and a desire for it. Such an "assertion of the natural" seemed to his critics to be the very antithesis of "the faith of the church, [which] makes a sharp distinction between the gifts of nature and the gifts of grace." For he equated "the gifts of divine grace" with "all the good things that are distributed to us in this life."

These were, Erigena added, "small when compared with the gifts of divine beatitude." But then, as he himself put it elsewhere, "what are we to say? Will the consequence of this not be that there remains no eternal death of misery, no punishment of the wicked," but universal salvation? His opponent Prudentius detected suspicious parallels between his eschatology and Origen's doctrine of "the restoration of all things." Erigena did not flinch from acknowledging this lineage, even to the point of stating a preference for Origen over Ambrose. Nothing less than the entire human race had been restored in the salvation brought by Christ. Confronted by the dilemma between the eternity of punishment and the universality of divine goodness, he did not hesitate: "If evil and death and its sting, which is sin, and all misery, as well as the last enemy, that is, the malice of the devil and all wickedness, will be abolished from the nature of things, what remains except that the whole of creation will remain alone, purged of all the filth of evil and wickedness, liberated from all the death of corruption, and set completely free?" Only then would the word of the apostle be fulfilled, that God would be "all in all," and that would include "not only all men, but the entire sensible creation." While his opponents insisted on the eternity of damnation as a counterpart to the eternity of bliss, Erigena looked for a resurrection in which evil, since it did not exist, would not be, and only "nature" in its goodness would abide forever. This meant that "God alone will be, but the world which is under the sun and which took its rise from the eternal causes will have returned to those causes" in God.

This vision of "theology as a kind of poetry," in which the data of revelation and the teachings of the fathers could be manipulated as symbols by the claims of reason, was indeed "an isolated phenomenon in the history of medieval learning, the most extravagant fruit of Caro-

Overbeck (1917) 109–10

Liebeschütz (1958) 79

C.Val. (855) *Can*.6 (Mansi 15:6)

Scot.Er.*Periph*.1.13 (*SLH* 7: 68)

Scot.Er.*Periph*.1.45 (*SLH* 7: 138)

See p. 99 above

Scot.Er.*Periph*.5.32 (*PL* 122: 949); Scot.Er.*Carm*.4.2.1 (*MGH Poet.* 3:545)

See pp. 242–45, 289–90 below

lingian culture," but it does not follow from this that "Scotus can be ignored in the history of medieval theology." For the congeries of issues to which his speculations had led Erigena would have to be dealt with also by more conventional theologians before the history of medieval theology was concluded. Even though most scholars would perhaps agree "that, generally speaking, Erigena's contemporary critics saw his position correctly," the condemnation of his answers in his own and in later times did not mean that his so-called "silly questions" had been eliminated. He was writing, Erigena said, especially with those in mind "who demand from catholics a rational account of the Christian religion," and he discussed the question of whether "an argument based on creatures" was sufficient to show what God was. Such a demand for a rational account was to be addressed to catholics again before very long, and with greater vigor. While most of his contemporaries drew their knowledge of classical philosophy "from the granary of the Lord's preaching" in the church rather than from the philosophers themselves, he was reading the texts, just as his more orthodox successors would have to do. On the other hand, his passing references to Islam would give way to the theological debate over the Muslim interpretation of Aristotle and its significance for Christian thought. When this happened, the very problematic on which his philosophy had come to grief—the relation between the eternity of God and the world—demanded the attention of theologians again. And by laying claim, however tenuously, to at least some share of the heritage of the fathers, he joined with his contemporaries of the Carolingian period in demonstrating for the periods that followed the necessity of going beyond the Augustinian synthesis.

3

The Plan
of Salvation

Waddell (1955) 60

Othl.*Tent*.2 (*PL* 146:56)

See p. 7 above

Kantorowicz (1957) 61

Ben.N.*Reg*.4.21 (*SC* 181:456–58)

Od.Clun.*V.Ger*.2.19 (*PL* 133:681); Rath.*Prael*.2.4.12 (*PL* 136:199)

Eadm.*V.Ans*.2.30 (Southern 107)

The tenth century produced no such flurry of theological and intellectual excitement as had the ninth, and "in the text-books it disputes with the seventh the bad eminence, the nadir of the human intellect." A monk who was born a decade or so after the close of the tenth century spoke of "seeing and hearing everywhere the destruction of the Christian religion." Even allowing for rhetorical exaggeration, which echoed similar jeremiads voiced in earlier centuries, we may see in this lament a recognition that scholarship and speculation were not flourishing as they had been during the Carolingian period. But scholarship and speculation, important as they have been in the development of Christian doctrine, are not the only index, and often not even the primary index, to that development. In the tenth and eleventh centuries there was being developed and articulated the characteristically Western understanding of Christ, so that "the monastic period from 900 to A.D. 1100" has been identified as "the uncompromisingly christocentric period of Western civilization"; it was christocentric for the very reason that it was monastic. The *Rule* of Benedict of Nursia had prescribed that one should "put nothing ahead of the love of Christ," and monastic writers vied with one another in extolling Christ as the source of all good.

Eventually, scientific theology would catch up with Benedictine piety. At the very close of the "christocentric period," in 1098, Anselm, the exiled archbishop of Canterbury, who was a Benedictine, composed his "remarkable book," *Why God Became Man,* on the purpose of the incarnation of Christ. Read as an essay in speculative

Ans.*Cur. d.h.*pr. (Schmitt 2: 42)

Rich.S.Vict.*Seir*.8 (*TPMA* 15: 269)
Eadm.*V.Ans*.2.30 (Southern 107)

Ans.*Cur d.h.*1.2 (*Schmitt* 2: 50)

Eadm.*V.Ans*.2.44 (Southern 122)

Ans.*Med*.3 (Schmitt 3:84–91)

Brun.S.*Inc.* (*PL* 165:1079–84)
Gisl.Crisp.*Jud.* (*PL* 159:1022–23)

Petr.Alf.*Dial*.10 (*PL* 157: 645–46); Hon.Aug.*Eluc*.1.16–18 (*PL* 172:1121–23)

Blum (1947) 56

Petr.Dam.*Serm*.73 (*PL* 144: 918)
Guib.Nog.*Vita sua*.1.17 (*PL* 156:874); Guib.Nog. *Mor*.pr. (*PL* 156:19)
Guib.Nog.*Inc*.3.2 (*PL* 156: 508–9)
Od.Cambr.*Pecc.orig.* (*PL* 160: 1071–1102)

Od.Cambr.*Jud.* (*PL* 160:1107–8)

Petr.Ab.*Rom*.2 (*CCCM* 11: 117)

Weingart (1970) 78

divinity, the treatise was a virtuoso performance with few rivals in the history of Christian thought, Eastern or Western; for it proposed to show, "without paying attention to Christ [remoto Christo]," that salvation was impossible except through someone who was simultaneously true God and true man. But in writing it he was "moved by his love of the Christian faith"; the origin, and therefore the goal, of his speculation was "what we believe and confess" in the catholic and orthodox "faith in redemption." Read as a reflective study of church doctrine, therefore, *Why God Became Man* was an effort to bring together a rational view of the person and work of Christ that was conformable to "the greater authority" of Scripture and dogma. That view, which Anselm set forth in a brief and nonspeculative epitome entitled *Meditation on Human Redemption,* was by no means his alone. It was, for example, summarized in the treatise *On the Incarnation of the Lord and His Burial* ascribed to his contemporary, Bruno of Segni, in a disputation against the Jews by Anselm's disciple, Gilbert of Crispin, and in other works of the time.

Another contemporary, Peter Damian, even though his sermonic works were not intended "exclusively to impart doctrine," used his writings to expound a christocentric devotion in which Christ would be the sole object of language and thought, of love and meditation. A younger contemporary and protégé, Guibert of Nogent, argued for the incarnation on the basis of a picture of the atonement that strongly resembled Anselm's. Similarly, Odo of Cambrai developed the doctrine of original sin as well as the doctrine of satisfaction through the sacrificial death of Christ in a manner that was decidedly "Anselmic." On the other hand, the analysis of the doctrine of the atonement in Peter Abelard's *Exposition of the Epistle to the Romans,* with its attack on the notion that "the death of his innocent Son was so pleasing to God the Father that through it he would be reconciled to us," was not intended to be "a comprehensive statement of a particular theory of the atonement, [but] an outline suggesting the motive for God's redemptive activity, the reasons for rejection of certain untenable soteriological interpretations, and the benefits and consequences of Christ's work." Therefore it would be a mistake to treat either Anselm's achievement or Abelard's critique, brilliant as they both are, in isolation from the many other witnesses of the tenth, eleventh, and twelfth centuries, or to concentrate on the differences between Anselm and Abelard at the expense of the exegetical and liturgical theology that went into the definition of the plan of salvation.

Already in the ninth century, a didactic poem on the themes of paradise lost and paradise regained spoke of Christ as "undergoing the cross, as was required by the plan of salvation [ordo salutis]." Similarly, Peter Damian referred to "the plan [ordo] of human restoration" and to "the plan required by human weakness," and Guibert of Nogent spoke of "the plan of the resurrection"; Anselm also used the term "plan," as did his successor as archbishop of Canterbury, Baldwin, in speaking of the events of salvation. Although "plan of salvation [ordo salutis]" did not yet have the technical significance that it was to acquire in the dogmatics of post-Reformation Protestantism, it did suggest a distinctive interpretation of the life, death, and resurrection of Christ as saving events. The relation between life, death, and resurrection —or the analogous, but not identical, relation between Christ as prophet, as priest, and as king—had not been formulated definitively in the dogmas of the church councils and creeds, but now Western theologians sought to make explicit what they took to have been implicit in those dogmas. Only in this sense would a "reconsideration of dogma" be seen as permissible in the tenth and eleventh centuries, not by a reopening of the question of the person of Christ, as "the Spanish heresy" of the ninth century had tried to do, but by an opening of the question of the salvific work of Christ the God-man.

The Paradox of Justice and Mercy

"God was in Christ reconciling the world unto himself, not imputing their trespasses unto them": this locus classicus on the salvific work of Christ had become an issue in the controversies of the ninth century, when Gottschalk, following the lead of Augustine, maintained that the term "world" in the passage referred only to the predestined, not to all men. Gottschalk's identification of the "many" for whom Christ had shed his blood with the elect alone continued to find support in this period; others took the word "many" to mean that the shedding

Marginal references:

Od.Clun.*Occup*.6.180; 6.440 (Swoboda 124; 132)
Petr.Dam.*Serm*.45 (*PL* 144: 744)
Petr.Dam.*Serm*.63 (*PL* 144: 858)
Guib.Nog.*Pign*.3.5.5 (*PL* 156: 664)
Ans.*Med*.3 (Schmitt 3:85); Ans.*Concept.virg*.6 (Schmitt 2:147)
Bald.*Sacr.alt*.2.1.2 (*SC* 93: 182)

See vol.1:141–55

See vol.2:293

Petr.Dam.*Opusc*.1.6 (*PL* 145: 29)

2 Cor.5:19

Aug.*Ev.Joh*.110.2 (*CCSL* 36: 623)

Goth.*Praed*.9.3 (Lambot 204)

Matt.26:28
ap.Guib.Nog.*Pign*.2.3.2 (*PL* 156:635)

Ps.Petr.Dam.*Exp.can.miss*.7 (*PL* 145:884)
See vol.1:303
Od.Clun.*Serm*.2 (*PL* 133:720)
Od.Clun.*Occup*.2 (Swoboda 25)
Matt.26:23
Othl.*Dial*.25 (*PL* 146:93)
Ans.*Conc*.2.2 (Schmitt 2:261)
Petr.Dam.*Omnip*.3 (*SC* 191: 396)
Ans.*Conc*.2.1 (Schmitt 2:260)
Petr.Dam.*Opusc*.9.3 (*PL* 145: 215)

of the blood of Christ was sufficient for all, but was efficacious only for those who were predestined. Augustine's language about "the fixed number of the predestined" was cited as orthodox teaching, but it was qualified by the standard distinction between predestination and foreknowledge. Similarly, it was maintained that Christ's prophecy that Judas would be the one to betray him did not constrain or predestine the act of betrayal. In the sense that an almighty God permitted evil to happen and did not prevent it, he could be said to have done it and therefore to have predestined evil as well as good; but in a stricter sense, since God could not will evil, he could not do evil either, not because something was impossible for God but because of his goodness. The paradox of free will and predestination—that "if predestination remains, free will amounts to nothing, but if we assert free will in some, predestination disappears in them"—carried over into the ethical realm, where God commanded the predestined to labor for the attainment of that which he had given them gratis.

Guib.Nog.*Inc*.3.3 (*PL* 156: 509)
Petr.Dam.*Serm*.45 (*PL* 114: 744–45)
Isa.28:21
Od.Clun.*Occup*.5.19–21 (Swoboda 95); Od.Clun.*Coll*. 3.52 (*PL* 133:637)
Od.Clun.*Serm*.4 (*PL* 133:738)
Ans.*Cur d.h*.2.20 (Schmitt 2: 131)

The consideration of the paradox of free will and predestination led once again to the even more fundamental paradox of justice and mercy. To carry out the salvation that his mercy had predestined, God had to undergo a death of which his divine nature was incapable. Mankind needed to produce both a high priest who was free of the sin that beset all men and a sacrifice that would atone for the sin. "What, then, was our high priest to do? Where was he to turn? What plan was he to find for our redemption? Where was the Mediator between God and men to obtain a sacrifice of propitiation by which to establish peace between God and man?" From the words of the prophet about an "alien work" of God there came a distinction between "the proper work of God," the work of salvation, which was appropriate to his nature, and the "alien work" of suffering and death, which was the necessary means to that end. The dilemma of the atonement lay in the need to face the contradiction between these two "works," that is, to describe "the mercy of God . . . as so great and so in keeping with [his justice]" that the paradox would be resolved.

Sometimes it seemed possible to explain the paradox by suggesting that justice was found in the Old Testament and grace in the New, but it was recognized that such a formula was too simplistic. For in the Old Testament it was said of God that even in his wrath he would not withhold his mercy. Elsewhere in the Psalter the task of comparing mercy and justice was enjoined by the words: "I will sing of mercy and judgment unto thee." What was needed was a way of defining the grace of God that would not nullify the justice of God, a way of stating his "benignity" without impairing his "dignity." The judgments of God as well as the mercies of God were too profound for the human mind to plumb. His goodness could not be exhausted, his mercy could not be consumed, his knowledge could not be incomplete, his power could not fail of its purpose. Mercy and justice both participated in the mystery of predestination and salvation, because the wicked who were to be saved could not be converted to good except by mercy, and the wicked who were to perish would not abide in their sins except by justice. Statements about consolation and statements about terror appeared together in Scripture "as a contradiction," so that men would prefer being saved by the kindness of God to being punished by his severity; "for God's clemency is so great that he exercises all his severity, which in our human way of speaking is called the wrath of God, against sinners in this world in such a way that in the world to come he may have mercy on them after they have been set straight from their wickedness." Justice and mercy came together in "the reconciliation of the human race," but how did this come about?

The answer could not be found in any way of speaking or thinking about God that ascribed either necessity or mutability to the divine nature. God was "that being which can subsist without the assistance of any other," by contrast with creatures, "whose total being consists in the power of Another." There was nothing that could exist at any time or at any place without the presence of God. The transcendence of God over nature and its laws meant that "the very nature of things has its own nature, namely, the will of God." What was called "necessity" and what was called "impossibility" were subject to that will and were defined by it. The "speaking" of God, as in the creation, was the same as his "willing." "I am that I am," the word from the burning bush, continued to serve as the proof text for the ontological abso-

---

Marginal references (left column):

Othl.*Dial*.8 (*Pl* 146:70)

Ps.77:9
Guib.Nog.*Vita sua*.1.1 (*PL* 156:838)

Ps.101:1

Od.Clun.*Occup*.2.50–51 (Swoboda 16)
Ans.*Cur d.h*.1.12 (Schmitt 2:70)

Od.Clun.*Coll*.3.37 (*PL* 133:619)

Ans.*Orat*.10 (Schmitt 3:35)

Rath.*Ot.serm*.2 (*CCCM* 46:158)

Othl.*Curs*.13 (*PL* 146:182–83)
Rath.*Serm.Asc*.2.3 (*CCCM* 46:186)

Othl.*Man*.1 (*PL* 146:245);
Petr.Ab.*Theol.S.b*.2.1 (*BGPM* 35–II:41)

Ans.*Inc*.7 (Schmitt 2:22)

Petr.Dam.*Omnip*.13 (*SC* 191:450)

Ans.*Cur.d.h*.2.17 (Schmitt 2:122)

Rem.Aux.*Gen*.1.3 (*PL* 131:55)
Ex.3:14
Petr.Dam.*Opusc*.1.1 (*PL* 145:22); Petr.Dam.*Omnip*. 17 (*SC* 191:476)

See vol.1:54

Guib.Nog.*Pign*.4.1.2 (*PL* 156:666)

Petr.Ab.*Serm*.1 (*PL* 178:386)

Jas.1:17
Petr.Dam.*Omnip*.10 (*SC* 191:430)

Guib.Nog.*Inc*.3.6 (*PL* 156:519)

Ans.*Cur. d.h*.1.8 (Schmitt 2:59)

Petr.Ab.*Dial*. (Thomas 111)

Ans.*Orat*.14 (Schmitt 3:55)

Ans.*Cas.diab*.4 (Schmitt 1:240)

Ans.*Concept.virg*.6 (Schmitt 2:147)
Ans.*Cas.diab*.18 (Schmitt 1:263)

Ans.*Concept.virg*.26–28 (Schmitt 2:169–71)

Rath.*Serm.Quad*.2.19 (*CCCM* 46:73)

Ans.*Cur d.h*.1.15 (Schmitt 2:73)

Ans.*Cur d.h*.1.15 (Schmitt 2:74)

luteness of the divine nature, as it had since patristic times. Of all the Old Testament, this text alone spoke "essentially," that is, unmetaphorically, about the nature of God. It taught that God "exists immutably, since only what is immutable has true being; for wherever a change takes place, being and nonbeing come together." The statement of the New Testament that there was in God "no variation or shadow due to change" meant that his immutability, abiding in itself, "disposes all things that are mutable." Those biblical passages in which God appeared to be mutable were a condescension to human mutability, intended to instruct and to inform. The transcendence of God "cannot in any way be brought down from its sublime height, nor does it labor in what it wills to do."

In the moral sphere, the transcendence of God was his justice; for "when we say that God is better than man, we mean nothing other than that He transcends all men." Therefore man had to confess not only that "He is most high and I am weak," but also that "He is most just and I am wicked," thus expressing not only the awe of the finite creature in the presence of the infinite Creator, but also the guilt of the sinner in the presence of the holy Judge. So just was God that the very presence of punishment was evidence of sin in the one being punished, since God could not condemn anyone unjustly. Even though "the absence of righteousness [justitia]" was not a positive reality but only the privation of a positive reality and therefore "nothing," it did not follow that when God punished sinners for the absence of righteousness, he was punishing them for nothing and hence unjustly. In short, "God cannot in any way do anything unjust." Although, in the eyes of men, infants who died before baptism had committed no sin and should not be condemned, God judged differently and condemned them justly, "not for Adam's sin but for their own." Nor was it legitimate automatically to "promise impunity to all who have been baptized," for the justice of God was not annulled even by baptism. There was no escape from his justice and his will: one who ran away from his "commanding will" came under his "punishing will" instead. The transcendence of God meant that no creature could add to the honor of God or detract from it "intrinsically," but such a term as "dishonoring God" was a way of

Ans.*Cur d.h.*1.13 (Schmitt 2: 71)

Petr.Ab.*Rom.*2 (*CCCM* 11: 117)

Ans.*Cur.d.h.*1.10 (Schmitt 2: 66)

Ans.*Conc.*3.13 (Schmitt 2: 285) ; Ans.*Cur d.h.*2.1 (Schmitt 2:97)

Guib.Nog.*Ord.serm.* (*PL* 156: 27)
Guib.Nog.*Vita sua.*1.1 (*PL* 156:838–39)

Ans.*Lib.arb.*11 (Schmitt 1:223)
Od.Clun.*Occup.*3.317 (Swoboda 40)

Guib.Nog.*Inc.*1.3 (*PL* 156: 494)
Petr.Dam.*Perf.mon.*6 (Brezzi 228)
Od.Clun.*Coll.*2.24 (*PL* 133: 568–69)
See p. 171 below
Hrot.*Asc.*18 (Homeyer 85)

Ans.*Concept.virg.*7 (Schmitt 2: 149)
Od.Clun.*Occup.*3.273 (Swoboda 39)

Od.Cambr.*Pecc.orig.*2 (*PL* 160:1084)

Ans.*Cur d.h.*1.11 (Schmitt 2: 170)
Ans.*Concept.virg.*27 (Schmitt 2:170)

Ans.*Concept.virg.*1 (Schmitt 2: 140)

Petr.Dam.*Omnip.*11 (*SC* 191: 436) ; Od.Clun.*Coll.*1.8 (*PL* 133:526)
Petr.Ab.*Sic et non.*143 (Boyer-McKeon 492–96) ;
Od.Cambr.*Pecc.orig.*1 (*PL* 160:1073–74)

Od.Clun.*Coll.*2.16 (*PL* 133: 563)

describing what happened when "a creature denies to the Creator the honor that is due him." In requiring either punishment or the restoration of that honor, God was not acting in a bloodthirsty manner, as some charged, but in a manner appropriate to his nature and consistent with his justice.

It was the intention of this just God in the act of creation "to make a just and blessed rational nature that would enjoy Him." The task of the proclamation of the Christian message, therefore, was to induce in the hearer an accurate self-knowledge; for through the knowledge of self one came to the knowledge of God. Self-knowledge revealed to man that "he cannot be turned back from sin and from its servitude except through another, that he cannot be turned away from rightness except through himself, and that he cannot be deprived of his freedom [of will] at all—either through another or through himself." Human nature was "divided": it continued to be the nature that God himself had created and that he did not despise; but on account of "the stains of marriage," "the sin that is committed in the hour of conception," everyone who was conceived in the usual way—even the Virgin Mary—was "conceived in iniquities and in sins," so that "the unclean seed" that gave him his existence also imposed on him the inevitability of sin. If nature had remained sinless, "as Adam was before his offense," it would have propagated itself without sin; but having become sinful in the fall, it now propagated itself in a sinful way. Sin could be defined simply as "not rendering to God what is due him"; original sin was the sin that was "present in the infant as soon as it has a rational soul," the term "original" referring not to the origin of the human race, which was pure, but to the origin of each individual person. The continuing goodness of God's creation, in spite of sin and the fall, implied that "evil of whatever kind . . . , even though it seems to exist, does not exist, because it does not come from God."

Although evil did not have an existence of its own but was only "the privation of good," there was nothing illusory about the fall of Adam and Eve into evil. It was possible to say that the transgression of Adam was not as grave as that of a later Christian, who sinned against the better knowledge that came through the law, the prophets, and the gospel; or one could treat the fall as a cautionary

Othl.*Man*.8 (*PL* 146:259)
Od.Clun.*Occup*.2.8 (Swoboda 14)

See vol.2:85

Othl.*Man*.8 (*PL* 146:258)

Othl.*Dial*.28 (*PL* 146:96)

Od.Clun.*Occup*.1.114 (Swoboda 6)
Ans.*Cas.diab*.4 (Schmitt 1: 241–42)

Rath.*Prael*.4.31 (*PL* 136:282)

Od.Clun.*Coll*.1.6 (*PL* 133:523)

Od.Clun.*Occup*.2.149 (Swoboda 19)

Ans.*Concept.virg*.9 (Schmitt 2:150–51)

Od.Cambr.*Pecc.orig*.2 (*PL* 160:1077)
Ans.*Concept.virg*.7 (Schmitt 2:148)

Ans.*Cur d.h*.1.11 (Schmitt 2:68–69)

Ans.*Concept.virg*.2 (Schmitt 2:141)

Guib.Nog.*Inc*.3.2 (*PL* 156:508–9)
Sent.Flor.30 (Ostlender 14); Rosc.*Ep.Ab*.5 (*BGPM* 8–V:67–68)
Rup.*Div.off*.6.36 (*CCCM* 7:222)

Ans.*Cur d.h*.1.12 (Schmitt 2:69)

tale, warning against the sin of presumption. But it was evident to all that it was much more. The idea of man as microcosm, which had figured in the christological discussions of the East, meant that the fall of man involved all the other creatures in man's fate. Created as the representative of all of humanity, Adam entered into battle against the enemy of mankind, the devil, and "he fell, conquered in the very first encounter of the battle." The devil, whose own fall had been caused by pride and by a desire to be God, indeed, to be more than God, persuaded Adam to despise the commandment of God. And thus "the devil and one's own will" were responsible for sin. Having sought to be free of the rule of God, Adam ended up instead placing himself, and all his posterity with him, into subjection to the rule of sin and temptation. As the poet lamented, "O unhappy father, the begetter and the curse of your progeny!" While it was sometimes suggested that if Eve alone had sinned and not Adam, this sin would not have been transmitted to later generations, since God could have created another woman as he had created Eve, later generations were said to "have sinned in Adam" even though they had not yet been in existence, because "we were all in Adam" and "we were going to come from him."

Such, then, was the predicament of fallen man as he stood before the justice of God. He owed God an obligation not to sin, which was "the righteousness or rightness that makes men righteous"; but in refusing obedience, man "dishonored" God by his sin, and therefore he owed God a "satisfaction" that was greater than the honor taken away by his sin. Man bore not only "the obligation of perfect righteousness," but also "the obligation of rendering satisfaction." Moses, David, and all the great men of God were "entangled in their own offenses" and could not take upon themselves the sins of others: "by what satisfaction, therefore, can anyone obtain release unless he has as his own faithful advocate the very one whom he has offended?" Most—but not quite all—theologians taught that for God to forgive man his sin without such satisfaction, by a simple fiat, was impossible, not because there was something that the Almighty was powerless to do, but because such an act of forgiveness would be a violation of the very justice it would be intended to uphold. This requirement of a satisfaction that exceeded the original obligation was supported by "the unchangeable truth" of revelation as well as by "the evident reason" of natural knowledge. And it was "just" to demand that the requirement be met by one who belonged to the same species that had committed the sin.

Such a description of the transcendence and the justice of God in relation to human sin, if carried to its logical conclusion, could seem to preclude any plan of salvation. What have been called the "seemingly Manichaean expressions" of Peter Damian could be taken to imply that human life as now constituted was beyond redemption. "Man could be saved either through Christ or in some other way or in no way," Anselm said, and went on to show that it would not be "in some other way." Thus it was either through Christ or not at all. Salvation must be possible as well as necessary; and as the discussion of divine justice had as its purpose to show that salvation was necessary, so the discussion of divine grace and mercy was directed to showing that salvation was possible through Christ. "Nothing was beyond the reach of his wisdom, nothing was too difficult for his power. . . . There was no way that the mystery [of the incarnation] could be ineffectual." Although the omnipotence and transcendence of God were expressed through his justice, it was also possible to argue that "he was not omnipotent if he could not be led by his faithfulness to redeem man, whom he had created well." The term "necessity," which, when applied to the relation between God and man, usually referred to the iron law of God's justice, could also become a synonym for grace and mercy, so that "it was necessary that [God] bring to perfection that in human nature which he had begun."

It was the accomplishment of "the gratuitous grace of God alone" that he inspired and made perfect anything on which he had mercy. The forgiveness that God granted in his mercy was extended to the sinner "whether I want it or not." No one could live and work in a manner that was truly the service of God "unless he has been led by the grace of God," in fact, "by the grace of God alone." All who were saved were saved "by the kindness of his grace alone," which transcended human thought and comprehension. So prominent was this theme of grace in Scripture that one could get the impression "that free

Ans.*Med*.3 (Schmitt 3:86–87)

Guib.Nog.*Inc*.3.3 (*PL* 156:509)

Blum (1947) 107

Ans.*Cur d.h*.1.25 (Schmitt 2:95)

Od.Clun.*Serm*.1 (*PL* 133:711)

Guib.Nog.*Inc*.1.3 (*PL* 156:493)

Ans.*Cur d.h*.2.4 (Schmitt 2:99–100)

Rath.*Prael*.6.5 (*PL* 136:320)

Rath.*Serm.Quad*.2.23 (*CCCM* 46:75)

Othl.*Curs*.17 (*PL* 146:200)

Othl.*Visib*. (*PL* 93:1120); Othl.*Tent*.1 (*PL* 146:30) Rath.*Prael*.2.13.33 (*PL* 136:214)

will does not contribute anything to salvation, but grace alone"; moreover, there were many who "assert that on the basis of experience they can prove that man is not sustained by any free will at all." The contradiction between the apostle Paul and the apostle James on faith and works could be resolved by noting that if faith without works was dead, a dead faith was no faith at all, and that if the righteous man lived by faith, someone without faith was dead; for "faith is the foundation of the entire good work." Similarly, the contradiction between "grace alone" and free will was resolved by showing that in the case of infants it was truly "by grace alone, with no action by the free will" that salvation came, while in more mature persons "the natural free will always assists" the gift of divine grace. Nevertheless, grace received the credit even here, for without it free will could not attain to salvation.

Therefore John Cassian, despite his contribution to monasticism, was to be censured for teaching "that there are some whom God saves through grace and others whom nature justifies through free will," and the answer to Cassian by Prosper of Aquitaine was to be commended as "a catholic book." "Who is converted to God," asked a manual of discipline for monks, "unless, having laid aside the blackness of his sins, he is made white through the grace of forgiveness?" According to another monastic writer, it was impossible for anyone to raise himself up to the divine heights by his own powers, "unless he is lifted up to them by the grace of him who for our sakes came down." Yet the same writer could also say that "heavenly gifts come only to those who, with the cooperation of the grace of God, have by their industrious action merited to attain to them." And elsewhere he warned that "although you cannot even will anything good, much less do it, without [the grace of God], still you must not believe that you will be saved regardless of your own effort." Failure was not due to being deserted by "the anticipating grace of God," but to being held back by "our own slothfulness." One could go so far as to say that human salvation had two causes, divine grace and human will, but even this statement was based on the principle that all human good was moved and inspired by grace, which conferred, also upon the free will, the capacity to do the good.

The relative roles of grace and free will in salvation

ap.Ans.*Conc.*3.1 (Schmitt 2: 263)

Jas.2:26
Rom.1:17

Ans.*Orat.*10 (Schmitt 3:36)

Ans.*Conc.*3.3 (Schmitt 2: 266)
Ans.*Conc.*3.4 (Schmitt 2: 267)
See vol.1:319–24

See vol.1:325–27
Bern.Reich.*Ep.*11 (PL 142: 1169)

Petr.Dam.*Perf.mon.*8 (Brezzi 244)

Rath.*Prael.*2.12.23 (PL 136: 206)

Rath.*Serm.Asc.*1.2 (CCCM 46: 50)

Rath.*Prael.*5.26 (PL 136:309)

Rath.*Serm.Pasch.*2 (CCCM 46: 180)

Od.Clun.*Occup.*2.428–31 (Swoboda 27)

See vol.1:318–31

See pp. 82–84 above

had been an issue in the fifth and sixth centuries, and again in the ninth century; and in the form of the controversy over justification by faith, the question was to dominate the debates of the sixteenth century. But here in this "uncompromisingly christocentric period" it was the doctrine of the person and work of Jesus Christ, rather than the doctrine of justification or even the doctrine of grace, that became the principal vehicle for affirming the character of salvation as a free and utterly unearned gift of God; and in the period of the Reformation, this medieval understanding of the person and work of Christ was to be a presupposition shared, at least in principle, by both sides in the dispute over justification by faith versus justification by faith and works, with each claiming that its idea of justification was the only one consistent with the doctrine of redemption through Christ.

The presupposition for the doctrine of redemption in our period was the orthodox christological dogma. So completely was this taken for granted that the formula of the decree of the Council of Chalcedon, that "the distinctive character of each nature [is] preserved" in the incarnation of the Logos, could be quoted, for example by Peter Damian or by Anselm, without the source of the quotation being cited by either author (or, for that matter, by the modern editor of either author). It was a repetition of the condemnation of "Apollinarism" when a tenth-century commentary on the Gospel of Matthew made a point of explaining that the incarnation involved a total human nature, consisting of soul as well as of flesh, or when a twelfth-century theologian repeated the Eastern motto that what Christ did not assume in the incarnation he did not save. The notion of "enhypostaton," as evolved in later christological controversies, served to answer those who maintained that because the Logos "was a hypostasis [persona] even before the assumption of a man . . . and the assumed man was a hypostasis, since every individual human being is acknowledged to be a hypostasis," it would be appropriate to speak of the incarnate one as "two hypostases"; this claim was erroneous because "in the term 'man' [as applied to Christ] only the [human] nature is meant," not a human hypostasis. Western theologians seem to have been somewhat less successful in appropriating the results of the Eastern controversies over one or two wills in Christ, as is evident in Anselm's statement

See vol.1:264

Petr.Dam.*Opusc.*1.3; 1.4 (*PL* 145:25; 26); Ans.*Cur d.h*.2.7 (Schmitt 2:102)

See vol.1:248

Rem.Aux.*Matt*.6 (*PL* 131: 898)

See vol.2:74–75
Petr.Ven.*Ep*.37 (Constable 119)

See vol.2:88–89

Ans.*Inc*.11 (Schmitt 2:28–29)

See vol.2:62–75

Ans.*Cur d.h.*1.9 (Schmitt 2: 63)

Ans.*Cur d.h.*1.10 (Schmitt 2: 64)

Hrot.*Mar.*29–30 (Homeyer 49)
Petr.Ab.*Serm.*12 (PL 178: 480)

Rad.Ard.*Hom.*1.12 (PL 155: 1342)
Att.Verc.*Serm.*2 (PL 134: 835)

Od.Clun.*Occup.*5.325–26 (Swoboda 103)

Ans.*Orat.*7 (Schmitt 3:23)

Guib.Nog.*Inc.*2.1 (PL 156: 499)
Rath.*Dial.conf.*15 (PL 136: 404)

Petr.Dam.*Serm.*3 (PL 144:521)

Rath.*Dial.conf.*27 (PL 136: 420)

Cyn.*Chr.*239–40 (Cook 10)

John 3:13 (Vulg.)

Gez.*Corp.*2 (PL 137:377)

Rup.*Div.off.*6.36 (CCCM 7: 224)

Ans.*Cur d.h.*2.17 (Schmitt 2: 124); Guib.Nog.*Inc.*3.2 (PL 156:509)
Od.Clun.*Coll.*3.53 (PL 133: 637)

Od.Clun.*Occup.*6.132 (Swoboda 123)

Od.Clun.ap.Joh.Saler.*V.Od. Clun.*1.5 (PL 133:46)

that "Christ came to do not his own will but that of the Father, because the righteous will that he had did not come from [his] humanity but from [his] divinity." Yet this did not imply the absence of a distinct human will in Christ.

It would be a mistake to conclude from the formal tone of such statements of adherence to christological orthodoxy that the content of the dogma had not entered into what was being believed, taught, and confessed. Latin theologians of this period reveled in the paradox of the incarnation, that "a woman conceived the Lord, so that a creature might give birth to the Creator," that "the pure [virgin] is purified, God is offered up, the Redeemer is redeemed," that "he whom the immensity of heaven cannot contain is confined to the narrowness of the manger," and that "he who is lying in the cradle sends a star from the constellations" to guide the Magi. Through his birth from Mary, "our God has become our brother," humbly taking upon himself everything that belonged to humanity. In his flesh, as now in the bread of the Eucharist, God himself lay hidden. He had been urged by his love to descend to earth, and "he who is consubstantial with the Father has through his love deigned to come to us." The very name "Jesus" was a title for "Savior," and those who were rescued from hell were "converted on account of the name of Jesus." The incarnate one was "the Wisdom that with the all-ruling God did shape the whole creation." When, according to the Vulgate text, Jesus said to Nicodemus that "the Son of man is in heaven," this proved that the Logos-made-flesh was present in heaven according to both natures while he was on earth. The hypostatic union of the divine and human natures in him made the atonement and satisfaction possible, in that "whatever was necessary to be done for the restoration of men, the divine nature did it if the human could not, and the human nature did it if it was not fitting for the divine."

Such was "Christ, the lover of humanity." The christocentric piety of this period multiplied titles and epithets for him, saluting him as "sacrifice, king, hero, judge, leader, altar, priest." Christmas Night, the feast of his nativity, was "that night in which peace was given back to angels and men." But his nativity was only the beginning of a chain of events that together made up the plan of salvation. "For Christ was born in order to suffer; he

Rath.*Serm.Pent*.1.5 (*CCCM* 46: 60); Bald.*Sacr.alt*.3.2.1 (*SC* 94:532)

Othl.*Dial*.33 (*PL* 146:101)
Rev.5:5
Brd.Clr.*Div*.57.1 (Leclercq-Rochais 6–I:286–87)

Ambr.*Is.et an*.4.31 (*PL* 14:513); Ambr.*Ps.118.6.6 (*PL* 15:1269–70)

Cyn.*Chr*.718–20 (Cook 27–28)

Alc.*Cant*.2.8 (*PL* 100:646–47); Petr.Dam.*Serm*.20 (*PL* 144:615)
Cyn.*Chr*.730–36 (Cook 28)

Brd.Clr.*Div*.60.2 (Leclercq-Rochais 6–I:291); Brd.Clr.*Nat*.5.2 (Leclercq-Rochais 4:267)

Petr.Ab.*Serm*.12 (*PL* 178:483)

See vol.1:142

Petr.Dam.*Lib.grat*.1 (*MGH Lib.lit*.1:19)

Petr.Ab.*Rom*.2 (*CCCM* 11:113)

died in order to rise again; he rose again in order to elevate to heaven the flesh that he had assumed from us for us; he took it with him there in order to make it immortal and happy forever." The economy of salvation included the incarnation, passion, and resurrection, which were to be taken together. The "seven seals" of the Apocalypse were the saving events of the life and death of Christ. A favorite metaphor for this chain of events in the economy of salvation, derived from Ambrose, was the idea of a series of "leaps." "He shall save the world," said the Anglo-Saxon poet Cynewulf, "and all that dwell therein by that noble leap. The first leap was when he came to the Maid." The list of further leaps varied from one theologian to another, but birth, crucifixion, and burial were in all of them. Significantly, Cynewulf included a graphic description of Christ's descent into hell as one of the leaps.

The birth and life of Christ, the crucifixion and death of Christ, the burial and resurrection of Christ—these three "leaps" provided the points of focus for the consideration of the atonement. Sometimes it was his humility and his summons to discipleship that served as the basis for his saving work; sometimes it was "the series of events in the Lord's passion" on the cross, and sometimes it was his restoration to glory as Lord of history and of the universe. As in patristic thought, so in the tenth and eleventh centuries, these "leaps" were not isolated from one another, but differences of emphasis did appear. It was recognized, moreover, that even as Redeemer and Lord, Christ had "retained the fullness of grace in himself" and had remained transcendent. But as this period set out to deal with "the question of what that redemption of ours through the death of Christ may be and in what way the apostle declares that we are justified by his blood," it worked within the presuppositions of its heritage about the being of God, about the nature of man, and about the mystery of the incarnation of the God-man. Each of these presuppositions had acquired definite form by this time, so that while there was no dogma of the atonement as such, no theory of redemption that overlooked any of these presuppositions, or appeared to slight one or another of them, would be deemed acceptable.

The Discipline of Jesus

The plan of salvation, as defined and refined in this period, did not restrict itself to the theory of redemption in the

See vol.1:142

narrow sense of that word. The "picture of Christ" under-lying it included not only the narrative of his suffering, death, and resurrection, but the entire account of his life and work, his miracles and parables as well as his cruci-fixion. The picture of man presupposed by the doctrine of salvation likewise required a comprehensive under-standing of what the coming of Christ had accomplished. "Man did not need only to be redeemed," according to this understanding of Christ's coming in search of the lost, "but also to be instructed about how he ought to

Od.Clun.*Coll*.3.52 (*PL* 133: 636)

live after redemption." Acceptance of such instruction was the hallmark of true discipleship. "To be truly a disciple of Jesus and one to whom Jesus speaks, one must love

Rath.*Ep*.16 (*MGH BDK* 1: 92)
Bald.*Sacr.alt*.2.1.2 (*SC* 93: 136)

the discipline of Jesus." Discipleship and discipline were inseparable in the Christian life, as were discipline and redemption in the delineation of the work of Christ. "The discipline of Jesus" included the total span of human experience as this was to be brought into conformity with the divine will that had been revealed through the incarnation of the Son of God in a fully human life, all of which was pertinent to the human lives that it was intended to redeem and renew.

Before the incarnation, there were many aspects of authentic human existence that had never been seen in a concrete person but "could be demonstrated only by rea-son, apart from experience." But now the very one "who was to redeem men and to lead them back from the way of death and perdition to the way of life and eternal blessed-ness" would at the same time be the one who lived as a man among men and who, "in this association with them, as he was teaching them by word how they ought to live,

Ans.*Cur d.h*.2.11 (Schmitt 2: 111–12)

would provide himself as an example for them." The dis-cipline of Jesus gave instruction to his followers "by

Petr.Ab.*Rom*.3 (*CCCM* 11: 212); Othl.*Dial*.16 (*PL* 146: 80)

teaching and by example." When the Son of God came in the flesh to receive all those who would take refuge with him, "he gave them instruction in the precepts of life and set forth an incorruptible and utterly sound pat-

Othl.*Dial*.23 (*PL* 146:90)

tern of new life." For example, the imperative of bearing with the weaknesses of others was inculcated "not only by precept but also by many examples," above all by that

Od.Clun.*Coll*.3.51 (*PL* 133: 635)

of "the humble Jesus." The combination of precept and example in the discipline of Jesus had its prototype in

Luke 10:38–42

the story of Mary and Martha. The two sisters represented the two commandments of that discipline, because "noth-ing else has been commanded us except that we either

Rath.*Serm.Mar.Marth*.6
(*CCCM* 46:150)
Rath.*Serm.Mar.Marth*.2
(*CCCM* 46:146)

Bern.Reich.*V.Udal*.6 (*PL* 142:
1189)

Od.Clun.*Serm*.2 (*PL* 133:
716–17)

Cyn.*Chr*.140–41 (Cook 6)

See vol.1:17–18; 38–39

Od.Clun.*Occup*.6.6–7
(Swoboda 119)

See vol.2:209–10; 238–40
Guib.Nog.*Inc*.2.4 (*PL* 156:
504)

John 14:6

Od.Clun.*Coll*.1.18 (*PL* 133:
531–32)
Joh.Saler.*V.Od.Clun*.1.18 (*PL*
133:51)

Od.Clun.*V.Ger*.1.8 (*PL* 133:
647)

Od.Clun.*V.Ger*.11 (*PL* 133:
650)

Rath.*Ep*.26 (*MGH BDK* 1:
141)

Rath.*Serm.Quad*.2.19 (*CCCM*
46:73)

Adalg.*Admon*.13 (*PL* 134:
931)

minister to Christ in his members," as Martha did, "or that we pay close attention to him in contemplating his will," as Mary did. Such hearing and such doing were the content of the Christian life. Thus it was said of one saint that "by day, with Martha, he ministered to the Lord in his members, but by night, with Mary, he sat at the feet of Jesus and listened to his word."

Listening to the word of Jesus was a way of describing "the sweetness of the contemplative life" symbolized by Mary. "He was," said the poet, "the bringer of laws, the giver of precepts." The conception of the gospel as a new law, which had come from the early church, continued to be a way to describe the commandments of Jesus as a fulfillment or an amendment of the old law. Although he was not merely a prophet, Christ as teacher of the new law could be identified as a prophet, too, and this in a treatise addressed to Jews. When Christ had said of himself, "I am the truth," this pertained not only to "the confession of Christ" as such, but to "the truth of justice" as it affected one's neighbor. It followed that anyone who denied the truth in the case of his neighbor for fear of offending those in power was "undoubtedly denying Christ" as truth incarnate. The author of these sentiments was himself identified as "the soldier of Christ," and in an account of someone who was literally a soldier as well as a soldier of Christ he saw the influence of "the love of Christ" on the battlefield, where the soldier "had no wish to assail the persons of the enemy, but only to check their audacity." The demands "of Christ, of peace, and of the common good" were uppermost in his mind, even as a soldier. Obedience to those demands was a defining characteristic of a Christian. Although it was said that "a Christian is one who does not oppose Christ in any way, while one who does not obey the sacred canons [of the church] is a rebel against Christ," the fundamental definition of a Christian was: "one who obeys the will of Christ."

Another way to put the same definition was to identify a Christian as one who read the Bible: "he who wishes to be with God always, must pray frequently and must read frequently; for when we pray, we speak with God, but when we read, God is speaking with us." The one resource that could preserve the equanimity of the wise man amid all the troubles of this world was meditation on Scripture,

Od.Clun.*Coll*.1.pr. (*PL* 133: 519)
Othl.*Tent*.1 (*PL* 146:39);
Othl.*Dial*.13 (*PL* 146:77)

Othl.*Curs.spir*.19; 23 (*PL* 146:207; 224)

Ps.23:5
Bern.Reich.*Dial*.8 (*PL* 142: 1098)

Rom.15:4

Othl.*Man*.4 (*PL* 146:251)

Ps.50:23
Rath.*Ep*.16 (*MGH BDK* 1:91)
Od.Clun.*Coll*.1.1 (*PL* 133: 520)

Othl.*Curs*.14 (*PL* 146:189)

Od.Clun.*Coll*.3.15 (*PL* 133: 601)

Rath.*Prael*.3.5.10 (*PL* 136: 225)

Eadm.*V.Ans*.1.7 (Southern 12)
Ans.*Cur d.h*.1.18 (Schmitt 2:82)

Ans.*Conc*.3.6 (Schmitt 2:271– 72)

Ans.*Inc*.1 (Schmitt 2:9–10)

which contained everything that there was to know about God and about the self. There was no weapon more effective against the wiles of the devil than citing Scripture. By this method those who read Scripture and meditated on it were able to put him to flight. When the psalmist said, "Thou preparest a table before me in the presence of my enemies," this was a reference to "the table of Holy Scripture . . . filled with various doctrines." But when the apostle said, "Whatever was written in former days was written for our instruction," these words "pertain especially to those who, being literate, can constantly recognize how they should govern themselves and those who have been entrusted to them"; therefore "it is incumbent especially on the clergy to pay supreme attention to what has been written." This duty could be identified as the most important thing that the clergy did. The "sacrifices of praise" that truly honored God in worship were the reading and teaching of the words of the divine law. Since it was the purpose of all of Scripture to act as a restraint against the evils of this present life, it addressed itself to the human condition in two ways, "either by consoling us or by warning us, for every divine pronouncement is set forth in this twofold fashion." The proclamation of the word of God consisted in the application of its consoling and warning message to the hearer.

As consolation and as warning, Scripture carried a unique authority, since it was the word of Christ. If anyone refused to heed this word, he showed that he was not on God's side. For those who were on God's side, it was enough that one "show proof from the divine Scriptures, and we believe him." It was said of Anselm, for example, that he reposed such trust in Scripture that everything in it was unquestionably true for him and he made it his supreme goal to conform his faith and thought to the authority of Scripture. He himself labeled as "false" and untenable whatever contradicted Scripture; and he explicitly put this as a check upon his speculation in such a way that if any conclusion of human reason was contradicted by Scripture it was not to be believed, while it if did not contradict Scripture it was to be accepted. A thinker must not bring his own philosophical preconceptions to the study of Scripture, but must "approach the questions of the Sacred Page with the utmost caution," something that "the dialecticians of our time, or rather the heretics of dialectic" failed to do. What made Anselm "the master of the entire Latin world" was his "strictness in the assertion of the Scriptures and of the faith" in opposition to these and other "heretics of this time."

Guib.Nog.*Mor*.pr. (*PL* 156: 19–20)

The authority of Scripture was supreme over that of reason; it was supreme over other authorities as well. God had so generously endowed the Old and New Testaments with his grace that "there is no need for us to add anything of doctrine to them nor to propound anything except what we have been taught by reading them." Although such a

Othl.*Dial*.1 (*PL* 146:62–63)

formulation of the authority of Scripture sounded as though it were isolated from the authority of the church and of the fathers, no such isolation was intended. The doctrine of authority in Ratherius of Verona may be regarded as typical. On the one hand, he could describe Scripture as a "labyrinth, utterly impenetrable to me" and

Rath.*Prael*.6.24 (*PL* 136:339)

open to access only through the writings of the fathers. Yet he could also, at least for the sake of argument, dispense with citations from the fathers, in favor of "the

Rath.*Prael*.2.13.30 (*PL* 136: 212)

more eminent authority" of Scripture. He even put the difference between the fathers and Scripture in the language of a distinction between "modern teachers" and "ancient ones," and admitted that he had "used them indiscriminately," since it had been through the "modern teachers" that God had made the ancient Scripture fruit-

Rath.*Prael*.6.24 (*PL* 136:338)

ful for him.

As the inspired word of God, Scripture was true and was consistent throughout. If something in one book of the Bible appeared to diverge from what was said in another, "they must all be understood as setting forth a single message, through the unity of him who is speaking

Petr.Dam.*Serm*.14 (*PL* 144: 573)

in all of them, the Holy Spirit." This unity brought together the New Testament and the Old Testament as the word of Christ. The very first verse of the very first

Ps.1:1
Othl.*Curs*.10 (*PL* 146:171)

psalm spoke "about the blessedness and the holiness" of Christ, as did many other portions of the Old Testament. It was suggested that originally the readings at the Christian liturgy had consisted only of the epistles of the apostle Paul, but that eventually other lessons were added,

Bern.Reich.*Miss.off*.1 (*PL* 142:1057)

not only from the New Testament but also from the Old. So central was the witness to Christ in the Old Testament

Hier.*Esai*.pr. (*CCSL* 73:1)
Bern.Reich.*Modul*.6 (*PL* 142: 1142)

that "Isaiah, as Saint Jerome says, should be called not so much a prophet as an evangelist and an apostle." The Song of Songs became "the book which was most read, and

Leclercq (1962) 90

Petr.Dam.*Serm*.34 (*PL* 144: 690)

Joh.Saler.*V.Od.Clun*.1.13 (*PL* 133:49)

Bald.*Sacr.alt*.1.1 (*SC* 93:80)

Guib.Nog.*Inc*.3.6 (*PL* 156: 519)

Othl.*Tent*.1 (*PL* 146:37)

Bern.Reich.*Dial*.3 (*PL* 142: 1091)

Rem.Aux.*Matt*.5 (*PL* 131: 892)

Matt.11:9

John 1:29
Rem.Aux.*Matt*.2 (*PL* 131: 877)

Rem.Aux.*Cel.miss*. (*PL* 101: 1251)

Othl.*Curs*.16 (*PL* 146:197)

most frequently commented in the medieval cloister" because it, as "a nuptial song," was suitable to the celebration of Christ and of his saints. Sometimes, it seems, the devotion in the medieval cloister to the Book of Psalms and related books was so intense that when the monks heard the reading of the Gospels, they exclaimed, "Stop it, and go back to the Psalms!" Despite their christological interpretation of the Old Testament, Christians sometimes argued, especially in their polemics against Judaism, that the law of Moses and the Old Testament promised only material blessings to the faithful, blessings such as wealth, children, and long life, but that "there is silence about eternal matters, and nothing is said about the rewards of heaven or the torments of hell." They recognized, moreover, that the christological interpretation of the Old Testament depended on the authority of Christ, and not vice versa, so that "even if you disbelieve something from all the proofs that have been adduced from the Holy Scriptures, either because they have been spoken in the shadow of the [Old Testament] law or by mere men, you will surely have to believe what has been said by the Lord Jesus Christ, who is God and man."

What had been said by Christ himself was, in a special and strict sense, what was contained in the Gospels. "Law and prophecy are recapitulated in the one gospel," because the words and deeds of Christ in the Gospels gave meaning to Moses and Isaiah. A prophet was not only one who predicted the coming of Christ as something in the future, but one who interpreted Scripture properly. Therefore John the Baptist was a prophet because he predicted what was to come, but "more than a prophet because with his finger he pointed at Him whom the other prophets had predicted as yet to come, and he said: 'Behold, the Lamb of God.'" This explicit recognition of the Christ whom the Old Testament had only adumbrated put the Gospels into a special category. "Gospel [evangelium], translated into Latin, means 'good news.' And what is better news than . . . the things that are said in the Gospel about the incarnation of the Son of God, about his miracles, his preaching, and his resurrection and ascension?" These events in the life of Christ, in fact "all the deeds of our Savior," were deserving of reflection and veneration, for "none of what is said or done in [the Gospels] is devoid of very beneficial mysteries." Although

Petr.Dam.*Serm*.49 (*PL* 144: 780)

Rab.*Inst.cler*.1.33 (Knoepfler 74–75); Joh.Abr.*Off.eccl.* (*PL* 147:32–35)

Rup.*Div.off*.1.37 (*CCCM* 7: 31)

Rem.Aux.*Cel.miss.* (*PL* 101: 1247)

Rom.*ord*.5.32–37 (Andrieu 2: 215–17)

Rom.*ord*.1.59–62 (Andrieu 2: 87–89)

Amal.*Off*.2.12.15 (*ST* 139: 226)

Amal.*Off*.2.18.13 (*ST* 139: 310)

Rem.Aux.*Cel.miss.* (*PL* 101: 1250)

Bern.Reich.*Miss.off*.2 (*PL* 142: 1058)

Petr.Dam.*Serm*.61 (*PL* 144: 847)

the Gospel of Matthew was the first and the Gospel of John the last, "nevertheless the holy evangelists are all one in authority and one in faith, not diverging from one another in any way."

The unique position of the Gospels within the Bible was shown also by their special place within the liturgy, where they were "the most important of all the things that are said in the office of the Mass." The order of service at the Mass did not begin with the reading of the lessons, but with songs and prayers, whose "sweetness and pleasantness would first soften the hearts of the hearers, so that the people, after hearing the melody of a pleasant song and having had their attention focused on spiritual things through the repentance of their minds, will take up the saving words of the Gospel with ardent interest." The reading of the Gospel was "more important" than the rest of the liturgy. According to a rite in use in the tenth century, the deacon at the Mass would kiss the Gospel, then take it in his hand, and proceed to the appointed place to read it; upon the announcement of the Gospel lesson, the clergy and all the faithful would turn to the east. It had been the custom even earlier to accompany the reading of the Gospel with incense and candles and with other signs of its central importance. It was fitting that the Gospel be read only by someone of the rank of deacon or higher, and from "a position of greater excellence" before the altar as an indication of "the preeminent doctrine proclaimed in the Gospel and its outstanding authority." Even the reading of the Epistle lesson had to yield to the Gospel, going before it not because of a greater worth but only in the way that the apostles walked ahead of Christ while he was on earth. The Gospel was supreme not only in the liturgy, but for the liturgy, determining liturgical practice even on such questions as omitting the Gloria during Lent.

As the word of Christ, the Gospels presented not only what he had said, but what he had been and done. In a Christmas sermon, for example, the recitation of formulas about the incarnation reminiscent of the creed of the Council of Chalcedon led direcly to a "common discussion about the humility of our Redeemer and what he accomplished for our salvation already in his very nativity." At his baptism, the Holy Spirit came in the form of a dove, because "the Lord who was coming in meekness

Rath.*Serm.Pent.*1.4 (*CCCM* 46: 59)

Matt.11:29
Od.Clun.*Occup.*5.559–62 (Swoboda 110–11)
Luke 22:47–48
Od.Clun.*Occup.*6.24–26 (Swoboda 120)

Isa.9:6

Od.Clun.*Occup.*5.696–98 (Swoboda 114)
Rem.Aux.*Matt.*11 (*PL* 131: 923–24)

Gez.*Corp.*7 (*PL* 137:381)

Od.Clun.*V.Ger.*1.42 (*PL* 133: 668)
Rad.Ard.*Hom.*1.30 (*PL* 155: 1421)

Petr.Dam.*Serm.*45 (*PL* 144: 746)

Othl.*Dial.*16 (*PL* 146:81)
Petr.Dam.*Serm.*32 (*PL* 144: 676)

Othl.*Prov.*D–68 (Korfmacher 19)

Od.Clun.*Serm.*2 (*PL* 133: 715)

Othl.*Visib.* (*PL* 93:1121);
Othl.*Prov.* S–75 (Korfmacher 79)

Matt.20:20–28

Rem.Aux.*Matt.*11 (*PL* 131: 926)

Joh.Saler.*V.Od.Clun.*2.12 (*PL* 133:68)

Od.Clun.*Occup.*5.528–30 (Swoboda 109)
Ans.*Sacr.eccl.*3 (Schmitt 2: 241)

Matt.10:38

wanted to have himself made manifest to men through a meek sign." He came to save the world from its pride, and "this he especially teaches by all the things that he does in utmost humility, saying, 'I am meek, all of you learn this from me.'" When Judas sought to betray him with a kiss, Jesus showed himself to be "meek and innocent." As the prince of peace, he was determined to exercise his reign through moderation and to change harsh actions into gentle ones. He who wanted to reign with Christ, therefore, must "first strive to suffer for him in humility." The humility of Christ was the nobility of his followers. They were truly worthy of him if they, like him, had grounds for pride and attained the height of power, but nevertheless remained humble. This was true even of Mary herself, "the unique, the incomparable Virgin, [who], if she had not followed the humility of Christ, would never have attained to the exaltation of Christ."

Like Mary, believers were to follow Christ, "who should be imitated in all respects, as far as possibility allows." If they claimed to abide in him, they must walk as he walked. For it was a basic rule of the Christian life that "he who wants to imitate Christ must continually go on learning." Following him today did not mean walking in his steps, but imitating his deeds. Since Christ was the head of the church, the eyes of all the faithful were to be intent on him, just as human eyes paid attention to the head of another person. When two of his disciples had been guilty of excessive ambition and the remaining ten had been guilty of resentment, Christ had not reproved either group, but had instead set himself forth to both as an example of the principle that "he who is the servant of all is truly the Lord." If the Virgin Mary herself was an imitator of the humility of Christ, then the imitation of the saints by believers was, in turn, an imitation of Christ; yet it was possible also to cite "the actions of our Lord Jesus" as a model for those "who object to" the examples of the saints. He had become a man so that human beings could imitate his human life and could not dismiss his virtues as something beyond the realm of possibility; "that was why he did not give them an archangel, but himself as a model." He was above all the model of how to bear the contempt of men as a reward for a life of righteousness.

In inviting men to follow his example, "he has lifted up the sign of the cross before the nations, and he declares:

Od.Clun.*Coll*.2.11 (*PL* 133: 558)
Petr.Dam.*Perf.mon*.3 (Brezzi 214); Ans.L.*Sent.Ans*.4 (Bliemetzrieder 108); Petr.Ven.*Ep*.145 (Constable 360)

Petr.Dam.*Perf.mon*.20 (Brezzi 300)

Southern (1953) 158

Od.Clun.*Occup*.5.788–90 (Swoboda 117)

Od.Clun.*V.Ger*.2.16 (*PL* 133: 679)

Gisl.Crisp.*V.Herl*. (Robinson 89)

Od.Clun.*V.Ger*.1.14 (*PL* 133: 652)
Od.Clun.*Coll*.3.7 (*PL* 133: 594)

Petr.Dam.*V.Rom*.25 (*FSI* 94: 54)

Petr.Dam.*Opusc*.43.6 (*PL* 145: 685)

Petr.Ven.*Ep*.20 (Constable 35)

Rom.13:14
Od.Clun.*Coll*.2.11 (*PL* 133: 558)

Od.Clun.*Serm*.2 (*PL* 133: 715)

Od.Clun.*V.Ger*.1.34 (*PL* 133: 662)

'He who does not take his cross daily and follow me is not worthy of me.'" The summons to "take up the cross of the Redeemer" was the core of the Christian life of self-mortification, in which one died to the world. This was the call to "follow him as your leader in the midst of the battle of temptations, as your guardian in the midst of peace and prosperity." Yet this call to follow Christ as leader was addressed to those who were in their "time of initiation" as recruits to the monastic life, rather than to lay Christians. Among lay Christians, moreover, "those who set themselves a higher standard than the ordinary looked to the monasteries for their examples." The exhortation to imitate "the example of the Lord" pertained to all who were his "followers." Nevertheless, when a layman gave evidence of a special "devotion to Christ," this was proof that "if one considers his desire [votum]," he was actually manifesting a "faithfulness to the monastic profession" even though his own circumstances prevented him from becoming a monk; and some laymen of this disposition did eventually enter the religious life.

The term "desire [votum]" in that description was apparently not yet being used in its technical sense of "monastic vow," but the three component elements of the doctrine of vows—poverty, chastity, and obedience—were clearly present in the specific ways in which Christ served as example. One who received the poor received Christ "in them," and one who heard their cries actually heard "Christ in the poor"; but those who renounced power and wealth to "take on a monastic habit" were said to have become "subject to Christ the pauper," and the ideal they followed was that of living "in the simplicity of Christ Jesus, the pauper and the crucified." "As a pauper and a pauper in spirit," an abbot exhorted a monk, "follow your Pauper-Lord." The ideal of chastity was likewise a part of following the example of Christ, the Son of the Virgin, who taught that "the one who takes up his cross is chaste in heart and in body and has never made provision for the flesh, to gratify its desires." As the Son of the Virgin, Christ not only rescued a Mary Magdalene "from the depths of the abyss" of her lusts; but he "imbued with the love of chastity" a lay believer, so that "he would not allow himself to be diverted from it even by the prospect of an excellent marriage." Such obedience to Christ de-

Matt.11:29–30
Od.Clun.*V.Ger*.3.8 (*PL* 133:
695)

Her.*V.Had*.5 (*PL* 139:1143)

Od.Clun.*Serm*.3 (*PL* 133:
724); Joh.Saler.*V.Od.Clun.*
1.29 (*PL* 133:56)

Othl.*Doctr.spir*.14 (*PL* 146:
280)

ap.Petr.Dam.*V.Rom*.24 (*FSI*
94:51)

Rem.Aux.*Matt*.9 (*PL* 131:
915)

Adalg.*Admon*.12 (*PL* 134:
930); Ael.*Spec.car*.3.5 (*PL*
195:582); Rad.Ard.*Hom*.2.10
(*PL* 155:1530)

Luke 23:34

Petr.Dam.*Opusc*.43.pr. (*PL*
145:679)

Petr.Dam.*Serm*.45 (*PL* 144:
745)

Od.Clun.*Coll*.3.43 (*PL* 133:
628)

Petr.Dam.*Opusc*.43.5 (*PL*
145:683); Petr.Dam.*Opusc*.50.2
(*PL* 145:734); Petr.Dam.*Serm.*
51 (*PL* 144:792)

Ans.*Cur d.h*.2.18 (Schmitt 2:
127)

Gilson (1960) 105

served to be called "bearing the yoke of Christ," but this "yoke" usually referred to monastic obedience. By contrast with Moses, who had coerced the Jews into obedience by using the rod of the law, Benedict of Nursia had "subjected the company of the monks to the sweet yoke of Christ." And the monk would say of himself that, in vowing obedience, he had promised Christ to bear "the monastic yoke."

The supreme vehicle of divine instruction and revelation through the discipline of Jesus, as the phrase "bearing the cross" indicated, was the passion and death of Christ. As the founder of the Camaldolese Order, Romuald, said, "If you bear the cross of Christ, it follows that you must not forsake the obedience of Christ." To obey and follow Christ implied that one hearken to his word and imitate his actions, but above all it meant that one "follow in the footsteps of his passion." If, for example, someone found it difficult to forgive his brother, he was to call up the memory of the sufferings of Christ, who prayed for his enemies even though he was dying an innocent death at their hands. An act of penance, such as fasting or flagellation, was, according to Peter Damian, "truly a sharing in the passion of the Redeemer," for by it the penitent was crucifying the allurements of the flesh in imitation of Christ on the cross. "Christ has given himself over to death for us," he admonished elsewhere, "and therefore let us, for the sake of his love, also mortify in ourselves every desire for earthly pleasure. By his willingness to undergo the suffering of the cross, he has shown us the road by which we can return to our fatherland." What Christ had suffered in himself as the head of the church, he continued to suffer in his members. The five wounds of Christ (two in his hands, two in his feet, and one in his side) corresponded to the five senses, each of which had its own special pleasures and needed to be cured of these. Anselm of Canterbury, in a treatise devoted to the doctrine of satisfaction by the death of Christ, also emphasized that "the injuries and insults and the death on the cross" served as "an example to men" of how they ought to bear their own sufferings.

This view of the cross as example received its classic formulation in the theology of Peter Abelard, "whose infallible instinct leads straight to dangerous questions and provoking replies." "In order to persevere bravely in the battle against our passions," he urged in a sermon for Palm Sunday, "we should always hold him before our eyes, and his passion should always serve as an example to

Petr.Ab.*Serm*.9 (*PL* 178:447)

us, lest we fall away." The words of the Gospel, "Greater love has no man than this, that a man lay down his life

John 15:13

for his friends," served him as a locus classicus for the understanding of the significance of the cross. They meant that "by the faith which we have concerning Christ love is increased in us, through the conviction that God in Christ has united our nature to himself and that by suffering in that nature he has demonstrated to us the supreme love of which he speaks"; through this love "we cling

Petr.Ab.*Rom*.2 (*CCCM* 11: 111–12)

to him and to our neighbor in an indissoluble bond of love for his sake." Again, these words meant that Christ had "persevered to the death for the doctrine of the preaching of the gospel and by dying had shown what

Petr.Ab.*Prob.Hel*.6 (*PL* 178: 686)

he could not have shown by being born." In yet another context he quoted these words to prove that Christ had "instructed and taught us perfectly" by his death and resurrection, "proposing an example" through the manner of his dying, "exhibiting a life of immortality" by his rising from the dead, and by his ascension "teaching us"

Petr.Ab.*Theol.chr*.4.62 (*CCCM* 12:292)

about eternal life in heaven. And on the basis of these words of Christ he could even define redemption itself as "that supreme love in us through the passion of Christ,"

Petr.Ab.*Rom*.2 (*CCCM* 11: 118)

replacing the fear of God with love for him.

This locus classicus provided Abelard with an interpretation for various traditional themes and pictures of salvation through the death of Christ. He was able to say, in a letter, that Christ "has purchased and redeemed you with his own blood. . . . The very Creator of the world

Petr.Ab.*Ep*.5 (*PL* 178:209–10)

has become the price for you." Christ was properly called "the highest King and the supreme Priest and the true

Petr.Ab.*Symb.Apost*. (*PL* 178: 622)
ap.Petr.Ab.*Apol*.2 (*CCCM* 11:359)

Savior." When challenged to vindicate the orthodoxy of his doctrine, Abelard declared: "I confess that the only Son of God became incarnate to liberate us from the servitude of sin and the yoke of the devil, and thus by his death to

Petr.Ab.*Conf*. (*PL* 178:105–6)

open for us the door of eternal life." A fairly extensive statement of his position appeared in a sermon bearing

Petr.Ab.*Serm*.12 (*PL* 178: 479–84)

the title "The Cross." Here the cross was set forth as a gift of "grace, by which we have been redeemed, since it is not of our own power to share in the passion of Jesus by our suffering and to follow him by carrying our own

Petr.Ab.*Serm*.12 (*PL* 178:484)

cross." On the cross Christ had been "physically cursed by God through punishment," which was "why he is said

Petr.Ab.*Serm*.12 (*PL* 179: 481)

Petr.Ab.*Rom*.2 (*CCCM* 11: 112); *Sent.Flor*.31–33 (Ostlender 15–16); Herm.Mag.*Epit*.23 (*PL* 178:1730–31)

Rom.8:32

to have taken upon himself or to have borne our sins, that is, to have accepted the punishment of our sins and thus in some way to have shared in our curse." Yet all of this language was put into the service of an interpretation of the cross as the means for God "to reveal his love to us or to convince us how much we ought to love him 'who spared not even his own Son' for us."

Brd.Clr.*Ep*.190.9.23 (*PL* 182: 1071); Wm.S.Th.*Disp.Ab*.3 (*PL* 180:325)

Brd.Clr.*Ep*.190.7.17 (*PL* 182: 1067)

Brd.Clr.*Ep*.190.9.25 (*PL* 182: 1072)

Brd.Clr.*Grat*.10.35 (Leclercq-Rochais 3:190)

Ans.*Cur d.h*.2.19 (Schmitt 2: 130)

To Abelard's opponents such a view of reconciliation through Christ was inadequate. Abelard was following "the Pelagian heresy" rather than "the Christian faith" by belittling the need for redemption. They took him to be saying that the significance of "human righteousness in the blood of the Redeemer" and the achievement of all the events of Christ's birth, life, death, and resurrection could be reduced to this, "that by his living and teaching, his suffering and dying he might impart to men a pattern of life and show to what limits love can go." If this were the entire purpose of his coming, then "he taught righteousness, but he did not grant it; he demonstrated love, but he did not infuse it." This was itself an inadequate and an unjust reading of Abelard's thought, one that has been perpetuated also by many modern scholars, but it did express the widely held "intuition" that, while Christ had taught righteousness, he had also granted it, and that he had infused love and had not merely exhibited it. Christ as teacher and pattern, even Christ crucified as example, needed to be related to the larger definition of Christ as Redeemer. He who provided the example of virtue must also provide the assistance of grace. "It would," according to Anselm, "be useless for men to be imitators of him if they were not participants in his merit."

The Cross as the Redemption of Mankind

Phil.2:7

Brd.Clr.*Ep*.190.9.25 (*PL* 182: 1072); Brd.Clr.*Div*.119 (Leclercq-Rochais 6–I:397)

Discipline, even "the discipline of Jesus," was a term for the effects of Christ upon the life and behavior of believers. There were, said Bernard of Clairvaux in refutation of Abelard, "three chief parts of our salvation: the form of humility, in which God 'emptied himself'; the measure of love, which extends to death, even death on a cross; and the mystery of redemption, for which he sustained the death that he bore." Humility and love were absolutely necessary, and the example of Christ was essential; but none of this "has a foundation nor even any reality if redemption is missing." Salvation must be more than discipline, more even than humility and love; it could not be less than all of these, but by itself the revelation of humility and love in Christ was not enough. Whether one called it reconciliation or the remission of sins or justification or redemption, what Christ had done had been accomplished "through his blood [per sanguinem]," not merely "through his word [per sermonem]." "We did not receive reconciliation in any other way except through the blood of Christ," one writer said. Perhaps nowhere was this intuition more movingly portrayed than in the anonymous Anglo-Saxon poem *The Dream of the Rood*. Here Christ was portrayed as "the Hero young—he was Almighty God," who, when "he wanted to redeem mankind," ascended to "the lofty gallows" of the cross. As another Anglo-Saxon poem put it, "the King redeemed them with his body." His intent was the redemption of mankind—not merely a redemption for humility and love, but a redemption from the power of the devil and the wrath of God. It was, moreover, a redemption of mankind as a whole, even though most men would reject it and perish. As a medieval proverb had it, "The cross and death of Christ constitute the restoration of the world." Only on that basis could the redemption be applied to believers, so that *The Dream of the Rood* could go on to say that by his suffering on the cross Christ had "ransomed us and given us life." It was this objective character of the redeeming work of Christ that Abelard's critics, rightly or wrongly, found to be missing in his answer to his own "question of what that redemption of ours through the death of Christ may be."

The doctrine of redemption had to be objective because redemption involved "a transaction between these three parties: mankind, God, and the devil." Although that particular statement was written about one-third of a century after the work of Anselm on the atonement, it was an apt summary of the perspective from which the theologians of the tenth and eleventh centuries viewed the saving work of Christ on the cross. Within the limits of the presuppositions summarized earlier in this chapter, the doctrine of redemption was based on an examination of how the relation of mankind to God and to the devil was changed by the death of Christ. What came out of the examination was a series of more careful formulations of the doctrine of redemption than had been worked out by patristic theology, together with a critique of meta-

Brd.Clr.*Ep.*190.8.20 (*PL* 182: 1069)

Rup.*Div.off.*9.3 (*CCCM* 7: 304)

Drm.*Rd.*39–41 (Swanton 91)
Cyn.*Chr.*1208–9 (Cook 46)

Othl.*Prov.*C–78 (Korfmacher 15)

Drm.*Rd.*145–47 (Swanton 96)

Petr.Ab.*Rom.*2 (*CCCM* 11: 113)

Hug.S.Vict.*Sacr.*1.8.4 (*PL* 176:307)

phors for the redemption that had come down from the fathers. The most comprehensive of these formulations, that of Anselm in *Why God Became Man,* was described by an early historian of doctrine as "almost the only point at which scholasticism brought about a truly healthy development." In it Anselm related the three parties to one another by means of a theory of "satisfaction" through the cross, giving systematic form to the biblical and liturgical identification of the work of Christ as sacrifice and producing "a doctrine of the atonement fully consonant with the matured sacramental system of the church."

Whatever metaphor or theory of the atonement one propounded, the death of Christ on the cross must be central to it. In the Latin text of the Nicene Creed, the incarnation of the Logos and all the events that followed it were said to have been "for the sake of us men and for the purpose of our salvation [propter nos homines et propter nostram salutem]," but the crucifixion was "for us [pro nobis]" in a more specific way. Whether this preposition "for [pro]" meant only "on our behalf" or whether it meant "in our stead," the creedal phrase did put the crucifixion into a special place within the economy of salvation through Christ. "For this he came into the world and for this he was born, that he might set us free by his passion," Peter Damian said. Christ was the Mediator and the Reconciler, but he was "the Mediator in his birth and the Reconciler in his death." Among all things under heaven, the sepulcher of Christ was second in importance only to the Virgin Mary. For "it was not by his nativity, but by the passion and the blood of Christ that original sin was removed." The theme of a twelfth-century Christmas sermon was: "Christ appeared [for the sake of] the redemption, cleansing, and satisfaction of the human race." Describing the birth and the life of Christ as "without guile," Othlo of Sankt Emmeram identified their purpose as that of perfecting what Christ had come to accomplish, which was to "suffer for the guilt of the world." Christ's "giving himself for us" was defined as "discharging the debt of our guilty death by his own death" and granting salvation. By the plan of the Father and with the cooperation of the Holy Spirit, Christ had redeemed the world from sin and eternal death by his voluntary dying.

The centrality of the crucifixion and death of Christ to the doctrine of redemption was betokened and con-

Thomasius (1876) 95

G.H.Williams (1960) 64

Symb.Nic.–CP (Schaff 2:59)

Petr.Dam.*Serm.*7 (*PL* 144: 543)

Rufin.As.*Bon.pac.*1.4 (*PL* 150: 1598)

Petr.Ven.*Serm.*2 (*PL* 189: 977)

Brun.S.*Sent.*5.3 (*PL* 165: 1026)

Rad.Ard.*Hom.ep.ev.*1.10 (*PL* 155:1700)

Othl.*Doctr.spir.*2 (*PL* 146: 266)

Od.Clun.*Occup.*3.130–33 (Swoboda 35)

Ans.*Orat.*3 (Schmitt 3:10)

See vol.2:110–11

See vol.2:156

Lib.Car.2.28 (MGH Conc.Sup.
2:89)

Ps.Alc.Div.off.18 (PL 101:
1210)

See pp. 236, 248 below

Petr.Dam.Serm.48 (PL 144:
766)

Othl.Dial.38 (PL 146:112)

Ans.Orat.4 (Schmitt 3:11);
Fulb.Hymn.12 (PL 141:345)

Hymn.lat.67 (Anal.Hymn.
50:74)

See vol.1:20
Rup.Div.off.5.1 (CCCM 7:
147); Rich.S.Vict.Edict.3
(Châtillon-Tulloch 72); Petr.
Ven.Ep.11 (Constable 17)

Petr.Dam.Perf.mon.20 (Brezzi
298)

Petr.Dam.Carm.A.93 (Lokrantz
71); Fulb.Hymn.12 (PL 141:
345)

Petr.Dam.Carm.A.59 (Lokrantz
64)
Petr.Dam.Carm.B.3.4 (Lokrantz
84)

Petr.Dam.Opusc.19.5 (PL 145:
432)

firmed by the cult of the cross. Among the Byzantine iconoclasts, the cross was the one exception to the rule that there were to be no images or symbols in the church. In the West also, the most vigorous attack on the use of images, *The Caroline Books* attributed to Charlemagne, nevertheless insisted that "it was through [the cross], not through [images], that the human race was redeemed," and that therefore only the cross, "not some image or another," was deserving of "servile supplication." For when the worshiper "prostrates himself bodily before the cross, he does so mentally before the Lord, venerating the cross through which we have been redeemed." Although the critics of the church, especially the Jews, accused the Christians of idolatry for adoring the cross, the defenders of the faith responded that such acts of adoration were not addressed to the material of the cross as such, but "only to the figure of the Lord's body that is placed on the cross." It was generally agreed that "adoration," in its technical sense as distinguished from "veneration," did belong to the cross; and Anselm was expressing this general agreement when he addressed a prayer to the cross: "O holy cross . . . , I adore, venerate, and glorify in thee that cross which thou dost represent to us, and in it our merciful Lord and what he has mercifully accomplished through it."

A widely used hymn by the sixth-century poet Venantius Fortunatus hailed "the royal banners" of the cross in procession and saluted the cross as the place where the price of the world's salvation was suspended; the hymn also made use of the Christian addition to the text of Psalm 96:10, "The Lord reigned from the tree." From this hymn the idea of the cross as a banner spread to medieval literature. Novices to the monastic vocation were to know that victory in the conflicts of their life would certainly be theirs, because the banner of the cross was leading the way. Hell would lament because it had been "conquered by thy banners," said a later hymn addressed to "the cross, the sole hope of mankind." Elsewhere, the poet spoke of the cross as "life to me and death to you, O enemy," and again as a "balance" on which the price of the world's redemption was weighed out. He also spoke of having frequently had a vision of Christ on the cross and of being transported by the vision to "the light of eternity." The mystery of the cross brought Old and New

Petr.Dam.*Serm*.18 (*PL* 144: 606)
Petr.Dam.*Serm*.48 (*PL* 144: 771)

Od.Clun.*Serm*.4 (*PL* 133:737–38); Petr.Dam.*Serm*.18 (*PL* 144:601–11)

Rab.*Inst.cler*.1.33 (Knoepfler 77); Rup.*Div.off*.2.15 (*CCCM* 7:48)
Rom.ord.5.60 (Andrieu 2: 221–22)
Ans.L.*Sent.Ans*.6 (Bliemetzrieder 114–15)

Seq.*trans*.120.16 (*Anal.Hymn*. 54:188)

Her.*V.Rem*.12 (*PL* 139:1159)

Petr.Ven.*Mirac*.2.20 (*PL* 189: 930–31); Rad.Ard.*Hom*.1.18 (*PL* 155:1372)

Rath.*Prael*.4.16 (*PL* 136:263)

Od.Clun.*Occup*.6.248–50 (Swoboda 126)

Ps.Petr.Dam.*Exp.can.miss*.8 (*PL* 145:884)
Petr.Dam.*Serm*.18 (*PL* 144: 602)

Rab.*Inst.cler*.2.37 (Knoepfler 130–31)

Testaments together into "one doctrine," for "the cross is the harmony of the Scriptures." But the use of the cross in worship was not confined to the Lenten season or to such festivals of the church year as the Invention of the Holy Cross, which was the occasion for some of these statements. The sign of the cross was an essential part of the liturgy of the Mass, coming as it did at all the important steps in the consecration and eucharistic sacrifice. At baptism, too, the several impositions of the sign of the cross were "sacraments" in their own right. No less essential was its function in popular piety, where its use was said to "repress the demons." When a Christian missionary came to a sacred spring dedicated to pagan worship, he adjured the demons by the name of Christ and made the sign of the cross; then the demons departed, and the spring was restored to its proper purpose of providing water for human use. Demons and lusts were driven away by the sign of the cross. Such works of literature as *The Dream of the Rood* were an expression in the vernacular of the cult of the cross.

In all these ways the cross and the crucifixion came to occupy a unique place in the life of Christ as the one event in which the plan of salvation achieved its fulfillment. The cross was the "tribunal" that Christ ascended on behalf of all, thus establishing "the reign of the church." Among the events in the Gospels, his passion and death clearly made the decisive difference; for before it happened, not even Abraham had been able to enter heaven, while after it happened, even the thief on the cross was able to gain entry. Not even the resurrection of Christ occupied this same place in the plan. Although the passion, the resurrection, and the ascension corresponded to faith, hope, and love, it was the cross that was the instrument of the victory of Christ over the devil. It would seem that one reason for rejecting what was taken to be Abelard's notion of the cross as primarily the decisive revelation of the love of God and the announcement, rather than the achievement, of redemption was that the resurrection of Christ performed this function of making known that the plan of salvation had been carried out in the crucifixion. Explaining why Good Friday was kept as a day of mourning, the liturgical theologian Rupert of Deutz asserted that "the joy of such a great salvation and of such a necessary redemption, of such a price by whose value the captivity of the world has been redeemed. . . . is to be deferred until the third day," namely, Easter Sunday; for by his resurrection "the Victor has announced his victory to us, has shown us in himself what we are to hope for about ourselves."

Rup.*Div.off.*6.3 (*CCCM* 7: 190)

Within the framework of this assumption about the cross even such a metaphor for the atonement as victory over the devil, in which crucifixion and resurrection were combined more successfully than in most others, could be interpreted almost exclusively on the basis of the suffering and death of Christ. The metaphor of victory had the great advantage that, by describing the "arena" into which God sent his Son to achieve the conquest of Satan, it was able to take seriously the role of the devil as the third party to the transaction that took place between God and man in the redemption of mankind. While the problem of the atonement was the reestablishment of the relation established in the creation of man and disrupted by his fall, nevertheless the devil, as the perpetrator of the disruption, must also belong in any complete account of the plan of salvation. He was the proud spirit, "always proud in relation to God and always malevolent in relation to us," who, being "more eminent" in his nature, believed that it was "better to reign in hell than serve in heaven [malles misere praeesse, quam feliciter subesse]" and who successfully tempted man into sharing his fate. Because man had "permitted himself to be so easily vanquished by him through sinning," he owed the devil something, namely, "to vanquish him in turn."

See vol.1:149–51

Hrot.*Asc.*7–10 (Homeyer 85)

Herb.Los.*Serm.*8 (Goulburn-Symonds 232–34)

Bald.*Sacr.alt.*2.3.1 (*SC* 93: 240)
Ans.L.*Sent.Ans.*2 (Bliemetzrieder 51)
Brd.Clr.*Grad.*10.36 (Leclercq-Rochais 3:44)

Ans.*Med.*3 (Schmitt 3:85–86); Ans.*Cur d.h.*2.19 (Schmitt 2: 131)

The suggestion that Christ had vanquished the devil on man's behalf by deceiving him had come down from the church fathers. On the basis of Job 41:1, the eleventh century could still see the redemption as a process by which God the Father caught the devil on a fishhook, with Christ as the bait, "in whom the passible flesh could be seen and the impassible divinity could not be seen," so that the devil was impaled on the hook. Shifting the metaphor from angling to snaring, an earlier medieval theologian could also say that "the devil was deceived by the death of the Lord, as a bird is." Vivid and homiletically useful though such analogies may have been, they could not withstand closer scrutiny. Did Christ carry out the work of redemption "so as to deceive the devil, who by deceiving man had cast him out of Paradise? But surely

See vol.1:355

Petr.Dam.*Serm.*46 (*PL* 144: 751); Rup.*Div.off.*3.19 (*CCCM* 7:91–92)

Isid.Sev.*Sent.*1.14.13 (*SPE* 2:265)

Ans.*Med*.3 (Schmitt 3:85)

the Truth does not deceive anyone." Any amount of critical reflection on the notion of salvation by deception had to lead to its rejection as unworthy of a just and holy God. In spite of the impressive array of theologians who could be cited in its support, the idea was self-contradictory and hence self-defeating; for it was not only "a fundamental principle of [Anselm's] whole argumentation," but an axiom of the church's teaching as a whole, that "where anything is proposed as unfitting to God as by faith we know Him to be, we must conclude that it is impossible."

Phelan (1960) 30–31

The strong point of the theory of deception lay in its ability to take seriously the role of the devil, but this role received what theologians found to be a more acceptable treatment in the image of Christ as victor, which had special association with the liturgical theology of the East, but which continued to enjoy wide support in the West. In this image, "the drama of Redemption has a dualistic background; God in Christ combats and prevails over the 'tyrants' which hold mankind in bondage." Thus *The Dream of the Rood* described Christ as resting in the grave, "feeble after his great strife." Christ was the great king who went forth into "the war of the passion against the devil, the prince of this world." In his true humanity he "destroyed death by dying, and he overcame the devil, who had the power of death." The work of Christ on the cross was a "battle," according to one of the sermons of Peter Damian; in a later sermon he described at some length the unique strategy of this warrior: "When our Redeemer entered the battlefield of this world to do battle," he wrote, "he equipped himself with a new kind of weapon, namely, that he brandished what was weak and concealed what was strong." Although this version of the image of Christ as victor still carried some overtones of the idea of deception, the theme of conflict between Christ and the devil predominated. Anselm himself could say that "he who was to assume humanity was to come to do battle against the devil." Yet it was, significantly, in poetry that the image found its most fitting expression. According to Odo of Cluny, "the One who died killed death and attacked hell." If he had yielded to the cries of his tormentors to come down from his cross, he would never have become "the victor, who arms" his followers against death. According to *The Dream of the Rood,* his cross

See vol.2:138–39

Aulén (1969) 55

Drm.Rd.64–65 (Swanton 93)

Rup.*Div.off*.5.1 (*CCCM* 7:146)

Heb.2:14
Petr.Dam.*Opusc*.1.3 (*PL* 145:24)

Petr.Dam.*Serm*.48 (*PL* 144:768)

Petr.Dam.*Serm*.66 (*PL* 144:884)

Ans.*Inc*.10 (Schmitt 2:26–27)

Od.Clun.*Occup*.5.64–66 (Swoboda 96)

Od.Clun.*Occup*.6.278–80 (Swoboda 127)

Drm.Rd.13 (Swanton 89)

Drm.Rd.67 (Swanton 94)

Seq.trans.7.3 (Anal.Hymn. 54:12)

Petr.Dam.Carm.B.26.2 (Lokrantz 115)
Petr.Dam.Carm.B.25.5 (Lokrantz 115)

Rath.Ep.25 (MGH BDK 1: 126)

Rath.Serm.Pasch.1.5 (CCCM 46:43)

Rath.Exh.prec. (PL 136: 450)

Bald.Sacr.alt.1.2 (SC 93:90)

Petr.Dam.Opusc.3 (PL 145: 58–59)
Petr.Dam.Serm.18 (PL 144: 607)

See vol.2:209
Rem.Aux.Gen.22.13 (PL 131: 95)

Rup.Div.off.11.18 (CCCM 7: 393)

Gen.14:18(Vulg.)

See vol.1:169

Rem.Aux.Gen.14.18 (PL 131: 85)

See pp. 188–90 below

was a "tree of victory," and even as he was being laid in the sepulcher his proper title was "the God of victory." The sequence hymn for Easter, "Lauds to the Paschal Victim," described a "wondrous duel" between life and death, after which "the leader of life who died now reigns alive."

Yet even in that hymn, as its very title indicates, the interpretation of Christ on the cross as the victor over man's enemies had to yield to the identification of Christ in his suffering and death as a sacrificial victim. Other hymns echoed the identification. The figure on the cross was "the victim who has drawn all to himself," "the victim who by his immolation purges the guilt of the world." The victim was a "paschal" victim "because he is immolated for us. Why immolated? So that he might die for us." The purpose of his immolation was "so that he himself might become our means of passing over to him, and might himself become our only joy." Because Christ, the Almighty, had become the sacrifice for the sins of all, his presence supported their own sacrifices in reparation for their sins. As sacrifice, Christ was the achievement of what had been perceived, however dimly, in the sacrifices of the Gentiles. The sacrifice of Christ was also the reason why Christians did not regard the ceremonial laws of the Old Testament as binding on them, for "whatever was carried out typologically in those sacrifices is completely fulfilled in the immolation of the Lamb that takes away the sins of the world"; Christ was "the unique sacrifice." Of such typological sacrifices in the Old Testament, the "binding of Isaac" was especially meaningful: Abraham symbolized God the Father, who sacrificed his only Son; but the death of Christ on behalf of a disobedient humanity was as though Isaac had been sacrificed to save Ishmael.

Another Old Testament "type" of the sacrifice of Christ was Melchizedek, who "offered bread and wine; he was priest of God Most High." Since early times this incident had been interpreted as a prefiguration of the Eucharist, and it continued to be seen this way. It was also a proof that "the true priesthood of Christ is older than the priesthood of the law." The sacrificial interpretation of the Eucharist, whose implication for the definition of the presence of the body and blood of Christ in the sacrament was soon to become a center of theological discussion, and the sacrificial view of the atonement, whose bearing on

Ans.*Sacr.eccl.*2 (Schmitt 2: 240)

Rup.*Job.*1.22 (*PL* 168:969)

Petr.Dam.*Serm.*72 (*PL* 144: 911)

Heb.9:24
Petr.Dam.*Lib.grat.*2 (*MGH Lib.lit.*1:20)
Hug.Bret.*Corp.* (*PL* 142: 1332); Dur.Tr.*Corp.*3.3 (*PL* 149:1381); Rath.*Serm.Cen. Dom.*5 (*CCCM* 46:102) *Thes.*Hymn.228.5 (*Anal. Hymn.*51:299)

Rom.*ord.*7.14 (Andrieu 2:300)

Gez.*Corp.*40 (*PL* 137:392)
Rem.Aux.*Matt.*8 (*PL* 131: 913)

Rem.Aux.*Cel.miss.* (*PL* 101: 1251–52)

Rup.*Div.off.*2.12 (*CCCM* 7: 46)

alternate views of redemption was now an issue, were mutually reinforcing; in the words of Anselm, "just as there is one Christ who sacrificed himself for us, so there is one offering and one sacrifice that we offer in the bread and wine." More precisely, it was Christ the Redeemer himself who "every day without interruption . . . sacrifices the burnt offering of his body and blood for us." Christ himself was the true priest, whose sacrificial ministry was carried out through "the visible priest" as his agent. All the forms of priesthood in the church were derived from his sacerdotal office, which he exercised when, as priest, he "entered into heaven itself," offering up the sacrifice of his own body and blood. In that ultimate act of sacrifice, Christ was the priest and the offering and the altar, all at the same time, as an early medieval eucharistic hymn had said.

The eucharistic prayer in a Frankish liturgy offered up the sacrifice of the Mass in continuity with the sacrifices of Abel, of Abraham, and of Melchizedek, in union with the true "immaculate sacrifice," which was Christ himself. The communicant who approached "the holy and terrible sacrifice" of the Mass without first being reconciled with his brother was to remind himself of the sacrifice of Christ on the cross, which had been intended for the reconciliation of all. Proceeding as he did from the identification of Christ as priest, the liturgical theologian saw in the mixture of wine and water in the chalice a symbol of the atoning sacrifice. The wine represented Christ, the water represented the people; "and if wine is offered without water, it seems to signify that the passion of Christ was of no benefit to the human race, while if water is offered without wine, it seems to signify that the people could have been saved without the passion of Christ." Both were needed to represent the full significance of the redemption. As the central act of Christian worship, the sacrifice of the Mass gave meaning to, and derived meaning from, the image of the suffering and death of Christ on the cross as atoning sacrifice.

If a theory of the atonement was to satisfy the demands of orthodoxy, it needed to be founded on the essential content of this image, which stood at the very center of the celebration of the Mass. According to Bernard's reply to Abelard, the answer to the question, "Where is the forgiveness of sins?" was given in the words of institution of the Eucharist: "This is the cup of the new covenant in my blood, which will be shed for you for the forgiveness of sins." This meant that the blood of Christ was indispensable to the redemption, which "we obtain through the intercession of the death of the Only-begotten, being justified freely in his blood." Although he did not understand the reason why this was so, Bernard stated, he did know as a fact that it was so: redemption and forgiveness came "through his blood." Also in a rebuttal of Abelard, William of Saint-Thierry, who stressed elsewhere that salvation had come "in the shedding of blood and the mystery of the paschal Lamb," ascribed to the blood of Christ such a value that "through his temporal death, which he did not owe, those who cling to Christ by faith will escape eternal death, which they do owe." The two steps of redemption were that Christ had taken the sins of mankind on himself and that he had made expiation for them. This expiation consisted in "the sacrifice of his flesh," whose effects were then applied to the sins of those who believed in him. Redemption, then, must involve some sort of "quid pro quo," in which, as philosophical theology had also recognized, Christ was given as "a general sacrifice for the sin of the whole world," as an offering in exchange for the salvation of mankind.

But "to whom did he make this offering? Was it perhaps to the one who had led men away captive and who held them in captivity? For to whom is a ransom for redemption usually offered except to the one who holds in captivity those who are to be redeemed?" The metaphors of redemption and ransom appeared to imply that the death of Christ was offered to the devil as the price for the release of the captives. If Christ was hanged on the cross "for the sins of mankind" and "with the ransom of his body purchased life for mankind," setting mankind free, the conclusion could easily be drawn that the ransom was paid to the devil, especially when the same source went on to say that Christ had shed his blood "so that through it you might be set free from the power of the devils." Such a conception of the exchange involved in the redemption did protect the doctrine of the immutability of God, which would be compromised if the ransoming death of Christ were thought of as changing God's mind or as appeasing his bloodthirsty demand for revenge. Abelard's confession "that the only Son of God

Brd.Clr.Ep.190.8.20 (PL 182: 1069)

Wm.S.Th.Cant.1.5.68 (SC 82: 170)

Wm.S.Th.Disp.Ab.7 (PL 180: 274)

Petr.Dam.Serm.46 (PL 144: 751)

Rich.S.Vict.Seir.14 (TPMA 15:276)

Scot.Er.Praed.9.4 (PL 122: 392)

Robt.Pull.Sent.4.14 (PL 186: 821)

Cyn.Chr.1093–99 (Cook 42)

Cyn.Chr.1449–50 (Cook 54)

became incarnate to liberate us from the servitude of sin and the yoke of the devil" gave his critics the opportunity for the unwarranted accusation that he was making "that sacred blood the price of redemption given to the devil." The notion that the death of Christ was a ransom paid to the devil was unacceptable for at least two reasons. Although the devil did exercise great de facto power over men, he had no claim de jure over them; and therefore neither God nor even man owed him anything. The idea also conflicted with the sacrificial interpretation of the cross. Offering a sacrifice to a creature rather than to the Creator would have been idolatry, and the only one to whom Christ could "offer the sacrifice of his passion was the One whom he was obeying by his suffering." The sacrifice pertained to God alone, to whom, then, the ransom was paid. Thus the definition of redemption and of ransom was determined by the image of sacrifice.

It was one of the historic achievements of Anselm's doctrine of the atonement to have translated the fundamental significance of the biblical and liturgical image of sacrifice—that the redemption of mankind by Christ was an act addressed to God, not to man or to the devil—into a form that was compatible with the immutability of God. The translation became possible by the interposition of the concept of "rightness [rectitudo]," which "lurks in the background of all Anselm's theology." In its basic religious and moral sense, "rightness of will, which makes men righteous or right in heart, that is, in will," was a quality of the creature in its relation to the Creator. The rightness of a physical creature "can be discerned by physical vision," but there was also a "rightness that is perceptible only by the mind." The biblical statement that the devil "did not abide in the truth" meant that "he forsook rightness and truth when he desired what he ought not to have desired." For this reason, "truth, rightness, and righteousness define one another." The rightness of a person or thing was synonymous with the "truth [veritas]" or reality of that person or thing. While rightness as justice was an attribute of persons as it pertained to their will, it was also an attribute that belonged to "the essence of things, because they are what they are in supreme truth." It was ultimately an aspect of reality, so that it would be possible to translate the term into English as "the moral order of the universe." And as only God could restore rightness to the disordered will, so also any restora-

Petr.Ab.*Conf.* (*PL* 178:105–6)

Wm.S.Th.*Disp.Ab.*7 (*PL* 180:274)

Ans.*Cur d.h.*2.19 (Schmitt 2:131); Ans.*Med.*3 (Schmitt 3:85–86)

Brun.S.*Inc.* (*PL* 165:1080)

Robt.Pull.*Sent.*4.14 (*PL* 186:821)

Heyer (1965) 39

Ans.*Cur d.h.*11 (Schmitt 2:68)

Ans.*Ver.*11 (Schmitt 1:191)
John 8:44

Ans.*Ver.*4 (Schmitt 1:180–81)
Ans.*Ver.*12 (Schmitt 1:192)

Ans.*Ver.*3 (Schmitt 1:180)

Ans.*Ver.*12 (Schmitt 1:194)

Ans.*Ver.*7 (Schmitt 1:186)

Ans.*Lib.arb.*10 (Schmitt 1:222)

tion of man to the rightness for which he was created had to conform to the rightness that stood at the center of the moral order itself.

The first disruption of the "rightness" of the creation had come with the fall of the devil and the other evil angels. As rational beings, they had received free will as a means for preserving their rightness. So firmly established was this rightness that while God, as the one who had created all things out of nothing, could annihilate them, he could not take away their rightness—unless they willingly surrendered it themselves. That is what happened in the disobedience of Satan. To "restore the number that had been diminished by the fall of Satan," the God of rightness and moral order created man. It was a long-established teaching, apparently based on the statement of the Septuagint (which was neither derived from the Hebrew nor carried over into the Latin) that "he fixed the bounds of the peoples according to the number of the angels of God," that "the number of the good angels, which was diminished after the fall of the evil angels, will be completed by the number of elect human beings, a number that is known only to God." Although there were some who maintained that God would have created man even if the devil and his angels had not disobeyed, it was a widespread belief among theologians that God had made the human race because the rightness of the moral order required that the number of the blessed ordained by him be completed. He "created men so that through them the empty places would be filled and the ruins of Jerusalem restored." When man, too, fell into sin, God could not simply restore him to bliss alongside the angels who had not sinned at all. Yet the angels needed the salvation of man as much as man himself did, for it was only through the salvation of the human race that the number of the angels could be brought to perfection.

Nevertheless, it would not have been fitting for any but a human being to have rendered satisfaction for what the human race had committed in the fall. Although it was customary in the language of the church to say that God "has redeemed us from sins and from His wrath and from hell and from the power of the devil," this needed to be understood in relation to the concept of "rightness." God did not require satisfaction as a means of appeasing his wrath, for he was impassible and therefore could not be

Ans.Lib.arb.3 (Schmitt 1:212)

Ans.Lib.arb.9 (Schmitt 1: 220)

Od.Clun.Occup.6.482 (Swoboda 133)

Deut.32:8(LXX)

Isid.Sent.1.10.13 (SPE 2: 250); Gr.M.Ev.34.11 (PL 76: 1252)

Ans.L.Sent.div.pag.4 (Bliemetzrieder 15)

Alex.III.Sent.Rol. (Gietl 271); Ans.Cur d.h.1.16 (Schmitt 2: 74)
Brd.Clr.Adv.1.5 (Leclercq-Rochais 4:164);
Brd.Clr.Cant.62.1.1 (Leclercq-Rochais 2:154)

Ans.Cur d.h.1.19 (Schmitt 2: 84)

Rem.Aux.Cel.miss. (PL 101: 1256)

Guib.Nog.Inc.3.3 (PL 156: 509)

Ans.Cur d.h.1.6 (Schmitt 2: 53)

Wm.S.Th.Disp.Ab.7 (PL 180: 274)

wrathful as men are. Instead of speaking of the "wrath" of God, therefore, Anselm spoke of his justice: the justice of God had been violated by the failure of man to render to God what he owed Him; the justice of God also made it impossible for God to forgive this sin by mere fiat, for this would have been a violation of the very order in the universe that God had to uphold to be consistent with himself and with his justice. Any scheme of human salvation, therefore, had to be one that would render "satisfaction" to divine justice and leave the "rightness" and moral order intact.

The choice lay between satisfaction and punishment: either man had to obey the violated honor of God by being punished eternally, or another way had to be found to vindicate divine justice. This was the fundamental dilemma to which the Anselmic doctrine of atonement by satisfaction addressed itself. For "without satisfaction, that is, without a spontaneous settlement of the debt, it is impossible for God to forgive a sin that has remained unpunished or for the sinner to attain to a beatitude such as the one he had before he sinned." If there were to be salvation, it was "necessary" that God should provide it. Yet the word "necessary" must not be taken to mean that "God had need of saving man in this fashion, but that human nature had need of rendering satisfaction to God in this fashion." God did not need to suffer on the cross, but man needed to be reconciled through such suffering. God was free of any "necessity." What the justice of God demanded, the mercy of God supplied: Because "the sinner has nothing . . . with which to make satisfaction," it was necessary that "the goodness of God come to its rescue, and the Son of God assume it into his own person" in order to provide the satisfaction that man needed to render and could not. The idea of "right order" implicit in the creation meant that it was not appropriate for God simply to replace fallen men by creating new ones, even through the miracle of virgin birth; for this would amount to writing off the creation of mankind in Adam as a total loss.

What was appropriate for God was the incarnation of the Son of God as man. It was impossible for a sinner to provide justification for another sinner. Therefore, "because no one owed satisfaction for guilt except man and because no one could render it except a merciful God,

Ans.*Med*.3 (Schmitt 3:86–87)

Rup.*Div.off*.11.18 (*CCCM* 7: 395)

Ans.*Cur d.h.*1.13 (Schmitt 2: 71)

Ans.*Cur d.h.*1.19 (Schmitt 2: 85)

Ans.*Med*.3 (Schmitt 3:86)

Rad.Ard.*Hom.ep.ev*.2.47 (*PL* 155:2108)

Ans.*Med*.3 (Schmitt 3:87)

Ans.*Concept.virg*.17 (Schmitt 2:158)

Ans.*Cur d.h.*1.23 (Schmitt 2: 91)

God became man, who, because he did not owe anything in his own name, discharged our debt by dying for us." Only man was liable for satisfaction, only God was capable of total satisfaction; therefore "it is necessary that a God-man render it." Because of the virgin birth, Jesus the man would have been sinless even without the incarnation. But if the one who offered the satisfaction had not been God but merely man, even a sinless man, he would still have had to be like the first man; and his obedience would have availed for himself alone. Yet if he had been only God and not man, he would not have been able to achieve salvation through satisfaction, since the divine nature was incapable of suffering or being humiliated, not to speak of dying. "Clearly," therefore, "the man we are looking for must be such that he dies neither of necessity (since he will be almighty) nor by obligation (since he will never have been a sinner), one who can die of his own free will because it will be necessary." The orthodox doctrine of the two natures in Christ came to the service of the doctrine of the atonement by describing one who was fully God and fully man, each of these for the sake of its contribution to salvation. Although the term "man," even after the adoptionist controversy, remained an appropriate one for the human nature of Christ, this nature was fundamentally different from that of all other men, because by his virgin birth Christ was the only one who had not been implicated in the fall of Adam. The theology of pre-existence, kenosis, and exaltation, based on Philippians 2:6–11, was taken as an assertion that the Son of God "together with the Father and the Holy Spirit determined that he would not manifest the sublimity of his omnipotence to the world in any other way than through death."

Because Christ did not have to die unless he willed to do so and because he was free of all sin, his voluntary acceptance of death and of the punishment that men had deserved was the means by which salvation was accomplished. He was capable of suffering simply because he wanted to be, not because he was under any obligation to suffer; and that made his suffering redemptive. The blood of the suffering God-man possessed infinite worth, far beyond that of any of the bloody sacrifices of the Old Testament. What gave it such worth was the utterly voluntary and spontaneous character of Christ's suffering, which was motivated not by any debt but by the honor of the

Rup.*Div.off*.6.2 (*CCCM* 7:189)

Ans.*Cur d.h*.2.6 (Schmitt 2:101)
Od.Cambr.*Pecc.orig.* (*PL* 160:1084)

Ans.*Concept.virg*.13 (Schmitt 2:155)

Ans.*Cur d.h*.1.8 (Schmitt 2:59)

Ans.*Cur d.h*.2.11 (Schmitt 2:111); Brun.S.*Gen*.22 (*PL* 164:199)

Ans.*Med*.3 (Schmitt 3:87–88)

Ans.*Cur d.h*.2.18 (Schmitt 2:127)

Ans.*Concept.virg*.23 (Schmitt 2:163)

See vol.1:256–58

Ans.*Cur d.h*.1.9 (Schmitt 2:62)

Wm.S.Th.*Disp.Ab*.7 (*PL* 180:274)

Guib.Nog.*Pign*.2.5 (*PL* 156:645)

Rich.S.Vict.*Apoc*.1.2 (*PL* 196:698)

Ans.*Med*.3 (Schmitt 3:87)

Ans.*Cur d.h*.1.8 (Schmitt 2:60)

Ans.*Cur d.h*.1.9 (Schmitt 2:62); Ans.*Med*.3 (Schmitt 3:88)

Guib.Nog.*Inc*.1.6 (*PL* 156:497)

Sacr.Gel.98.541 (Mohlberg 84)

Ans.*Cur d.h*.1.21 (Schmitt 2:89)
Ans.*Cur d.h*.2.14 (Schmitt 2:114)
Ans.*Cur d.h*.2.17 (Schmitt 2:124)

Isa.53:7(Vulg.)

Brd.Clr.*Purif.Mar*.3.2 (Leclercq-Rochais 4:343)

Hrot.*Abr*.7.12 (Homeyer 317); Isid.*Orig*.6.19.73 (*PL* 82:258); Rab.*Inst.cler*.2.30 (Knoepfler 116) Tert.*Paenit*.5.9 (*CCSL* 1:328) Brd.Clr.*Conv*.4.6 (Leclercq-Rochais 4:77); Brd.Clr.*Div*.40.4 (Leclercq-Rochais 6–I:237–38)

Ans.*Cur d.h*.1.20 (Schmitt 2:86–87)

Od.Cambr.*Jud*. (*PL* 160:1109); Rad.Ard.*Hom*.2.25 (*PL* 155:1589–90)

Rath.*Exh.prec*. (*PL* 136:450)

Petr.Dam.*Serm*.72 (*PL* 144:911)

Ans.*Med*.3 (Schmitt 3:88)

Father and the plight of mankind. The Father did not force him to undergo such suffering and death, but Christ took it upon himself. His "obedience" in doing so was addressed to the justice of God, which could not prevail without his dying, not to any necessity imposed upon him. When theologians celebrated the gift of salvation in Christ as exceeding what had been lost in the fall of Adam, this was an adaptation of the liturgical affirmation that what God had marvelously created, he had even more marvelously redeemed. But in Anselm's doctrine of the atonement this doxology became the basis for the assertion that the worth of the death of Christ far exceeded what man owed, because his "life is more deserving of love than sins are deserving of hate." As the God-man and as the one who died voluntarily, "he was offered because he himself wanted to be," which meant that "he was offered not because he needed to be or because he was subject to the edict of the law, but because he chose to be."

Although historians have looked for the origins of this idea of satisfaction in Germanic customs such as "wergild," whereby a crime against a person must be atoned for in accordance with the station of that person, or in feudal law, the most obvious and immediate source of the idea would appear to be the penitential system of the church, which was developing just at this time. The earliest of Latin theologians had already spoken of penance as a way of "making satisfaction to the Lord," and the term "satisfaction" had become standard. When Anselm came to speak of what was required as a consequence of human sin, the satisfaction offered in penance was a natural analogy, but one that was inadequate because, even in rendering such satisfaction, man was giving God only what he owed him. But the satisfaction offered by the death of Christ possessed infinite worth, and thus the redemption on the cross could be seen as the one supreme act of penitential satisfaction. "Satisfaction," then, was another term for "sacrifice," and Christ's sacrificial act of penance made even human acts of satisfaction worthy, since of themselves they were not. It also gave authority to the pronouncement of absolution by a "visible priest," for Christ as the true priest had earned such absolution for all sinners. It was fitting, then, that the act by which "our Christ has redeemed us through the cross" should be appropriated by the individual through penance.

Although it is technically accurate to say that "never once does Anselm explain Christ's death as substitutionary," the treatise *Why God Became Man* was in fact an effort "to discover the reason why Jesus' death could justly be counted by God as vicarious." It was standard practice to speak of "the vicarious suffering of the Lord." Summarizing his argument, Anselm asserted that he had shown the necessity for the completion of the heavenly city through the salvation of men and the impossibility of such salvation except through one who was both God and man; "therefore we have clearly come to Christ, whom we confess to be both God and man and to have died on our behalf." Although the style of his argument was his and his alone, its doctrinal content was shared with the tradition in which he stood. In a remarkable passage of an Easter sermon on the "judiciary game [ludus judiciarius]" that had been played on the cross, Peter Damian described the cross as the tribunal where Christ, "our Advocate," confronted the devil, who claimed possession of the human race as a consequence of sin. But Christ contested this claim on the grounds that he had created humanity and was now reclaiming his heritage. This he did in his cross and resurrection, bringing the claims of the devil to naught and restoring mankind to its place under God. Beyond his own speculative achievement, Anselm was above all giving voice to the common conviction that the cross was the redemption of mankind.

The Lord of History

The climax of "the uncompromisingly christocentric period" of reflection on the work of Christ was the celebration of "the Logos as king" in the theology of Bernard of Clairvaux, just as the climax of "the plan of salvation" itself was the reign of Christ within and beyond the ages of human history. While the title "king before all ages" could, of course, be applied also to God, "king" was usually a way of speaking about Christ. As in other places and periods, the royal office of Christ was joined to his priestly office or to his prophetic office. The name "Christ" meant "the anointed one," identifying him as the true king and priest. As king, he was descended from the royal line of David; as priest, he offered up the sacrifice of himself for mankind. The first of these offices was the theme of the

---

Margin notes:

Hopkins (1972) 211–12
Petr.Dam.*Serm*.66 (*PL* 144: 887)

Ans. *Cur d.h*.2.15 (Schmitt 2: 115–16)

Petr.Dam.*Serm*.12 (*PL* 144: 566–67)

Brd.Clr.*Cant*.85.4.10 (Leclercq-Rochais 2:314)

Brd.Clr.*Grat*.13.43 (Leclercq-Rochais 3:196)
Brd.Clr.*Cant*.42.7.10 (Leclercq-Rochais 2:39); Rup.*Div.off*.9.6 (*CCCM* 7:319)
See vol.2:293

Rem.Aux.*Cel.miss*. (*PL* 101: 1253); Herm.Mag.*Epit*.30 (*PL* 178:1744)

Petr.Dam.*Serm*.46 (*PL* 144: 755)

Petr.Dam.*Serm*.49;53 (*PL* 144: 782; 805)
Rem.Aux.*Gen*.47.22 (*PL* 131: 122); Od.Clun.*Serm*.1 (*PL* 133:711)
Rem.Aux.*Matt*.3 (*PL* 131: 883)
Petr.Dam.*Serm*.46 (*PL* 144: 755)

Od.Clun.*V.Ger*.3.12 (*PL* 133: 698)

Bald.*Sacr.alt*.2.1.2 (*SC* 93: 180)
Rem.Aux.*Matt*.7 (*PL* 131:902)
Od.Clun.*Occup*.5.425 (Swoboda 106)
Od.Clun.*Occup*.6.1 (Swoboda 119)
Brd.Clr.*Cant*.83.1.1 (Leclercq-Rochais 2:298)
Rup.*Div.off*.12.22 (*CCCM* 7: 415)
Wm.S.Th.*Cant*.2.pr.146 (*SC* 82:308)

Brd.Clr.*Cant*.23.2.4 (Leclercq-Rochais 1:141)

Brd.Clr.*Cant*.62 (Leclercq-Rochais 2:154)

Brd.Clr.*Dil*.3.10 (Leclercq-Rochais 3.127)

Brd.Clr.*Cant*.68.2.4 (Leclercq-Rochais 2:199)

Heb.11:40

Brd.Clr.*Cons*.5.7.16 (Leclercq-Rochais 3:480)

Brd.Clr.*Grad*.7.20 (Leclercq-Rochais 3:131)

Gospel of Matthew, the second was that of the Gospel of Luke. But it was as king that Christ exercised his rule also over the priests of the church. It was likewise Christ the king who exercised the prophetic office.

Although Christ, too, was "king before all ages," the historical character of his incarnation meant that the primary locus of his reign was human history. He was "Christ, the Lord of history [dispositor saeculorum]." By his guidance the entire arrangement of events and times in human history had been directed to the one end of the salvation of mankind. The kings of the earth were subject to his sovereignty, as the Magi acknowledged and as Herod should have acknowledged. He was "King Jesus," the king of the angels, "Christ the evangelical king," and "the king of eternal peace." The ages of history over which Christ was sovereign were, for Bernard, three: creation, reconciliation, and "the reparation of heaven and earth." During the present age of history, a time of pilgrimage, the church "looks to the past and to the future," to the consummation and beatitude of heaven in the future and to "the memory of the passion of Christ" in the past. That memory was the source of consolation from generation to generation, for it sustained the elect in their hope of the glory to come and provided a key to the understanding of the history through which they were passing. On the other hand, "the end of all things depends on the state and consummation of the church," and therefore the patriarchs and prophets and even the angels and the saints could not attain their perfection until the final age of human history, since "apart from us they should not be made perfect." In this way the memory of Christ as the Lord of history also helped to make sense of the Christian hope, and the meaning of history depended on the mystery of the incarnation.

The content of the mystery was defined for Bernard by the orthodox dogmas of the Trinity and the person of Christ. These dogmas were the unquestioned—and unquestionable—premise for everything said about Christ and about salvation. "My God," he said, "is what the catholic faith confesses him to be." The trinitarian confession was fundamental not only to Christian faith, but also to Christian life, for each person of the Trinity bore a special relation to the disciple of Christ. With apologies

Brd.Clr.*Dil*.4.13 (Leclercq-
Rochais 3:130)

for the inadequacy of any such language, Bernard could
say that "the entire Trinity loves" the child of God. The
necessary condition for genuine Christian love was a refusal to allow any deviation, whether by heretics or by

Brd.Clr.*Cant*.20.5.9 (Leclercq-
Rochais 1:120)

demons, "from the purity of what the church believes."
When some of his contemporaries were raising dialectical
questions in relation to the dogma of the Trinity that

See pp. 263–67 below
Brd.Clr.*Cons*.5.7.15 (Leclercq-
Rochais 3:479)

appeared to cast doubt on the orthodox faith, Bernard
vigorously reaffirmed the teachings of the Nicene Creed,
including the Western elaboration of those teachings, the
idea that the Holy Spirit "is the strong bond, the indivisi-

Brd.Clr.*Cant*.8.1.2 (Leclercq-
Rochais 1:37); Brd.Clr.*Dil*.12.
35 (Leclercq-Rochais 3:149)

ble love, and the indissoluble unity between the Father and
the Son." Not only the creeds and confessions of the

Brd.Clr.*Cant*.71.3.7 (Leclercq-
Rochais 2:219)

church, but also its liturgies and hymns served as an expression of this orthodox and catholic faith.

Only an impeccably orthodox doctrine of the Trinity
could guarantee that the Savior was God in a complete

Brd.Clr.*Cant*.76.2.5 (Leclercq-
Rochais 2:257)

and unequivocal way. Conversely, it was only through the
Savior that one had the right to speak of God; "as a man, I

Brd.Clr.*Cant*.22.1.3 (Leclercq-
Rochais 1:131)
Brd.Clr.*Cant*.31.1.1 (Leclercq-
Rochais 1:219–20)

speak of him as a Man to men." In his essence God was
immutable and absolute, beyond time and suffering; because of the incarnation it was possible to know that "al-

Brd.Clr.*Cant*.26.3.5 (Leclercq-
Rochais 1:173)
Ex.3:14
Brd.Clr.*Cons*.5.6.13 (Leclercq-
Rochais 3:477)

though God is not capable of passion, he is capable of
compassion." The word to Moses, "I am who I am," proved
that God was "the first principle" of all creatures; the
same passage provided support for the complete equality

Brd.Clr.*Cant*.51.3.7 (Leclercq-
Rochais 2:87)

of Christ, as Son of God and Logos, with the Father.
Christ was the image of God by his essence, while men

Brd.Clr.*Cant*.80.2.3 (Leclercq-
Rochais 2:278–79)

were the image of God by their creation. By becoming the
Son of man as well as the Son of God, he was able to serve

Brd.Clr.*Cant*.2.3.6 (Leclercq-
Rochais 1:11)

as the Mediator between God and man. This did not
imply that the being of God had been changed through
the incarnation; that would be unthinkable. Rather, it
was through Christ that God had shown himself to be
present and participating in his creatures in such a way
that "one need not fear to say that he is one with our spirit,
although he is not one with our person, nor one with our

Brd.Clr.*Cons*.5.5.12 (Leclercq-
Rochais 3:476)

substance." The doctrine of the Trinity was not a speculative construct, or an exercise in dialectical subtlety, but a
soteriological necessity.

This applied particularly to the doctrine of the two
natures in Christ. Although "the entire Trinity loves"
and the Holy Spirit could be identified as "the indivisible

Brd.Clr.*Dil.*11.33 (Leclercq-Rochais 3:147)

Brd.Clr.*Cant.*2.2.3 (Leclercq-Rochais 1:9–10)

Brd.Clr.*Grad.*3.12 (Leclercq-Rochais 3:25)

Heb.2:9

Brd.Clr.*Cant.*48.2.4 (Leclercq-Rochais 2:69)

Brd.Clr.*Cant.*45.6.9 (Leclercq-Rochais 2:55)

Brd.Clr.*Cons.*5.9.21 (Leclercq-Rochais 3:484)

See vol.2:83–84

I John 1:7

Brd.Clr.*Cant.*16.2.2 (Leclercq-Rochais 1:90)

Brd.Clr.*Adv.*1.8 (Leclercq-Rochais 4:167)

See pp. 128–29 above

Brd.Clr.*Div.*60.1 (Leclercq-Rochais 6–I:290–91)

love between the Father and the Son," it was nevertheless in the Son of God, incarnate as a man, that saving love had come. He was the source of love for the believing soul. As the Logos assuming humanity, he bestowed divine love on behalf of God; as humanity being assumed by the Logos, he accepted it on behalf of man. In the unity of his person he "has two natures, one by which he has always existed and the other by which he begins to exist." As a consequence, he could be "lower than the angels" according to his human nature, while at the same time, according to his divine nature, he remained sovereign over the angels. Such a distinction between the two natures must not be permitted to jeopardize the union of the natures in the single person of the God-man, a union so intimate and indissoluble that one could and should, "in a true and catholic sense," predicate of his one person the properties belonging to each nature and "call God man and call man God." Although it had been worked out in greater detail by Eastern than by Western theologians, the idea of "the communication of properties," according to which each nature imparted its own characteristic properties to the person of the incarnate Logos, so that the New Testament could properly speak of the blood of the Son of God, was here put into the service of the Western effort to understand the plan of salvation.

The status accorded to the humanity of Christ through the incarnation imparted a unique force not only to his life and work, but also to his teachings. He was "this great prophet, mighty in deed and in word," but he was different from all the other prophets because he alone had "descended from heaven." For all of his insistence, in his polemics against Abelard, that it was heretical to reduce the work of Christ to that of a teacher and example, Bernard was able to say that "our Lord and Savior Jesus Christ, wanting to teach us how to ascend into heaven, himself became what he taught, that is, he ascended into heaven." He had, moreover, assumed human nature in order to be able to teach this lesson and to "show us the way by which we, too, may ascend." As the teacher who had come from heaven and who showed the way to heaven, Christ spoke words that were "living and powerful" and that imparted "the revelation of secrets," far

Brd.Clr.*Cant*.2.1.2 (Leclercq-
Rochais 1:9)

John 6:63
John 6:60
Brd.Clr.*Div*.5.1 (Leclercq-
Rochais 6–I:98–99)

Brd.Clr.*Cant*.30.5.11 (Leclercq-
Rochais 1:217)

Brd.Clr.*Div*.121 (Leclercq-
Rochais 6–I:398); Rad.Ard.
Hom.2.20 (*PL* 155:1564)

Brd.Clr.*Div*.40.1 (Leclercq-
Rochais 6–I:234–35)

Brd.Clr.*Cant*.6.1.4 (Leclercq-
Rochais 1:27)

Brd.Clr.*Sanct*.1.6 (Leclercq-
Rochais 5:331)

Brd.Clr.*Grad*.1.2 (Leclercq-
Rochais 3:18)

Brd.Clr.*Cant*.30.5.10 (Leclercq-
Rochais 1:217)

Brd.Clr.*Apol*.3.5; 6.12
(Leclercq-Rochais 3:85; 92)
Brd.Clr.*Cant*.51.1.2 (Leclercq-
Rochais 2:85)

Heb.5:8

Brd.Clr.*Grad*.3.6 (Leclercq-
Rochais 3:21)

Isa.53:3(Vulg.)

surpassing in their power any vision or dream. The words of Christ were "spirit and life" to those who were his true followers, while to others they seemed to be "a hard saying" from which they could not derive any consolation. True believers were those who clung to the teachings of Christ and accepted his word as the guide and norm of their lives. They learned their lessons in "the lecture hall of Christ."

"We are in the school of Christ," Bernard would say. The school of Christ was on earth, and his lecture platform was in heaven; his disciples came to him as to their teacher, and those who were ill came to him as to their physician, but he was the physician who healed "by the word alone." Even as physician, then, he was the teacher. As the one who from eternity had been the teacher of the angels "in silence," he had through his incarnation become the teacher of his disciples when "he opened his mouth on the mountain" and taught them in the Sermon on the Mount. In the Old Testament the revelation of the will of God had come through Moses on Mount Sinai; so likewise in the New Testament it was on a mountain that the new and complete revelation had been given. Therefore Christ the teacher, like Moses the teacher, could be called "the lawgiver." Yet he stood apart from all the lawgivers and teachers of history; for while they taught their followers how to live and how "to preserve the life of the soul in the body," he taught his disciples how "to lose this life," as he himself would lay down his life for them as not only their teacher but their "Savior." The disciples of Christ were those who heard his teachings in contemplation and heeded them in action; thus both Mary and Martha were examples for the disciple to imitate, belonging together in the full life of devotion to Christ the teacher.

Christ the teacher had, however, himself been a pupil first. The paradox of the incarnation meant that the events of the human life of Christ became a source of knowledge for him. For not only did he "learn obedience"; he also "learned mercy. Not that he did not know how to be merciful already, he whose mercy is from everlasting to everlasting, but what he had known by nature from eternity, he learned through temporal experience." Since he was, according to the prophet, "one who knows infirmity," he must have used his human feelings and sense experiences as a means of access to the human condition, becoming compassionate through personal acquaintance with the misery and weakness of man; and so, as man, "he learned that which he already knew," as God. It was as God that he was able to cure human infirmities, but it was as man that he had experienced them himself; "I would not say that he has been made wiser through this experience, but he does seem to be nearer" to the children of Adam. He only "seemed" to be nearer because, as God, he was omnipresent in his holiness and in his compassion and thus could not come any nearer. Similarly, while the holiness of Christ was "spread abroad by thy conception as well as by thy life," this, too, was only in the eye of the beholder. For the persistent crux of interpretation in orthodox christology, the statement of the Gospel that "Jesus increased" in wisdom and in grace, must be understood to refer "not to what he was, but to what he seemed to be," since he was, as the Son of God, already perfect in wisdom and in grace.

Although such "increasing" was in this sense an illusion rather than a reality, that did not in any way make the human life of Christ an illusion, as it had been in ancient heresy. A "principal cause" of the incarnation was the need of man to have, in concrete historical form, the embodiment of the invisible God in the real events of a human life, "either in his birth or in his infancy, either in his teaching or in his death, either in his resurrection or in his ascension." These events, "collected from all the anxieties and bitter experiences" of the life of Christ, were a source of instruction and of consolation to the believer, who was sustained by "the example of our Savior" in his sufferings and in his life. Each event had a special message: his virgin birth was a disclosure of purity, his life revealed "the sinlessness of his character," his teaching conveyed "unalloyed truth," his miracles taught purity, his sacraments manifested "the hidden power of his faithfulness," his suffering proved his willingness to undergo the cross, his death made it clear that he suffered voluntarily, his resurrection inspired the martyrs with fortitude, and his ascension vindicated his promises. The chronological sequence of events in his life also served the purpose of his "passing through every stage" of human life, so that every age from infancy to maturity might have access to him.

Marginal references (left column):

Brd.Clr.*Cant*.56.1.1 (Leclercq-Rochais 2:115)

Brd.Clr.*Grad*.3.9 (Leclercq-Rochais 3:23)

Brd.Clr.*Cant*.22.3.8 (Leclercq-Rochais 1:134)

See vol.1:251

Luke 2:52(Vulg.)

Brd.Clr.*Laud.Virg*.2.10 (Leclercq-Rochais 4:28); Ans.L.*Sent.div.pag*.6 (Bliemetzrieder 40)

See vol.1:89–90

Brd.Clr.*Cant*.20.5.6 (Leclercq-Rochais 1:118)

Brd.Clr.*Cant*.43.2.3 (Leclercq-Rochais 2:42) Brd.Clr.*Grad*.3.6 (Leclercq-Rochais 3:21)

Brd.Clr.*Cant*.70.4.7 (Leclercq-Rochais 2:212)

See vol.1:144–45 Brd.Clr.*Cant*.66.4.10 (Leclercq-Rochais 2:185)

Brd.Clr.*Cant*.23.3.6 (Leclercq-Rochais 1:142)

It was through such a "discipline" of Christ that one learned to be a "disciple" of Christ. To reveal "the law of life and of discipline," God had sent Christ as "the leader and guide" who would train others as he had trained him-

Brd.Clr.*Cant*.21.2.3 (Leclercq-Rochais 1:124)

self in "the way of wisdom." Christ set himself forth to others as the example of humility and as the model of gentleness, so that by following him they might find

Brd.Clr.*Grad*.1.1 (Leclercq-Rochais 3:16–17)

"the way that leads to truth." The discipline of following Christ consisted in taking one's cross. Those who "took the cross," for example, by entering the religious life, but failed to follow the humility of Christ were betraying the

Brd.Clr.*Apol*.1.2 (Leclercq-Rochais 3:82)

very ideal to which they had committed themselves; the same would also be true of those who "took the cross" in the sense of embarking on a crusade, but who did not imitate the example of Christ. For "this can serve as a definition of humility: Humility is that virtue by which, through a knowledge of himself, a person becomes worth-

Brd.Clr.*Grad*.1.2 (Leclercq-Rochais 3:17)

less in his own estimation." The doctrine of the two natures in the God-man lent a special poignancy to the imitation of Christ. Not only did "Jesus, as a boy, set forth to saintly boys a pattern of how to obey," but he did so as the incarnate Son of God, which meant that he who was the Logos and wisdom of God followed a carpenter and his wife and that he who was the Master obeyed

Brd.Clr.*Cant*.19.3.7 (Leclercq-Rochais 1:113)

those who were in fact his disciples. His unique standing gave a divine authority to the example he set forth, but it also endowed it with this paradoxical character.

Example though he was, also and especially in his suffering, Christ was always more than an example—especially in his suffering. Christ had come "not only to us [ad nos], but for our sakes [propter nos]." In doing so,

Brd.Clr.*Adv*.7.1 (Leclercq-Rochais 4:195)
Brd.Clr.*Cant*.22.3.8 (Leclercq-Rochais 1:133)

"what is there that he should have done that he has not done?" Without separating any of these from the others,

Brd.Clr.*Div*.119 (Leclercq-Rochais 6–I:397); Brd.Clr.*Ep*.190.9.25 (*PL* 182:1072)

it was possible to distinguish three basic purposes of the incarnation: "the pattern of humility, the proof of [divine] love, and the mystery of redemption." The pattern of humility, since it was provided by "the Media-

1 Tim.2:5

tor between God and men," was not like the humility of an ordinary man, who became worthless in his own estimation because that was his true condition. The humility of Christ came about through "the condescension of God to men, proceeding completely from the fountain of divine goodness," so that it was more appropriately called

Wm.S.Th.*Cant*.1.9.108 (*SC* 82:242)

"humiliation" than merely "humility." Those who imi-

Isa.53:3; Matt.11:29
Wm.S.Th.*Am*.11.34 (*PL* 184: 401); Alex.III.*Sent.Rol.* (Gietl 158–59)

Brd.Clr.*Dil*.4.11 (Leclercq-Rochais 3:128)

Bald.*Tract*.1 (*PL* 204:412)

Bald.*Tract*.11 (*PL* 204:517)

Brd.Clr.*Cant*.15.4.6 (Leclercq-Rochais 1:87)

Brd.Clr.*Laud.Virg*.3.14 (Leclercq-Rochais 4:45–46)

Brd.Clr.*Cant*.22.3.7 (Leclercq-Rochais 1:133)

Ps.24:10(Vulg.)
Brd.Clr.*Cant*.13.1.1 (Leclercq-Rochais 1:68)

1 Cor.1:24
Brd.Clr.*Grat*.8.26 (Leclercq-Rochais 3:184)

Brd.Clr.*Cant*.61.2.4 (Leclercq-Rochais 2:151)

Brd.Clr.*Dil*.3.7 (Leclercq-Rochais 3:124)

John 13:1
Wm.S.Th.*Med*.10 (*PL* 180: 236)

1 Cor.1:30
Brd.Clr.*Cant*.22.4–5 (Leclercq-Rochais 1:135–36)

Brd.Clr.*Cant*.62.4.6 (Leclercq-Rochais 2:159)

tated his humility as "a man of sorrows" and who took his yoke upon them and learned from him would thereby follow him through humiliation to glory. They followed the example of his death on earth and would hereafter reign with him in eternal life. It would be "ridiculous" if, while the Lord was suffering for the servant, the servant would surrender himself to the pleasures of the flesh; for the Lord had "suffered on the cross so that through the mystery of the cross the virtue of patience might be confirmed in us." As man and God in one person, he was an example according to his humanity and a source of assistance according to his divinity, to be imitated in his gentleness and depended upon in his power. The admonition was therefore to "learn his humility, imitate his gentleness, embrace his love, have communion with his sufferings, be washed in his blood, and offer him up as the propitiation for our sins." "The pattern of a holy life" was inseparable from "the price of satisfaction"; both were the gift of the cross of Christ.

At the same time Christ was the proof of divine love. Being himself "the Lord of virtues," he was the one who imparted every virtue and every kind of knowledge; being himself the wisdom of God, he was the one through whom true wisdom about God and man came to men. Above all this was the wisdom about the love of God for mankind, which showed that "there is no greater compassion than this, that one should lay down his life for those who had been sentenced and condemned." True believers knew how much they needed the cross of Christ when they "admired and embraced transcendent love in him." This was the effect of the redemption, that men had learned to love. But because they were sluggish in their love, it was necessary to set forth to them the picture of Christ the crucified, who seemed to be saying from the cross: "When I loved you, I loved you to the end." Some were drawn by their desire for wisdom, some by their need for forgiveness, some by the example of his life, and some by the remembrance of his passion; so it was that Christ was made "for us wisdom, righteousness, sanctification, and redemption." But for each of these groups and for all levels of men, it was the crucifixion that served as the revelation of the way and will of God, even for those who were not able to penetrate the mysteries of that will. Anyone who reviewed the events of the passion story one by one and

Brd.Clr.*Dil.*3.7 (Leclercq-
Rochais 3:124)

Ael.*Spec.car.*3.5.14 (*CCCM*
1:112)

Brd.Clr.*Cant.*70.1.2 (Leclercq-
Rochais 2:208)

Brd.Clr.*Cant.*20.1.2 (Leclercq-
Rochais 1:115)

Brd.Clr.*Cant.*11.2.3 (Leclercq-
Rochais 1:56)

Brd.Clr.*Dil.*5.14 (Leclercq-
Rochais 3:130)

Brd.Clr.*Cant.*66.4.9 (Leclercq-
Rochais 2:184)
Brd.Clr.*Dil.*7.22 (Leclercq-
Rochais 3:137)

Brd.Clr.*Ep.*190.5.14 (*PL* 182:
1065)

Brd.Clr.*Cant.*20.2.3 (Leclercq-
Rochais 1:115–16)

Ael.*Spec.car.*1.5.14 (*CCCM*
1:18)

Phil.2:7
Brd.Clr.*Cant.*11.2.3 (Leclercq-
Rochais 1:56)
Brd.Clr.*Dil.*10.28 (Leclercq-
Rochais 3:143)

See vol.2:10–12

Rup.*Div.off.*9.6 (*CCCM* 7:
317); Alg.*Sacr.*1.2 (*PL* 180:
745)

Petr.Dam.*Serm.*46 (*PL* 144:
749)

Od.Clun.*Occup.*6.344
(Swoboda 129)
Herb.Los.*Serm.*7 (Goulburn-
Symonds 152)
Rup.*Div.off.*3.13 (*CCCM* 7:
79)

considered "what he underwent, who it was that underwent it, and how," would be filled with love, even toward his enemies. Christ, who had been "love itself" from eternity, would always be the subject of love, but through his incarnation and crucifixion he became the object of love.

Yet what "makes thee, O good Jesus, lovable to me" both as an example of humility and as proof of divine love was "the work of our redemption. . . . It is this that charmingly attracts and rightly demands our devotion." This work of redemption was "the chief and the greatest of his benefits." Through it God showed himself to be not only the generous benefactor, faithful comforter, and loving ruler of all, but above all the Redeemer and Savior. His redeeming work was "abounding," universal in its saving will and comprehensive in its results. Christ gave himself to provide merit for those who had been captives. Their captivity to the devil was, according to Bernard, a just one, and the power of the devil had a valid claim, "not one that had been legitimately acquired, but one that had been wickedly usurped, nevertheless one that had been justly permitted" by God; therefore when Christ came "to set men free," he freed them from a genuine captivity. His death was the means of "rendering satisfaction to the Father," it was "the price of our redemption," and it was the device "by which he deceived the tyrant." All these various metaphors for redemption could be used together to describe the mystery of salvation through the cross. What made it possible was "the self-emptying of God"; what it made possible was "the opportunity to fill ourselves with him." To be filled with God through redemption was "to be deified." The definition of salvation as deification, although more familiar in Eastern than in Western thought, did appear in Latin theology also, as did the term "deified man" for the humanity of Christ, so that, quoting 2 Peter 1:4, one could say that Christ "ascended in order to make us participants in his divinity."

The resurrection and the ascension of Christ had an essential part in the plan of salvation. In fact, Easter could be called "that happy day on which [Christ] redeemed all the ages," a festival with a special "prerogative," and it could even be said that "the victory of Christ was achieved in the resurrection." What Christ as the Re-

Petr.Dam.*Serm*.20 (*PL* 144: 616)

Brd.Clr.*Cant*.33.3.6 (Leclercq-Rochais 1:237)

Drm.*Rd*.101–2 (Swanton 95)

Brd.Clr.*Div*.57.2 (Leclercq-Rochais 6–I:287)

Ps.62:11–12

Rom.4:25
Brd.Clr.*Dil*.3.9 (Leclercq-Rochais 3:126)

Od.Clun.*Occup*.6.355–56 (Swoboda 129)

Brd.Clr.*Dil*.3.8 (Leclercq-Rochais 3:125–26)

Heb.4:14
Brd.Clr.*Cant*.79.1.3 (Leclercq-Rochais 2:273)

Cyn.*Chr*.613–18 (Cook 24)

Rath.*Serm.Asc*.1.5 (*CCCM* 46:53)

See pp. 134–36 above

Hrot.*Asc*.1–22 (Homeyer 85)

deemer had signaled during the period of the Old Testament and had accomplished in his cross and passion, "he suddenly made known only in the glory of his resurrection and ascension." The whole life of Christ had been "an aurora, and even that somewhat indistinct," until the full light dawned in his resurrection. "After drinking the cup of death, the Lord arose in his mighty power, a succor to mankind." The paradox of Good Friday—that the impassible God suffered on the cross and that the immortal Son of God died and was buried—was resolved on Easter Day, when "he who had been a lamb in his passion became a lion in his resurrection." Because both "power" and "mercy" were said to belong to God, the death of Christ and his resurrection were proof of these two divine attributes, of mercy in his "dying for our sins" and of power in his "being raised for our justification," but of both in the life of believers and of the church. The gift and power of the resurrection of Christ could be seen in the joyful renewal not only of human nature, but of all nature— flowers, birds, and all creatures—in the new life conferred by his conquest of death. In similar fashion, the flowers and fruits of the new life of believers were the consequence of "the glory of his resurrection."

As the enumeration of the "leaps" in the life of Christ suggested, it was characteristic of the piety and theology of this period that the resurrection of Christ was inseparable from his ascension into heaven. For "if my Lord Jesus had indeed risen from the dead, but had not ascended into heaven, it could not be said of him that he had 'passed through,' but only that he had passed away." Even the passion of Christ and even his resurrection could be subordinated to his ascension, and it could be said that "he has granted salvation to us at his ascension to be our hope, when he dispelled that woe which we had endured before and when the only-begotten King appeased, on behalf of mankind, that great feud with his dear Father" —all this through the ascension. It was such a feast of celebration because "today our flesh has ascended into heaven together with Christ," so that "our soul can follow it with its desire." Although the crucifixion was sometimes viewed as the victory of Christ over the devil and other enemies—and the descent into hell and the resurrection even more—the ascension was especially suited to this theme. Having carried out his mission on earth, Christ

Att.Verc.*Serm*.10 (*PL* 134: 845–46)

Od.Clun.*Hymn*.4.2 (*Anal. Hymn*.50:268)

See vol.1:150–51

Ildef.*Cog.bapt*.49 (*SPE* 1: 287–88)

Isid.Sev.*Sent*.1.14.15 (*SPE* 2: 266)

Herb.Los.*Serm*.8 (Goulburn-Symonds 236–46)

Cyn.*Chr*.558–60 (Cook 22)

Cyn.*Chr*.1059–61 (Cook 44)

Od.Clun.*Occup*.6.298–300 (Swoboda 127–28)
Od.Clun.*Hymn*.2.21–22 (*PL* 133:515)

Cyn.*Chr*.20 (Cook 2)
1 Cor.16:22
Cyn.*Chr*.243–44 (Cook 10)

Drm.*Rd*.150–56 (Swanton 96–97)

Eph.4:8
Brd.Clr.*Dil*.3.7 (Leclercq-Rochais 3:125)

Brd.Clr.*Div*.11.3 (Leclercq-Rochais 6–I:126)

now ascended triumphantly into heaven, and he took with him the spoils of his conflict with hell and death. As he had made the earth bright by his incarnation and birth, so now he also "adorns the heavens" by his ascension.

Standing in close relation to the resurrection and the ascension was the descent into hell, which was part of the text of the Apostles' Creed and therefore had to be dealt with by Western theologians as a part of the plan of salvation. Because it stood in the creed between the burial of Christ and the resurrection, they ascribed it to the soul of Christ, since his body was in the grave and his deity was in heaven. Its purpose was "to open a way of return to heaven for those who were being detained [in hell] for other reasons than punishment," that is, for the patriarchs of the Old Testament who had been awaiting the coming of Christ to be set free. From this body of Western teaching about the descent into hell came the theme of "the harrowing of hell," which, long before the late medieval dramatic poem of that title, caught the imagination of poets and artists. Christ, "the holy one, has now harrowed hell of its tribute, of all that it had of old swallowed up unjustly into that house of torment." In response to his invasion, "hell, the avenger of sin, perceived that the Creator, the all-wielding God had come." While his suffering was "for the sake of our salvation," the descent into hell burst "the infernal chains" and set the captives at liberty. Then he rose "with victory from hell." The *Christ* of the Anglo-Saxon poet Cynewulf was a celebration of that victory, opening with the prayer, "Vouchsafe victory to us," and paraphrasing the ancient prayer, "Our Lord, come," to read: "Come, thou Victor-Lord, shaper of man." *The Dream of the Rood* described the heavenward journey of the "triumphant" Son of God, accompanied by the angels and liberated saints. Bernard described how the church "sees death dead and the author of death defeated. It sees captivity led captive from hell to earth and from earth to heaven," and he prayed that the triumph of Christ over hell and death would set men free from sin and damnation and grant them liberty and salvation.

The intense subjectivity of these poems and prayers, in which Bernard shared, would seem to suggest that, despite his attack on Abelard's teaching about redemption for its neglect of the objective element, Bernard's own

Brd.Clr.*Cant*.62.4.7 (Leclercq-Rochais 2:159)
Brd.Clr.*Cant*.61.2.3 (Leclercq-Rochais 2:150)
Brd.Clr.*Cant*.22.3.8 (Leclercq-Rochais 1:134)

Brd.Clr.*Dil*.4.12 (Leclercq-Rochais 3:129)

Cyn.*Chr*.1428-32 (Cook 53)

Brd.Clr.*Div*.96.1 (Leclercq-Rochais 6-I:355)

Brd.Clr.*Cant*.15 (Leclercq-Rochais 1:82-88)

Isa.7:14; Matt.2:23

Seeberg (1953) 133

Brd.Clr.*Cant*.32.3.7 (Leclercq-Rochais 1:230)

Brd.Clr.*Laud.Virg*.4.11 (Leclercq-Rochais 4:57)

Brd.Clr.*Cant*.84.1.3 (Leclercq-Rochais 2:304)

Brd.Clr.*Grat*.14.51 (Leclercq-Rochais 3:203)

Brd.Clr.*Cant*.61.2.5 (Leclercq-Rochais 2:151); Bald.*Comm. fid*. (PL 204:587)

view of the work of Christ expressed itself in a piety that had a thoroughly personal and profoundly mystical cast. "What," he could ask, "is so effective for the healing of the wounds of conscience and for the purification of the intention of the soul as constant meditation on the wounds of Christ?" The "wounds of the Savior" were the only refuge of the weak and weary, his passion "the last refuge and the only remedy." The faithful soul could enjoy the presence of Christ and could look forward in hope to the vision of the glory of God by glorying in the ignominy of the cross. Of this exchange of glory for ignominy, the crucified and risen Christ said to the sinner: "I suffered ... so that you might acquire a winsome beauty like mine." "And so instead of the Paradise that we had lost, Christ the Savior has been regained." Together with the cross, it was the name "Jesus" that became the object of mystical contemplation. God himself had changed his name from one that connoted his "majesty and power" to one that represented his "kindness and grace," that is, the name "Immanuel." From such language as this it has been concluded that "Bernard and Abelard, in their doctrine of reconciliation, ultimately came to very similar forms of subjectivism."

Such a conclusion, however, fails to do justice to the relation between objective and subjective factors in the ecclesiastical doctrine of reconciliation, including Bernard's version of that doctrine. Even when he spoke of the experience of the heart, he emphasized the necessity of "a proper distinction between what comes from God and what comes from ourselves"; this he did in opposition to those whom he called "the enemies of grace," who overlooked the objectivity of divine action and spoke only of the subjectivity of human action. The merits that God required of men were those that he, by his prevenient grace, had already given to them. "The soul," said Bernard, "seeks the Logos, but it had previously been sought by the Logos." What seemed to be "our merits" were in fact "nurseries of hope, incentives for love, signs of a hidden predestination, and foretokens of future bliss," but not a ground for the divine act of justification, whose basis lay in God, not in man. Therefore "my merit consists in the mercy of the Lord." Justification meant that "thou art not only righteous, but art called 'righteousness,' a

Brd.Clr.*Cant*.22.3.8 (Leclercq-
Rochais 1:134)

righteousness that justifies." The relation between the
righteousness (or justice) that was an attribute of God
and the act of justification which conferred righteousness
could be summarized in the axiom: "The righteousness of
God consists in his not sinning, but the righteousness of

Brd.Clr.*Cant*.23.6.15 (Leclercq-
Rochais 1:149)

man consists in his being forgiven by God." A baptized
infant already possessed merits, but they were the merits

Brd.Clr.*Cant*.68.3.6 (Leclercq-
Rochais 2:200)

of Christ. And so if one asked what free will contributed
to salvation, the answer was: "It is saved. Take away free
will, and there is nothing that needs to be saved; take away

Brd.Clr.*Grat*.1.2 (Leclercq-
Rochais 3:166)

grace, and there is no way to save it."

A further guarantee of the objectivity of salvation was
the reality of the Last Judgment. At his return to judg-

Brd.Clr.*Cant*.73.2.4 (Leclercq-
Rochais 2:235); Rup.*Div.off.*
7.16 (*CCCM* 7:243)

ment, Christ would "appear in that form in which he was
born," but by his return to judgment he would transform
the very basis of knowledge and experience that had prevailed before. Even the souls of the blessed departed,
wrapped in the light of eternity, could not attain the
perfection for which they were intended until death was

1 Cor.15:54
Brd.Clr.*Dil*.11.30 (Leclercq-
Rochais 3:144–45)

swallowed up in victory and history had passed over into
the kingdom of God. As for the godless, they were giving
themselves over to "consumption" and enjoyment, when

Brd.Clr.*Dil*.7.19 (Leclercq-
Rochais 3:135)

what was awaiting them was "consummation" and judgment. For both the blessed and the wicked, then, subjective
experience must be corrected by the eschatological objectivity of the final and eternal order. This was true even
of one's experience of oneself; for what the apostle said
about the believer's knowledge of Christ, that "though
we have known Christ after the flesh, we know him so no

2 Cor.5:16

longer," applied to self-knowledge as well: a knowledge
based on the flesh and its necessities had to yield to the
true knowledge of the spirit, when "the love of the flesh

Brd.Clr.*Dil*.15.40 (Leclercq-
Rochais 3:153)

is absorbed by the love of the spirit." Such a way of
contrasting history and eschatology was consistent with
widespread usage. After the Last Judgment the "form of

Phil.2:7
Guib.Nog.*Pign*.3.2.5 (*PL* 156:
657)

the servant" in which Christ would appear would be
"totally transformed into a divine form." The knowledge
of God vouchsafed to believers would likewise be trans-

Petr.Dam.*Omnip*.3 (*SC* 191:
394)

formed from the mediated knowledge granted to them
now "to the contemplation of the Divinity" itself. Christ
would be seen as "the Victor-Judge," as "the King of

Cyn.*Chr*.1060; 1228; 1516
(Cook 40; 46; 56)

Victory," as "the warden of victory." The "mass" of those
who had refused to acknowledge him on earth would

Od.Clun.*Occup*.6.328
(Swoboda 128)

have to suffer "an endless hell," and they would not be

Cyn.*Chr*.1571–72 (Cook 58)
Od.Clun.*Coll*.3.43 (*PL* 133: 627)
Guib.Nog.*Pign*.4.3 (*PL* 156: 673)

Ans.*Pros*.9 (Schmitt 1:108);
Bald.*Comm.fid*. (*PL* 204: 575)

Ans.*Med*.1 (Schmitt 3:79)

Brd.Clr.*Cant*.55.1.1 (Leclercq-Rochais 2:112)
Brd.Clr.*Grad*.10.33 (Leclercq-Rochais 3.42)
Brd.Clr.*Div*.87.1 (Leclercq-Rochais 6–I:329); Brd.Clr.*Cant*.6.3.8 (Leclercq-Rochais 1:30)

Brd.Clr.*Dir*.90.1 (Leclercq-Rochais 6–I:337)

Brd.Clr.*Cant*.14.1.1 (Leclercq-Rochais 1:76)

Brd.Clr.*Cant*.23.5.12 (Leclercq-Rochais 1:146)

Brd.Clr.*Cant*.23.6.15 (Leclercq-Rochais 1:148)

Brd.Clr.*Cant*.6.3.9 (Leclercq-Rochais 1:30)
Brd.Clr.*Cant*.73.2.4 (Leclercq-Rochais 2:235)

Brd.Clr.*Dil*.15.40 (Leclercq-Rochais 3:154)

granted any "time for repentance" any more. The Lord of history, "the kind Judge," would establish a new earth on which the resurrected saints would dwell.

Although it was ultimately true that "Thou art merciful because thou art supremely just," still only the Last Judgment would bring a resolution of the paradox of justice and mercy, for it was ultimately resolved only in Christ. "He whose name is called 'Savior,' . . . he himself is the Judge, in whose hands I tremble for fear. . . . O sinner, hope in him of whom you are afraid, flee to him from whom you have fled." Only because Christ was both Judge and Savior, both just and merciful, could he be truly either one. Only a mercy that was just was a genuine virtue, in God as well as in man. Mercy without justice would make the sinner presumptuous, justice without mercy would make him despondent. Seen in the light of Christ, "mercy and judgment are the two feet of God," both of which had to leave their print in the soul if it was to be saved. Throughout human history, they would be equally familiar to Christ the Judge, who would dispense them both equitably. History would contain evidences of "the vengeance, most severe and most secret, of God the just Judge, who is terrible in his counsels regarding the children of men," hardening the reprobate who defied his will. Only rarely and only briefly could the eyes of faith discern within history the God who was "tranquil and in repose," whose essential attribute was mercy. And so it would be throughout time, with "thy two justifications," mercy and judgment, side by side, "until mercy having been exalted high above judgment, my miserable state shall cease" at the end. For "in the time of judgment [he] will exalt mercy above judgment." Once mercy had accomplished this end, its mission would be completed. "Only the justice of God will be remembered, and there will be no place for misery and no time for mercy," because the paradox would be resolved.

4 The Communication of Grace

Southern (1970) 34

During the century that followed the writing of Anselm's *Why God Became Man* in 1098, the social, political, and intellectual situation of Latin Christendom altered significantly. In a series of changes, which, taken together, constitute "the most remarkable fact in medieval history," Christian Europe made the transition that was to take it into the High Middle Ages. Doctrinally, too, the twelfth century may be seen as a time of accelerating movement, as our quotations from that period in the preceding chapter have already suggested. It was a time when questions that had been either neglected or left unanswered in the "Augustinian synthesis" and that had been raised but not resolved in the "Carolingian renaissance" came once more to theological attention, and in such a way that this time they had to be faced.

The clarification and codification of what Western Christian doctrine meant by salvation through Christ served to make a consideration of these questions necessary. What has been said of the development of doctrine in the early centuries would apply even more accurately to the twelfth century: "The Incarnation is the antecedent of the doctrine of Mediation, and the archetype both of the Sacramental principle and of the merits of Saints. From the doctrine of Mediation follow the Atonement, the Mass, the merits of Martyrs and Saints, their invocation and *cultus*." The declaration of the Council of Nicea

Newman (1949) 86
See vol.1:201

See vol.1:261

that the Son of God was homoousios with the Father was followed a century later by the declaration of the Council of Ephesus that his mother was Theotokos, the Mother of God. In the early centuries the doctrine of the means of

See vol.1:155–56

grace had developed much more rapidly than the doctrine of grace itself, with consequences that fundamentally shaped the history of Augustinian theology. Now it was to be the achievement of a definitive doctrine of grace and salvation, in the christological and soteriological teachings of such theologians as Anselm, that would help to bring about a more decisive view of the communication of grace, as formulated in the teachings of such churchmen as Baldwin of Canterbury, Anselm's successor in that see. In a treatise devoted to the doctrine of Mary, Baldwin spoke of God incarnate in Christ as one "who participates in our nature and is a communicator of his grace [communicans naturae nostrae, et communicator gratiae suae]."

Bald.*Tract*.7 (*PL* 204:473)

The communication of grace was, as he and his contemporaries saw it, the chief content of the doctrine of Mary and the other saints. It was also, according to Lanfranc (Anselm's immediate predecessor as archbishop of Canterbury) and his followers, the chief issue in the debates over the Eucharist and the other sacraments.

The doctrine of Mary and the doctrine of the Eucharist, with their corollaries, had been brought to the center of theological attention through the writings of Paschasius

Radb.*Corp*.12 (*CCCM* 16:76–77)
Alg.*Sacr*.1.21 (*PL* 180:802);
Petr.Ab.*Sic et non*.117.83 (Boyer-McKeon 400)

Radbertus, which had so worked their way into the literature that a quotation from Radbertus on the Eucharist was regularly attributed to Augustine. Both these doctrines were, moreover, closely tied to worship and devotion, where the ancient principle obtained that "the rule of

See vol.1:339

prayer should lay down the rule of faith." And so the stock argument in the consideration of these doctrines would be the implication of the rule of prayer as documented in the liturgy, often introduced with some such formula as: "Lest anyone suppose that I have thought up this idea on my own, I have cited the preface that is used on every Lord's Day throughout almost the entire Latin

Guit.Av.*Corp*.1 (*PL* 149:1434)

world, between Epiphany and Septuagesima." The formal language of the prescribed liturgy simultaneously reflected and shaped the piety of the worshipers, above all in their attitude toward the communication of grace through the saints, especially Mary, and through the sacraments, especially the Eucharist; and the theologians of the church "yielded, out of deference to the devotion that came from

Brd.Clr.*Ep*.174.9 (Leclercq-Rochais 7:392)

a simple heart and from a love for the Virgin." Even those who were advancing the current trends in devotion recognized that the forms of popular interest in miracles some-

Brd.Schol.*Mirac.Fid*.pr. (*PL* 141:131)

Guib.Nog.*Pign*.1.1 (*PL* 156: 615)
Brngr.Tr.ap.Guit.Av.*Corp*.2 (*PL* 149:1447)

Brngr.Tr.*Ep.Adel*. (Montclos 534); Brngr.Tr.*Coen*.20; 35 (Beekenkamp 35; 93)

Rem.Aux.*Cel.miss*. (*PL* 101: 1264)

Ans.*Concept.virg*.pr. (Schmitt 2:139)

Simson (1956) 159–82
See p. 69 above

Schapiro (1964) 71

Curtius (1953) 123

Guib.Nog.*Vita sua*.2.1 (*PL* 156:895)

Acts 17:23

times served to cast doubt on miracle stories; the more moderate among those who attacked these trends urged that at least the clergy should rebuke the dangerous excesses of folk piety; and the more extreme of the critics repudiated the authority of the lives of the saints and identified as their "adversaries the common people and those who share the madness of the common people, Paschasius, Lanfranc, and whoever else may interpret the matter this way." For both proponents and opponents, then, saints and sacraments developed together in the church's teaching, since it was "in the community and unity" of the saints that "we perform these mysteries" of the sacraments.

Mary as Mediatrix

The connection between the doctrine of salvation and the doctrine of Mary was direct and explicit. As Anselm himself pointed out, his treatise on the atonement had helped to provoke the question of "how it was that God assumed a man from the sinful mass of the human race without sin." In Christian iconography as well as in Christian literature, there was a new attention to the significance of Mary: a painting of Ildefonsus, celebrated for his devotion to her, constitutes "one of the oldest expressions of the cult of the Virgin, which was then beginning to pervade Christian piety." Why it was beginning to do so just at this time, is not clear, and many of the answers probably lie beyond the scope of this work. Thus when it is suggested that in the mariology of Bernard of Clairvaux, "as through an opened sluice, the fertility cult of the earliest ages flows once again into the speculation of the Christian West," this is an explanation that is at least as much psychological as it is historical. Contemporaries were aware of the parallels between the cult of the Virgin and "the fertility cult of the earliest ages." There was, for example, the legend of an ancient temple "dedicated to a woman not yet born, who was to give birth to one that would be both God and man. It was therefore devoted to the future Mother of God, yet to be born." Such parallels were seen as an anticipation of the Virgin Mary, analogous to anticipation of the true God represented by the Athenian statue to the unknown god. But Mary was not only the fulfillment of ancient intui-

Petr.Dam.*Carm*.D.4.19
(Lokrantz 143)
Guib.Nog.*Inc*.1.1 (*PL* 156:
491)
Bern.Reich.*V*.*Udal*.14 (*PL*
142:1195)

tions and legends; she was also the woman who conquered worldly wisdom through the miracle of the virgin birth, as well as the one who conquered the false teachings of the heretics and resisted the incursions of the barbarians.

Considerations of this kind were part of a process that strove to identify the place of the Virgin in the economy of salvation. As one scholar has noted, somewhat ruefully, "scientific Mariology. . . . , enjoying the status of a distinct and quasi-autonomous tract within theology, with its several theses systematically organized and connected under the control of one master principle and various secondary principles, did not exist in the Middle Ages."

Shea (1955) 285

Therefore the detailed classification of her "merits," "privileges," and "prerogatives" had not yet developed, but the beginnings of the process were evident in this

Brd.Clr.*Ep*.174.5–7 (Leclercq-Rochais 7:390–92)

period. It was an anticipation of later language about her when Peter Damian referred to her "singular privilege of merits, so that as thou dost not know a peer among human

Petr.Dam.*Off*.*B*.*V*.*M*. (*PL* 145:935)

beings, thou dost also surpass the dignity of the angels."

Petr.Dam.*Carm*.B.44.9
(Lokrantz 129)

Elsewhere, too, he praised her "merits" for granting release from "our debts." Speaking of the relation between her maternity and her virginity, another writer conceded that "a privilege is to be ascribed to her as mother," yet in such a way that her virginity also shared in the honor paid to her. The relation between maternity and virginity

Guib.Nog.*Virg*.5 (*PL* 156:586)

was likewise the basis for partisans on both sides of the

Brngr.Tr.*Apol*. (Matronola 118)
Guit.Av.*Corp*.1 (*PL* 149:1443)

eucharistic controversy to speak about her "privilege" or about her "singular prerogative," namely, that she gave birth as other mothers do, yet without pain and without the loss of her virginity. Merits, privileges, and prerogatives were all a way of affirming that, as the Mother of God, she was unique not only among human beings, but among all creatures.

Her uniqueness was the subject of the titles that were bestowed on her, and it was in these, more than in a systematic delineation of "marian prerogatives," that this period expressed its estimate of her importance. As in the

See vol.2:139–41

East so in the West, poets and theologians vied with one

Guib.Nog.*Vita sua*.1.16 (*PL* 156:871)

another in elaborating distinctive appellations for the Virgin. For she was "the standard-bearer of piety," whose life of prayer the faithful imitated in their own. She served as a model to them because she was "courageous in her resolution, temperate in her silence, prudent in her ques-

Brd.Clr.*Div*.52 (Leclercq-
Rochais 6–I:276)
Ans.*Orat*.7 (Schmitt 3:18);
Goff.Vind.*Serm*.1 (*PL* 157:
237)
Brun.S.*Luc*.1.1.4 (*PL* 165:
346)
Brun.S.*Sent*.1.5 (*PL* 165:
915)
Goff.Vind.*Serm*.7 (*PL* 157:
266)
Petr.Dam.*Ep*.6.32 (*PL* 144:
431)
Ans.*Orat*.2 (Schmitt 3:8)
Brun.S.*Sent*.5.1 (*PL* 165:
1021)
Petr.Dam.*Serm*.46 (*PL* 144:
753); Petr.Dam.*Carm*.B.1.17
(Lokrantz 78)

Brd.Clr.*Laud.Virg*.2.3
(Leclercq-Rochais 4:23)

Cyn.*Chr*.275–76 (Cook 11)

Bald.*Tract*.7 (*PL* 204:472)
Rich.S.Vict.*Serm.cent*.47; 55
(*PL* 177:1029; 1061)

See p. 70 above

Brun.S.*Laud.Mar*.5 (*Anal.
Hymn*.23:73)
Hrot.*Mar*.274–76 (Homeyer
58)
Brun.S.*Sent*.3.1 (*PL* 165:944)

Num.24:17

Curtius (1973) 129

Rich.S.Vict.*Serm.cent*.4 (*PL*
177:910–11); Rich.S.Vict.
Except.2.10.4.3 (*TPMA* 5:
384–85)

Hier.*Hebr.nom*.Matt.M; Ex.
M (*CCSL* 72:137; 76)

Isid. Sev.*Orig*.7.10.1 (*PL* 82:
289)

Thes.Hymn.123.1 (*Anal.Hymn*.
51:140)
Od.Clun.*Serm*.2 (*PL* 133:
721); Petr.Dam.*Serm*.1 (*PL*
144:508); Fulb.*Serm*.4 (*PL*
141:321–22)
Guib.Nog.*Inc*.3.3 (*PL* 156:
514)
Fulb.*Hymn*.11 (*PL* 141:345);
Petr.Dam.*Carm*.A.94; B.1.2
(Lokrantz 71; 76)
Petr.Dam.*Serm*.46 (*PL* 144:
753); Fulb.*Serm*.4 (*PL* 141:
321); Brun.S.*Sent*.5.1 (*PL* 165:
1021–22)
Num.17:8
Brun.S.*Num*.17 (*PL* 164:486)
Isa.11:1(Vulg.)

Isa.7:14

tioning, and righteous in her confession." As "the Queen of angels, the ruling Lady of the world, and the mother of him who purifies the world," she could acquire such names as these: "mother of truth"; "mother and daughter of humility"; "mother of Christians"; "mother of peace"; "my most merciful Lady." She was also called, in a term reminiscent of Augustine, "the city of God." The paradox that a creature had become the mother of her Creator justified such terms as "the fountain from which the living fountain flows, the origin of the beginning." Therefore she was "the woman who uniquely deserves to be venerated, the one to be admired more than all other women," in fact, "the radiant glory of the world, the purest maid of earth." Thus she excelled all others, "more beautiful than all of them, more lovable than all of them, supersplendid, supergracious, superglorious." The glory of her name had filled the entire world.

Two of the titles often used for Mary in this period involved metaphors that depended at least in part on tricks of language. One was the identification of the Virgin as "Mary, the star of the sea [Maria maris stella]," a name that was said to have been given her from on high. The name was thought to have been prophesied in the oracle, "A star shall come forth out of Jacob." Because "this class of [nautical] metaphor is extraordinarily widespread throughout the Middle Ages," the image of Mary as the star guiding the ship of faith was an especially attractive one. Its origins seem to lie in Jerome's etymology for the name "Mary" as "a drop of water from the sea [stilla maris]," which he preferred to other explanations. This etymology was taken over by Isidore of Seville, but in the process "drop [stilla]" had become "star [stella]." On that basis, apparently in the ninth century, an unknown poet composed an influential hymn, hailing Mary as "the star of the sea." Soon the title became a part of the homiletical language about the Virgin, as well as of theological literature; but it was especially in poetry that the symbol of Mary as the lodestar of voyagers through life found expression. The other such title was based on the assonance of the words "virgin [virgo]" and "rod [virga]." The miracle by which the rod of Aaron had sprouted was a type of the miracle of the virgin birth, and the prophecy that "a rod shall come forth from the root of Jesse, and a flower shall arise from his root" was fulfilled, as Isaiah

Brd.Clr.*Adv*.1.11 (Leclercq-Rochais 4:169);
Brd.Clr.*Laud*.*Virg*.2.6 (Leclercq-Rochais 4:25)
Cyr.H.*Catech*.12.28 (Reischl-Rupp 2:38)
Rich.S.Vict.*Comp*. (*PL* 196:1031–32)

Brd.Clr.*Cant*.47.2.5 (Leclercq-Rochais 2:64)

Herb.Los.*Serm*.3 (Goulburn-Symonds 80)

Brd.Clr.*Assump*.4.5 (Leclercq-Rochais 5:248)

Brd.Clr.*Vig*.*Nat*.3.9 (Leclercq-Rochais 4:218)
Petr.Dam.*Carm*.D.4.3 (Lokrantz 141)
Petr.Dam.*Serm*.45 (*PL* 144:747)

Brd.Clr.*Vig*.*Nat*.1.1 (Leclercq-Rochais 4:198)
Brd.Clr.*Laud*.*Virg*.3.8 (Leclercq-Rochais 4:41)

Guib.Nog.*Inc*.1.1 (*PL* 156:491)

Guib.Nog.*Inc*.3.7 (*PL* 156:523)

Goff.Vind.*Serm*.1; 3; 4 (*PL* 157:237; 244; 259); Rem.Aux.*Matt*.4 (*PL* 131:891)
Brd.Clr.*Vig*.*Nat*.4.4 (Leclercq-Rochais 4:223); Herb.Los.*Serm*.1 (Goulburn-Symonds 8)

Luke 2:7

Rup.*Div*.*off*.3.20 (*CCCM* 7:93)

Ezek.44:1–2
Cyn.*Chr*.317–25 (Cook 13); Guib.Nog.*Laud*.*Mar*.4 (*PL* 156:543–47)
Robt.Pull.*Sent*.3.22 (*PL* 186:795); Petr.Dam.*Carm*.A.1; B.1.7 (Lokrantz 53; 77)
Bern.Reich.*Modul*.9 (*PL* 142:1147–48)
Zen.Ver.*Tract*.1.13.10 (*PL* 11:352)

Rath.*Metr*.8 (*CCCM* 46:21)

himself had said, in the Virgin, who was the rod and the flower. Although the title was present also in Greek theology, where the play on words was not present, the paronomasia in Latin made it especially attractive, as when Bernard of Clairvaux, with his ear for language, called Christ "a virgin born of a rod that was a virgin [virgo virga virgine generatus]."

By far the most important language about Mary was, of course, that which referred to her virginity and to her maternity, and to the two together. It was in the combination of these two titles, as "Virgin Mother," that her uniqueness was to be found. She was the only one in whom the fertility of motherhood and the purity of virginity had ever come together. As "virgin, mother, and bearer," all at the same time, she was miraculous not only in the way she conceived, but also in the way she believed. "A virgin believes, a virgin conceives by faith, a virgin gives birth and remains a virgin. Who would not be amazed?" Thus she was "a fertile virgin and a chaste childbearer." Any questioning of the virgin birth was an act of blasphemy against the Holy Spirit. The doctrine of the virgin birth had long since included not only the teaching that the conception of Christ was different from that of other men, but also the idea that in the act of being born Christ had been unique, since he had left his mother's virginity intact. For "not only was her conception without shame and her giving birth without pain, but she is a mother without corruption." Her perpetual virginity was not inconsistent with the biblical identification of Jesus as her "firstborn," since this did not necessarily imply that there were any children after him. The prophecy that "this gate shall remain shut, for the Lord, the God of Israel, has entered by it" was unanimously accepted as proof that Mary had remained a virgin after the birth of Christ. For he had been born of a womb that remained closed in the act of giving birth. Yet this was not to be taken to mean that Mary had conceived "though her ear," as some patristic theories had evidently suggested, even though theologians did insist that her "hearing remained utterly inviolable."

One obvious corollary of the doctrine of the virgin birth was the emphasis on virginity and on clerical celibacy. "Because the Lord's body grew together in the temple of the Virgin's womb, he now requires of his

Petr.Dam.*Opusc*.18.1 (*PL* 145:
388)

Petr.Dam.*Opusc*.17.3 (*PL*
145:384)

Petr.Dam.*Serm*.35 (*PL* 144:
691)

Guib.Nog.*Virg*.4 (*PL* 156:
584)

Guib.Nog.*Inc*.2.5 (*PL* 156:
505)

Guib.Nog.*Virg*.4 (*PL* 156:
585)

Brd.Clr.*Laud.Virg*.2.1
(Leclercq-Rochais 4:21)

Guib.Nog.*Virg*.5 (*PL* 156:
586)

Guib.Nog.*Laud.Mar*.2 (*PL*
156:539)

Luke 1:28(Vulg.)
Petr.Ven.*Ep*.94 (Constable
236-37)
Brun.S.*Sent*.2.5 (*PL* 165:915)

Rom.4:2
Brd.Clr.*Assump*.6.1 (Leclercq-
Rochais 5:260-61)
Brd.Clr.*Laud.Virg*.1.5
(Leclercq-Rochais 4:17-18)
Rath.*Prael*.2.9.18 (*PL* 136:
202)
Rup.*Div.off*.8.6 (*CCCM* 7:
276)
Bern.Reich.*V.Udal*.10 (*PL*
142:1193)

See p. 71 above

Luke 2:22-39
Fulb.*Serm*.3 (*PL* 141:319);
Brd.Clr.*Purif.Mar*.3.1
(Leclercq-Rochais 4:341);
Herb.Los.*Serm*.3 (Goulburn-
Symonds 82);
Goff.Vind.*Serm*.7 (*PL* 157:
262)

Rich.S.Vict.*Edict*.3
(Châtillon-Tulloch 60-62)
Petr.Ven.*Ep*.94 (Constable
238-39)

See vol.1:314

ministers the purity of sexual continence." Christ had not
only remained a virgin himself and chosen to be born of a
virgin, but he had even selected as his guardian and puta-
tive father one who was also a virgin; "by whom then, I
ask you, does he want his body to be governed" on earth
except also by virgins? Christian virgins shared in Mary's
reversal of the victory that "the ancient foe" had achieved
over Eve in the fall. Her virginity served as a model and
an incentive for anyone who was "wavering in his resolve
to preserve his own virginity" and who, by contemplating
"the sublime dignity of the way she gave birth," would
be moved to follow in her footsteps. As his birth from a
virgin was the only fitting way for Christ to assume human
nature, since it was the purest and the most excellent way,
so he also urged on his followers, though he did not
require it, a life of virginity and continence in imitation.
Another title for Mary, consequently, was "Queen of
virgins," since she was the one in whose purity other
Christian virgins shared and in whose dignity they participated to such an extent that the angels venerated them
together with her. Even such encomia of Mary's virginity,
however, were usually counterbalanced by the recognition that it was above all her maternal office, not her
virginal state, that gave her a special place in the economy
of salvation.

The same recognition underlay the assertion that when
Mary was called "full of grace" by the angel of the annunciation, this was because of her humility, not simply
because of her virginity; "for virginity without humility
may perhaps 'have something to boast about, but not before God.'" One could, after all, be saved without virginity, but not without humility. Mary was "the standard
of humility," in fact, "the Queen of the humble," so that
the poor and oppressed of the world could be called "the
family of Saint Mary." The humility of Mary was part of
her holy and sinless life. As earlier medieval theologians
had maintained also, the Gospel account of her purification did not imply that she needed to be purified in accordance with the Mosaic law, but was evidence of her
"humility and obedience," as well as a means of protecting
her reputation among those who were not aware of the
special circumstances. The question of whether, and in
what sense, she was free of original sin was an issue on
which Augustine had not come to a definite conclusion;

Brd.Clr.*Ep*.174.5 (Leclercq-
Rochais 7:390)
Brd.Clr.*Assump*.2.8 (Leclercq-
Rochais 5:237)

Guib.Nog.*Laud.Mar*.5 (*PL*
156:550–51)

Luke 1:42
Bald.*Tract*.7 (*PL* 204:476)

Andr.Cr.*Or*.4 (*PG* 97:865)

Paul.Diac.*Homil*.45 (*PL* 95:
1496)

Brd.Clr.*Adv*.2.5 (Leclercq-
Rochais 4:174)

Petr.Dam.*Serm*.45 (*PL* 144:
741)

and there was no unanimity on it during the twelfth century, or even later. It was, however, widely held, even by those who did not accept the idea of her immaculate conception, that "it was fitting for the Queen of virgins, by a singular privilege of sanctity, to lead a life that was free of all sin." It was therefore "the pious thing to believe that Mary did not have any sin of her own." Sometimes it was suggested that since she was "full of grace" and grace was synonymous with the forgiveness of sins, she must have had sins that needed to be forgiven. But this interpretation was not able to stand up against the dominant belief that a special "immunity" had been conferred on her and that this was what made her "full of grace" and "blessed among women."

Most of this could have been—and had been—said centuries earlier. What sets the devotion and thought of this period apart from the development leading up to it was the growing emphasis on the office of Mary as "mediatrix." The title itself seems to have appeared for the first time in Eastern theology, where she was addressed as "the mediatrix of law and of grace." Whether from such Eastern sources or from Western reflection itself, the term then came into Latin usage, apparently near the end of the eighth century. It was, however, in the eleventh and twelfth centuries that it achieved widespread acceptance. It was a means of summarizing what had come to be seen as her twofold function: she was "the way by which the Savior came" to mankind in the incarnation and the redemption, and she was also the one "through whom we ascend to him who descended through her to us . . . , through [whom] we have access to the Son . . . , so that through [her] he who through [her] was given to us might take us up to himself." The term "mediatrix" referred to both of these aspects of her mediatorial position.

In the first instance, it was a way of speaking about her active role in the incarnation and the redemption. There seemed to be a direct and irrefutable inference from the universally accepted thesis that "it would have been impossible for the redemption of the human race to take place unless the Son of God had been born of a Virgin" to the corollary thesis that "it was likewise necessary that the Virgin, of whom the Logos was to be made flesh, should herself have been born." Thus she had become "the gate of Paradise, which restored God to the world

Petr.Dam.*Carm*.B.23.2
(Lokrantz 112)

Brd.Clr.*Assump*.4.8 (Leclercq-
Rochais 5:250)

Fulb.*Serm*.9.5 (*PL* 141:338)

Ans.*Orat*.7 (Schmitt 3:21)

See p. 140 above

Petr.Dam.*Serm*.46 (*PL* 144:
752)

Brd.Clr.*Laud.Virg*.2.3
(Leclercq-Rochais 4:23)

1 Pet.2:9
Petr.Dam.*Carm*.B.42.2
(Lokrantz 126)

Bald.*Tract*.7 (*PL* 204:473)

Guib.Nog.*Pign*.3.5.5 (*PL* 156:
664)

Gen.3:15(Vulg.)

See p. 71 above

Brd.Clr.*Laud.Virg*.2.4
(Leclercq-Rochais 4:23–24);
Fulb.*Serm*.4 (*PL* 141:320);
Goff.Vind.*Serm*.3 (*PL* 157:
247)

Ans.*Orat*.6 (Schmitt 3:16)

Ans.*Orat*.7 (Schmitt 3:20)

and opened heaven to us." By her participation in redemption she had filled heaven with the saved and had emptied hell of those who would have been condemned except for her. It was her assent to the word and will of God that had made the incarnation and therefore the redemption possible. "O woman marvelously unique and uniquely marvelous," Anselm prayed, "through whom the elements are renewed, hell is redeemed, the demons are trampled under foot, men are saved, and angels are restored!" The reference to the restoration of the angels was an allusion to the idea that the number of elect would make up for the number of the angels who had fallen; Mary was seen as the one through whom "not only a life once lost is returned to men, but also the beatitude of angelic sublimity is increased," because through her participation in salvation the hosts of angels regained their full strength. In the same sense she wrought reparation for what man's first parents had done, and she brought life to all their posterity. Through her, then, the "royal priesthood" spoken of by the apostle had truly come into being in the Christian church. All of this made her "the minister and cooperator of this dispensation, who gave us the salvation of the world."

Mary's cooperation in the plan of salvation helped to explain the puzzling circumstance in the Gospel narratives, that after his resurrection Christ had not appeared first to his mother: "Why should he have appeared to her when she undoubtedly knew about the resurrection even before he suffered and rose?" An index of the increasingly important part being assigned to her in the plan of redemption was the ease with which the words of God to the tempter that "she [ipsa] shall crush your head," which had not been taken in this sense by most earlier exegetes, came to be applied to the Virgin; for "to whom is this victory to be attributed, if not to Mary? Without a doubt it was she who crushed the venomous head." She was the virginal human being of whom was born the divine human being who was to save the sinful human being. She was "the sanctuary of the universal propitiation, the cause of the general reconciliation, the vessel and the temple of the life and the salvation of all men." Such praises as these by Anselm of the Virgin's place in the history of salvation, voiced in the setting of prayers, as so much of the language about her was, could

Brd.Clr.*Assump*.2.2 (Leclercq-Rochais 5:233)

Fulb.*Serm*.9.1–2 (*PL* 141:336–37); Rich.S.Vict.*Em*.1.10 (*PL* 196:618)

Petr.Dam.*Serm*.46 (*PL* 144:758)

Bald.*Tract*.7 (*PL* 204:473)

Od.Clun.*Occup*.6.367–68 (Swoboda 129–30)

Od.Clun.*Serm*.2 (*PL* 133:721)

Ans.*Orat*.16 (Schmitt 3:65)

Rup.*Div.off*.8.11 (*CCCM* 7:285)

Gen.3:16
Brd.Clr.*Vig.Nat*.4.3 (Leclercq-Rochais 4:222)
Brd.Clr.*Laud.Virg*.2.3 (Leclercq-Rochais 4:22–23)

Cyn.*Chr*.95–99 (Cook 4–5)

Brd.Clr.*Cant*.85.3.8 (Leclercq-Rochais 2:313)

Guib.Nog.*Laud.Mar*.14 (*PL* 156:577)

Brd.Clr.*Assump*.4.8 (Leclercq-Rochais 5:249)

only mean, in the words of Bernard, that "she is our mediatrix, she is the one through whom we have received thy mercy, O God, she is the one through whom we, too, have welcomed the Lord Jesus into our homes."

As mediatrix, Mary was also the Second Eve, just as Christ was the Second Adam. As it had been through a woman that the earth had come under the curse of sin and death, so it would be through a woman that blessing would be restored to the earth. The curse of Eve had been a consequence of her pride and disobedience, the blessing of Mary a consequence of her humility and obedience. The status of Mary as the Second Eve could even be said to confer a special eminence on her namesake, Mary Magdalene; for "just as through Saint Mary the Virgin, who is the only hope of the world, the gates of Paradise have been opened to us and the curse of Eve has been canceled, so through Saint Mary Magdalene the shame of the female sex has been undone, and the splendor of our resurrection, which arose in the Lord's resurrection, has been granted to us by her." Mary Magdalene was celebrated as "the blessed bride of God" and as a type of the church that had been drawn from the paganism of the heathen to the source of grace. The canceling of the curse of Eve through the Virgin Mary was especially evident in the birth of Christ, which took place without the pain that was the result of that curse. Mary, the daughter, had taken away the shame and guilt of Eve, the mother, by being obedient rather than disobedient in her response to the word of God. Mary, "David's beloved kinsmaid," cast out the curse of Eve and elevated the status of woman. Eve had been the instrument through which folly had been mediated to her descendants, but through Mary wisdom had once more been mediated to the human race.

The title "mediatrix," however, applied not only to Mary's place in the history of salvation, but also to her continuing position as intercessor between Christ and mankind, as the one whose "virginity we praise and whose humility we admire; but thy mercy tastes even sweeter, and it is thy mercy that we embrace even more fondly, think of even more often, and invoke even more frequently." It was the remembrance of Mary's "ancient mercies" that aroused in a believer the hope and confidence to "return to thee [Mary], and through thee to God the Father and to thy only Son," so that it was possi-

Guib.Nog.*Vita sua*.1.3 (*PL* 156:843)

ble to "demand salvation of thee [Mary]." The consummation of the believer's glory was the awareness that Mary
stood as the mediatrix between him and her Son; in fact,
she had been chosen by God for the specific task of plead-

Guib.Nog.*Laud.Mar*.14 (*PL* 156:577)

ing the cause of men before her Son. And so she was
"the Mother of the kingdom of heaven, Mary, the Mother

Guib.Nog.*Vita sua*.1.19 (*PL* 156:881)

of God, my only refuge in every need." Mary was addressed as the one who could bring cleansing and healing

Petr.Dam.*Carm*.B.37.3 (Lokrantz 124); Ans.*Orat*.5 (Schmitt 3:14) Rad.Ard.*Hom*.1.16 (*PL* 155: 1359)

to the sinner and as the one who would give succor against
the temptations of the devil; but she did this by mediating
between Christ and humanity. "By thy pious prayer, make

Petr.Dam.*Carm*.B.38.2 (Lokrantz 124)

thy Son propitious to us," one could plead; or again:
"Our lady, our mediatrix, our advocate, reconcile us to
thy Son, commend us to thy Son, represent us to thy Son.
Do this, O blessed one, through the grace that thou hast
found [before God], through the prerogative that thou
hast merited, through the mercy to which thou hast given

Brd.Clr.*Adv*.2.5 (Leclercq-Rochais 4:174) Hrot.*Mar*.13–16 (Homeyer 48); Od.Clun.*Serm*.2 (*PL* 133: 721); Fulb.*Serm*.9.5 (*PL* 141: 338) Brd.Clr.*Laud.Virg*.2.4 (Leclercq-Rochais 4:23–24) Brun.S.*Laud.Mar*.1 (*Anal. Hymn*.23:73) Guib.Nog.*Vita sua*.1.19 (*PL* 156:881)

birth."

Such terms for Mary as "the only hope of the world,"
"the one who crushed the venomous head" of the serpent,
the one through whom death was conquered, and "my
only refuge in every need" raised the question of the
relation of Christ and Mary. "As we make a practice of
rejoicing at the nativity of Christ," one preacher exhorted,

Petr.Dam.*Serm*.46 (*PL* 144: 753); Fulb.*Serm*.4 (*PL* 141: 320)

"so we should rejoice no less at the nativity of the mother
of Christ." For it was a basic rule that "whatever we set
forth in praise of the Mother pertains to the Son, and on
the other hand when we honor the Son we are not drawing

Brd.Clr.*Laud.Virg*.4.1 (Leclercq-Rochais 4:46) Guib.Nog.*Laud.Mar*.9 (*PL* 156:563–64)

back from our glory to the Mother." Christ was pleased
when praise was offered to the Virgin Mary; conversely,
an offense against either the Son or the Mother was an

Ans.*Orat*.6 (Schmitt 3:16)

offense against the other one as well. It was particularly the
intercessory implication of the title "mediatrix" that
could be interpreted as taking something away from
Christ, who was "the High Priest so that he might offer

Hug.S.Vict.*Verb*.5.3 (*SC* 155: 76)

the vows of the people to God." The countervailing force
against what could be construed as "Mariolatry" was the
recognition that she had been "exalted through thy omnipotent Son, for the sake of thy glorious Son, by thy

Ans.*Orat*.7 (Schmitt 3:19)

blessed Son." The portrayal of "the coronation of the
Virgin," which became a standard part of the iconography
of Mary during the twelfth century, regularly depicted her
as sitting at Christ's right hand, and it was a continuation
of this understanding when later painters showed Christ

Mâle (1958) 254–58

Bald.*Tract*.6 (*PL* 204:458);
Rad.Ard.*Hom*.2.25 (*PL* 155:
1588)

Brd.Clr.*Ep*.174.2 (Leclercq-
Rochais 7:388)

Petr.Dam.*Carm*.D.8.6–8
(Lokrantz 156); Goff.Vind.
Serm.8 (*PL* 157:269)

Petr.Dam.*Serm*.45 (*PL* 144:
743)
Guib.Nog.*Laud.Mar*.1 (*PL*
156:537)

Guib.Nog.*Virg*.5 (*PL* 156:
585)

Cant.parth.202 (*Anal.Hymn*.
20:160–61)

Petr.Dam.*Carm*.B.22.3
(Lokrantz 111)

Petr.Dam.*Serm*.46 (*PL* 144:
752)

Brd.Clr.*Ep*.174.2 (Leclercq-
Rochais 7:389)
Petr.Dam.*Ep*.6.29 (*PL* 144:
419)

Ans.*Orat*.7 (Schmitt 3:21)

Ans.*Pros*.2 (Schmitt 1:101)

Ans.*Concept.virg*.18 (Schmitt
2:159)

Ans.*Orat*.5 (Schmitt 3:13)

Joh.Lod.*V.Petr.Dam*.15 (*PL*
144:132); Petr.Dam.*Ep*.6.29
(*PL* 144:419); Rup.*Div.off*.
7.25 (*CCCM* 7:255); Brd.Clr.
Ep.174.2 (Leclercq-Rochais 7:
388–89)

or God the Father or the entire Trinity investing her with the crown. It was, moreover, a consensus that Mary had been saved by Christ, so that, while she lamented his death because he was her Son, she welcomed it because he was her Savior. Extravagances of devotion and rhetoric were curbed by the principle that "the royal Virgin has no need of any false honor."

It was perceived as an appropriate honor and an authentic expression of her position in the divine order when Mary was acclaimed as second in dignity only to God himself, who had taken up habitation in her. The ground of this dignity was the part she had taken in the redemption, more important than that of any other ordinary human being. Through her Son she had been exalted "above all creatures" and was worthy of their veneration. This applied to all earthly creatures, but it included all other creatures as well, so that "there is nothing in heaven that is not subject to the Virgin through her Son." Echoing the language of the *Te Deum* about the praise of God, as other Marian hymns were to do later in the Middle Ages, a poem of Peter Damian proclaimed: "The blessed chorus of angels, the order of prophets and apostles affirm thee to be exalted over them and second only to the Deity." For none of them—"neither the chorus of the patriarchs for all their excellence, nor the company of the prophets for all their powers of foretelling the future, nor the senate of the apostles for all their judicial authority"— deserved to be compared with the Virgin. Since she was the one who held first place among the entire celestial host, whether human or angelic, she, next to God himself, should receive the praises of the whole world. There was, in short, "nothing equal to Mary and nothing but God greater than Mary." As the greatness of God could be defined as "that than which nothing greater can be imagined," so the purity of the Virgin could be defined as "that than which, under God, nothing greater can be thought." Among all that could be called holy, save God, Mary possessed a holiness that was unique.

Therefore it was also fitting that veneration and prayer should be addressed to her. Although there had long been such worship of the Virgin, various leaders of the church during these centuries systematically encouraged and nourished her cult. In a revealing autobiographical memoir, one Benedictine abbot described how, when his

Guib.Nog.*Vita sua*.1.3 (*PL* 156:842)

Bern.Reich.*Ep*.7 (*PL* 142: 1164); Bern.Reich.*V.Udal*.pr. (*MGH Scrip*.4:381)

Ans.*Orat*.6;7 (Schmitt 3:16; 25)

Oesch (1961) 42

Rath.*Ep*.26 (*MGH BDK* 1: 154)

Petr.Dam.*Opusc*.10.10 (*PL* 145:230)
Petr.Dam.*Opusc*.33 (*PL* 145: 565–66)

Petr.Dam.*Opusc*.10.10 (*PL* 145:230)

Hrot.*Mar*.243–49 (Homeyer 57)
Rad.Ard.*Hom*.1.34–35 (*PL* 155:1439–47); Petr.Bl.*Perf. Jud*.12 (*PL* 207:841)
Petr.Dam.*Serm*.45 (*PL* 144: 741)

See pp. 179–81 below

Petr.Dam.*Opusc*.33.3 (*PL* 145: 564–65)

Guib.Nog.*Laud.Mar*.10 (*PL* 156:564–68)

Guib.Nog.*Vita sua*.1.16 (*PL* 156:871)

Guib.Nog.*Pign*.3.3.4 (*PL* 156: 659–60)

Petr.Dam.*Serm*.45–46 (*PL* 144:740–61)

Herm.Torn.*Rest.Mart*.57 (*MGH Scrip*.14:299)

mother was in great pain at his birth, "this vow was made . . . that if a male child should be born, he would be given over to the service of God and . . . offered to her who is Queen of all next to God." Another Benedictine abbot made it a practice to refer to himself as "the slave of the Mother of God." And yet another Benedictine abbot of this period, who went on to higher things, had the practice of addressing prayers simultaneously to "my good Lord and my good Lady," saying to them: "I appeal to you both, devoted Son and devoted Mother." What has been called "the glowing reverence for Mary" of one of these Benedictines was characteristic of them all. Prayers to Mary were cited as support for admonitions and arguments on behalf of her cult, and it was urged that such prayers would gain the succor of "the Mother of the Judge in the day of need." The very day of the Sabbath was said to have been dedicated to Mary, and those who appealed to her as "the gate of heaven, the window of Paradise" when they were plagued by the guilt of their sins received full absolution.

It was no exaggeration of the importance of Mary in the devotion and worship of the church when the festival of her nativity, announced by an angel, was celebrated and was asserted to be "the beginning of all the festivals of the New Testament . . . , the origin of all the other festivals." As was inevitable with any saint, and a fortiori with her, it became a standard expression of piety to attribute to Mary the performance of various miracles. A few of these may have taken place during her earthly life, but others were continuing to take place long afterward, up to the very present. A special form of the devotion to her miracles was the cultivation of her relics. At Chartres, for example, according to one writer, "the name and the relics of the Mother of God [above all, her "sacred tunic"] are venerated throughout almost all the Latin world." Yet when a particular church claimed to possess such relics, that claim was met by the same writer with the response that if "she, through the same Spirit by whom she conceived, knew that he to whom she gave birth by faith was to fill the entire world," she would not have kept such mementos of his childhood as her own mother's milk. A more appropriate way of celebrating her memory was the commemoration of her nativity or the recitation of the Ave Maria, whose cultic repetition became characteristic of piety during this period and whose exposition eventually provided a basis for the articulation of her special place in the history of salvation.

The doctrinal authority derived from the practice of addressing worship to the Virgin had as its counterpart a certain caution about those expressions of devotion to her for which there was no basis in the received forms of the church's worship, especially because certain heretics were propounding the theory "that the Blessed Virgin was created in heaven, and of a heavenly nature, and that therefore Christ assumed a heavenly flesh from the Blessed Virgin." One such devotional expression was the commemoration of her immaculate conception, which did not have a fixed place in the liturgical calendar. Therefore, Bernard argued, "if it is appropriate to say what the church believes and if what she believes is true, then I say that the glorious [Virgin] conceived by the Holy Spirit, but was not also herself conceived this way. I say that she gave birth as a virgin, but not that she was born of a virgin. For otherwise what would be the prerogative of the Mother of God?" It was widely believed that the "special novelty of grace" by which Mary had given birth to Christ did not affect in any way the manner by which she herself had been born, which did not differ from the usual method of conception and birth. On the other hand, the virgin birth of Christ from one who had herself been conceived and born in sin did not seem to resolve the question of how he could be sinless in his birth if his mother was not. Such argumentation seemed to lead to the notion of an infinite regress of sinless ancestors, going back presumably to Adam and Eve, all of whom had been preserved free of sin in order to guarantee the sinlessness of Christ and of Mary. A certain kind of "superflous curiosity" could then begin to inquire into Mary's parentage as a means of explaining how she had given birth through how she herself had been born. For if, as was universally assumed, those who were conceived and born in the normal way were infected by original sin, then Mary must have been unique in some way. It remained to be determined "how it was that the Virgin was purified before the conception" of Christ; this could not have been "otherwise than by him" to whom she gave birth, since he was pure and she was not. A feast devoted to the commemoration of her conception, therefore, was not appropriate, since it was not how she had been conceived, but how she herself had conceived, that set her apart.

Marginal notes (left column):

Bald.*Tract*.7 (*PL* 204:467–78)

Petr.Ven.*Ep*.94 (Constable 244)

ap.Alan.Ins.*Haer*.1.33 (*PL* 210:335); ap.Rain.Sacc. *Cathar.* (Dondaine 76); ap. Petr.Mart.*Patar*.6 (*AFP* 17:323); ap.Monet.Crem.*Cathar*. 3.2.1 (Ricchini 232)

Brd.Clr.*Ep*.174.7 (Leclercq-Rochais 7:391–92)

Petr.Dam.*Serm*.46 (*PL* 144:761)

Ans.*Cur d.h*.2.16 (Schmitt 2:116–17)

Brd.Clr.*Ep*.174.6 (Leclercq-Rochais 7:390–91); Hug.Bret.*Corp*. (*PL* 142:1330) Petr.Dam.*Serm*.46 (*PL* 144:754)

Rich.S.Vict.*Cant*.26 (*PL* 196:482)

Bald.*Tract*.7 (*PL* 204:475–76) Ans.*Concept.virg*.18 (Schmitt 2:159); Fulb.*Serm*.6 (*PL* 141:326); Herb.Los.*Serm*.1 (Goulburn-Symonds 2–4); Rich.S.Vict.*Em*.2.26–27 (*PL* 196:660–61) Ans.*Cur d.h*.2.16 (Schmitt 2:119); Ans.L.*Sent.div.pag*.5 (Bliemetzrieder 39)

Brd.Clr.*Ep*.174.9 (Leclercq-Rochais 7:392)

Brd.Clr.*Ep*.174.3 (Leclercq-Rochais 7:389); Brun.*S.Apoc*.5.14 (*PL* 165:686); Brun.S.*Laud.Mar*.10 (*Anal.Hymn*.23:74); Petr.Ven.*Mirac*.2.30 (*PL* 189:949)

Luke 10:38–42

Guib.Nog.*Laud.Mar*.7 (*PL* 156:557)

Ps.68:18; Eph.4:8

Brd.Clr.*Assump*.1.2 (Leclercq-Rochais 5:229)

John 12:26

Hrot.*Asc*.83–89 (Homeyer 87–88)
Att.Verc.*Serm*.17 (*PL* 134:856)

Brd.Clr.*Assump*.1.1 (Leclercq-Rochais 5:229)

Petr.Dam.*Carm*.B.24.3 (Lokrantz 113)

Brd.Clr.*Assump*.4.1 (Leclercq-Rochais 5:244)

Gen.5:24; 2 Kings 2:11

Luke 2:35

Rath.*Metr*.12 (*CCCM* 46:26)
Att.Verc.*Serm*.17 (*PL* 134:857)
Petr.Ven.*Ep*.94 (Constable 248)

If the immaculate conception of Mary (which did not become dogma until 1854) was not yet an established part of the worship and teaching of the church, her assumption (which did not become dogma until 1950) had a much firmer hold on faith and practice; and there was a specific feast in the church year, fixed by this time at August 15, that commemorated "the day when she was assumed from the world and entered into heaven." The story of Mary and Martha, the sisters of Lazarus, served as the Gospel pericope for that feast, apparently because its closing words, "Mary has chosen the good portion, which shall not be taken away from her," seemed to fit the mother of Jesus even better than they did the sister of Lazarus. By a similar transposition of reference, a text such as "When he ascended on high . . . he gave gifts to men," which had been applied to the ascension of Christ, also seemed to suit the assumption of Mary, through which gifts had been distributed to mankind. Or when Christ promised, "If any one serves me, he must follow me, and where I am there shall my servant be also," there was no one among mortals who had served him in so special a way as Mary had, and therefore, in accordance with his promise to her before his ascension, she had also followed him into heaven. By her presence not only the entire world, but even "the heavenly fatherland shines more brightly because it is illuminated by the glow of her virginal lamp." Her assumption had elevated her above all the angels and archangels, and even all the merits of all the saints were surpassed by those of this one woman. Thus the assumption of the Virgin meant that human nature had been raised to a position superior to that of all the immortal spirits.

One question raised by the doctrine of the assumption was whether Mary had ever died or had, like Enoch and Elijah, been taken up alive into heaven. The prophecy of Simeon to her, "And a sword will pierce your own soul also," seemed to imply that she would die. As it stood, the prophecy spoke only of "sorrow, not the martyrdom of death." But this was not an adequate ground to "arouse doubt concerning her death," since she was by nature mortal. The prophecy did, moreover, appear to disprove the pious feeling of some that she who had given birth without pain should also have died without pain; for "by what authority can one suppose that she did not suffer

Petr.Dam.*Opusc*.55.1 (*PL* 145: 800–801)

Fulb.*Serm*.5 (*PL* 141:325)
Petr.Dam.*Serm*.64 (*PL* 144: 870); Herb.Los.*Serm*.12 (Goulburn-Symonds 352)
Rich.S.Vict.*Em*.1.12 (*PL* 196: 619)

Att.Verc.*Serm*.17 (*PL* 134: 856–57)

Guib.Nog.*Pign*.1.3 (*PL* 156: 623–24)

Rich.S.Vict.*Diff.sacr.* (*PL* 196: 1043)
Luke 1:28(Vulg.)

Acts 6:8

Col.2:9

Brd.Clr.*Laud.Virg*.3.2 (Leclercq-Rochais 4:36–37)

Rem.Aux.*Cel.miss.* (*PL* 101: 1259)

Petr.Dam.*Carm*.B.24.3 (Lokrantz 113)

Petr.Dam.*Serm*.46 (*PL* 144: 752); Rich.S.Vict.*Serm.cent*. 34 (*PL* 177:980)

Ans.*Orat*.5 (Schmitt 3:13)

Rup.*Div.off*.3.13 (*CCCM* 7: 80)

Ecclus.24:10(Vulg.)

Bald.*Tract*.5 (*PL* 204:446)

Ps.68:35(Vulg.)
Brd.Clr.*Laud.Virg*.1.9 (Leclercq-Rochais 4:20)

pain in her body? . . . But whether at her death she did not feel pain, which God could grant, or whether she did feel it, which God could permit," the conclusion seemed to be that "the Blessed Virgin did undergo the vexation of the flesh by dying." Mitigating this conclusion was the widely held belief of "Christian piety" that her death had been followed immediately by a resurrection, which was followed in turn by her assumption; for she was "the firstfruits of [human] incorruptibility." Yet it was recognized at the same time that "we do not dare to affirm that the resurrection of her body has already taken place, since we know that this has not been declared by the holy fathers." Although it was "wicked to believe that the chosen vessel" of Mary's body had been subject to corruption, still "we do not dare to say that she was raised, for no other reason than that we cannot assert it on the basis of evident proof."

The special place of Mary in the history of salvation served to enhance the place of all the saints, but at the same time it called attention to her uniqueness among them. For while her prerogative of being "full of grace" was matched by that of Stephen, the first martyr, who was also said to be "full of grace," she was the only saint to whom the words originally spoken of Christ, "In him the whole fulness of deity dwells bodily," could be literally applied. Because it was through her that all believers, including all other saints, had been accounted worthy of receiving the Author of life, she occupied the first place in any commemoration of the saints. Yet her worthiness was so much more than theirs—and so much more than that of the heavenly host—that she was utterly unique. The apostles, patriarchs, martyrs, and fathers did not deserve to be compared with the Virgin. She exceeded the angels in purity and surpassed the saints in piety. Although other saints, by preaching the word of God and composing the books of the Bible, had served as gates to heaven, nevertheless this title, too, belonged to Mary in a distinctive sense, since it had been only through her that the Logos, the Word of God in person, had become flesh. Similarly, the words, "He who created me rested in my tabernacle," applied to all the righteous, but Mary had a special right to appropriate them for herself. And when the psalm said that "God is marvelous in his saints," this, too, applied a fortiori to her.

Only of Mary could it be said that she had never, even for a moment, suffered an interruption in her beatific vision of God. Other saints had had the grace to overcome their lusts, but she, perhaps alone among them all, had been spared the lusts themselves. For to other saints grace had been given, bountifully and yet in measure, but to Mary it had been granted without measure or limit. In short, while God was present in all his creatures, and more particularly in his rational creatures, and most particularly of all in those who were good and holy, he was present in Mary as in no other; for only of her could it be said that Christ had been formed "of [God's] substance and of hers." When she was said to be "more precious than any, more holy than all," or when she was hailed as an example for all the saints, this made it necessary to clarify not only her unmatched eminence in the divine plan, but also the general category of sainthood, to which she belonged even when she transcended it. That clarification, too, was a theological task to which this period set its hand.

The Communion of Saints

The Virgin Mary was mentioned in the Apostles' Creed (as was Pontius Pilate), but only as an actor in the drama of salvation: Jesus Christ was "born of the Virgin Mary, suffered under Pontius Pilate." But as an object of faith she was simply included with all the other saints in the confession: "I believe in the Holy Spirit, the holy catholic church, the communion of saints." The precise meaning of the phrase, "the communion of saints [communio sanctorum]," had not been specified in the patristic era and remained ambiguous in medieval theology. Because the substantively used adjective "saints" could be either masculine or neuter both in the Greek and in the Latin version, "we may take the word 'saints [sanctorum]' as a neuter, that is, as a reference to the sanctified bread and wine in the Sacrament of the Altar"; but it could also refer to "that communion by which saints are made or are confirmed in their sanctity (that is, by participation in the divine Sacrament), or to the common faith of the church, or to a union in love." In the latter sense it meant "the communion and society of the saints" in which the sacrifice of the Mass was offered, "the communion of saints [which] we have received" in joining the church. Sometimes it took a specifically eschatological connotation when "saints" were

Guib.Nog.*Laud.Mar*.7 (*PL* 156:561)

Bald.*Tract*.11 (*PL* 204:526); Rich.S.Vict.*Em*.2.31 (*PL* 196: 664)

Guib.Nog.*Laud.Mar*.1 (*PL* 156:539)

Brd.Clr.*Laud.Virg*.3.4 (Leclercq-Rochais 4:38) Brd.Clr.*Adv*.2.4 (Leclercq-Rochais 4:173) Petr.Dam.*Carm*.D.8.1 (Lokrantz 155)

Symb.Apost. (Schaff 2:45)

Petr.Ab.*Symb.Apost.* (*PL* 178:630; 629)

Rem.Aux.*Cel.miss.* (*PL* 101: 1259) Brd.Clr.*Cant*.62.1.1 (Leclercq-Rochais 2:154)

defined as "those who, in the faith that we have received, have migrated from this present world to God" and with whom believers had "an association and a communion of hope." These various significations were not contradictory, but complementary, as when "the communion of saints" was defined as "the reality of the sacraments of the church, in which the saints who have migrated from this life in the unity of the faith have had communion."

The "communion," too, had a many-layered meaning. Its metaphysical ground lay in the inner nature of God, who, as Trinity, was "neither singular nor solitary," but had "a common essence" and "a common life," whose very existence as Three in One was an existence in communion. Through the incarnation of the Second Person of the Trinity, this communion was extended to a human nature, and through it to human nature as such. The person of Christ was the link between the divine communion of the hypostases in the Trinity and the human communion of the saints in the church, for in a theology whose "central point" was "communion with God" Christ was "the common prize" of the saints, as he had been "the common price" of their redemption. That communion had now become the characteristic of the church, extending even to a communion of goods, which was "the form of the primitive church." The true saints were endowed with "such a communion, such a harmony of love, that in spiritual things their heart and mind are one and even in physical things nothing is private property but all things are common property." Even now, when the communion of goods was being practiced only by those in the monastic life, all Christians could still "have communion" not only with one another but with the sufferings of Christ, although it remained true that the martyrs "have had communion with the death and the blood of Christ" in a special way.

The communion of the saints and the communion with the saints meant that believers were "fellow citizens and comrades of the blessed spirits." As such, they were united with the saints in the society of faith, and the saints served them as "a mirror and an example, and indeed as a seasoning of human life on earth." Their footsteps were there to be imitated and followed. A saint was a hero of the faith and "an athlete of Christ." Such a hero could be described as "utterly pure in thought, helpful and discreet in speech,"

Alc.*Disp.puer*.11 (*PL* 101: 1142)

Iv.*Serm*.23 (*PL* 162:606)

Bald.*Tract*.15 (*PL* 204:546)

Rup.*Div.off*.9.6 (*CCCM* 7: 319)

Whitney (1932) 104

Petr.Dam.*Carm*.B.32.2 (Lokrantz 120)

Petr.Dam.*Opusc*.27.2 (*PL* 145: 506–7)

Rup.*Div.off*.9.6 (*CCCM* 7: 318)

Brd.Clr.*Laud.Virg*.3.14 (Leclercq-Rochais 4:45)

Rup.*Div.off*.7.5 (*CCCM* 7: 229)

Brd.Clr.*Sanct*.5.5 (Leclercq-Rochais 5:365)
Rich.S.Vict.*Serm.cent*.6 (*PL* 177:914)

Brd.Clr.*V.Mal*.pr. (Leclercq-Rochais 3:307)
Petr.Dam.*Carm*.B.32.2 (Lokrantz 120)
Petr.Dam.*Serm*.13 (*PL* 144: 568)

Her.*Episc.Leod*.12 (*MGH Scrip*.7:170)

Her.*V.Rem*.4 (*PL* 139:1154)
Rath.*Metr*.13 (*CCCM* 46:27); Petr.Ven.*Ep*.53 (Constable 170)

Rem.Aux.*Gen*.42.9 (*PL* 131:119)

Brd.Clr.*Sanct*.2.4 (Leclercq-Rochais 5:345)

Petr.Ven.*Jud*.2 (*PL* 189:521) Alan.Ins.*Haer*.1.73 (*PL* 210:374)

Ps.150:1(Vulg.) Brun.S.*Sym*.1 (*MGH Lib. lit*.2:546); Brun.S.*Sent*.6.1.5 (*PL* 165:1043)

Brd.Clr.*Cant*.13.5.6 (Leclercq-Rochais 1:72)

ap.Her.*V.Rem*.21 (*PL* 139:1166)

Ans.*Orat*.13 (Schmitt 3:51)

Ans.*Orat*.9 (Schmitt 3:32)

Ans.*Orat*.10 (Schmitt 3:38) Ans.*Orat*.12 (Schmitt 3:47–48)

Brd.Clr.*Sanct*.5.5 (Leclercq-Rochais 5:364)

Rem.Aux.*Cel.miss*. (*PL* 101:1259); Gisl.Crisp.*Jud*. (*PL* 159:1014)

dedicated wholeheartedly both to the active and to the contemplative life, and again as "angelic in his appearance, steady in his gait, holy in his activity, sound in his body, smart in his mind, circumspect in his work, outstanding in his genius, great in his counsel, catholic in his faith, patient in his hope, and universal in his love." The saint in his virtues was a reflection of the virtues of Christ, as the stars were a reflection of the light of the sun. "The perfection of the saints, the splendor of the church" worshiped Christ in his glory. Already now, even before the general resurrection, they shared his bliss in their spirits, as they would eventually share it in their bodies as well.

The close identification between Christ and his saints made it possible, and even mandatory, for believers who prayed to God to invoke the saints also, since the saints prayed for them in turn. The opening verse of the Latin version of the last of the psalms read: "Praise the Lord in his saints"; this was a favorite text about the saints. It meant that "if I discern something in the saints that is worthy of praise and admiration, I find, when I examine it in the clear light of truth, that though they appear to be admirable and praiseworthy, it is Another than they who is really so, and I praise God in his saints." On this basis it was possible, for example, to dedicate a monastery "to God and to his saints." Conversely, sin was an offense not only against God, but against all the saints, and the penitent sinner appealed to God and to the apostle Peter: "O God and thou, the greatest of his apostles, how great would be my misery if the immensity of the mercy of both of you did not prevail against it!" Similar prayers could be addressed to "both of you," meaning Christ and Paul, and to Christ and the apostle John together. Such invocation and veneration of the saints was "not for their benefit, but for ours," since "the saints have no need of our honors, nor do they gain anything as a result of our devotion." The potential threat of such a practice to the integrity of monotheistic worship, though not a prominent element in the hagiographic literature, did not go unnoticed. The cult of the martyrs did not imply that "the church offers sacrifices to the martyrs, but only to the one God, the God of the martyrs and our God. . . . The sacrifice is the body of Christ, which is not offered to them." The possible excesses of devotion to a particular saint

Brd.Clr.*Sanct*.1.1 (Leclercq-
Rochais 5:327)

Brd.Clr.*Cant*.13.5.6 (Leclercq-
Rochais 1:72)

Brd.Clr.*Sanct*.5.1 (Leclercq-
Rochais 5:361)

Petr.Dam.*Serm*.49 (*PL* 144:
778)

Od.Clun.*Hymn*.3.17–18 (*PL*
133:515)

Od.Clun.*Serm*.4 (*PL* 133:746)

Ans.*Orat*.15 (Schmitt 3:64)
Goff.Vind.*Serm*.11 (*PL* 157:
276)

Od.Clun.*Serm*.3 (*PL* 133:722)
Petr.Dam.*Perf.mon*.6 (Brezzi
234)

Ans.*Orat*.15 (Schmitt 3:62)
Od.Clun.*Serm*.3 (*PL* 133:722)

Petr.Dam.*Perf.mon*.3 (Brezzi
216)

Bern.Reich.*V.Udal*.4 (*PL* 142:
1187)

Petr.Ven.*Ep*.16 (Constable 23)

were also counteracted by the observation that the virtues pertaining to one saint were in fact less significant than the glory of all the saints together, and by the reminder that these virtues had their origin in God, not in the saints themselves.

It was nevertheless to individual and special saints that a cultus would come to be attached. While the development of such a cultus for this or that particular saint is not our business here, we do need to take note of the phenomenon as such. It was based on the belief that there were differences between one saint and another, differences not so much in the quantity of holiness or sainthood as in its quality. For example, Matthew, as the writer of the first Gospel on whom the other three evangelists were dependent, had a position of such preeminence that there was "no one after Christ to whom the holy universal church owes more than to him." Yet some nonbiblical saints, too, could stand out more than others. Martin of Tours, patron saint of France, was "a peer of the apostles," one to whom more churches were dedicated than to any other saint with the exceptions of Mary and Peter. As the founding father of Western monasticism, Benedict of Nursia was the object of special devotion, particularly among members of his order, who revered him as "the advocate of monks" and "the holy discoverer of our second regeneration." He had been chosen by God to be "among the supreme and elect fathers of the holy church," one whose *Rule* was inspired by the Holy Spirit. Not only those who had "vowed to live in accordance with the Rule" and "not only the rustics, but even city people" honored Benedict, "the new Joshua" who had led the people of God into the Promised Land. Other saints, too, had their special devotees, and often their cultus was confined to only one locality, at least initially.

No locality could be in the same class with Rome, because Rome was the seat of so many Christian martyrs and saints. Ulrich of Augsburg—the first, as far as is known, to become a saint through formal canonization, in 993 —had himself gone to Rome "in order to be able to commend himself more attentively to the prayers of [the martyrs] and of the other saints" there. The graves of martyrs became special shrines. What made the martyrs special was that they had been put to death for Christ as Christ had first been put to death for them, "the Lord for

Petr.Dam.*Serm*.39 (*PL* 144:712)

Rup.*Div.off*.7.5 (*CCCM* 7:229)

Brd.Clr.*Cant*.61.3.7 (Leclercq-Rochais 2:152)
Rich.S.Vict.*Serm.cent*.28 (*PL* 177:960–64)

Matt.5:10
Brd.Clr.*Sanct*.1.15 (Leclercq-Rochais 5:341)

Petr.Dam.*Serm*.65 (*PL* 144:881)
Guib.Nog.*Pign*.1.3 (*PL* 156:622)

Her.*Episc.Leod*.21 (*MGH Scrip*.7:173)

Petr.Dam.*Serm*.54 (*PL* 144:807)

Brd.Clr.*Sanct*.5.2 (Leclercq-Rochais 5:362)

Brd.Clr.*V.Mal*.pr. (Leclercq-Rochais 3:309)

Brd.Clr.*V.Mal*.16.37 (Leclercq-Rochais 3:343)

Brd.Clr.*V.Mal*.pr. (Leclercq-Rochais 3:308)

Joh.Abr.*Off.eccl*. (*PL* 147:59)

the servant and the servant for the Lord." Through the Eucharist all believers had communion with the body and blood of Christ and with his death, but the martyrs "have had communion with the death and the blood of Christ at much greater cost." Their martyrdom was "a glorious likeness of the death" of Christ, from whose wounds there came "the endurance of martyrdom [and] the utter confidence" that enabled the martyr to face death. The words of the Beatitudes, a lesson for All Saints' Day, "Blessed are those who are persecuted for righteousness' sake, for theirs is the kingdom of heaven," applied with unique force to the martyrs, though not exclusively to them. For while it was a great thing to die for Christ, it was no less glorious to live for him. Besides, the heretics and schismatics had also had their martyrs, as had to be pointed out even in a recital of the lives of orthodox bishops who had been martyred by the barbarians.

Because the definition of sainthood had to a considerable degree been shaped by the veneration of the martyrs, it was necessary to broaden the definition by reminding believers that "even we, who cannot die in defense of the faith, obtain the consummation of victory if we strive to live a life of saintly virtues, so that we may be directly translated to that kingdom whence they merited their martyrdom." In addition to the martyrs, apostles, and other saints venerated by the church, there was another category of saint, "but a hidden one. For there are saints who are still battling, still fighting," but the final outcome of whose lives was known only to God; they were saints according to the mystery of divine predestination. Even among one's personal acquaintances, therefore, it was possible to have had a genuine saint as one's "special friend." "In my own lifetime," Bernard of Clairvaux said of Malachy, the Irish saint, whose death he had attended, "I have had the privilege of seeing this man. I have been refreshed by his appearance and by his words, and I have taken delight in them as in all his riches." Yet the very recollection of this contemporary saint gave him the opportunity to contrast the golden age of the martyrs and saints with the present, when "the best man today is one who is not excessively evil."

The growing devotion to saints and martyrs did not meet with completely unanimous approval from theologians. Everyone continued to be opposed to "excesses"

in the commemoration of the saints and to "the superstitions of sacrilegious observances" such as auguries and
incantations, and everyone would have agreed that it
was a distortion when "what is beautiful is admired more
than what is holy is venerated" in the images of the saints;
but for most Christian thinkers the veneration of the
saints itself did not merit rebuke, but praise. Nevertheless,
there were some who "make it a cause of ridicule against
us that we baptize infants, that we pray for the dead, and
that we entreat the help of the saints." Thus Berengar of
Tours, best known for his views on the Eucharist, also refused to accept the authority of saints' lives as historical
arguments for a doctrine, especially of course for a eucharistic doctrine. Above all, it was Guibert of Nogent, the
critic of the superstitions and abuses connected with
the traffic in the relics of the saints, who also protested
against certain other aspects of their cultus. "If you pray
to someone whom you do not know to be a saint," he insisted, "you are thereby sinning." For loyalty to the truth
was an essential component of the true worship of God,
and anything that was said in praise of God but in contradiction of the truth was an act of dishonor to God. Sometimes the people gave their devotion to so-called saints
the outcome of whose life was evil or at best obscure.
When that happened, it was the responsibility of their
priests to set them straight.

As the hagiographic literature made amply evident,
there were many believers for whom the most important
events in the lives of the saints were the miracles that the
saints had performed. "Praise be to the true and living
God," a hymn said, "for the miracles of his glorious
saint." In fact, miracles seemed to be the touchstone for
distinguishing between who was a saint and who was
not; as Scripture said in speaking of the "saint [beatus],"
"He has done miraculous things [mirabilia] in his life."
But the very writers on the saints who quoted this passage
in connection with miracles could also use it to remind
their readers that one should not "seek signs" and that
"those who do miraculous things in their life are those
who live in Christ miraculously." What has been said
of the first of these writers could be said of much of the
literature, that "in one sentence Odo seems to repudiate
miracles as a witness to sanctity and in the next to appeal
to them." Elsewhere, too, he denounced "inquisitors of

Rath.*Prael.*1.4.7 (*PL* 136:152)

Brd.Clr.*Apol.*12.28 (Leclercq-Rochais 3:105)

Brd.Clr.*Cant.*66.4.9 (Leclercq-Rochais 2:183)

ap.Guit.Av.*Corp.*2 (*PL* 149:1447)

Guib.Nog.*Pign.*1.3 (*PL* 156:623)

Guib.Nog.*Pign.*3.1.1 (*PL* 156:649–50)

Guib.Nog.*Pign.*1.1 (*PL* 156:615)

Fulb.*Hymn.*6 (*PL* 141:343)

Ecclus.31:9(Vulg.)

Od.Clun.*V.Ger.*2.pr. (*PL* 133:670)

Bald.*Comm.fid.* (*PL* 204:606)

Sitwell (1958) 132

miracles, who judge every one of the holy fathers as powerful or powerless" on the basis of the number of miracles he had performed, and he contrasted "those who are always looking for miracles" with the apostle Paul, who did not think of them as very important. Yet he also argued that "if God, who did miraculous things for the fathers, even in our time deigns to work miracles in order to revive enthusiasm for downtrodden religion, . . . it ought not to seem incredible."

Such references to the "fathers" indicated that a fundamental issue in the consideration of miracles was the contrast between the early centuries of the church and the present, when miracles had become "unfruitful and superfluous." The apostles, as "new ministers" of a "new message," also had to perform "new signs." So great had been the miraculous power of those times that even those who were morally unworthy of acting as revealers of divine power had performed miracles. The promise of Christ to the apostles that they would do marvelous deeds had been fulfilled in them in a physical manner, as the church averred against the heretics, but during later periods of the church "the ones who drive out demons in the name of Christ are those who by his power drive away from their hearts the vices that the demons suggest." In a literal sense, therefore, that promise did not pertain to all believers in all times, but specifically "to those to whom it was granted in the beginning, while the church was being born, to perform miracles." By the age of Benedict, this power was waning, but this did not necessarily imply that "his power or his piety is any less than if he had abounded in miracles." It did not necessarily imply such a contrast, but one could also blame the decline of miracles on "the neglect of the service of God" and "the incorrigible malice" of the people. The prophecy that "before [Leviathan's] face there will be destitution" had long been taken to mean that before the coming of Antichrist the gift of performing miracles would be taken away from the church. This continued to serve as an explanation of the contrast. But a corollary of this line of thought was that whenever it was necessary to produce miracles again, God would grant the power to his church for a time. In his narrative of the miracles of a contemporary saint, therefore, the biographer could insist that "in the present, too, there are many signs occurring in our midst," no less than in the past.

Od.Clun.Serm.3 (PL 133:723)

Od.Clun.Serm.4 (PL 133:737)

Od.Clun.V.Ger.1.42 (PL 133:668)

Herb.Los.Serm.8 (Goulburn-Symonds 212)
Od.Clun.Occup.6.642 (Swoboda 138)

Petr.Dam.Serm.65 (PL 144:876)

Mark 16:17–18

Monet.Crem.Cathar.1.9 (Ricchini 98)

Rath.Serm.Asc.1.3 (CCCM 46:50)

Bald.Comm.fid. (PL 204:605)

Od.Clun.Serm.3 (PL 133:723)

Othl.V.Bonif.2.32 (MGH Scrip.Ger.50:215)

Job 41:22 (Vulg.)

Gr.M.Mor.34.3.7 (PL 76:721)

Od.Clun.Coll.1.25 (PL 133:536); Od.Clun.Serm.3 (PL 133:722); Od.Clun. V.Ger.2.10 (PL 133:676)

Od.Clun.V.Ger.3.12 (PL 133:698)

Brd.Clr.V.Mal.22.48 (Leclercq-Rochais 3:353)
Her.V.Land.1.3.17 (PL 139:1120–21); Petr.Ven.Mirac.1.25 (PL 189:898)

Even amid such a narrative, however, would come the reminder that "in my judgment his first and greatest miracle was he himself." The grace of converting men from evil to good was far superior to the power of performing miracles, even of raising the dead. The ambiguity of the word "power [virtus]" as simultaneously one of the technical terms for "miracle" and the term for "virtue" allowed a biographer to disparage "the people famous for miracles [virtutibus]" and then to praise his subject as "the exemplar of all virtues [virtutum]." One could also speak of "miracles" and "merits," sometimes citing the former as evidence for the presence of the latter, but sometimes pointing out that doing something great in "miracles" was not the same as being something great in "merits." As the Gospel noted, John the Baptist did not perform any overt miracles; neither, for that matter, did the Virgin Mary. Yet both of these saints merited the highest praise. Gregory the Great had reminded his readers that those who excelled in virtue were not in any way inferior to those who were noted for their miracles, and this reminder served as an explanation for the relative brevity of miracle accounts in certain saints' lives. In the words of the proverb, "the proof of those who are true members of the family of God is not miracles, but true love." While miracles supported the preaching of the gospel and thus supported faith, faith itself was the greatest miracle of all. A miracle without faith was empty; but even if the miracle should prove to be inauthentic, Guibert asserted, faith would obtain the object of its hope.

As Guibert's attitude indicated, a special class of miracles performed by saints consisted of those that were attributed to their relics. Although he was highly sensitive to the dangers of gullibility and superstition in the quest for miracles and extremely critical of the abuses to which the cult of relics was subject—tendencies that increased through the Crusades—even he felt obliged to admit that when relics were carried from one place to another, "the gracious Judge who comforts with his pity [in heaven] those whom he reproved [on earth] showed many miracles where they went." The arrival of a relic in a new site would be the occasion for miracles of healing and other signs to take place. Similarly, the construction of a basilica in which the bodies of saints were enshrined would set off a series of miracles that continued long after the building had been completed. The "translation of a

Brd.Clr.*V.Mal.*19.43 (Leclercq-Rochais 3:348)

Rich.S.Vict.*Ben.min.*44 (*PL* 196:33)

Petr.Dam.*Serm.*65 (*PL* 144:876)

Joh.Saler.*V.Od.Clun.*1.14 (*PL* 133:49)
Her.*Episc.Leod.*28 (*MGH Scrip.*7:176); Her.*V.Land.*1.1.5 (*PL* 139:1114–15)

Petr.Dam.*Serm.*24 (*PL* 144:639)
John 10:41
Herb.Los.*Serm.*10 (Goulburn-Symonds 290); Bald.*Comm.fid.* (*PL* 204:604)
Petr.Dam.*V.Rad.Dom.Lor.*11 (*PL* 144:1020)

Gr.M.*Dial.*1.12 (*PL* 77:213)
Petr.Dam.*V.Rom.*pr. (*FSI* 94:10); Od.Clun.*V.Ger.*pr. ·(*PL* 133:642); Fulb.*V.Aut.*4 (*PL* 141:359–60)

Othl.*Prov.*F–41 (Korfmacher 26)
Her.*Episc.Leod.*9 (*MGH Scrip.*7:169); Rich.S.Vict.*Ben.maj.*4.3 (*PL* 196:137)
Bald.*Comm.fid.* (*PL* 204:606); Gisl.Crisp.*V.Herl.* (Robinson 92)

Guib.Nog.*Pign.*3.5.2 (*PL* 156:663)

Guib.Nog.*Pign.* 1.1 (*PL* 156:613)
Guib.Nog.*Pign.*1.4 (*PL* 156:626–30)
Guib.Nog.*Gest.*1.5 (*PL* 156:695)

Guib.Nog.*Vita sua.*3.12 (*PL* 156:938)

Her.*V.Land.*2.5 (*PL* 139:123); Fulb.*V.Aut.*14 (*PL* 141:367)

Petr.Dam.*V.Rom.*28 (*FSI* 94:64)

Petr.Dam.*Serm*.2 (*PL* 144: 515)

Her.*V*.*Land*.1.2.7 (*PL* 139: 1115)
Bern.Reich.*Ep*.9 (*PL* 142: 1167)

Petr.Dam.*V*.*Rom*.70 (*FSI* 94: 113)

Her.*V*.*Rem*.21 (*PL* 139: 1168); Petr.Ven.*Serm*.4 (*PL* 189:1003)

Petr.Ven.*Serm*.4 (*PL* 189: 999–1000)

Brun.S.*Sacr.eccl.* (*PL* 165: 1100); Brun.S.*Sent*.1.7 (*PL* 165:898)

Od.Clun.*V*.*Ger*.4.9 (*PL* 133: 701)

Od.Clun.*V*.*Ger*.1.25 (*PL* 133: 657)

Od.Clun.*V*.*Ger*.3.3 (*PL* 133: 691)

holy body" was an occasion for joy, because through it "the things that happened a long time ago . . . somehow seem recent and new." Therefore the relics of the saints had to be protected against violation by hostile and pagan forces, for through the relics of his body the saint acted as "patron" of the place where they reposed. If the power of God had manifested itself in the life of a saint through the miracles that he executed, the relatively unimportant event that was his death did not mean a cessation of that power, which now worked through the remains of his body rather than through his personal presence. In fact, it was the purpose of such miracles done by the relics of a saint "to give testimony that he is alive with the Lord."

The power of the relic, then, was, strictly speaking, the power of the saint—or, to be even more correct, the power of God granted to the saint during his earthly life and still continuing now that his earthly life was over. In answer to the question, "What is the point of honoring lifeless corpses?" one could reply that it was to pay respect to the body, which had been the servant of God, and that it was an expression of faith in the resurrection of that body. The relics in the altar had as their counterpart "the relics in the heart," that is, the honoring of the memory of the saint by cherishing his words and imitating his example. When the issue arose whether miracles of healing were to be ascribed to relics or to the merits of Gerald of Aurillac, the saint who had employed the relics in performing the miracles, his biographer, Odo of Cluny, replied that, in his opinion, "the benefits of health are conferred through the holy relics in such a way as not to deny the cooperating virtue of Saint Gerald." That reply suggests that in many ways Odo's *Life of Saint Gerald* was not typical of the hagiographic genre: both its literary quality and the distinctiveness of its subject (who was a layman, albeit a celibate layman) set it apart. For that very reason, however, its treatment of relics may be taken as indicative of the common faith. As the count of his region, Gerald took many official journeys, but not without being accompanied by relics of the saints. He also collected relics for the churches under his guardianship, and so avidly that there was a surplus, which could be sold off. When he was about to die, Gerald "foresaw all that would be necessary for the future inhabitants [of the

Od.Clun.*V.Ger*.3.1 (*PL* 133: 690)

monastery he had established] and took care to provide for them in relics of the saints, in ornaments and vestments for the church, and in the produce of the fields," all of these being necessary for their welfare.

The zeal for collecting relics did not content itself with those of the saints, but extended itself to relics associated with Christ. One group of such relics consisted of those that had, in one way or another, been involved in the history of his life. Among these were the cords that had

Guib.Nog.*Vita sua*.2.1 (*PL* 156:896–97)
Guib.Nog.*Vita sua*.3.12 (*PL* 156:938–39)

bound him after his capture, as well as such items as the sponge that was lifted to his mouth on the cross. These were affirmed to be authentic even by critics whose general attitude to relics was somewhat skeptical. But when some overzealous preachers claimed that "within this vial

ap.Guib.Nog.*Pign*.1.2 (*PL* 156: 621)

is contained a portion of the bread that the Lord chewed with his very own teeth," the skepticism became much more pronounced. It became most vigorous when the relic of Christ being advertised was not merely something that had come into some sort of contact with him during his earthly life, but an actual portion of his body itself. Thus one community of monks maintained that they had one of the milk teeth of Christ, which he had shed in

Guib.Nog.*Pign*.3.1.2 (*PL* 156:651)

the course of growing up. There were others who had in their possession what they professed to be the foreskin of Christ after his circumcision or other relics of his very body, thus fulfilling the warning of "the great Origen" against those who "are not ashamed to write books even

Guib.Nog.*Pign*.2.1 (*PL* 156: 629)

about the Lord's circumcision."

When it came to such relics as these, the basic issue was no longer merely the question of credulity or even of superstition. For if there was somewhere an authentic relic of the historical body of Jesus Christ, this would constitute a threat to the belief that in the consecrated bread and wine of the Eucharist the church possessed the true (and historical) body of Christ. Hence "Christ could not have left behind any corporeal mementos for

Guth (1970) 94

us." Or, to put it the other way, if Christ had established the mystery of the Lord's Supper as a means of providing the consolation of his presence to the church, such relics

Guib.Nog.*Pign*.3.2.2 (*PL* 156: 656–57)

had to be regarded as "superfluous portions of his body." For what was the need of these additional relics when one had in the body and blood of the Eucharist the true presence of Christ himself? The vision of the seer of the

Guib.Nog.*Pign*.2.1 (*PL* 156: 630–31)

Apocalypse, who "saw under the altar the souls of those

Rev.6:9

Petr.Dam.*Serm*.72 (*PL* 144: 908)

who had been slain for the word of God and for the witness they had borne," could be used to associate the relics of the bodies of the saints with the body of the Lord on the altar. But there was also a tradition, repeated by various authors, according to which relics of the bodies of saints had sometimes been in rivalry with the body of Christ in the Eucharist. In a church where miracles had repeatedly taken place, the relics of the patron saint had been placed on the altar, with the result that "suddenly the miracles ceased." The explanation of this phenomenon came in the words of the patron saint, that "my relics are lying on the altar of the Lord, where the majesty of the divine mystery

Od.Clun.*Coll*.2.28 (*PL* 133: 573); Gez.*Corp*.58 (*PL* 137: 402)

should be celebrated all by itself." When the offending relics were removed, "the miracles of faith resumed." Apparently the presence in the Eucharist was "the principal reality," with which relics, even and especially so-

Guib.Nog.*Pign*.2.1.1 (*PL* 156: 630)

called relics of the body of Christ, could not be allowed to compete. But this raised again the question that had been asked, but not answered, in the ninth century, whether the body present on the altar for the sacrifice of the Mass and present for the communicant in the liturgy was substantially identical with the body born of the Virgin Mary and sacrificed on the cross. To this question, inevitably, theology had to return.

The Real Presence

Although the communion of saints and communion with the saints, above all with the Virgin Mary, held a prominent place in the developing views of the communication of grace during the eleventh and twelfth centuries, the special sense of the words "communion" and "communicate" came from their application to the Eucharist, through which, as through the other sacraments, grace was believed to be communicated. "To communicate"

Petr.Dam.*Opusc*.34.pr. (*PL* 145:573)

meant to receive the Eucharist. There were some who argued that Scripture did not use the term "communion" for the Eucharist, only the term "communication," but

Brngr.Tr.*Coen*.8 (Beekenkamp 10)
Bald.*Sacr.alt*.2.4.3 (*SC* 94: 358); Herb.Los.*Serm*.11 (Goulburn-Symonds 304)
John 6:54
Brd.Clr.*Ps*.90.3.3 (Leclercq-Rochais 4:394)
ap.Hug.Am.*Haer*.1.14 (*PL* 192:1271); Hug.Sper.ap.Vac.*Err*.20.7 (*ST* 115:539)

the general usage of the church supported the legitimacy of both terms. The words of Scripture about eating the flesh of Christ and drinking his blood, according to Bernard of Clairvaux, referred to "communicating with his sufferings" through the Eucharist.

Except for certain heretics, there was general agreement

that the proper celebration of the Eucharist and the proper understanding of it lay at the center of the Christian faith. Among all the actions of the church, the Mass was "the supreme sacrament." Nothing else, not even the episcopacy or the sacrament of chrism, could be compared with the body and blood of the Savior in importance. Although certain sacramental actions, such as ordination and confirmation, were reserved to the bishop, nevertheless "that sacrament which is the most excellent of them all, namely, the body and blood of Christ, is consecrated daily by priests as well as by bishops, and it is no holier when done by the latter than when done by the former." "The holy mystery of the Lord's body" was the greatest of all the benefits granted to mankind, "because the entire salvation of the world consists in this mystery." To be sure, it was only in this life that the Sacrament was needed, but it was needed desperately. There were, accordingly, three necessities in life: the Trinity (including the incarnation), baptism, and the Eucharist; for "the sum total of our faith is this, to know Christ in the Father, Christ in the flesh, and Christ in the participation of the altar." Consequently, a correct interpretation of the Eucharist was essential to the integrity of the Christian faith itself, and without such an interpretation "the entire discipline of the Christian confession will perish."

That ominous warning about what was at stake in the doctrine of the Eucharist came in response to the reopening in the eleventh century of the controversy about the nature of the eucharistic presence that had originally erupted in the ninth century. In the interim the two principal figures in the discussion during the Carolingian era had been treated in two quite different ways by subsequent generations of theologians. Odo of Cluny, who was born about two decades after the death of Radbertus, drew extensively from his treatise on the Eucharist in his own exposition of the meaning of the Sacrament, concluding with the observation that "if anyone reads these things, even though he may be a smatterer, he will learn much." Odo's younger contemporary, Ratherius of Verona, incorporated "some excerpts from the works of a certain Paschasius Radbertus on this subject" (apparently the whole of Radbertus's treatise) into his writings. Another tenth-century theologian, Gezo of Tortona, also took over "almost the entire book of Paschasius," making Radbertus's

Rup.*Div.off.*1.17 (*CCCM* 7: 15); Rich.S.Vict.*Serm.cent.* 94 (*PL* 177:1193)

Petr.Dam.*Opusc.*26.1 (*PL* 145:500)

Bern.Reich.*Miss.off.*2 (*PL* 142:1061)

Od.Clun.*Coll.*2.28 (*PL* 133: 572)

Brd.Clr.*Cant.*33.2.3 (Leclercq-Rochais 1:235)

Fulb.*Ep.*5 (*PL* 141:197)

Bald.*Sacr.alt.*2.3.2 (*SC* 93: 270)

Dur.Tr.*Corp.*1.1 (*PL* 149: 1377)

Od.Clun.*Coll.*2.30–32 (*PL* 133:575–77)

Rath.*Dial.conf.*42 (*PL* 136: 444)

Gez.*Corp.*pr. (*PL* 137:373)

Gez.*Corp*.14–35 (*PL* 137: 387)

Her.*Corp*. (*PL* 139:187)

Dur.Tr.*Corp*.4.10 (*PL* 149: 1389)
Rich.S.Vict.*Serm.cent*.94 (*PL* 177:1193); Wm.Mon.*Henr. Mon*.6 (Manselli 53)

Sig.*Vir.ill*.95 (*PL* 160:569)

Her.*Corp*.1 (*PL* 139:179)

Dur.Tr.*Corp*.9.33 (*PL* 149: 1423)
Brngr.Tr.*Ep*.7 (Sudendorf 211); Brngr.Tr.*Coen*.7 (Beekenkamp 9)

Lanf.*Corp*.4 (*PL* 150:413)

Goz.*Ep.Val*.34 (*PL* 143:902)
Dur.Tr.*Corp*.5.12; 1.1 (*PL* 149:1393; 1378)

Her.*Corp*.1 (*PL* 139:179)

Adel.*Ep.Brngr*. (Heurtevent 288)

Heurtevent (1912) 288
Gez.*Corp*.8 (*PL* 137:383);
Hug.Am.*Haer*.2.10 (*PL* 192: 1281); Petr.Ven.*Petrob*.169 (*CCCM* 10:101)

Brngr.Tr.*Apol*. (Matronola 120)
Brnld.*Brngr*.2 (*PL* 148:1454)
Hug.Met.*Ep*.4 (*PL* 188:1274)

Goz.*Ep.Val*.32 (*PL* 143:901)
Guit.Av.*Corp*.1 (*PL* 149: 1431–32)

ideas his own. And yet another theologian of the tenth century, in his treatise on the Eucharist (if indeed it is actually his), also came to the support of Radbertus. Radbertus came to be celebrated as "the most diligent of investigators of the divine Sacrament and its catholic expositor," and he went on being cited as a standard authority on eucharistic theory and practice. The name of Ratramnus, on the other hand, had largely passed into oblivion. He was said to have "written a book for King Charles" against Radbertus; but when the controversy broke out again, it seems that his book, which was accused as the source of false doctrine about the Eucharist, was being attributed to John Scotus Erigena by its champions as well as by its detractors, who eventually had it condemned and destroyed at a synod held in Vercelli in 1050.

The occasion for the synod and for the condemnation of Ratramnus under the name of Erigena was the doctrine of the Eucharist set forth by Berengar of Tours. His opponents claimed that everything had been peaceful until he and his adherents came along with their theories, these "inciters of modern heresy." As one of these opponents summarized the situation, there were "some who say that what is eaten from the altar is the same as what was born of the Virgin, while others deny this and say that it is something else." "Using the language of [your opponents]," a contemporary wrote to Berengar, "you are accused of saying that [the Eucharist] is not the true body of Christ nor his true blood, but some sort of figure and likeness." As this statement indicates, "for his contemporaries the question comes down to an expression of doubt about Berengar with regard to the real presence . . . , not transubstantiation." According to the defenders of the real presence, Scripture left "no room for ambiguity on the reality of the flesh and blood" in the Eucharist. According to Berengar, however, the alternatives were false, since "whatever is said to be the case spiritually is truly the case." Nor was he alone in his espousal of this position; he had "his supporters," in fact "many of them," so that "the whole church everywhere has been infected . . . with this poisonous leaven," even though there was great variety among them.

We cannot (and need not) settle the chronological, psychological, and political problems still remaining in the historical understanding of the controversy. Berengar himself complained that his adversaries had been harassing him "for a hundred years," and they claimed, near the end of his life, that he had been condemned by various councils and synods (fourteen in all) "for almost forty years." Among his opponents, the ones mentioned most often were "Lanfranc, Guitmond, and Alger," although modern scholars regard it as "very doubtful" that the last of these was writing against Berengar. It has largely been from quotations supplied by his opponents that later scholars have been obliged to reconstruct Berengar's thought; for he himself consigned his books to the flames, and when, some time later, he wrote another treatise setting forth his views, Lanfranc destroyed that in turn. But in the process of replying to it, Lanfranc excerpted it so copiously that the main lines of Berengar's doctrine do become evident; Lanfranc also reproduced other documents from the controversy, notably Berengar's recantation of 1059 at Rome (subsequently repudiated by Berengar), which was incorporated into other treatises against Berengar as well. And then, after "remaining hidden from the sight of mankind for seven centuries," Berengar's book *On the Holy Supper* was discovered by Gotthold Ephraim Lessing in 1770 and eventually published in 1834. There are also letters and, if one accepts it as authentic, an apologia written for the Roman council of 1079.

In his recantation of 1059 Berengar was coerced into affirming that "the bread and wine which are placed on the altar are, after the consecration, not only a sacrament, but the true body and blood of our Lord Jesus Christ." Just what it meant for something to be "only a sacrament," or a sacrament at all, was still quite unclear from the Augustinian tradition; and the twelfth century was to be the time when the definition, as well as the number, of the sacraments achieved final specification. Whatever it was that made matrimony a sacrament and the Lord's Prayer not a sacrament, there apparently had to be even more to the Eucharist than this; it had to be "not only a sacrament, but the true body and blood of our Lord Jesus Christ." The "more" in the Eucharist was identified in various ways. Sometimes theologians had followed Augustine in distinguishing between the sacrament and its "power [virtus]," but this did not permit an adequate

Brngr.Tr.*Apol.* (Matronola 117)

Brnld.*Brngr*.9 (*PL* 148:1456–57)
Petr.Ven.*Petrob*.153 (*CCCM* 10:87–88)
Häring (1958) 51

Lanf.*Corp*.1 (*PL* 150:409)

Lanf.*Corp*.5 (*PL* 150:415)

Brngr.Tr.*fr*.ap.Lanf.*Corp*.2 (*PL* 150:410–11)
ap.Brnld.*Brngr*.5 (*PL* 148:1455); ap.Alg.*Sacr*.1.19 (*PL* 180:796–97); ap.Iv.*Decr*.2.10 (*PL* 161:160–61)
Beekenkamp (1941) 12

Brngr.Tr.*fr*.ap.Lanf.*Corp*.2 (*PL* 150:411)

See vol.1:304–6

Aug.*Ev.Joh*.26.11 (*CCSL* 36:265)

Rab.*Inst.cler*.31 (Knoepfler 62)

distinction between the Eucharist and the other "sacraments," all of which were, as Cyprian had already said, "spiritually abundant in power [in virtute]." A potentially more precise Augustinian formula for specifying the "more" was the distinction between the sacrament and "the matter of the sacrament [res sacramenti]," as when Bernard of Clairvaux described someone who "presumed to say that in the Eucharist there is only the sacrament and not the matter of the sacrament, that is, only sanctification and not the reality of the body."

The "reality of the body" of Christ offered up as a sacrifice in the Mass set it apart from all the other sacraments. All the sacraments, including the Eucharist, were means of grace to the recipient; the Eucharist alone was not only a sacrament, but also a sacrifice. "Although this sacrifice is also a sacrament," explained one prominent canonist, "it is evident that it differs in many ways from the remaining sacraments, for it alone . . . is repeated every day." Berengar's opponents charged him with "teaching otherwise than the catholic faith holds concerning the body and blood of the Lord, which is sacrificed daily throughout the world," but they recognized that he, too, affirmed that Christ "is immolated every day in the Sacrament." Indeed, the sacrificial understanding of the Mass was so dominant over all other aspects of the Eucharist that a theologian of the late twelfth century felt obliged to say: "This sacrifice was instituted by the Lord not only to be offered, but also to be eaten." Later he combined the sacrifice of Christ, the eating of Christ, and the imitation of Christ as the themes of the eucharistic celebration. Because the Mass was "the new and true sacrifice that the holy church offers," what it offered was "not only bread and wine." For if it were, "if it consisted only in the sacrament, that is, in bread and wine that has been consecrated but not changed, there would be no reason why the sacrifice of the New Testament would be superior to that of the Old Testament."

The superiority of the Eucharist, as the distinctive sacrifice of the New Testament, to the entire system of Levitical sacrifices in the Old Testament served to reinforce the idea that there was not only a new ritual, but a new reality, in Christian worship. The Eucharist was "the end of the Old Testament and the beginning of the New Testament." There was still a priesthood, as there had

Cypr.*Domin.orat*.9 (*CSEL* 3: 272)

Aug.*Ev.Joh*.26.18 (*CCSL* 36: 268)

Brd.Clr.*V.Mal*.26.57 (Leclercq-Rochais 3:360–61)

Deusd.*Inv.sym*.2.7 (*MGH Lib.lit*.2:325)

Adel.*Ep.Brngr*. (Heurtevent 288)

Brngr.Tr.*Opusc*.ap.Lanf.*Corp*. 15 (*PL* 150:425)

Bald.*Sacr.alt*.2.1.2 (*SC* 93: 138)

Bald.*Sacr.alt*.2.2.2 (*SC* 93: 226)

Rup.*Div.off*.2.2 (*CCCM* 7: 33–34)

Alg.*Sacr*.2.3 (*PL* 180:815)

Brun.S.*Sent*.4.9 (*PL* 165:1001)

Rab.*Inst.cler*.2.1 (Knoepfler 79)

Isid.Sev.*Orig*.7.12.17 (*PL* 82:291–92)

Petr.Dam.*Opusc*.17.3 (*PL* 145: 384)

Bern.Reich.*Miss.off*.5 (*PL* 142:1068)

Rem.Aux.*Matt*.8 (*PL* 131: 909)

Bald.*Sacr.alt*.2.4.2 (*SC* 94:338)

See pp. 136–37 above

Gen.14:18(Vulg.)

Sent.Flor.62 (Ostlender 29)
Rab.*Inst.cler*.1.31 (Knoepfler 61)

Montclos (1971) 335

Brngr.Tr.*Coen*.29 (Beekenkamp 62)

Bald.*Sacr.alt*.3.1.pr. (*SC* 94: 416)

Petr.Lomb.*Serm*.18 (*PL* 171: 511)

Ps.66:15

Adalg.*Admon*.9 (*PL* 134:925)

Ps.27:6

Rup.*Div.off*.2.2 (*CCCM* 7:32–33)

been in the Old Testament, and therefore still a sacrifice for which the priest had primary responsibility. The responsibility implied that "the priest [sacerdos], whose task it is to give over that which is sacred [sacrum dare], that is, to offer the sacrifice to God," ought to pay attention to his own relation to God. The moral and cultic imperatives addressed to the Old Testament priest now pertained to the priest who offered the sacrifice of the Mass. The true "holy of holies" was "the sacrifice of the body and blood of our Lord Jesus Christ" on the cross, in which the sacrifice of the Mass participated directly but the sacrifices of the Old Testament had participated only by anticipation. The Old Testament believers who shared in the manna and the New Testament believers who shared in the Eucharist were the same in what they received with their hearts, but they were different in what they received with their mouths. Among all the "types" of the Eucharist set forth in the Old Testament, it was the offering of Melchizedek, who "offered bread and wine" to Abraham, and thus was "the first who celebrated this Sacrament," that helped to fix the content of the eucharistic sacrifice. Even though "Berengar and his disciples were able to make use of the argument from the comparison between Christ and Melchizedek" as proof that bread and wine remained in the sacrifice also after the consecration, since that was what the Book of Genesis called them, most interpreters regarded Melchizedek's sacrifice as a "prefiguration" of the New Testament sacrifice of the body and blood of Christ in the Eucharist.

Perhaps the most influential such prefiguration, however, was provided by the references in the cultic portions of the Old Testament to sacrifice, burnt offering, and the like. Although some of these references pertained in particular to the total offering of oneself to God, specifically as this was characteristic of the monks, the sacrificial interpretation of the Mass meant that the words of the Psalmist, "I will offer in his tabernacle sacrifices of joy," were fulfilled when "the holy catholic church offers the true Logos of God, the true Son of God, to her Creator, and at the same time offers bread and wine." Those closing words suggest that the relation of the "body" sacrificed in the Mass to the elements of bread and wine and its relation to the body sacrificed on the cross continued to be the two chief problems. The sacrifices that had preceded Calvary were an anticipation of it, but were the sacrifices that followed Calvary an extension of it, a repetition of it, or simply a reminder of it?

The offering of the Mass on behalf of the faithful departed, although rejected by certain heretics, appeared to assume that "the precious blood that was shed for many for the forgiveness of sins avails not only for the salvation of the living, but also for the salvation of the dead." Therefore the identity between the sacrifice of the Mass and the sacrifice of Calvary could seem to be obvious, since "our altar is the altar of Christ, on which we celebrate his sacrifice, in fact, on which we offer him up to the Father in the Sacrament of his very own body and blood." For if the daily sacrifice of the church were other than the sacrifice offered once and for all on the cross, "it would not be true but superfluous," since the only sacrifice that truly availed was that offered on Calvary and an effective sacrifice in the Mass had to be identical with it. The two sacrifices were one sacrifice, and both were the body "taken from the Virgin." It was helpful, but not really correct, to relate the incarnation and the atonement to each other by saying that "as he is being sacrificed daily, so long as we announce his death, thus also he appears to be born, so long as we faithfully re-present his nativity." It was correct, but not particularly helpful, to observe that on the cross Christ had been sacrificed by unbelievers, while in the Mass he was sacrificed "by believers with piety." Or, because of the chronology of the Passion story in the Gospels, it was likewise correct to note that Christ had been "sacrificed for the life of the world first in the Sacrament" and then in the crucifixion, when "the Son of God ascended the gallows of the cross and offered himself, as both priest and victim, to his Father as a sacrifice." Yet there remained the statement of the New Testament that the sacrifice of the cross had been "once and for all." From it there appeared to follow the thesis that the crucifixion of Christ could not be repeated "as a punishment," but only as a re-presentation of the mystery. The notion of "sacrifice," therefore, while it was the basis for a definition of the real presence, could not of itself yield such a definition, which had to come from a consideration of the meaning of the word "body" as it was applied to the Eucharist and to the historical Christ.

Consideration of that issue was complex because the

ap.Petr.Ven.*Petrob*.225; 229 (*CCCM* 10:134; 136)

Rem.Aux.*Cel.miss.* (*PL* 101: 1263)

Petr.Ab.*Serm*.10 (*PL* 178:449)

Alg.*Sacr*.1.16 (*PL* 180:786)

Wm.S.Th.*Sacr.alt*.10 (*PL* 180: 358); Petr.Ven.*Petrob*.167 (*CCCM* 10:99–100)

Lanf.*Corp*.15 (*PL* 150:425)

I Cor.11:26
Brd.Clr.*Vig.Nat*.6.6 (Leclercq-Rochais 4:239)

Brun.S.*Ex*.29 (*PL* 164:357)

Dur.Tr.*Corp*.3.3 (*PL* 149: 1381)

Heb.9:28; 1 Pet.3:18

Guib.Nog.*Pign*.2.6.1 (*PL* 156: 646–48); Petr.Ven.*Petrob*.200 (*CCCM* 10:118)

Adel.*Ep.Brngr.* (Heurtevent 298); *Sent.Flor.*66 (Ostlender 30)

term "body of Christ" in Scripture and in patristic usage had "multiple" meanings. The fathers had spoken "in various, though not in contradictory ways on this matter. . . . Therefore, since the body of Christ in human form, the body of Christ in the Sacrament, and the body of Christ in the church are three different ways [of using the term "body of Christ"], those who are unable to distinguish among these ways in the Holy Scriptures fall into great

Alg.*Sacr.*1.17 (*PL* 180:790–91); Wm.S.Th.*Sacr.alt.*12 (*PL* 180:361–62)

confusion, so that what is said about one 'body of Christ' is taken to refer to another." The problem of distinguishing between the latter two of these three ways of using the term lay in the language of Scripture itself, as when the apostle Paul wrote: "The bread which we break, is it not the communion of the body of Christ? For we being many are one bread and one body, for we are all partakers

1 Cor.10:16–17

of that one bread." Christian exegetes of all periods in the history of the church, including the modern period, have had difficulty deciding whether "the communion of [or: participation in] the body of Christ" referred to the Eucharist or to the church or to both. Even when he was distinguishing between the sacrament and the "matter of the sacrament," Augustine defined the latter as "the unity of the body and blood of Christ," which he appeared to equate with "the society of his body and members, which is the holy church in those who have been pre-

Aug.*Ev.Joh.*26.15 (*CCSL* 36:267)

destined and called." The presence of this difficulty in the writings of the fathers continued to be a source of perplexity in the controversy over the Eucharist during the eleventh and twelfth centuries.

A far deeper perplexity in this controversy, however, was the relation between the first and the second of the meanings of "body of Christ," that is, "the body of Christ in human form" and "the body of Christ in the Sacra-

Alg.*Sacr.*1.17 (*PL* 180:791)

ment." Even before the controversy had broken out, the line of thought that had come down from Radbertus and that relied on his ideas was urging that when, in the distribution of communion, the recipient heard the phrase "the body of Christ," he was "to consider what is being spoken of, and about whom, and to whom. What is being spoken of? The same body of the Lord. If you ask about which Lord it is being spoken, why, it is about the one who, in the flesh that he assumed for you, the flesh in which he suffered much for you, was crucified, died, buried and raised, the flesh that he elevated to heaven—

Rath.*Dial.conf.*15 (*PL* 136: 403)

Rup.*Div.off.*2.2 (*CCCM* 7: 34–35); Herb.Los.*Serm.*7 (Goulburn-Symonds 180–88)

Robt.Pull.*Sent.*8.5 (*PL* 186: 965)

Her.*Corp.*1 (*PL* 139:179)

Brngr.Tr.*Ep.Adel.* (Montclos 533)

Wm.S.Th.*Sacr.alt.*1 (*PL* 180: 345–46)

2 Cor.5:16

Ambr.*Spir.*3.17.122 (*CSEL* 79:202)

Brngr.Tr. *Coen.*21; 37; 41; 42 (Beekenkamp 44; 110; 137–38; 143)

Brngr.Tr.*Coen.*27 (Beekenkamp 58)

Acts 3:21

Brngr.Tr.*Coen.*47; 37 (Beekenkamp 163; 108)

Brngr.Tr.*Coen.*21; 39 (Beekenkamp 44; 119)

Brngr.Tr.*Coen.*47; 21; 9 (Beekenkamp 164; 43; 13–14)

who in that flesh now enters you, to whom this is being spoken." The solution of the perplexity that eventually won out in the debate was the insistence that "there are not two bodies, that which is received from the altar and that which was received from the womb of the Virgin, . . . [but] one and the same body" in both. It was "no other flesh than that which he took to heaven for us, no other blood . . . than that which flowed from his side." This identification of the human, physical body of Christ with the body in the Eucharist was the issue in the debate.

It was this identification that Berengar attacked. In one of his earliest public statements he argued that "the fathers proclaim that the body and blood are one thing and the sacraments of the body and blood are something else." In his major work, the treatise *On the Holy Supper,* his campaign against the identification of the bread and wine in the Eucharist with the historical body and blood of Christ became central. His locus classicus, which was something of an embarrassment to his adversaries, was the word of the apostle: "Even if we have known Christ according to the flesh, henceforth we know him no more." The passage was combined several times with the statement of Ambrose that the resurrected and ascended Christ could not be wounded any more and therefore was immune to any change. The words of the apostle stood as a refutation "of anyone who says: 'The empirical [sensualis] bread consecrated on the altar is, after the consecration, truly the body of Christ that exists above.'" Because the heavens had received the historical body of Christ "until the time of the restitution of all things," what the priest held in his hand and the communicant chewed with his teeth in the Eucharist could not be that body; for even if Christ had been known according to the flesh, he would be known so no longer. These words meant, furthermore, that it was an error to suppose that "a portion of the flesh [of Christ] that never existed before the celebration of the Lord's Table begins to exist in the celebration of the Lord's Table, and that it comes from the body of Christ, of which no part at all can be denied to have been in existence already for a thousand years and more." To "know Christ according to the flesh" was to know him as subject to time and change; but the exalted Christ was no longer temporal or mutable, nor could his body come into being anymore.

See pp. 219–20 below

Ambr.*Myst*.9.53 (*SC* 25–II: 186–88)

Guit.Av.*Corp*.3 (*PL* 149:1473)

Hug.Bret.*Corp*. (*PL* 142:1328)

Dur.Tr.*Corp*.4.7; 4.9 (*PL* 149: 1385; 1387)

Lanf.*Corp*.18 (*PL* 150:431)

Brngr.Tr.*Coen*.36 (Beekenkamp 99–105)

Petr.Dam.*Serm*.45 (*PL* 144: 743)

Brun.S.*Sent*.4.9 (*PL* 165:1006)

Acts 3:21

Brngr.Tr.*Opusc*.ap.Lanf. *Corp*.17 (*PL* 150:426); Brngr.Tr.*Coen*.31 (Beekenkamp 77) Aug.*Fid.et symb*.6.13 (*PL* 40: 188)

Rup.*Div.off*.9.8 (*CCCM* 7:325)

Although Berengar sought to reinforce his argument with the quotation from Ambrose about the impassibility of the exalted body of Christ, his opponents laid claim to Ambrose as the champion of their insistence upon the identity of the historical and the sacramental body. "That which we confect," Ambrose said, arguing for the parallel between the virgin birth and the Eucharist, "is the body born of the Virgin." After quoting these words against Berengar, one of his critics asked: "What, I ask, are you looking for that would be said better or more clearly? If the sacraments on the altar were merely a shadow and a figure of the Lord's body, what would be happening here that goes beyond nature?" The virgin birth went beyond nature, and so did the confecting of the body of Christ in the Sacrament; for the body in both was the same. Ambrose was saying that the eucharistic body was the body that was "born, not one that is similar to something." The quotation from Ambrose became a commonplace in the conflict with Berengar. When Lanfranc in his polemic cited it as a refutation of Berengar, Berengar replied by attempting to prove from the context that Ambrose did not support Lanfranc's position but was, despite the passage in question, making a distinction between the body confected in the Sacrament and the body born of the Virgin. But the identification of the two was already a given for most theologians. "What the catholic faith holds, what the holy church faithfully teaches" was that "the very body of Christ that the blessed Virgin bore . . . this very body, I say without any doubt, and no other, we now receive from the holy altar." For if the bread was changed into the flesh of Christ, it had to be into "that which he received from his Virgin Mother, since he does not have any other."

Yet the flesh and body that Christ had received at birth from his Virgin Mother was the flesh and body that he took into heaven at his ascension. There it would remain "until the times of the restitution of all things," which Berengar took to mean that it would be eternally immortal, incorruptible, and "incapable of being summoned down." Although theologians repeated the warning of Augustine that speculative inquiry into the state of the ascended body of Christ at the right hand of God in heaven was useless, some answer to this argument seemed necessary; for if Christ could not come down from heaven,

Guit.Av.*Corp*.2 (*PL* 149:1466)
Aug.*Fid.et symb*.7.14 (*PL* 40:188)

Rup.*Div.off*.9.8 (*CCCM* 7:323)

Gez.*Corp*.70 (*PL* 137:406);
Rem.Aux.*Cel.miss*. (*PL* 101:1260)

Hug.Met.*Ep*.4 (*PL* 188:1274)

Alg.*Sacr*.1.14 (*PL* 180:781–82); Wm.S.Th.*Sacr.alt*.1 (*PL* 180:347); Hug.S.Vict.*Sacr*.2.8.11 (*PL* 176:469)

Brngr.Tr.*Coen*.37 (Beekenkamp 110)

Guit.Av.*Corp*.2 (*PL* 149:1466)
Rem.Aux.*Cel.miss*. (*PL* 101:1260); Gez.*Corp*.70 (*PL* 137:406); Hug.Am.*Haer*.1.14 (*PL* 192:1272)

Petr.Dam.*Opusc*.11.8 (*PL* 145:238); Alex.III.*Sent.Rol.* (Gietl 222)

Guit.Av.*Corp*.2 (*PL* 149:1434)

Sent.Flor.70 (Ostlender 31)
Gisl.Por.*Ep.Matt*. (*PL* 188:1256)

then he was not reigning there, but was a prisoner. Besides, as Augustine had added, "the right hand of God" did not refer to a physical location, but to a judicial authority and power. Because the human nature of Christ, and thus his physical body, was inseparable from his divine nature through the hypostatic union, "the divinity of the Logos of God, which is one and which fills all things and which is total everywhere, brings it about . . . that there is one body of Christ, identical with that which he received from the Virgin's womb." Even in his days on earth, the body of Christ had not been subject to the limitations of space, but had, through its union with his divinity, transcended the laws of nature; so it did also by being present in the Sacrament. After the ascension, "the flesh of Christ, which has been exalted by God above all creatures . . . is present everywhere, wherever it pleases, through the omnipotence that has been given to it in heaven and on earth." Therefore, if Christ willed it, his body could be present, completely and truly, in heaven and in the Sacrament at one and the same time.

The reference to the presence of the body "completely" in both was also an answer to another of Berengar's objections to the identification of the sacramental with the human—and now heavenly—body of Christ. "A portion of the flesh of Christ," he urged, "cannot be present on the altar . . . unless the body of Christ in heaven is cut up and a particle that has been cut off from it is sent down to the altar." Rejecting such an understanding of what was implied by the ascension, Berengar's critics refused to "speak of Christ's being sacrificed or eaten on earth in such a way that he would meanwhile have to desert heaven, for he is totally in heaven even while his body is being truly eaten on earth." The reason was that "there are not many bodies of Christ . . . but only one body of Christ" at the right hand of God and on the altar. It was likewise a single body that was received by communicants wherever they were in the world. Therefore "the entire host is the body of Christ, but in such a way that each separate particle is the entire body of Christ." It was "the entire body of Christ" that was received by the communicant, so that even if he received only the bread or only the cup he received the entire Christ. This was true even though the body and the blood in the Eucharist were a way of showing that Christ had redeemed both

Brun.Col.*1.Cor*.10 (*PL* 153:176)
Guit.Av.*Corp*.1 (*PL* 149:1434)

Herm.Mag.*Epit*.29 (*PL* 178:1741)
Guib.Nog.*Pign*.2.2.2 (*PL* 156:633)

Ps.Petr.Dam.*Exp.can.miss*.4 (*PL* 145:882)

Macdonald (1930) 173

Guit.Av.*Conf*. (*PL* 149:1500)

Guit.Av.*Conf*. (*PL* 149:1497);
Ans.L.*Sent.div.pag*.1 (Bliemetzrieder 4)

John 6:51,54

Brd.Clr.*Ps*.90.3.3 (Leclercq-Rochais 4:394)

Bald.*Sacr.alt*.2.3.2 (*SC* 93:258)

the flesh and the soul, for "he who receives only the blood or only the body, receives everything." What he received was, ultimately, not a thing, not bits of the body of Christ, but a person, "the true body of Christ, indeed Christ himself," complete in his humanity and in his divinity. In sum, "where there is consecrated bread, there is the entire Christ in the entire species of the bread."

Anyone who identified the eucharistic body with the historical body of Jesus Christ had to specify how that body was present in the Sacrament. When Guitmond of Aversa, whose "contribution to the development of eucharistic doctrine . . . far outweighs those of the other" opponents of Berengar, confessed the "total and complete" presence of that body even in "the most minute" fragment of the consecrated bread, he did so in the context of a statement of faith in which he also spoke of the "total" presence of God the Creator even in "the most minute" of his creatures. The difference between the two kinds of presence, however, was that the creature in which God the Creator was declared to be present was not said to be, or to have been changed into, God himself, while the eucharistic bread in which the body of Christ was affirmed to be present was thought to have undergone a transformation. Another difference, in the judgment of many, was that the presence of the body and blood of Christ in the Eucharist was conditional on the faith of the recipient in that presence, by contrast with the presence of the Creator in the creature, which was an objective reality, regardless of whether the creature had faith or not.

The source of this latter view of the sacramental presence was the eucharistic interpretation of the words of Jesus: "I am the living bread which came down from heaven. . . . He who eats my flesh and drinks my blood has eternal life, and I will raise him up at the last day." Commenting on these words, Bernard of Clairvaux asked: "What does it mean to eat his flesh and drink his blood but to communicate with his sufferings? . . . Therefore this refers to the undefiled Sacrament of the Altar, where we receive the body of the Lord." Another commentator on these words explained that "Christ is the bread of life to those who believe in him. To believe in Christ is to eat the bread of life, to have Christ in oneself, to have eternal life." From such language it was not a far distance to the idea that since faith was the truest and deepest meaning of "eating" the flesh and body of Christ, it was a matter of only secondary importance whether that faith was accompanied by a physical act of eating or not. Some such idea seemed to have been part of Augustine's thinking, as some of his interpreters had to acknowledge. But those who were defending his eucharistic theology in the conflict with Berengar explained that he had had in mind both a spiritual eating by which "Christ is received in our heart by faith" and "the eating and use and perception of his very body and blood within us"; the first conferred "the presence of the divinity by which we were created," but the second conveyed "the presence of the body by which we were redeemed."

Was the second kind of eating, and therefore the second kind of presence, dependent on the first? Conversely, were the body and blood of Christ present in the Sacrament even when the communicant did not have faith? The answer to this question was bound up with the warning of the apostle Paul: "Whoever, therefore, eats the bread or drinks the cup of the Lord in an unworthy manner will be guilty of the body and blood of the Lord. For any one who eats and drinks unworthily, eats and drinks judgment upon himself, not discerning the body." If these words were taken together with the words of Jesus about the eating of his flesh as the means of granting eternal life, they appeared to imply that "only true believers" received the heavenly food of the body of Christ, while the unworthy received "nothing else than mere bread." For "if that bread were to have nothing sacred about it beyond what common bread has, but he who ate it regarded it as the body of the Lord and took it upon himself to receive it shamelessly, he would undoubtedly be subject to no less a judgment than if it were, in utter reality, the body of Jesus." He would be condemned for his subjective state, regardless of the objectivity of the presence. The test case was that of Judas Iscariot at the Last Supper. The church fathers had not been able to agree whether or not Judas had received communion before betraying Christ, and the question continued to agitate the theologians of this period as well, without leading to much more of a consensus than had been achieved earlier. Adding to the concern now was the campaign of the eleventh-century reformers against abuses

See vol.1:305

Herm.Mag.*Epit*.29 (*PL* 178:1741); Hug.Met.*Ep*.4 (*PL* 188:1273)

Bald.*Sacr.alt*.2.3.2 (*SC* 93:272); Lanf.*Corp*.15 (*PL* 150:425)

Hon.Aug.*Eluc*.1.30 (*PL* 172:1132)

Rup.*Div.off*.2.9 (*CCCM* 7:42)

I Cor.11:27, 29

Guit.Av.*Corp*.3 (*PL* 149:1491)

Guib.Nog.*Pign*.2.3.9 (*PL* 156:641); Joach.*Art.fid.* (*FSI* 78:28)

Guib.Nog.*Pign*.2.3.3 (*PL* 156:636); Rath.*Ep*.16 (*MGH BDK* 1:94)

Guib.Nog.*Corp*.1 (*PL* 156:529)

Gez.*Corp*.38 (*PL* 137:389); Herb.Los.*Serm*.7 (Goulburn-Symonds 196); Bald.*Sacr.alt*.2.1.2 (*SC* 93:138–40); Herm.Mag.*Epit*.29 (*PL* 178:1741); Hug.S.Vict.*Sum.Sent*.6.7 (*PL* 176:143); Alex.III.*Sent.Rol.* (Gietl 229–30)

in the church, which was raising the issue of the sacramental validity of ordination through simony.

See pp. 212–13 below

What finally determined the answer to the problem of
those who "eat the flesh of Christ but are not members of
Christ," who "do not become the body of Christ although
they eat the body of Christ," was the application to the
eucharistic presence of the concept of sacramental objectivity originally formulated by Augustine in his response to the claim that the apostasy or moral impurity
of a catholic bishop invalidated his administration of the
sacraments: the validity of the sacrament was dependent
neither on the minister nor on the recipient, but on the
institution of Christ. Now it was recognized, however, that
whereas Augustine had used the concept to defend the
doctrine of baptism, it had been extended by Radbertus
to the doctrine of the Eucharist. Therefore "even if someone confesses that he is unworthy, he should believe and
say that what he is receiving is the body of Christ"; otherwise an unworthy priest celebrating a private mass as
the sole communicant would nullify the institution of
Christ and the faith of the church in the presence of the
body and blood of Christ. Even those who pointed out the
difficulties of maintaining that the unworthy communicant received the true body and blood of Christ to his
own damnation acknowledged the force of the pastoral
argument that, since a communicant often doubted his
own worthiness, he would be deterred from communion
by his dread of judgment, and they concluded that the
sacraments of the church were "common to the reprobate
and to the elect."

There were various possible corollaries that could follow
from this view of the objectivity of the presence of the
body of Christ, several of them belonging to the area of
casuistry or of speculation. For example, if what was
present in the bread of the Eucharist was nothing other
than the true body of Christ, the question arose: "What
does a mouse eat" by nibbling a consecrated host? Although a denial that the mouse ate the true body appeared
to cast doubt on the reality of the presence, "the reverence
. . . for the body of the Lord made the thought intolerable
that [it] . . . could get into a situation that was incompatible with its sublimity," and most theologians rejected
the suggestion that an animal could eat Christ's body.
Another implication could conceivably be that the true

Hug.Met.*Ep*.4 (*PL* 188:1273)
Wm.S.Th.*Sacr.alt*.7 (*PL* 180:
354)

Alg.*Sacr*.1.21; 3.3 (*PL* 180:
798–803; 834–36)

See vol.1:131

See p. 76 above
Petr.Dam.*Lib.grat*.9 (*MGH*
Lib.lit.1:27)

Guit.Av.*Corp*.3 (*PL* 149:1483)

Guib.Nog.*Pign*.2.4.1 (*PL* 156:
642)

Guib.Nog.*Ord.serm*. (*PL* 156:
23)

Guib.Nog.*Pign*.2.2.2 (*PL* 156:
633)
Bald.*Sacr.alt*.2.1.3 (*SC* 93:
206)

Guit.Av.*Corp*.2 (*PL* 149:
1448)

Landgraf (1952) 3–II:222
Guib.Nog.*Pign*.2.3.8 (*PL* 156:
640); Herm.Mag.*Epit*.29 (*PL*
178:1743–44)

Acts 2:31

Brngr.Tr.*fr*.ap.Guit.Av.*Corp.*
2 (*PL* 149:1445)

Fulb.*Ep*.3 (*PL* 141:193)

Geiselmann (1933) 78

Brngr.Tr.*fr*.ap.Lanf.*Corp*.2
(*PL* 150:411)

John 20:27

Guit.Av.*Corp*.1 (*PL* 149:1432)

Herb.Los.*Serm*.7 (Goulburn-
Symonds 194–96)

Lanf.*Corp*.11 (*PL* 150:422)

John 6:52

Robt.Pull.*Sent*.8.5 (*PL* 186:
966); Abb.*Fract*. (*PL* 166:
1344); Hug.S.Vict.*Sum.Sent.*
6.8. (*PL* 176:144–45); Hug.
S.Vict.*Sacr*.2.8.11 (*PL* 176:
469–70); Herm.Mag.*Epit*.29;
(*PL* 178:1742); Vac.*Err*.19.1
(*ST* 115:523)

Brngr.Tr.*Coen*.21 (Beekenkamp
43)

Brngr.Tr.*Coen*.42 (Beekenkamp
140)

Brngr.Tr.*Opusc*.ap.Lanf.
Corp.9 (*PL* 150:419)

Brngr.Tr.*fr*.ap.Guit.Av.*Corp.*
1 (*PL* 149:1431)

body of Christ, being incorruptible, was not subject to
deterioration; as Berengar pointed out, however, the elements of the Eucharist could decay, and it was out of regard for this problem that church custom dictated the
consumption of the reserved host within forty days. The
most notorious corollary of the real presence was expressed in Berengar's confession under duress in 1059,
probably written for him by Humbert of Silva Candida,
perhaps also with the East in mind: "The bread and wine
are the true body and blood of our Lord Jesus Christ . . .
handled and broken by the hands of the priests and
ground by the teeth of the faithful." There were some for
whom these words were no different from the report in
the Gospel that Thomas touched the wounds in the body
of the risen Christ, provided that one preserved the teaching that "the immortal and incorruptible body of Christ
is not subject to any corruption." Others, because of the
aversion to the grossly physical notion of "eating Christ"
attributed to his hearers in Capernaum (and therefore
labeled "Capernaitic" in later polemics), made such language part of the paradox that "the body of Christ seems
to be broken and is not broken, seems to be ground by the
teeth and is not ground, since surely the grinding and
breaking affect the appearance [species], not the reality
[res]."

Such particulars aside, the fundamental difference between Berengar and his opponents over the real presence
lay in the interpretation of the "conversion" that took
place through the consecration of the bread and wine.
Berengar, who preferred to use the word "change," pointed
out that "it is not a simple matter to say what the word
'to be converted' means," since a thing could be "converted" by its objective and physical transformation into
something that it had not been before, whereas "through
the consecration at the altar bread and wine become the
Sacrament of faith, not by ceasing to be what they were,
but by remaining what they were and being changed into
something else" in addition. If it was claimed that in the
Eucharist bread and wine were destroyed and were replaced by the body and blood of Christ and yet that they
retained all the qualities of bread and wine, "this is a
change that nature cannot undergo." As Saul of Tarsus
was changed into Paul the apostle by remaining what he
was and yet becoming something else, so it was with the

Brngr.Tr.*Coen*.31 (Beekenkamp 75)

Brngr.Tr.*Apol*. (Matronola 118); Brngr.Tr.*Coen*.21 (Beekenkamp 46)

Alg.*Sacr*.1.6 (*PL* 180:754)

ap.Guit.Av.*Corp*.1 (*PL* 149: 1430)

Hug.Bret.*Corp*. (*PL* 142:1327)

ap.*V.Mauril*.11 (*PL* 143: 1383)
Adel.*Ep.Brngr*. (Heurtevent 291); Goff.Vind.*Opusc*.1 (*PL* 157:213)

Gen.1:3

Alg.*Sacr*.1.9 (*PL* 180:768)

Joach.*Art.fid*. (*FSI* 78:24–25)

Alg.*Sacr*.1.6 (*PL* 180:755)

Guit.Av.*Corp*.3 (*PL* 149:1482)

Rup.*Div.off*.2.2 (*CCCM* 7:32)
Bald.*Sacr.alt*.2.1.3 (*SC* 93: 204); Rem.Aux.*Cel.miss*. (*PL* 101:1260)

Rath.*Ep*.13 (*MGH BDK* 1:69)
Adel.*Ep.Brngr*. (Heurtevent 294); Brun.S.*Lev*.16 (*PL* 164: 436)
Brngr.Tr.*Apol*. (Matronola 114); Hug.Bret.*Corp*. (*PL* 142:1330); Brun.S.*Job*.1.6.19 (*PL* 165:502)
Ambr.*Sacr*.4.4.20 (*SC* 25-II:112)

elements in the Sacrament. And "as the Logos of God became flesh by assuming what he was not and remaining what he was, thus also the bread . . . becomes the body [of Christ] by remaining what it was and assuming what it was not." This analogy between the Eucharist and the incarnation led to a theory labeled (whether by the Berengarians themselves or by their critics) "impanation," by which the substance of the bread and wine remained, but "the body and blood of the Lord are contained there in a manner that is true but hidden."

All of these efforts by Berengar and his followers to explain—or explain away—the miracle of eucharistic change were unacceptable. Either the bread stopped being bread, or there was no point in calling it the body of Christ. Therefore "before the consecration the bread set forth on the Lord's table is nothing but bread, but in the consecration, by the ineffable power of the Divinity, the nature and substance of the bread are converted into the nature and substance of the flesh" of Christ. As for the bread, nothing remained except its outward appearance. Despite the parallel that could be drawn between creation by the word, "Let there be light," and the new creation by the word, "This is my body," the change in the Eucharist differed from the original creation ex nihilo precisely because, "by a manner that is new and unheard-of," the bread was changed into the body of Christ, but the body of Christ did not cease being what it had always been. That was also why the analogy between the incarnation and the Sacrament broke down, for the Logos did not cease to exist but assumed the body to himself, while the bread did cease to exit as bread when it was changed into the body. Hence the theory of "impanation" was misguided. None of these theories sufficed, in the judgment of Berengar's critics, to describe "the work of truth by which the bread and the wine are transformed into the true body and blood of the Lord." The transformation was "true and mystical," both at the same time. For the Eucharist remained a mystery of faith also for those who had the right doctrine about the presence. The body of Christ remained invisible in the Sacrament, partly to exercise the faith of the communicants and partly, as Berengar and his opponents agreed on the basis of Ambrose, to avoid "horror at the blood."

Only with a doctrine that asserted the "true and mystical" transformation of the bread and wine into the body and blood of Christ would the rule of faith be conformable to the rule of prayer. Although Berengar also quoted the authority of the canon of the Mass and other liturgical texts in support of his views, the import of the belief that liturgical words and actions "contain the mysteries [sacramenta] of heavenly secrets" was clearly working against him. Even the prayer "that what we now do in an outward sign [specie], we may take hold of in reality [in rerum veritate]," which seemed to contrast the outward sign of bread and wine in the Sacrament with the reality of the body and blood, to be grasped in the future, became instead a proof that it was the true body of Christ present both in the Sacrament now and in the celestial vision eternally. For if the bread and wine were only an outward sign of the body and blood, analogous to other symbols of Christ, there would be no reason to venerate the eucharistic elements as the worship of the church did or for the eucharistic prayer to ask that they be placed on God's heavenly altar by the hands of an angel. Within the eucharistic prayer, it was increasingly the words of institution—understood as literally true, in opposition to Berengar's view that they were not meant "literally [proprie]"—to which Western theologians attributed the power of transforming bread and wine into body and blood. There contined to be echoes of the characteristically Eastern idea that the transformation took place through the invocation of the Holy Spirit. But as the emphasis shifted from "being filled with the Spirit" to "making the body and blood present," the words of institution came to be seen in isolation from the rest of the eucharistic prayer, including the invocation of the Spirit. "Before the words of Christ, the chalice is full of wine and water; when the words of Christ have been spoken, then the blood that redeemed the people is produced." Unless these words were spoken, there would be no transformation of the elements. Although the priest spoke the words of institution at the celebration of the Mass, it was Christ himself who did the consecrating. Thus the words of institution were "the essence [substantia] of the Sacrament"; everything else was merely decoration.

The formal rule of prayer in the liturgy was reinforced by the informal rule of prayer in the piety of the people. Above all, it was through "miracles that are congruous to

Brngr.Tr.*Coen*.46 (Beekenkamp 159–62); Brngr.Tr.*fr*.ap.Guit. Av.*Corp*.2 (*PL* 149:1467)

Rup.*Div.off*.pr. (*CCCM* 7:5); Ps.Petr.Dam.*Exp.can.miss*.9 (*PL* 145:885)

Sacr.Gel.229.1231 (Mohlberg 189)

Lanf.*Corp*.20 (*PL* 150:436)

See p. 79 above Guib.Nog.*Corp*.3 (*PL* 156:531)

Brngr.Tr.*Coen*.20 (Beekenkamp 37)

See vol.2:277–78 Rath.*Dial.conf*.14 (*PL* 136:402); Fulb.*Ep*.3 (*PL* 141:195); Brun.S.*Ex*.29 (*PL* 164:357–58)

Geiselmann (1933) 256–57

Steph.Aug.*Sacr.alt*.15 (*PL* 172:1293)

Dur.Tr.*Corp*.5.15 (*PL* 149:1397)

Othl.*Dial*.48 (*PL* 146:128); Rem.Aux.*Cel.miss*. (*PL* 101:1260) Od.Clun.*Coll*.1.21 (*PL* 133:533); Gez.*Corp*.40 (*PL* 137:391); Bald.*Sacr.alt*.2.4.3 (*SC* 94:358) Ps.Isid.Sev.*Ep.Red*.2 (*PL* 83:905–6) Alex.III.*Sent.Rol*. (Gietl 232)

Lanf.*Corp*.19 (*PL* 150:435);
Alg.*Sacr*.1.13 (*PL* 180:779)
Brngr.Tr.*Coen*.7 (Beekenkamp 9)

Guit.Av.*Corp*.3 (*PL* 149:1479–80)

Gez.*Corp*.pr. (*PL* 137:373)

Petr.Dam.*Opusc*.34.pr. (*PL* 145:573)
Herb.Los.*Serm*.1 (Goulburn-Symonds 30–32); Guib.Nog.
Pign.1.2 (*PL* 156:616); Gez.
Corp.41 (*PL* 137:393); Hug.
Met.*Ep*.4 (*PL* 188:1275)
Petr.Ven.*Mirac*.1.2 (*PL* 189:
853–54); Alan.Ins.*Haer*.1.62
(*PL* 210:365)
Brd.Clr.*V.Mal*.5.11 (Leclercq-Rochais 3:320); Petr.Ven.
Mirac.2.2 (*PL* 189:911–12)

Od.Clun.*Coll*.2.32–34 (*PL* 133:
577–81); Bern.Reich.*V.Udal*.
8 (*PL* 142:1191); Hrot.*Dion*.
171–74 (Homeyer 199); Dur.
Tr.*Corp*.8 (*PL* 149:1418–21)

Browe (1933) 17

Brngr.Tr.*Opusc*.ap.Lanf. *Corp*.
20 (*PL* 150:436)

Guib.Nog.*Corp*.3 (*PL* 156:
531)

Eph.2:20; 1 Pet.2:6
Brngr.Tr.*Opusc*.ap.Lanf.*Corp*.
6 (*PL* 150:415–16)

Bald.*Sacr.alt*.2.1.2 (*SC* 93:
142–44)
Her.*Corp*.4 (*PL* 139:182)
Lanf.*Corp*.6 (*PL* 150:416)

Att.Verc.*Serm*.8 (*PL* 134:
843); Bald.*Comm.fid*. (*PL*
204:627–28); Bald.*Sacr.alt*.
3.1.1 (*SC* 94:418)
See pp. 75–76 above
Gez.*Corp*.41 (*PL* 137:393)

this faith of ours" in the real presence that the doctrine was confirmed. Although Berengar criticized Radbertus for his credulity in repeating tales of eucharistic miracles, his adversaries used "very well-known miracles" as proof in "rational confutation" of his teachings. Through these miracles God had revealed to his faithful not only what glories awaited them in heaven, but also "what a gift he left for them here on earth" in the Eucharist. A primary purpose of the miracles was to "show the visible reality of the body of the Lord." Sometimes this happened through a special revelation by which a spectator at Mass saw a human form, often the form of a child, replace the form of the consecrated host. Then there were miracles that served as the means of calling someone to repentance after he had profaned the sacrament. The presence and power of Christ in the Eucharist was even able to raise someone from the dead. In hagiographic literature and in theological polemics, the accounts of eucharistic miracles served the purposes of edification and of correction, especially against Berengar's denial of the real presence. The vindication of the real presence against him was, in turn, responsible for "the rise of a eucharistic devotion" devoted to the adoration of the consecrated host apart from the celebration of the Mass.

For so massive a reality as this, the very presence of the body and blood of Christ, born of Mary, the language of "likeness, figure, and sign," for all its patristic support, was inadequate. If the presence amounted to no more than a figure or a memorial, it would be "perfunctory." When Berengar sought to put the presence on the same level with such statements as "Christ is the chief cornerstone," he failed to comprehend the difference between this figure of speech and the words of institution, "This is my body," which "no one should suppose to have been set forth figuratively by him through some sort of signification," since what was involved was not a "figure," but "reality." It was not "body," but "bread," that was used figuratively, since "we sometimes call things by the names of the things from which they have been made." The proper distinction between figure and reality in this area lay between the figure of the Eucharist in the Old Testament and the reality of Christ in the New. As Radbertus had pointed out, Christ did not say, "This is the figure of my body," for the body and blood made of bread and wine

John 2:1–11
Rath.*Ep*.13 (*MGH BDK* 1:
68–69)

Ps.Haim.Halb.*Corp*. (*PL* 118:
817); Dur.Tr.*Corp*.7.25 (*PL*
149:1417)

Southern (1948) 40

Aug.*Trin*.7.4.7 (*CCSL* 50:
255)
Radb.*Matt*.2.1 (*PL* 120:107);
Sent.Flor.6 (Ostlender 3);
Brngr.Tr.*Apol*. (Matronola
116–17)

Matt.6:11 (Vulg.)

Alc.*Ep*.28 (*MGH Ep*.4:70)

Radb.*Corp*.4 (*CCCM* 16:28)

Radb.*Corp*.8 (*CCCM* 16:42)

Radb.*Ep.Fr*. (*CCCM* 16:149–
50)

Ratr.*Corp*.30 (Brink 42)

Ratr.*Corp*.49 (Brink 46)

John 15:5

Ratr.*Corp*.8 (Brink 35)

Ratr.*Corp*.10 (Brink 35)

in the Eucharist were no more figurative than was the wine made of water at Cana of Galilee. When such church fathers as Augustine spoke of the Eucharist as a "figure," they were calling it a figure not of the real body of Christ, but of the church.

If the language of "figure" was no longer an appropriate way of speaking about the real presence, the language of "substance" now became appropriate, for this "was the new factor about the discussion on the Eucharist from this time on." The term "substance [substantia]" had been used in patristic Latin for the divine essence or "ousia," and it continued to carry that meaning in medieval theology. The Latin fathers do not appear to have made use of the word in speaking of the eucharistic presence, although the Vulgate did translate the fourth petition of the Lord's Prayer as "Give us this day our supersubstantial [supersubstantialis] bread." When an eighth-century theologian spoke of "consecrating the elements of bread and wine into the substance of the most holy body and blood of Christ," he was apparently not introducing "substance" in a technical or precise philosophical sense. That lack of philosophical precision in employing such terminology became evident in the exchange between Radbertus and Ratramnus. According to Radbertus, the body and blood of Christ were "produced from the substance of bread and wine" when "the substance of bread and wine is changed into the flesh and blood of Christ, efficaciously and inwardly" and "the invisible Priest converts his visible creatures into the substance of his body and blood." For his part, Ratramnus could also speak of "bread and wine that have been converted into the substance of [Christ's] body and blood," but he equated the "invisible substance" of the eucharistic elements with "the power of the divine word" by which this change was wrought. He also insisted, after quoting the words of Christ, "I am the vine, you are the branches," that "substantially the bread is not Christ, nor is the vine Christ, nor are the branches the apostles." And he even spoke of "taste, smell, and color" as "the substance of the wine" that remained after the consecration, thus using the word in a sense opposite to that which it was to have here in the eleventh and especially the twelfth centuries.

What now gave the term "substance" an increasingly specific meaning was the expansion of philosophical learn-

Grabmann (1957) 2:65

See vol.1:167

Rup.*Div.off*.2.9 (*CCCM* 7:41)

Brngr.Tr.*fr*.ap.Lanf.*Corp*.2 (*PL* 150:411)

Herb.Los.*Serm*.7 (Goulburn-Symonds 186)

Lanf.*Corp*.18 (*PL* 150:430)

Bald.*Sacr.alt*.2.1.3 (*SC* 93: 210)

Rath.*Ep*.13 (*MGH BDK* 1:69)

Scot.Er.*Periph*.1.63 (*SLH* 7: 182); Othl.*Dial*.33 (*PL* 146: 102–3)

Lanf.*Corp*.18 (*PL* 150:430) Robt.Pull.*Sent*.8.5 (*PL* 186: 966) Othl.*V.Wolf*. (*MGH Scrip*. 4:538)

Guit.Av.*Corp*.2 (*PL* 149: 1450); Alg.*Sacr*.1.7 (*PL* 180: 756–57)

Ps.Petr.Dam.*Exp.can.miss*.7; 14–16 (*PL* 145:883; 888–89)

Alex.III.*Sent.Rol*. (Gietl 231)

Steph.Aug.*Sacr.alt*.13; 14 (*PL* 172:1291; 1293)

ing, which "took place partly through a more general distribution and use of sources that had hitherto been known very little, partly through the translation of philosophical authors who had been unknown until now." Although Rupert of Deutz, echoing a formula of Irenaeus's, spoke of an "earthly" and a "divine substance" in the Eucharist as in the incarnation, and equated the latter substance with the Logos, this sounded too much like the Berengarian theory of "impanation." It was necessary to believe, in the words of Berengar's recantation of 1079, that the bread and wine "are substantially converted" into the very body of Christ. That became the accepted way of describing the change: "not in a phantasy, but substantially"; "earthly substances . . . are changed into the essence of the Lord's body"; "the substance of the bread is changed into the substance of the flesh of Christ." The problem of the color, taste, and smell of the eucharistic elements remained to be dealt with; not only Ratramnus, but his severe critic, Ratherius, referred to these qualities as the "substance" of the elements. Although the Aristotelian distinction of "substance" and "accidents" had been known to Erigena and others, those who were quite ready to speak of "substance" in the Eucharist would still refer to "outward appearances and certain other qualities" or to "properties," but not to "accidents."

When "accidents" also became part of the standard vocabulary, with the treatise of Guitmond, the way was prepared for the definitive statement of the doctrine of the real presence, which took the form of the dogma of transubstantiation. The first use of this word has been attributed to various theologians of the period, often to Peter Damian, until the *Exposition of the Canon of the Mass* under his name, where the word occurs, was shown to be a later work. It now seems that Rolando Bandinelli, who eventually became Pope Alexander III, was the first to speak of "transubstantiation," in a work prepared about 1140, although it also appears in a work ascribed to Stephen of Autun from about the same time. Three-fourths of a century later, the Fourth Lateran Council in 1215 promulgated the dogma that "the body and blood [of Jesus Christ] are truly contained in the Sacrament of the Altar under the outward appearances of bread and wine, the bread having been transubstantiated into the

CLater. (1215) Const.1
(Alberigo 206)

Petr.Pict.Sent.5.12 (PL 211:
1247); Bald.Sacr.alt.2.1.2 (SC
93:148)

CTrid. (1545–63) 13.Cap.4
(Alberigo 671)

Brngr.Tr.Opusc.ap.Lanf.Corp.
20 (PL 150:436)

Wm.S.Th.Sacr.alt.11 (PL 180:
359)

Rup.Div.off.pr. (CCCM 7:5)

Bald.Sacr.alt.2.4.2 (SC 94:
348)

I Cor.13:13

Herm.Mag.Epit.1 (PL 178:
1695); Alex.III.Sent.Rol.
(Gietl 1)
Brd.Clr.Cant.66.5.11 (Leclercq-
Rochais 2:185)

Hug.S.Vict.Sacr.1.9.2 (PL 176:
317)

Steph.Aug.Sacr.alt.12 (PL 172:
1284); Bald.Sacr.alt.2.4.2;
2.4.3 (SC 94:322–24; 360)

See vol.1:163–66

body and the wine into the blood." Theologians continued to recognize that the fundamental content of the dogma of transubstantiation was the doctrine of the real presence, rather than a particular philosophical definition of substance and accident. Even after the upheaval of the Reformation, the Council of Trent in 1551 reaffirmed transubstantiation with the statement: "This change [of bread and wine into body and blood] has conveniently and appropriately been called transubstantiation by the holy catholic church."

The Grace of the Sacraments

In the controversy over the real presence, Berengar was attempting to explain the doctrine of the Eucharist on the basis of a general definition of likeness, figure, sign, and sacrament, but by the time the controversy had ended the doctrine of the Eucharist had decisively affected the definition of sacrament itself. Even his severest critics had to acknowledge that he had inadvertently brought about a clarification of sacramental theology by raising questions that had been neglected by the fathers. Theologians and churchmen discovered that they had not paid sufficient attention to these questions, and they concluded that "celebrating the sacraments without understanding them is like speaking a language without knowing what it means." It was incumbent especially on the clergy to penetrate into the mysteries of the sacraments they were administering. Paraphrasing the apostolic formula of faith, hope, and love, theologians opened their treatises on doctrine with the statement: "The sum of human salvation consists of three things: faith, love, and the sacraments." For a denial of the sacraments was tantamount to a denial of the church itself. The sacraments were that important because each sacrament "contains a certain spiritual grace," and it was through the several sacraments that the grace of the forgiveness of sins, life, and salvation was communicated.

During the patristic era and even beyond it, the paradigm for the understanding of the sacraments as means of grace had been baptism. In the West, the founder of Latin theology, Tertullian, had summarized the catholic doctrine of baptism in a form that was to remain constant for most of the following centuries. When the issue of the validity of the sacraments arose, Augustine turned to baptism as the

See vol.1:302–4; 311

Ans.L.*Sent.div.pag*.5
(Bliemetzrieder 42–43);
Hrot.*Gall*.2.9.1 (Homeyer
263)

Rath.*Prael*.4.21 (*PL* 136:269);
Brd.Clr.*Cant*.69.2.3 (Leclercq-
Rochais 2:204)

Alg.*Mis.et just*.1.55 (*PL* 180:
882); Alg.*Sacr*.3.6 (*PL* 180:
838); Ans.L.*Sent.div.pag*.5
(Bliemetzrieder 44); Alex.III.
Sent.Rol. (Gietl 206–7)

Brun.S.*Sym*.11 (*MGH Lib.lit.*
2:555)

Luke 23:42

Alex.III.*Sent.Rol.* (Gietl 8;
208–10); Rich.S.Vict.*Apoc.*
7.8 (*PL* 196:883)

Guib.Nog.*Inc*.1.2 (*PL* 156:
493)

Ans.L.*Sent.div.pag*.5
(Bliemetzrieder 42–43)
Bald.*Sacr.alt*.2.4.2 (*SC* 94:
324); Brngr.Tr.*Coen*.32
(Beekenkamp 80–81)
Petr.Dam.*Lib.grat*.9 (*MGH
Lib. lit*.1:27)

John 19:34

See p. 137 above

I Cor.10:1–4
Od.Clun.*Occup*.5.727–28
(Swoboda 115); Rup.*Div.off.*
3.24 (*CCCM* 7:100)

Guib.Nog.*Pign*.1.1 (*PL* 156:
613); Robt.Pull.*Sent*.8.1 (*PL*
186:959)

Alg.*Sacr*.3.8 (*PL* 180:840)

Guib.Nog.*Corp*.3 (*PL* 156:
532)

key to a resolution of the issue. Even here in the eleventh and twelfth centuries, when the Eucharist was moving into this paradigmatic role, baptism continued to be seen as fundamental, sometimes even as "chief among the sacraments that Christ instituted in the church," because it alone was necessary for salvation. So necessary was it that unbaptized children, even those of believing parents, were condemned, albeit to a punishment milder than that imposed on obdurate adults. Because of its necessity, baptism could, in cases of extreme emergency, be administered by a layman or even by a pagan or an infidel. This was because of the principle, defended by Augustine, that "baptism is good regardless of who gives it, because it does not depend on the faith of the one giving it." Yet the necessity of baptism did not deny salvation to those who, like the thief on the cross, had the desire, but not the opportunity, for the sacrament.

Although this period, then, continued to teach that "without the faith [conferred] in baptism, the other sacraments are annulled," there appears to have been a shift in emphasis from baptism to the Eucharist, such that one could perhaps call baptism fundamental but no longer central, at least not so central as it had been. Outweighing the statement that baptism was "chief among the sacraments that Christ instituted in the church" were other statements in which it was one of the "two chief" or "three chief" sacraments. The other "chief sacrament" was the Eucharist, with ordination sometimes added as the third. The blood and the water that flowed from the side of Christ on the cross, while sometimes used to justify the liturgical practice of mixing water with wine at the consecration of the elements, became, together with the Pauline typology of the manna in the desert and the cloud through which Israel passed, biblical proof for the two sacraments of Eucharist and baptism. These two were universal throughout Christendom and essential for salvation. Of the two, however, the Eucharist was "the greater" and was "not only on a par with baptism, but its foundation and its completion." Baptism was carried out "through nothing more than the invocation of the Trinity," but the Eucharist was "confected by the very Logos of God." While the water of baptism had its power of forgiving sins only for a brief moment and then flowed away, "this host [in the Eucharist] is always borne up to

Guib.Nog.*Pign*.2.3.1 (*PL* 156: 634–35)

Deusd.*Inv.sym*.2.7 (*MGH Lib. lit*.2:325)

Ambr.*Sacr*.4.4.20 (*SC* 25–II: 112)

Lanf.*Corp*.20 (*PL* 150:439)

ap.Alg.*Sacr*.pr. (*PL* 180:739)

Alg.*Sacr*.1.8 (*PL* 180:761)

Adel.*Ep.Brngr*. (Heurtevent 292)

Petr.Dam.*Lib.grat*.9 (*MGH Lib.lit*.1:27)

Lanf.*Corp*.20 (*PL* 150:437); Alg.*Sacr*.1.4 (*PL* 180:752)

the throne of glory and will never perish." For although "the sacrament itself is transitory and is therefore repeated every day, the divine power [virtus] that is eaten in it is eternal."

As sacraments, baptism and the Eucharist possessed certain similarities, but it was easy—and dangerous—to press these too far. Thus Ambrose had drawn a parallel between the two sacraments by declaring: "As you have assumed the likeness of the death [of Christ], so you also drink the likeness of [his] precious blood." The trouble with the parallel was that because "there is not a true death of Christ in baptism," someone might conclude that "therefore it is not his true blood in this sacrament" either. There were those among the followers of Berengar who maintained, on the basis of the parallel, that "the bread and wine are not changed, but are merely a sacrament, like the water of baptism," and hence that the body of Christ in the Eucharist was figurative, not real. But the difference that this ignored was a basic one: "The water of baptism . . . does not contain the Holy Spirit essentially, but only figuratively; only the Sacrament of bread and wine is changed in such a way that in substance it is not what it used to be before." The significance of the parallel became even more obscure when an opponent of Berengar, seeking to make the point that it was the ever-present Christ who "baptizes men through men and consecrates whatever is consecrated through men," went on to assert a kind of real presence of Christ in the water of baptism, because "whenever a body is immersed in water with the invocation of certain solemn words, He Himself makes the dead soul alive by remitting its sins." One aspect of the parallel that did prove useful in this period was the argument that not only baptism, but also the Eucharist had an objective validity, so that both of "these mysteries are not better when administered by good priests nor worse when administered by evil ones."

The consideration of the Eucharist and of its relation to other "sacraments," especially baptism, brought about a more precise consideration of the idea of sacrament as such. It was recognized by Lanfranc, and on the basis of Lanfranc by Alger, that "the term 'sacrament' is not found to be used with a uniform meaning in the divine writings." From the statement of the New Testament that "manifestly the sacrament of piety [pietatis sacramentum]

1 Tim.3:16(Vulg.)

Rich.S.Vict.*Em*.1.13 (*PL* 196: 622)

Alex.III.*Sent.Rol.* (Gietl 157; 194); *Sent.div.*4.pr. (Geyer 52)

Lanf.*Corp*.14 (*PL* 150:424)

Brun.S.*Matt*.2.11.43 (*PL* 165:172)

Od.Clun.*Coll*.1.21 (*PL* 133: 533)

Alg.*Sacr*.1.16 (*PL* 180:789)

Bald.*Sacr.alt*.3.2.1 (*SC* 94: 352)

Rath.*Prael*.4.22 (*PL* 136:271); Lanf.*Corp*.13 (*PL* 150:423)

Guib.Nog.*Pign*.2.3.6 (*PL* 156: 638)

Hug.S.Vict.*Sacr*.1.9.7 (*PL* 176: 327)

Rab.*Inst.cler*.1.31 (Knoepfler 58); Brun.S.*Matt*.2.8.25 (*PL* 165:141); Ratr.*Corp*.50 (Brink 46)

Fulb.*Ep*.5 (*PL* 141:197)

Alg.*Sacr*.2.8 (*PL* 180:826)

Häring (1958) 72

Alex.III.*Sent.Rol.* (Gietl 155)

is great, that which was manifest in the flesh," the term "the sacrament of the incarnation" established itself permanently in theological usage; it was "the well-known chief sacrament, the incarnation of the Logos," from which the understanding of "the other sacraments" proceeded. Thus "Christ is the sacrament of Christ" himself, and it was Christ who disclosed the meaning of the sacraments. His consecration, not that of the priest apart from him, made the sacraments efficacious, granting to the recipients of the sacraments the grace of being "cosacramental with Christ." Even after the controversy over the sacraments had, at least in principle, been settled, it was still possible to speak of "the four sacraments, namely, the nativity, the passion, the resurrection, and the ascension of Christ." Another usage of the word, going back to pre-Christian Latin, was as a term for an oath, especially an oath of allegiance or an oath confirming the truth of a statement. Taking account of this classical definition of the word as well as of Christian definitions, Guibert of Nogent posited a threefold significance for the term: "as an oath, as a thing that has been consecrated, and as a mystery." A different sort of threefold significance was that proposed by Hugh of Saint-Victor: "those sacraments in which salvation principally consists and is received"; "others which, while not necessary for salvation, contribute to sanctification"; and "yet other sacraments which appear to have been instituted for the sole purpose of somehow preparing and sanctifying the things that are necessary for the sanctification and institution of the other sacraments." An illustration of the lack of clarity in the usage was the widespread designation of the Eucharist as "sacraments" in the plural, "the two sacraments of life, namely, the body and the blood of the Lord," even though in their signification the two were one.

Nevertheless, the issues raised by Berengar made it obligatory to introduce greater specificity into the church's language about the grace of the sacraments, for "when Berengar proposed his definitions of *sacramentum* and used them to argue his point, the theologians opposing him were not sufficiently prepared to discuss the speculative value of those definitions." One of the most widely employed ways of defining "sacrament" had come from Augustine: "as Augustine says, a sacrament is the visible sign of an invisible grace." A variation on this definition

Wm.S.Th.*Sacr.alt*.9 (*PL* 180:
356); Wm.Mon.*Henr.Mon*.5
(Manselli 52)

Isa.7:14; Luke 2:12

Guit.Av.*Corp*.2 (*PL* 149:1458);
Bald.*Sacr.alt*.2.1.2 (*SC* 93:
110); Bald.*Tract*.16 (*PL* 204:
564)
Hug.Met.*Ep*.4 (*PL* 188:1274);
Ans.L.*Sent.Ans*.7
(Bliemetzrieder 117)

Ghellinck (1930) 88
Alex.III.*Sent.Rol*. (Gietl 215–
16)

Geiselmann (1933) 235–36
Petr.Lomb.*Sent*.4.1.1.2
(Quaracchi 4:8); Thos.Aq.
Sent.4.1.16
(Mandonnet 4:9)

See p. 188 above

Alg.*Mis.et just*.1.62 (*PL* 180:
884)

Ans.L.*Sent.Ans*.6
(Bliemetzrieder 114)
Herm.Mag.*Epit*.28 (*PL* 178:
1739)

Ans.L.*Sent.Ans*.10
(Bliemetzrieder 134)

Ans.L.*Sent.div.pag*.
(Bliemetzrieder 46)

Bald.*Sacr.alt*.2.1.2 (*SC* 93:
122)

Brun.S.*Sacr.eccl*. (*PL* 165:
1094)

was simply to say that " a sacrament is the sign of a sacred reality." The biblical use of the word "sign" as a term for Christ himself made it possible (and necessary) even for those who were arguing that the sacraments, in particular the Eucharist, could not be adequately defined as signs, to acknowledge that the term was appropriate, if insufficient. Another definition, also attributed to Augustine, was that "a sacrament is the visible form of an invisible grace." But the formula as usually quoted does not seem to appear in the authentic writings of Augustine, and Berengar "is, as far as we know, the first author who ever employed this definition." These two definitions—sometimes with the addition of the formula "sacred secret" or mystery—were to "dominate the theology of the twelfth century in its determination of what a sacrament is," and even Peter Lombard and Thomas Aquinas still built their own discussions of the matter around these definitions.

The requirement that, in order to qualify as a sacrament, a sacred action had to involve the visible "form" or "sign" of an invisible reality present there seems to have come from a consideration of the Eucharist, where the notion of "presence" was fundamental; it was much more difficult to apply to such a sacrament as penance, where there was no presence and no obvious visible sign. It was likewise from eucharistic theology that other elements in the definition of sacrament were derived. Thus the distinction between the sacrament and "the matter of the sacrament," which had been thought to apply only to the Sacrament of the Altar, and not to the other sacraments, now served to explain baptism, where the matter of the sacrament was "the justification of a man" or his "inward washing," as well as matrimony, whose "matter is the process of becoming a member of Christ." It was true of all the sacraments that some received only the sacrament, some only the matter of the sacrament, and some both of these. The stress on the necessity of the words of institution in the Eucharist also carried over to baptism, which was not valid "without the solemn form of the words"; the suggestion that "without the invocation of the Trinity no sacrament takes place in the church" moved in the opposite direction, from baptism to the Eucharist and the other sacraments, but it did not take hold.

With the shift to the words of institution as the constitutive force in a sacrament came an emphasis on insti-

Hug.S.Vict.*Sacr*.1.9.2 (*PL* 176:317)

Geyer (1918) 332

Rup.*Div.off*.10.18 (*CCCM* 7:353)

Joach.*Ev*.1 (*FSI* 67:198–99)

Matt.26:26–28; Mark 14:22–24; Luke 22:19–20; 1 Cor. 11:23–25

Alex.III.*Sent.Rol.* (Gietl 198–99); Ans.L.*Sent.div.pag*.5 (Bliemetzrieder 43)

Sent.div.5.1 (Geyer 110)

John 3:5

Matt. 28:20
Rup.*Div.off*.3.24; 5.31 (*CCCM* 7:100; 185)

John 19:34

Joach.*Ev*.1 (*FSI* 67:198–99)

Matt.3:2
Ans.L.*Sent.Ans*.8 (Bliemetzrieder 121)

Alex.III.*Sent.Rol.* (Gietl 213)

Goff.Vind.*Opusc*.9 (*PL* 157:227); Hug.S.Vict.*Sum.Sent.* 6.15 (*PL* 176:153); Hug.S. Vict.*Sacr*.2.15.2 (*PL* 176:577); Alex.III.*Sent.Rol.* (Gietl 262)

CTrid. (1545–63) 14.*Unct. Cap*.1 (Alberigo 686)

Rab.*Inst.cler*.1.33 (Knoepfler 77)
Isid.Sev.*Orig*.6.19.39 (*PL* 82:255)

Radb.*Corp*.3 (*CCCM* 16:24)
Ps.Petr.Dam.*Serm*.69 (*PL* 144:897–902)

tution itself as the warrant for the sacrament. It was apparently with Hugh of Saint-Victor that "institution by Christ is for the first time taken over formally into the definition of a sacrament." Although it continued to be "the Holy Spirit who is the author and the power of this sacrament [the Eucharist] and of all the sacraments," the certification of that power came through the proof that the sacrament had been properly instituted. But while there were four accounts in the New Testament of the institution of the Eucharist, the institution of the other sacraments was more difficult to establish. For the institution of baptism it was possible to cite at least three separate occasions: the baptism of Christ in the Jordan by John; the statement of Christ to Nicodemus about the necessity of being born again through water and the Spirit; the command of Christ to his disciples to go and baptize. Another possibility sometimes cited was the flowing of water from the wounded side of Christ on the cross. The status of other sacraments was even more ambiguous. It could be said, for example, that John the Baptist had instituted the sacrament of penance with his call to repentance. On the basis of the Book of Acts it seemed that confirmation had been instituted by the apostles, not directly by Christ. During this period there was general agreement that the anointing of the sick or "extreme unction," too, owed its origins to an apostolic institution; but in the sixteenth century the Council of Trent was to insist that it had come from Christ himself, "through James, the apostle and brother of the Lord."

This fluctuation in the definition of the grace of the sacraments and in the requirements for a sacrament was reflected inevitably in the list of actions qualifying as sacraments. One of the most widely accepted formulas spoke of "four sacraments," which were, on the basis of Isidore: "baptism; chrism; the body of the Lord; the blood." But the number varied widely, from the two on which everyone agreed to twelve and even more. It is not clear where the notion of seven as the number of the sacraments began, although the anonymous *Sentences of Divinity* from about 1145 may have been the first to list the seven that were to become canonical: the five sacraments common to all Christians (baptism, confirmation, penance, the Eucharist, and extreme unction); and two that were not shared by everyone (marriage, which was only for the laity, and ordination, which was only for the clergy). That distinction, together with the number seven, achieved acceptance within a decade or two. Perhaps because of the number seven, with its biblical and other sacred associations, the number was accepted even by those contemporaries whose actual lists varied from these. But this list was the one that Peter Lombard took over into his *Sentences;* and "for the further development of the doctrinal concept the *Sentences* of Peter Lombard were decisive. . . . It is significant that . . . his doctrine of the sacraments, especially the number seven, finds universal acceptance." The commentators on the compilation of canon law by Gratian almost all listed seven sacraments, because of the influence of Peter Lombard, even though Gratian himself did not.

So it came about that a definition of "the sacraments in general" determined the understanding of the individual sacraments: "the sacrament of the body and blood of Christ, and the sacrament of baptism, and all the other sacraments of the church." Of these other sacraments, the most important (despite the ambiguity of its having been instituted not by Christ, but already in the Old Testament or perhaps by John the Baptist) was probably penance, which was fundamental not alone to a full understanding of sacramental doctrine, but to the pastoral and disciplinary life of the church. "Without it," said a cardinal and reformer of the early twelfth century, "none of the sacraments is of any use to sinners." There was, said an earlier cardinal, nothing standing between penance and the kingdom of heaven. Therefore it received far lengthier treatment in manuals of theology than, for example, confirmation or the anointing of the sick. Penance was instituted as a means of grace because those who had received the forgiveness of sins through baptism went on to sin again and needed "a second refuge after this shipwreck" to reconcile them to the church, from which they were alienated by their transgression. It was defined as consisting of a vow to avoid sin, an act of confession, and an act of satisfaction. The seven steps of penance were, as enumerated by Bernard of Clairvaux and his disciple Nicholas: "the knowledge of oneself; repentance; sorrow; oral confession; mortification of the flesh; correction [or satisfaction] by a work; perseverance." Satisfaction, which provided Anselm with the fundamental metaphor

Margin notes:

*Sent.div.*5.pr.2 (Geyer 108–9)
Petr.Pict.*Sent.*5.3 (*PL* 211:1229)

Petr.Lomb.*Sent.*4.2.1 (Quaracchi 4:47)

Geyer (1918) 342

Gillmann (1909)

Bald.*Tract.*3 (*PL* 204:421)

Petr.Pict.*Sent.*3.13 (*PL* 211:1071)
Ans.L.*Sent.Ans.*8 (Bliemetzrieder 121)

Goff.Vind.*Serm.*2 (*PL* 157:241)

Petr.Dam.*Serm.*50 (*PL* 144:783)
Alex.III.*Sent.Rol.* (Gietl 237–55)
Alex.III.*Sent.Rol.* (Gietl 212–14; 261–64)

Ans.L.*Sent.Ans.*8 (Bliemetzrieder 120)
Robt.Pull.*Sent.*5.30 (*PL* 186:851); Petr.Dam.*Perf.mon.*6 (Brezzi 232)

Rup.*Div.off.*5.19 (*CCCM* 7:173)

Rich.S.Vict.*Pot.lig.solv.*5 (*TPMA* 15:83); Petr.Ab.*Eth.* (Luscombe 76)

Brd.Clr.*Div.*40 (Leclercq-Rochais 6-1:234–43); Nicol.Clr.*Serm.*58 (*PL* 144:831–33)

See p. 143 above

for his theory of redemption, consisted in reparation or restoration of that which one had taken away by sinning and was the public witness to the church of one's contri-

Alex.III.*Sent.Rol.* (Gietl 244)

tion and absolution.

Confirmation and extreme unction were probably the least clearly defined and the least specifically developed of the seven sacraments in the thought of this period.

Herm.Mag.*Epit.*28 (*PL* 178: 1740)

Confirmation was "greater" than baptism in the sense that the administration of it was reserved to bishops while baptism could be administered by priests or even by laymen. Sources from earlier periods of the history of the church showed that priests had performed confirmations then, but such testimony "is to be understood on the basis of the times, namely, the primitive church, when it was permissible for priests to do so because of the rarity of

Alex.III.*Sent.Rol.* (Gietl 214)

Brun.S.*Sacr.eccl.* (*PL* 165: 1102); Hrot.*Pel.*243–46 (Homeyer 140)

Goff.Vind.*Opusc.*9 (*PL* 157: 226)

bishops." Although "the fullness of the entire mystery of the Christian religion" was present in confirmation, the identification of the special grace it conferred did not come until after the Middle Ages, if then. Extreme unction likewise suffered from lack of clarity in medieval theology. It was "a great sacrament," but the question of its institution seemed to be more interesting than the question of the special grace that it conferred. For example, Bruno of Segni, generally acknowledged as one of the leading exegetical scholars among medieval theologians, "does not even make an allusion either to marriage or to extreme

Grégoire (1965) 309

unction as a sacrament." When theologians did discuss extreme unction, they were hard pressed to identify any

Herm.Mag.*Epit.*30 (*PL* 178: 1744)

ways in which it contained any different "sacramental matter" from that of the other sacraments.

*Sent.div.*5.pr.2 (Geyer 108)

The two sacraments that were "not common to all" believers were matrimony and ordination: priests did not receive the first (although widowers could be ordained), and laymen did not receive the second. It was characteris-

Ans.L.*Sent.Ans.*10 (Bliemetzrieder 129); Alex. III.*Sum.Rol.* (Thaner 113)

tic of both of these sacraments that canon law dominated the discussion of them even on the part of theologians. Thus the oft-repeated observation that "while the institution of the other sacraments took place through human beings on this earth of sin and misery and on account of the variety of sins, this sacrament [matrimony] was in-

Alex.III.*Sent.Rol.* (Gietl 271); Rad.Ard.*Hom.ep.ev.*1.21 (*PL* 155:1742)

stituted by the true and living God in the joys of Paradise at the beginning of time" could serve as the preamble to a detailed catalog of consanguinity, affinity, and other impediments to marriage, where the sacramental defini-

Alex.III.*Sent.Rol.* (Gietl 271–313)

Herm.Mag.*Epit*.31 (*PL* 178:1745)
Isid.Sev.*Sent*.2.40.2 (*SPE* 2:382)

Goff.Vind.*Serm*.11 (*PL* 157:280)

Eph.5:32 (Vulg.)
Herm.Mag.*Epit*.31 (*PL* 178:1747)

Wm.Mon.*Henr.Mon*.7 (Manselli 55)

Sent.div.5.pr.2 (Geyer 108)

Hug.S.Vict.*Sacr*.1.9.7 (*PL* 176:327)

Hon.Aug.*Eluc*.1.30 (*PL* 172:1131)

Petr.Dam.*Opusc*.30.2 (*PL* 145:526)

Seekel (1933) 69

tion of matrimony played no role at all. The problem was that "marriage, although it is of course a sacrament, does not confer any particular gift [of grace], as the other sacraments do, but is a remedy for evil." Another ambiguity was that, in a formula received from Isidore, marriage was good but virginity was better, and yet virginity was not a sacrament while marriage was. In fact, marriage was the only one of the sacraments to be explicitly called a sacrament in the New Testament; "this is," the apostle declared, "a great sacrament [sacramentum hoc magnum est]," adding: "I am, moreover, speaking in Christ and in the church." On the basis of this passage, matrimony was "the sacrament of Christ and the church," and the relation between spouses was a sign of the relation of the church to Christ as his bride. Despite this connection with the church, however, matrimony was the only sacrament that was constituted "without any celebration . . . and without the institution of the church," on the basis of "only the consensus of certain persons."

The other of the two sacraments "not common to all" was ordination. It, like matrimony, belonged to the category of those sacraments "in which salvation principally consists and is received"; unlike matrimony, however, it had been "instituted for the sole purpose of somehow preparing and sanctifying the things that are necessary for the sanctification and institution of the other sacraments." The sacrament of holy orders, therefore, was basic to the other sacraments, which were, as a rule, dependent on it for their valid administration. The validity or invalidity of ordination, consequently, had implications for the grace of every sacrament. When the reform of the church during the eleventh and twelfth centuries, directed as it was against the twin abuses of simony and lay investiture, reopened the question of the validity of ordinations obtained by illegal means, these implications were unavoidable. As in the discussions of matrimony, this was a problem in canon law that impinged upon theology. The Augustinian emphasis on the objectivity of baptism could serve as the basis for the generalization of Peter Damian that "the divine power truly effects its sacrament," regardless of the merit of the priest. Radbertus had transferred this principle from baptism to the Eucharist; and now, in support of the objectivity of the real presence, Damian transferred it "to a third, namely, to ordination."

The development in the thought of Alger of Liège, presumably under Damian's influence, is illustrative of the doctrinal problem. He believed that "in the celebration of the sacraments of Christ" one must follow the institution of Christ, to assure that "what we perform is true by His power and legitimate by His authority." Originally this led him to maintain that sacraments administered by a priest who had been invalidly ordained were "as far as their effects are concerned, neither true nor holy," but eventually he concluded that the Mass was the sacrifice of the church even when it was offered by such a priest.

The definitive list of the seven sacraments was an exclusive as well as an inclusive one, eventually disqualifying certain sacred acts that had at one time or another been called sacraments or that had at any rate participated in the sacramental system. Monastic vows, for example, had long been identified as a "second baptism," and occasionally they joined the list of sacraments. "The dedication of a church in which all the other sacraments are celebrated" could assume the dignity of a sacrament itself. The sign of the cross accompanying sacramental actions likewise seemed to merit the title. Although matrimony was one of the seven sacraments to attain official recognition, there were those who defined the mutual fidelity of the spouses as "the sacrament that is appropriate to marriage." Similarly, while baptism was a sacrament on everyone's list, the faith accompanying it could also be one. Together with the sign of the cross, the blessing of Easter candles belonged to "those sacraments in the church from which, even though salvation does not actually consist in them, salvation is enhanced insofar as devotion is exercised"; these were too numerous to mention. On some lists, "the sacrament of the anointing of a king" was able to claim a place. On the other hand, the consecration of a bishop, on which the ordination of a priest depended in much the same way that the other sacraments in turn depended on ordination, was sometimes called a sacrament, but it did not achieve sacramental status. Only after this period was the idea of "sacramentals" fully evolved to include some of these actions.

The principle that each of the sacraments contained and conveyed a special grace, combined with a more detailed and precise definition of what a sacrament must be and must do, helped to establish the normative list of

Alg.*Sacr*.3.14 (*PL* 180:854)

Alg.*Mis.et just*.3.2 (*PL* 180: 932)

Alg.*Sacr*.3.9 (*PL* 180:842)

Petr.Dam.*Perf.mon*.6 (Brezzi 232); Petr.Dam.*Opusc*.16.8 (*PL* 145:376)
Ps.Petr.Dam.*Serm*.69 (*PL* 144: 901)
Brun.S.*Sacr.eccl*. (*PL* 165: 1090); Hug.S.Vict.*Sacr*.2.5.1 (*PL* 176:439)

Ans.L.*Sent.Ans*.4 (Bliemetzrieder 110)

Rath.*Prael*.2.3.7 (*PL* 136:195)
Herb.Los.*Serm*.8 (Goulburn-Symonds 210)

Hug.S.Vict.*Sacr*.2.9.1 (*PL* 176:471)

Ps.Petr.Dam.*Serm*.69 (*PL* 144: 899–900)

Goff.Vind.*Lib*.7 (*MGH Lib. lit*.2:695)

Hug.S.Vict.*Sacr*.1.9.2 (*PL* 176:317)

seven sacraments. More importantly, it served to integrate
the sacraments with one another—and to integrate all
of them as a system with the communion of the saints in
the church—in such a way as to bring the entirety of
human life, literally from the cradle to the grave, under
the sway of divine grace. Sacramental theology and its
corollaries thus became the most thoroughly articulated
application of the ancient principle that "the rule of prayer
should lay down the rule of faith."

See vol.1:339

5   The One True Faith

The application of the principle that "the rule of prayer should establish the rule of faith" to the doctrine of the saints and the doctrine of the sacraments confirmed the doctrinal authority of "the rule of prayer," but in the process it also called attention to the need for a further and more fundamental inquiry into "the rule of faith." At no time in the period covered by this volume would there have been any substantial denial of the assertion that there was one true faith, the faith set forth in the unchanging and unchangeable consensus of the catholic centuries. Yet the disputes and developments of the eleventh and twelfth centuries, in particular the eucharistic controversy and its repercussions, made it impossible to identify or to assert the one true faith as simplistically as its spokesmen had been doing before the complexity and ambiguity of such an assertion came clearly into view.

In part this complexity was due to the understanding of the nature of faith itself. "The invisible things of God," according to Hugh of Saint-Victor, "can only be believed, but cannot in any way be comprehended." They transcended all analogy and likeness, whether of body or of soul, and therefore "their very substance is the faith by which they are believed." Faith was "the certain comprehension of unchangeable truth, confirmed by the surest authority," a comprehension that "exceeds all the experience of the senses and transcends all the conjectures of human reason" and that deserved to be called "knowledge" in the fullest sense, since it was a confident trust in the God who was truth itself. Again, it was "a certitude of the

Hug.S.Vict.Sacr.1.10.2 (PL 176:328–29)

Bald.Comm.fid. (PL 204:583)

Hug.S.Vict.*Sacr*.1.10.2 (*PL* 176:330); Alex.Hal.*Sent*.1.3.13 (*BFS* 12:44)

Petr.Lomb.*Serm*.26 (*PL* 171: 436–37)

Guit.Av.*Corp*.3 (*PL* 149: 1485)

Bern.Reich.*Dial*.1 (*PL* 142: 1089); Brun.S.*Az*. (*PL* 165: 1985)

Brun.S.*Apoc*.5.16 (*PL* 165: 693)

mind concerning matters that are not present, above opinion but below knowledge." Different though these definitions were in emphasis, they were agreed in viewing the true and catholic faith as "only one," by contrast with the "vain credulity" of false believers, which was inconstant and varied. Although there was a "diversity of customs," this did not affect "the one faith of our holy catholic mother, the church." Standing over against "the foolish wisdom of heretics and of philosophers" was "the true and catholic faith," which was distinct from the knowledge that came from sense experience or through reason. What made it distinct was its origin in divine grace and its ground in the supernatural authority of divine revelation. In the twelfth and thirteenth centuries the implications of these truth claims needed to be drawn in relation to tradition, in opposition to schism and heresy, in response to other religions, and in comparison with the claims of reason.

The Problem of Patristic Consensus

Alan.Ins.*Haer*.1.59 (*PL* 210: 363)

In the course of the conflict over the nature of the eucharistic body, the central issue often appeared to come down to the question of authority, especially because so much of the tradition, including the ecumenical creeds, had been silent on the matter. When it was discovered that among "the authorities there are some who seem to say clearly that this is the true body" while others seemed

Sent.*Flor*.73 (Ostlender 32)

to say the opposite, that represented a potential threat to the identification of "our faith" as "solidly established on

Bald.*Sacr.alt*.2.1.3 (*SC* 93: 208)

the firm rock of divine authority" rather than on "the uncertainty of human opinions." Berengar made the question of authority basic to his argument. When his opponents claimed the support of the majority in the church for their view of the presence, he countered that the majority was not always in the right, and cited as

1 Kings 19:18
Brngr.Tr.*Coen*.12 (Beekenkamp 19)

Brngr.Tr.*Coen*.27 (Beekenkamp 56)
Brngr.Tr.*Coen*.9 (Beekenkamp 13)
Brngr.Tr.*Coen*.8 (Beekenkamp 10)

Brngr.Tr.*Coen*.15 (Beekenkamp 25–26)

proof the seven thousand who, in the days of Elijah the prophet, had not bowed to Baal. It was better to stand with the few in the defense of the truth than to err with the many. Nor did he accept the charge that he had been condemned by a church council; for there had been councils before in the history of the church that had erred, and the true church council was one that confessed the truth, that is, one that taught as he did. In sum, he declared to his adversaries, "as you have nothing of truth, so also

Brngr.Tr.*Coen*.38 (Beekenkamp 110)

Lanf.*Corp*.23 (PL 150:442)

Guit.Av.*Corp*.3 (PL 149:1480)
See vol.1:333

Bald.*Sacr.alt*.2.1.2 (*SC* 93: 144)

Guit.Av.*Corp*.3 (PL 149: 1489)

See vol.1:334
Aug.*Parm*.3.4.24 (*CSEL* 51: 131)
Lanf.*Corp*.1 (PL 150:407)

Brngr.Tr.*Coen*.27 (Beekenkamp 57)

Brngr.Tr.*Coen*.6 (Beekenkamp 7)

Brngr.Tr.*Coen*.25 (Beekenkamp 54)

Lanf.*Corp*.22 (PL 150:440–41)

Guit.Av.*Corp*.3 (PL 149: 1474)

Her.*Corp*.1 (PL 139:180)

Lanf.*Corp*.22 (PL 150:441)
Lanf.*Corp*.8 (PL 150:419)

you have nothing of authority." They in turn accused him and his followers of claiming: "Only in us and in those who follow us has the holy church remained on earth."

The need to be in agreement with the church, whatever the definition of the church might be, made it imperative to identify what had been taught "everywhere over such a long period of time," for this was a norm of catholic truth. When it came to eucharistic doctrine, "that understanding of these words of Christ is to be preferred . . . which is acknowledged to belong to the interpretation of the church, which has the support of the authority of the orthodox fathers, and which has the commendation of the faith of the catholic and apostolic church." What the catholic church believed was what Christ had wanted it to believe and what the Holy Spirit had led it to believe, and this was the true faith that it had handed down by tradition to subsequent generations. "The universal faith of the church" was "not recent, not a matter of this or that man, but of the whole world." Echoing the Augustinian formula that "the judgment of the whole world is reliable," Berengar's critics attacked him for setting himself "against the whole world," but he refused to equate "the confession of the church throughout the whole world" with "the madness of the fools in the church" who taught otherwise than he did. Indeed, if his teaching were labeled as heresy, then "without this heresy no one has ever been or ever will be a catholic." His opponents had no right to claim "the ancient faith of the church" as their authority.

But "if what you believe and affirm about the body of Christ is true," they replied, "then what is believed and affirmed by the church throughout the nations is false," and they challeged him to ask anyone in the Latin world or, for that matter, anyone among the Greeks or Armenians about the doctrine of the real presence. East and West, "all the principal doctors of the church, both Greek and Latin, teach" this doctrine. All of them, as part of the catholic church, taught the same thing, and "there is no schism" among them. For if this doctrine was not an ecumenical one and if "the faith of the universal church has been a false one, then either there has never been a catholic church or it has perished"; neither of these conclusions was possible. It was "incumbent on a member of the church not to deviate from the church." So deeply

See vol.1:236–38

Lanf.*Corp*.17 (*PL* 150:427–28)

Lanf.*Ep*.50 (*PL* 150:543)

Hil.*Trin*.8.13–14 (*PL* 10:245–47)

Her.*Corp*.7 (*PL* 139:184); Dur.Tr.*Corp*.3.3 (*PL* 149:1382)

Petr.Dam.*Opusc*.47 (*PL* 145:712); Petr.Dam.*Opusc*.50 (*PL* 145:735); Petr.Dam.*Ep*.2.11 (*PL* 144:277–78)

Hug.Met.*Ep*.4 (*PL* 188:1275)

See p. 186 above

Brngr.Tr.*Ep*.7 (Sudendorf 211–12)

Brngr.Tr.*Coen*.44 (Beekenkamp 149–53)

Guit.Av.*Corp*.3 (*PL* 149:1469)

Dur.Tr.*Corp*.7.26 (*PL* 149:1417)

Rup.*Ev.Joh*.ep.ded. (*PL* 169:202)

Guit.Av.*Corp*.1 (*PL* 149:1430)

Guit.Av.*Corp*.3 (*PL* 149:1470)

embedded was the doctrine of the real presence in the faith of the universal church that both the heretic Nestorius and the ecumenical Council of Ephesus that condemned him in 431 had been agreed on it, even though they drew from it contradictory teachings about the person of Christ. In the previous century, Hilary of Poitiers—whom Berengar was accused of attacking on other grounds as well—had been able to take an orthodox doctrine of the Eucharist for granted even among those who denied that the Son was homoousios with the Father, and he had "proved what was in doubt [the homoousion] on the basis of what was beyond doubt [the real presence], even for the heretics." Not only Eastern theologians and heretics, but Satan himself was a witness to the doctrine of the real presence, who, "whether he wants to or not, accepts the reality of the body and blood of the Lord."

Within the tradition of the universal church, it was above all Augustine who was the "patron" for the critics of the developing doctrine of the real presence. They argued that when the Synod of Vercelli in 1050 had condemned what it took to be a heretical doctrine of the Eucharist, that doctrine was in fact "the teaching of Saint Augustine." To prove this, they compiled catenae of quotations from the writings of Augustine that seemed to reject the notion of a physical presence of the historical body of Christ in the elements of the Sacrament. The champions of the real presence themselves recognized that "the origin of almost the entire scandal seems to have come from Saint Augustine," whose language about the Eucharist was so "subtle" that "certain perverse individuals have fallen into the labyrinth of error on account of this great doctor's ways of speaking and have striven obstinately to draw others in after them." Nevertheless, they charged that it was "altogether false" to identify Augustine with the doctrines of Berengar. The only way to achieve such an identification was "to spin out some pathetic rationalizations and then to support them from certain of the statements of Saint Augustine." But if instead one took the pains to understand him rather than to blame him for teachings he had never espoused, one would find that in his writings there was "nothing embarrassing, nothing ambiguous."

There were, however, more than a few passages in the Augustinian corpus that did seem somewhat ambiguous and that were therefore also quite embarrassing. When Berengar quoted passages that described the Eucharist as a "figure" and a "sign," the response was that "Augustine . . . never called the food on the altar of the Lord a 'sign' or a 'figure,' but he did say that the celebration of the Lord's body is a 'sign.'" Other passages were more troublesome. One such was the oft-quoted statement, "Why are you preparing your teeth and your stomach? Believe, and you have already eaten." This could be dismissed on the grounds that Augustine was speaking "about one mode of eating, that according to which Christ is eaten through faith by the righteous." It was not so easy to dismiss another familiar Augustinian paraphrase of the words of Jesus, "Understand spiritually what I have said. You are not to eat this body which you see, nor to drink that blood which will be shed by those who are to crucify me," especially if these were taken to be authentic words of Christ himself. Berengar found his teachings substantiated in these words, which became for him "the foundation of [his] defense." "If, then," he argued, "it is not that body or that blood, it follows that what is eaten from the altar is merely a shadow and a figure of the body and blood." In their responses to the quotation from Augustine, his opponents cited, as had Berengar himself, other words of Augustine in the same commentary: "He received flesh from the flesh of Mary. . . . He walked here in that very flesh and gave us that very flesh to eat for our salvation." It was a "calumny" to twist Augustine's words and to transform "this pillar of the church, this foundation of the truth" into a heretic.

Nevertheless, the only way for Augustine to stand as a pillar of the church and a foundation of the truth in his eucharistic teachings was with the support of other catholic doctors, notably Ambrose. As had become evident already in the ninth century, Ambrose was a far more explicit witness to the real presence than Augustine, and it was from his definition of the eucharistic body as the body born of the Virgin that the defenders of the real presence had derived their doctrine. His exposition of the change that took place in the Eucharist provided the documentation for their position. Even when he was being quoted alongside such fathers as Hilary and Augustine, Ambrose was said to "possess the principal authority in the catholic church, next to that of the apostles," and he

Brngr.Tr.*Coen*.9 (Beekenkamp 13)

Guit.Av.*Corp*.2 (*PL* 149: 1455)

See vol.1:305
Alg.*Sacr*.1.8 (*PL* 180:762);
Iv.*Pan*.1.136 (*PL* 161:1075);
Aug.*Ev.Joh*.25.12 (*CCSL* 36: 254)

Bald.*Sacr.alt*.2.3.2 (*SC* 93:270–72)

Aug.*Ps*.98.9 (*CCSL* 39:1386)

Petr.Lomb.*Serm*.23 (*PL* 171: 803)
Brngr.Tr.*Coen*.43 (Beekenkamp 146)

Lanf.*Corp*.18 (*PL* 150:433)

Brngr.Tr.*fr*.ap.Guit.Av.
Corp.2 (*PL* 149:1462)
Alg.*Sacr*.1.11 (*PL* 180:773–74); Guit.Av.*Corp*.2 (*PL* 149: 1462)
Brngr.Tr.*Coen*.43 (Beekenkamp 146)

Aug.*Ps*.98.9 (*CCSL* 39:1385)

Lanf.*Corp*.18 (*PL* 150:433–34)

See pp. 192–93 above

Lanf.*Corp*.18 (*PL* 150:430–32)

Dur.Tr.*Corp*.4.6 (*PL* 149: 1384)

Her.*Corp*.4 (*PL* 139:183)

Brngr.Tr.*Ep*.12 (Sudendorf 220)
Ambr.*Spir*.3.17.122 (*CSEL* 79: 202)

Brngr.Tr.*Coen*.27 (Beekenkamp 58)

Brngr.Tr.*Coen*.29 (Beekenkamp 62)

Lanf.*Corp*.9 (*PL* 150:419)

Her.*Corp*.1 (*PL* 139:179–80); Anast.Clun.*Ep.Ger*. (*PL* 149: 435–36)

Brnld.*Brngr*.11 (*PL* 148:1458)

Guit.Av.*Corp*.2 (*PL* 149:1463)

Alg.*Sacr*.1.7 (*PL* 180:756)

Guit.Av.*Corp*.2 (*PL* 149: 1464)

was an important witness to the ecumenical character of orthodox doctrine because "no other Latin [theologian] seems to have followed the Greeks" as much as he. Berengar, too, demanded to have his ideas put "under the judgment . . . of Saint Ambrose," claiming Ambrose's statement that the body of Christ could not be wounded again as substantiation of his contention that the true body could not be broken by the hands of the priest nor torn by the teeth of the communicant. He could cite Ambrose "with complete justification and with no injury" to his teaching. But he was, replied his opponents, "presumptuous in summoning Ambrose as a witness," for an examination of his "*On the Sacraments* or of all the other books written by Ambrose that are now in use in the church" would not produce any passages in which he had taught what Berengar claimed to have derived from him. And so, whether one took Ambrose or Augustine or Jerome, it would be evident that "these great men do not disagree and that everyone in the catholic church should think one and the same thing, and that there is no schism among them."

All the parties in the controversy would probably have agreed that "everyone in the catholic church should think one and the same thing," but it was by no means as clear that "these great men do not disagree." The assumption that there was such a thing as patristic consensus on the question of the eucharistic presence was difficult to substantiate, even for the opponents of Berengar. They could "simply put forward the testimonies of the holy fathers about the body of the Lord," but that did not remove the problem. For the best they could do sometimes was to acknowledge that, for example, some of Augustine's statements about the Sacrament, "although they are somewhat ambiguous, do not support their [the Berengarians'] side any more than they do ours." Even in the case of Ambrose, there were some passages that had to be interpreted in a particular way, "lest he contradict his own authority and that of the other saints." Still there were statements in the fathers that did not lend themselves to such harmonization; in such cases the father in question "either is not to be accepted or is to be believed on the basis of many of his statements rather than only of one." Sometimes it was possible to attribute the contradictions to differences in language, specifically to the con-

Goz.*Ep.Val.*30 (*PL* 143:900)
Bald.*Sacr.alt.*2.1.2 (*SC* 93:148)

trast between the fathers, who had observed a reverent silence about the mysteries of the faith, and later generations, which had felt obliged to invent new terminology "for the sake of a devout confession of the faith." When none of these techniques of explanation availed, "it is safer for the reader, in dealing with very difficult passages in the holy fathers, ... to say that he does not know than ...

Lanf.*Ep.*50 (*PL* 150:544)

to define things in a way that is contrary to the faith."

Underlying all such attempts to cope with the contradictions among the church fathers was the recognition that the writings of the fathers were only part of a larger and more comprehensive system of doctrinal authority.

See vol.1:119

An individual passage from an individual father on such an issue as the eucharistic presence needed the context of "Scripture itself ... and the message of the gospel and

Guit.Av.*Corp.*2 (*PL* 149:1463)

the authority of the universal church" to be interpreted in an orthodox manner. It is not surprising that the dispute over the real presence brought the problem of patristic consensus into sharper focus; "nor," on the other hand, "was it accidental that when the Eucharistic controversy

Smalley (1964) 92

revived in the eleventh century," the questions of the exegesis of Scripture and the authority of Scripture once more became prominent. This was not only because Berengar and his followers were seen as "despising the histo-

Guit.Av.*Corp.*3 (*PL* 149:1480)

ries of the fathers as well as contradicting the gospel," but also because his opponents made the literal truthfulness of the words "This is my body" dependent on the trustworthiness of the entire Gospel narrative of the institution of the Eucharist, including the statement that Christ "broke" the bread, so that "anyone who does not concede that the body of Christ 'is broken' has done everything he can to break the entire [article of] faith concerning this

Abb.*Fract.* (*PL* 166:1344)
Brd.Clr.*Cant.*72.3.6 (Leclercq-Rochais 2:229)

Sacrament." If even the most trivial details in Scripture were fraught with meaning, much more so was its language about such an important matter as this.

Among the defenders of the doctrine of the real presence in the twelfth century, Baldwin of Canterbury was outstanding for his recognition that the doctrine of the unique inspiration and supreme authority of Scripture was crucial to the orthodox doctrine of the Eucharist. While he acknowledged that in doctrinal and even in liturgical questions "the authority of the ancient [church

Bald.*Sacr.alt.*2.1.2 (*SC* 93:116)

fathers] ought to be reason enough for us" and while he could speak as though "the words of the law and the prophets, of the apostles and evangelists, of the orthodox fathers, and of individuals who have been faithful in the confession of the faith" were all on the same level, the church fathers and the church itself bore such authority only because the church had "accepted the word of faith, which is the word of God, in the apostles" and in the apostolic Scripture of the New Testament. For example, the monastic life had the standing it did in the church because it had been established "by the apostles themselves," without whom it would have no authority. It was "extremely dangerous to let in any false opinion about God," who was "his own witness to himself" in Scripture, which "is divinely inspired [and in which] the form of faith is written down for us." Because God had "seen fit to reveal the truth about God in the Sacred Scriptures, a faith that believes worthily about God ought to be a faith in the words of God." It followed from this that "the foundation of our faith can be reduced to the authority of Sacred Scripture: if this is true, the witnesses of the faith are true, the testimonies of the faith are true, and consequently the faith itself is true."

Like his contemporaries, Baldwin was troubled by discrepancies between various biblical accounts, for example in chronology, but faith did not depend on how one resolved such discrepancies, "so long as we believe without any doubt what the deeds or words say [in] the Gospel narrative." For there could not possibly be any contradiction between the Gospels and the writings of the Old Testament prophets, since both had been inspired by the same Holy Spirit. Accordingly, when theologians made the correct understanding of Scripture dependent on a prior acceptance of faith in Christ or when they argued that the Gentile world "accepts the authority of the [Old Testament] Scriptures because it has first come to believe in Christ," this was in no way a diminution of the authority of Scripture. In fact, in a consideration of the Gospel account of the transfiguration of Jesus, at which Moses and Elijah appeared on either side of him, Richard of Saint-Victor drew a distinction between those teachings of Christ "which I am able to confirm on the basis of my own experience" and those that dealt with sublime and transcendent truth; when the teachings of Christ spoke of these latter, "I will not accept Christ without a witness, nor can any revelation, regardless of its verisimilitude,

Bald.*Comm.fid.* (PL 204:620)

Bald.*Sacr.alt.*2.1.2 (SC 93:144–46)

Bald.*Tract.*15 (PL 204:545)

Bald.*Tract.*9 (PL 204:487)

Bald.*Comm.fid.* (PL 204:575)

Bald.*Comm.fid.* (PL 204:621)
Rich.S.Vict.*Tabern.*3 (PL 196:241)

Bald.*Sacr.alt.*2.1.2 (SC 93:174)

Rich.S.Vict.*Em.*1.7 (PL 196:613)

Bald.*Comm.fid.* (PL 204:628)

Petr.Ven.*Jud.*4 (PL 189:592)

Matt.17:1–8

Rich.S.Vict.*Ben.min.*81 (*PL* 196:57)

1 John 5:7

Bald.*Comm.fid.* (*PL* 204:614)

Her.*Ep.Hug.* (*PL* 139:1129)

Rich.S.Vict.*Serm.cent.*99 (*PL* 177:1205)

Rich.S.Vict.*Tabern.*1.pr. (*PL* 196:211–12)

Brd.Clr.*Laud.Virg.*4.11 (Leclercq-Rochais 4:58)

Rich.S.Vict.*Ben.maj.*1.1 (*PL* 196:63); Guib.Nog.*Ord.serm.* (*PL* 156:29)

Rich.S.Vict.*Except.*2.pr. (*TPMA* 5:213)

See vol.2:76

be valid without the attestation of Moses and Elijah, that is, without the authority of the Scriptures." Hence "the authority of the faith" was established by the testimony that the Father bore to Christ in revealing "the Son in the Scriptures" and "the Son in us."

Although it was still appropriate to link Scripture and the fathers as two parts of a unified system of authority, there was a qualitative difference, not merely a quantitative one, between the authority of the two. A contradiction among the fathers was perplexing, a contradiction within Scripture was unthinkable. Moreover, what made a church father such as Augustine great was that he was "filled with the Spirit of the prophets and apostles"; for the fathers saw themselves, and wanted others to see them, as interpreters of Scripture. As such, they had "treated many great and profound matters with all diligence, expounding many things historically or allegorically or tropologically in a wondrous way." Therefore it was not to seem "surprising if they left behind a less adequate exposition of some passage" and if, as a result, "we are able, in one or another passage, to add something that could make a contribution to a greater insight or a clearer understanding." It was necessary to make this point "for the sake of those who refuse to acknowledge anything except what they have received from the most ancient fathers." What was important was that the things one said "after the fathers" not be "contrary to the fathers," even though they themselves may not have said these things. Such an addition was not an act of presumption or of "temerity," but of faithfulness to the heritage of the fathers. It was better, in the study of Scripture, to draw on "one's own experience" than merely on the opinions of others.

To dramatize the qualitative distinction between the authority of Scripture and the authority of the fathers, Peter Abelard compiled a chrestomathy of passages, whose very title, *Yes and No* [*Sic et non*], suggested that the inconsistencies and downright contradictions in the patristic tradition, together with methods of dealing with these, were to be its theme. Such compilations ordinarily served the purpose of documenting the patristic consensus on issues of Christian doctrine and practice. In addition to providing methodological suggestions for discovering such a consensus behind the discrepancies, Abelard purposed to "introduce certain passages from the Scriptures, [which would] arouse the reader and draw him to an inquiry into the truth, all the more so when the authority of Scripture itself is given greater emphasis." The canonical Scripture of the Old and New Testaments was the norm of true doctrine, and dissent from it was heretical. The same did not apply to the church fathers, who, as "commentators" on Scripture, did not merit the "undoubting faith" appropriate to the writers in the biblical canon. Augustine had warned his readers: "Do not be willing to yield to my writings as to the canonical Scriptures." These and other quotations from Augustine provided Abelard with proof that the greatest loyalty to the fathers consisted in subjecting them to the authority of the Bible, as they themselves had demanded.

Although there were other theologians who also emphasized that there was no obligation to give to any church father, regardless of how learned and catholic he was, the same deference that belonged to the canonical Scripture, it is clear that "in this differentiation between Scripture and the fathers Abelard sets himself apart from his theological contemporaries." Yet the fundamental tendency of his book was one that he shared with them, as well as with those among his contemporaries whose primary concern was not with theology, but with canon law. For the legal scholars, too, "their firm belief that the authors of the canons acted under the inspiration of the Holy Spirit also rendered more acute the inherent difficulties of sifting and interpreting the so disparate elements in the monuments of canonical tradition." It was "a great insult to the Holy Spirit himself" if one did not attempt to achieve a consensus among the statements that he had inspired. In their procedures for harmonizing these elements of patristic tradition, the expositors of doctrine and the expositors of law made use of the same methods, but they were also aware that there was a basic difference between the two areas; for "the catholic fathers have from the beginning established the limits of true faith and sound doctrine, which it is altogether forbidden to transgress," while in such areas of custom as fasting or liturgical practice the rules set down by the fathers and councils had not been intended to carry the same weight of authority. It was possible to speak of "a change of the law brought about by necessity," but not of a change of doc-

Petr.Ab.*Sic et non*.pr. (Boyer-McKeon 104)

Petr.Ab.*Sic et non*.pr. (Boyer-McKeon 101)

Petr.Ab.*Sic et non*.pr. (Boyer-McKeon 103)

Aug.*Trin*.3.pr.2 (*CCSL* 50: 128)

Petr.Ab.*Sic et non*.pr. (Boyer-McKeon 100–101)

Petr.Ven.*Ep*.94 (Constable 245)

Grabmann (1957) 2:210

Ryan (1956) 138

Bernl.Const.*Lib*.10 (*MGH Lib.lit*.2:139)

Bern.Reich.*Miss.off*.7 (*PL* 142: 1073)

Iv.*Prol*. (*PL* 161:57)

trine. In spite of this difference, however, lawyers and theologians faced many of the same problems in dealing with the tradition of the church, and they formulated many of the same solutions. For "it is by this sublime disregard of history (or, we may say, by the primacy of reason over history) that the medieval lawyers [as well as the medieval theologians] were able to make a system out of the conflicting data they found in the experience of reality."

Kuttner (1960) 35

Abelard's first rule for handling contradictions was to decide whether there had been "a false identification of the title or a corruption of [the text of] the writing itself." During some of the controversies of medieval theology, the question of authenticity had been an important factor, and various parties had exchanged accusations of tampering with the text of the fathers. The right did not lie infallibly with any of the parties, but there had been instances—for example, in the conflict over predestination —in which the Pseudo-Augustine had been able to prevail over the real Augustine. Recognizing the problem, interpreters of Augustine urged that "when Augustine contradicts himself," one possible explanation was that "his manuscripts could have been corrupted by some falsifier." In addition, entire works or individual pieces of legislation could carry the name of a church father but not have come from him at all; for "many things have been falsely attributed to the statutes of the holy fathers," both in law and in doctrine. This had happened, Abelard pointed out, even in the text of Scripture itself, and it was understandable if the works of the fathers had not been immune to corruption. The diagnosis and correction of these errors could serve to separate the wheat of patristic teaching from the chaff of later accretions.

Petr.Ab.*Sic et non*.pr. (Boyer-McKeon 91)

See pp. 63–65 above

See p. 86 above

Guit.Av.*Corp*.2 (*PL* 149:1464)

Bernl.Const.*Lib*.15 (*MGH Lib.lit*.2:157)

If the authorship of the document and its text were beyond challenge, the next step was "to pay attention . . . to whether elsewhere . . . [such statements] were retracted by them and corrected, once they had recognized the truth." In dealing with canon law, "a comparison of diverse statutes with one another is very helpful to us, because one [statute] often elucidates another" by clarifying it or even correcting and retracting it. The most illustrious example of this self-correction was, of course, Augustine himself, whose *Retractations,* written near the end of his life, had reviewed his books one by one and

Petr.Ab.*Sic et non*.pr. (Boyer-McKeon 92)

Bernl.Const.*Lib*.10 (*MGH Lib.lit*.2:139)

See vol.1:307–8

Petr.Ab.*Sic et non*.pr. (Boyer-McKeon 94)

Petr.Ab.*Sic et non*.pr. (Boyer-McKeon 96)

Iv.*Prol.* (*PL* 161:50)

Bernl.Const.*Lib*.10 (*MGH Lib.lit*.2:139)

Petr.Ab.*Sic et non*.pr. (Boyer-McKeon 96)

Iv.*Prol.* (*PL* 161:47)

See pp. 212–13 above

Bernl.Const.*Lib*.4 (*MGH Lib.lit*.2:90)

made detailed revisions and explanations. In the course of "retracting and correcting" various of his earlier statements, Augustine had also "acknowledged that he had taken many of these positions more on the basis of the opinions of others than from his own convictions." In his works or in those of any other father, therefore, it was necessary also to be aware of the places where he was quoting or paraphrasing someone else, often for the purpose of considering alternatives rather than of setting forth his own ideas.

"When diverse things are said on the same issue," Abelard continued, "one must also investigate what was intended [by each] . . . , so that we may find a solution of the difficulty on the basis of a diversity of intentions," specifically the diversity between general rules and particular legislation. Among the precepts and the prohibitions of church law, "some are movable, some are immovable." Sometimes the apparent conflict between various parts of the tradition could be traced to this difference. For "the holy fathers instituted [some things] as a matter of prudent administration [dispensatorie], to be observed only temporarily," while other rules were meant "to be kept universally and for all time." Abelard pointed out that some legislation had been intended to carry "the force of precept," while in other cases the intention had been to mitigate the demands of the rule. If some canons had been "based on rigor and others on moderation, some on justice and others on mercy," that would lead to apparent contradictions. Obviously, this means of coping with contradictions was better suited to canon law than to theology, where it was not permissible to make adjustments for the sake of "rigor" or of "moderation" and where the tension between "justice" and "mercy" had been resolved not by legislation but by the atoning death of Christ. Yet such a question as that of sacramental validity, which was under discussion in this period, belonged both to doctrine and to canon law, so that, for example, Alger of Liège, who was simultaneously a theologian and a canonist, did make such adjustments in his teaching; and a contemporary of his, faced with the same question, drew a distinction between the "effect" of baptism, which could never be outside the church, and the "reality" of the sacraments, which was objectively true regardless of the status of minister or recipient.

Petr.Ab.*Sic et non*.pr. (Boyer-McKeon 96)

Underlying any such adjustment or distinction was the historical recognition, especially in the case of decrees and canons, that "one must distinguish between times," since "what has been allowed at one time is found to have been prohibited at another." For example, the requirement of clerical celibacy had been dispensed for the English church, on the grounds that the marriage of priests, while less desirable than celibacy, was preferable to promiscuity; but "when the necessity ceases, the dispensations also ought to cease, nor should one regard as law what utility

Iv.*Prol.* (*PL* 161:58)

has urged or necessity has required." A failure to pay attention to these historical differences, according to Bernold of Constance, could lead a careless observer to the hasty conclusion that different canons were "absurd or contrary," when "a consideration of the times, the places, or the persons" would show that the diversity was to be attributed to the special circumstances surrounding the cases and that there was no real contradiction between

Bernl.Const.*Lib*.10 (*MGH Lib.lit*.2:139)

them. When Bernold pointed out, in this same connection, that "the original causes" that had provoked the statutes could illumine the specific intention of the legislation, he was enunciating a principle of historical interpretation that could be applied to the original causes, often the teachings of heretics, that had been the provocation for dogmatic legislation as well.

Abelard was less interested in these historical solutions of the contradictions than in the proposal that "an easy solution of many controversies will be found if we can demonstrate that the same words have been used by

Petr.Ab.*Sic et non*.pr. (Boyer-McKeon 96)

different authors in different senses." As he had said earlier, "the greatest impediment to our understanding [of the fathers] is our unfamiliarity with their way of speaking and with the diverse significance of many of

Petr.Ab.*Sic et non*.pr. (Boyer-McKeon 89)

the same terms." Sorting out these various meanings and learning that the same word had been used in various ways and that various terms could be used for the same thing would lead to a clarification of ambiguous texts and so to a harmonization of the discordant statements that had come from the tradition. It was a standard principle of theological method that "similar terms, when applied to dissimilar objects, are to be understood in differing ways, and they should not always be understood in one or the other way even though they sound the same." As that principle applied to Scripture, it provided a way of preserving orthodox doctrine even when—as, for example, in many passages that spoke of (a or the) "son of God"— biblical writers had not used a term univocally. But it could also justify the procedure of comparing patristic quotations with a view to analyzing how various terms had been employed. Thus even so crucial a trinitarian term as "substance" had been employed in differing ways by the fathers, especially if one compared Greek and Latin usage, but this did not compromise their doctrinal orthodoxy.

Although these techniques would take care of many, perhaps of most, contradictions, there would inevitably be some "that cannot be resolved by any device." In such a case, "the authorities should be compared, and that which has the stronger witness and the greater support should be given preference." In canon law likewise, "if there happens to be a patent opposition, the lesser authority will have to yield to the greater." In effect, this moved the entire process back to where it had begun, for the issue of choice among authorities had been the fundamental problem all along—not only the choice between Scripture and the fathers, but the choice among the fathers themselves. Even those who maintained that the contradictions within the tradition were often apparent rather than real had to concede that the tradition was less than uniform on many questions. Such was the case on relatively minor issues such as whether or not the bodies in which angels appeared were their own, or whether hell was an actual place or only the condition of eternal damnation. But it had to be admitted that "not only those who assemble [passages] with the intention of starting an argument, but also those who would like to use them in support of the catholic faith" found the statements of the fathers on such a central question as the Eucharist "so doubtful and so troublesome and sometimes so downright mutually contradictory" that some comparison of their relative authority was unavoidable.

Such a comparison was not an easy assignment, at least partly because there was such a large number of traditions to take into consideration. The reverence for Christian antiquity had brought about an attitude that was better informed about the events and ideas of a millennium before than about those that were only forty or fifty years old. But everyone was committed to the effort of harmonizing the tradition and achieving a patristic

Petr.Ven.*Jud*.1 (*PL* 189:511)

Petr.Ab.*Sic et non*.9 (Boyer-McKeon 136–39)

Petr.Ab.*Sic et non*.pr. (Boyer-McKeon 96)

Deusd.*Coll.can*.pr. (Glanvell 3)

Bernl.Const.*Lib*.15 (*MGH Lib. lit*.2:156)

Brd.Clr.*Cant*.5.2.7 (Leclercq-Rochais 1:24)
Petr.Ab.*Dial*. (Thomas 153–59)

Wm.S.Th.*Sacr.alt*.11 (*PL* 180:359)

Petr.Cant.*Verb.abbr*.79 (*PL* 205:233)

Petr.Ven.*Mirac*.2.pr. (*PL* 189:908–9)

Scot.Er.*Periph*.5.17 (*PL* 122:
889); Hug.S.Vict.*Sacr*.1.1.2
(*PL* 176:187)

Petr.Ab.*Sic et non*.pr. (Boyer-
McKeon 89)

1 Cor.6:2

Prov.22:28

See vol.2:172

Bernl.Const.*Lib*.15 (*MGH Lib.
lit*.2:159)

Bern.Reich.*Dial*.2 (*PL* 142:
1089)

consensus. It had been customary for centuries to warn against "temerity" in dealing with apparent contradictions in that tradition, and Abelard made use of the very same word in the opening sentence of his preface to *Yes and No,* warning that "one should not judge with temerity concerning those by whom the world is to be judged." The warning, "Do not cross the boundaries which your fathers have set," which Western theologians were constantly quoting against the East, was applicable here as well: disputation was not to proceed so far as to give the impression that it was crossing those boundaries, and "the statutes of those who have precedence over us in age and in wisdom" were the boundary that it was not legitimate to cross. But the task of creating—or, as they would have put it, of discovering—harmony among these statutes and traditions was one that had to wait until the end of the twelfth and the beginning of the thirteenth centuries for its successful completion.

Schism, Sect, and Heresy

Bald.*Tract*.15 (*PL* 204:552)

Wm.Mon.*Henr.Mon*.3
(Manselli 47)

See vol.1:69

Hug.Am.*Haer*.3.7 (*PL* 192:
1294)

Gisl.Crisp.*Sim*. (Robinson 112)

Petr.Ven.*Petrob*.247 (*CCCM*
10:146)

Brun.S.*Ep*.1 (*PL* 165:1139)

Vac.*Err*.31.5 (*ST* 115:569–
70)
Petr.Ven.*Sect.Sar*.pr.11
(Kritzeck 225)

Hug.Am.*Haer*.pr. (*PL* 192:
1255–56)

The twelfth century witnessed a resurgence of schism, of sect, and of heresy, as well as of movements that qualified for more than one of these names. Because the one true faith had as its necessary corollary the doctrine that there was only one true church, a defender of the catholic faith against "a schismatic" had to make "the unity of the church" a central theme of his exposition. The patristic distinction between "heresy" and "schism" implied that, in strict usage, a heretic was one who persisted in defending error, one who "with a pertinacious mind refuses to cling to the unity of that faith which the universal church of Christ believes and holds." Such a false teacher was distinct from a faithful catholic who fell into error or doubt, but who did not "resist the church publicly and pertinaciously." While it was historically valid to assert that certain teachings "are specifically called 'heresies' because they have been judged and condemned in the councils" of the church, "the legal definition" of a heretic applied also to an errorist on whom a council had not yet passed judgment. For the example of the ancient councils and fathers showed that "no heresy is to be overlooked." Now that there were "new heretics emerging" along with the same "old heresies," as Hugh of Amiens put it, it was time to defend the one true faith again.

One of the first of "the heresies of his own time" against

which this twelfth-century heresiologist contended was the refusal to recognize that because "the Holy Spirit proceeds from the Father and is sent from the Son," it followed that "being sent from the Son, he also proceeds from him"; this had to be asserted "against the heretics," by whom he evidently meant Eastern Christians. The doctrinal differences between the two parts of Christendom have been treated in some detail in the second volume of this work and need not be rehearsed here. But the schism with the East was also a significant part of the theological atmosphere within the Western church itself during the twelfth century, when there developed "a lively . . . curiosity about the heritage of Eastern Christianity," past and present, partly as a consequence of the intensified contact with the East through the Crusades and other forms of travel and commerce. Among the noblest products of this contact was the irenic activity of Anselm of Havelberg, and particularly the dialogues he held with Nicetas of Nicomedia at Constantinople in 1135.

Unlike Hugh of Amiens, Anselm of Havelberg was careful not to label the Byzantines as heretics, but as dissenting catholics. He acknowledged, in a prefatory epistle to Pope Eugenius III, that many of his Latin co-religionists had misunderstood the teachings of the Greeks, "supposing that they affirm what they do not affirm and that they deny what they by no means deny." It was his concern to identify "how the church of God, while she is one in and of herself, is multiform as far as her sons are concerned, those whom she has formed and continues to form in diverse laws and institutions." Despite some passing attention to such differences as the Greek rejection of the Latin custom of mingling water with the wine at the Eucharist, Anselm and his fellow disputant concentrated on the fundamental points of divergence: the problem of the Filioque and the locus of authority in the church. On the first, Anselm urged that they avoid "a quarrel about words" and stick to the substantive issues. He also took pains to refute the suggestion that the idea of Filioque was introducing the notion of more than one principle of being within the Godhead. Therefore the Holy Spirit was said to proceed from the Son as well as from the Father, "not according to his essence, which is common [to all three persons], nor according to his person, which is unto itself, but according to his relation" to both the Father and the Son.

Hug.Am.*Haer.*1.2 (*PL* 192: 1258–59)

See vol.2:146–98

Chenu (1966) 289

See vol.2:180–81

Ans.Hav.*Dial.*3.22 (*PL* 188: 1248)

Ans.Hav.*Dial.*pr. (*PL* 188: 1141)

Ans.Hav.*Dial.*1.2 (*PL* 188: 1143)

Ans.Hav.*Dial.*3.20 (*PL* 188: 1241–45)

Ans.Hav.*Dial.*2.1 (*PL* 188: 1164)

Ans.Hav.*Dial.*2.2 (*PL* 188: 1166)

Ans.Hav.*Dial.*2.10 (*PL* 188: 1178–79)

Eventually, of course, even the problem of the Filioque came down to the question of authority. In support of the Western theory of the procession of the Holy Spirit, Anselm cited the authority of various Eastern fathers whom he took to be espousing the doctrine of Filioque. When Nicetas appealed to an ecumenical council as the proper forum of authority for adjudicating this and other doctrinal differences, Anselm agreed: "I, too, earnestly desire that there be a universal council." To be sure, his definition of what constituted an ecumenical and orthodox council had at its center the stipulation that the pope must validate such an assembly for it to have universal authority over the church. By going its own way on various questions, the Eastern church had separated itself "from obedience to the most holy Roman church and from its unity with this great communion." Yet it was Rome alone that had "always remained unshaken" by heresies, while all the other sees of Christendom had, at one time or another, succumbed to error. More than any of them, Constantinople had "always been fermenting with innumerable heresies." Although this view appeared to the Greeks to be substituting the authority of the pope for that of Scripture and tradition, it was, even more than the Filioque, the one point on which it was impossible for Rome to compromise.

Policy toward Byzantium was only one of the forces—political as well as theological, domestic as well as foreign—that led the defenders of church authority at this time to place even greater emphasis on the legitimacy and objectivity of the structures of the church. As we have noted repeatedly, the conflict with the Eastern church and the conflict with the Western empire had long been responsible for evoking affirmations from Rome and its spokesmen about the nature of the church and its authority. The new factor in the twelfth century was the rise of sectarian movements, which, taking as their target of protest the corruption of the church and of its leaders, repudiated the institutional structure, the liturgical order, and even the sacramental system of catholic Christianity. Around the beginning of the century it may have been possible to exult that "the catholic faith has fought and has crushed, conquered, and annihilated the blasphemies of the heretics, so that either there are no more heretics or they do not dare to show themselves," but the situation changed rapidly and drastically. Bernard complained that "heresy

Ans.Hav.*Dial*.2.24 (*PL* 188: 1204)

ap.Ans.Hav.*Dial*.2.27 (*PL* 188: 1209–10)
Ans.Hav.*Dial*.3.22 (*PL* 188: 1248)

Ans.Hav.*Dial*.3.12 (*PL* 188: 1226–28)

Ans.Hav.*Dial*.3.3 (*PL* 188: 1211)

Ans.Hav.*Dial*.3.5 (*PL* 188: 1214)

Ans.Hav.*Dial*.3.6 (*PL* 188: 1215)

See vol.2:167

Herb.Los.*Serm*.14 (Goulburn-Symonds 418)

Ecb.*Cathar*.1.1 (*PL* 195:13); Bonac.*Manif*.pr. (*PL* 204: 778)

Brd.Clr.*Cons*.3.1.4 (Leclercq-
Rochais 3:434)

Brd.Clr.*Cant*.66.1.2 (Leclercq-
Rochais 2:179)
Wm.Mon.*Henr.Mon*.pr.
(Manselli 44); Petr.Ven.
Petrob.8 (*CCCM* 10:12)

Guib.Nog.*Vita sua*.3.17 (*PL*
156:951–52); Ecb.*Cathar*.1.1
(*PL* 195:14)

Herib.*Haer.* (*PL* 181:1271);
Ebr.*Antihaer*.20 (*MBP* 24:
1564–65)

ap.Hug.Am.*Haer*.3.5 (*PL*
192:1291)
Alan.Ins.*Haer*.1.63 (*PL* 210:
365); Hug.Am.*Haer*.3.4 (*PL*
192:1288); Ebr. *Antihaer*.7
(*MBP* 24:1544–47)

ap.Wm.Mon.*Henr.Mon*.10
(Manselli 60)

Rad.Ard.*Hom.ep.ev*.2.19 (*PL*
155:2011)

Hug.Sper.ap.Vac.*Err*.14.4
(*ST* 115:515)
Matt.21:13

Petr.Mart.*Patar*.14 (*AFP* 17:
329)

Hug.Am.*Haer*.3.2 (*PL* 192:
1284)

Vac.*Err*.14.1 (*ST* 115:513)

is creeping in clandestinely almost everywhere" and expressed his amazement that while earlier heretical groups
had taken their names from those of their founders, he
was now confronting a series of movements that were
anonymous. Some of the founders were in fact identified
by their orthodox opponents, and others have come to be
known in other ways; but more important are the parallels
between men and movements who seem not to have had
any direct connection.

What many of them had in common was "the boast that
they maintain the apostolic life," and that no one else
could lay claim to it. "In the region of Périgueux," according to one account, "a great many heretics have arisen
who say that they are leading the apostolic life." The content of this so-called apostolic life, it continued, was a
thoroughgoing asceticism: "They do not eat meat; they
do not drink wine, except very moderately every third
day; they genuflect a hundred times a day; they do not
accept money." If their critics are to be believed, these
groups did not extend their asceticism to the area of sex
and marriage. They were said to oppose the catholic exaltation of celibacy and at the same time to reject the
catholic definition of matrimony as a sacrament. Nevertheless, there would appear to be some indications that
some of them urged absolute sexual continence. It was
apparently the ideal of Christian poverty that they exalted
above other virtues as the essential criterion of the apostolic life. This ideal applied in particular to the clergy:
"The bishops and priests," they argued, "should not have
either honors or money." In the name of their "apostolic
life," some of them "say that they do not lie, nor do they
take any oaths whatever," and "under the pretext of
abstinence and continence they condemn the eating of
meat as well as marriage."

All of this was in contrast to the life of the bishops and
clergy in the catholic church. The church had become for
them a "den of thieves." On the doctrine of the one, holy,
catholic, and apostolic church "all [the heretics] suffer
shipwreck." Apparently it was "especially those who
have fallen away from the clergy and gone over to heresy"
who led the campaign against the ecclesiastical structure.
The "chief motivation" of the heretics, according to their
opponents, was hostility "against our priests," whom they
attacked "as though all of them were filled with crimes."

They were, to be sure, not alone in their belief that a fundamental reform of life and morals was necessary. Bernard of Clairvaux lamented that "now that we have peace from the pagans and peace from the heretics, there is still no peace from the false sons [of the church]. . . . Almost all Christians are looking after their own interests, not those of Jesus Christ." The offices of the church had become a matter of shameful profit and shady dealing, and the pastor who served the Lord for the Lord's sake was exceedingly rare. Hence it was not only the heretics but also faithful believers who, "as catholics," were concerned about the church of God. Their "lukewarm" attitude to the church and their hesitancy about involvement with its moral corruption did not brand them as heretics, for their opposition was "neither public nor pertinacious."

The heretics were distinct from such faithful catholics by their reiteration of the question: "How can someone who is accursed consecrate?" Rejection of the catholic doctrine of penance was one of the things on which all heretics agreed. They repudiated the absolution pronounced by priests, on the grounds that "the priests of our own time do not have the power to bind and loose [sins], for they have been deprived of that power by their own sins." They even went so far as to argue that it had not been a commandment of the Gospels at all that one should go to a priest to confess. Baptism likewise suffered from the general corruption of church and clergy and, when it was administered by an immoral or hypocritical priest, was invalid. It was above all the Eucharist that had lost its efficacy through the corruption and apostasy of the catholic clergy. Quite simply, "the body of Christ is not confected by an unworthy minister," and only "if he who does it is found to be worthy" could the body of Christ be called into being at the Mass. "The power of the sacraments," according to Tanchelm, "depends on the merits and the holiness of the ministers." Otherwise, if the Mass were celebrated by an adulterer, God would be associated with a sinner in the confecting of the body of his Son. The words of Christ contrasting the true shepherd with the thief and robber meant that "only he enters through the door who approaches with a true and a pure heart, to govern the people of God for the sake of righteousness and truth."

Beyond these attacks on the sacramental ministry of

Phil.2:21
Brd.Clr.*Ps*.90.6.7 (Leclercq-Rochais 4:410); Joach.*Ev*.3 (*FSI* 67:244–46)

Rad.Ard.*Hom*.2.24 (*PL* 155: 1585)

Hug.Am.*Haer*.3.9 (*PL* 192: 1297)

Petr.Ven.*Petrob*.247 (*CCCM* 10:146)

Hug.Sper.ap.Vac.*Err*.10.1 (*ST* 155:502)

Petr.Mart.*Patar*.17 (*AFP* 17: 329)

ap.Wm.Mon.*Henr.Mon*.8 (Manselli 56)
ap.Alan.Ins.*Haer*.1.52 (*PL* 210:356); ap.Wm.Mon.*Henr. Mon*.9 (Manselli 58); ap.Ebr. *Antihaer*.4 (*MBP* 24:1537)

ap.Vac.*Err*.9.1 (*ST* 115:499)

ap.Wm.Mon.*Henr.Mon*.6 (Manselli 53)

ap.*Ep.Traj*. (Fredericq 16)

ap.Vac.*Err*.10.1 (*ST* 155:501); ap.Rad.Ard.*Hom.ep.ev*.1.5 (*PL* 155:1681)

John 10:1–18

ap.Vac.*Err*.2.1 (*ST* 155:488)

See vol.1:308–13

Alan.Ins.*Haer*.1.66 (*PL* 210: 369)

Hug.Am.*Haer*.1.13 (*PL* 192: 1269)

See vol.1:316–18

Hug.Am.*Haer*.1.11 (*PL* 192: 1266); Alan.Ins.*Haer*.1.39 (*PL* 210:345)

Mark 16:15–16

ap.Petr.Ven.*Petrob*.10 (*CCCM* 10:12–13)

Heb.11:6

Hug.Sper.ap.Vac.*Err*.13.2 (*ST* 115:511); Petr.Mart.*Patar*.25 (*AFP* 17:332) ap.Hug.Am.*Haer*.1.12 (*PL* 192:1268)

ap.Wm.Mon.*Henr.Mon*.4 (Manselli 47)

Hug.Sper.ap.Vac.*Err*.16 (*ST* 115:518)

Wm.Mon.*Henr.Mon*.4 (Manselli 50); Petr.Ven.*Petrob*. 12 (*CCCM* 10:14)

Petr.Mon.*Hist.Alb*.2 (*PL* 213: 546)

Petr.Ab.*Int.theol*.2.4 (*PL* 178:1056)

Vac.*Err*.19–20 (*ST* 115:521– 44)

Ghellinck (1913) 1242

the catholic church, which were strongly reminiscent of Donatism, the sectarians of this period directed an even more fundamental criticism at the catholic understanding of the sacraments as such. When the defenders of the church reasserted the Augustinian doctrine that "baptism suffices, regardless of time or age or condition or gender, for the forgiveness of sins, for righteousness, for the reception of grace, and for eternal life, once it has been properly received in Christ from anyone whatsoever and through anyone at all," they were also reaffirming the correctness of infant baptism, which Augustine, in his critique of Donatism, had been able to take for granted. But now "the heretics . . . say that the sacraments are of benefit only to those who know about them, not to ignorant adults, and that they do not confer anything at all on little children. Therefore they condemn the baptism of little children and infants." Because the command of Christ had required that, to be saved, one both believe and be baptized, "infants, even though they are baptized by you, are simply not saved, because their age prevents them from believing." Since it was impossible to please God without faith and "an infant cannot believe or know anything," it followed that "a faith that he cannot have does not do him any good." Christ himself had been baptized as an adult, not as an infant. Not only was it impossible for infants to be saved through a faith not their own; it was also "unjust for someone to be condemned through a sin not his own." Infants who had not sinned themselves were said to be punished because of their parents' sin. This was as unacceptable to the sectarians as the catholic doctrine that children were saved through the faith of the church.

Those who depreciated infant baptism likewise refused to see anything special about the Eucharist. Thus Tanchelm "compelled many to be rebaptized . . . and declared that the Sacrament of the Altar should no longer be celebrated." Significantly, the longest section of the defense of the orthodox faith against various errors by the theologian and jurist "Master Vacarius" near the end of the twelfth century was devoted to an exposition of the doctrine of the real presence in the Eucharist. "The principal affirmation of the sects was directed against the conversion of the bread and wine into the body and blood of Jesus Christ." These sectarians seemed to be even worse than

Petr.Ven.*Petrob.*153 (*CCCM* 10:87–88)
Hild.*Ep.*47 (*PL* 197:232)
Alan.Ins.*Haer.*1.57 (*PL* 210:360); Bonac.*Manif.*7 (*PL* 204:782)
ap.Vac.*Err.*20.5 (*ST* 115:537–38)
ap.Ermeng.*Tract.*11 (*PL* 204:1251); ap.Monet.Crem.*Cathar.*4.3.1 (Ricchini 296); ap.Alan.Ins.*Haer.*1.61 (*PL* 210:364)

ap.Vac.*Err.*20.4 (*ST* 115:535)
ap.Hug.Am.*Haer.*1.14 (*PL* 192:1272)

Petr.Ven.*Petrob.*106 (*CCCM* 10:63)

ap.Vac.*Err.*19.f. (*ST* 115:530)
ap.Vac.*Err.*20.2 (*ST* 115:533)

Brd.Clr.*Cant.*66.4.11 (Leclercq-Rochais 2:185)

See vol.1:355–56

Hug.Am.*Haer.*3.3 (*PL* 192:1287–88)

ap.Petr.Ven.*Petrob.*211 (*CCCM* 10:126)

Petr.Ven.*Petrob.*215 (*CCCM* 10:128)

ap.Vac.*Err.*19.1 (*ST* 115:522)

Berengar had been in their denial of the real presence, for he at least had continued to affirm that the Eucharist was a sacrament and a figure, which they were now denying. They were attacking not only "the holiness of the body and blood of Christ" in the Eucharist, but the presence. One group said that the words "This is my body" meant "This is the sign and the remembrance of the suffering of my body," another that the words referred to the body of Christ seated at table with his disciples. Sharing in the body and blood of Christ meant sharing in his love, not in his true body. As a real presence was unnecessary, so also was a sacrifice. The heretics "despise this sacrifice of ours and deny altogether that [a sacrifice] exists now in the church." Either the sins of the communicants had already been forgiven (in which case they did not need a sacrifice), or they had not (in which case they were eating and drinking unworthily). "Otherwise," they argued, "the Lord would have died twice."

Underlying the attack on the sacrifice of the Mass was not only the general opposition to the sacramental ministry of clergy who were deemed unworthy, but also, at least in some cases, a denial of the doctrine of purgatory, to which the sacrificial interpretation of the Eucharist had been closely connected. It was charged among the orthodox that some of the sectarians had gone so far as to reject the doctrine of the resurrection of the dead. It does seem clear, in any event, that, for example, Peter de Bruys and his followers contended "that the sacrifices of the altar, offerings, prayers, alms, and other good deeds of the good who are still living cannot be of any benefit to the good who are dead." If there was nothing that the church terrestrial could do to improve the state of those who had died, this negated the belief that it could "pray for the rest or the glory of those of its members who have been translated into the other life," and even more the belief that those who needed further cleansing from their sins could profit from the offering of the body and blood of Christ in the Mass. Hence Hugh of Speroni asserted "that neither in the law nor in the prophets nor in the New Testament do we hear the statement that Christ 'dies mystically'" in the Mass.

The repudiation of the catholic priesthood and the catholic sacraments could be broadened into a repudiation of the entire liturgical life of the church. The Petrobrusians

Petr.Ven.*Petrob*.273 (*CCCM* 10:162); Ermeng.*Tract*.10 (*PL* 204:1250)

Petr.Ven.*Petrob*.27 (*CCCM* 10: 24); Ebr.*Antihaer*.4 (*MBP* 24:1536)

Wm.Mon.*Henr.Mon*.12 (Manselli 61)

ap.Vac.*Err*.19.c (*ST* 115:526)

ap.Vac.*Err*.20.13; 27.1 (*ST* 115:543; 533)
See vol.2:110–11

ap.Herib.*Haer*. (*PL* 181:1722)

ap.Peter.Ven.*Petrob*.114 (*CCCM* 10:68); ap.Ebr. *Antihaer*.17 (*MBP* 24:1560–62)

Petr.Ven.*Petrob*.120 (*CCCM* 10:71)

Petr.Ven.*Petrob*.100 (*CCCM* 10:60–61)

Hug.Am.*Haer*.1.9 (*PL* 192: 1263); Petr.Ven.*Petrob*.9 (*CCCM* 10:12)

ap.Hug.Am.*Haer*.3.7 (*PL* 192: 1294)
See vol.2:146
Wm.Mon.*Henr.Mon*.6 (Manselli 53)

Petr.Ven.*Petrob*.11 (*CCCM* 10: 13)

Vac.*Err*.20.5 (*ST* 115:538)

and others were opposed to the use of hymns and music, on the grounds that the proper worship of God was internal and spiritual. They also scorned church buildings, which they refused to call "churches" because that name was appropriate "not to a structure with walls, but to the congregation of the faithful." Henry the Monk, a sectarian leader, made the matter of "churches constructed of wood or stone" the first item on his agenda of grievances. Hugh of Speroni similarly asked: "Who is it that has taught our people to build towers, to ring bells, to draw pictures, to set up crosses, to fabricate, worship, adore, and kiss idols?" He did not believe that "sanctifying things made of wood" had anything to do with God, and he took issue with catholic practice in building altars and celebrating festivals. Even the cross, which Eastern iconoclasts had continued to worship when they rejected the use of images, was not immune from attack: "Oh, how miserable are those who adore you!" they said of the cross and of the image of Christ. It was, they charged, "foolish and profane to adore or venerate the cross, because the tree that tortured the members of Christ deserves to be crushed or burned rather than venerated or adored." To this the orthodox responded that there was nothing in all creation that had not somehow served as an instrument of torture, so that "all of humanity would have to rise up against all of the world" in indignation. Besides, religion had need of objects and of holy places, where it could venerate what was sacred.

Concentrating as they did on the institutions and practices of catholic Christianity rather than on its dogma, such sectarians did nevertheless diverge from the church in some fundamental doctrinal ways, so that they were "heretics" as well as "schismatics." They professed to be loyal to the church, if only they could find the true church and receive an answer to their question: "What is the church of God, and where is it, and why is it?" But they were tearing asunder the "seamless robe" of Christ by creating division in the church. In their repudiation of infant baptism they acted as though the entire church had been in error for a thousand years or more, and in their repudiation of the real presence in the Eucharist they acted as though in the words of institution "the Lord Jesus and the apostle had chosen such words as to deceive the whole world, except for you." Quoting Acts 5:29

ap.Wm.Mon.*Henr.Mon*.pr.
(Manselli 44); ap.Alan. Ins.
Haer.2.2 (*PL* 210:380–81)

against the established church, they declared their intention to obey God rather than the bishops. They claimed to accept only the primitive gospel but to reject subsequent tradition as a betrayal of the message of Christ, even though, according to catholic teaching, the gospel, the church, and the apostolic tradition had all come from the same source and had been transmitted through the

Petr.Ven.*Petrob*.29; 231
(*CCCM* 10:25; 137–38)
Brd.Clr.*Cant*.66.5.12 (Leclercq-
Rochais 2:186–87)

same channels. The defenders of the faith, urging that "faith should come by persuasion, not by imposition" and that heresy should be overcome "not by force of arms but

Brd.Clr.*Cant*.64.3.8 (Leclercq-
Rochais 2:170)

by force of argument," nevertheless charged the bishops of the church with the responsibility of using "preaching and even, if need be, armed force through laymen" in

Petr.Ven.*Petrob*.ep.ded.1
(*CCCM* 10:3)

government to overcome heresy. The contradictions in that attitude, while not in the strict sense a part of the history of Christian doctrine, were to be a source of consternation to theologians and churchmen throughout the twelfth century and well beyond it.

While it is probably sound to insist, with the leading historian of these movements, that "the idea of Christian

Grundmann (1961) 21

poverty and of the apostolic life . . . is the essential content of the heresy" and that "the question of the authentic Christian life in accordance with the gospel as the way of salvation is more important and more vital than all

Grundmann (1961) 496–97

theological and cosmological questions of doctrine," there was one heretical group in which questions of doctrine dealing with theology and cosmology occupied a prominent place. These were, as they referred to themselves,

ap.Ecb.*Cathar*.5.6 (*PL* 195:
31)
Lib.princ. (Dondaine 144)

"the Cathari, that is, the pure," or, as they also called themselves, "the true Christians." Many of the emphases for which they acquired a reputation as heretics were those that they shared with other heretical movements of the time, but their espousal of radically dualistic theories of cosmology, with all the implications of such theories, set them apart from other critics and even from other heretics.

Together with other groups, these "Manichean here-

Rad.Ard.*Hom*.2.19 (*PL* 155:
2011)

tics . . . make the false claim that they hold to the apostolic life," even though, according to their opponents, "they are contrary to the holy faith and the sound doctrine that has been handed down to us by tradition from the holy

Ecb.*Cathar*.1.1 (*PL* 195:14)

apostles and from the Lord and Savior himself." Their claim of adhering to a truly apostolic life, which led them

ap.Ebr.*Antihaer*.15 (*MBP* 25:
1556–58)
ap.Monet.Crem.*Cathar*.5.13.3
(Ricchini 513)

to repudiate capital punishment and to oppose "all war as illicit," was their way of differentiating themselves from

ap.Monet.Crem.*Cathar*.5.3.1 (Ricchini 412–13)

ap.Ecb.*Cathar*.4.1 (*PL* 195: 25)

See vol.1:309–10

Rain.Sacc.*Cathar*. (Dondaine 69–70)

ap.Monet.Crem.*Cathar*.3.4.2 (Ricchini 263)

2 Thess.2:3

ap.Ermeng.*Tract*.17 (*PL* 204: 1267); ap.Monet.Crem. *Cathar*.4.9.5 (Ricchini 374–75)

ap.Ermeng.*Tract*.8 (*PL* 204: 1249)

ap.Ebr.*Antihaer*.12 (*MBP* 24: 1553)

ap.Petr.Mart.*Patar*.14 (*AFP* 17:329)

Rain.Sacc.*Cathar*. (Dondaine 65)

Alan.Ins.*Haer*.pr. (*PL* 210: 307–8)

Monet.Crem.*Cathar*.5.2.2 (Ricchini 411)

the institutions of the catholic church; for they believed that since the days of the apostles there had been a fall of the church from apostolic purity. As a consequence of this fall, catholics were unable to do genuine good works, and therefore the sacraments administered by their priests were invalid. Like the ancient Donatism which it resembled, this position left the Cathari open to the argument that on the very same grounds they could never be sure of the objective efficacy of their own sacraments, but had to "labor under very great doubt and danger." In their charge that the church had fallen, some went so far as to identify Sylvester I, who was the pope when the emperor Constantine was converted, as the Antichrist prophesied in the New Testament. The Cathari objected to the catholic practice of prayers for the dead, as well as to its corollary, the idea that the saints in heaven were praying for the living on earth. Setting themselves in opposition to the catholic belief that churches and shrines could be called "holy places" and "the house of God," they denounced the practice of pilgrimages to the so-called holy places of Christ and the saints. They brushed aside the sacramental system of the church, asserting "that there are not more than two sacraments," namely, confirmation and ordination, both administered by the laying on of hands. In place of the catholic practice of the Eucharist they practiced a breaking of bread at table, during the noon meal and again during the evening meal.

Extreme though such doctrines were in how they carried out the implications of more generally held views, these teachings of the Cathari could be seen as no more than a part of the general heretical attitudes that we have been summarizing. But the Cathari and their catholic opponents agreed on one conclusion, if on very little else: that the doctrine of the Cathari went far deeper in its divergence from catholic orthodoxy than even the most radical of attacks on the church and its structures, penetrating to the very center of Christian monotheism, including the doctrines of the Trinity and the person of Christ. It had amalgamated the ideas of various earlier heresies into "a single general heresy." When catholic polemics charged that "the church of the Cathari has taken its origin . . . from the heathen or from the Jews or from apostate Christians" or when their teachings were connected to those of the Gnostics, the Muslims, the

See vol.2:230

Haer.Cathar. (*AFP* 19:306)
Rain.Sacc.*Cathar.* (Dondaine 76)

See vol.2:216–17
Ecb.*Cathar.*1.3 (*PL* 195:16–17)

Rain.Sacc.*Cathar.* (Dondaine 64); Bonac.*Manif.*pr. (*PL* 204:775); Petr.Mart.*Patar.*9 (*AFP* 17:324–26)

Lib.princ. (Dondaine 83)
Monet.Crem.*Cathar.*1.1.1 (Ricchini 7); Alan.Ins.*Haer.*1.35 (*PL* 210:337)

Ebr.*Antihaer.*5 (*MBP* 24:1540)

Ermeng.*Tract.*2 (*PL* 204:1237)

See vol.1:73

See vol.2:219

Matt.7:18; Luke 6:43

Lib.princ. (Dondaine 81); Alan.Ins.*Haer.*1.4 (*PL* 210:309); Monet.Crem.*Cathar.*1.1.2 (Ricchini 10)

Bonac.*Manif.*pr. (*PL* 204:775)

ap.Petr.Mart.*Patar.*1 (*AFP* 17:320)

Lib.princ. (Dondaine 117)

Lib.princ. (Dondaine 127–28)
See pp. 111–12 above

Alan.Ins.*Haer.*1.4 (*PL* 210:310)

Nestorians as well as the Monophysites, and the Apollinarists, this could be no more than the regular practice of attacking a heresy by identifying it with some previous movement already condemned by the orthodox church. But such charges implied more than that, and accurately. The Cathari stood in a succession, episcopal as well as doctrinal, with the Bogomils of Bulgaria, and through them—whatever the historical connection may have been —with the ancient Manichean heresy. At the same time catholic theologians recognized that the Cathari were not a homogeneous group doctrinally, but contained a considerable variety of opinion on various issues.

Both the confessional literature of the Cathari themselves and the writings of catholics against them identified the dualistic view of God as their primary tenet. "They say that there are two gods," catholic theologians reported, or, amplifying the report, "they say that there are two gods, one of them omnipotent and the other malignant." Ever since Marcion, Christian dualists such as the Bogomils of the East had been quoting the saying of Jesus that a good tree cannot bear evil fruit. Evidently that saying became a locus classicus for the Cathari as well, who found support in it for their contention that an evil world could not have been the work of a good Creator. Some of them taught that God had been the original Creator of the elements of the world, while others attributed their creation to the devil; but they were agreed that the devil had divided the elements and was their lord. As one of them stated their creed, "God created and made all good things . . . by which I understand only those things that are invisible to the physical eye; the other things were created and made by the devil." The irreconcilable antithesis between the notion of a good Creator and the reality of evil in the world led them to the conviction that "there is undoubtedly another creator or maker who is the source and the cause of death, perdition, and all that is evil." Such acts as murder and fornication could not be the work of the good Creator, but had to be the result of the activity of another deity, the evil god. The catholic response to this assertion of the Cathari was the familiar idea that because God was the Creator only of all things good, evil was the absence of good and therefore did not truly exist.

Among the many heretical corollaries that seemed to the orthodox to be derived from this primary tenet of

Ecb.*Cathar*.5–13 (*PL* 195:26–98)

ap.Petr.Mart.*Patar*.3 (*AFP* 17:321)

Alan.Ins.*Haer*.1.19 (*PL* 210:321)

See vol.1:89–90

ap.Ermeng.*Tract*.7 (*PL* 204:1243)

Petr.Mart.*Patar*.8 (*AFP* 17:324)

Alan.Ins.*Haer*.1.32 (*PL* 210:334)

ap.Ebr.*Antihaer*.9 (*MBP* 24:1549)

Alan.Ins.*Haer*.1.23 (*PL* 210:324)

ap.Rain.Sacc.*Cathar*. (Dondaine 75)

ap.Alan.Ins.*Haer*.1.27 (*PL* 210:328)

dualism, the most crucial doctrinally were those that imperiled the two central dogmas of the catholic faith—not only the Trinity, which was obviously jeopardized by the assertion that there were two gods, but also the person of Christ. If the good God could not be the Creator of a visible world in which sin and evil took place, it had to follow that the human nature of Christ could not partake of such a world. He must have had "only one nature," which was not involved in a sinful creation. Therefore "some of the heretics say that the Son of God presented to men only the shadow of a human nature, not the reality," because a fully real humanity would have been unable to avoid contamination by the physical world, whose origin was the malignant god or the devil. Some of the Cathari apparently extricated themselves from this difficulty by resorting to the ancient docetic heresy that the humanity of Christ was only an illusion; thus "Christ was not born of a woman, did not have genuine flesh, did not truly die, and did not suffer but only gave the appearance of suffering." Despite the efforts of catholic heresiologists to trace the lineage of these christological ideas to various ancient systems of false doctrine, the fundamental dilemma of the Cathari, as understood by their catholic critics, was between the divine sonship of Christ and his true humanity, one of which had to give. Of course, whichever way the dilemma was resolved would be unacceptable to orthodox Christianity.

It was likewise a corollary of the dualism of the Cathari that the traditional Christian doctrine of the resurrection of the body was unacceptable: "We shall rise in another body, and God will give us a new body." For if the human body, together with all things visible in the world, had come from the devil rather than from the good God, "by whom will the bodies of the saints be glorified on the Day of Judgment? Certainly not by the devil, nor, so it seems, by God; for God will not glorify an evil nature. And therefore it seems that the saints will not rise in bodies that have been glorified." At least one of the sects of the Cathari appears to have taught a doctrine of the transmigration of souls, according to which "the souls of God are transmitted from one body to another and they are all finally liberated from punishment and guilt." On the other hand, there seem also to have been those who asserted that the soul was mortal and perished with the

See vol.1:134–36

ap.Petr.Mart.*Patar*.11 (*AFP* 17:327–28)

ap.Alan.Ins.*Haer*.1.9 (*PL* 210: 316)

ap.Petr.Mart.*Patar*.22 (*AFP* 17:330–31); ap.Monet.Crem. *Cathar*.2.5.1 (Ricchini 138–41)

Alan.Ins.*Haer*.1.35 (*PL* 210: 337); Ermeng.*Tract*.3 (*PL* 204:1237)

ap.Monet.Crem.*Cathar*.2.7.1 (Ricchini 196–203)

Ecb.*Cathar*.pr. (*PL* 195:13–14)

Luke 24:44

ap.Ebr.*Antihaer*.2 (*MBP* 24: 1530); ap.Alan.Ins.*Haer*.1.37 (*PL* 210:341)

ap.Petr.Mart.*Patar*.5 (*AFP* 17:322–23)

ap.Petr.Mart.*Patar*.7 (*AFP* 17: 323); ap.Ebr.*Antihaer*.13 (*MBP* 24:1554–55); ap. Ermeng.*Tract*.6 (*PL* 204:1242–43)

Ecb.*Cathar*.2.1 (*PL* 195:18)

Bonac.*Manif*.pr. (*PL* 204:777)

death of the body. Still others, echoing ideas of Origen, identified the resurrection bodies with those that were defeated in the prehistoric battle between Satan and the good angels, bodies that were destined to rise at the end of the world. This was apparently related to the belief, also reminiscent of the theology of Origen, that human souls were fallen angels, condemned to do penance for a time in human bodies. The contempt for the physical body expressed in this attitude toward the resurrection asserted itself as well in the strict rules of fasting enforced by the Cathari.

The "second article of the heresy" of the Cathari, according to the defenders of the catholic faith, was their assertion "that the law of Moses was given by the prince of darkness, that is, by the malignant god, while the law of the gospel was given by the prince of light, that is, by the merciful god." This was consistent with their dualism, "so that as there are two principles of reality, there are likewise two testaments derived from them." The contrast between the morality of the Old Testament and that of the New was due to the origin of the former in the evil god. Attacking the Cathari for their arbitrary method of quoting proof texts from Scripture, the catholics cited the authority of Christ, who taught his disciples that "the law of Moses and the prophets and the psalms" had been written about him. A particular feature of the hostility of the Cathari to the Old Testament was the belief that "the patriarchs . . . and all those who died before the passion [of Christ] were damned." When such New Testament passages as the eleventh chapter of the Epistle to the Hebrews spoke of the patriarchs as having been saved, this referred to "certain other celestial beings having the same names." John the Baptist came in for special condemnation from some of the Cathari as "the one who had been sent by the devil to impede the way of Christ" and who had been damned.

Nor was it only those who had lived before Christ whom the Cathari repudiated; they also put themselves in opposition to the catholic tradition after Christ, claiming "that the truth of the Christian faith is known only to [them] and has been hidden with [them] alone." The fathers of the catholic church—whether Ambrose or Gregory, Augustine or Jerome—"these and others they universally condemn." To the catholics such an attitude toward tradition and the church fathers was self-contradictory. Setting the apostolic Scriptures in antithesis not only to the Old Testament but also to the church undermined the authority of Scripture, which was validated by the church. Therefore the heretics "should believe [the church] in the very same way as [they] believe the apostles themselves." What they rejected as having come from Augustine came from the Gospels, and there was no contradiction possible between the church and Scripture in their authority. The conflict with dualistic heresy, like the conflicts with Eastern schismatics and with Western sectarians, finally came down to the defense of the one true and apostolic faith as confessed by the one true and apostolic church, which defined itself as the legitimate "successor" of the apostles.

The Encounter with Other Faiths

While the theologians of the twelfth century were engaged in a renewed conflict with heresy, they also encountered, more intensely and more systematically than had any of their medieval predecessors, the spokesmen for other faiths. Although they believed that "the gospel has been broadcast throughout the world through the preaching of the apostles," they gradually discovered the continuing power of alternatives to the gospel. "The three greatest enemies of holy Christendom in our times, namely, the Jews, the heretics, and the Saracens," all called forth the defense of the faith in the twelfth century, as well as the enterprise of "comparing [our doctrine] with all other doctrines." Thus when Alan of Lille wrote a treatise entitled *On the Catholic Faith against the Heretics of His Time,* he devoted the first two books to the Christian heretics, the third to the Jews, and the fourth to the Muslims. Whereas Alan identified the Saracens as "pagans," Peter the Venerable recognized "four varieties of sects in the world in our days, namely, the Christians, the Jews, the Saracens, and the pagans." Peter spoke of "the heresy of Mohammed" as "the dregs of all heresies," which exceeded "all the heresies that have been aroused by the diabolical spirit in the 1,100 years since the time of Christ."

The encounter of Western Christendom with "the heresy of Mohammed" reached a climax in this period for a variety of reasons, chief of which was, of course, the

---

Petr.Ven.*Petrob*.27 (*CCCM* 10:24)

Petr.Ven.*Petrob*.69 (*CCCM* 10:43)

Wm.Mon.*Henr.Mon*.5 (Manselli 51)

Rad.Ard.*Hom*.1.1 (*PL* 155: 1305)

Petr.Pict.*Ep.Petr.Ven.* (Kritzeck 216)

Petr.Ab.*Dial.* (Thomas 86)

Alan.Ins.*Haer.* (*PL* 210:305–430)
Alan.Ins.*Haer*.4.1 (*PL* 210: 421)

Petr.Ven.*Petrob*.161 (*CCCM* 10:94)
Petr.Ven.*Ep*.111 (Constable 294)

Petr.Ven.*Sect.Sar*.pr.12 (Kritzeck 226)

action by which "the enemies of Christ occupied the temple and the sepulcher of Christ, together with Jerusalem itself, that divine and royal city." The campaign of "the Latin world" aimed at "expelling these enemies of the Christian name" and the counterattacks of the Muslims in "subjugating the Holy Land" made the confrontation between Christianity and Islam principally a military one during these centuries. Islam had "shrouded the name of Christendom," managing to conquer more Christian territory than had any of the heresies, even more than Arianism had. Indeed, it had assumed control of "almost one-third of the human race, by an inscrutable judgment of God." But the Crusades, whose military progress does not in itself belong to the history of the development of Christian doctrine, did oblige the thinkers of the Latin church to take Islam more seriously as a theological issue as well. Except for some occasional references in earlier medieval literature, which varied "between the ridiculously inaccurate and the unpleasantly absurd," the Christian case against the Muslims had been the business principally of theologians in the East such as John of Damascus and Theodore Abu Qûrra, who formulated the standard apologetic arguments; these need not be repeated here. Although "none of the teachers of the [Western] church have written against" Mohammed, it now fell to scholars in the Occident to defend the faith against the religion of the prophet, even as their armies were defending it against the Saracens. The most important of these scholars was Peter the Venerable, whose works, including the translation of the Koran into Latin, were to remain "the major source of informed European Christian knowledge of Islam since the twelfth century," at least until the writings of Raymond Lully and of Ricoldus de Monte Croce in the fourteenth century.

With their colleagues in the East, Western commentators on Islam were impressed by the way it had "mixed the good with the bad and confused the true with the false." In that respect it seemed to deserve being called a Christian heresy, for it had, "after the manner of the heretics, accepted some things from the Christian faith and rejected others." Such affinities with Christian heresy were understandable historically, since Mohammed had derived his knowledge of Christian doctrines from hereti-

Petr.Ven.*Jud*.4 (*PL* 189:601)

Guib.Nog.*Gest*.1.1 (*PL* 156: 685)
Petr.Ven.*Ep*.130 (Constable 327)

Guib.Nog.*Gest*.1.4 (*PL* 156: 692)

Petr.Ven.*Sect.Sar*.pr.12 (Kritzeck 225–26)

Petr.Ven.*Sum.Sar*. (Kritzeck 205)

Daniel (1960) 5–6

See vol.2:227–42
Guib.Nog.*Gest*.1.3 (*PL* 156: 689)

Kritzeck (1964) viii

Petr.Ven.*Ep*.111 (Constable 297)

Petr.Ven.*Sect.Sar*.pr.13 (Kritzeck 227)

Petr.Alf.*Dial*.5 (*PL* 157:600);
Petr.Ven.*Ep*.111 (Constable 296)

See vol.2:105–17; p. 236 above
Alan.Ins.*Haer*.4.11 (*PL* 210: 427)

Petr.Ven.*Ep*.111 (Constable 297)

Hild.Tr.*Mah*.pr. (*PL* 171: 1346)

Alan.Ins.*Haer*.4.1 (*PL* 210: 421)

Petr.Ven.*Petrob*.161 (*CCCM* 10:94)

Petr.Ven.*Sum.Sar*. (Kritzeck 204)

See vol.1:286–90

Alan.Ins.*Haer*.4.3 (*PL* 210: 423–24)

Petr.Ven.*Sum.Sar*. (Kritzeck 204)

Petr.Ven.*Ep*.111 (Constable 296)

cal sources, specifically from a Nestorian monk, who had converted him from heathenism to heresy, to which, then, some elements of Judaism were added. Like the Jews and like certain Christian heretics, the Muslims attacked the Christian worship of images as a form of idolatry. Erroneous though this charge was in Christian eyes, it did express the affirmation of monotheism and the rejection of idolatry to which Mohammed had come as a result of his conversion, but to Christian apologists it illustrated the propensity of the prophet and his followers to let "a new error expel previous errors." Probably the most dramatic instance of that propensity was the Muslim view of the person of Christ.

"They assert," a Christian tract against the Muslims noted, "that Christ was born of a virgin, that Mary remained a virgin, and that Christ was conceived by the Spirit of God, that is, by the breath of God." What is more, Christ was believed by the Muslims to have been not only "born of a holy virgin by the divine breath," but "to have taught what is true and to have performed miracles." Yet because "according to them no one can be a father without sexual intercourse, they deny that God the Creator is the Father" of Christ. Consequently, "although they believe that Christ was conceived by the Holy Spirit, they do not believe that he is the Son of God, nor that he is God." Instead he was, according to them, "a good prophet and a most truthful one, free of all lies and of all sins, the Son of Mary, born without a father." As the Christian polemicists saw it, therefore, the doctrine of the virgin birth, which was to them a guarantee of the true humanity of Christ, became for Muslim theology a means of ascribing to him less than a complete human nature. The Christians attributed to Muslim teaching the belief that Christ "had never died, since he was not deserving of death; but when the Jews were intent on killing him, he escaped from their hands and ascended to the stars, where he now lives in his flesh in the presence of the Creator, until the coming of Antichrist." Therefore, although Mohammed "confesses that [Christ] is the messenger of God, the Word of God, and the Spirit of God, he does not understand or confess by the terms 'messenger,' 'word,' and 'spirit' what we do." Such misreadings of the traditional christological terminology vitiated the orthodox appearance of the Muslim confession about the person of Christ.

The other favorite object of criticism by the Christian apologists was Muslim eschatology. As the promises of the Koran about the life to come appeared to Christians, they were completely materialistic, setting the hopes of Muslim believers on the attainment of the objects of all the physical appetites that had not been fully satisfied in the present life. Even in the present life the morality of the Gospels had been modified to make concessions to the flesh; likewise, eternal life was not patterned after "the angelic society, nor the divine vision, nor the highest good, 'which eye has not seen, nor ear heard, neither has entered into the heart of man,' but actually the sort of thing that flesh and blood, indeed the dregs of flesh and blood, have desired and yearned to attain." Here again the Muslim tendency to accept and then to distort orthodox Christian belief was manifest. Thus they affirmed the validity of miracles, but proceeded to lay claim to miracles "by antiphrasis," that is, by using the term for acts that were devoid of "either reason or authority." To Christian apologists this was evidence that in their faith, as in their hope, the Muslims were mixing the good with the bad and confusing the true with the false.

The encounter of the twelfth century with Muslim teaching was important for yet another reason. It served to put the entire question of the relation between Christianity and Judaism into a different light. On the one hand, Christians could say to Jews that their two faiths were at least agreed on the reality of the crucifixion and death of Christ, while Muslims regarded these events as an illusion. At the same time Christians laid claim to an agreement with the Muslims about the virgin birth over against the teachings of the Jews, who, because they were "not far away from us, but in our very midst, are much worse than the Saracens" (although the heretics were even worse than the Jews). Presumably it was an expression of some such judgment when Crusaders, on their way to make war against the Muslim infidel in the Holy Land, interrupted their journey to massacre Jews in Europe. In other ways, too, Islam provided a foil for the disputes between Jews and Christians. A convert from Judaism to Christianity could be challenged to explain

Petr.Alf.*Dial*.5 (*PL* 157:599)

Alan.Ins.*Haer*.4.5 (*PL* 210: 424)

Hild.Tr.*Mah*.9 (*PL* 171:1357)

1 Cor.2:9

Petr.Ven.*Ep*.111 (Constable 296–97)

Alan.Ins.*Haer*.4.14 (*PL* 210: 429)

Petr.Ven.*Ep*.111 (Constable 297)

Petr.Alf.*Dial*.5 (*PL* 157:606)

Petr.Ven.*Ep*.130 (Constable 328)
Petr.Ven.*Petrob*.97 (*CCCM* 10: 57–58)

Guib.Nog.*Vita sua*.2.5 (*PL* 156:903)

Petr.Alf.*Dial*.5 (*PL* 157:597)

ap.Petr.Ven.*Jud*.4 (*PL* 189:589)

See vol.1:63; vol.2:235–36

Rup.*Ann*.pr. (*PL* 170:561–62)
Gualt.Torn.*Jud*.pr. (*PL* 209:425)

See vol.1:16

Petr.Bl.*Perf.Jud*. (*PL* 207:825–70)

Od.Cambr.*Jud*. (*PL* 160:1112)

Ps.Wm.Camp.*Dial*. (*PL* 163:1045)

Petr.Alf.*Dial*. (*PL* 157:535–672)
Petr.Bl.*Perf.Jud*.28 (*PL* 207:861)
Herm.Sched.*Conv*.2 (*PL* 170:807); Brd.Clr.*Cant*.60.1.3 (Leclercq-Rochais 2:143)

Miccoli (1959) 9

Joach.*Ev*.1 (*FSI* 67:82; 95);
Joach.*Jud*. (*FSI* 95:3)

why he had not become a Muslim instead, and in response he articulated the distinctiveness of the Christian gospel in contrast to both of these options. Another Jewish disputant took the rise of Islam as an occasion to ask his Christian interlocutor: "If the Christian era, now established, . . . could not believe without miracles, how is it that . . . the Mohammedan heresy . . . has infected such large portions of the world without performing any miracles?" As it had before, the Christian encounter with other faiths compelled an examination of the prior question of the relation between Christianity and Judaism.

The twelfth century, therefore, seems to have produced more treatises of Jewish-Christian disputation than any preceding century of the Middle Ages, perhaps as many as all those centuries combined. Some of the treatises were obviously literary creations, not reports of genuine encounters; in at least one case, the "dialogue" was between two Christians rather than between a Christian and a Jew. The ancient Christian practice of compiling "testimonies" from the Old Testament to prove the superiority of Christianity to Judaism was also continued. Other treatises, however, were based on meetings that had actually taken place, as in the conversation between Odo of Cambrai and a Jew named Leo on the way to Poitiers, a conversation whose conclusion was an exchange in which the Christian asked, "Why then do you not believe?" and the Jew replied, "Because I do not dare to surrender the truth of our tradition to these words of yours." Despite the failure to effect conversions, the disputations could be carried on in an "amicable" atmosphere, and even a discussion between a Jew and a convert from Judaism to Christianity dealt principally with the theological issues. Christian spokesmen did repeat atrocity stories about Jewish ritual, as well as the stock charges of Jewish commercialism; nevertheless, the treatises of this period stand out from the literature summarized earlier, not only quantitatively but also qualitatively.

Although, in the twelfth century as in earlier centuries, "the themes of anti-Jewish polemics are in large part a step-by-step repetition of the usual 'authorities' of Christian apologetics," the existential situation between spokesmen for Judaism and spokesmen for Christianity had changed. There were even some Christians who believed that the time for the conversion of all Israel was at hand.

Southern (1963) 88–91

Gisl.Crisp.*Jud*.pr. (*PL* 159: 1005–6)

Alan.Ins.*Haer*.3 (*PL* 210:399– 422); Ebr.*Antihaer*.27 (*MBP* 24:1578–79)

See vol.1:19; vol.2:206 Petr.Alf.*Dial*.7 (*PL* 157:613– 17); Rich.S.Vict.*Em*.1.6 (*PL* 196:612–13); Gualt.Torn.*Jud*. 1.2 (*PL* 209:426–27); Gisl. Crisp.*Jud*. (*PL* 159:1027)

Rich.S.Vict.*Em*.pr.; 1.2 (*PL* 196:601–2; 607)

See vol.2:201

Petr.Ven.*Petrob*.126 (*CCCM* 10:74); Paulin.Aquil.*Fel*.1.12 (*PL* 99:363)

Gez.*Corp*.39 (*PL* 137:390)

See vol.2:200–215

Deut.6:4 ap.Ps.Wm.Camp.*Dial*. (*PL* 163:1056–58); Rup.*Ann*.3 (*PL* 170:604); ap.Alan.Ins.*Haer*. 3.1 (*PL* 210:401); Joach.*Jud*. (*FSI* 95:21) Gisl.Corp.*Gent*. (Webb 64; 73)

1 Cor.8:6

Petr.Ven.*Jud*.2 (*PL* 189:521) Petr.Bl.*Perf.Jud*.2 (*PL* 207: 828)

Hil.*Trin*.4.16; 4.33 (*PL* 10: 109; 121)

Gisl.Crisp.*Jud*. (*PL* 159:1018)

See vol.1:181; 197 Gualt.Torn.*Jud*.2 (*PL* 209: 437–50)

Jews were playing a new role in provoking Christian theological discussions, for example in the circle surrounding Anselm of Canterbury; and in a report on such a discussion with a Jew, one of Anselm's disciples gave an account of a dialogue that was fair and substantive in its argumentation on both sides. The prominence of the Jewish question in Christian discourse may be gauged from the works of Alan of Lille and Ebrard of Béthune, both of whom incorporated a polemical tract against Judaism into a general heresiology. So imposing was the encounter with Judaism that on such perennial issues as the proper translation and interpretation of the word "virgin" or "young woman" in Isaiah 7:14, which continued to engage attention on both sides, it became necessary for defenders of orthodoxy to warn against a "Judaizing" tendency among some Christian theologians to concede that Jewish exegesis had been correct. Following established custom, Christian heresiologists were quick to label as "Jewish" the implications of false teaching, especially on the doctrine of the person of Christ. They likewise warned that "heretics or pagans, and especially Jews," were to be excluded from attending Christian worship.

Of the conventional topics for dispute between Jews and Christians, the question of "Trinity and Shema," the charge that the dogma of the Trinity contradicted the oneness of God, continued to be prominent. Repeatedly the words of the Shema appeared as the basis for a Jewish critique of trinitarianism, or even for a pagan critique. The Christian response to this critique was to quote the New Testament formula "There is one God, the Father, from whom are all things and for whom we exist, and one Lord, Jesus Christ, through whom are all things and through whom we exist" and to argue that although God was "one," that did not mean that he was "solitary"; both of these responses were drawn from Hilary's exposition of the unity of God affirmed in the Shema. "Trinity" did not imply "triplicity." In defense of trinitarian monotheism, Christian exegetes repeated the standard interpretations of various Old Testament "passages of distinction," to prove that the doctrine of the Trinity was present already there. Peter Alfonsi, a convert from Judaism, went even further, setting forth a fanciful explanation of the Tetragrammaton from Exodus 3:14 as a mystical

Petr.Alf.*Dial*.6 (*PL* 157:611)

Petr.Ven.*Jud*.1 (*PL* 189:519)

Gisl.Crisp.*Jud*. (*PL* 159:1017)
Rup.*Ann*.3 (*PL* 170:601);
Herm.Sched.*Conv*.3 (*PL* 170:811)

Petr.Alf.*Dial*.12 (*PL* 157:670); Gisl.Crisp.*Jud*. (*PL* 159:1034–35)

Petr.Alf.*Dial*.12 (*PL* 157:656)
Ps.Wm.Camp.*Dial*. (*PL* 163:1046)

Jer.2:8 (Vul.)

Petr.Ven.*Jud*.4 (*PL* 189:574)

Ps.Wm.Camp.*Dial*. (*PL* 163:1048–50)

ap.Gisl.Crisp.*Jud*. (*PL* 159:1007)
ap.Alan.Ins.*Haer*.3.6 (*PL* 210:407); ap.Petr.Dam.*Opusc*.3 (*PL* 145:57–59)

ap.Petr.Ab.*Dial*. (Thomas 52)

Rup.*Ann*.2 (*PL* 170:588–91)

Rich.S.Vict.*Edict*.2 (Châtillon-Tulloch 46)

Gisl.Crisp.*Jud*. (*PL* 159:1010)

Ps.Wm.Camp.*Dial*. (*PL* 163:1047)

Gisl.Crisp.*Jud*. (*PL* 159:1010)

Jer.31:31
Gualt.Torn.*Jud*.1.7 (*PL* 209:430–31); Petr.Ven.*Jud*.4 (*PL* 189:572–73)
Petr.Ab.*Dial*. (Thomas 85)

Ps.Wm.Camp.*Dial*. (*PL* 163:1051)

Petr.Ab.*Dial*. (Thomas 53)

symbol of the Trinity; this was an extension of the belief shared by Jews and Christians that "the name of God" was God himself. As part of this defense, Christians also had to specify that it was not the man Jesus as such who was the object of Christian faith, but the preexistent Son of God incarnate in him. Otherwise, the worship of Jesus would be idolatry, as would the worship of images and statues, including the image of the cross; but Christian apologists maintained that "when we genuflect before the cross, we are not adoring that cross nor the image affixed to it, but rather God the Father and his Son, Jesus Christ."

In that light, Christians could assert that they were as faithful to the law of Moses as Jews were, in fact much more faithful. Quoting the words of the prophet, "While keeping every law, they did not know Me," they charged that Judaism had substituted the observance of the law for the knowledge of God, but that Christianity proceeded through the study of the law to the knowledge and the worship of God. As it was impossible to eat a nut that was still in its shell, so the true observance of the law had to penetrate to its kernel. "We observe the Law given by God," the Jews replied, "and we implicitly follow Moses the lawgiver," and they recited the various commandments of Moses that Christians flouted. Everyone knew that "practically all delicious foods are forbidden" to Jews. They also made the law of the Sabbath an issue in their exchanges with Christians. To the Christians, such citations of the Mosaic law ignored the fundamental purpose of the Old Testament dispensation, which was "to go on from things that were good to things that were even better." Therefore some of the provisions of the law of Moses were temporary, and "what the old law had decreed temporarily, that the new law has fulfilled eternally." The symbols and requirements of the Mosaic law were intended to prepare for the coming of Christ, but with that coming they were to cease. The prophets of the Old Testament themselves had promised that there would be a "new law" written in the heart, to replace the law written on stone, and the law that was more recent would supersede the earlier and less perfect law. The more recent law was also the recovery of the original natural law, which had preceded the promulgation of the written law. The patriarchs of the Old Testament, including Abraham, had had to be content with this natural law.

The law of Moses came after the natural law and before the evangelical law; it was valid for its own time, but not for all time.

The contention over the validity and the interpretation of the law of Moses was part of the larger dispute about the authority and the exegesis of Scripture as a whole.

Petr.Ven.*Jud*.5 (*PL* 189:650)

"We have overcome you with the Holy Book" was the Christian claim, to which the Jewish response was said to have been: "All the things you say belong to me, and you have taken them over from my books. Where did you get these things? What business do you have with my

ap.Rup.*Ann*.1 (*PL* 170:566)

Scriptures?" The reason for this reliance on the Jewish Bible in Christian apologetics was obvious: Christians were attempting to make their case on the basis of an authority that they had in common with Jews, urging the

Petr.Ven.*Jud*.pr. (*PL* 189:509)

Jews to "believe your own Scriptures, not someone else's." Ultimately this authority rested on faith rather than on

Petr.Ab.*Dial*. (Thomas 48)

proof, and the Christian appeal to Jewish hearers was predicated on the assumption that acceptance of the Old Testament led inevitably to acceptance of the New, so that as the Christians believed the Jewish prophets, the

Petr.Ven.*Jud*.4 (*PL* 189:588)

Jews should believe the Christian apostles.

Upon closer scrutiny, the premise of a common authority was open to some question. For one thing, the Christians did feel competent to go beyond the text of the Old Testament, as when they "added what Isaiah does not

Isa.7:14

add, namely, that after the birth [of Christ, Mary] re-

Ps.Wm.Camp.*Dial*. (*PL* 163:1054)

mained a virgin." The rabbis also noted that Christians often quoted as sayings of the law and the prophets various passages that did not appear in canonical Jewish Scripture,

ap.Gisl.Crisp.*Jud*. (*PL* 159:1026)

for example, from the Book of Baruch. These "deutero-canonical books" stood alongside the Jewish canon in the

Petr.Ven.*Petrob*.65–66 (*CCCM* 10:41)

Christian version of the Old Testament. Charged as they were with having canonized more than the legitimate books of the Bible, the Christians accused the Jews of elevating the authority of the Pentateuch over that of

Rup.*Ann*.2 (*PL* 170:581)

the Psalms and the prophets, books that were essential sources for the Christian arsenal. Moreover, Judaism, too, had gone beyond the canon of the Old Testament, "beyond

Petr.Ven.*Jud*.5 (*PL* 189:627)

the law and beyond the prophets," by raising the Talmud to the level of Scripture or even regarding "this egregious doctrine of yours, this Talmud, as preferable to the books

Petr.Ven.*Jud*.5 (*PL* 189:602)
Joach.*Jud*. (*FSI* 95:23)

of the prophets and all the authentic" books of the Bible. The Christian message was not "a new faith." To the accusation of having tampered with the canon and the text of the Old Testament Christians indignantly responded that "because Christ is the truth, the faith of Christ does not need any falsehood, nor is there any place in the church of Christ for falsehood." The church had received the law and the prophets from Judaism, and "what it received from you, it has preserved unchanged through so many centuries to the present time."

Not only had Christians "preserved intact and preserved uncorrupted" the books of the Old Testament that they had received from the Jews; they had also been responsible for bringing these books to the Gentiles, by translating them into the languages of the nations as part of the Christian mission, so that "the Latin, the Greek, and the barbarian have from these books whatever you as a Jew have," whereas the original Jewish impulse that had been responsible for the translation of the Bible into Greek had not continued and Christians had taken over the responsibility for teaching the law and the prophets to other peoples. The Jewish translation of the Bible into Greek, the Septuagint, became a sore point in itself. Despite the dependence of Christian exegesis on the translations (or mistranslations) of the Septuagint, Christians, following Jerome, still accused the Jewish translators of having suppressed evidence for the doctrine of the Trinity when they rendered the Hebrew into Greek. Yet it remained true in most cases that the Jewish participants in the debate did not know the Septuagint, while the Christian participants did not know the Hebrew text. That situation would, of course, change when the Christian partner in the conversation was a convert from Judaism; but it was also becoming less surprising than it had been when a Christian theologian, even one who had not been born a Jew, could claim at least some grasp of the original language of the Old Testament.

The disputes over the canon, text, and language of the Old Testament were all directed toward the real issue between Jews and Christians in their use of the Bible, which was the interpretation of the crucial passages. "To Judaize according to the letter" was a standard way for Christians to derogate the Jewish methods of exegesis. The Jewish interpretation of a favorite Christian locus classicus such as Psalm 2 was "tortuous." Jewish disputants reciprocated by accusing Christian exegetes of "speaking as you wish,

Margin notes:

Gisl.Crisp.*Jud.* (PL 159:1027)

Petr.Ven.*Jud.*4 (PL 189:582)
Joach.*Jud.* (FSI 95:98)
See vol.1:20

See vol.2:206–7
Hon.Aug.*Eluc.*2.27 (PL 172:1154)

Hier.*Hebr.quaest.*pr. (CCSL 72:2)

Bern.Reich.*Modul.*2 (PL 142:1132)

Gisl.Crisp.*Jud.* (PL 159:1027–28)

Petr.Alf.*Dial.*pr. (PL 157:539)

Herm.Sched.*Conv.*2 (PL 170:808)

Petr.Ab.*Dial.* (Thomas 146); Petr.Ven.*Petrob.*77 (CCCM 10:47)

Petr.Ven.*Jud.*1 (PL 189:512)

ap.Rup.*Ann*.1; 7 (*PL* 170: 573; 597)

Petr.Alf.*Dial*.1 (*PL* 157:553)

Ps.Wm.Camp.*Dial*. (*PL* 163: 1048)

See vol.1:18

Petr.Ven.*Jud*.1 (*PL* 189:513–18); Joach.*Jud*. (*FSI* 95:8)

Gen.49:10
See vol.1:55–67
Fulb.*Jud*. (*PL* 141:306–18); Petr.Lomb.*Serm*.2 (*PL* 171: 376–81)
Alan.Ins.*Haer*.3.12 (*PL* 210: 411–12)

Gisl.Crisp.*Jud*. (*PL* 159:1010)

Rup.*Ann*.1 (*PL* 170:564)

Petr.Dam.*Opusc*.2.1 (*PL* 145: 46)

Rich.S.Vict.*Except*.1.4.13 (*TPMA* 5:141)

Ans.*Cur d.h*.1.18 (Schmitt 2: 78); Joach.*Jud*. (*FSI* 95:76–77)

Ps.Wm.Camp.*Dial*. (*PL* 163: 1055)

citing the terms of the Scriptures in accordance with your own intention and twisting them any way you want." The hermeneutics of the Christians was guided by the belief that the writings of the Old Testament prophets were obscure in themselves and needed a principle of interpretation beyond themselves to make sense. The books of the Old Testament were filled with "many things that are diverse and even contradictory, which cannot stand if they are interpreted literally," and therefore a spiritual interpretation was called for. For example, Psalm 110, which had been a favorite proof text in the New Testament and in the early fathers of the church, did not, as Jewish scholars claimed, refer to Abraham, but to "Jesus Christ as God and man at the same time," who was authorized to be seated at the right hand of God the Father. The same was true of many other passages of the Old Testament.

Among such passages, the prophecy of Jacob to Judah continued to provide the most comprehensive guide to the history of Israel. Sometimes it was the sole subject of a tract against the Jews, but it also played a prominent part in the total argument. It was used to prove to the Jews that the figures of the Old Testament law could no longer claim to be valid, now that the object of their symbolism had come. That object was Jesus Christ, who was, as the text of Genesis 49:10 stated, "the expectation of the nations." For if it was true that Jews had been living for a thousand years without a king and under the domination of alien nations, that was the fulfillment of the prophecy that "a leader shall not fail from Judah, nor a ruler from his thighs, until that which has been laid up for him shall come; and he shall be the expectation of the nations." As a twelfth-century chronicle of world history put it, "when the legitimate unction of the Jewish nation came to an end, there was imminent, according to the prophetic word, the expectation of the nations, our Lord Jesus Christ." Of course, God would have called the Gentiles even if all the Jews had believed, but the Jewish rejection of Christ became the historical occasion for the call to be extended to other nations. To make this kind of historical sense of the prophecy, however, it was necessary for an exegete to study not only the text of Genesis itself, but also "historical annals." Such study would show that the reign of Herod was the time when the prophecy was ful-

Petr.Ven.*Jud.*4 (*PL* 189:559–63)

See vol.2:212–13

Rup.*Ann.*3 (*PL* 170:606)

Guib.Nog.*Inc.*3.7 (*PL* 156:522)

Petr.Ab.*Dial.* (Thomas 50)

Petr.Bl.*Perf.Jud.*13 (*PL* 207:843)
Alterc.syn. (Blumenkranz 55)

Rup.*Ann.*2 (*PL* 170:591–92)

Joach.*Jud.* (*FSI* 95:72)

Petr.Ab.*Dial.* (Thomas 76)

Petr.Alf.*Dial.*2 (*PL* 157:581)

Petr.Ab.*Dial.* (Thomas 58)

Od.Cambr.*Jud.* (*PL* 160:1103)

Petr.Alf.*Dial.*3 (*PL* 157:581–82)

Petr.Ven.*Jud.*3 (*PL* 189:539)
Petr.Dam.*Opusc.*2.4 (*PL* 145:55)

ap.Od.Cambr.*Jud.* (*PL* 160:1103)

Jul.Tol.*Aet.sext.*1.8 (*PL* 96:545)

See vol.2:211

Isa.2:4

filled, and once again Christians relied on Josephus as the primary historical source for their argument.

The narrative of Josephus was read as proof that the Roman conquest of Jerusalem and the Holy Land was an act of divine judgment. Specifically, the destruction of the temple showed that Judaism, valid for its own time, had now come to an end as a dispensation of God. A calamity of such proportions could not have come upon the Jewish nation "except by the most extreme wrath of God" and by his "righteous vengeance," brought on by "no other cause than their sin against Jesus Christ." All the "prerogatives" of Judaism had been annulled. Above all, "the land that they had received, they lost on account of their sins," but the land had not been "the whole of the promise, only a sort of bonus added on." Yet it was the loss of the land and of the city of Jerusalem that was the most acute reminder of the captivity of Israel. It was a captivity from which they would not be set free until the Jews began to believe what their fathers in the time of Christ had refused to believe. The promises given to the people of Israel in the Book of Deuteronomy had ignored "spiritual blessing" and had concentrated exclusively on earthly blessings, including the promise of the land. These were blessings that Christians interpreted as "heavenly" in their intent rather than "earthly." The same was true of eschatological hopes. Thus the Jews hoped that after the resurrection their faithful would inhabit the Promised Land, where the true believers "from everywhere would congregate." Yet after so many years of captivity, such hopes were absurd.

A significant component of that Jewish hope was the expectation not only that "all kingdoms will be subjected to us" in the Messiah, but also that "under him we shall have perpetual peace." Using the same passages of the Old Testament, Christians had also been claiming for a long time that with the advent of Christ "wars have come to an end throughout the world." The realities of political and military history, as in the East so also in the West, seemed to Jewish critics to belie the promise. Above all, it was the prophetic vision of a world in which "they shall beat their swords into plowshares, and their spears into pruning hooks; nation shall not lift up sword against nation, neither shall they learn war any more" that seemed to be a long way off, even though such events "without doubt are to be completed after the coming of Christ. Yet to the present day the nations are battling against one another." The Christian response that these prophecies did not pertain to "what the nations are going to do, but to what Christ is going to command" was not altogether satisfying. The Jewish complaint that "the military order in our time is not yet beating its swords into plowshares nor its spears into pruning hooks," but that rather "there are scarcely enough smiths or enough iron for the manufacture of military weapons" seems to have been sufficiently forceful to be quoted verbatim in two Christian tracts separated by about a century. To Christians, all of this unrest, whether foreign or domestic, was a sign of the impending end.

Nevertheless, as one Jewish disputant put it, "even if we have disposed of all these matters, we come to Christ, in whom the entire point at issue in the questioning and in the controversy consists." All the other issues in the controversy were a function of this one. The dispute over the Trinity was ultimately a conflict over the appropriateness of ascribing such titles as "God" and "Lord" to Christ. When Jews and Christians were contending over the status of the Mosaic law, it was the temporary validity of the "old law" given by Moses by contrast with the eternal permanence of the "new law" given by Christ that Christians were seeking to establish. Although differences of opinion on exegetical matters were common within each of the two communities, the differences of biblical interpretation between the two communities had to do basically with the application of Old Testament texts to the person of Christ as the incarnate Son of God. And the dominant theme of the clash over the loss of the Promised Land was the Christian claim to have "proved beyond all doubt that this captivity has lasted so long on account of the death of Christ and [Jewish] malevolence toward him," together with the correlative principle that the promises about the land, which Judaism applied to itself, actually dealt with the Christian "hope in Christ."

Throughout the disputations, therefore, the fundamental difference between the Jew and the Christian was, as one Christian stated it, that "I say, 'He has come,' while you say, 'He will come.'" For if he had already come, the Jews asked, why was it that the prophecies of the universality of the messianic kingdom had not been fulfilled?

Petr.Alf.*Dial*.9 (*PL* 157:636)

ap.Gisl.Crisp.*Jud*. (*PL* 159: 1012); ap.Alan.Ins.*Haer*.3.11 (*PL* 210:410–11)

Ebr.*Antihaer*.27 (*MBP* 24: 1578)

ap.Gisl.Crisp.*Jud*. (*PL* 159: 1011)

Petr.Ven.*Jud*.2 (*PL* 189:521)

Ps.Wm.Camp.*Dial*. (*PL* 163: 1047)

Petr.Ven.*Jud*.1 (*PL* 189:517–18)

Petr.Alf.*Dial*.2 (*PL* 157:581)

Od.Cambr.*Jud*. (*PL* 160:1103)

Petr.Ven.*Jud*.4 (*PL* 189:558)

Isa.2:2–3

ap.Alan.Ins.*Haer*.3.11 (*PL*
210:410)

ap.Gisl.Crisp.*Jud*. (*PL* 159:
1011)

Joach.*Jud*. (*FSI* 95:9–17)

Zech.9:9; Matt.21:5
Petr.Bl.*Perf.Jud*.15 (*PL* 207:
844–45)

Petr.Ven.*Jud*.2 (*PL* 189:529);
Gisl.Crisp.*Gent*. (Webb 67)

Petr.Ven.*Jud*.3 (*PL* 189:541)

Petr.Ab.*Dial*. (Thomas 50)

Petr.Ab.*Dial*. (Thomas 53)

Sent.Flor.50 (Ostlender 23)

See vol.1:11–67

It was still only the Jewish nation that was saying, "Come, let us go to the mountain of the Lord," whereas the Christians said, "Let us go to the Church of Saint Peter or of Saint Martin." Specifically, it was the Christian belief that Jesus was the promised Messiah that defined the difference between Judaism and Christianity. Even when a Jew found it possible to pay a high tribute to Jesus, declaring, "I believe that Christ is a prophet, most excellent in his possession of all virtues, and I shall believe Christ [Christo credam]," he was obliged to add: "But I do not believe in Christ [in Christum], nor shall I ever do so, because I do not believe in anyone but in God, and in one God." The Jews could not identify the "angel of the Lord" with the Lord himself. As the Christians saw it, the stumbling block for Jews was the paradox foretold by the prophet and fulfilled on Palm Sunday, that "your king comes to you . . . humble." Others had been humble and lowly, for that was the human condition, which the Jews "regard as vile and unworthy of the name or the honor of the Divine Majesty." It seemed to them "incongruous" for the sublime glory of God to be present personally in so humble a man. And yet, the Christians countered, if Jesus Christ was not the humble king promised in such Old Testament prophecies, who else could it be?

The Christian conflict with Judaism over the necessity of Christ raised with special poignancy the question of the possibility of revelation and of salvation apart from Christ. Christians did share with Jews and with Muslims, and for that matter with other rational men, a commitment to monotheism and an abhorrence of polytheism and idolatry. From this common ground, however, each religious tradition went its own particular way in "believing that it is serving God and supposing that it does what is pleasing to him." Yet this did not imply that one should give approval to all the religious traditions indiscriminately, as though the differences between them were meaningless. Just such indifference was thought to be one of the errors of Muslims, who "say that everyone can be saved in his own faith." Within Christendom, too, the problem could not simply be dismissed, especially because of the encounters with Judaism and now also with Islam. The standard view, which had come out of the early church in its disputes with Jewish and with classical thought, continued to be the principle that "from the beginning no one has been saved without faith in Christ," but that for some this had been a faith in Christ as "the one who was to come," while for Christians it was a faith in "the past events" of his life, death, and resurrection. That principle appeared to be too firmly established in the faith of the church to be open to question.

Yet there did arise some who, it was reported, "assert that many who came before the incarnation of God were saved and redeemed through his passion, even though they never believed either his incarnation or his passion." Peter Abelard, while rejecting this idea as heretical and arrogant, was willing to consider the case of someone who "has refused to give honor to Christ, not through malice but through error." He could not accept the simple answer that such a person would be damned for an "invincible ignorance [that] makes him similar to those for whom the Lord in his passion or Stephen prayed." Rather, he found it "consonant with piety as well as with reason" to believe that those who strove to please God according to their best lights on the basis of the natural law would not be damned for their efforts. But since salvation must be through Christ, God would disclose the saving truth of "what is to be believed about Christ" to such heathen, either through a special messenger or by direct inspiration. With this proposal he safeguarded the tenet that there was no salvation except through Christ, without having to consign the invincibly ignorant to a state that was beyond the reach of the grace and mercy of God. In effect, he accomplished this by shifting the question from the topic of salvation to the topic of revelation, asking not, "How can one be saved without Christ?" but, "How can one know of God, and how much can one know, without Scripture and the church?" The answer to that question could come only through a new consideration of the relation between faith and understanding.

Faith in Search of Understanding

The defense of the faith against heresy and against the truth claims of other faiths inevitably raised the question of how the authority of revelation within the church was related to other ways of knowing. Even if the relation between reason and revelation had not been forced on the attention of the interpreters of the faith by these challenges, moreover, the imperatives of Christian thought

Hug.S.Vict.*Sacr*.1.10.6 (*PL* 176:336)

ap.Petr.Ab.*Theol.chr*.4.78 (*CCCM* 12:302)

Luke 23:34; Acts 7:60

Petr.Ab.*Prob.Hel*.13 (*PL* 178: 696)

Petr.Ab.*Eth*. (Luscombe 64–66)

See vol.1:27–55

See pp. 95–105 above

Alan.Ins.*Haer*.pr. (*PL* 210: 307)

Monet.Crem.*Cathar*.1.1.3 (Ricchini 23)

Ans.*Ep*.136 (Schmitt 3:280–81)

Ecb.*Cathar*.pr. (*PL* 195:13–14)

Petr.Ven.*Petrob*.153 (*CCCM* 10:87–88)

Macdonald (1930) 98

Brun.S.*Lev*.7 (*PL* 164:404)

itself would have compelled them to address the problem of faith and understanding. There was, then, both an inner and an outer necessity to reopen a perennial discussion that had been going on since patristic times and that had been raised for medieval theology by the probing speculations of John Scotus Erigena.

"The catholic faith," according to one heresiologist of the twelfth century, "is based not only on the foundation of divine reasons, but also on that of human reasons," even though "it stands invincible because of its irrefutable theological authorities." The rise of the "new heretics," who were reviving ancient heresies and "philosophical speculations," made it incumbent on him "to give a reasoned account of a rational faith on the basis of clear reasons." The Cathari, for example, were said to "rely not only on the testimonies of the Scriptures, but also on certain reasons that appear to them to be natural or logical, although they are in fact sophistic." Anselm drew a distinction between "the impious" and "those who admit that they take delight in the honor of the name 'Christian'"; it was proper to direct a rational defense of the faith only against the former group. But Anselm would have included the various heretics of his time among "the impious," not among those who could lay claim to "the honor of the name 'Christian,'" and therefore would have found it appropriate to "demonstrate rationally to them how irrational it is for them to despise us." The orthodox refutation of heresy could not content itself with arguments based on the interpretation of Scripture, but had to be concerned with questions of philosophy and reason as well.

To no heresy did this apply more fully than to the denial of the real presence in the Eucharist, which the sectarian radicals of the twelfth century shared with Berengar of Tours. "The foundation of the whole system of Berengar's exegesis" is said by a modern scholar to have been an "application of the dialectical method, in order to supplement the authority of tradition, whether Scriptural or patristic." At the time, however, Berengar seemed to be supplanting, not merely supplementing, traditional authority. "By disputing philosophically about the body and blood of Christ, he has led us to impossible conclusions," one of his opponents declared. His most prominent opponent, Lanfranc of Bec, accused Berengar of "leaving the

Lanf.*Corp*.7 (*PL* 150:416)

Lanf.*1 Cor*.1.11 (*PL* 150:157)

Gisl.Crisp.*V*.*Herl*. (Robinson 95)

Sig.*Vir.ill*.155 (*PL* 160:582)

Adel.*Ep.Brngr*. (Heurtevent 294–96)

Bald.*Sacr.alt*.pr. (*SC* 93:74)

Bald.*Sacr.alt*.2.1.3 (*SC* 93: 206)

Dur.Tr.*Corp*.6.17 (*PL* 149: 1401); Rem.Aux.*Cel.miss*. (*PL* 101:1262); Petr.Ven.*Petrob*. 189 (*CCCM* 10:112)

Petr.Ven.*Petrob*.97 (*CCCM* 10:57–58)

Petr.Alf.*Dial*.6 (*PL* 157:606); Petr.Ven.*Jud*.4 (*PL* 189:571)

Rich.S.Vict.*Seir*.8 (*TPMA* 15: 266–67)

sacred authorities behind and taking refuge in dialectic."
Yet Lanfranc himself was not averse to the use of dialectic, which, he said, "does not oppose the mysteries of God, but, when the subject requires it, supports and confirms them, provided that it is held in line." Lanfranc was celebrated as a scholar and a master of the liberal arts, even by the Greeks, and soon after his death it was said of him in a biobibliography of ecclesiastical writers that "Lanfranc, the dialectician and the archbishop of Canterbury, expounded Paul the apostle, and, wherever the opportunity presented itself in the passages of the text, he set forth propositions, assumptions, and conclusions in accordance with the laws of dialectic." Other critics of Berengar also used their polemics against him as occasions to distinguish among the ways of knowing and to analyze the relation of faith to sense experience and to reason. After warning in the preface to his work on the Eucharist that "the conjectures of human reason" could not deal adequately with the mystery of the eucharistic presence, another archbishop of Canterbury went on, in a later chapter of the work, to find that he could not altogether avoid dealing with such philosophical concepts as form and matter or species and substance. His warnings were a commonplace of eucharistic theology, which repeatedly urged that this mystery was meant to be believed and venerated rather than discussed and debated. Nevertheless, the discussion and debate went on.

While bad Christians such as heretics were in some ways worse than unbelievers, they both deserved to be met on their own chosen field of battle, which was reason. In the encounter with other faiths, whether Jewish or Muslim, the spokesman for the Christian faith "refuted both of them, sometimes on the basis of reason and sometimes on the basis of authority." Reliance on reason as a defensive weapon against rival systems of belief was all the more necessary when those systems, unlike Judaism and Islam, had no biblical authority in common with Christianity. It had been "with reason as their guide" that the Gentiles had "understood the anticipations of divine revelation," including even some aspects of "the mystery of our reparation," which they awaited with yearning. And then, when the Christian gospel came into the world, it succeeded in converting the most rational of men, the Greek philosophers, to its message; this was proof that the gospel

Petr.Ab.*Dial.* (Thomas 85–86
was not to be dismissed as irrationality and "insanity." Since it was obvious that the differences between the several faiths were due to the differences of authority on which they were based, rather than to "reason, which is

Petr.Ab.*Dial.* (Thomas 94);
Gisl.Crisp.*Gent.* (Webb 60)
by nature prior to" all of these authorities, it was the function of reason to analyze how those who "acknowledge that we are all worshipers of one God" could nevertheless each adhere to "a diverse [form of] faith and life," be it that of the Christian or that of the Jew or

Petr.Ab.*Dial.* (Thomas 41)
that of the philosopher.

The confutation of false doctrine, which professed Christianity but was not faithful to the tradition, and the response to alternative faiths had often been the occasion for a consideration of the relation between revelation and

See vol.2:242–43
reason. It was a distinctive characteristic of this period in the growth of medieval theology that in addition to continuing and intensifying the "rational defense of our faith against the impious," whether heretics or infidels, it took upon itself the task of beginning with the confession of faith and the "pledge made at baptism" and of moving on from it, by "advancing through faith to understanding, rather than proceeding through understanding

Ans.*Ep.*136 (Schmitt 3:281)
See pp. 5–6 above
to faith." In the history of the development of Christian doctrine (and of "theology" in this sense of the word) as distinct from the history of medieval philosophy (and of "theology" in this sense of the word), the discovery of this imperative that faith must move on to understanding is perhaps the most important aspect of the intellectual changes that took place during the twelfth and thirteenth centuries. For this discovery shaped the development of several fundamental doctrines in ways that were to determine their future course for centuries to come.

A decisive source of the change, as well as a helpful index to it, was—together with the often-quoted admoni-

Ghellinck (1948) 279–84
tion of the New Testament to "be ready always to give a

1 Pet.3:15(Vulg.)
reason" for the faith—the use of an early Latin translation of Isaiah 7:9, based on the Septuagint but not incorporated into the Vulgate: "Unless you believe, you will not understand." Although he knew the Vulgate's rendering of the words as "Unless you believe, you will

Aug.*Doctr.christ.*2.12.17 (*CCSL*
32:43)
not abide," Augustine quoted the older version in his treatise *On the Trinity* to show that "faith seeks, but understanding finds," so that it was necessary to seek

Aug.*Trin.*15.2.2 (*CCSL* 50:
461)
understanding on the basis of faith; he also quoted it to

Aug.*Trin*.7.6.12 (*CCSL* 50: 267)

Ildef.*Cog.bapt*.137 (*SPE* 1: 372)
Scot.Er.*Prol.Ev.Joh*.3 (*SC* 151: 214)

Ans.*Pros*.1 (Schmitt 1:100)
Petr.Ab.*Theol.chr*.3.51 (*CCCM* 12:215)
Herm.Sched.*Conv*.11 (*PL* 170: 823)

Rich.S.Vict.*Trin*.1.1 (*SC* 63: 64)

Éthier (1939) 52

See vol.2:31

Ecclus.3:21–22

Fulb.*Ep*.5 (*PL* 141:196);
Petr.Lomb.*Serm*.1 (*PL* 171: 374)

Herb.Los.*Serm*.7 (Goulburn-Symonds 196); Lanf.*Corp*.17 (*PL* 150:427)
Petr.Ven.*Petrob*.189 (*CCCM* 10:112); Guit.Av.*Corp*.1 (*PL* 149:1441); Abb.*Fract*. (*PL* 166:1345); Wm.S.Th.*Sacr.alt*. pr. (*PL* 180:345); Bald. *Sacr. alt*.2.3.2 (*SC* 93:298–300)

Ans.*Mon*.pr. (Schmitt 1:8)

Alc.*Elip*.4.11 (*PL* 101:294)

John 6:69
Aug.*Ev.Joh*.27.9 (*CCSL* 36: 274)

Beat.*Elip*.1.20 (*PL* 96:905)
Rath.*Prael*.2.12.24 (*PL* 136: 206–7)

show that until understanding came, it was essential to hold to faith. Thus the passage continued to be used in the Old Latin form even after the general acceptance of the Vulgate. John Scotus Erigena quoted it in support of the principle that faith had to precede understanding. The classic interpretation of the words of Isaiah was the one formulated by Anselm in the first chapter of his *Proslogion*: "I yearn to understand some measure of thy truth, which my heart believes and loves. For I do not seek to understand in order to believe, but I believe in order to understand. For I believe even this: that I shall not understand unless I believe." Abelard likewise used it to justify his argumentation, as did Herman of Scheda in his discussion of Christian apologetics toward Judaism. Richard of Saint-Victor also quoted it in the opening chapter of his treatise *On the Trinity*, where it provided the justification for his position that "faith, the attraction for every kind of fruitful investigation and the foundation of every good, nevertheless occupies an inferior place in our ascent to God" in comparison with understanding. The traditional proof text on faith and understanding was the warning: "Seek not what is too difficult for you, nor investigate what is beyond your power. Reflect upon what has been assigned to you, for you do not need what is hidden." This warning continued to be quoted, being especially applicable to the mystery of the real presence in the Eucharist. Yet even the mystery of the Eucharist lent itself to the use of the verse from Isaiah as proof that "faith is not the fruit of understanding, but understanding is the fruit of faith" in the presence.

The idea of faith in search of understanding, together with the use of Isaiah 7:9 to support it, came from Augustine, to whose thought Anselm, in the context of his apologetic writings, acknowledged his continuing debt. This element of the Augustinian synthesis had never disappeared from medieval theology. Alcuin, for example, in his attack on Elipandus, quoted the formula of Augustine: "We have not known and believed, but have 'believed and have come to know.' For we believed in order to understand." Writing against the same opponent, Beatus of Liébana likewise elaborated the Augustinian schema of a faith that led to understanding. Other medieval theologians echoed the phraseology. For all of them Augustine was "the greatest philosopher" among Chris-

Petr.Ab.*Dial.* (Thomas 109; 102); Bald. *Tract.*6 (*PL* 204: 451–52)

Rich.S.Vict.*Trin.*3.1 (*SC* 63: 164–66)

Gen.1:26
Aug.*Trin.*14.19.25 (*CCSL* 50: 456)

Ans.*Mon.*31 (Schmitt 1:49); Hon.Aug.*Inev.* (*PL* 172:1203)

Ans.*Pros.*1 (Schmitt 1:100)

Ans.*Mon.*32 (Schmitt 1:51)

Ans.*Mon.*68 (Schmitt 1:78–79

tians, who had come from pagan philosophy to Christian truth. His speculations about the "traces of the Trinity" in the human mind were the outstanding example of faith in search of understanding. Yet the thinkers of the twelfth century went well beyond such speculations in their investigation of the role of understanding and reason in relation to faith and revelation, and they were aware that in doing so they were engaged in an enterprise for which there were very few precedents in the writings of the church fathers. It was not until the Christian tradition stood virtually unchallenged that it could undertake the task of determining how much of its contents could be known without faith.

As the foundation for Augustine's speculations about the trinitarian structure of the mind was the biblical plural, "Let us make man in our image, after our likeness," so it was also the idea of creation in the image of God that provided the justification for the effort to confirm by reason what was already known by revelation. Every creature of God reflected to some degree the nature of the Creator. Merely by being, it participated in the being of God. But the Creator was the living God, and therefore those creatures that were living resembled him more than those that were not. Since the living God was at the same time one who perceived all things, the perceiving among his living creatures had a special likeness to him. But among the creatures that perceived other creatures, those that were able to reason about this perception were in a unique position in relation to the divine Origin and bore his image in a special way. Therefore "that which is rational [bears the likeness of the supreme nature] more than that which is incapable of reasoning." God had put his image into man so that man might be aware of him, ponder him, and love him. Man could not do this, because of his sin, unless God "renewed and reformed" the image. And yet the rational mind continued to be created "according to the likeness" of the supreme wisdom of God. Therefore it was incumbent on any "rational creature . . . to express by its voluntary activity this image that has been impressed on it by natural power." This it did when it applied all of its powers to "remembering, understanding, and loving the Summum Bonum."

Scripture itself acknowledged the validity of the activity of reason when it left to the choices of reason the

Rich.S.Vict.*Tabern*.1.7 (*PL* 196:216–17)

Ans.*Mon*.pr. (Schmitt 1:7)

Ans.*Mon*.1 (Schmitt 1:13)

Rich.S.Vict.*Trin*.1.4 (*SC* 63:70)

Hug.S.Vict.*Did*.2.1 (Buttimer 24)

Hug.S.Vict.*Scrip*.1 (*PL* 175:9)

Petr.Ab.*Dial*. (Thomas 88–89)

Rom.10:9
Ans.*Inc*.1 (Schmitt 2:7);
Gisl.Crisp.*Gent*. (Webb 77)

Ans.*Pros*.2 (Schmitt 1:101)

Gisl.Crisp.*Gent*. (Webb 60)
Petr.Ab.*Dial*. (Thomas 106)

Ans.*Mon*.1 (Schmitt 1:13)

See vol.1:52–53

Eadm.*V.Ans*.1.19 (Southern 29)

questions that it defined as "undetermined" by its own authority. Even those matters that were determined by the authority of Scripture, moreover, could also fall within the purview of "rational necessity" to deal with on its own terms. On this level such matters could be treated "by reason alone," which could produce its own kind of certainty about such questions as the existence of God and the reality of the divine nature. The certainty to which rational demonstration led came from "not merely probable, but necessary" arguments in support of ultimate truth. It was the responsibility of philosophy to "investigate the reasons of all things, whether divine or human," although logic, mathematics, and physics were incapable of penetrating to "that truth in which the salvation of the soul lies." One basic different between philosophical and theological reasoning was that the former proceeded from ethics to theology and metaphysics, while the latter started with a consideration of the nature of God and then went on to "good works." Beginning, then, with "the truth of that which the catholic church believes in its heart and confesses with its mouth," the Christian mind was to "seek to discover the reason why this is true." At least in principle, there was no aspect of that truth to which the believing mind could not turn in its search for understanding.

The most important of these aspects of the truth for the Christian thinkers of the period was the existence of God. The logical validity of Anselm's "ontological argument" for the existence of God (defined as "that than which nothing greater can be imagined") is not our concern here, but the definition itself is. Significantly, it was a definition that Anselm shared, not only with his own disciples, but with Abelard, whatever other theological differences they may or may not have had. At the heart of Anselm's reasoning was the conception of "one nature, highest of all the things that are, alone sufficient unto itself in its eternal beatitude." The traditional Christian view of the absoluteness of God, which had long been understood not only as the explicit assertion of divine revelation but at the same time as an axiom of natural philosophy, thus became once more a principle whose demonstration did not depend on an acceptance of the authority of Scripture and tradition, but was shared by all who could think clearly, Christian or not. From this principle it followed by reason that all other realities existed through this one ultimate reality, and that there could not be a multiple source of things, but only one source. Quite apart from the authority of revelation, then, "there are many ways by which we can prove that there is no God but one." As the words of the apostle Paul said, the evidence of the works of creation had led the Gentile philosophers to recognize not only the existence, but also the oneness of God.

Yet "once a Christian thinker gets to this point, nothing could prevent him from applying the same method to each of the Christian dogmas," not merely to the existence and the oneness of God but also to the Trinity and the incarnation. Anselm's most complete statement of his doctrine of the atonement was not his *Meditation on Human Redemption,* based on Scripture and tradition, but his *Why God Became Man,* which set out to prove the doctrines of sin and redemption within the limits of reason alone, "putting into parentheses, so to speak, the historic fact of Christianity, the dogmatic imperative of revelation, and, all the more, the authority of the fathers and doctors" of the church. In this enterprise he was followed by Richard of Saint-Victor, who maintained that "it is demonstrated on the basis of reason that the Mediator between God and men must be true God and true man." Richard did recognize that there were some articles of faith to which it would be almost impossible to hold if the catholic tradition had not transmitted them. While there were doctrines that were "above reason but not beyond reason," such as those dealing with the oneness of God, other doctrines "are above reason and seem to be beyond reason or even contrary to reason," such as "almost all the things that we are commanded to believe about the Trinity of persons."

Almost all such things in the dogma of the Trinity had to come either "through revelation" or "solely by authority," but not quite all of them. For the creation of man according to the image of God, which was used to validate this effort to move from faith to understanding through the use of reason, was, by general agreement, a creation "according to the image of the Trinity." Augustine taught, moreover, that through an understanding of the nature of true love one would come to a knowledge of the Trinity. His analysis of love led to the conclusion

Ans.*Mon.*3 (Schmitt 1:16)

Rich.S.Vict.*Trin.*2.14 (*SC* 63: 136)
Rom.1:20

Herm.Mag.*Epit.*11 (*PL* 178: 1712)

Gilson (1938) 26

Roques (1962) 24–25

Rich.S.Vict.*Seir.*8 (*TPMA* 15: 269)

Rich.S.Vict.*Trin.*2.1 (*SC* 63: 110)

Rich.S.Vict.*Ben.maj.*1.6 (*PL* 196:72)

Rich.S.Vict.*Ben.maj.*4.2 (*PL* 196:136)

Brd.Clr.*Div.*45.1 (Leclercq-Rochais 6–1:262); Petr.Ab. *Theol.schol.*45–46 (*CCCM* 12: 418); Petr.Ab.*Theol.chr.*1.12 (*CCCM* 12:76)
Aug.*Trin.*14.19.25 (*CCSL* 50: 456)

Aug.*Trin.*8.7.10 (*CCSL* 50: 284–85)

Aug.*Trin*.9.2.2 (*CCSL* 50: 294)

that "there are these three: the one who loves, the one who is loved, and the love itself." On the basis of this analysis Richard of Saint-Victor proceeded to a consideration of the Trinity on the basis of love, "but Richard's conception is quite different: his attention is directed entirely to the personal relations" between human beings as well as

Dumeige (1952) 90

within the Trinity. As a consequence, Richard concentrated on the implications of love as a natural proof for the doctrine of the Trinity. There could be no love where there was only one person; since God was supremely good and only God was deserving of absolute love, it followed that the infinite love which was God must always have had

Rich.S.Vict.*Trin*.3.2 (*SC* 63: 168–70)

an infinite object even when there were no creatures. Therefore a rational consideration of the nature of love, without the aid of revelation, led to the conclusion that

Rich.S.Vict.*Trin*.3.11 (*SC* 63: 194)

"the fulfillment of love requires a Trinity of persons." Augustine's idea of "traces of the Trinity" in the mind,

Ans.*Mon*.67 (Schmitt 1:77–78)

as interpreted by Anselm, had served Richard's mentor, Hugh of Saint-Victor, as a justification for the claim that "to some degree the human reason has the power" to

Hug.S.Vict.*Sacr*.1.3.28 (*PL* 176:230)

penetrate to the truth of the Trinity, but Richard carried the effort to prove the Trinity rationally to further lengths. In this effort he was joined by those who found evidence

Petr.Ab.*Theol.chr*.1.121; 2.12 (*CCCM* 12:123; 137–38); Herm.Mag.*Epit*.12 (*PL* 178: 1714–15)

for the doctrine of the Trinity in the ancient Gentile philosophers.

If it was permissible to apply the methods of rational speculation to the mystery of the Trinity, even to the point of proving the doctrine of the Filioque on the

Rich.S.Vict.*Trin*.5.8 (*SC* 63: 318–24); Ans.*Mon*.50 (Schmitt 1:65)

basis of reason alone, without the authority of Scripture or tradition, what was to prevent someone from beginning with the same rational method but coming to conclusions that did not accord with the orthodox doctrine? Richard

Rich.S.Vict.*Ben.maj*.2.2 (*PL* 196:80)

spoke out against logicians and "pseudophilosophers," who cared more about novelty than about truth, as well as against stylists, who were more fearful of violating the

Rich.S.Vict.*Ben.min*.46 (*PL* 196:34)

rules of the grammarian Priscian than of sinning against the rule of Christ. The widespread revival of interest in logic and grammar during the twelfth century and the application of these disciplines to theology, specifically to trinitarian theology, set off a series of disputes and speculations on the Trinity, some of which he seems to

See vol.1:221–22

have had in mind in his attacks. From the Cappadocian fathers to Hegel and beyond, the Nicene dogma has fascinated the metaphysically minded among its expositors, especially when, as in the twelfth and thirteenth centuries, a recovery of acquaintance with earlier systems of philosophy stimulated new interest in long-neglected questions. The doctrinal implications of these movements of thought, as distinct from their dialectical principles as such, had a direct bearing on what the church was believing, teaching, and confessing about the Trinity.

As in the trinitarianism of the Cappadocians, the relation between the Three and the One in the Godhead was bound up with the question of universals. Roscellinus of Compiègne seems to have discussed the doctrine of the Trinity within the context of a theory of universals according to which "universal substances are only vocal sounds," so that, for example, color had no reality of its own as distinct from a colored object. It was, according to his opponents, an application of this theory when Roscellinus also taught that "in God, either the three persons are three realities, [existing] in separation from one another (as do three angels) and yet [existing] in such a way that there is one will and power; or else the Father and the Holy Spirit were incarnate" as well as the Son. From the only work of his that has survived, a letter to Abelard, it is clear that Roscellinus did argue from the well-known confusion between Greeks and Latins in trinitarian terminology, by which the Greeks spoke of "three substances [hypostases]," while the Latins, using "substance" for "ousia," spoke of "one substance." Roscellinus took this to mean that one could say: "Nothing else is the substance of the Father except the Father himself, and nothing else is the substance of the Son except the Son himself." Therefore there were "three substances" in the Trinity. Indeed, Roscellinus apparently went so far as to say that the Three "could truly be called three Gods if usage permitted it." Quoting a phrase of Isidore's, Roscellinus found the oneness of the Trinity in "a community of majesty" rather than in "a singularity of majesty."

The trinitarianism of Abelard was diametrically opposed to that of Roscellinus, against whom he composed a treatise on the doctrine of the Trinity. Although there was no discerning Christian who forbade rational discussion of the faith, Roscellinus was twisting dialectic into sophistry by his argumentation. Abelard attacked the notion that "the diversity of persons" in the Trinity implied diverse "realities," as Roscellinus contended. Nor, on the

Rosc.ap.Ans.*Inc.*1 (Schmitt 2:9)

Rosc.ap.Ans.*Ep.*136; *Ep.*129 (Schmitt 3:279; 271)

Aug.*Trin.*7.4.7 (*CCSL* 50: 255); Petr.Ab.*Sic et non.*9 (Boyer-McKeon 136–39)

Rosc.*Ep.Ab.*10 (*BGPM* 8-V: 74)

Rosc.ap.Ans.*Ep.*136 (Schmitt 3:279)
Isid.Sev.*Orig.*7.4.2 (*PL* 82: 271)

Rosc.*Ep.Ab.*13 (*BGPM* 8-V: 77)

Petr.Ab.*Ep.*14 (*PL* 178:356–57)

Petr.Ab.*Dial.* (Thomas 97)
Petr.Ab.*Theol.chr.*3.4 (*CCCM* 12:195)

Petr.Ab.*Theol.chr.*3.90 (*CCCM* 12:230)

Petr.Ab.*Theol.schol*.50 (*CCCM* 12:420)

Petr.Ab.*Theol.chr*.3.109 (*CCCM* 12:235) Petr.Ab.*Theol.chr*. 3.69 (*CCCM* 12:223)

Petr.Ab.*Theol.chr*.1.8 (*CCCM* 12:75)

Petr.Ab.*Theol.chr*.3.60 (*CCCM* 12:219)

Buytaert (1974) 131

John 3:5

Petr.Ab.*Theol.schol*.50 (*CCCM* 12:420)

Petr.Ab.*Theol.chr*.1.7 (*CCCM* 12:74)

Petr.Ab.*Theol.chr*.1.52 (*CCCM* 12:216) See vol.1:349–50

Gisl.Por.*Com.Eut*.pr.7 (Häring 234)

Joh.Salis.*Hist.pont*.8–14 (*MGH Scrip*.20:522–30) ; Ot.Fr.*Gest. Frid*.1:50–57 (*MGH Scrip*.20: 379–84)

Häring (1951) 4–5

other hand, would he admit that the alternative was to say that the Father and the Holy Spirit were incarnate, too. The doctrine that the Father had begotten the Son from eternity did not imply, as Roscellinus contended, that "substance begets substance." For there was only "one substance and one reality" in the Trinity of three persons, since God was "trine, not according to a diversity of substance but according to the properties of the persons." In opposition to the statements of Roscellinus about "three Gods" and about "a community of majesty" rather than "a singularity of majesty" in the Trinity, Abelard declared that the Christian faith "consistently proclaims and believes a singularity of unity, except for what pertains to the distinction of the three persons. . . . not three Gods or Lords"; thus "the three persons are somebody different without being something different." If Roscellinus inclined toward tritheism by his theories, Abelard stressed the unity of the Godhead in such a way as to seem to imperil the distinction of persons, which was a matter of attributing to one of the divine persons a work that "in accordance with the union of their nature we do not question as belonging to all of them." Although "the assumption of flesh is assigned only to the Son, and we are said to be born again 'of water and the Spirit' alone, not of water and the Father or the Son, yet the activity of the entire Trinity was present in these [works]." It was in this sense that power was predicated of the Father, wisdom of the Son, and love of the Holy Spirit.

In his philosophical exposition of the doctrine of the Trinity, Abelard knew that he was drawing heavily on what had been "handed down to us by Boethius alone." It was also on Boethius, "a catholic by virtue of his sound faith in the things that are not seen, a philosopher by virtue of his true knowledge of realities," that Gilbert de La Porrée based his trinitarian speculations. These speculations, according to contemporary accounts, led Gilbert into a dispute over the distinction between God and his essence and between nature and person in the Godhead. It has been suggested that "one principle dominates in his writings and is truly the key to Gilbert's system, namely, that there is no true knowledge of a concrete material object or *id quod*, unless the mind succeeds in establishing the cause or *id quo* of each and every reality in the *id quod* and classifies it according to the ten Aristotelian categories." That principle could, however, be applied

Gisl.Por.*Com.Eut*.4.36
(Häring 294)

Gisl.Por.*Com.Trin*.1.4.28; 2.1.
34 (Häring 120; 170)

M.E.Williams (1951) 78

Gisl.Por.*Com.Trin*.1.4.82; 2.1.
28 (Häring 131; 168)

Gisl.Por.*Com.Trin*.2.1.31
(Häring 169)

Gisl.Por.*Com.Trin*.2.2.68
(Häring 177)

Gisl.Por.*Com.Trin*.2.1 17–19
(Häring 166)
Gisl.Por.*Com.Trin*.1.5.38
(Häring 147)
Aug.*Trin*.5.8.9; 7.1.2; 7.6.11
(*CCSL* 50:215–16; 245; 262)

Häring (1951) 14

Gualt.S.Vict.*Lab*.pr. (Glorieux
201)

Iv.*Ep*.7 (*PL* 162:17)

Petr.Ab.ap.Rosc.*Ep.Ab*.2
(*BGPM* 8–V:64–65)

See pp. 127–29 above

Brd.Clr.*Ep*.191.1 (*PL* 182:
357)
Petr.Ab.*Theol.chr*.4.100
(*CCCM* 12:314–15)

CSen. (1140)*Cap*.1 (Mansi 21:
568)

Brd.Clr.*Cons*.5.7.15 (Leclercq-
Rochais 3:479) ; Brd.Clr.*Cant*.
80.4.8 (Leclercq-Rochais 2:282–
83)

"only to created things," while "in theological matters some things are [to be treated] similarly, but others differently." The language of theology was not as precise and rich in its capacity for discrimination among synonyms as was the language of philosophy, but to some degree the basic principle and distinction of Gilbert's thought was appropriate also in theology, since "the problem for him is in origin one of predication and logic." For it was true also of God that "there is one single, undivided, simple, and solitary essence by which the Eternal One was, is, and will be God." It was that single essence by which also the three persons of the Trinity were one, so that the essence was "predicated of the Three communally, separately, and collectively." But because there was only one divinity that belonged to the Three, they were "one God by [this] unity." Each of them was "substance" in his own right, but because "the same substance is predicated of the Three collectively, . . . there is truly one substance." They were "one by the property of the essence, simple and without any composition." Despite parallels that could be quoted from Augustine, this distinction between "that which is" and "that by which it is" in the Trinity inevitably aroused suspicion.

The application of categories that were "logical rather than theological" to the dogma of the Trinity by Roscellinus, Abelard, and Gilbert led to quite divergent theological conclusions, but the application was suspect in each case and in each case led to official condemnation by the church. Roscellinus was condemned at the Synod of Soissons in 1092 for teaching tritheism, and he recanted. Abelard, who cited the condemnation of Soissons against Roscellinus as proof of heresy, was himself prosecuted for his doctrine of the Trinity, as well as for his other theological ideas, by Bernard, who accused him of "attempting to bring the merit of the Christian faith to naught because he supposes that by human reason he can comprehend all that is God." Specifically, he was accused, despite his insistence on the equality of the three persons in the Trinity, of ascribing "power" only to the Father, not to the Son or the Holy Spirit, and thus of denying the catholic doctrine of the Trinity. Gilbert also earned the opposition of Bernard, who charged him with teaching "that there is some thing by which God is what he is, but which is not God," while Bernard's pupil charged that Gilbert af-

firmed "a form in God by which God is what he is, but
which is not God." With such forces arraigned against
him, Gilbert was condemned at the Synod of Reims in
1148, which decreed "that no reason in theology should
make a division between nature and person [in the Trin-
ity]" nor between God the Trinity and his essence.

Whether or not these condemnations disposed of the
challenges to the received form of the dogma of the Trinity, they did not resolve the underlying questions raised
by these three dialecticians. For each of them had, in his
own way, reopened the problem of the relation between
traditional doctrine and theological speculation, or, more
fundamentally, the problem of theological method, and
the problem could not be disposed of by simply urging
that "the teachers of the church should follow the divine
arts, not the liberal arts, and imitate the apostles, not the
philosophers." For the logical, grammatical, and dialectical
inquiries of the twelfth and thirteenth centuries would
eventually go their way, with results that were to affect the
history of philosophy permanently; but the preservation
and cultivation of the catholic tradition of doctrine had
its own task of administering the patristic heritage in a
way that was intellectually respectable. The very legitimacy of this task was called into question by all the issues
with which we have been dealing here: the contradictions
among the fathers, the challenges of other interpretations
of Christian doctrine, the encounters with other systems
of faith, and the questions raised by reason. If the tradition of the church and the faith and worship of the
church were to be affirmed, it would be necessary to find
a method of theology that could do justice to the claims
of reason without capitulating to them and that could at
the same time come to terms with the other counterclaims
of the age. The thirteenth century represented a distinctive
combination of all those counterclaims and of the theological capacity to address them.

Goff.Clr.*Lib*.6 (*PL* 185:597)

CRem. (1148)*Act.* (Mansi 21:
726)

Gualt.S.Vict.*Lab*.4.1 (Glorieux
270)

6   Summa Theologica

Walsh (1907)

Whether or not it was the "greatest of centuries," the thirteenth century does hold a special place in the history of Christendom. It was the age of Pope Innocent III and Emperor Frederick II, of Saint Dominic and Saint Francis of Assisi, of Albertus Magnus and Roger Bacon, of Thomas Aquinas and Bonaventure, of Giotto and Dante, of the Fourth Crusade and the Fourth Lateran Council. It began with the papacy in almost unchallenged control of European society; it ended with the papacy in disarray, about to flee to Avignon. Probably never before, and perhaps never again, did the Christian view of the world and of man play so decisive a role in the life of the mind. Philosophical reflection, long overshadowed, came into its own again, and scientific questions once more demanded serious attention. Systems of speculative divinity, literally by the dozens, were published and debated, among them the *Summa Theologica* of Thomas Aquinas (less commonly, but more accurately called *Summa Theologiae*), which continues to be the only such work on virtually every list of great books. In the history of "theology" understood as systematic theology, the thirteenth was undeniably one of the most important of all centuries.

Paradoxically, it was far less important in the history of the development of Christian "doctrine" as we have been defining it in this work, and in the history of "theology" as we have defined it in this volume. At the Fourth Lateran Council in 1215, the doctrine of the real presence of the body and blood of Christ in the Eucharist achieved its definitive formulation in the dogma of transubstantiation; but this was the doctrinal achievement more of the

See vol.1:1
See pp. 5–6 above

See pp. 203–4 above

268

twelfth than of the thirteenth century. At the Council of Lyons in 1274, the doctrinal issues in dispute between East and West were debated and resolved, if only temporarily, but very little was changed by the actions of the council. Although the scholastics speculated extensively about the nature of angels, church doctrine continued to be reticent on the subject, contenting itself with a reaffirmation of the opening statement of the Nicene Creed, that God was the Creator of "all things invisible and visible," which meant "both the angelic and the earthly" creatures. The reality of the church as an institution was more impressive than was the doctrine of the church as an object of faith during the thirteenth century. As we shall have occasion to observe, the twelfth century summarized the full scope of the medieval doctrine of the church more effectively than the thirteenth did; on the other hand, it was only in the fourteenth century that the doctrine began to develop: "the first treatise on the church in the history of theology," that of James of Viterbo, appeared in 1301–1302, followed almost immediately by those of Giles of Rome and John of Paris. It was significant that the term "summa" was becoming increasingly popular as a way of describing and often entitling a work of theology, for the principal contribution of this period to the history of doctrine was to be summarization and systematization, not further development.

Still, as the examples of Gregory the Great and of Maximus Confessor show, it also deserves to be called a form of doctrinal development when an era summarizes into a systematic whole the doctrines that have developed in preceding centuries. Those two examples suggest, moreover, that such an achievement often goes on to serve the following period as a starting point for further development. So it was to be with the thirteenth century. A critical reexamination of its systems during the fourteenth and fifteenth centuries, and above all during the sixteenth, brought on far-reaching changes in the life and teachings of the church. The reintegration of the catholic tradition achieved by the thirteenth century continued to take it for granted, as catholic theology in East and West had done since the early church, that the authentic witness of tradition and the authentic message of the Bible would always be in accord. But what would happen when, with varying degrees of radicalism and with varying degrees

See vol.2:271; 276–77

CLater. (1215) *Const*.1 (Alberigo 206)

Arquillière (1926) 10

Petr.Ab.*Int.theol*.pr. (*PL* 178: 979); Hug.S.Vict.*Sacr*.pr. (*PL* 176:183)

See vol.1:333–39; 349–57
See vol.2:8–36

of consistency, Protestantism would pit Scripture against tradition and reject first the authority and eventually much of the content of this catholic tradition? In relation to the developments of the Middle Ages as well as to the developments of the Reformation, this century was to be "a watershed in religious history" and in the history of doctrine, a time of "summa theologica" not only in the book bearing that title but in what was believed, taught, and confessed by many different spokesmen of the church, despite important differences among them in philosophical outlook and in systematic formulation.

Knowles (1960) 1:3

The Reintegration of the Catholic Tradition

At no time during the growth of medieval theology had there been a threat in principle to "the integrity of the catholic tradition" that was its foundation, except from certain heretics who acquired that label because of their rejection of the authority of tradition. But the controversies of the Carolingian period disclosed that the tradition was considerably less integrated than everyone had been assuming, and the clarification of the doctrine of the real presence had as its by-product the recognition that citing the authority of Augustine and other church fathers was not adequate to adjudicate a doctrinal conflict. Abelard's exposé of inconsistencies in the tradition, while not intended to discredit its authority, did serve to call attention to the problem. It was likewise Abelard who, together with several of his contemporaries, brought the status of the doctrinal tradition up for discussion in another way, by opening again the investigation of the dogma of the Trinity. The reintegration of the catholic tradition, therefore, consisted in the clarification of the norms of orthodox doctrine and in the reassertion of the most hallowed of its tenets. Both of these were made possible by the compilation of quotations from the fathers in the work of Peter Lombard, "the Master of the *Sentences*," and by the work of the Sententiaries, more than a thousand in number, who commented on his book.

Stegmüller (1947)

Fundamental to the program of the *Sentences,* and to that of its commentators during the twelfth and thirteenth centuries, was the reaffirmation of Augustine. In Lombard's compilation "Augustine is quoted most often, in about 950 passages, or, if one includes the quotations from the writings that are certainly ascribed to him falsely, in

Baltzer (1902) 2

Bon.*Brev*.3.5;3.6;3.8 (Quaracchi 5:235;235;237)

Bonav.*Quaest.disp*.4 (Quaracchi 5:23)

Gilson (1926) 117–18

Thos.Aq.*S.T*.1.39.5 ad 1 (*Ed. Leon*.4:405)
Thos.Aq.*Graec*.pr. (*Ed.Leon*. 40:71)

Aug.*Praed.sanct*.1.2 (*PL* 44: 961)

See vol.1:318–31

See pp. 93–94 above

more than a thousand passages, i.e., more than twice as often as all other fathers combined." That reliance on Augustine continued to dominate the thirteenth century. Bonaventure's systematization of Christian doctrine, the *Breviloquium,* concluded one chapter after another with what he took to be "Augustine's opinion, which is to be believed," what "Augustine truly says," and what "the eminent doctor Augustine explains." Augustine was, without a doubt, "the most authentic doctor among all the expositors of Sacred Scripture." To carry out his criticism of Augustine, Thomas Aquinas appealed from tradition to tradition and proceeded "to reestablish the truth by rescuing Saint Augustine from the compromising context" of his Platonism and yet keeping the orthodox substance of the Augustinian doctrine intact. It was in response to a troubling quotation from Augustine that Thomas formulated his general principle: When "the holy doctors have at times gone beyond the bounds of precise language . . . , we must not expand on their expressions, but interpret them in a correct sense," although elsewhere he made it applicable to other fathers as well. There was no doctrine of the Christian faith for which this reaffirmation of the Augustinian-catholic tradition was not appropriate, but both the ambiguities of Augustinism itself and the earlier history of medieval theology made certain questions unavoidable.

The most obvious of such questions was the doctrine of predestination. Already during his own lifetime Augustine had faced certain "brethren" who feared the consequences of his predestinarian views, and in response he wrote his treatises (which may be two parts of a single treatise) *On the Predestination of the Saints* and *On the Gift of Perseverance.* The controversies of the following hundred years left the question of predestination unresolved, and it remained for the ninth century to bring it back into open discussion. That discussion had likewise concluded ambiguously, with no clear identification of an orthodox doctrine on the issues in dispute. One of the fundamental issues in the predestinarian conflict of the ninth century was the relation between the justice of God and the mercy of God. The doctrine of redemption through the vicarious satisfaction rendered to the "rightness [rectitudo]" of God by the death of Christ the God-man—elaborated by Anselm in his *Why God Became*

Ans.*Cur d.h.*1.18 (Schmitt 2: 76–84)

Anc.*Conc.*2.2 (Schmitt 2:261)

Ans.*Conc.*1.1 (Schmitt 2:246)

See pp. 86–87 above

Ans.*Conc.*1.5 (Schmitt 2:254); Hon.Aug.*Eluc.*1.4 (*PL* 172: 1112)

Ans.*Conc.*2.2 (Schmitt 2:261); Hon.Aug.*Inev.* (*PL* 172:1199)

Ans.*Conc.*2.3 (Schmitt 2:262)

See p. 16 above

Hon.Aug.*Inev.* (*PL* 172:1197)

Hon.Aug.*Inev.* (*PL* 172:1200)

Man, but shared by other spokesmen for the theology of the church in the twelfth century—was a way of treating the relation between justice and mercy; but because of its emphasis on divine election as the basis of the creation and redemption of man, the Anselmic doctrine of the atonement compelled further consideration of the Augustinian doctrine of predestination.

Anselm himself was the one who began to provide a basis for the consideration. By his recognition that there was a sense in which God could be said to have predestined evil deeds, but only because he caused them as deeds and not because he caused the evil in them, Anselm formulated a principle for explaining away those statements of Augustine and other fathers, and even of Scripture, that spoke of God as having predestined something evil. He resolved the paradox of man's free will and God's predestination with the aid of a resolution of the more general paradox of man's free will and God's foreknowledge. Freedom and foreknowledge were not incompatible even in the case of human sin, because the precise way of stating their relation was: "God foreknows that it is without necessity that I am going to sin." Because there was neither past nor future in God but only an eternal present, it was—as had been pointed out in the predestinarian controversy—inaccurate to speak as though God had known in the past what was going to happen in the future, for "in eternity is present immutably all truth and only truth." So likewise God did not in fact predestine anything, since "all things are present to him at once." It was a reasonable conclusion from the analysis of foreknowledge to argue that "all the considerations by which I have shown above that free choice is not incompatible with foreknowledge show equally that it is compatible with predestination."

Soon, by a process noted earlier, Anselm joined the list of authorities on the question. Within a generation or so, an essay on predestination could observe that "outstanding theologians have composed many treatises on this subject" and then, without mentioning him (or any other of these "outstanding theologians") by name, quote Anselm's definition of "free choice." Although Peter Lombard does not himself seem to have included any of Anselm's discussion of predestination in his compilation of quotations on that question, the commentators on his

Alex.Hal.*Sent*.1.40.20 (*BFS* 12:412)

Thos.Aq.*S.T.*1.63.3 resp. (*Ed. Leon*.5:126)

Bonav.*Sent*.1.40.2.1 (Quaracchi 1:708–9)
Bonav.*Sent*.2.7.1.2.2 (Quaracchi 2:186)

John 6:37; Rev.3:20
Aug.*Ev.Joh*.1.19 (*CCSL* 36:11)
Ans.*Cas.diab*.3 (Schmitt 1:239)

Bonav.*Sent*.1.40.4.2 (Quaracchi 1:720–21)

Thos.Aq.*Sent*.1.40.4.2 (Mandonnet 1:955)

Gand.*Sent*.1.144 (Walter 96–97)

Alb.M.*Sent*.1.40.10 sol. (Borgnet 26:317)

Thos.Aq.*S.T.*1.14.13 resp. (*Ed.Leon*.4:186)

Thos.Aq.*Sent*.1.40.3 (Mandonnet 1:950)

Sentences did draw upon Anselm for their explication of the Lombard's distinctions. Anselm's books on the fall of the devil and on the harmony of free will with the foreknowledge, predestination, and grace of God figured in the discussion of predestination by Alexander of Hales and in the explanation offered by Thomas Aquinas for the fall of the devil, as well as in Bonaventure's account of why divine foreknowledge and divine predestination did not impose any constraint on the free will of men and did not destroy the free will even of demons. Bonaventure enumerated authorities—two quotations from the New Testament, one from Augustine, and one from Anselm—in support of the teaching that God was not himself the Author of the hardening of the heart of a sinner. Addressing the same issue in his own commentary on Lombard's *Sentences,* Thomas Aquinas cited as his authority the consensus of "what the saints say in common," namely, Dionysius, Augustine, and Anselm: "that the reason why someone does not have grace is that he refused to accept it, and not that God refused to grant it."

The pattern set by Anselm for the treatment of predestination was visible in these commentators in other ways as well, most notably in their concentration on the question of divine foreknowledge as the key to predestination. Augustine showed, according to one compilation of *Sentences,* "that predestination and reprobation cannot be without foreknowledge." If "foreknowledge is construed strictly," according to Albertus, "there is no predestination without foreknowledge." In particular it was God's knowledge of future contingents—"not successively . . . , as we [know them], but simultaneously"—whose implications for predestination concerned them. In a discussion of the certainty of predestination, Aquinas rejected the suggestion "that God does not know future contingents except in accordance with what they are, namely, that he knows them to be contingent," for this would mean "that God does not know any more about the salvation of men than man does." Bonaventure's answer to the question of the certainty of predestination was also based on a consideration of foreknowledge. Although it had to be admitted, on the basis of the distinction between contingency and reality, "that there is no greater certainty about the number of the elect than there is about the number of other future contingents," still, "be-

Bonav.*Sent.*1.40.2.2
(Quaracchi 1:712)

Bonav.*Brev.*1.8 (Quaracchi
5:217)
Alb.M.*Sent.*1.40.12 ad 1
(Borgnet 26:321)

Bonav.*Sent.*1.40.2.2 (Quaracchi
1:712)

Thos.Aq.*S.T.*1.23.7 resp. (*Ed.
Leon.*4:282)

Petr.Pict.*Sent.*1.14 (*PMS* 7:
132)
Aug.*Praed.sanct.*15.30 (*PL* 44:
981)
Alex.Hal.*Quaest.disp.*12.4.40
(*BFS* 19:158); Petr.Lomb.*Coll.
Rom.*1.4 (*PL* 191:1309)

Thos.Aq.*S.T.*1.23.1;2;3;4;6;8
(*Ed.Leon.*4:271;273;274;275;
281;285)

Bonav.*Sent.*1.40.1.2
(Quaracchi 1:704–5)

Bonav.*Sent.*1.41.1.2 (Quaracchi
1:733)

Bonav.*Sent.*1.41.1.2
(Quaracchi 1:732);
Alex.Hal.*S.T.*1.228 (Klumper
1:322–23)

cause divine foreknowledge is infallible and therefore things always turn out as he has foreknown them," predestination to salvation was completely certain. From the fundamental axiom that God, as first principle, "knows all things perfectly through his own self" it followed that he "knows contingent things infallibly" and that therefore predestination was sure.

Bonaventure did not, however, ground the certainty of predestination only in the infallibility of God's foreknowledge, but in the unchangeability of his "plan and ordinance." For, as Thomas Aquinas put the matter, "the number of the predestined is said to be certain to God, not only by reason of his knowledge, that is, because he knows how many will be saved—for in this way the number of drops of rain and the number of the sands of the sea are certain to God—but by reason of his election and determination." Aquinas's emphasis on election and determination rather than on foreknowledge had been anticipated in the teaching that the cause of justification was not what God had known from eternity in his mind but what he had planned from eternity in his mercy, and in the Augustinian teaching that "Christ Jesus is the brightest light of predestination." In keeping with this emphasis, Aquinas, in the main body of almost every article of his examination of the doctrine of predestination, connected this doctrine closely with the doctrine of divine providence. It was all the more striking that he should do so, since he maintained that predestination belonged chiefly to the divine intellect while Bonaventure assigned it chiefly to the divine will. At the same time, Bonaventure warned against defining the will of God as an arbitrary "cause of causes and reason of reasons," which elected whomever it pleased simply because it pleased to do so; for "in wanting to exalt the will of God, we may rather be diminishing it instead" by removing the mystery from the doctrine of predestination.

The warning came during the defense of a statement on predestination that included the provision that predestination "does not have its cause in [human] merit." For the temptation was to avoid the impression of arbitrariness in predestination by basing it on God's foreknowledge of how men were going to act. It was a temptation to which Augustine himself had succumbed. In a commentary on the passage, "Jacob I loved, but Esau

Mal.1:2–3; Rom.9:13

Aug.*Rom*.60–61 (*PL* 35:2079)

Aug.*Retract*.1.22.2 (*CSEL* 36: 107–8);
Aug.*Praed.sanct*.3.7 (*PL* 44: 964–65)

Gand.*Sent*.1.148 (Walter 98–99)

Hug.S.Vict.*Sum.Sent*.1.12 (*PL* 176:63)

Petr.Lomb.*Sent*.1.41.2.1 (*Spic. Bon*.1–II:289)

Aug.*Praed.sanct*.19.38 (*PL* 44: 988)

Bonav.*Sent*.1.41.1.2 (Quaracchi 1:732)

Chenu (1964) 54

Hon.Aug.*Inev*. (*PL* 172:1215–16)

I hated," he had suggested that the basis for the difference lay in the divine foreknowledge of the two. Later, however, having struggled through the Pelagian controversies, Augustine retracted that suggestion, because any such differentiation between the saved and the damned would be a negation of the priority of grace. Augustine's mature judgment became a standard part of the various compilations of patristic theology, as well as an inducement to deeper study. The *Sentences* of Gandulph of Bologna documented Augustine's change of mind, and Hugh of Saint-Victor, attributing to "some" theologians the idea that God had selected Jacob on the basis of the foreknowledge that Jacob would be faithful, quoted Augustine in refutation. Whatever his sources may have been, Peter Lombard summarized— again with a reference to "some" who had believed otherwise—Augustine's eventual stress on election by grace without any consideration of foreknown merit. On this basis the commentators on the *Sentences* could find in Augustine's *On the Predestination of the Saints* declarations to the effect that "God chose us not because he knew that we would be such men, but in order that we might be such men." Beyond that, "no doubt it was the repeated reading, one prolonged beyond the florilegia, of the *De praedestinatione sanctorum* and of the *De dono perseverentiae,* which led Saint Thomas to discovering the historical existence of semi-pelagianism, and thus to underscoring with much greater emphasis, from the *Contra Gentiles* onward, God's initiative in the preparation for grace." Augustine, not as a distant authority but as a continuing force, became the inspiration for a transition from a speculative to a soteriological view of grace—even though he had in fact been the source of both.

The stumbling block in the Augustinian view of grace remained, as it had been in the fifth and ninth centuries, his doctrine of reprobation, implying as it did a grace that was less than universal. The hardening of the heart of Pharaoh, over which Gottschalk and Hincmar had contended, was still a problem. The compilers and commentators of the twelfth and thirteenth centuries strove to explain Augustine's language on the issue. Peter of Poitiers attributed a statement to Augustine that does not seem to be present in his authentic writings, to the effect that "as the reprobation of God is his not wanting to have mercy,

Petr.Pict.Sent.1.15 (PMS 7: 149)
Bonav.Sent.1.40.4.2 (Quaracchi 1:720)

See p. 86 above

Petr.Lomb.Coll.Rom.9.18 (PL 191:1462)

Ps.Aug.Hypomn.6.6.8 (PL 45:1661–62)

Schupp (1932) 142

Gand.Sent.1.128 (Walter 87)
Petr.Lomb.Sent.1.40.2 (Spic. Bon.1–II:286–87)

Aug.Praed.sanct.6.11 (PL 44: 968–69)
Alex.Hal.Sent.1.41.1 (BFS 12: 413–14); Alex. Hal. S.T.1.239 (Klumper 1:333)

Hon.Aug.Inev. (PL 172:1199); Hon.Aug.Eluc.2.9 (PL 172: 1140)

Aug.Civ.21.12 (CCSL 48:778)
Bonav.Sent.1.41.1.2 (Quaracchi 1:733)

Rom.11:33

Aug.Praed.sanct.8.16 (PL 44: 972–73); Aug.Persev.11.25; 12.30 (PL 45:1007; 1011)

so his hardening [of the human heart] is his not having mercy"; reprobation, therefore, was not a positive act of divine election, but a negative act of divine "permission." It was similarly from a work attributed to Augustine but not composed by him—this time the *Memorandum against the Pelagians and Celestians,* on which Hincmar had relied in his dispute with Gottschalk—that Peter Lombard, who taught that "the hardening of the heart is merited by the sin of the entire condemned mass [of humanity]," quoted the alleged principle of Augustine, which had also been quoted by Hincmar: "This rule must be inviolably observed, that sinners have been foreknown in their sins, but not predestined, but that their punishment has been predestined." But in quoting it to support a "sharp emphasis" on the distinction between predestination and foreknowledge, both Gandulph of Bologna and Peter Lombard identified its location as Augustine's tract *To Prosper and Hilary,* that is, *On the Predestination of the Saints,* which was the source for some of the very statements about reprobation that had so frequently caused difficulty for Augustine's defenders. The same confusion regarding Augustine's authorship appeared in Alexander of Hales.

Even this endorsement of Hincmar's (and Pseudo-Augustine's) solution for the problem of reprobation was linked to a repetition of Augustine's (and Gottschalk's) conclusions about the mystery of double predestination. Isidore's summary of Augustine was quoted in the declaration: "Predestination is double." Augustine had defended divine justice in reprobation on the grounds that "if all had remained under the punishment of just condemnation, the mercy of redeeming grace would not have been visible in anyone, but if all had been transferred from darkness to light, the severity of retribution would not have been made manifest in anyone." Quoting this argument in a paraphrase, Bonaventure reinforced the "need for the concealment" of the ways of God, as proclaimed in a passage from Romans that Augustine had cited over and over at decisive points in his statements of the mystery of double predestination against the Pelagians: "O the depth of the riches and wisdom and knowledge of God! How unsearchable are his judgments and how inscrutable his ways!" Thomas Aquinas attempted to harmonize the love of God with the fact of divine reproba-

Thos.Aq.*S.T.*1.23.3 ad 1 (*Ed. Leon.*4:274)
Thos.Aq.*S.T.*1–II.79.3 (*Ed. Leon.*7:79–80)

1 Tim:2:4

See vol.1:321
Thos.Aq.*S.T.*1.19.6 ad 1 (*Ed. Leon.*4:241)
Alex.Hal.*Sent.*1.40.21 (*BFS* 12:413); Alex.Hal.*Quaest.disp.* App.2.18 (*BFS* 21:1372)
Thos.Aq.*S.T.*1.23.4 ad 3 (*Ed. Leon.*4:275); Bonav.*Sent.* 1.40.3.1; 1.41.1.1 (Quaracchi 1:714; 728)

Rom.3:19
Bonav.*Sent.*1.41.1.2 (Quaracchi 1:734)

See pp. 59–61 above

Alex.Hal.*S.T.*1.445 (Klumper 1:637–40); Thos.Aq.*S.T.*1.31.1 ad 5 (*Ed.Leon.*4:344)

See vol.2:183–98

See pp. 263–67 above

Schneider (1961) 5

tion by maintaining that in loving all men and wishing them all some good, God did not wish the same good to all of them; "insofar, therefore, as he does not wish [some of them] this particular good—namely, eternal life—he is said to hate or to reprobate them." This withholding of his grace was "of his own accord." As for the statement of the New Testament that God "desires all men to be saved," which had been so vexing for Augustine, it was to be explained by the various devices that Augustine had proposed. In addition, this statement was to be understood according to "his antecedent will," by which he willed things relatively, depending on how men responded, rather than according to "his consequent will, which is to will absolutely." The conclusion of the whole matter was yet another quotation from Augustine about the remoteness of divine judgment from our senses, together with the no less Augustinian admonition: "And so the discussion of predestination must be closed in the insufficiency of our understanding, 'so that every mouth may be stopped, and the whole world may be held accountable to God,' whose judgments are not open to our scrutiny, but are to be revered with awesome silence." When Thomas Bradwardine, John Wycliffe, Martin Luther, and John Calvin reopened the question of double predestination, it was with this neo-Augustinism that they began.

There was a second constituent of the Augustinian legacy whose interpretation had been reopened for discussion by Gottschalk in the ninth century; it was then reintroduced during the debates of the twelfth century, and needed to be restated in the summae of the thirteenth, where the echoes of Gottschalk's dispute with Hincmar over the "trine" in God could still be heard. In spite of its standing as the most utterly unchangeable of all the unchangeable dogmas of the one true faith, the doctrine of the Trinity had reappeared on the roster of disputed questions, not only because of the conflict with the East over the procession of the Holy Spirit, but because of the speculations of "the labyrinths of France," particularly those of Peter Abelard and Gilbert de La Porrée, as well as those of Roscellinus. The response to this phenomenon was "an enrichment of theological speculation specifically in the area of the doctrine of the Trinity," which in turn served to bring about the reappropriation of Augustine's doctrine and the reintegration of the catholic tradition in

Petr.Lomb.*Sent.*1.24.1.1
(*Spic.Bon.*1–II:187);
Alex.Hal.*S.T.*1.365 (Klumper 1:541)

Vignaux (1935) 31–32
Alex.Hal.*Quaest.disp.*1.8
(*BFS* 19:9)

Chenu (1964) 274–75

Stohr (1923) 167

Bonav.*Sent.*1.34.1.3 resp.
(Quaracchi 1:592)

Petr.Pict.*Sent.*1.25 (*PMS* 7: 203–4); Alex.Hal.*Sent.*1.8.34
(*BFS* 12:112)

Häring (1957) 124

Gand.*Sent.*1.96 (Walter 65);
Bonav.*Sent.*1.33.2.2 ad 1
(Quaracchi 1:575)
Gand.*Sent.*1.21 (Walter 13–16)

Alex.Hal.*Sent.*1.34.5 (*BFS* 12: 341); Petr.Lomb.*Sent.*1.25.2.5
(*Spic.Bon.*1–II:194)

the light of this trinitarian perspective. The grammatical and logical implications of calling God "Trinity," as raised in the twelfth century, obliged Peter Lombard and his commentators, up to and including Martin Luther, to address once more the question of "how the three persons are one," and to do so "by aligning these missions [of the three persons] with the properties of the one or the other person who is sent" in the trinitarian relation. Eventually, however, "in accordance with the riches he reaps from Augustine's analyses, [Thomas Aquinas] brings to the fore the original relationship of subject to known and loved object in a mind capable of knowing and loving God." And Bonaventure, who in his view of the Three and the One "is more dependent on Alexander [of Hales] then he is almost anywhere else," systematized this view in what must be called a trinitarian ontology with few parallels in the history of Christian doctrine.

First it was necessary to dispose of the challenges from the logicians and dialecticians. Often without being mentioned by name, they helped to define the areas of discussion on the doctrine of the Trinity. Thus, for example, the identification of the Father as "power," for which Abelard had been condemned by Bernard, was acknowledged as legitimate so long as it referred to the "order" or the origin of the persons in the Trinity, since the Father was the only one of the three persons who did not come from another. The suggestion that the trinitarian distinctions were little more than a manner of speaking, connected explicitly with Roscellinus but present also in the thought of other critics, was met with the objection that ancient heretics had similarly dismissed the issues in the dogma of the Trinity as a question merely of names. The references were often anonymous because "the doctrines being refuted were not the specific property" of any one party, even though the doctrines of Gilbert de La Porrée were, perhaps more often than not, the explicit object of the anathema. Gilbert's effort to draw a distinction between "that by which the Father is God" and "that by which the Father is Father" was rejected, as was his distinction between "that which is God" and "that which is in God." Despite its association with Roscellinus the identification of the three hypostases as "three realities" could be legitimate, so long as it was remembered that "they are one and the same supreme reality," for

Augustine had spoken of Father, Son, and Holy Spirit as "realities" in the plural and yet in the singular. Peter Lombard's most consistent response to Gilbert's questions was to refer, usually by means of a quotation from Hilary, to the transcendence and incomprehensibility of truth about God. His commentators defended his appeal to Hilary and identified Gilbert as the object of his criticism, and the Fourth Lateran Council in 1215 took the unusual step of declaring: "We believe and confess with Peter [Lombard]" on trinitarian questions raised by Gilbert de La Porrée and by Joachim of Fiore (in a book since lost).

At least partly because of these challenges but also because of an intensified study of the catholic tradition, the thirteenth century came to a deepened awareness of the centrality of the doctrine of the Trinity as (together with its corollary, the doctrine of the incarnation) the fundamental teaching of the Christian faith. Richard of Saint-Victor called "the most sacred and most secret mystery of the Trinity" "the supreme article of our faith." Peter Lombard, quoting Augustine, declared that "the Trinity is the one and only true God." Consequently, the central message of biblical religion, whether in the Old Testament or in the New, which was the oneness of God as confessed in the Shema, was dependent for Christians on the confession of the Trinity, since "without faith in the Trinity the faith in one God is not complete, because the Trinity is the one God." Thomas Aquinas summarized this trinitarian confession. "The recognition of the Trinity in unity," he affirmed, "is the fruit and the goal of our entire life." The result of his reappropriation of Augustine and the catholic tradition on the doctrine of the Trinity was a series of articles in the *Summa Theologica* that were "unrivalled as precise statements of the Christian faith." For his own system as well as for the reintegration of the tradition, the dogma of the Trinity became determinative, so that "the doctrine of the Trinity is the key to the whole theology of the *Summa.*"

Two specific issues for which Thomas Aquinas drew upon Augustine to achieve this fuller statement of the trinitarian faith were the Filioque and the image of God. Among the various objections of Eastern theologians to the Latin idea of Filioque, none was more sensitive than the charge that by introducing the notion of a procession of the Holy Spirit from the Son as well as from the Father

---

Aug.*Doctr.christ.*1.5.5 (*CCSL* 32:9)

Hil.*Trin.*2.5; 8.21–22 (*PL* 10: 53–54; 252–53)

Petr.Lomb.*Sent.*1.33.1.8; 1.34.1.1 (*Spic.Bon.*1–II:242; 247)
Bonav.*Sent.*1.33 dub.1 (Quaracchi 1:580–81)
Alex.Hal.*S.T.*1.476 (Klumper 1:677–78); Thos.Aq.*Sent.* 1.33.1.1 (Mandonnet 1:764); Thos.Aq.*S.T.*1.28.2 resp. (*Ed. Leon.*4:321)
CLater.(1215)*Const.*2 (Alberigo 208)

Rich.S.Vict.*Trin.*4.5 (*SC* 63: 238)
Aug.*Trin.*1.2.4 (*CCSL* 50:31)
Petr.Lomb.*Sent.*1.2.1.1 (*Spic. Bon.*1–II:61)

Deut.6:4

Bald.*Sacr.alt.*2.3.2 (*SC* 93: 268)

Thos.Aq.*Sent.*1.2 exp.text. (Mandonnet 1:77)

Knowles (1962) 267

Velecky (1965) xx

Petr.Pict.*Sent*.1.30 (*PMS* 7: 239–61)

See vol.2:197

See vol.2:188

Hil.*Trin*.2.29 (*PL* 10:69)

Alex.Hal.*S.T*.1.311; 1.493 (Klumper 1:453; 695–96); Bonav.*Sent*.1.29.2.2 (Quaracchi 1:515–16) Alb.M.*Sent*.1.29.5 (Borgnet 26:9)

Thos.Aq.*Sent*.1.11.1.4 sol. (Mandonnet 1:284) Alan.Ins.*Reg.theol*.24 (*PL* 210:632)

Thos.Aq.*S.T*.1.36.4 ad 7 (*Ed. Leon*.4:384)

Thos.Aq.*S.T*.1.36.4 s.c. (*Ed. Leon*.4:384)

Aug.*Trin*.5.14.15 (*CCSL* 50: 223) Alex.Hal.*Quaest.disp*.7.1.2 (*BFS* 19:60) Aug.*Trin*.4.20.29 (*CCSL* 50: 200)

Thos.Aq.*S.T*.1.33.1 resp. (*Ed. Leon*.4:358)

Thos.Aq.*S.T*.1.39.5 obj.6 (*Ed. Leon*.4:404) Alex.Hal.*Quaest.disp*.8.3.34 (*BFS* 19:77)

Thos.Aq.*S.T*.1.33.1 ad 2 (*Ed. Leon*.4:358)

the West was making the Son a second "source" or "principle" or "cause" within the Trinity and was thereby jeopardizing the unity of the Godhead. It did not help matters that so influential a Western expositor of the doctrine of the Trinity as Hilary of Poitiers could be quoted in evidence of the charge, for he had said that the Holy Spirit proceeded "from the Father and the Son as his authors [(a) Patre et Filio auctoribus]." On the basis of Hilary's formula some thirteenth-century theologians were saying that the Father and the Son were both "spirators" of the Holy Spirit, and Thomas himself was initially willing, perhaps because of Albertus Magnus, to assert that the Father and the Son "are spirating and are spirators." Eventually he altered this position and, following a suggestion made also by Alan of Lille, found only the participle acceptable, not the noun: "The Father and the Son are two spirating . . . , but not two spirators."

It was from Augustine that Thomas drew this defense of the Filioque against the accusation of teaching two principles in the Godhead. In his reply to a series of objections containing the quotation from Hilary, he quoted, though not quite verbatim, what "Augustine says, that the Father and the Son are not two principles, but one principle of the Holy Spirit." Augustine's *On the Trinity* was also the source of the axiom, quoted by others as well, "The Father is the principle of the entire Godhead," which formed the basis for Thomas's discussion of the appropriateness of referring to the Father, and only to the Father, as "principle." The same axiom then appeared again in a later question, in which Thomas identified the sense in which it was true that the Father was the principle both of the Son and of the Holy Spirit by begetting the former and spirating the latter. As part of his counterattack against the East, Thomas, like Alexander of Hales, was also able to point out an imprecision in Greek trinitarian terminology as compared with that of Augustine. "The Greeks use the noun 'cause' and the noun 'principle' indiscriminately in speaking of God, whereas Latin theologians do not use the noun 'cause,' but only the noun 'principle.'" The reason was that "cause," if applied to the relation between the Father and the Son, could not avoid the taint of subordinationism.

The thought of Augustine was also the source for Aquinas's teaching that the image of God, according to which man had been created, was the image of the Trinity. The exegesis of the plural in Genesis 1:26, "Let us make man in our image, after our likeness," in the light of the orthodox doctrine of the Trinity was a speculative idea of far-reaching "historical importance." It was a universal patristic consensus among both Latins and Greeks that the plural was a reference to the Trinity, but it has been pointed out "that among Greek Christian writers there is no precedent to be found for the trinitarian analogies of Augustine." Thomas sought to reflect the consensus when he quoted John of Damascus and Gregory of Nyssa as authorities on the image of God, following this with a quotation from Hilary to the effect that man had been created "after the common image" of Father, Son, and Holy Spirit, namely, their common deity, which was single, rather than after the image of their distinctness, which was trine. Therefore the trinitarian interpretation of the image of God, as distinct from the standard trinitarian interpretation of the creation narrative itself, was dependent on Augustine, who had almost single-handedly turned Western theology in this direction.

In Thomas's interpretation of the image of God, there were many passages from Augustine to be considered, more, in fact, than from all other Christian writers put together. These passages dealt with almost all the various aspects of the image of God. Although Thomas gave little or no attention to the place of the doctrine of creation after the image of God as an issue between Augustine and his Pelagian opponents, he did comment on Augustine's interpretations of the creation story. There was only one reference to Augustine's *City of God,* not the familiar passage in the twelfth book in which Augustine had summarized the general teaching of the church on creation after the image of God, but a less common passage in the eleventh book, in which Augustine had made explicit his characteristic idea that "we recognize in ourselves the image of God, that is, of the supreme Trinity," and that therefore there was a trinity in the image, one of being what we are, of knowing what we are, and of loving what we are. An examination of the many quotations on this subject from Augustine's *On the Trinity* in Thomas's discussion of the image, some of which had appeared in Peter Lombard and in Alexander of Hales, suggests that he put his reading of this treatise to several uses, the most

Gilson (1960) 219

See vol.1:197; vol.2:203–4

Schindler (1965) 44

Thos.Aq.*S.T*.1.93.5 obj.1 (*Ed. Leon*.5:405)

See vol.1:313–16

Thos.Aq.*S.T*.1.93.2 s.c.; 1.93.4 ad 1; 1.93.6 obj.4 (*Ed.Leon.* 5:402–7)

Aug.*Civ*.12.24 (*CCSL* 48:381)
Aug.*Civ*.11.26 (*CCSL* 48:345)

Thos.Aq.*S.T*.1.93.7 obj.1 (*Ed. Leon*.5:409)

Alex.Hal.*Quaest.disp*.26.5.22 (*BFS* 19:475)

Schmaus (1927)
Aug.*Trin*.9.12.18 (*CCSL* 50: 310)
Aug.*Trin*.10.12.19 (*CCSL* 50: 332)

Protois (1881) 128

D'Arcy (1957) 169
Petr.Lomb.*Serm*.14 (*PL* 171: 856)

1 John 2:16

Petr.Lomb.*Serm*.9 (*PL* 171: 848)

Petr.Pict.*Sent*.2.9 (*PMS* 11:50)

Bonav.*Trip*.pr.1 (Quaracchi 8:3)

Bonav.*Red.* (Quaracchi 5: 317–25)

Bonav.*Hex*.3.1 (Quaracchi 5: 343)

Bonav.*Hex*.22.16–17 (Quaracchi 5:440)

typically Augustinian of which was "the psychological doctrine of the Trinity" as "mind, knowledge, and love" or as "memory, understanding, and will."

Our account of the place of the doctrine of the Trinity in the twelfth and thirteenth centuries would not be complete without at least some attention to the manner in which "the number three sometimes inspires in Peter Lombard ingenious combinations out of which there rise currents of high spirituality." This, too, was a way of appropriating the Augustinian tradition, where "numbers ... exist apart, a kind of galaxy in the mind's firmament." Lombard manipulated threes of all kinds in his sermons, even to the point of using the warning of the New Testament about "the lust of the flesh and the lust of the eyes and the pride of life" as the basis for a discussion of a trinity of evil, corresponding to the Augustinian trinity of "memory, understanding, and love." "Therefore the tempter has proposed three things," he concluded, "so that he might by three devices separate from God a man who clung to God in three ways; thus he who by a trinity was similar to the Trinity would by a trinity become dissimilar to it." Various of the commentators on the Lombard engaged in such numerological speculations inspired by the doctrine of the Trinity, but it would seem that for none of them were such trinitarian discussions as central as they were for Bonaventure.

"Since every science," Bonaventure wrote, "and particularly [though not only] the science contained in the Holy Scriptures, is concerned with the Trinity before all else, every science must necessarily present some trace of this same Trinity." In his treatise, *The Reduction of the Arts to Theology,* Bonaventure applied this trinitarian method to the several fields of study. His *Collations on the Hexaemeron* not only followed the patristic consensus in finding evidence for the Trinity in the creation story of Genesis and other passages of the Old Testament, but its very outline and method of presentation went through one natural trinity after another, with trinities within trinities, all as signs of the divine Trinity; even the three orders in the church—laymen, prelates, and contemplatives—corresponded to the three persons of the Trinity. The chapters on the Trinity in Bonaventure's *Breviloquium* were an adaptation of the dogma in the technical vocabulary of scholastic theology. Perhaps the supreme instance

Rich.S.Vict.*Stat.hom*.pr. (*PL* 196:1116)

Bonav.*Trip*.2.1.2 (Quaracchi 8:8)

Bonav.*Trip*.3.6.9 (Quaracchi 8:15)

Bonav.*Trip*.pr.1 (Quaracchi 8:3)

Bonav.*Trip*.3.2 (Quaracchi 8: 12)

Hellmann (1974)

Bonav.*Itin*.1.3 (Quaracchi 5: 297)

Riquet (1926) 118

Bonav.*Itin*.2.7 (Quaracchi 5: 301)
Bonav.*Itin*.6.2 (Quaracchi 5: 311)

Bonav.*Sent*.1.3.4 conc. (Quaracchi 1:76)

of this trinitarian tendency was his treatise *On the Three-fold Way,* where, following the lead of Peter Lombard and Richard of Saint-Victor, he even had to formulate the results of the fall of Adam as "guilt incurred, grace wasted, and glory lost," and where he urged that "because of original sin, three things, namely, sorrow, gratitude, and conformity, are necessary requirements for any person," while before the fall only the latter two had been needed. Bonaventure's idea of "the threefold way" was based on a trinitarian interpretation of the traditional steps of mysti-cal ascent—purgation, illumination, and union—which were then spun out in further series of triplets.

Although there were other examples of numerology in Bonaventure, as there had been in Augustine, which were not directly related to the Trinity, his generalized trini-tarianism was more than this. It was, rather, the funda-mental structure or "order" of created as well as of un-created reality. It would not be going too far to say that Bonaventure, on the basis of Augustine, had developed a trinitarian ontology, according to which there was a "triple existence of [created] things: existence in physi-cal reality, in the mind, and in the 'eternal art' " or wisdom of God. In setting forth such a trinitarian ontology, Bona-venture was continuing the thought of Augustine, who had translated the doctrine of the Trinity from the liturgi-cal and the dogmatic understanding of the Creator to the metaphysical and the psychological understanding of the creature. Although this Augustinian tour de force had been the basis for the doctrine of the image of God in Aquinas, it does seem that in this respect as in others Bonaventure's "Augustinian traditionalism" went further than Thomas was willing to go. Bonaventure carried his identification of the created trinities throughout the universe into "manifest" evidences of the uncreated Trinity, and he argued from the trinity in the mind to the Trinity in God (and not merely from the divine Trinity to a human trinity) with a confidence in the analogy that went even beyond that of Augustine, although he also asserted that, strictly speaking, the unaided mind could not know "the Trinity of persons, but only the trinity of unity, truth, and goodness as attributes [appropriata]." Such a reintegration of the catholic tradition, however, was incomplete and indefensible without a careful analy-sis of the method of argument and proof. The relation be-

tween proof from tradition and proof from reason, and
therefore the relation between believing and knowing,
was an indispensable part of the restatement of Augustinian theology.

Natural Theology and the Scholastic Method

The attempt of certain Christian thinkers to prove the
dogma of the Trinity by natural reason brought the
question of the method of theology into the center of attention, including its relation to the method of philosophy.
Because our concern here is not with scholastic philosophy, but only with scholastic theology, and even with
this only as a statement of what the church believed,
taught, and confessed, the problem of theological method
is pertinent to our narrative only as it affected the
content of that statement, not as it affected its forms.
The search for a valid method of stating Christian doctrine
was also an issue in the reintegration of the catholic tradition through the repossession of the church fathers, especially of Augustine. For, as Abelard's review of the contradictions in the tradition had suggested and as the
cautionary example of John Scotus Erigena had already
shown, one could sometimes resolve such contradictions
by transposing them into the province of philosophical
discourse. Method, in this way, was a matter of vital
doctrinal concern.

  The doctrinal basis for a method that sought to prove
the Trinity by reason was a proposition shared even by
those who rejected such an attempt, namely, that man
had been created after the image of the Trinity. More
fundamental was the belief in creation after the image of
God as such, which provided the basis for the effort to
prove the existence of God, but not the doctrine of the
Trinity. But the doctrine of the image of God—be it
the image of the Trinity or, more generally, the image of
the one God in the human mind—had an even more
fundamental doctrinal basis, which was essential to the
Christian case for the use of rational demonstration in
the treatment of the articles of faith. This was the familiar

See vol. 1:278–331
Augustinian distinction between nature and grace. For
only if the state of nature, after the fall and despite the
fall, had retained some of its integrity and rationality,
could it proceed, by rational steps and without the aid of
revelation, to demonstrate the reality and the oneness of

God. Conversely, only if the state of nature were now devoid of the superadded gift of grace, could one contend, on Christian grounds, that certain mysteries of the faith, notably the Trinity and the incarnation, were beyond the reach of nature and of reason.

In clear recognition of these connections, Thomas Aquinas, in the very first question of the *Summa Theologica,* stated the entire rationale for the use of proofs as a theological enterprise, as distinct from his clarifications elsewhere, for example in his commentaries on Aristotle, of the philosophical significance of such proofs. Having laid down the axiom that when treating of the doctrine of God "we make use of his effects, either of nature or of grace, rather than of a definition," he went on to take up the question of "whether sacred doctrine proceeds by argument." The answer to the question required a precise distinction between the method of "sacred doctrine ["theology" in the modern sense]" and the methods appropriate to other sciences. In the other sciences the argument from authority was the weakest form of proof; but here it was the strongest of all, because it argued not from human reason but from divine revelation. Therefore the warnings of the church fathers against relying on arguments in support of faith were meant to rule out argumentation that would seek to prove the articles of faith from reason, but an argumentation that proceeded from the articles of faith to their necessary corollaries was legitimate. As for the use of argument "to confute those who contradict" the faith, this was valid if it argued on the basis of the articles of faith against false Christians, but confined itself to the refutation of false arguments, avoiding proof, against those who did not accept the Christian revelation at all.

Thomas Aquinas justified this determination of theological method by appealing, beyond the principles of epistemology, to the doctrines of creation and redemption and thus to the relation between nature and grace. "Since grace does not abolish nature, but completes it," he asserted, it followed that "natural reason should minister to faith, just as the natural inclination of the will ministers to the love [created by grace]." The possibilities as well as the limitations of rational argument in sacred doctrine were derived from the axiom that grace did not abolish nature, but completed it. Nature and grace were

Thos.Aq.*S.T*.1.1.7 ad 1 (*Ed. Leon*.4:19)

Tit.1:9

not identical; else the same methods of proof would obtain in both. Nor were they equal, for nature without grace was imperfect, and a knowledge based only on nature and on reason was inadequate in matters of salvation and revelation; therefore "Sacred Scripture has no science that is superior to it." Nor, on the other hand, were nature and grace antithetical, but grace affirmed and sustained nature even as it completed and perfected it; hence, "since faith rests upon infallible truth, and since the contrary of a truth can never be demonstrated," the defense of the faith could and should resort to rational arguments in confutation of objections that were raised against the articles of faith. Only by a correct demarcation of the scope and territory of both nature and grace could the respective functions of reason and of revelation and the use of each of these in theology be defined.

Thos.Aq.*S.T.*1.1.8 (*Ed.Leon.* 4:21–22)

This way of discriminating between reason and revelation on the basis of the relation between nature and grace was the culmination in the thirteenth century of a process going back to the beginning of the twelfth century, when the question of whether or not the truth of the doctrine of the Trinity was subject to rational proof gained the attention of theologians. Apparently alluding to Abelard's exploration of this question, Peter Lombard, in his exegesis of the standard passage of Scripture on the natural knowledge of God, cited the opinion of those who took "the invisible things" in that passage to refer to the Father, "virtue" to refer to the Son, and "divinity" to refer to the Holy Spirit, all as part of what had been "understood through the things that have been made." His reply was that the heathen philosophers "did not have, and could not have had, this distinction [between the persons] of the supreme Trinity, which the catholic faith professes, without the teaching [of the church] or the revelation of an inner inspiration." (Elsewhere he explained that inspiration could take place either "through dreams and visions" or "by the impulse of the Holy Spirit alone, without any external means.") He took this reply over almost verbatim into his *Sentences*. The interpretation of Romans 1:20 as proof for a natural knowledge of the Trinity, indeed the very effort to assert such a knowledge, was rejected by his contemporaries as well, but the presence of this discussion in the *Sentences* provided the occasion for continuing study of it, particularly

Rom.1:20(Vulg.)

See vol.1:27

Petr.Lomb.*Coll.*Rom.1.20 (*PL* 191:1328)

Petr.Lomb.*Ps.*pr. (*PL* 191:55)
Petr.Lomb.*Sent.*1.3.1.9 (*Spic. Bon.*1–II:71)

Brun.S.*Sent.*4.1 (*PL* 165:977)
Gand.*Sent.*1.34 (Walter 25–26)

because the trinitarian definition of the image of God, when combined with the belief that the image had not been lost in the fall, could be taken to indicate that a natural knowledge also of this mystery was still possible. As we have noted, Bonaventure seems to have come close to positing such a possibility, at least in some passages of *The Journey of the Mind to God.*

In his *Commentary on the Sentences,* on the other hand, he denied that it was possible to rise from a knowledge of creatures to a knowledge of the Trinity of persons in the Godhead. On the basis of Peter Lombard, Thomas Aquinas rejected the suggestion that the heathen philosophers could have known the Trinity by the use of natural reason; and, noting the passages from Richard of Saint-Victor that appeared to be affirming such a natural knowledge of the Trinity, he declared that "if the statement of Richard is taken in a universal way to say that everything true can be proven by reason, it is obviously false," although it could be interpreted differently. He spoke out even more strongly in the *Summa Theologica,* charging that the attempt to prove the Trinity by reason detracted from the faith by diminishing the dignity of faith and by subjecting it to the ridicule of its despisers. For "it is impossible to attain to the knowledge of the Trinity by natural reason." If it were possible, the distinction between nature and grace would be meaningless, for only by grace and revelation could man know those things about God that did not pertain to him as "the principle of all things." The effort of Alexander of Hales to assert a natural proof for the doctrine of the Trinity on the basis of the natural knowledge of the goodness of God was also misguided, according to Thomas, for it failed to distinguish with sufficient precision between nature and grace. "The supreme goodness of God," Aquinas maintained, "as we understand it now through its effects [in creation], can be understood without the Trinity of persons," for this was in the realm of nature; "but as understood in itself, and as seen by the blessed, it cannot be understood without the Trinity of persons," for this was in the realm of grace.

By nature, then, one could know the existence of God, and even the supreme goodness of God. The words of Romans 1:20, whose application to the doctrine of the Trinity was rejected as false, were the first sentence of

Petr.Lomb.*Sent.*2.39.1.1 (*Spic. Bon.*1–II:553)

Thos.Aq.*Sent.*1.3.1.4 (Mandonnet 1:97–99)

Thos.Aq.*S.T.*1.32.1 resp. (*Ed. Leon.*4:349)

Alex.Hal.*S.T.*1.295 (Klumper 1:414)

Thos.Aq.*S.T.*2–II.2.8 ad 3 (*Ed.Leon.*8:35)

Petr.Pict.*Sent.*1.1 (*PMS* 7:6)

Petr.Lomb.*Sent.*1.3.1.1 (*Spic. Bon.*1–II:68–69)

Petr.Lomb.*Sent.*2.1.4.1 (*Spic. Bon.*1–II:332)

Petr.Lomb.*Sent.*2.24.5.2 (*Spic. Bon.*1–II:454)

Petr.Lomb.*Sent.*2.25.9.1 (*Spic. Bon.*1–II:469)
Petr.Lomb.*Sent.*2.39.3.1 (*Spic. Bon.*1–II:555)

Petr.Lomb.*Ps.*4.7 (*PL* 191:88)

See pp. 139–40 above
Alex.Hal.*Sent.*2.24.1 (*BFS* 13:207)

Thos.Aq.*Sent.*2.24.3.3 ad 3
(Mandonnet 2:624)

Thos.Aq.*Sent.*2.39.3.1 s.c.
(Mandonnet 2:996)

Thos.Aq.*Sent.*2.24.2.2 ad 3
(Mandonnet 2:607)

1 Cor.13:12
Bonav.*Sent.*1.3.1.3 conc.
(Quaracchi 1:74)

the first chapter of the first book of the *Sentences* of Peter of Poitiers, where they were paraphrased to mean that "when man sees that this machine of the world, so great and spacious, could not have been made by some other creature, he understands that it was Another who produced this beautiful and spacious work, and thus, with the guidance of reason, he comprehends God very well and very surely." Peter Lombard's exegesis of the passage in his own *Sentences* identified two factors that helped in this process of understanding: "[human] nature, which was rational; and the works of God." God had made a rational creature that would be able by its reason to understand him as the Summum Bonum and to love him. Man's reason was that which he did not have in common with the beasts but did have in common with the angels. As a consequence of the fall of Adam, man lost his holiness and thus his freedom from sin; but he did not lose his rationality and his freedom to act without necessity. For the first of these was "by grace," but the second was "by nature." In this sense it was even possible to say that man "by nature wills the good." Reason was able to conclude from the creation that there was a Creator, because reason belonged to nature, not to grace, and, although "deformed," continued after the fall.

On the basis of Peter Lombard, theologians of the thirteenth century continued and developed the arguments from Christian doctrine for the validity of a natural theology. The distinction between nature and grace implied that even "rightness [rectitudo]," which had been central in the soteriology of Anselm, was "of two kinds, namely, that which is by nature and that which is by grace." When applied to the question of a knowledge of God based on creation, natural rightness implied the use of reason to demonstrate the existence of God. For although it was true that "a corrupted reason is not reason" to the extent that it was corrupted, still it also remained true that "that which is natural is not abolished as a result of sin," and "therefore the spark of reason is not extinguished as a result of sin." Even after the fall, human reason "both includes and is more than that part of the mind in which the image [of God] consists." As a consequence of the fall, however, the knowledge of God through his creation, which had been "as though in a mirror clearly," had now become "in a mirror dimly"; yet as far as it went, it was valid. Such knowledge or demonstration of the existence of God could not comprehend God as he was in himself, because demonstration dealt either with sense experience or with understanding, neither of which was capable of grasping a God who had no body and no form, but who was characterized most fully in the self-definition: "I am who I am."

Alan.Ins.*Reg.theol*.36 (*PL* 210: 638)

That self-definition from Exodus 3:14, in combination with the standard proof text for natural theology from Romans 1:20, provided Thomas Aquinas with the necessary biblical support for undertaking to prove the existence of God by reason. Hence it was by the authority of revelation that the theologian proceeded to argue even apart from revelation that God could be known from his creation. First, what "the apostle says, 'The invisible things of [God] are clearly seen, being understood through the things that have been made'" was cited to show that the existence of God could be known and proved "from those of his effects that are known to us." Then the word spoken "in the person of God" to Moses became the ground for the "five ways" by which Thomas, with the aid of Aristotle, proved the existence of God. For "since the name of his God was 'I am,' any Christian philosopher had to posit 'I am' as his first principle and supreme cause of all things, even in philosophy," and therefore "his philosophical first principle had to be one with his religious first principle." The equation of the God of Abraham, Isaac, and Jacob with the first principle of being permitted the theologian, charged as he was with the task of expounding the doctrinal tradition, to engage also in the philosophical enterprise of measuring the capacity of reason to establish the truth of the divine being; and in this sense he was obliged to state a natural theology.

Rom.1:20 (Vulg.)

Thos.Aq.*S.T*.1.2.2 (*Ed.Leon.* 4:30)

Thos.Aq.*S.T*.1.2.3 s.c. (*Ed. Leon*.4:31)

Gilson (1941) 41

The alternative to such an equation of the philosophical first principle with the religious first principle was a doctrine of double truth, by which something could be true theologically and false philosophically or vice versa. Believing (mistakenly, as it now seems) that some of his contemporaries were espousing such a doctrine, Thomas condemned a position that would "necessarily conclude by reason" that one thing was true, but "firmly hold the opposite by faith." A few years after Thomas's death, these thinkers were condemned by the bishop of Paris for proceeding in their philosophizing "as though there were

Thos.Aq.*Un.int*.5.122 (Keeler 79)

two contradictory truths and as though there were in the
sayings of the accursed heathen a truth that is contrary
to the truth of Holy Scripture." The object of these condemnations was the effort of several thirteenth-century
Christians, notably Siger of Brabant and Boetius of Dacia,
to adapt to the purposes of Christian thought the interpretations of Aristotle that had been created by the
twelfth-century Muslim philosopher Averroës (Ibn-
Rushd), who was understood to have preserved his Islamic
orthodoxy by means of a theory of double truth. Since it
was through Latin translations of Arabic translations of
the Greek original that many of Aristotle's writings came
to be known in the Western church during the thirteenth
century, together with the commentaries of Averroës and
other Muslim thinkers, it became necessary, for the purposes of the theological use of Aristotle, to disengage his
thought from the accretions of "Averroism" and to produce translations of his works directly from the Greek.
In the process Averroës was condemned, along with his
Christian followers, but Aristotle was exonerated of
the guilt by association that had attached itself to his
philosophy.

Whatever these actions may have meant philosophically, the condemnation of Averroism and the exoneration
of Aristotelianism were both direct corollaries of the
theological principle that "grace does not abolish nature,
but completes it." It followed from this principle that although "the truth of nature" and "the truth of faith"
were not coextensive, they did stand in the kind of continuity that enabled the truth of nature to be true as far as
it went. There could not be a contradiction between one
kind of truth and another; for if there were, grace would
not be able to complete nature, but would have to destroy
and replace it. The tension between the two kinds of truth
became especially troublesome in the case of those doctrines on which Scripture and Aristotle had both spoken
explicitly but in opposite ways. Of these, the eternity of
the world was perhaps the most serious; for "Thomas
Aquinas recognized that Aristotle had advanced the doctrine that neither the world nor time had a beginning, but
he defended Aristotle against the contemporary Augustinians on the grounds that no demonstrative reasons are
conclusive for or against the eternity of the world, and
creation is an article of faith." This did not imply that

the eternity of the world was true philosophically while creation ex nihilo was true theologically, but rather that creation ex nihilo could be known only by revelation and that therefore the question lay beyond the competence of reason and of philosophy to decide. Reason and philosophy were competent to conclude from the order and motion of the universe that there was a First Cause and an unmoved Mover. Revelation did not abolish this conclusion, but completed it by disclosing that the First Cause was in fact the Trinity of Father, Son, and Holy Spirit, and that the universe had not existed forever, but had, together with time itself, come into being ex nihilo.

The most influential presentation of this doctrine of the relation between reason and revelation was probably not that of any of the theologians with whom we have been dealing, but that of Dante Alighieri. Although his epitaph acclaimed him as "Dante the theologian, not lacking in any doctrine," it is evident that this was "a poetical eulogy," for he was not a theologian in the technical sense. On the other hand, although "the Thomism of Dante is an exploded myth," it is no less evident that he "was at home in the intellectual world of the Latin Middle Ages," so that it is quite proper to speak of the "Augustinism" of Dante. The identification of the role of Vergil in the *Divine Comedy* as, among other things, that of reason leading to revelation and of nature being completed but not abolished by grace is, despite the objections of some Dante scholars, warranted by the words of the poem as well as by its very structure. "I can speak to you," Dante had Vergil say, "only as far as reason sees; beyond that, you must wait for Beatrice, for that is the business of faith [opra di fede]." In that realm the natural reason represented by Vergil was no longer able to be of service, since he could "see no further"; and only the grace of revelation, represented, at least in part, by Beatrice, could suffice. The messianism of the Fourth Eclogue qualified Vergil to be the one through whom the Roman poet Statius had been converted to Christianity. Yet Vergil himself admitted that he had lived in an age of idolatry, and that he had not known and worshiped the true God "as was due him." Having been present in the inferno at the time of the harrowing of hell, he had witnessed the victory of Christ; it was perhaps for that reason that Vergil was able to quote the familiar hymn of Venantius

Thos.Aq.*S.T*.1.46.2 resp. (*Ed. Leon.*4:481)

Thos.Aq.*S.T*.1.2.3 resp. (*Ed. Leon.*4:31)

Gilson (1963) 289

Curtius (1953) 595
Curtius (1953) 360

Dant.*Purg*.18.46–48

Dant.*Purg*.27.129

Dant.*Purg*.15.76–78
See vol.1:64
Dant.*Purg*.22.73
Dant.*Inf*.1.131

Dant.*Inf*.1.131; 4.37–39
See p. 154 above
Dant.*Inf*.4.52–54
See p. 132 above

Dant.*Inf.*34.1
Bergin (1965) 237

Dant.*Purg.*27.139

Gilson (1963) 187

2 Cor.5:17

Fortunatus about the "banner" of the cross. But "doctrinal necessity" required that Vergil, the spokesman for the capacities of nature at their highest, take leave of the poet with no further "word or sign" when they came to the gates of Paradise. And that doctrinal necessity was the necessity that came from the doctrine of the relation between nature and grace; for Dante "knew, having derived the notion from St. Thomas, whose fundamental thesis it is, that the peculiar effect of grace is not to vindicate nature or to suppress it, but to perfect it."

That Thomistic—and basically Augustinian—thesis was to come under attack from several directions during the centuries that followed the period being covered in this volume. In its criticism of scholastic theology for being too generous toward nature and reason, the theology of the sixteenth-century Reformers sometimes threatened to denigrate not only reason and philosophy, but nature and creation itself, and to verge on determinism and dualism. Grace did not abolish nature, nor did it complete nature; it seemed to replace nature with a "new creation" that was radically discontinuous with the old creation. "Magisterial Reformers" such as Luther and Calvin resisted this tendency, but in the writings of their followers (and sometimes in their own writings) it continued to appear. Most of the time, however, intellectual history since the end of the thirteenth century has been dominated by the opposite emphasis: the exaltation of nature over grace. If Thomas and Bonaventure argued that nature needed grace to be complete and could not attain perfection by its own powers, the more recent champions of nature found grace to be less and less necessary for the perfection—or, at any rate, for the progress toward perfection—of man in his natural state. In the same way, the corollary of the scholastic hierarchy of nature and grace, which was the hierarchy of reason and revelation, was increasingly unacceptable to those who found that, despite the warnings of the scholastics, unaided reason could and did lead to ultimate truth about man and the universe, or at least to as much of it as was needed; the truths of revelation, on the other hand, diminished in importance when the questions to which they were intended to be answers lost their hold on human minds and hearts. For the scholastics of the twelfth and thirteenth centuries, natural theology was a necessary task for church theology to engage in, but for some of the rationalists of the eighteenth and nineteenth centuries it was the only task and thus it became a substitute for church theology.

The Celestial and Ecclesiastical Hierarchies

Collins (1947) x

Two areas of doctrine that are conventionally associated with the thirteenth century are angels and the church. Even without the help of "the hoary canard about medieval disputation being chiefly concerned with the number of angelic occupants of the point of a pin," for which there is no documentation in the texts, the impression is widespread that during this period angelology established itself as a central topic of official church teaching. Similarly, the institutional dominance of the church over the culture of the thirteenth century has seemed to indicate that ecclesiology occupied a prominent place in the doctrinal thinking of the time. There is in fact little said about either doctrine in the pronouncements of what the church believed, taught, and confessed, even though the speculative systems of theologians and philosophers did deal extensively with the first and the administrative statements and actions of prelates and popes did give voice to an explicit understanding of the second.

See vol.1:344–49; vol.2:141–42

Bonav.*Sent.*2.9 (Quaracchi 2:238)
Bonav.*Hex.*21.22 (Quaracchi 5:435)

See pp. 282–83 above
Bonav.*Hex.*21.18 (Quaracchi 5:434)

Thos.Aq.*Sent.*2.9.1.1 sol. (Mandonnet 2:226)

Collins (1947) 220

The two doctrines were in some ways closely related, for both of them were based on a hierarchical definition of reality. The parallel between the celestial hierarchy and the ecclesiastical hierarchy had achieved classic formulation in the mystical theology of Pseudo-Dionysius. After quoting various definitions of "hierarchy" from Dionysius, Bonaventure proposed a definition that would "apply not only to the angelic hierarchy, but also to the ecclesiastical or human hierarchy," namely: "A hierarchy is an ordered power of sacred and rational realities, which preserves for those who are subordinate [in the hierarchy] their proper authority [over others]." There was "a concordance of hierarchies." It is not surprising, in the light of his trinitarianism, that for him any hierarchy had to be threefold in its structure. Commenting on these same texts from the first book of *The Celestial Hierarchy* by Dionysius, Thomas Aquinas also set forth a generalized view of hierarchy, which was based "upon a hierarchical view of reality as proceeding from the divine goodness in orderly and graded fashion." In his commentary on the *Sentences*

Bonav.*Hex*.22.2 (Quaracchi 5: 438)
Dion.Ar.*C.h*.1.3 (*PG* 3:123)

Thos.Aq.*Sent*.2.9.1.3 obj.5 (Mandonnet 2:233);
Thos.Aq.*S.T*.1.108.4 obj.3 (*Ed. Leon*.5:498)

Thos.Aq.*S.T*.1.112.2 resp. (*Ed. Leon*.5:521)

Bonav.*Hex*.22.27 (Quaracchi 5:441)

Bonav.*Brev*.2.8 (Quaracchi 5: 226)

Thos.Aq.*S.T*.1.50.1 resp. (*Ed. Leon*.5:4)

Bonav.*Brev*.2.6 (Quaracchi 5: 224)

Gilson (1965) 241

Petr.Pict.*Sent*.2.5.4 (*PMS* 11: 24)

Bonav.*Sent*.2.9.1.2 (Quaracchi 2:244)
Thos.Aq.*S.T*.1.108.4 resp. (*Ed. Leon*.5:498)

Hug.S.Vict.*Sacr*.1.5.19 (*PL* 176:254)

Thos.Aq.*S.T*.1.1.8 ad 1 (*Ed. Leon*.4:22)

and again in the *Summa* he quoted with approval (as did Bonaventure) the principle of Dionysius that the ecclesiastical hierarchy was modeled after the celestial, even though he disapproved of some of the uses to which that principle was being put. Nor was hierarchy confined to angels and the church, for "the entire universe" was ordered hierarchically. This was a corollary of the fundamental tenet discussed earlier, that grace did not abolish nature but completed it, which implied a "hierarchization of grace over nature."

In this hierarchical universe, the celestial hierarchy of angels, who "move and are moved within a hierarchical order," held a special place. According to Thomas, the perfection of such a universe required that between a Creator who was pure spirit and a creature who was compounded of body and spirit there should be a creature who was pure spirit; according to Bonaventure, the Creator made not only physical nature, but also that nature which was "closest to his own, the spiritual and immaterial." Despite the differences between a "linear" view of this hierarchy in Aquinas and a "more complicated" view in Bonaventure, therefore, they were agreed on the place of the angelic hierarchy within the hierarchical universe. Although there were some theologians who held that "the orders of angels were not distinguished this way from the beginning of their creation," it became the prevalent view to hold that the distinction between the orders of angels was by nature as well as by grace; yet it remained "principally by grace" among the angels, while within the church such a distinction was entirely by grace. The participation of the angels in divine grace made them a proper topic in Christian doctrine. "There are many other questions about this spiritual nature, from which the curiosity of the human mind cannot manage to find rest"; but most of these questions, for example, the angels' means of locomotion or even their mode of cognition, were not articles of faith, any more than similar questions about human beings would be, but at most were inferences drawn from articles of faith. Our attention here is directed only to questions that pertained directly to the creed of the church and to its message of creation and salvation.

The two most important questions of this kind with reference to the angels were the creation of the evil angels and the confirmation of the good angels. The Christian

See vol.1:35-37

Thos.Aq.*Sep.sub*.94 (Lescoe 138)

Thos.Aq.*S.T*.1.61.1 obj.1 (*Ed. Leon*.5:106)

Gen.1:1
Gand.*Sent*.2.5 (Walter 161–62)

Thos.Aq.*S.T*.1.61.2 resp. (*Ed. Leon*.5:107)

Bonav.*Sent*.2.2.1.2.3 conc. (Quaracchi 2:68)

Thos.Aq.*S.T*.1.61.2 resp. (*Ed. Leon*.5:108)

See p. 239 above

Bonav.*Sent*.2.3.2.1.1 conc. (Quaracchi 2:113); Thos. Aq. *Sent*.2.3.2.1 sol. (Mandonnet 2:110): Thos.Aq. *S.T*.1.63.5 resp. (*Ed.Leon*.5:130)

John 8:44
Gen.1:1

doctrine of creation, as it had been stated by the earliest spokesmen for the church against classical thought, rejected the idea that the world or matter or time had always existed. This assertion of creation ex nihilo could not be established by reason, but the scholastics made it a fundamental part of their doctrine of angels. For it was contrary to the catholic faith to teach, as some philosophers had, that spiritual beings such as angels had always existed, since "the catholic faith maintains the assertion that they began to exist after they had previously not existed." To be sure, there was no mention of the angels in the creation narratives of the Book of Genesis, which could be taken to mean that they did not belong to the order of creatures. But the comprehensive term "heaven and earth" included them together with all other temporal reality, since "the catholic faith holds without doubting that God alone, Father, Son, and Holy Spirit, is from eternity." Because of the silence of Genesis, there was some question about when the angels had been created, especially since some of the Greek fathers had taught that the angels were made before the physical world. Bonaventure identified four creatures—time, matter, the empyrean heaven, and the angelic nature—as the first among all things to have been created; Aquinas, despite his regard for the Greek patristic tradition, preferred to hold that the angels had not been created before the physical world.

Such questions as these about the creation of the angels provided the backdrop for the consideration of the creation of the devil and the other angels who fell, an issue made even more vital by the recrudescence of various kinds of cosmological dualism. In this consideration, as distinct from some other questions of angelology, the faith of the church definitely was at stake, so that both Bonaventure and Thomas Aquinas, who elsewhere in the discussion of angels spoke about "the more prevalent" or "the more reasonable" or "the more probable" opinion, resorted here to the word "heretical." Yet, by the authority of Christ himself, the devil had been "a murderer from the beginning." If this was the same beginning spoken of in Genesis, the conclusion seemed to be that the devil had been created evil. Augustine appeared to be drawing that very conclusion from the passage when he said that "it is not groundless to suppose that the devil fell by pride from the beginning of time and never lived in peace and

Aug.*Gen.ad litt*.11.16 (*CSEL* 28–I:349)

Bertola (1957) 42
Petr.Lomb.*Sent*.2.3.4 (*Spic. Bon.*I–II:344); Petr.Pict.*Sent.* 2.3 (*PMS* 11:4–5)

Hug.S.Vict.*Sacr*.1.5.19 (*PL* 176:254); Bonav.*Brev*.2.7 (Quaracchi 5:224–25)
Alb.M.*Sent*.2.3.14 (Borgnet 27:86–87)

Thos.Aq.*S.T.*1.63.5 resp. (*Ed. Leon*.5:130)
Bonav.*Sent*.2.3.2.1.2 (Quaracchi 2:116)

Gen.1:31

See vol.1:85–89; vol.2:220–23

CLater. (1215) *Const*.1 (Alberigo 206)

Hug.S.Vict.*Sacr*.1.5.19 (*PL* 176:254)

Thos.Aq.*Sent*.2.4.1.3 (Mandonnet 2:136–39)

See vol.1:329

Alex.Hal.*S.T.*2.1.100 (Klumper 2:126)

blessedness with the holy angels, but apostatized from his Creator at the very outset of his creation." "By a very analytic procedure and with a very precise terminology," Peter Lombard and Peter of Poitiers both cited this explanation, but went on to show, in the words of the latter, that the words of Christ in John 8:44 had meant "from the beginning of time, that is, after the beginning" of creation referred to in the opening words of the Bible. Hugh of Saint-Victor and Bonaventure, quoting the Augustinian and anti-Manichean axiom that "the supremely good First Principle does not make anything that is not good," concluded that all the angels, including the ones that fell, must have been created good. Supported by a reference to Albertus Magnus and other authorities, Thomas asserted: "It is clear that the sin of the [fallen] angel was an act subsequent to his creation." Bonaventure, too, posited an interval, albeit "a very brief interval [morula]," between creation and fall. No one who wanted to hold to the catholic faith could suggest that anything created by God had been created evil, for "God saw everything that he had made, and behold, it was very good." Alluding to these words of the creation story, the Fourth Lateran Council reaffirmed the doctrine that orthodoxy had been defending against dualism since the conflicts with Gnosticism and Manicheism: "The devil and the other demons were created naturally good by God, but they became evil by their own doing."

But if all the angels were created good and if some of them fell, it followed, according to Hugh of Saint-Victor, that their "goodness, righteousness, and blessedness were of the kind that nature received as it was beginning, not of the kind that it itself achieved or that it merited by the achieving." They were sinless and holy, not perfect, since perfection belonged to the completion and consummation of a creature, not to its beginning. Were then the angels, including those that eventually fell, created with grace? This was a question on which orthodox theologians could disagree, and did. It was, Aquinas conceded, "the more prevalent" opinion that the angels had, to use the Augustinian terms, received the "natural endowment" but not the "superadded gift." Alexander of Hales thought that "it seems better to say that [the apostate angel] never had that grace which makes one pleasing to God [gratia gratum faciens]." In this interpretation

Bonav.*Sent*.2.4.1.2 conc.
(Quaracchi 2:133–34)

Thos.Aq.*Sent*.2.4.1.3 sol.
(Mandonnet 2:138)

Gen.1:11

Thos.Aq.*S.T*.1.62.3 resp. (*Ed.
Leon*.5:112)

Petr.Lomb.*Sent*.2.11.1 (*Spic.
Bon*.1–II:380); Thos.Aq.*S.T*.
1.113.2 S.C. (*Éd.Leon*.5:526)

Matt.18:10

Hier.*Matt*.18.10 (*CCSL* 77:
159)
Hon.Aug.*Eluc*.2.28 (*PL* 172:
1154)

Thos.Aq.*Sent*.2.11.1.3 ad 1
(Mandonnet 2:275–76); Bonav.
Sent.2.11.1.2 conc.
(Quaracchi 2:279)

Bonav.*Brev*.2.8 (Quaracchi 5:
225)

of the original state of the angels Hugh of Saint-Victor and Alexander of Hales were joined by Bonaventure, who identified it as "the more prevalent" view and who accepted it as "the more probable" one. Although this opinion was "more prevalent," the opinion that the angels were created with grace was, according to Thomas, "more true," because "it harmonizes more completely with the opinion that maintains that at the beginning of creation all things were distinguished according to species"—an opinion that did have "more authorities of the saints" in support of it. Once again, he was appealing from an explicit statement in the tradition to the implications of the main body of the tradition. In the *Summa* he reiterated this opinion, supporting it from the relation between nature and grace and arguing that "sanctifying grace stands in the same relation to blessedness as the seedlike form does to the natural effect in the order of nature," where God had created the separate species as "seedlike forms."

The dispute over the presence of grace in the angels at their creation was closely related to an idea for which there was no explicit biblical warrant but such widespread support in the catholic tradition and such theological and even pastoral necessity that it was to survive in Protestant dogmaticians who claimed to rely on Scripture alone: the confirmation of the good angels after the fall of the evil angels. A major source of this idea was the belief in guardian angels, in support of which theologians quoted the saying of Jesus that "in heaven [children's] angels always behold the face of my Father who is in heaven," together with Jerome's comment: "Great is the dignity of souls, for each one to have an angel assigned to guard it from its birth." Honorius of Autun had systematized the view of individual guardian angels, which seems to have been deeply rooted in piety and devotion. Even before the fall of Adam and Eve angels had been given this assignment. But after the fall of Adam and Eve, preceded and brought on as it had been by the fall of the apostate angels, the guardianship of the angels over the individual soul required that "those angels who turned toward [God after the fall of the evil angels] were at once confirmed in their choice through grace and glory," since otherwise the angel and the soul it was guarding would be even more vulnerable. The confirmation was not an act of the "operating grace" of God, by which he worked on men to convert them from sin to grace, but of his "cooperating grace," by which he worked with men after their conversion. Although the confirmed angels, like the saints in glory, were not able to sin (non posse peccare), they did not lose the essence of free choice thereby, any more than the saints—or, for that matter, God himself—did.

As the belief in guardian angels and the idea of the confirmation of the good angels suggest, much of the doctrine of angels—including, according to Hugh of Saint-Victor and Peter Lombard, the names of the various angelic ranks—was "on our account." Likewise, the celestial hierarchy was, according to Dionysius, the model after which the ecclesiastical hierarchy had been patterned. Therefore in Bonaventure's angelology the illumination of the Trinity passed successively through the angelic hierarchies, which consisted of three hierarchies of three members each, and "through all of them to the ecclesiastical" hierarchy. In spite of the parallel, however, the scholastic theologians of the twelfth and thirteenth centuries, who discoursed so extensively about the celestial hierarchy, wrote relatively little about the ecclesiastical hierarchy or even about the nature of the church in general. During these two centuries we must look not primarily to the systematic theologians and summists, nor to the canonists and lawyer-popes, but to the monastic exegetes and expository preachers for a comprehensive doctrine of the church. Above them all, Bernard of Clairvaux, simultaneously (or alternately) a reflective mystic and an éminence grise, articulated a vision of the church that was "extremely spiritual" and yet included its spotted actuality. His younger contemporary, Joachim of Fiore, who was also a monastic exegete and a mystic, had his own vision of the church, one in which all of human history was "the progressive assimilation of society to the mystical body of Christ." The contrasts—and the affinities—between these two visions of the church and of the ecclesiastical hierarchy may well be interpreted as representing the range of ecclesiological doctrine in this period.

The analogy of the celestial and the ecclesiastical hierarchy implied for Bernard not only a parallel between the orders of "angels and archangels arranged under their one head, who is God" and the orders of clergy and prel-

---

Petr.Pict.*Sent.*2.4 (*PMS* 11:8)

Petr.Lomb.*Sent.*2.7.1 (*Spic. Bon.*1–II:359)
Gand.*Sent.*2.19–22 (Walter 171–73)
Bonav.*Sent.*2.7.1.2.1 conc. (Quaracchi 2:184)

Hug.S.Vict.*Sacr.*1.5.32 (*PL* 176:261); Petr.Lomb.*Sent.* 2.9.3 (*Spic.Bon.* 1–II:372)

Dion.Ar.*C.h.*1.3 (*PG* 3:123)

Bonav.*Hex.*21.21 (Quaracchi 5:435)

Congar (1953) 154

Bloomfield (1957) 265

ates arranged "under one supreme pontiff," but a unique status for the church as a society that "has God as its Author and that derives its origin from heaven." There was therefore, strictly speaking, a single church of angels and of men, which was, taken together as a unit, "the bride of Christ." It was also "the body of Christ," more precious to him than his own physical body. This was "the church of the elect," which, by the mystery of divine predestination, had always existed as a reality in the mind of God. The God who governed and administered the entire universe was nevertheless especially concerned with the well-being of this "church of the elect" as with nothing else in all creation. The object of this special care was the church as a whole, "not I as an individual nor you apart from me nor someone else without both of us, but all of us at the same time." Even the saints could not enter the church triumphant without the believers on earth. For when God had "wrought salvation in the midst of the earth," this was not the salvation of "the individual soul, but of the great number of souls which he intended to gather into the one church."

In such a high view of the church and of its place in the divine scheme of things, "the unity of the Spirit in the bond of peace" within the church was the essential presupposition for the salvation of any individual. If the individual was to belong to the church "not only without strife, but with grace," he must assiduously cultivate that unity. Therefore "woe to that man who is responsible for breaking the sweet bond of unity!" Out of the many tribes and languages of the human race this one catholic church gathered men together into the unity of the one true faith. Those such as Jews, heretics, and heathen, who did not participate in this unity, did not receive the support of the church's prayers; and when they did, as in the special intercessions appointed for Good Friday, the church still omitted from its petitions those who had separated themselves from its fellowship and had therefore been excommunicated. Yet it would be a mistake to equate the unity of the church with uniformity. The church was "wrapped around with varieties" of custom, order, age, and gender. "Whether Cluniacs or Cistercians or regular clergy or even faithful laymen [sive etiam laici fideles]"—the church was "one out of all" of these. If "the authority of the prelates, the proper conduct

Brd.Clr.*Cons*.3.4.18 (Leclercq-Rochais 3:445)

Brd.Clr.*Cant*.27.4.6 (Leclercq-Rochais 1:186)
Brd.Clr.*Cant*.12.4.7 (Leclercq-Rochais 1:65)
Brd.Clr.*Ps*.90.6.7;7.10 (Leclercq-Rochais 4:411;420)

Brd.Clr.*Cant*.78.2.3; 62.1.1 (Leclercq-Rochais 2:268; 154)

Brd.Clr.*Cant*.68.1.2 (Leclercq-Rochais 2:197)

Brd.Clr.*Apol*.4.7 (Leclercq-Rochais 3:87)
Brd.Clr.*Sanct*.3.1 (Leclercq-Rochais 5:349–50)

Ps.74:12

Brd.Clr.*Cant*.68.2.4 (Leclercq-Rochais 2:198)

Eph.4:3
Brd.Clr.*Apol*.4.7 (Leclercq-Rochais 3:87)

Brd.Clr.*Vig.Nat*.3.6 (Leclercq-Rochais 4:216)
Brd.Clr.*Cant*.29.2.3 (Leclercq-Rochais 1:204)

Brd.Clr.*Cant*.78.2.5 (Leclercq-Rochais 2:269)

Brd.Clr.*Grad*.22.56 (Leclercq-Rochais 3:58)

Ps.45:14 (Vulg.)

Brd.Clr.*Apol*.3.5–7 (Leclercq-Rochais 3:85–87)

of the clergy, the discipline of the people, and the peaceful devotion of the monks" were united amid all their variety, the unity of the church would be preserved. But if those who had just been "converted" to the monastic life fell away or if the monks attacked the secular clergy and the prelates for doing what they had to do in society, the unity of the church was in jeopardy.

The emphasis on catholic unity also held together the "extremely spiritual" image of the church as the bride of Christ or the body of Christ and the institutional understanding of the church as consisting of the pope, the prelates, the clergy, the monks, and "even faithful laymen." In the name of the catholic unity of the body of Christ Bernard involved himself in the practical issues of the institutional church and the papacy. He equated "apostolic sanctions" and "the decrees of the holy fathers" with "the practices of the holy Roman church," whose authority as "the apostolic see" was to be enforced in all the churches. The pope was "the prince of bishops, the heir of the apostles, Peter according to his authority and Christ according to his anointing." On such a question as the observance of the nativity of the Virgin Mary and even, apparently, the doctrine of her immaculate conception, for example, he was prepared to defer to the judgment of Rome. Yet he also warned Pope Eugenius III, in a treatise on discipline written especially for him, that "the holy church of Rome . . . is the mother of churches, not their mistress," and that the pope himself was "not the lord of bishops, but one of them, in fact, a brother." Possession and dominion over the earth belonged to God alone, and the pope merely had the responsibility of caring for it. There were many aspects of the papacy, especially its temporal wealth and power, in which the pope was "not the successor of Peter, but of Constantine." The word of the psalm about meditating on the law of the Lord day and night had come to refer not to the laws of the Lord, but to those of Justinian. The chief business of the pope had become litigation, not the upbuilding of the spiritual welfare of the church.

Such criticism of the spotted actuality of the institutional church was not the same as the repudiation of the church by sectarians and heretics, for here it was a matter of "carrying on a contest against the church, even in a hostile spirit, but with a pain that is constructive." The church not only deserved this kind of criticism, but needed

Brd.Clr.*Cant*.46.1.4 (Leclercq-Rochais 2:57)
Brd.Clr.*Cant*.63.3.6 (Leclercq-Rochais 2:164)

Brd.Clr.*Cant*.12.6.9 (Leclercq-Rochais 1:66)

Brd.Clr.*V.Mal*.3.7 (Leclercq-Rochais 3:315–16)
Brd.Clr.*V.Mal*.15.33 (Leclercq-Rochais 3:340)

Brd.Clr.*Cons*.2.8.15 (Leclercq-Rochais 3:423)

See p. 171 above

Brd.Clr.*Ep*.174.9 (Leclercq-Rochais 7:392)

Brd.Clr.*Cons*.4.7.23 (Leclercq-Rochais 3:466)

Brd.Clr.*Cons*.3.1.1 (Leclercq-Rochais 3:432)

Brd.Clr.*Cons*.4.3.6 (Leclercq-Rochais 3:453)

Ps.1:2
Brd.Clr.*Cons*.1.4.5 (Leclercq-Rochais 3:399)

Brd.Clr.*Cons*.1.3.4 (Leclercq-Rochais 3:397)

Brd.Clr.*Cant*.30.1.1 (Leclercq-Rochais 1:210)

Brd.Clr.*Cant*.33.7.14–15
(Leclercq-Rochais 1:243–44)

Brd.Clr.*Cons*.1.10.13
(Leclercq-Rochais 3:409)
See p. 232 above
Matt.21:13

Brd.Clr.*Cant*.25.1.2 (Leclercq-
Rochais 1:164)

Brd.Clr.*Cant*.27.7.12 (Leclercq-
Rochais 1:190)

Brd.Clr.*Cant*.26.1.2 (Leclercq-
Rochais 1:170)

Eph.5:27

Brd.Clr.*Cant*.25.2.3 (Leclercq-
Rochais 1:164)

Joach.*Ev*.3 (FSI 67:251)

Joach.*Ev*.1 (FSI 67:52)

Isa.1:21
Joach.*Ev*.1 (FSI 67:96–97)
Rev.17:18

Joach.*Apoc*.6 (191r)

it. While the great threat to the primitive church had been persecution, the new enemy was hypocrisy and greed. "The church," Bernard complained, "is filled with ambitious men," and he even echoed the language of the heretics in speaking of a "den of thieves." He recognized that there were wicked men who shared in the church's confession of faith and in the sacraments and who for such reasons as these were called members of the church and "children of Jerusalem." It remained true that the church on earth was a pilgrim church, which, though it already possessed spiritual treasures and had spiritual members, was still far from its goal. As such, the church, having passed through "the struggle of its laborious warfare," bore the stains and the scars of that experience. Yet this church, so spotted and stained, was the very same reality of which the apostle spoke as "a glorious church, not having a spot or a wrinkle or anything of the kind, but holy and immaculate."

The tension between the church as an object of faith and hope and the church as an object of criticism, which Bernard manifested but did not resolve, could be resolved by a more radical doctrine. That came in the ecclesiology of Joachim of Fiore, who incorporated his interpretation of the institutional church and of the ecclesiastical hierarchy into an eschatology in which the nature of the church was to be transformed by being "resurrected, as it were, from the grave." Like Bernard, Joachim lamented the present state of the church and its loss of spiritual vitality. In contrast with "the perfection of the primitive church," whose prelates had "begun to cross over from vices to virtues," there stood "the church of the present time," to which it was appropriate to apply the words of the prophet about Jerusalem: "How has the faithful city become a harlot!" The harlot of Babylon described in the Apocalypse of John, "the great city," had been identified by the catholic fathers as Rome—"not because of the church of the righteous, which carried on its pilgrimage in the midst of [Rome], but because of the multitude of the reprobate, who by their wicked words blaspheme and harm the pilgrim church in their midst." From these words themselves, as well as from their context, it appears that by "Rome" Joachim may not have been referring to the ancient pagan city with a minority church in its midst, but to the capital of catholic Christendom, in which the true church was still (or again) a minority.

Joachim's criticism of the corruption of the church was

part of a total interpretation of church history. The doctrine of the Trinity, which provided other thinkers of the
twelfth and thirteenth centuries with a scheme of organi-
zation for their view of the world, became the basis for a
See pp. 282–84 above division of history into three ages: "the first, in which we
were under the law; the second, in which we were under
grace; the third, which we expect very soon, under a more
ample grace." The stages of church history were bounded
Joach.*Conc.*5.84 (112r) by various notable events. The conversion of Constantine,
"when the church of Peter, or rather of Christ, was es-
tablished as the mistress of the whole world," closed the
Joach.*Conc.*4.25 (54r); first stage; the second had endured for fourteen genera-
Joach.*Ev.*3 (FSI 67:308–9) tions; and the third was now about to close. The signs of
Joach.*Ev.*1 (FSI 67:106) the end announced in the Gospels were being fulfilled,
and a new epoch would soon begin. In this third stage a
new church would be born of the old church, and "the
Joach.*Conc.*pr. (i) order of clerics" would reach its consummation and its
conclusion. Stating the theme of this apocalyptic hope at
the beginning of his book *The Harmony of the New and
the Old Testaments,* Joachim declared: "It is our intention
Joach.*Conc.*4.34 (57r); ... to comprehend the end of the temporal realm, which is
Joach.*Ev.*1 (FSI 67:32) properly called Babylon, and to disclose in the clearest
possible words that which is near, the birth of the church,
which will take place at the same time."
Joach.*Conc.*1.1 (1r)   The vision of a new spiritual church that was yet to be
did not invalidate the institutional church that had pre-
ceded it. The older form of the church was like John the
Baptist, worthy of respect even though it was being
Joach.*Conc.*2.2.7 (22v) superseded. "For even if, with the substitution of the
things that are new, the things that are old were to pass
away, this was not as though these things had not in their
own time been instituted by God for righteousness, but
rather because lesser things are to be left behind so that
more powerful mysteries might be given to the faithful
Joach.*Ev.*1 (FSI 67:176) for their salvation." A "new [form of] religion, which
will be altogether free and spiritual," was to replace the
obsolete "ecclesiastical order, which struggles over the
Joach.*Conc.*5.65 (95v) letter of the Gospel." As Christ rose from the dead on
the third day, so in this third age of history the church
Joach.*Ev.*3 (FSI 67:251) would be raised. What would rise, as from the grave of
the old church, was a new "spiritual church," into which
the true "lovers of Christ" would pass over just as some
Jews, those who believed in Christ, had passed over from
Joach.*Conc.*4.37 (58r-v) the synagogue to the church; in this restored spiritual

Joach.*Ev*.1 (*FSI* 67:95)

Joach.*Ev*.3 (*FSI* 67:292–92)
Joach.*Conc*.4.31 (564)

Wendelborn (1974) 166

Joach.*Conc*.5.74 (103r)

McGinn (1971)

See vol.1:302–4; pp. 42, 91–93, 299 above

Thos.Aq.*S.T*.1.23.7 ad 3 (*Ed. Leon*.4:283)

church all the Jews would finally be converted to Christ. With "the coming again of the Lord in the Holy Spirit," there would come a basic change of attitude, for in the spiritual church "men will cease being zealous for those institutions that have been established temporarily [pro tempore et ad tempus]." Thus there would have to arise "a new leader, a universal pontiff of the new Jerusalem," which would seem to mean quite explicitly "that the papacy in the form it has had hitherto cannot continue and cannot even provide from within itself the spiritual leaders of the future." Even the sacraments of the church would be replaced, just as they in their turn had replaced the observances of the Old Testament. The institutional church would be transformed into the spiritual church, and the kingdoms of this world would yield to the kingdom of God.

Despite the response that Joachim's dichotomy between the institutional church of the present and the spiritual church of the future evoked in the thirteenth century, even from Bonaventure and Thomas Aquinas, it could not prevail against the dominance of an ecclesiology like that of Bernard of Clairvaux in which the spiritual and the institutional were ultimately inseparable. Only when the state of the institutional church made it increasingly difficult to apply spiritual attributes to it would the dichotomy begin to gain widespread support. The publication of the first theological treatises devoted to ecclesiology in the fourteenth century and the demands for reform of the ecclesiastical hierarchy (as well as for a new form of its relations with the nation-state) in the fourteenth and fifteenth centuries gave fresh currency to views that had appeared eccentric or even dangerous in the twelfth and thirteenth centuries. Augustine's notion of a "church of the predestined," which had recurred throughout the history of medieval theology, became, in the hands of Wycliffe and Hus, an instrument to call the institutional church to account in the name of the true church.

The Vision of God

The culmination of the history of the church was the vision of God. It was not, strictly speaking, a doctrine, but it was the consummation of all doctrine. The vision of God was the content of eternal bliss, transcending the common state of nature, as God was "above all things"

Is.St.*Serm*.20 (*PL* 194:1757)

Petr.Ab.*Sic et non*.48 (Boyer-McKeon 217–22)
Thos.Aq.*Gent*.3.48 (*Ed.Leon.* 14:130–32)

1 Cor.13:12(Vulg.)
Petr.Lomb.*Serm*.20 (*PL* 171: 362)

Brd.Clr.*Cant*.3.1.1 (Leclercq-Rochais 1:14)

Brd.Clr.*Cant*.74.2.5 (Leclercq-Rochais 2:242)

Rich.S.Vict.*Erud.hom*.1.2 (*PL* 196:1235)

Rich.S.Vict.*Erud.hom*.2.10 (*PL* 196:1309)

Bald.*Tract*.11 (*PL* 204:528)

Guib.Nog.*Vita sua* (*PL* 156: 837–962)

in his singularity, simplicity, and constancy. As such, it was a blessing that the saints in glory shared with the angels, and it was not attainable in its fullness here on earth. For although here man's vision of God was "through a mirror in an image," the vision in glory would be "face to face." Nevertheless, there were anticipations of the vision vouchsafed to some in the experience of this present life. It was another characteristic of the doctrinal reflection of the twelfth and thirteenth centuries that it began once more to relate the dogmas of the tradition to subjective experience and that it thus served to introduce a new element into the interpretation of the faith. A brief consideration of this element of subjectivity in the medieval understanding of the content of Christian doctrine may well serve as a conclusion to this volume.

"We shall read today," Bernard told his monastic confreres, "in the book of experience. Turn your minds inward upon yourselves, and let each of you examine his own conscience in regard to those things that are to be mentioned." He himself had frequently been granted a personal experience of the presence of Christ the Logos, when he "felt that He was present." Richard of Saint-Victor carried the reading "in the book of experience" even further than Bernard had. There was, he taught, "nothing better, nothing more certain, and nothing more sublime" that the human mind could know than what it learned by experience. The practice of prayer was especially conducive to such experience, when "the light of illumining grace" would come over the mind and enable it "to penetrate profound mysteries by the inspiration [of grace]." Experience joined with the consciousness of faith and with the events of the history of salvation to teach man about his nature as a being who was both physical and spiritual. The exploration of subjectivity was a constituent part of the Augustinian tradition, and even though the manuscripts of Augustine's *Confessions* were not distributed as widely in monastic libraries as were those of some of his other major works, this unique history of a soul sounding its own depths to know a God who transcended the antithesis of subject and object continued to find echoes in medieval literature and thought. In the early twelfth century, Guibert of Nogent composed an autobiographical work in the Augustinian mode, upon which we have drawn repeatedly in this book. The data of his life and experience served as a way toward the knowledge of self and of God.

Yet the most remarkable statement in these two centuries of what we have called "the identification of personal religious experience as an epistemological principle in theology" came neither in the *Sermons on the Canticles* of Bernard of Clairvaux nor in the meditative books of the Victorine mystics nor in the autobiography of Guibert of Nogent, but in *The Journey of the Mind to God,* written by Bonaventure and inspired by Francis of Assisi. As we have seen, Bonaventure found traces of the Trinity throughout the "macrocosm" of the universe, but the created trinities came into the sharpest focus when one turned to a consideration of the "microcosm" of the mind. The mirror of the external world was dark and useless until one had polished the mirror of that internal world. From philosophy there came the method of speculation on the basis of the outer world, but one had to learn to speculate about the inner world from Scripture. The introspective method of speculation was, Bonaventure maintained, "superior" to the method that began with externals, for by introspection it was possible to "enter our own self, that is, our own mind, in which is reflected [God's] very own image," and the mind was enabled to "reenter its own inner world, there to see God 'in the splendor of the saints.' " The celestial and ecclesiastical hierarchies had their counterpart in "the hierarchy of our mind." If one wanted to enter into the celestial hierarchy or the heavenly Jerusalem, it was necessary not only that he participate in the sacraments administered by the ecclesiastical hierarchy, but that he "first descend, by grace, into his own heart." Thus he would be "transported in ecstasy above the intellect" to the beatific vision of God.

As the paradigm for this theology of experience, Bonaventure pointed to "the example of our most blessed father Francis," who had been "transported out of himself" and had thereby become "a model of perfect contemplation, a second Jacob," through whom God was to "invite all truly spiritual men" to the same experience, not by what Francis had said or taught but by what he had done and by what had been done to him. Among those who followed in the footsteps of Francis—almost literally—was Bonaventure himself, who, "at a time close to the thirty-third anniversary of the blessed man's departure," had traced the

See vol.2:259

Bonav.*Itin.*2.2 (Quaracchi 5: 300)

Bonav.*Itin.*pr.4 (Quaracchi 5: 296)

Bonav.*Itin.*4.5 (Quaracchi 5: 307)

Bonav.*Itin.*4.1 (Quaracchi 5: 306)

Bonav.*Itin.*3.1 (Quaracchi 5: 303)

Ps.110:3(Vulg.)

Bonav.*Itin.*4.6 (Quaracchi 5: 307)

Bonav.*Itin.*4.4 (Quaracchi 5: 307)
Bonav.*Itin.*1.7 (Quaracchi 5: 298)

Bonav.*Itin.*pr.2 (Quaracchi 5: 295)

Bonav.*Itin.*7.3 (Quaracchi 5: 312)

Bonav.*Itin*.pr.2 (Quaracchi 5: 295)

Bonav.*Itin*.6.2 (Quaracchi 5: 310)

See p.261 above

Bonav.*Itin*.pr.3 (Quaracchi 5: 296)

Bonav.*Itin*.3.6 (Quaracchi 5: 305)
Bonav.*Itin*.7.4 (Quaracchi 5: 312)

Bonav.*Itin*.7.6 (Quaracchi 5: 313)

path of Francis to the top of Mount Alverno, where he had worked out the contents of *The Journey of the Mind to God*. Although he could not presume to match Francis in the quality of his experience, what he learned there was a way of reflection that drew upon such experiences as those of Francis and even on his own experiences. This meant that Bonaventure as a person provided data for Bonaventure as a theologian. The method of pressing experience to extract from it the truth of doctrine enabled one to probe the imagination in such a way as to "see and understand that the 'best' is . . . that than which nothing better can be imagined." In Bonaventure's treatment of it, this rendition of the Anselmic and originally Augustinian argument for the existence of God became a way for what he called "the flash of intuition" to come to the truth of being and of goodness. The Augustinian combination of objective and subjective truth led Bonaventure to assert that "when the soul speculates on its triune Principle by means of the trinity of faculties which makes it the image of God, it is assisted by the lights of knowledge, which perfect and inform it and which represent the blessed Trinity in a triple manner." It was an experience of the mind that transcended the mind, going beyond doctrine to grace and beyond intellectual understanding to existential desire.

Profoundly Augustinian and thoroughly medieval though this theology of experience was in Bonaventure, it was to become something quite different in later centuries. As the natural theology of the scholastics eventually lost its connection with the traditional doctrine out of which it had come, so the experiential theology of Bonaventure and of Augustine was transformed into an autonomous source of truth. In Bonaventure, the Augustinian method of introspection within the context of divine grace led, through experience and reflection, to a transcendent Goodness than which nothing better could be imagined, the God whose mercy, made known in Christ, made it possible for one to sound the depths of his own experience and to affirm himself in nature as well as in grace. In Descartes, on the other hand, despite its undeniable ancestry in Augustine, Anselm, and Bonaventure, the "cogito" led through doubt to thought and from thought to the affirmation both of the self and of God. Although the piety of Descartes undoubtedly stood in the catholic tradition, the Cartesian method of philosophy by introspection did not stand or fall with the truth-claims of Christian faith, but increasingly compelled such truth-claims to justify themselves, if they could, by its canons. That transposition of experience from one key to another will play a major part in our subsequent narrative.

Selected Secondary Works

GENERAL

Arquillière, Henri Xavier. *L'augustinisme politique: Essai sur la formation des théories politiques du moyen-âge.* 2d ed. Paris, 1955.

Auerbach, Erich. *Literary Language and Its Public in Late Latin Antiquity and in the Middle Ages.* Translated by Ralph Manheim. New York, 1965. The first chapter, entitled "Sermo Humilis" (pp. 25–81), is especially pertinent to our narrative.

———. *Mimesis. The Representation of Reality in Western Literature.* Translated by Willard R. Trask. Princeton, 1971.

Bach, Joseph von. *Die Dogmengeschichte des Mittelalters.* 2 vols. Vienna, 1874–75. An early effort to identify the distinctive features of the history of doctrine during the Middle Ages.

Blaise, Albert. *Manuel du latin chrétien.* Strasbourg, 1955.

———. *Dictionnaire latin-français des auteurs du moyen-âge.* Turnhout, Belgium, 1975. A companion volume to the series *Corpus Christianorum. Continuatio Mediaevalis* (See "Editions and Collections" above).

Bloch, Marc. *Feudal Society.* 2 vols. Translated by L. A. Manyon. Paperback edition. Chicago, 1964.

Bloomfield, Morton Wilfred. *Essays and Explorations: Studies in Ideas, Language, and Literature.* Cambridge, Mass., 1970. Includes "Distance and Predestination" and "Some Reflections on the Medieval Idea of Perfection."

Chenu, Marie-Dominique. *La théologie comme science au XIIIe siècle.* Paris, 1957.

———. *La théologie au douzieme siècle.* 2d ed. Paris, 1966. Works of great learning and profound insight.

Curtius, Ernst Robert. *European Literature and the Latin Middle Ages.* Translated by Willard R. Trask. Princeton, 1953. The "excursuses," which form about a third of the volume, are at least as important as the text.

Díaz y Díaz, Manuel C. *Index scriptorum latinorum medii aevi hispanorum.* 2 vols. Salamanca, 1958–59.

Du Cange, Charles Dufresne. *Glossarium mediae et infimae Latinitatis.* 10 vols. Niort, 1883–87. Originally published three hundred years ago, this work remains indispensable.

Durant, William James. *The Age of Faith.* New York, 1950.

Franz, Adolf. *Die Messe im deutschen Mittelalter.* Freiburg, 1902. Based on extensive study of manuscript sources.

Geyer, Bernhard. *Die patristische und scholastische Philosophie.* Reprint edition. Basel, 1951. The medieval volume of Ueberweg's *Grundriss der Geschichte der Philosophie.*

Ghellinck, Joseph de. *Littérature latine au moyen âge.* 2 vols. Paris, 1939.

———. *L'essor de la littérature latine au XIIe siècle.* 2 vols. Paris, 1946.

———. *Le mouvement théologique du XIIe siècle.* 2d ed. Paris, 1948.

Gilson, Étienne. *The Spirit of Medieval Philosophy.* Translated by Alfred Howard Campbell Downes. New York, 1940. The Gifford Lectures for 1931.

———. *History of Christian Philosophy in the Middle Ages.* New York, 1955.

———. "Historical Research and the Future of Scholasticism." In *A Gilson Reader.* Edited by Anton Charles Pegis, pp. 156–67. Garden City, N. Y., 1957.
These works, together with others by the same author listed under various chapter headings below, have been fundamental to the modern study of medieval thought.

Gordon, George Stuart. *Medium Aevum and the Middle Age.* London, 1925.

Grabmann, Martin. *Mittelalterliches Geistesleben.* 3 vols. Munich, 1956. An inexhaustible source of information.

———. *Die Geschichte der scholastischen Methode.* 2 vols. Reprint edition. Graz, 1957.
Despite its title, this work concerns itself with far more than method.

Harnack, Adolf von. *Lehrbuch der Dogmengeschichte.* 3 vols. 5th ed. Tübingen, 1931–32.

Hefele, Carl Joseph. *Histoire des conciles d'après les documents originaux.* Translated by Henri Leclercq. 10 vols. in 19. Paris, 1907–38.

Jungmann, Josef Andreas. *The Mass of the Roman Rite: Its Origins and Development.* Translated by Francis A. Brunner. 2 vols. New York, 1951–55.

Kamlah, Wilhelm. *Apokalypse und Geschichtstheologie: Die mittelalterliche Auslegung der Apocalypse vor Joachim von Fiore.* Berlin, 1935.

Kantorowicz, Ernst Hartwig. *The King's Two Bodies: A Study in Mediaeval Political Theology.* Princeton, 1957. There is almost no aspect of medieval thought and faith that is not illumined by this analysis.

Klibansky, Raymond. *The Continuity of the Platonic Tradition during the Middle Ages.* London, 1939.

Knowles, David. *The Evolution of Medieval Thought.* London, 1962. Dependent on the work of Grabmann, Geyer, and Gilson, the account that Knowles has fashioned is a balanced and learned telling of the story.

Landgraf, Artur Michael. *Dogmengeschichte der Frühscholastik.* 4 vols. Regensburg, 1952–56. These four double volumes rest almost completely on manuscripts in various archives, and thus they are a unique collection of source material.

Leclercq, Jean. *The Love of Learning and the Desire for God: A Study of Monastic Culture.* Translated by Catherine Misrahi. Paperback edition. New York, 1962.

Lopez, Robert Sabatino. Introduction to *Age of Faith,* by Anne Fremantle. New York, 1965.

Lot, Ferdinand. *The End of the Ancient World and the Beginnings of the Middle Ages.* Translated by Philip and Mariette Leon. Introduction by Glanville Downey. Paperback edition. New York, 1961.

Lubac, Henri de. *Corpus mysticum: L'eucharistie et l'église au moyen âge. Étude historique.* 2d ed. Paris, 1949.

———. *Exégèse médiévale: Les quatre sens de l'Écriture.* 2 vols. in 4. Paris, 1959–64.
Many of the thinkers dealt with in our account are also the subjects of this erudite and profound work.

Manitius, Max. *Handschriften antiker Autoren in mittelalterlichen Bibliothekskatalogen.* Leipzig, 1935.

————. *Geschichte der lateinischen Literatur des Mittelalters.* 3 vols. Reprint edition. Munich, 1965.

Mirbt, Carl. *Die Stellung Augustins in der Publizistik des gregorianischen Kirchenstreits.* Berlin, 1888.

Overbeck, Franz Camillo. *Vorgeschichte und Jugend der mittelalterlichen Scholastik: Eine kirchenhistorische Vorlesung.* Edited by Carl Albrecht Bernoulli. Basel, 1917.

Pickman, Edward Motley. *The Mind of Latin Christendom.* New York, 1937.

Raby, Frederic James Edward. *A History of Christian Latin Poetry.* 2d ed. Oxford, 1953.

Rand, Edward Kennard. *Founders of the Middle Ages.* Cambridge, Mass., 1929.

Seeberg, Reinhold. *Die Dogmengeschichte des Mittelalters.* Volume 3 of *Lehrbuch der Dogmengeschichte.* Basel, 1953.

Smalley, Beryl. *The Study of the Bible in the Middle Ages.* Paperback edition. Notre Dame, Ind., 1964. Especially helpful for its discussion of the Victorines and for its account of the revival of Christian interest in Hebrew.

Southern, Richard William. *The Making of the Middle Ages.* New York, 1953.

————. *Western Views of Islam in the Middle Ages.* Cambridge, Mass., 1962.

————. *Western Society and the Church in the Middle Ages.* Baltimore, 1970. Volume 2 of "The Pelican History of the Church."

Stegmüller, Friedrich. *Repertorium commentariorum in sententias Petri Lombardi.* 2 vols. Würzburg, 1947.

Thomasius, Gottfried. *Die Dogmengeschichte des Mittelalters und der Reformationszeit.* Erlangen, 1876. Volume 2, published posthumously, of his *Die Christliche Dogmengeschichte als Entwicklungs-Geschichte des kirchlichen Lehrbegriffs.*

Thompson, James Westfall. *The Literacy of the Laity in the Middle Ages.* Berkeley, 1937.

————. *The Medieval Library.* Reprint edition, with a supplement by Blanche B. Boyer. New York, 1957. The preservation and transmission of learning, both Christian and classical.

Troeltsch, Ernst. *Augustin, die christliche Antike und das Mittelalter.* Berlin, 1915. An attempt at definition.

Vacant, Jean-Michel-Alfred, et al., eds. *Dictionnaire de théologie catholique.* 15 vols. Paris, 1903–50. Usually the first place to turn, and often the last.

Waddell, Helen. *The Wandering Scholars: The Life and Art of the Lyric Poets of the Latin Middle Ages.* Reprint edition. Garden City, N. Y., 1955.

Williams, A. Lukyn. *Adversus Judaeos: A Bird's-Eye View of Christian "Apologiae" until the Renaissance.* Cambridge, 1935.

Young, Karl. *The Drama of the Medieval Church.* 2 vols. Oxford, 1933.

1. The Integrity of the Catholic Tradition

Altaner, Berthold. "Der Stand der Isidorforschung: Ein kritischer Bericht über die seit 1910 erschienene Literatur." In *Miscellanea Isidoriana: Homenaje a San Isidoro de Sevilla,* pp. 1–32. Rome, 1936. "The theological writings of Isidore, including the exegetical works, are practically unknown territory as regards the investigation of their sources."

Arnold, Franz. *Das Diözesanrecht nach den Schriften Hinkmars von Rheims.* Vienna, 1935. A study in canon law.

Beeson, Charles Henry. *Isidorstudien.* Munich, 1913.

Betz, Karl-Ulrich. *Hinkmar von Reims, Nikolaus I., Pseudo-Isidor: Fränkisches Landeskirchentum und römischer Machtanspruch im 9. Jahrhundert.* Bonn, 1965.

Bischoff, K. "Wendepunkte in der Geschichte der lateinischen Exegese im Frühmittelalter." *Sacris Erudiri* 6 (1954): 189–281.

Braegelmann, Sister Athanasius. *The Life and Writings of Saint Ildefonsus of Toledo.* Washington, 1942.

Burch, George Bosworth. *Early Medieval Philosophy.* New York, 1951.

Capelle, Bernard. "Le rôle théologique de Bède le Vénérable." *Studia Anselmiana* 6 (1936): 1–40.

Carlson, Charles P. *Justification in Earlier Medieval Theology.* The Hague, 1975. A study of Pauline commentaries.

Carroll, Mary Thomas Aquinas. *The Venerable Bede: His Spiritual Teachings.* Washington, 1946.

Cascante Dávila, J. M. *Doctrina Mariana de S. Ildefonso de Toledo.* Barcelona, 1958.

Duckett, Eleanor Shipley. *Anglo-Saxon Saints and Scholars.* New York, 1947.

Ellard, Gerald. *Master Alcuin, Liturgist.* Chicago, 1956.

Fontaine, Jacques. *Isidore de Séville et la culture classique dans l'Espagne wisigothique.* 2 vols. Paris, 1959. The fundamental work on the subject.

Fröhlich, Karlfried. *Formen der Auslegung von Mt. 16:13–18 im lateinischen Mittelalter.* Tübingen, 1963. The locus classicus on Peter and the church.

Göller, Emil. *Die Staats- und Kirchenlehre Augustins und ihre Fortwirkung im Mittelalter.* Freiburg, 1930.

Hillgarth, Jocelyn Nigel. "El *Prognosticon futuri saeculi* de San Julián de Toledo." *Analecta Sacra Tarraconensia* 30 (1957): 5–61.

―――――. "The Position of Isidorian Studies: A Critical Review of the Literature since 1935." In *Isidoriana: Colección de estudios sobre Isidoro de Sevilla, publicados con ocasión del XIV centenario de su nacimiento,* edited by Manuel C. Díaz y Díaz, pp. 1–74. León, 1961.

Iserloh, Erwin. "Die Kontinuität des Christentums beim Übergang von der Antike zum Mittelalter im Lichte der Glaubensverkündigung des heiligen Bonifatius." *Trierer theologische Zeitschrift* 63 (1954): 193–205. A provocative essay on the meaning of "medieval."

Kleinclausz, Arthur Jean. *Alcuin.* Paris, 1948. Especially pertinent is the discussion of "Alcuin contre l'hérésie," pp. 71–90.

Laistner, Max Ludwig Wolfram. *Thought and Letters in Western Europe A.D. 500–900.* Paperback edition. Ithaca, N.Y., 1966.

Levison, Wilhelm. *England and the Continent in the Eighth Century.* Oxford, 1946.

McNeill, John Thomas, and Gamer, Helena Margaret, eds. *Medieval Handbooks of Penance: A Translation of the Principal "Libri Poenitentiales" and Selections from Related Documents.* New York, 1938.

Meyer, Hans Bernhard. "Alkuin zwischen Antike und Mittelalter: Ein Kapitel frühmittelalterlicher Frömmigkeitsgeschichte." *Zeitschrift für katholische Theologie* 81 (1959): 306–50, 405–54.

Mullins, Sister Patrick Jerome. *The Spiritual Life according to Saint Isidore of Seville.* Washington, 1940.

Murphy, Francis Xavier. "Julian of Toledo and the Condemnation of Monotheletism in Spain." In *Mélanges Joseph de Ghellinck, S.J.,* 1:361–73. Gembloux, 1951.

Ogara, Florentino. "Tipología bíblica, según S. Isidoro." In *Miscellanea Isidoriana,* pp. 135–50. Rome, 1936.

Schubert, Hans von. *Geschichte der christlichen Kirche im Frühmittelalter.* Tübingen, 1921.

Stout, D. *A Study of the "Sententiarum libri tres" of Isidore of Seville.* Washington, 1937.

Tiralla, Hugo. *Das Augustinische Idealbild der christlichen Obrigkeit als Quelle der "Fürstenspiegel" des Sedulius Scotus und Hincmar von Reims.* Greifswald, 1916. The early medieval use of Augustine's *City of God.*

Wallach, Luitpold. *Alcuin and Charlemagne: Studies in Carolingian History and Literature.* Ithaca, N. Y., 1959.

Winandy, Jacques. *Ambrose Autperte moine et théologien.* Paris, 1953.

2. BEYOND THE AUGUSTINIAN SYNTHESIS

Amann, Émile. "L'adoptionisme espagnol du VIIIe siècle." *Revue des sciences religieuses* 16 (1936): 281–317.

―――. *L'époque carolingienne.* Paris, 1934. Volume 6 of Fliche, Augustin, and Martin, Victor, eds., *Histoire de l'Église depuis les origines jusq'à nos jours.*

Balić, Carlo. "The Mediaeval Controversy over the Immaculate Conception up to the Death of Scotus." In *The Dogma of the Immaculate Conception: History and Significance,* edited by Edward Dennis O'Connor, pp. 161–212. Notre Dame, Ind., 1958.

Beeson, Charles Henry. *Servatus Lupus as Scribe and Text Critic.* Cambridge, Mass., 1930.

Boshof, Egon. *Erzbischof Agobard von Lyon: Leben und Werk.* Cologne, 1969.

Brink, J. N. Bakhuizen van den, ed. Ratramnus. *De corpore et sanguine Domini.* Amsterdam, 1954.

Browe, Peter. *Die Verehrung der Eucharistie im Mittelalter.* Munich, 1933. "The rule of prayer" on the Eucharist.

―――. *Die eucharistischen Wunder des Mittelalters.* Breslau, 1938.

Canal, J. M. "La virginidad de Maria según Ratramno y Radberto, monjes de Corbie. Nueva edición de los textos." *Marianum* 30 (1968): 53–160.

Cappuyuns, Maïeul. *Jean Scot Érigène: sa vie, son oeuvre, sa pensée.* Reprint edition. Brussels, 1964. Probably the most important single work on Erigena.

Cristiani, Marta. "La controversia eucaristica nella cultura del secolo IX." *Studi medievali* 9 (1968): 167–233.

Dörries, Hermann. *Zur Geschichte der Mystik: Erigena und der Neuplatonismus.* Tübingen, 1925.

Fahey, John Francis. *The Eucharistic Teaching of Ratramn of Corbie.* Mundelein, Ill., 1951.

Geiselmann, Josef Rupert. *Die Eucharistielehre der Vorscholastik.* Paderborn, 1926. Geiselmann's investigations of the history of medieval eucharistic doctrine, including those listed under chapter 4 below, have been decisive for our understanding of the development.

Giannoni, Carl. *Paulinus II. Patriarch von Aquileia: Ein Beitrag zur Kirchengeschichte Österreichs im Zeitalter Karls des Groszen.* Vienna, 1896.

Gordillo, Mauricio. *La Asunción de Maria en la Iglesia Española (siglos VII–XI).* Madrid, 1922.

Graus, František. *Volk, Herrscher und Heiliger im Reich der Merowinger.* Prague, 1965. A social-political interpretation of the cult of the saints.

Halphen, Louis. *Charlemagne et l'empire carolingien.* Paris, 1947. Includes (pp. 213 ff.) a discussion of Charlemagne and theology.

Häring, Nicholas Martin. "Character, Signum und Signaculum: Die Entwicklung bis nach der karolingischen Renaissance." *Scholastik* 30 (1955): 481–512; 31 (1956): 41–69, 182–212.

Hauck, Albert. *Kirchengeschichte Deutschlands.* Vol. 2. 4th ed. Leipzig, 1912. Especially important for its sections on doctrine and theology (pp. 297–349, 623–88).

Heil, W. "Der Adoptianismus, Alkuin und Spanien." In *Karl der Grosze: Lebenswerk und Nachleben,* edited by B. Bischoff, 2:95–155. Düsseldorf, 1965.

Helfferich, Adolf. *Der westgothische Arianismus und die spanische Ketzer-Geschichte.* Berlin, 1860. Still useful.

Jolivet, Jean. *Godescalc d'Orbai et la Trinité.* Paris, 1958. An original and illuminating monograph.

Kolping, Adolf. "Amalar von Metz und Florus von Lyon: Zeugen eines Wandels im liturgischen Mysterienverständnis in der Karolingerzeit." *Zeitschrift für katholische Theologie* 73 (1951): 424–64.

Lopez, Robert Sabatino. *The Tenth Century: How Dark the Dark Ages?* New York, 1959. A judicious selection of sources, in English translation.

Mathon, Gérard. "L'utilisation des textes de saint Augustin par Jean Scot Érigène dans son *De Praedestinatione.*" In *Augustinus Magister,* 3:419–28. Paris, 1954.

Mauguin, Gilbert. *Veterum auctorum qui a IX. saeculo de praedestinatione et gratia scripserunt opera et fragmenta.* 2 vols. Paris, 1650. Still the handiest collection of source materials.

Menéndez y Pelayo, Marcelino. *Historia de los heterodoxos españoles.* 2d ed. 3 vols. Madrid, 1912–19. The unique role of Spanish theology throughout most of the Middle Ages.

Meyvaert, Paul. "The Exegetical Treatises of Peter the Deacon and Eriugena's Rendering of the 'Ad Thalassium' of Maximus the Confessor." *Sacris Erudiri* 14 (1963): 130–48.

Morrison, Karl Frederick. *The Two Kingdoms: Ecclesiology in Carolingian Political Thought.* Princeton, 1964.

O'Meara, John J., and Bieler, Ludwig, eds. *The Mind of Eriugena: Papers of a Colloquium, Dublin, 14–18 July 1970.* Dublin, 1973.

Peltier, Henri. *Pascase Radbert, abbé de Corbie.* Amiens, 1938.

Quadrio, G. "Il trattato 'De Assumptione beatae M. V.' dello pseudo-Agostino." *Analecta Gregoriana* 52 (1951): 149–62.

Sage, Carlton M. *Paul Albar of Cordova.* Washington, 1943.

Scheffczyk, Leo. "Die Grundzüge der Trinitätslehre des Johannes Scotus Eriugena." In *Theologie in Geschichte und Gegenwart: Michael Schmaus zum sechzigsten Geburtstag,* edited by J. Auer and H. Volk, pp. 497–518. Munich, 1957.

———. *Das Mariengeheimnis in Frömmigkeit und Lehre der Karolingerzeit.* Leipzig, 1959.

Schrörs, Heinrich. *Hinkmar, Erzbischof von Reims: Sein Leben und seine Schriften.* Freiburg, 1884.

Severus, Emmanuel von. *Lupus von Ferrieres: Gestalt und Werk eines Vermittlers antiken Geistesgutes an das Mittelalter im 9. Jahrhundert.* Münster, 1940.

Sheldon-Williams, Inglis-Patric. "A Bibliography of the Works of Johannes Scottus Eriugena." *Journal of Ecclesiastical History* 10 (1959): 198–224.

Solano, Jesús. "El Concilio de Calcedonia y la controversia adopcionista del siglo VIII en España." In *Das Konzil von Chalkedon: Geschichte und Gegenwart,* edited by Aloys Grillmeier and Heinrich Bacht, 2:841–71. Würzburg, 1951–52.

Van der Meer, Frederik. *Augustine the Bishop.* Translated by Brain Battershaw and G. R. Lamb. New York, 1961.

Vielhaber, Klaus. *Gottschalk der Sachse.* Bonn, 1956. Even though the personal elements in Gottschalk's story are the most fascinating, Vielhaber devotes a significant part (pp. 68–82) of his narrative to Gottschalk's doctrine.

Walker, George Stuart Murdoch. "Erigena's Conception of the Sacraments." In *Studies in Church History,* edited by Geoffrey John Cuming, 3:150–58. Leiden, 1966.

Wilmart, Henri-Marie-André. "L'ordre des parties dans le traité de Paulin d'Aquilée contre Félix d'Urgel." *Journal of Theological Studies* 39 (1938): 22–37. Wilmart proposes, on the basis of manuscript evidence, a different sequence of the sections of Paulinus's treatise. His argument is persuasive, but for the sake of convenience we have in our citations followed the conventional order.

3. The Plan of Salvation

À Cluny. Congrès scientifique, fêtes et cérémonies en l'honneur des saints abbés Odon et Odilon, 9–11 juillet 1949. Dijon, 1950.

Aulén, Gustaf. *Christus Victor: An Historical Study of the Three Main Types of the Idea of Atonement.* Translated by A. G. Hebert. Reprinted with an introduction by Jaroslav Pelikan. New York, 1969.

Blomme, Robert. *La doctrine du péché dans les écoles théologiques de la première moitié du XIIe siècle.* Louvain, 1958.

Blum, Owen J. *St. Peter Damian: His Teaching on the Spiritual Life.* Washington, 1947.

Bourgin, Georges, ed. *Guibert de Nogent. Histoire de sa vie (1053–1124).* Paris, 1907.

Clerck, D. E. de. "Droits du démon et nécessité de la rédemption: Les écoles d'Abélard et de Pierre Lombard." *Recherches de théologie ancienne et médiévale* 14 (1947): 32–64.

Dubois, Marguerite-Marie. *Les éléments latins dans la poésie religieuse de Cynewulf.* Paris, 1942.

Fairweather, Eugene Rathbone, ed. *A Scholastic Miscellany: Anselm to Occam.* Philadelphia, 1956. Important texts in English translation, with a spirited and informative introduction.

————. " 'Iustitia Dei' as the 'Ratio' of the Incarnation." In *Spicilegium Beccense,* 1:327–35. Paris, 1959.

Franks, Robert Sleightholme. *A History of the Doctrine of the Work of Christ in Its Ecclesiastical Development.* 2 vols. London, 1918. Volume 1:147–350 deals with "the mediaeval theology."

Gilson, Étienne. *Heloise and Abelard.* Translated by Leonard K. Shook. Ann Arbor, Mich., 1960.

Gottschick, Johannes. "Studien zur Versöhnungslehre des Mittelalters." *Zeitschrift für Kirchengeschichte* 22 (1901): 378–438.

Gross, Julius. *Entwicklungsgeschichte des Erbsündendogmas im nachaugustinischen Altertum und in der Vorscholastik (5.–11. Jahrhundert).* Munich, 1963.

Heyer, George S. "St. Anselm on the Harmony between God's Mercy and God's Justice." In *The Heritage of Christian Thought: Essays in Honor of Robert Lowry Calhoun,* edited by Robert E. Cushman and Egil Grislis, pp. 31–40. New York, 1965.

Hiss, Wilhelm. *Die Anthropologie Bernhards von Clairvaux.* Berlin, 1964.

Hopkins, Jasper. *A Companion to the Study of St. Anselm.* Minneapolis, 1972. Together with the author's translations of Anselm into English, a significant contribution to the literature.

Kahles, Wilhelm. *Geschichte als Liturgie: Die Geschichtstheologie des Rupertus von Deutz.* Münster, 1960.

Kuttner, Stephan Georg. *Kanonistische Schuldlehre von Gratian bis auf die Dekretalen Gregors IX systematisch auf Grund der handschriftlichen Quellen dargestellt.* Rome, 1935.

Leclercq, Jean. *Saint Bernard mystique.* Paris, 1948. The christocentrism of Bernard's devotion and thought.

————. *Saint Pierre Damien, ermite et homme d'église.* Rome, 1960.

McIntyre, John. *St. Anselm and His Critics: A Reinterpretation of the "Cur Deus Homo."* Edinburgh, 1954. A defense against Aulén and others.

Macrae-Gibson, O. D. "Christ the Victor-Vanquished in *The Dream of the Rood."* *Neuphilologische Mitteilungen* 70 (1969): 667–72.

Monticelli, Giuseppe. *Raterio vescovo di Verona (890–974).* Milan, 1938.

Ott, Heinrich. "Anselms Versöhnungslehre." *Theologische Zeitschrift* 13 (1957): 183–99.

Patch, Howard Rollin. "Liturgical Influence in *The Dream of the Rood."* *Publications of the Modern Language Association* 34 (1919): 233–57.

Phelan, Gerald Bernard. *The Wisdom of Saint Anselm.* Latrobe, Pa., 1960.

Rivière, Jean. *Le dogme de la rédemption au début du moyen âge.* Paris, 1934.

Schmitt, Franciscus Salesius. "La 'Meditatio redemptionis humanae' di san Anselmo in relazione al 'Cur deus homo.'" *Benedictina* 9 (1955): 197–213.

Schwark, Bruno. *Bischof Rather von Verona als Theologe.* Königsberg, 1915.

Stevens, William Oliver. *The Cross in the Life and Literature of the Anglo-Saxons.* New York, 1904.

Strijd, Krijn. *Structuur en Inhoud van Anselmus' "Cur Deus Homo"* [The structure and content of Anselm's *Cur Deus Homo*]. Assen, 1957.

Weingart, Richard Ernest. *The Logic of Divine Love: A Critical Analysis of the Soteriology of Peter Abailard.* Oxford, 1970. An examination of the charge of "subjectivism."

Williams, George Huntston. *The Norman Anonymous of 1100 A.D.* Cambridge, Mass., 1951. "Christocentrism" in political thought.

————. *Anselm: Communion and Atonement.* Saint Louis, 1960. Baptism and the Eucharist as models for the doctrine of the atonement.

4. THE COMMUNICATION OF GRACE

Beekenkamp, Willem Hermanus. *De avondmaalsleer van Berengarius van Tours* [The eucharistic doctrine of Berengar of Tours]. The Hague, 1941.

Beissel, Stephan. *Die Verehrung der Heiligen und ihrer Reliquien in Deutschland bis zum Beginne des 13. Jahrhunderts.* Freiburg, 1880.

————. *Geschichte der Verehrung Marias in Deutschland während des Mittelalters.* Freiburg, 1909.

Bover, José María. "Maria Mediatrix." *Ephemerides theologicae Lovanienses* 6 (1929): 439–62. A compilation of quotations from Eastern and Western sources.

Brommer, Ferdinand. *Die Lehre vom sakramentalen Charakter in der Scholastik bis Thomas von Aquin inklusive.* Paderborn, 1908.

Courtney, Francis. *Cardinal Robert Pullen: An English Theologian of the Twelfth Century.* Rome, 1954.

Dooley, Eugene A. *Church Law on Sacred Relics.* Washington, 1931.

Eynde, Damien van den. *Les définitions des sacrements pendant la première période de la théologie scolastique (1050–1240).* Rome, 1950.

Forsyth, Ilene H. *The Throne of Wisdom: Wood Sculptures of the Madonna in Romanesque France.* Princeton, 1972. Illustrations of "the rule of prayer" as expressed in art.

Geiselmann, Josef Rupert. "Die Stellung des Guibert von Nogent (†1124) in der Eucharistielehre der Frühscholastik." *Theologische Quartalschrift* 110 (1929): 66–84, 279–305.

———. "Der Abendmahlsbrief des Anselm von Canterbury ein Werk des Anselm von Laon." *Theologische Quartalschrift* 111 (1930): 320–49.

———. *Die Abendmahlslehre an der Wende der christlichen Antike zum Frühmittelalter: Isidor von Sevilla und das Sakrament der Eucharistie.* Munich, 1933. Fundamental for an understanding of the transition from patristic to medieval interpretations of the Eucharist.

Geary, Patrick J. *Furta Sacra: Thefts of Relics in the Central Middle Ages.* Princeton, 1978.

Geyer, Bernhard. "Die Siebenzahl der Sakramente in ihrer historischen Entwicklung." *Theologie und Glaube* 10 (1918): 324–48.

Ghellinck, Joseph de. *Pour l'histoire du mot sacramentum.* Paris, 1924.

———. "Un chapitre dans l'histoire de la définition des sacrements au XIIe siècle." In *Mélanges Mandonnet,* 2:79–96. Paris, 1930.

Gillmann, Franz. *Die Siebenzahl der Sakramente bei den Glossatoren des Gratianischen Dekrets.* Mainz, 1909.

Grégoire, Réginald. *Bruno de Segni exégète médiéval et théologien monastique.* Spoleto, 1965.

Guth, Klaus. *Guibert von Nogent und die hochmittelalterliche Kritik an der Reliquienverehrung.* Augsburg, 1970.

Häring, Nikolaus Martin. "A Study in the Sacramentology of Alger of Liège." *Mediaeval Studies* 20 (1958): 41–78.

Heurtevent, Raoul. *Durand de Troarn et les origines de l'hérésie bérengarienne.* Paris, 1912.

Jorissen, Hans. *Die Entfaltung der Transsubstantiationslehre bis zum Beginn der Hochscholastik.* Münster, 1965.

Kemp, Eric Waldram. *Canonization and Authority in the Western Church.* London, 1948.

Korošak, B. *Mariologia S. Alberti Magni eiusque coaequalium.* Rome, 1954. The doctrine of Mary in Dominican theology.

Lebon, J. "Sur la doctrine eucharistique d'Hériger de Lobbes." In *Studia mediaevalia in honorem . . . R. J. Martin,* pp. 61–84. Bruges, 1948.

Macdonald, Allan John. *Berengar and the Reform of Sacramental Doctrine.* New York, 1930. A sympathetic account.

Mâle, Émile. *The Gothic Image: Religious Art in France of the Thirteenth Century.* Translated by Dora Nussey. Paperback edition. New York, 1958.

Montclos, Jean de. *Lanfranc et Bérenger: La controverse eucharistique du XIe siècle.* Louvain, 1971. For some time to come, the definitive monograph.

Newman, John Henry. *An Essay on the Development of Christian Doctrine.* Edited by Charles Frederick Harrold. New York, 1949.

Poschmann, Bernhard. *Busse und letzte Oelung.* Freiburg, 1951. Part of the sacramental section of the *Handbuch der Dogmengeschichte.*

Rahner, Karl. "Die Gegenwart Christi im Sakrament des Herrenmahles." In *Schriften zur Theologie,* 4:357–85. 3d ed. Einsiedeln, 1962. On the distinction—and the connection—between "real presence" and "transubstantiation."

Rogers, Elizabeth Frances. *Peter Lombard and the Sacramental System.* New York, 1917. Includes a translation of the text of the Lombard's discussion of the sacraments.

Rosati, M. *La teologia sacramentaria nella lotta contro le simonia e l'investitura laica del secolo XI.* Tolentino, 1951. An important, but little-known investigation of a significant question.

Saxer, Victor. *Le culte de Marie-Madeleine en Occident des origines à la fin du moyen-âge.* Paris, 1959.

Schapiro, Meyer. *The Parma Ildefonsus: A Romanesque Illuminated Manuscript from Cluny, and Related Works.* New York, 1964.

Seekel, Friedrich. *Geistige Grundlagen Petrus Damianis untersucht am "Liber gratissimus."* Jena, 1933.

Shaugnessy, P. *The Eucharistic Doctrine of Guitmund of Aversa.* Rome, 1939.

Shea, George W. "Outline History of Mariology in the Middle Ages and Modern Times." In *Mariology,* edited by Juniper B. Carol, 1:281–327. Milwaukee, 1955.

Sheedy, Charles Edmund. *The Eucharistic Controversy of the Eleventh Century against the Background of Pre-Scholastic Theology.* Washington, 1947.

Simson, Otto von. *The Gothic Cathedral: Origins of Gothic Architecture and the Medieval Concept of Order.* New York, 1956. According to von Simson (p. 172), "the age was indeed the age of the Virgin."

Sitwell, Gerard, ed. *St. Odo of Cluny.* London, 1958.

Somerville, Robert. "The Case against Berengar of Tours—A New Text." *Studi Gregoriani* 9 (1972): 53–75.

Southern, Richard William. "Lanfranc of Bec and Berengar of Tours." In *Studies in Medieval History Presented to Frederick Maurice Powicke,* edited by Richard William Hunt et al., pp. 27–48. Oxford, 1948.

Whitney, James Pounder. *Hildebrandine Essays.* Cambridge, 1932.

5. The One True Faith

Altaner, Berthold. "Zur Geschichte der anti-islamischen Polemik während des 13. und 14. Jahrhunderts." *Historisches Jahrbuch* 56 (1936): 227–33.

Barth, Karl. *Fides quaerens intellectum: Anselms Beweis der Existenz Gottes im Zusammenhang seines theologischen Programms.* Munich, 1931. An analysis that many will reject but none can ignore.

Bligh, J. "Richard of St. Victor's *De Trinitate:* Augustinian or Abelardian?" *Heythrop Journal* 1 (1960): 118–39.

Blumenkranz, Bernhard. *Juifs et chrétiens dans le monde occidental, 430–1096.* Paris, 1960.

———. *Les auteurs chrétiens latins du moyen âge sur les Juifs et le Judaïsme.* Paris, 1963.

Borst. Arno. *Die Katharer.* Stuttgart, 1953. Identified by Grundmann (see below) as "probably the definitive presentation in its substance."

Buytaert, Éloi Marie. "Abelard's Trinitarian Doctrine." In *Peter Abelard: Proceedings of the International Conference Louvain, May 10–12, 1971,* edited by Éloi Marie Buytaert, pp. 127–52. The Hague, 1974.

Daniel, Norman. *Islam and the West: The Making of an Image.* Edinburgh, 1960.

Denifle, Heinrich. "Die Sentenzen Abälards und die Bearbeitungen seiner Theologie." *Archiv für Literatur- und Kirchengeschichte des Mittelalters* 1 (1885): 402–69, 584–624.

Dräseke, Johannes. "Bischof Anselm von Havelberg und seine Gesandschaften nach Byzanz." *Zeitschrift für Kirchengeschichte* 21 (1901): 160–85.

Dumeige, Gervais. *Richard de Saint-Victor et l'idée chrétienne de l'amour.* Paris, 1952.

Éthier, Albert Marie. *Le "De Trinitate" de Richard de Saint-Victor.* Paris, 1939.

Gammersbach, Suitbert. *Gilbert von Poitiers und seine Prozesse im Urteil der Zeitgenossen.* Cologne, 1959.

Gauss, Julia. "Anselm von Canterbury und die Islamfrage." *Theologische Zeitschrift* 19 (1963): 250–72.

———. "Anselm von Canterbury: Zur Begegnung und Auseinandersetzung der Religionen." *Saeculum* 17 (1966): 277–363.

Ghellinck, Joseph de. "Eucharistie au XIIe siècle en Occident." *Dictionnaire de théologie catholique,* edited by Jean-Michel-Alfred Vacant et al., 5:1233–1302. Paris, 1913.

Gilson, Étienne. *Reason and Revelation in the Middle Ages.* New York, 1938.

Grundmann, Herbert. *Religiöse Bewegungen im Mittelalter.* 2d ed. Darmstadt, 1961. Still the best overall introduction to medieval sects and heresies.

Häring, Nikolaus Martin. "The Case of Gilbert de la Porrée, Bishop of Poitiers, 1142–54." *Mediaeval Studies* 13 (1951): 1–40.

Kritzeck, James. *Peter the Venerable and Islam.* Princeton, 1964.

Kuttner, Stephan Georg. "Zur Frage der theologischen Vorlagen Gratians." *Zeitschrift der Savigny-Stiftung für Rechtsgeschichte, Kanonistische Abteilung* 23 (1934): 243–68. On Alger of Liège as canonist and theologian.

———. *Harmony from Dissonance: An Interpretation of Medieval Canon Law.* Latrobe, Pa., 1960.

Leclercq, Jean. *Pierre le Vénérable.* Saint-Wandrille, France, 1946.

———. "Simoniaca Haeresis." *Studi Gregoriani* 1 (1947): 523–30.

———. "Les formes successives de la lettre traité de Saint Bernard contre Abélard." *Revue Bénédictine* 78 (1968): 87–105.

Lerner, Robert Earl. *The Heresy of the Free Spirit in the Later Middle Ages.* Berkeley and Los Angeles, 1972.

McGinn, Bernard. *The Golden Chain: A Study in the Theological Anthropology of Isaac of Stella.* Washington, 1972.

Manselli, Raoul. *Studi sulle eresie del secolo XII.* Rome, 1953.

Miccoli, Giovanni. *Due note sulla tradizione manoscritta di Pier Damiani: "Antilogus contra Iudaeos epistola."* Rome, 1959.

Milano, Ilarino de. "Le eresie popolari del secolo XI nell' Europa occidentale." *Studi Gregoriani* 2 (1947): 43–89. Stresses heresy as a folk movement.

Roques, René. "La méthode de Saint Anselme dans le 'Cur Deus homo.'" *Aquinas: Ephemerides thomisticae* 5 (1962): 3–57.

Ryan, John Joseph. *Saint Peter Damiani and His Canonical Sources: A Preliminary Study in the Antecedents of the Gregorian Reform.* Toronto, 1956.

Schmidt, Martin. *Gottheit und Trinitaet, nach dem Kommentar des Gilbert Porreta zu Boethius, "De Trinitate."* Basel, 1956.

Southern, Richard William. *Saint Anselm and His Biographer.* New York, 1963.

Synan, Edward Aloysius. *The Popes and the Jews in the Middle Ages.* New York, 1965.

Thomas, Rudolf. *Der philosophisch-theologische Erkenntnisweg Peter Abaelards im "Dialogus inter Philosophum, Judaeum, et Christianum."* Bonn, 1966.

Williams, Michael E. *The Teaching of Gilbert Porreta on the Trinity.* Rome, 1951.

6. SUMMA THEOLOGICA

Arquillière, Henri Xavier. *Le plus ancien traité de l'Église: Jacques de Viterbe "De regimine christiano."* Paris, 1926.

Baltzer, Otto. *Die Sentenzen des Petrus Lombardus: Ihre Quellen und ihre dogmengeschichtliche Bedeutung.* Leipzig, 1902.

Benz, Ernst. *Ecclesia spiritualis: Kirchenidee und Geschichtstheologie der franziskanischen Reformation.* Stuttgart, 1934.

Bergin, Thomas Goddard. *Dante.* New York, 1965.

Bertola, Ermenegildo. "Il problema delle creature angeliche in Pier Lombardo." *Pier Lombardo* I-II (1957): 33–54.

Bloomfield, Morton Wilfred. "Joachim of Flora: A Critical Survey of His Canon, Teachings, Sources, Biography and Influence." *Traditio* 13 (1957): 249–311.

Bonnefoy, Jean-François. *Le Saint-Esprit et ses dons selon Saint Bonaventure.* Paris, 1929.

————. *Une Somme Bonaventurienne de théologie mystique: Le "De triplici via."* Paris, 1934.

Bougerol, J. Guy. *Introduction to the Works of Bonaventure.* Translated by José de Vinck. Paterson, N. J., 1964.

Chenu, Marie-Dominique. *Toward Understanding Saint Thomas.* Translated by A.-M. Landry and D. Hughes. Chicago, 1964.

Chesterton, Gilbert Keith. *St. Thomas Aquinas.* London, 1933. A work of serious thought and great charm.

Collins, James Daniel. *The Thomistic Philosophy of Angels.* Washington, 1947.

Camparetti, Domenico Pietro Antonio. *Virgilio nel medio evo.* 2d ed. by Giorgio Pasquali. Florence, 1955.

Congar, Yves. "L'ecclésiologie de S. Bernard." In *Saint Bernard Théologien*, pp. 136–90. Rome, 1953.

Courtès, C. "La peccabilité de l'ange chez saint Thomas." *Revue Thomiste* 53 (1953): 133–63.

D'Arcy, Martin Cyril. "The Philosophy of St. Augustine." In *Saint Augustine,* pp. 155–96. Paperback edition. Cleveland, 1957.

Delhaye, Philippe. *Pierre Lombard: Sa vie, ses oeuvres, sa morale.* Montreal and Paris, 1961.

Geenen, G. "L'usage des auctoritates dans la doctrine du baptême chez saint Thomas d'Aquin." *Ephemerides theologicae Lovanienses* 15 (1938): 278–329.

Gilson, Étienne. "Pourquoi saint Thomas a critiqué saint Augustin." *Archives d'histoire doctrinale et littéraire du moyen âge* 1 (1926): 5–127.

————. *God and Philosophy.* New Haven, 1941.

————. *The Christian Philosophy of St. Thomas Aquinas.* Translated by Lawrence K. Shook. New York, 1960.

————. *The Christian Philosophy of Saint Augustine.* Translated by L. E. M. Lynch. New York, 1960.

————. *Dante and Philosophy.* Translated by David Moore. Paperback edition. New York, 1963.

————. *The Philosophy of St. Bonaventure.* Translated by Illtyd Trethowan and Francis Joseph Sheed. Paterson, N. J., 1965.

González, Justo Luis. "The Work of Christ in Saint Bonaventure's Systematic Works." In *S. Bonaventura 1274–1974,* pp. 371–85. Rome, 1974.

Grabmann, Martin. *Thomas Aquinas: His Personality and Thought.* Translated by Virgil Michel. New York, 1928.

———. *Introduction to the "Theological Summa" of St. Thomas.* Translated by John S. Zybura. Saint Louis, 1930.

———. *Die Werke des heiligen Thomas von Aquin: Literarhistorische Untersuchung und Einführung.* 3d ed. Münster, 1949.

Grundmann, Herbert. *Studien über Joachim von Fiore.* 2d ed. Stuttgart, 1966.

Guardini, Romano. *Die Lehre des heil. Bonaventura von der Erlösung: Ein Beitrag zur Geschichte und zum System der Erlösungslehre.* Düsseldorf, 1921.

———. *Systembildende Elemente in der Theologie Bonaventuras.* Leiden, 1964. The centrality of the doctrine of the Trinity in Bonaventure's thought.

Häring, Nikolaus Martin. "Petrus Lombardus und die Sprachlogik in der Trinitätslehre der Porretanerschule." In *Miscellanea Lombardiana,* pp. 113–27. Novara, 1957.

Hellmann, J. A. Wayne. *Ordo: Untersuchung eines Grundgedankens in der Theologie Bonaventuras.* Munich, 1974.

Knowles, David. *The Religious Orders in England.* 3 vols. Cambridge, 1960.

Lonergan, Bernard. *Verbum: Word and Idea in Aquinas.* Notre Dame, Ind., 1967. One of the most important modern studies of Aquinas.

Lortz, Joseph, ed. *Bernhard von Clairvaux, Mönch und Mystiker.* Vienna, 1955.

McGinn, Bernard. "The Abbot and the Doctors: Scholastic Reactions to the Radical Eschatology of Joachim of Fiore." *Church History* 40 (1971): 30–47.

McKeon, Richard Peter. "Aristotelianism in Western Christianity." In *Environmental Factors in Christian History,* edited by John Thomas McNeill et al., pp. 206–31. Chicago, 1939.

Mandonnet, Pierre. *Siger de Brabant et l'Averroïsme latin au XIIIe siècle.* 2 vols. 2d ed. Louvain, 1908–11.

Pannenberg, Wolfhart. *Die Prädestinationslehre des Duns Skotus im Zusammenhang mit der scholastischen Lehrentwicklung.* Göttingen, 1954.

Pelikan, Jaroslav. "Imago Dei." In *Calgary Aquinas Studies,* edited by Anthony Parel. Toronto, 1978.

Principe, Walter Henry. *The Theology of the Hypostatic Union in the Early Thirteenth Century.* 4 vols. Toronto, 1963–75. A major work of original scholarship, which has contributed to our discussion of the Trinity.

Protois, Félix. *Pierre Lombard évêque de Paris dit le maitre des "Sentences": Son époque, sa vie, ses écrits, son influence.* Paris, 1881.

Reeves, Marjorie Ethel. *The Influence of Prophecy in the Later Middle Ages: A Study of Joachimism.* Oxford, 1969.

Riquet, Michel. "Saint Thomas d'Aquin et les 'auctoritates' en philosophie." *Archives de philosophie* 3-II (1926): 117–55.

Schaefer, Alexander. "The Position and Function of Man in the Created World according to Saint Bonaventure." *Franciscan Studies* 20 (1960): 261–316; 21 (1961): 233–382.

Schindler, Alfred. *Wort und Analogie in Augustins Trinitätslehre.* Tübingen, 1965.

Schlenker, Ernst. *Die Lehre von den göttlichen Namen in der Summe Alexanders von Hales: Ihre Prinzipien und ihre Methode.* Freiburg, 1938.

Schmaus, Michael. *Die psychologische Trinitätslehre des heiligen Augustinus.* Münster, 1927.

Schneider, Johannes. *Die Lehre vom dreieinigen Gott in der Schule des Petrus Lombardus.* Munich, 1961.

Schupp, Johann. *Die Gnadenlehre des Petrus Lombardus.* Freiburg, 1932.

Stohr, Albert. *Die Trinitätslehre des heiligen Bonaventura.* Freiburg, 1923.

Tavard, George Henri. *Expérience et théologie: Essai sur la nature de la théologie d'après le "Commentaire des Sentences" de Saint Bonaventure.* Lyons, 1949.

Velecky, Ceslaus, ed. *Summa Theologiae.* Blackfriars Edition, vol. 6. London, 1965.

Vignaux, Paul. *Luther commentateur des "Sentences."* Paris, 1935.

Walsh, James Joseph. *The Thirteenth—Greatest of Centuries.* New York, 1907.

Weisheipl, James Athanasius. *Friar Thomas D'Aquino: His Life, Thought, and Work.* New York, 1974. A biography for the septecentenary of Thomas Aquinas.

Wendelborn, Gert. *Gott und Geschichte: Joachim von Fiore und die Hoffnung der Christenheit.* Vienna, 1974.

Index

Biblical

General

THE CHRISTIAN TRADITION, Volume III

Designed by Joseph Alderfer.
Composed by Typoservice Corporation
in Linotype Garamond with display lines
in Foundry American Garamond.
Printed by Halliday Lithograph Corp.
on Warren's Olde Style.
Bound by Halliday Lithograph Corp. in Joanna Arrestox
Vellum and stamped in purple and gold.

The symbol on the cover is adapted from the Ruthwell
Cross, dating from the seventh or eighth century, on
which there appear, in runic inscription, portions of the
Old English poem *The Dream of the Rood.*